PLATE 1

House of Abraham Ackerman
Hackensack

This is an outstanding example of a type of architecture developed by the Dutch in America. It was built in 1704 by Abraham Ackerman with the aid of his sons David and Gerrit. It was the home of the Ackerman family until 1825, of the Brinkerhoff family from 1825 to 1899, and of descendants of both families from 1906 to the present time.

PRE-REVOLUTIONARY
DUTCH HOUSES
AND FAMILIES

IN NORTHERN NEW JERSEY
AND SOUTHERN NEW YORK

BY

ROSALIE FELLOWS BAILEY

❖

WITH A NEW FOREWORD BY THE AUTHOR

WITH AN INTRODUCTION BY
FRANKLIN D. ROOSEVELT

PHOTOGRAPHY BY
MARGARET DE M. BROWN

DOVER PUBLICATIONS, INC.
NEW YORK

Published in Canada by General Publishing Company, Ltd.,
30 Lesmill Road, Don Mills, Toronto, Ontario.
Published in the United Kingdom by Constable and Company, Ltd.,
10 Orange Street, London WC 2.

This Dover edition, first published in 1968, is an unabridged and
unaltered republication of the work originally published by William
Morrow & Company in 1936 in a limited edition of 334 copies for the
Holland Society of New York.
This edition contains a new Foreword by the author.

Library of Congress Catalog Card Number: 68-26053

Manufactured in the United States of America

DOVER PUBLICATIONS, INC.
180 Varick Street
New York, N. Y. 10014

FOREWORD TO THE DOVER EDITION

I HAVE always been intrigued by the rich historical background and folklore of the Hudson River Valley, where I was raised. This fascination is no doubt due in part to close personal ties with the region, for my ancestors—Dutch, English, German, Walloon, Flemish, French, Scottish and Scandinavian—have lived in this area for more than three centuries. In my youth I used to love to explore the countryside, and this led to a life-long interest in the genealogy of various old families and in the beautiful native Dutch colonial style of architecture, of which there were many fine local examples. These gracious and well-built houses were little appreciated in those days, and I came to feel the need to record them for posterity, for future generations that would not be able to take them for granted. Hence this book, which was originally published in 1936 under the sponsorship of The Holland Society of New York.

In the early 1930's it was still possible to study and compare such materials as maps, land surveys and district road records, and then to ferret out—in strips and corners of land that had been cut off in the process of straightening colonial roads—many pure examples of this style of building. Here my background and training in property archives and as a professional genealogist were indispensable to me, for owners usually described their property boundaries in terms of their neighbors' lands. When lecturing on houses or teaching genealogy, I stress that documents may be very useful today for a reason different from that for which they were originally executed.

Had the research for this book not been done in the troubled times of the Depression, the opportunity for such thorough coverage would have been lost forever. The post-World War II proliferation of highways and gigantic real estate developments would make such a task extremely difficult, perhaps impossible, today, and of course the end result would be much less rewarding, since the recent prosperity has led to the destruction of many of the buildings illustrated in this book. I particularly mourn the loss of two houses, both in Hackensack—the beautiful Ackerman homestead (shown in the frontispiece), razed for a supermarket, and the imposing Terheun house (Plate 100), torn down to make a parking lot that was later developed into a city park.

Today some of the few houses left standing are being threatened with destruction. For example, New Jersey's historic Old Mine Road and its houses (Plates 167, 169, 170, and 171) are currently endangered by the Federal recreation and reservoir project to dam the Delaware River. However, in recent years this native school of domestic architecture has been widely acclaimed, and state and municipal governments, as well as private organizations and individuals, have become increasingly interested in preserving and restoring our colonial heritage.

A forerunner of this trend was the Washington Rocky Hill Headquarters Association, organized to purchase from a quarry company in 1897 Judge Berrien's home in Somerset County (Plate 128), where Washington wrote his Farewell Address to the Army. During the Depression, it was acquired by the State of New Jersey, was later moved again, and recently reopened with the cooperation of the Rockingham Association. An early endeavor in New York was that sponsored by the Grand Lodge, Free and Accepted Masons, which in 1930 purchased for a memorial shrine the De Wint house in Tappan, Rockland County (Plate 48), on several occasions George Washington's temporary headquarters and the reputed site of the signing of Major André's death warrant. The building is still open to the public, but somewhat altered; in particular, the original gracefully free-flowing roofline has been awkwardly squared off. Since 1965 it has been part of an 85-acre historic zone created by the Town Board of Orangetown. This town was the first to act under the new enabling law, recently passed by the State of New York.

The State of New Jersey, with laws dating from 1931 and 1945, had been in the vanguard of the movement to preserve historic sites. As early as 1928 it purchased the house at New Bridge, North Hackensack, which had been the State's gift to Baron von Steuben (Plate 113). In the light of recent research, in 1967 the building was officially renamed the Ackerman-Zabriskie-von Steuben house. The Passaic County Commission continues its intelligent care of the Dey Mansion (Plate 144) and, after finding foundations of its milk-cooling house, recently reconstructed it.

The City of New York has actively supported the Staten Island Historical Society's restoration project known as Historic Richmondtown, for which I was research consultant. A 100-acre site around the Island's oldest buildings was acquired by city condemnation in 1952, and the Britton-Cubberly house (Plate 26) is now being rebuilt there, while the Guyon-Lake-Tysen house (Plate 31) has already been carefully restored there, along with the oldest known schoolhouse in America, dating from 1695. Still situated elsewhere on the Island, the Stillwell-Britton-Perine house (Plate 38) has been documented as earlier in date and has had the roof of its early portion raised steeply to accord with the slant of its original timbers when uncovered, and its jambless fireplace restored.

In 1966 the Landmarks Preservation Commission of the City of New York, of which I am now Senior Landmarks Preservation Specialist, designated some houses in Kings and Queens Counties as official historical landmarks, among them the Lefferts homestead (Plate 10), the Wyckoff house (Plate 23) and the Lent homestead (Plate 24). It also designated the important Van Wyck homestead, built about 1735 at Douglaston, unfortunately unknown to me when I wrote this book.

Individuals too have become interested in this attractive building style, and many have approached me for advice on how to restore old homes that they have purchased. A member of the Luyster family recently opted for twentieth-century surroundings, but has thoughtfully kept the original homestead in Middletown (Plate 125) intact as a private museum wing. The De Wolf house at Old Tappan (Plate 89) remains in very good condition under the careful attention of the present owner, a descendant of the original builders. The Schenck house (Plate 13) was purchased by a private concern, then donated to the Brooklyn Museum, where it has been reerected within the museum walls. At my earnest behest as researcher for the project, the steeply pitched roof, which was to be omitted from the exhibit, was restored. Unfortunately, when the first Demarest house in Bergen County (Plate 82) was moved and rebuilt in 1955, the steep pitch of the roof was modified, thereby destroying one of the principal indications of the building's great age. In recent years such roofs have been recognized as historically and esthetically important, and have been carefully preserved. Architects are becoming more and more sensitive to the distinctive and characteristic features of this regional style of building, and are consequently restoring old homes with greater fidelity to the past.

Numerous architects have spoken to me of this book's usefulness, and indeed one can now see the influence of this style in some of the recent custom and mass produced housing. I like to feel that my book has made a direct and practical contribution to beautifying the countryside.

I am much encouraged to find evidence of increasing consciousness of this rich heritage on the part of private organizations, individuals and civic organizations, and it is my hope that the republication of this book will further and deepen interest in all aspects of our colonial background.

ROSALIE FELLOWS BAILEY
Member of the Society of Architectural Historians
Fellow of The American Society of Genealogists

New York City
June, 1968

THE HOLLAND SOCIETY
OF NEW YORK

·

Special Committee on

PRE-REVOLUTIONARY DUTCH HOUSES IN NORTHERN NEW JERSEY
AND SOUTHERN NEW YORK

·

FRANKLIN D. ROOSEVELT
CHAIRMAN

J. WILSON POUCHER, M.D.
VICE-CHAIRMAN

CHARLES L. SCHENCK   WALTER L. SUYDAM (deceased)

EDWARD DE WITT   CHARLES M. DUTCHER

WILFRED BLANCH TALMAN, *Secretary*

·

Ex Officio

The Officers of The Holland Society of New York

JOHN de C. VAN ETTEN, *President*

WALTER M. MESEROLE, *Secretary*

ARTHUR R. WENDELL, *Treasurer*

INTRODUCTION

ALL COLLECTORS know the great number of ambitious, definitive publications which end with Volume I. It is, therefore, a great satisfaction to all of us who are deeply interested in the history of the early days of New York and New Jersey to see the completion of the survey of early Dutch Houses which was undertaken several years ago.

We are concerned, however, not merely as antiquarians. The architecture, the decorations, the furniture of our early settlers have a very definite relationship to the arts of today. It is true that our modern life calls for conveniences unthought of in seventeenth century New Amsterdam; but the charm of line, the judgment of location and the spirit of simplicity of the homes of our ancestors are all a good influence on a civilization which to some of us seems to be reverting to the more humble and honest ideals.

FRANKLIN D. ROOSEVELT

HYDE PARK
DUTCHESS COUNTY
NEW YORK

April 27, 1936

A WORD FROM THE BOOK COMMITTEE

IT is with great satisfaction that the members of this committee of The Holland Society see the completion of this volume which has been prepared for the committee by Miss Rosalie Fellows Bailey of New York, and which assures to future generations a knowledge of many early Dutch houses in New Jersey, on Long Island and Staten Island and in Rockland County, New York. The book is a companion volume to *Dutch Houses in the Hudson Valley before 1776*, which was prepared under the auspices of this committee by Helen Wilkinson Reynolds of Poughkeepsie and published in 1929.

In the selection of authors for these two volumes the committee has been fortunate and it desires to record here its appreciation of the able way in which Miss Reynolds and Miss Bailey have carried through a monumental task. Also, the committee would offer its thanks to all those who in many ways have cooperated in its project and helped to make that project a success.

Miss Bailey, Vassar graduate and professional genealogist, is descended from most of the well known families of New Amsterdam and early New York. She is in her third year as a member of the board of directors of the Daughters of the Cincinnati, and is also a member of the Colonial Dames of America and of the Colonial Lords of Manors in America. Her name heads the list of genealogists recognized by the National Society of Colonial Dames in New York, and she has recently been appointed a member of the publication committee of the New York Genealogical and Biographical Society.

The plan for these two volumes was first conceived in conversation between Miss Helen W. Reynolds, Mr. Franklin D. Roosevelt and Dr. J. Wilson Poucher at Mr. Roosevelt's home in Hyde Park, New York, but has been realized only through the generous enthusiasm of the following gentlemen, members of The Holland Society of New York, who as a board of underwriters made it possible financially: Edward De Witt, Franklin D. Roosevelt, De Witt Van Buskirk,* William A. Simonson, J. Wilson Poucher, E. Covert Hulst, James S. Polhemus,* Walter M. Meserole, William L. Brower, Henry Van Dyke,* Charles L. Schenck, Henry D. Lott, Wyllis Van Metre, Joseph F. Simmons, Samuel V. Hoffman, Charles A. Ryder, George B. Cortelyou, Charles M. Dutcher, Albert V. B. Voor-

---

* Deceased.

hees, Col. Cleveland Coxe Lansing, Arthur R. Wendell, R. J. Wortendyke, E. P. Hoes,* G. Payn Quackenbos, James H. Pinckney, W. G. Van De Water, F. W. Suydam, Herbert M. Waldron, I. E. Ditmars,* J. C. Traphagen, Jeremiah R. Van Brunt, Dorville S. Coe, John W. Morrell, Willis D. Van Brunt, Gerrit Y. Lansing, George B. Wendell, Cecil B. de Mille, Frank J. Le Fevre, Robert C. Pruyn,* John S. Van Riper, Henry E. Ackerson, Jr., Lindell T. Bates, Arthur D. Benson, William E. Bruyn, Henry B. Decker, William E. Decker, Bruyn Hasbrouck, Francklyn Hogeboom, H. M. O'Bleness, Walter S. Rapelje, Edwards F. Schermerhorn, Wilfred B. Talman, John de C. Van Etten, Ottomar H. Van Norden, William Van Wyck.

HON. FRANKLIN D. ROOSEVELT, Chairman
J. WILSON POUCHER, Vice-Chairman
JOHN de C. VAN ETTEN, President, ex officio
ARTHUR R. WENDELL, Treasurer, ex officio
WALTER M. MESEROLE, Secretary, ex officio
CHARLES L. SCHENCK
EDWARD DE WITT
WALTER L. SUYDAM*
CHARLES M. DUTCHER
WILFRED BLANCH TALMAN, Secretary
Publication Committee.

---

*Deceased.

CONTENTS

CONTENTS

ILLUSTRATIONS

ILLUSTRATIONS

WESTERN NEW JERSEY, including Essex, Passaic, Hunterdon, Morris, Sussex and Warren Counties

PREFACE

VAN WICKLE—SUYDAM HOUSE
INTERIOR

PREFACE

THIS book on pre-revolutionary Dutch houses and families is an attempt to re-create and record for posterity the manner of life of the early Dutch settlers in this country. Emphasis has been given to their homes because so many of them are being torn down or have fallen into decay and will soon disappear, but this is not primarily a book on architecture and technical discussion will not be found along this line. A large part of the text is devoted to the builders and inhabitants of these houses, to their births, marriages and deaths, to the size of their families, and to the important events of their lives, in other words to the genealogical side with occasional biographical sketches.

The classification of a house as Dutch has been determined largely by the conditions, circumstances and early history of the country. The Dutch government of New Netherland lasted for only forty years. Only a small portion of the territory under discussion was settled during this period and very few houses remain which were built before the English conquest of 1664. Nevertheless, the field survey undertaken for this book has revealed that wherever the Dutch or their descendants settled, the Dutch culture prevailed, absorbing all other elements in the community. Thus houses will be found in this book which were built in the Dutch style by men of Scotch, English, French, German, Polish and Scandinavian descent. These men of other nationalities had for the most part emigrated to this country while it was under Dutch government; they were political or religious refugees or adventurers seeking opportunities of advancement and were attracted by the liberal and flourishing commerce. In return for asylum and opportunity and the kindly feelings of their Dutch neighbors (which remained a factor long after their rule ended), the emigrants of the various races adopted the language and manner of living of the Dutch and chose their wives from among them, so that the second and third generations were as much Dutch in outlook and breeding as though they were one hundred per cent Dutch in blood.

This broad qualification, covering the cosmopolitan period of Dutch sovereignty, has been the standard used for the inclusion of a house in this work for another reason also. This volume has been written under the auspices of the Holland Society of New York. Eligibility to the Society is based on descent in the male line from an inhabitant of New Netherland, regardless of his original nationality.

The present work was planned as a companion volume to *Dutch Houses in the Hudson Valley before 1776*, by Helen Wilkinson Reynolds, which was published in 1929 under the auspices of The Holland Society of New York. Miss Reynolds dealt with the houses and lives of the people in the Hudson River Valley, on the east side as far south as Westchester County and on the west side down to Orange County. No better and fuller account can be given of the manner of life, background, customs, traditions and homes of the Dutch than in her book, to which the author urgently refers the reader who wishes to acquire an adequate background of the life of the times. The genealogical stress gives a different slant to the present volume.

The territory covered is that of Southern New Netherland, the Dutch settlements not treated in Miss Reynolds' work. The Province of New Netherland included, as well as New York, the whole of the present State of New Jersey. The southern half of New Jersey has been omitted from this volume because it was principally settled by the English and Scotch, and no Dutch influence was ever prevalent there. Rockland County on the west side of the Hudson River is included in this rather than in the former work, because in topography, type of houses and families it is more akin to Bergen County, New Jersey, than to the other Hudson River counties in New York. The Dutch settlements in Kings, Queens and Richmond Counties in New York are also treated. New Amsterdam has been omitted because the pre-revolutionary Dutch houses there have disappeared many years ago, and it was felt that very little new material could be found.

An attempt has been made to photograph and give the early history of all existing Dutch houses within the territory mentioned, which were found to be only slightly altered. This is in keeping with the aim to record for posterity the appearance of the houses as they were when inhabited by the Dutch. The history has also been given of a few houses which have recently disappeared and of some others which have been too much altered for a photograph to convey the desired impression. Reference has been made to other photographs and prints of these houses which have been published, so as to enable the reader to study other views.

This work establishes the fact that the average pre-revolutionary Dutch house was a farmhouse, inhabited by the farmer and militiaman of the day. It will be noticed that there are not many historical houses and very few that can be dignified by the term of mansion. The hardships of nature inherent in the opening up of a new country operated alike on rich and poor, with the result that their homes were very similar with only minor differences in size and detail.

A field survey was made of Greater New York in 1925, and many of the houses chosen and photographed then have since disappeared; the mainland was surveyed in 1932 and 1933. The colonial and Revolutionary roads in these regions were found with the aid of old maps (those of Robert Erskine, Surveyor General under Washington, proved invaluable) and located among the present-day roads. These were intensely scoured by motor, the houses thus found were examined, their owners, old residents and local historians interviewed, and a large volume of correspondence initiated, resulting in very welcome aid. The information thus garnered supplied the clues for an intensive study in various libraries, among the county histories, family genealogies, church records and wills. Where possible, the land deeds and conveyances were examined at the county seats. A complete abstract of title to every property could not be compiled in a volume of this type, but enough material has been furnished to direct further research by those interested in any particular property. An attempt has been made to give a genealogical sketch of the families of the builders and early owners. Original research work on over two hundred families was of course impossible in the short amount of time allotted; therefore published and manuscript genealogical accounts have been resorted to wherever they were available and seemed reliable. The entries in many family Bibles, still in private ownership, were copied; asterisks against dates in this volume are used to denote this valuable source.

The author is deeply grateful for the hearty cooperation of the present owners in showing their homes and placing their records at her disposal. So many people have been of aid in the preparation of this volume that it is impossible to enumerate them here. Particular thanks are due to Dr. Frank L. Van Cleef, the Rev. Lefferd Haughwout, Loring McMillen, Lewis D. Cook, Cornelius C. Vermeule, Judge and Mrs. Henry E. Ackerson, Jr., Miss Mary A. Demarest, Louis L. Blauvelt, M. Montgomery Maze, George H. Budke, J. Elting Sloat and Wilfred Blanch Talman. The advice of Howard Stelle Fitz Randolph, then associate editor of the New York Genealogical and Biographical Society, and of Walter M. Meserole, Secretary of The Holland Society of New York, have been invaluable, also the encouragement of Miss Helen Wilkinson Reynolds and Dr. J. Wilson Poucher. The author has had access to the manuscript records and collections of The Holland Society of New York, the New York Genealogical and Biographical Society, the New York Historical Society, the New York Public Library, the Staten Island Institute of Arts and Sciences, and the Rutgers University Library. This work could not have been accomplished without the photography of Miss Margaret De M. Brown, who has succeeded so well in portraying the homes and living atmosphere of the Dutch period in her plates.

ADDENDA

AN IMPORTANT CONTEMPORARY DESCRIPTION

Not until this book was on the press was the following contemporary description discovered. It is an interesting account not heretofore quoted in connection with the Dutch life of the period.

James Thacher, a surgeon's mate, in his *Military Journal of the American Revolution*, p. 156, thus described a regiment's march on Nov. 28-Dec. 2, 1778, to King's Ferry, across the Hudson River to New Jersey, and on through Kakiat, Paramus and Acquackanonk: "These towns are inhabited chiefly by Dutch people; their churches and dwelling houses are built mostly of rough stone, one story high. There is a peculiar neatness in the appearance of their dwellings, having an airy piazza supported by pillars in front, and their kitchens connected at the ends in the form of wings. The land is remarkably level and the soil fertile; and being generally advantageously cultivated, the people appear to enjoy ease and happy competency. The furniture in their houses is of the most ordinary kind, and such as might be supposed to accord with the fashion of the days of Queen Anne. They despise the superfluities of life, and are ambitious to appear always neat and cleanly, and never to complain of an empty purse."

The chief importance of this account is the description of the piazza as supported by pillars. Heretofore it has been presumed that the pillars were added under the influence of the Classic style at the end of the eighteenth century. The houses of the late period generally had pillars, whereas the overhanging roofs of many of the earlier houses are left in balanced suspension to this day. The above account, however, shows that columns were in common use as early as the Revolutionary period. Statements throughout this volume of the subsequent addition of the pillars must therefore be accepted only after study of the particular house in question.

PRE-REVOLUTIONARY DUTCH HOUSES
IN NORTHERN NEW JERSEY AND SOUTHERN NEW YORK

Land Titles

A GROUP of Amsterdam merchants received in 1614 from the States General of the United Provinces a charter, which granted them the exclusive right to trade in the Hudson country of New Netherland. The Dutch West India Company was incorporated by the States General in 1621, the charter granting almost regal powers to colonize, govern and protect New Netherland. The company was organized and the first group of permanent settlers sent over in 1624. A charter of Freedoms and Exemptions was adopted in 1629, granting large patroonships to individuals founding colonies of fifty adults. As this Act did not sufficiently encourage colonization, a new charter of Freedoms and Exemptions was adopted in 1640, whereby patroonships were limited to four miles of river frontage, and 200 acres were allowed to every colonist bringing over five others. A proclamation was issued offering every emigrant as much land as he could properly cultivate; a quit rent of a tenth was reserved for the company, thus assuring legal estates of inheritance to the grantees. Each grantee was required to sign a pledge of obedience to the officers of the West India Company, acting in subordination to the States General. The occupation of the Dutch settlers was always sanctioned by ground brief (patent) from the West India Company and a confirmatory patent was issued after the land was under cultivation. Prior to this the rights of the Indians to the lands had to be extinguished; although a few individuals purchased directly from the Indians, the greater part of the country was bought by the West India Company and in general had to be purchased several times from various groups of Indians.

Charles II of England, without competent authority, granted the Province of New Netherland to his brother James, Duke of York, who conquered the Colony by force in 1664. The Province of New York was ruled as his personal demesne and it became a royal province upon his accession to the throne. All Dutch grants had to be turned in under penalty of forfeiture and were confirmed for a moderate fee. Patents (that is, confirmations of title to original purchasers) were issued to individuals or groups by the governor, as the representative of the Duke and later of the kings. As heretofore, these titles were based on the extinguishment of Indian rights.

The Province of New Jersey was sold by the Duke of York on June 24, 1664 to John, Lord Berkeley and Sir George Carteret. They formed a constitution for the colony and appointed Philip Carteret as Governor. Under the Concessions of the Proprietors, land could only be taken up under a warrant from the governor, who gave a confirmatory deed after the land had been purchased from the Indians. Such favorable terms were offered to settlers that they came in large numbers. Prior titles to land under cultivation were readily confirmed. However, Carteret and especially the later Proprietors contested the early immense grants and were generally able to restrict them to land actually in occupation. The Province was divided into East and West Jersey on July 1, 1676. Berkeley had sold his undivided share (West Jersey) in 1674 to John Fenwicke in trust for Edward Byllinge, both members of the Society of Friends. Byllinge assigned his share to William Penn and other Quakers, and Fenwicke likewise sold interests to others. West Jersey was divided among the Proprietors into hundredths. Carteret's widow and trustees sold East Jersey in 1680 to William Penn and eleven others, but later the ownership was enlarged and East Jersey was owned and ruled by twenty-four Proprietors. New Jersey became a royal province on April 17, 1702, when the Proprietors of East and West Jersey surrendered to Queen Anne the power of government, retaining for themselves the title to the soil. The Proprietors thus became an association of land-owners. They were tenants in common. Warrants were issued from time to time according to their respective rights, authorizing them to survey and appropriate tracts. Such a warrant did not convey title of the property to one of them, as he had that before; it authorized him to sever it from the common stock and so operated as a release to him, allowing him to sell it to others. The lands in New Jersey were gradually sold in this manner, and no grants were ever made in New Jersey by the King to individuals.

All these transfers of authority were bound to cause grave disturbances in certain areas. Gov. Nicolls granted the Monmouth patent immediately after the English conquest, before learning of the transfer of the New Jersey province. Settlement was commenced under this patent, which gave the right of local government, but the patentees resisted Carteret's claim to rights of ownership and government, and it was not until 1683 that the matter was finally settled in favor of the Proprietors. The partition line between East and West Jersey was long in dispute; it was first drawn in 1676 and finally drawn in 1743. In the meantime the border land was granted to various settlers by both the East Jersey and West Jersey Proprietors. The consequent land troubles were severest in western Essex County, the Horseneck or Fairfield region, and resulted in many of the actual settlers being ousted if they could not repurchase their lands. A large slice of the northern counties in New Jersey was for many years claimed by the Province of New York and several New York patents extended far into New Jersey. Similarly some of the early patents issued by the New Jersey Proprietors were for lands later found to be in New York. It was not until 1772 that the present line was accepted.

Location of Settlements

The Dutch settled principally in the plains and along rivers and creeks. New Amsterdam was established in 1624 on the tip of Manhattan. The level plains and large numbers of bays and inlets of Long Island attracted them almost immediately and five Dutch towns were established or gradually grew up in the present Kings County—New Amersfoort or Flatlands, Breuckelen, Midwout or Flatbush, New Utrecht, and Bushwick or Woodtown. These and the English town of Gravesend, where many of the Dutch also lived, were organized under the government of New Netherland. The present Queens County was almost entirely settled by the English from New England but a number of Dutchmen opened up plantations along Bouwery Bay, where the East River joins the Sound. Several unsuccessful attempts were made at an early date to settle Staten Island where the first permanent colony was formed in 1661. The early farms on the Jersey shore of the Hudson River were likewise laid waste by the Indians, and the palisaded village of Bergen, erected in 1660, was the first successful development. From these older villages came the settlers who gradually opened up the northeast corner of the province of New Jersey, which was watered by the Hackensack, Passaic, Saddle, Pequannock and Ramapo Rivers, and now comprises the counties of Hudson, Bergen, Passaic and parts of Essex and Morris. A small village grew up at Old Hackensack, now Ridgefield Park, another at Acquackanonk, now Passaic, and a third at Second River, now Belleville; the whole country was studded with farms. Rockland County to the north had a similar development, its main community was started in 1683 at Tappan. The English settled a large territory in central New Jersey, the present Union County, most of Morris and Essex, and parts of Middlesex and Somerset Counties. Another Dutch stronghold was established in the 1680s south of the English, along the Raritan and Millstone Rivers, which water parts of Somerset and Middlesex Counties. There were two villages here, Raritan, now Somerville, and New Brunswick, the latter being part Dutch and part English. Monmouth County was mainly settled by the English and Scotch but a small group of Dutchmen sailed south from Kings County in and about 1695 and opened up farms in the rolling valleys around Holmdel. Most of Hunterdon County in West Jersey was settled in the early eighteenth century by Quakers and Germans from Pennsylvania, but a Dutch settlement grew up around Readington after 1700. The Minisink country, along the Delaware River in the extreme northwestern corner of the province, was settled in the opening years of the eighteenth century by Dutchmen who drifted down from Esopus in Ulster County, New York.

The Builders

There were few trained architects and professional builders among the Dutch in the sense that we employ these terms. The average Dutch farmhouse was erected by the owner, with the help of his wife, grown sons and the neighboring farmers, sometimes under the supervision of a local tradesman, who was generally called a carpenter in the records but whose manner of life was similar to that of his farmer neighbors. These substantial houses, especially the stone houses, are the result of the abundant and inexpensive slave labor of the times, the Proprietors of New Jersey granting 75 acres for every slave brought into the colony. It is exceedingly doubtful if the stone would have been so extensively quarried, cut, dressed, carried and laid if there had been no slaves.

Types of Houses

The term "Dutch Colonial house" has often been used for the type of one and a half story house developed here by the Dutch, which flourished to perfection especially in Bergen County, New Jersey. The name is really a misnomer for it came into existence after the fall of the New Netherland government and reached its greatest height in the half century after the American Revolution. It is a distinctive architecture and our only indigenous form until the coming of the modern skyscraper.

The earliest houses of the Dutch were temporary shelters, which were of two types. There were dugouts, which were excavations in the earth, lined with bark and covered with rude roofs of sod or reeds. There were also crudely built houses with sapling framework covered and lined with bark. The first permanent homes were small, one story buildings of roughly cut stone or wood, with straw thatched roofs, narrow windows with only two panes of glass, stone fireplaces and ovens, and chimneys of boards plastered inside with mortar or mud; in the interior rough shelves were used for cupboards and benches for beds. The wing of the Swaert—Van Brunt house at New Utrecht, built 1657-75 (plate 20), belongs to this very early period in type. Its low, rough stone walls, steep roof, absence of overhanging eaves, and small number and size of windows are characteristic features. As soon as practical the houses were modeled after those of the Fatherland, of good size, substantial and comfortable; their very steep roofs and stepped gables are familiar to us in prints of early New Amsterdam.

Gradually there arose a native style which had no prototype in Europe. This development cannot be divided into definite periods as it was a slow, steady growth, and the earlier types continued to be built along with the newer. The most striking change was in the roofline.

In the middle of the seventeenth century the roof was extended to overhang the front and often the rear wall, and generally this projection was curved slightly to avoid the windows and prevent a top-heavy appearance. The protection of the clay and mud mortar from the rain is the reason generally advanced for this development. Since the change came about in the frame houses also, a desire to divert the rain from the foundations may also have been a factor. Examples of this in conjunction with the early steep roofs are to be seen in the Varleth—Sip house, built 1664 (plate 107), the Mill Island Schenck house, built 1676 (plate 13), the Demarest house, built 1678-80 (plate 82) and the De Clark—De Wint house, built 1700 (plate 48). When the curved overhanging eaves came into vogue, they were added in many instances to houses already standing. Numerous examples of this are found on Staten Island.

The pitch of the roofline was gradually lowered. Early examples of the more moderately sloped roof without overhanging eaves are the wing of the Schuyler—Colfax house, built 1695-1712 (plate 148), the rear wing of the Stynmets—Sip house, built 1694-99 (plate 149), the Stillwell—Britton house, built in 1680 and 1713 (plate 38), and the wing of the Ackerman—Brinkerhoff house, built about 1728 (plate 72). Except on Staten Island, the roofs of the later houses usually had a moderate slope with curved overhanging eaves. A few examples of the straight overhang are the Luyster house, built 1728-30 (plate 125), the Van Wickle—Suydam house, built about 1722 (plate 140), and the Hendrickson house, built 1730-50 (plate 124).

The gambrel roof came into use in the opening years of the eighteenth century. This is a roof with two slopes, the line being broken at an obtuse angle. It is found in Europe and was also used in early New England, but the Dutch combination of slopes and curved overhanging eaves is the most beautiful gambrel known. The early New England gambrel was broken near the middle, the top slope was at an angle of 30 degrees and the lower slope at 60 degrees, resulting in a steep roof with ample room in the attic story. This type was used by the Dutch, especially at first. However, the typical Dutch gambrel was broken near the ridgepole, the upper slope was short and fairly flat, at an angle of about 22 degrees, and the long lower slope extended at an angle of 45 degrees (these are averages). The curve or flare at the bottom of the roof is characteristic; sometimes there was a gentle curve and at other times there was a break with a third pitch. The result was a beautiful, comparatively low gambrel roof of good proportions and graceful sweep, which blended with the rural surroundings. There was less bedroom space under this type of gambrel but this was of no consequence to the Dutch who lived on the first floor and used the open garret for storage purposes and workshop. One of the most beautiful gambrels is one of the earliest erected, that on the house of Abraham Ackerman, built in 1704 (plate 71). In this roof the entire lower slope is one long, gentle curve. As a general rule the lower slope was straight, the curve commencing shortly above or at the line of the walls and extending beyond to form the overhanging eaves. The degree of steepness and length of the slopes also varied slightly: compare the Haring house, built about 1704 (plate 89), the Demarest house, built before 1720 (plate 83), the Brinkerhof house, built about 1735 (plate 79), the Vanderbilt house, probably built about 1730 (plate 67), the Mabie house dating from the third quarter of the eighteenth century (plate 54), the Durie house, believed to have been built during the Revolution (plate 86), the Nagel house, built about 1780 (plate 98), the Van Houten house, possibly not built until 1795-98 (plate 106), and the Terhuen house of unknown date (plate 100). The Housman house, built 1773 (plate 95), has one of the few gambrels without overhanging eaves. The Brickman—Ackerson house, built about 1747 (plate 78), is the only gambrel with straight overhanging eaves; it has not the suggestion of a curve. The well-known and so-called "Dutch Colonial" houses belong to this type, with the low gambrel roof and curved overhanging eaves.

The modest one and a half story farmhouses of the gable and gambrel roof types were prevalent throughout southern New Netherland; houses of two stories and more were common in New Amsterdam but not in the country nor in the villages. Only on the farms of the Raritan and Millstone River section were two-story houses popular. Their architecture may have been influenced by the style of the English houses in the vicinity of Trenton and Princeton, and in some instances it is possible that the wealth and prominence of the builders were factors in the erection of more pretentious houses. The resultant style is totally dissimilar to the Dutch houses in other regions and has less individuality of character and beauty of line. The Van Campen house on the Delaware River (plate 170) and the Dey house at Preakness (plate 144) are the only two-story houses in the balance of the territory covered by this volume.

Varied Building Materials

A notable feature of the Dutch style is the combination of various building materials—stone, shingle, clapboard, brick and iron were often used in one house to form a beautiful composition, with each element contributing its share and adding life and scale by its individual quality.

In the construction of the walls, the Dutch used stone, brick or wood. Stone was preferred where it was easily available: thus, although forests and sandstone quarries were both abundant in Bergen and Rockland Counties, the houses were all built of the native stone which was generally quarried on the property. In the early days the stones were used in the irregular shapes in which they were taken from the ground and were laid in rough courses. Free use was made of chips and rubble (plates 62, 68, 78 and 147). The binding was mud or clay, strengthened by straw or hogs' hair. Straw may still be picked out of the mortar in the old wing of the Packer house (plate 99), and likewise hogs' hair from the Brickman—Ackerson house (plate 78). This binding was used for even the later houses and is not so crude as it sounds, for the New Jersey clay is impervious to moisture although liable to erosion by strong rains. The stones were roughly faced at an early date but irregular shapes continued in use into the nineteenth century for the side and rear walls. The corners of the houses were usually laid with larger and better finished stones, accurately joined together. The custom arose of emphasizing the front wall of the house which was generally built of regular, well-dressed and carefully laid stones (plates 46, 85 and 149). Life and variety were added by the varied color and texture of the masonry (plates 79 and 105), by the use of occasional rows of stone chips (plates 72 and 94), and by the contrast of long and short blocks in the same course (plates 96 and 110) which later developed into a pattern (plates 65 and 95). These slight variations in the masonry have become more perceptible in the present day as the use of white lime mortar for repointing has replaced the old clay binding, which was about the color of the stones. These stone walls were built from one and a half to three feet thick. They were sometimes covered with a sand and lime wash and frequently whitewashed or painted.

On the wooded plains of Long Island and other places where stone was rare, wood was used for the construction of the walls. Frames of lathwork were built on sills and, when completed, all the neighboring farmers joined in raising them to their vertical position, making use of the occasion for a bit of merrymaking. The framework was filled with a clay and straw mortar and was then covered with shingles or, less frequently, with broad clapboarding. The shingles were hand hewn from the wood of the cypress tree; they were often 42 inches long and were laid with about 14 inches exposed.

Occasionally houses were built of brick. This material was used to a greater extent around Albany than in the southern part of New Netherland. The common tradition that the bricks were brought from Holland as ballast is improbable due to the prohibitive cost of such freight and the need for transportation of more important supplies in the limited number of ships. The tradition is readily explained by the terms Holland brick and English brick which were used as standards of measurement. As the De Clark—De Wint house, built 1700, was the home of the leader of the little community, in this instance the tradition may be correct that the house was built of brick brought from Holland. It was a Dutch custom to build the front walls of more carefully finished materials. A logical development was the use of brick for the front walls of the houses, as in the De Clark—De Wint house (plate

48), the Dey mansion, built in 1740 with brick fired on the property (plate 144), and the Ryerson house, built about 1738 (plate 160). In the territory covered by this volume, the only houses extant built completely of brick are found in Somerset County: the two story Van Vechten house, built in or shortly after 1715 (plate 139), the Lane—Brokaw farmhouse (plate 132), and the Frelinghuysen house, built about the time of the Revolution (plate 133).

The contrasting building materials, so characteristic of Dutch houses, are found in the smaller areas. When the houses were of brick, the gables were of the same material. Otherwise the gables were shingled or occasionally clapboarded. It is believed that this was the custom with the stone houses in order to minimize the amount of unprotected stone and clay mortar to be repaired on the ends. The appearance of these gable ends varied with the height to which the masonry was carried; generally it ended at the line of the eaves, occasionally a trifle higher (plate 58), sometimes it was carried up beyond the attic windows (plates 44 and 54), and in very rare instances the whole gable end was of stone (plate 155). The roofs were generally shingled, whether the house was of brick, stone or wood, and the overhanging eaves were sheathed beneath with a boxed wooden cornice, 5 to 6 inches deep at the outer edge. In the houses of the seventeenth and the first half of the eighteenth century, the courses of small-sized stones were continued directly over the door and window openings. Lintels came into use before the Revolution. These took many forms: occasionally they were long, oblong blocks of stone (plates 63 and 65), more generally they were long stones of trapezoidal form (plate 46), sometimes they were made of the same sized stones as the walls of the house but placed on end (plates 134 and 167). Brick was frequently used and was laid on end to form the same shape as the trapezoidal stone lintels (plate 52); large blocks of wood were often marked and sanded to represent either stone or brick. Occasionally the doors and windows had shallow arch heads, built of stone or of brick with the space beneath sometimes filled in with a wooden plank; this style was common in West Jersey (Hunterdon County plates) and is found as early as 1699 in the stone Vechte house at Gowanus. Handwrought iron pieces, occasionally seen on the outer walls (plates 105, 154 and 160), are generally the ends of tie rods which were extended through the building to strengthen the structure. They were occasionally shaped so as to record the date of erection (plate 131). The local blacksmiths wrought the various standardized forms of hinges, locks, cranes and cooking utensils found inside the house.

Size and Plan of Houses

The following contracts disclose many characteristics of Dutch houses throughout the seventeenth and eighteenth centuries. Ambrose London, a speculator, contracted with Michah Jure to build a house and to pay him 40 guilders for it, a skipple of corn at the time he began, 10 guilders at the raising, and the balance at the finishing; the house to be 22 feet by 12 feet and 8 feet high with a partition in the middle and a chimney, to lay both rooms with "joice," cover the roof and make up both gable ends with clapboards, also two windows and a door. London soon sold this house and made a contract for a second house with John Hawes, builder: the house to be upon sills of 26 feet by 16 feet and 10 feet high, two chimneys in the middle, two doors and two windows, clapboard only the roof and dobe the balance; price to be 110 guilders or one Dutch cow. These houses were erected at Gravesend shortly after it was founded in 1643.

There was a gradual growth in the size of the house, as the community became better settled and as the family grew in numbers and wealth. The early homes were generally one room houses, occasionally with a narrow bedroom, not much more than a closet, at the rear, such as the wing of the Swaert—Van Brunt house, built after 1657 (plate 20). This type was also used for the houses first built in a newly opened territory, for the homes of the young men throughout the eighteenth century, such as the central unit of the Blauvelt house, dated 1741 (plate 43), and the wing of the Ackerman house, built 1750-60 (plate 75). Another early type of house was twice the size and consisted of two adjoining main rooms each with its outside door; a beautiful example is the Demarest house, built 1678-80 (plate 82). These houses often had narrow bedrooms at the rear, which varied in size, and opened directly into the front main rooms, thus eliminating the need of a central hallway, as the Varleth—Sip house, built 1664 (plate 107), the Haring house, built 1704 (plate 89), and the Blauvelt house, built 1710 (plate 42). A hallway, running the depth of the building, became characteristic of the larger Dutch houses. Generally, the hall ran through the center of the house, with two rooms opening from it on either side, but sometimes it was placed at the end of the main house, with two rooms on one side and a one room wing on the other. A small central hall is occasionally found in as narrow a building as the Blauvelt house, built 1763 (plate 44); it gives access only to the main room on either side, for the narrow back bedrooms open directly into the front rooms.

As the family grew in wealth and numbers, additions were made to the house. Back bedrooms were often added by increasing the depth at the rear. The Wyckoff house in Flatlands and the Van Pelt house in New Utrecht were altered thus. Such a change only shows from the exterior if the house is of stone, as the Blauvelt—Hogencamp house (plate 47). A view of the Garret Schenck house in Beekman's *Early Settlers*, p. 12, emphasizes this type of addition even better as the newer part is of frame. Additions made at the side of the original unit were often similar in type

25

and size, as in the Blauvelt house (plate 43), the central unit of which is dated 1741, the west unit 1752, and the east unit somewhat later. Other examples are the Acker-man—Naugle and Schuyler—Colfax houses (plates 73 and 148). The size of the De Pew house (plate 49) was more than doubled as the addition included a central hallway; the position of the chimneys in the Dongan—Christopher and Van Duyn houses (plates 30 and 166) emphasizes the difference in size of otherwise similar additions. Occasionally a large house, consisting of two rooms on either side of a central hallway, was developed from the original one room unit. The thick walls of one room of the Ackerman—Brinkerhoff house (plate 71) and the absence of cellar under one room of the Van Buskirk house (plate 103) are signs of an integral change of this sort. The central portion of the Staats house (plates 6 and 136) was built at different times, the east rooms and hall erected in 1738-40 and the west rooms not until about 1800 in spite of the unity of the exterior. Occasionally the main unit of the house was the original structure and the wings were later; this was especially the case on Staten Island. The most usual form of addition was the erection of a larger and deeper house at the side and the conversion of the original unit into a kitchen wing with slave quarters. Upon the marriage of a son of the family, a wing was often erected on the other side for his menage or for the use of the grandparents. Such houses are found especially in Bergen County. Thus a beautifully balanced composition gradually grew from the needs of the family rather than from any pre-conceived ideas. It was not until the nineteenth century that wings were built at the same time as the main building, such as the Lott house, in which the main unit and west wing were erected in 1800 (plate 11). Few of the three unit houses are com-pletely pre-revolutionary in date, the newer wing and sometimes the main unit being erected after the war, as in the Westervelt houses (plates 109, 110 and vignette).

The small two room houses consisted of the kitchen, which was also the dining and living room, and the parlor, which was also the best bedroom. The larger houses had bedroom closets or narrow bedrooms at the rear. With the erection of an addi-tion, the living and bedroom quarters were transferred here and the original unit became the kitchen wing and slave quarters. Occasionally the kitchen was in a sepa-rate building, as in the Dey house at Preakness. Slaves slept in the cellar, as in the Van Wickle house (plate 140), in the garret over the kitchen or in separate outbuild-ings. Occasionally one wing was given over completely to the slaves, with a separate kitchen for them in the end room, a larder or workroom in the inner room, and sleeping quarters in the garret. Generally the second wing was set apart for a younger or older generation of the family. The attic floor of the main house was left unfin-ished and unpartitioned, and was used for storage purposes, for a workshop (the large weaving looms were kept here) and for children's sleeping quarters. The Haring house (plate 89) has an open garret to this day.

26

Architectural Details

The development of the characteristic rooflines was traced above, under types of houses. The gable roof was commonly used on the small and narrow houses and on the wings. It had a steep or moderate slope depending upon the period, and often had curved overhanging eaves. A frequent variation was the asymmetrical balance of a curved overhang in front with a long, straight slope in the rear extending almost to the ground, and covering a narrow bedroom (plates 66 and 97) or a lean-to (plates 16 and 143). Many of the deeper houses were likewise covered by a broad gable roof with overhanging eaves (plates 15, 53, 125 and 154). However, the majority of the larger houses were covered by a gambrel roof, the long, lower slope of which continued in a gentle and graceful curve to form a deep overhang. A combination of the two rooflines was frequent, especially in Bergen County where the main house with a gambrel roof was generally flanked by wings with gable roofs. The overhanging eaves are found only over the front and rear walls. The gable end was always flat, the roof never extended beyond it (plates 71 and 105); the projection of the roof beyond the gable end is a late nineteenth or twentieth century change (plates 94 and 96). The amount of overhang varied with the size of the house; in the large houses it was generally three or more feet deep. These projecting eaves hung in a beautiful and balanced suspension; no columns were necessary and none were added for their support until the influence of the Classic style was felt in the nineteenth century.*

The only relief of the plain exterior of the house was the Dutch "stoep" or front stoop, which was an important feature in olden days. It was a platform in front of the door, with railings and backless benches at either side, and was popular as a gathering place in the evenings. Very few of these stoops still exist. The Stoothoff—Baxter house has four stoops, one at the front and rear of each unit (plate 18 and vignette); the broad main stoop has lost in character since the removal of the benches. Many of these stoops were not much wider than the doorway, as in the Van Wagening house (plate 154). A late nineteenth century lithograph of the Vanderbeck house in Hackensack shows a long, narrow stoop under the overhanging eaves, extending in front of the door and two of the four windows; it was two steps above the ground and had railings and benches on either side (Black, p. 250).

The doorway was planned for utility rather than effect. The Dutch doors were double, the upper half opening separately. They were massively built and strengthened on the inside by a second set of boards, often narrow strips of wood laid obliquely side by side. The upper half of the door was generally panelled in the form of a cross; typical panelling is shown in plates 14, 31, 62, 147 and 160. The original door in the Cornelius Couwenhoven house (plate 121) was a very beautiful specimen; it was painted on the inside with an Amsterdam scene in the upper panel

27

---

* See addenda at end of introduction.

and spreading tulips in the lower panel. Bull's eyes of thick bottle glass were often set in inside doors and are occasionally found in outside doors (plates 83, 127 and 136). In the thick stone houses, the doors were often placed at the inner line of the walls, and the depth of the wall was cased with wooden planking (plate 155) which was often panelled (plates 46, 65 and 100). Simple, oblong fanlights extended over the doors. Judging by the existing examples, there were three types in common use: four or five panes of glass in a row side by side without any decoration (plates 98, 124 and 140), similarly laid panes with arched tops (plates 68 and 84), and panes cut in a sunrise design (plates 54 and 96). Often there was no fanlight at all (plates 43 and 44). The elaborate doorway, flanked by long, narrow windows and topped by oblong or arched fanlight with fancy moldings, belongs to the post-revolutionary and early nineteenth century periods. An early example is in the Lefferts house, probably built shortly after the Revolution (plate 10).

The houses, almost without exception, had cellars which were reached from the outside. Sloping hatches under one, and sometimes two, of the windows covered a short flight of stone steps down to the cellar. These hatches were generally at the front of the house but had no embellishment.

The size, shape and placing of the windows varied and are to a certain extent an indication of the age of the house. The early windows were small for better protection from cold, for economy of glass, and for greater safety from the Indians. Double hung windows were used extensively throughout the Colonial period, but the earlier style of casement window is found in some houses built before 1700. Until a comparatively late date, sashes of six panes were in common use. A type prevalent throughout the eighteenth century was the large upper sash of twelve panes (three rows of four panes each) combined with a lower sash of eight panes (two rows), as in the Demarest house (plate 83). In the Varleth—Sip house, built 1664, and the Demarest house, built 1678-80 (plates 107 and 82), the windows are large, both sashes being of twelve panes each, but these large windows did not become characteristic until the eighteenth century. A combination of several sizes was frequent; smaller and fewer windows were the rule for the rear bedrooms, regardless of the date of erection, and the windows of the wings were generally smaller than in the main house. In the early period the arrangement of the windows varied greatly (plates 27, 36, 38, and 100), but later under the influence of the balanced classic form they were symmetrically placed with reference to the doorway. The open garret was generally lighted at the gable ends with two or three windows near the floor level and a small window at the apex of the gable. In early days this was square but in the eighteenth century a semi-circular shape came into vogue and later two quarter lunars. The panes themselves were small in size due to the crude glass manufacture of the day. Many of the original sashes have since been superseded by modern sashes of two or three larger panes. The shutters on the windows were of solid wood, occasionally they were battened, more often they consisted of two or three simple panels resembling those on the nearby double door.

The chimneys of the Dutch were always built on the inside of the houses. The large, rectangular brick or stone areas, which are so characteristic of the first floor of many gable ends, are the backs of the deep fireplaces, and form the only portion of the chimney seen in the wall from the outside (plates 8 and 12). A chimney built on the exterior of the house (plates 63 and 121) is modern and such a type was never erected by the Dutch. Occasionally their chimneys were in the center of the house (plate 128), but were more generally placed at the gable ends (plate 24). There were fireplaces as a rule in both main rooms. In large houses, especially those of the late eighteenth century, one or both back bedrooms were often equipped with fireplaces (plates 7, 31, 141 and 142). Double chimneys are frequently found, the flues for the fireplaces in one main room and in the bedroom behind curving and joining in the garret into one chimney outlet at the roof. Sometimes the fireplaces were built diagonally across the corners of adjoining rooms so that one chimney fed both (plate 6). A bake oven was generally built at the back of the kitchen fireplace and protruded beyond the outer wall of the house (plates 129 and 138); most of these ovens have been demolished in recent years. In the cellars of the stone houses are stone arches which have the appearance of fireplaces, but which have no flues; they are structural foundations to support the weight of the gable wall and the chimney above, and incidentally have been useful as cupboards.

The Dutch had a praiseworthy custom of recording the date of erection on the house. The year, sometimes the month and day, and often the initials of the builder and his wife were cut into some large, flat stone. There was no general rule for the position of this stone; sometimes it was in the center of the wall (plate 71), under the eaves (plate 43) or in the foundations, at the corner (plate 159) or by the side of the door, and occasionally the door or window lintels were thus inscribed. In the De Clark—De Wint house, the date is worked across the front wall in large brick figures, the "0" of which can be seen by the window in the accompanying view (plate 48). These dates are not found so frequently as we could wish. Care must be used in accepting them, for the dated stone may have been originally in a demolished wing and later inserted in the main house, or it may apply only to a part of the present house.

There were no stairways in many of the early houses; the garret was reached from one of the rooms by a ladder and trap door. A ladder is still the means of communication in the humble Haner—Ryder house (plate 51) and was used until the end of the nineteenth century in the Ackerson house, which was erected about 1747 (plate 78). The average Dutch house of the colonial period had boxed stairs, which were built in the corner of the kitchen if there was no hallway. The stairway was enclosed, with a door at the bottom, to keep the heat generated by the fires in the living quarters of the first floor. Many of these narrow enclosed stairways still exist, for example in the houses photographed in plates 44, 83, 97, 119 and 164, which were built respectively in 1763, before 1720, before 1745, 1738-40 and about 1720-30. Some of the later houses had open stairways with contrasting treads and banisters (plate 4). The hallway generally ran the depth of the house from front to rear and had a double Dutch door at either end. Access to the cellar was only from the outside by means of a short flight of stone steps covered by sloping hatches.

There was little variation in the treatment of the interior (see plates 2, 3 and 4). The massive hand-hewn beams supporting the attic floor were left exposed; sometimes their edges were chamfered or molded. In the simpler houses the walls were plastered and the only decoration was a narrow chair rail. More generally the lower part of the wall, below the chair rail, was wainscotted. The fireplace wall of the main rooms was emphasized; usually the chimney was in the center, flanked by cupboards, and the whole wall was panelled. The early fireplaces were often large enough to contain seats on one side as well as space to walk to the oven door at the back, and their lintels were immense beams. The fireplaces were frequently framed with glazed blue Delftware tiles, which were imported from Holland and often depicted Biblical scenes. The chimney breast was panelled in as early an example as the Demarest house, built 1678-80 (plate 82), and we find a panelled wall in as primitive a house as the Titsworth house, built about 1710 (plate 168). The type of panelling depended on the period of erection but it was always very simple. Most of the early mantels had no shelf. The cupboards were of many sizes, running the gamut from full length closets to small apertures in the side of the chimney wall. In general, they had solid, panelled wooden doors, hung on various types of hand-wrought hinges. There were also corner cupboards with shell-shaped tops and butterfly shelves. We find very little carving until the Revolutionary period. About the time of the war, various forms of sunburst decoration came into favor. They were made with a gouge by itinerant carpenters to embellish the fireplace lintels and the trim over the doorways. This typical sunburst decoration can be seen over the front door of the Lefferts and Tallman houses (plates 10 and 64).

The seventeenth and eighteenth century farmhouses of the Dutch were austere and severely plain, depending completely for their effect on beauty of line and blending of varied building materials. Houses continued to be built in the same style until about 1835. The Revolution stimulated the interchange of ideas between the various colonies and broke down the isolation of the separate communities. The Dutch houses built in the post-revolutionary era and early nineteenth century were often influenced in the interior by the late Georgian and Classic styles. The exterior modifications were minor and took the form of decoration—an occasional dentil cornice, architectural trim around the windows, columns under the overhanging eaves,* lunar attic windows in the gables, and the front doorway emphasized and flanked by long narrow windows, elaborate fanlight, moldings and carved wood trim.

The main nineteenth century changes in the houses were brought about by a desire for greater comfort, especially for more commodious sleeping quarters. The narrow back bedrooms, which were often not larger than closets, were not considered adequate. Improvement was made in two ways, by alteration or by structural addition. In those houses and wings which were covered by a gable roof, the space in the attic was often inadequate for bedrooms, so the roof was raised and an additional half story erected. This was generally of frame and is therefore especially noticeable in the stone buildings, such as the Van Buskirk and Parlaman houses (plates 103 and 165) and the wings of the Packer and Westervelt houses (plates 99 and 109). This half story was lighted by low windows near the floor level, which from their position acquired the name of "lie-on-your-stomach windows"; those on the wing of the Packer house are the usual type (plate 99). There was more garret space under the gambrel roof, so no extensive alteration was required in these houses. Partitions were built from time to time under the sloping roof when there was need for more bedrooms. In the Westervelt house (plate 110) there still exists, under the gambrel slope, a small, windowless bed closet which was considered adequate since fresh air was not deemed necessary in the nineteenth century. The different ceiling levels of the bedrooms in the Ackerman house (plate 71) are evidence that the garret was not improved all at one time. The attic of the Ryerson house (plate 160) was not modernized until the twentieth century. Most of the garrets have been improved in the last hundred years and dormers added to give air and light to the bedrooms; one of the few attics still in its original condition is the open garret of the Haring house (plate 89). The sloping dormer was probably added in some instances at an early date (plates 32 and 34). It continues the line of the upper slope of gambrel roofs (plate 52) and merges with gable roofs. Thus this early type of dormer blends well with the lines of the house and does not form such a complete break and unpleasant interruption as the later dormer and gable windows.

Other nineteenth century changes center about the porch. The most popular type was the continuation of the roof overhang one or two more feet and the addition of columns of various forms for its support;* several more or less successful examples

---

* See addenda at end of introduction.

of this are to be seen in plates, 10, 13, 21, 75, 81, 91, 92, 99, 100 and 101. Small roofed platforms in front of the door were common, some of them similar to roofed examples of the early stoops. The most prevalent of these had a small, square single pitch roof, with a moderate slope away from the house, as in plates 26, 31, 109, and 127, the first two being at the rear of the house and the latter two at the front. A porch running the length of the house was added as a rule to houses of two stories; an early example of this is the Van Buskirk house (plate 103), in which the early stone flagging has not been replaced by wood flooring.

Outbuildings

The farms had many outbuildings, of which the barn, smokehouse and corn crib were the most important. The smokehouse was built like a small one room house. One of the few still existing is photographed in plate 114. It is of stone, covered by a gable roof, and the end is completely filled by a mammoth chimney.

The barn was a very large building, several times the size of the house. Many of them stood until a few years ago along the country roads. A typical example is reproduced in Miss Reynolds' work (plate 9). The ridgepole is very high, so that the roof covers a large area although it has a steep pitch; the side walls are low. Most of the barns were of frame. A barn of this type existed in perfect condition on the Zabriskie—Board property (see plate 112) until it was remodelled for a clubhouse in 1933. A stone barn with a wide gambrel roof is shown in plate 61. Sketches of barns which stood until recently on the Tallman properties (see plates 64 and 65) show large frame structures, each with a very high door at the center of the gable end and smaller doors nearer the eaves; the barns were flanked on either side by hovels, open front buildings of massive oak timbers. The Dutch barn had many uses. Grain and hay were stored in the loft, and horses and cows had their quarters on either side under the eaves. The barns stood a short distance behind or at the side of the houses.

Kitchens were sometimes placed in separate buildings (see plates 75 and 144).

The well with its long sweep was located at the front of the house, generally a little to one side. Once a characteristic feature, it has almost completely disappeared. Two examples are photographed in plates 89 and 145.

A Contemporary Description

Peter Kalm, the Swedish naturalist, travelled through the American Colonies in 1748 and 1749. In his account of his journey from Trenton to New Brunswick, he recorded his impression of the barns of the locality and gave a description of the village of New Brunswick. The houses and barns of other regions were probably very similar except in the more abundant use of stone.

"... The barns had a peculiar kind of construction hereabouts, which I will give a concise description of. The whole building was very great, so as almost to equal a small church; the roof was pretty high, covered with wooden shingles, declining on both sides, but not steep: the walls which support it were not much higher than a full-grown man; but on the other hand the breadth of the building was the more considerable: in the middle was the threshing floor, and above it, or in the loft or garret, they put the corn which was not yet threshed, the straw, or anything else, according to season: on one side were stables for the horses, and on the other for the cows, and the small cattle had likewise their particular stables or styes; on both ends of the buildings were great gates, so that one could come in with a cart and horses through one of them and go out at the other: here was therefore under one roof the threshing floor, the barn, the stables, the hay loft, the coach house, etc. This kind of building is chiefly made use of by the Dutch and Germans; for it is to be observed that the country between Trenton and New York is inhabited by few Englishmen, but, instead of them, by Germans or Dutch, the latter of which especially are numerous."

"... About noon we arrived at New Brunswick, a pretty little town in the province of New Jersey in a valley on the west side of the river Rareton; ... (it had four churches which were of stone or of wood) ... Some of the other houses were built of bricks, but most of them are made either wholly of wood or of bricks and wood; the wooden houses are not made of strong timber but merely of boards or planks, which are within joined by laths: such houses as consist of both wood and bricks have only the wall towards the street of bricks, all the other sides being merely of planks. ... The houses were covered with shingles; before each door there was an elevation, to which you ascend by some steps from the street; it resembled a small balcony, and had some benches on both sides on which the people sat in the evenings, in order to enjoy the fresh air, and have the pleasure of viewing those who passed by. The town has only one street lengthways, and at its northern extremity there is a street across; both of these are of considerable length. The river Rareton passes hard by the town and it is deep enough for great yachts to come up. ... One of the streets is almost entirely inhabited by Dutchmen who came hither from Albany, and for that reason they call it Albany Street. These Dutch only keep company among themselves, and seldom or ever go amongst the other inhabitants, living as it were quite separate from them. New Brunswick belongs to New Jersey; however, the greatest part, or rather all its trade is to New York, which is about forty English miles distant. ... Several small yachts are every day going backwards and forwards between these two towns. ..." *

33

---

* See addenda at end of introduction for contemporary description of another region.

Comparison between Counties

One of the most important factors in the development of the Dutch style of houses was that America was a new, unsettled and undeveloped country. Difficulties of travel formed an efficient barrier against any large degree of intercourse with New England, the South and even Pennsylvania. The Dutch and those whom fortune cast with them lived in an isolated manner, uninfluenced by the styles and thoughts of the other colonies, and they developed an individual architecture, not only unlike that of their far neighbors but also unlike that of their forebears. The opening of a new country, the cold of winter and heat of summer, the difficulty of obtaining supplies from the Mother country and the need of making most of their own necessities—all these natural hardships and conditions inherent in an undeveloped country affected alike the rich and poor, the talented and obscure, with the result that a homogeneous architecture was created by the Dutch. These same conditions separated the various settlements of the Dutch and acted on them in different degrees. The young men opened up new territories and only maintained casual connections with their old homes, forming new and self-sufficient communities; they married their neighbors' daughters and gradually there grew up a new tradition based on the solidarity of family and pioneer life in their locality. Thus the houses in each community were built alike, varying mainly in size and finish, and differing from the houses in other sections, even though fundamentally they were based on the same architectural style and conditions of living.

Most of the houses on Long Island were built of wood because the country lacked the abundant sandstone quarries of northeastern New Jersey and had a plentiful supply of timber. They could be built with less heavy labor than those of stone but were less durable. Consequently on Long Island when new houses were built, the old ones were often discarded instead of being used as kitchen and slave wing. In Bergen County the homes represent the building activity and social life of several generations, but this is rarely the case on Long Island. A different type of roof was popular in the two sections. The gambrel roof never took a deep hold on the imaginations of the inhabitants, as in northeastern New Jersey. The gable roof remained in great favor; it was used for the deep houses with rear bedrooms, and in the nineteenth century when bedrooms were desired upstairs, the additional space was acquired by building the ridgepole at a greater height. The overhanging eaves were a characteristic feature but the curve of the roofline was very moderate.

The Staten Island (Richmond County) houses were generally long and narrow, only one room in depth. Their apparent narrowness, when contrasted with houses of other sections, is increased by the absence of overhanging eaves. Most of them were built of irregular stones gathered in the fields rather than of quarried stone and therefore little attempt was made to lay the walls in courses. The steep gable roof was exceedingly popular and the windows were small and few in number. Unlike the houses elsewhere, the large section was generally the original unit.

The Rockland County houses, with few exceptions, were built of the local sandstone, cut and drawn from the nearby quarries. More than half belong to the small and unpretentious type prevalent on Staten Island, but they were built at a much later date and therefore the stones of the front walls were cut in more regular shapes, the houses were deeper, generally having rear bed closets, and there were more and larger windows. About two-thirds of the houses are covered by gable roofs, many with curved overhanging eaves in front. Three of the deep houses have gable roofs in the manner popular on Long Island but the slope is much steeper. The other third of the houses in Rockland County are large and deep, and covered by gambrel roofs, generally with a curving overhang; they belong to the Bergen County type. In fact, although Rockland County was known until the nineteenth century as Orange County under the Mountains, it was thoroughly akin to Bergen County in its families and homes.

In Bergen County the roof with curved overhanging eaves was developed to its greatest perfection and used on most of the houses, whether the roofs were of the gable or gambrel type. The gambrel roof was very prevalent and was almost always employed for the large, deep houses. In Bergen County we find the greatest number of balanced compositions: some of the main gambrel roofed houses were flanked on one side by an earlier wing with gable roof and on the other side by a similar wing of later date. The frequent addition to the wings of half stories of frame in the early nineteenth century emphasizes the composition. The houses built in the century before the Revolution were all of sandstone blocks from the local quarries, and varied in finish and size with the wealth and prominence of the builders.

The territory adjoining Bergen County on the west belonged to different civil divisions at various times; originally a part of Essex County, more than half of it was a part of Bergen County in the eighteenth century, and in the nineteenth Passaic County was formed from both divisions. Passaic County (the lower half) and the adjoining reaches at the upper end of the present Essex County were settled by the Dutch, most of whom came from Bergen. It is therefore to be expected that the styles of these counties should be similar. Actually no homogeneous architecture was developed in this territory. Almost every house still standing has its individual character, although fundamentally it belongs to the style developed by the Dutch throughout the country; characteristics prevalent in Bergen, Rockland, Kings and Richmond Counties are seen in different houses; even the arched window tops of

West Jersey are found in two of the dwellings. One of the houses is a two story mansion situated in the rolling country, miles from any village; it is dissimilar to the Dutch farmhouses in most of its aspects, although the varied use of building materials is characteristic. The sizes, type of roofs and grouping of units differ with each building. All were built of the local stone, but their treatment varied greatly and included two with front walls of brick. The pre-revolutionary units, whether they are narrow or of great depth, are covered by gable roofs, and in the sections which belonged at one time to Bergen County the curved overhanging eaves are more prevalent.

The Dutch settlements in Morris County were grouped in the northeastern part adjoining Passaic and Essex Counties. The houses resemble the simple type popular especially in Rockland County. They are small, narrow buildings covered by moderately steep gable roofs with or without overhanging eaves. The stone prevalent in this locality varies considerably in color and texture from the red sandstones of the eastern counties, and the difference in quality may be the cause for the larger sizes in which it was generally cut. Interesting variety is achieved in the buildings by the colors of the stones and the use of large blocks surrounded by stone chips.

In Monmouth County the Dutch located in the rolling valleys around Holmdel. The shingled houses built here bear great resemblance to their former homes on Long Island. They are covered by gable roofs, usually with steep slopes and with or without overhanging eaves. The steepness and straightness of the roofs tend to emphasize their length and make them the predominant feature.

Middlesex County was settled mainly by the English, but the Dutch built homes in the southern and western portions. Their one and a half story farmhouses, similar to those in the adjoining Somerset County, are clapboarded or shingled and covered by moderately steep gable roofs with no overhanging eaves. The Georgian style influenced two of the houses which are large two story buildings, totally dissimilar to those in Somerset County.

Along the Raritan and Millstone Rivers of Somerset County, many of the houses erected in the mid-eighteenth century are totally unlike the Dutch homes in the country elsewhere. They are large two story houses located on farms of at least several hundred acres. They are built of brick, of clapboards or shingles, and differ in size and dimensions. Two of them were the homes of prominent men, who dignified their estates by naming them, and others were the homes of large land-owning farmers. Each of these houses has its individual character, of which only an occasional feature has its prototype in the more humble farmhouses of the Dutch. Most of the one and a half story farmhouses in Somerset County are reminiscent of the houses on Long Island; they are covered with clapboards or shingles and have gable roofs of varying degrees of steepness; only two have overhanging eaves and these have the very straight slope occasionally seen in Monmouth County. A few houses are covered with gambrel roofs of English proportions. One house is unusual in that it is built completely of brick and has a gable roof of very moderate pitch. Two houses have the window arches characteristic of West Jersey and two others have the long, round-edged shingles very occasionally seen elsewhere.

The settlers of Hunterdon County in West Jersey belonged to several different nationalities, the Dutch locating near Somerset County. The extant houses are built of the local stone, cut in irregular blocks. The rooflines varied; two gambrel roofs have the deep, curved overhanging eaves so characteristic of Bergen County, but the upper slopes are long, similar to those in Somerset County. The most characteristic and interesting feature of the West Jersey houses is the arch head over the doors and windows. It is a shallow arch of bricks or stones set on end, and sometimes has a shaped wooden plank in the space between the arch and the frame. This feature is also occasionally seen in other sections of the country.

Sussex County in West Jersey formerly stretched along the Delaware River to the Water Gap and included the present Warren County. The Dutch settled in the Minisink regions. The average building seems to have been a long, narrow one of limestone blocks, covered by a gable roof of varying degrees of steepness, and without overhanging eaves. Each of the houses that remains has an individual character, the most unusual being a small, square house with a steep roof. There is a two story mansion built of limestone, which does not resemble the few other two story houses. It has arched window tops on the first floor and a roof of unusual steepness for this type.

Possibilities in Modernization of Old Houses

The majority of the pre-revolutionary Dutch houses existing to this day are still used as farmhouses. Many of them have been allowed to fall into decay and only a few have been improved and reconditioned according to modern standards. The alterations made in the Victorian age destroyed much of the beauty of the old houses. The old wooden mantels and the twelve pane window sashes were torn out, large gables and porches added, and other unfortunate changes made. The houses which have not been thus altered offer the greatest possibilities of restoration to the original style and conversion into modern residences. The solid construction and beautiful lines of the old houses, their interesting panelling and woodwork, are sound foundations for intelligent alterations, complying with present-day standards of comfort and taste. The associations, age and history of the houses cannot help but enhance their value for cultured owners.

The maximum charm and quaintness are achieved through a strict restoration, with the preservation of the original layout. However, as a large living room is the modern desideratum and as the rooms in Dutch houses are comparatively small, two of them may be thrown together. The partition is generally torn out between the old best room and the narrow bedroom behind it, making a large room extending the depth of the house, with windows on both ends and sometimes on the long side. The location of the chimney may be an objection. If there are two fireplaces they will be on the side of the room. Generally there is only one, which will then be off center on the long wall. Such a living room may seem unbalanced to many unless another center of interest is cleverly created at the other end. Where the hall running through the center of the house is not considered a necessary feature, a large living room can be made successfully by throwing the two main rooms into one, thus creating a living room extending the width of the main house, with windows the length of the long wall and fireplaces on either end. This has been done very well in the Van Wickle—Suydam house (plates 2 and 140). The large number of windows and two fireplaces give a feeling of space, a wealth of light, and great warmth and comfort. The fireplace wall of the best room is often completely panelled as in this case, and usually has wall or corner cupboards. The second main room is generally treated in a simpler manner; originally it may have been the combined kitchen and living room, and a mantel piece added when the kitchen was moved into a wing, or it may always have been a living room. The different treatment gives a pleasing variety to the ends of the new large, living room. In the Van Wickle—Suydam house, one fireplace wall has a panelled chimney breast, a simple mantel with no shelf, and on either side cupboards of different sizes with panelled doors (plate 2); the wall on the opposite end of the long room has a wide, low fireplace, a mantel piece of simple proportions with a high lintel and a narrow shelf, a plastered chimney breast, on one side a set of bookshelves with cupboards below, and on the other side a door into the dining and kitchen wing (see vignette).

Structural change is seldom necessary in the hallway (plate 4). The stairway is generally narrow and steep, especially when enclosed, but its alteration destroys more in individuality than it achieves in comfort. The hall is often dark, as there is frequently no fanlight over the back door and light from the fanlight over the front door is obscured by the deep overhanging eaves or porch. In restorations the upper halves of the double Dutch doors have been treated like the old windows, with rows of four small glass panes (plates 2, 4, and 73), thus affording the desired light. Many of the halls are not so wide and therefore not so important a feature as the one photographed here, and the enclosed stairways in vogue detract from their size and decorative quality. In these cases, an attractive and successful treatment is one which has been used in the Van Wickle—Suydam house. The rear has been changed to the front of the house, the former front portion of the hall has been included in the new, large living room, leaving the former rear portion as an entrance hall with the box stairs going up one side. In small houses which have no hallway, the rear of the house can be changed to the front and an entrance made directly into one of the former narrow bedrooms, which would be converted into a small reception room. In very narrow houses with neither hallway nor back bedrooms, the front door must perforce lead directly into the living room, unless a structural addition is made or the wing is converted into an entrance unit.

The rooms on the first floor can be easily adapted to the varying needs of the modern owner. In the Ackerman house, one of the back bedrooms has been successfully converted into a den or small library (plate 3). Rows of bookshelves cover one long wall above and on either side of the window, and panelled cupboards have been placed below them. The window sill has been deepened to the line of the cupboards and conceals a radiator below. This treatment gives the wall a uniform surface in a useful and interesting manner. The size of the small room does not appear to be greatly diminished by an integral change of this sort.

Most of the garrets of the Dutch houses are already divided into bedrooms. These may be of pleasant proportions, or the existing partitions may have to be knocked out in order to form attractive bedrooms with the closets and bathrooms required by modern standards. Frequently dormers are necessary. The sloping form (plates 52, 98 and 148) gives as much light and air as other types and blends considerably better with the lines of the roof.

Overhead beams, old windows, double doors, wooden mantels, glazed fireplace tiles, cupboards, panelling, chair rails and wainscotting are all characteristic features of the old Dutch houses. The hand-hewn beams supporting the second floor should be left exposed as they add considerably to the character of the house. Some are very massive, some show the axe marks and others have chamfered or molded edges (plates 2, 3, and 4). In the nineteenth century these beams were often covered with a plaster ceiling, the removal of which will add considerable height as well as charm. Occasionally large vertical beams in the side wall may be uncovered to advantage (plate 2). If the many-paned windows and wooden mantels have been taken away, these should be replaced if possible with old examples or reproductions. The old mantels have good proportions and blend better with the interior than the marble mantels of the Victorian era. The old many-paned windows have quaintness and charm and increase the coziness of the interior by excluding the outside world more completely than the modern ones. In these old windows, the large upper sash was immovable and the lower sash was raised and fastened with pegs. Greater ventilation can be easily obtained by placing these sashes on hinges so that they open upward and outward. In many houses the interior has not been altered and only renovation is needed.

The treatment of the interior of the rooms depends largely on the tastes of the owner. The unpanelled walls may be left plastered (plate 2) or covered above the chair rail with old-fashioned wallpaper (plates 3 and 4). The beams may be stained, or painted to match the balance of the woodwork. The white painted panelling and the various browns of the beams and furniture (plate 2) make a pleasing room that does not seem lacking in color. Certain bright hues are characteristic of the colonial period. Occasionally a more definite color scheme may be worked out, thus in the library (plate 3) the woodwork is painted the yellow of sunshine, the ends of the bookshelves are picked out in red and the frames of the old prints and maps hanging on the wall are red or black. All informal styles of furniture will blend well with the old backgrounds. A few large pieces are good, like the upholstered wing chair by the fireplace (plate 2), and the high secretary desk (just off the photograph) which extends almost to the ceiling and balances the height of the windows on the opposite side of the room. Windsor and ladder back chairs are placed to advantage in front of panelled walls as none of the panelling is lost behind them. In the small rooms special care should be taken to choose small scale furnishings.

The exterior of the houses should be restored as much as possible to the original lines in order to preserve their charming individuality. Nineteenth century roofs extending beyond the gable end and supported by heavy brackets can be eliminated easily and the characteristic flat gable end restored. The requisite dormers should be of a simple type, carefully designed and placed so as not to break the roofline more than necessary. The sloping form of dormers blends best with the roof (plates 52, 98 and 148). Overhanging eaves, which in some cases have been cut off, should be replaced as the lines are so graceful. These eaves can be made over five feet deep and simple columns added for their support to form a porch in the late eighteenth century style (plate 75). However, if a porch is not deemed necessary, the beautiful lines of the overhanging eaves show to best advantage when left in balanced suspension, as originally planned. The ground beneath the eaves was often paved with stone flagging; a modern version of this is the stone terrace (plate 140), which creates an outdoor living room and links the house with the garden. The old Dutch stoop should not be allowed to fall into oblivion. Successful adaptations have been achieved in recent restorations: in one case (plate 54) two open slat-backed benches stand on either side of the platform, thus combining the backless bench and railings of the olden days; in another case (plate 158) the doorway is flanked by two very high, solid-backed benches, which are of the so-called Colonial type although actually of modern design. A more typical Dutch stoop has been covered with a modern trellis (plate 136); the small hood over another doorway (plate 164) has beautiful proportions.

Some judicious planting about the foundations, trees and a rolling lawn (plates 75, 107, 155, 117, 164 and 141) accomplish to a great extent the change from Dutch farmhouse to modern residence as far as the outward aspect is concerned.

Preservation of the Houses

The Dutch in America created an individual and charming architecture which should be preserved. In villages and in the open country many of the houses can be converted easily into modern residences with attractive surroundings. Where growing land values, new roads or reservoirs doom these old houses to extinction, they can be preserved only if the public interest is aroused. Unfortunately there is at present little hope unless the house has a historic past or is intimately connected with the growth of a city. In this case associations are formed for its upkeep and if necessary it is moved to another site. The patriotic societies have done good work along this line and have converted some of the old houses into museums or chapter houses. However, there is little general interest in the Dutch houses from the architectural standpoint, although they form the only indigenous architecture prior to the modern skyscraper. The Brooklyn Institute of Arts and Sciences is a pioneer in this respect; in its section devoted to American architecture are to be found several houses from various parts of the country brought together for comparison, and among them is the Schenck house formerly at Canarsie on Long Island. It is to be hoped that this example will be followed in various communities.

PLATE 2

*Van Wickle—Suydam House
Interior*

Symen Van Wickle built his house along the Raritan River about 1722. The exterior is reproduced in plate 140. The hallway and two main rooms have been recently thrown together to form one large living room with a fireplace at each end, extending the length of the house. This view shows that part of the living room which was originally the best room and the back door which was formerly the front door. The other end of the large room is shown in the vignette.

PLATE 3

House of Abram Ackerman
Interior

The exterior view of the house of Abram Ackerman at Saddle River can be seen in plate 75. The two interiors reproduced here are in that part of the house which, although pre-revolutionary in style, was not built until 1781. This view shows one of the narrow back bedrooms on the main floor which has been recently converted into a small library.

PLATE 4

House of Abram Ackerman
Interior

This is another interior of the house of Abram Ackerman at Saddle River. It was customary in Dutch houses for the hallway to run the depth of the house. This view, taken from the front door, shows the hall and its present treatment. No architectural changes have been made.

Mid-Nineteenth
Century

1925

1932

PLATE 5

House of Barent and John Nagel at Closter
Stone Unit Built by Barent Before 1745 for One of His Children

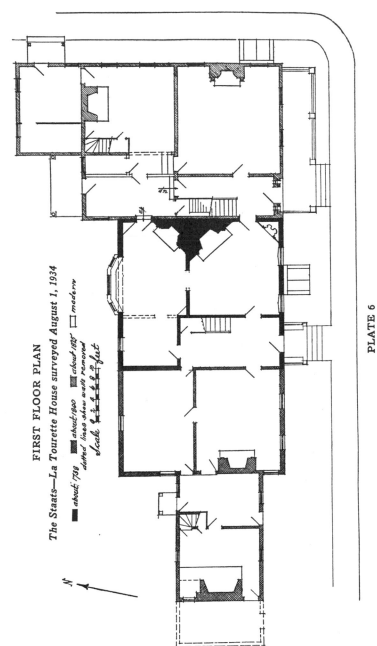

FIRST FLOOR PLAN

The Staats—La Tourette House surveyed August 1, 1934

PLATE 6

HOUSE OF HENDRICK AND ABRAHAM STAATS

The exterior view of the central portion is reproduced in plate 136 and the house as a whole in the Somerset Co. vignette

KINGS AND QUEENS COUNTIES

REAR OF STOOTHOFF—BAXTER—
KOUWENHOVEN HOUSE

KINGS AND QUEENS COUNTIES

Kings County

THE southwestern end of Long Island, which extends some distance south of Manhattan, became Kings County when counties were organized in 1683 and is now co-terminous with the Borough of Brooklyn in Greater New York. Except in the vicinity of the ridge of hills, where the land was stony, the settlers found good farming lands and in the southeastern part large grass plains devoid of forests. The Dutch commenced to come here shortly after they had formed the first permanent settlements at New Amsterdam and Beverwyck (Albany). The first purchases of land in Kings County were made by the individual settlers directly from the Indians and the lands confirmed to them by the Dutch authorities. However, in 1638 and 1639 the Dutch West India Company acquired from the Indians the title to nearly all land in Kings and Queens Counties.

One English and five Dutch towns were organized while the country was still a part of New Netherland. Attracted by the large open flats or plains, scattered settlements are believed to have been made as early as 1624 at New Amersfoort or Flatlands. This town is in the southeastern part of the county fronting on Jamaica Bay. An Indian path led from Fulton Ferry to Bergen Island in Jamaica Bay along the old line of Flatbush Avenue and Mill Lane. The palisaded village of Flatlands was erected at Flatbush Avenue and the King's Highway. A Dutch Church was organized in 1654 and a house of worship erected in 1663. A mill was started on Mill Island in 1664-66. The maize lands at the north end of the town on Canarsie Neck were not cultivated until a later date. The next center-of settlement was in the town of Breukelen along the East River, where plantations were granted at Gowanus in 1636 and at the Wallabocht in 1637. A public ferry connecting the Island with New Amsterdam was soon established by Cornelius Hooglandt, and the group of houses around the slip came to be known as The Ferry. In the interior along Fulton Avenue the village of Breukelen was settled in 1645 and another hamlet grew up in the Clove at Bedford. A Dutch Church was organized in 1660. No pre-revolutionary houses remain in these densely populated sections. The town of Midwout or Flatbush is believed to have had scattered settlements as early as 1634-36, although no patent to the town was issued until 1651. Its sloping wooded plains are very fertile and covered the central part of Kings County, separated from Breukelen by the ridge of hills. Individual settlers located first in the south part of the town along the Indian path, now Flatbush Avenue. The center of the village was at the intersection of Church Street. A Dutch Church was organized and built in 1654. As late as 1697 the Labadist travellers remarked that the road from Flatbush over the hill to Breukelen was only a trail through a dense forest and was very stony. Consequently the best way to New Amsterdam was by boat from Gravesend Bay or by the shore road via Flatlands, New Utrecht and Gowanus. Both Flatbush and Flatlands had been purchased from the Canarsie Indians. Another tribe, the Rockaways, claimed the ownership of part of Flatbush; the town was repurchased from them in 1670 and its eastern boundary established. The settlement made here shortly afterwards was known as Oostwoud (East Woods) or the New Lots of Flatbush; it was later organized as the independent town of New Lots, now East New York. The land along the Narrows and part of Gravesend Bay was known as the Nyack tract. It may have been settled as early as 1643. In 1652 Cornelius Van Werckhoven, schepen of Utrecht in Holland and member of the Dutch West India Company, obtained a grant from the government and repurchased the Nyack tract from the Indians. He intended to plant a patroonship here but died in 1655-56. Jacques Cortelyou, the learned tutor to his children and manager of his estates, later obtained a large part of the tract for the debts he had paid in behalf of his employer. In 1657 he laid out the village of New Utrecht, consisting of twenty village plots in a square surrounded by the same number of 50-acre farms. The village was guarded by palisades and a blockhouse. A disastrous fire in 1675 destroyed most of the settlement. A Dutch Church was organized in 1677. Wood-town or Bushwick was the last town formed in Kings County. Scattered plantations were cleared in 1641-50 by a few Swedes and Normans along the East River south of Newtown Creek. No attempt at an organized settlement was made until 1660 when the Indian troubles caused the governor to order the farmers to concentrate. A village was erected on the Wallaboght in the present Williamsburg district. The village of Bushwick was organized on Bushwick Avenue above Grand Street, mainly for the French settlers in the vicinity. Another center developed at the Crossroads, where Bushwick Avenue intersected the Road from the Ferry to Newtown (Flushing Avenue). The only English settlement was made at Gravesend, on the sandy but productive soil of the extreme southern part of the county. A patent was obtained for these lands in 1643 by Lady Moody who immediately started an English colony for the free enjoyment of religion. It was almost wiped out by the Indians in the first year of its existence. It was laid out in accordance with a definite plan, consisting of a 16-acre village square of forty house plots, fortified by palisades, and surrounded radially by forty planters' farms.

The five Dutch towns in Kings County were organized into a district in 1661, to which was assigned a schout fiscal and secretary responsible to the general government, and to whom the village schepens were subordinate. The English town of Gravesend was allowed greater independence. After the capture of New Netherland in 1664 by the English, the province of New York became the personal property of the Duke of York, later James II. At the Convention of town delegates gathered in 1665 at Hempstead by order of Gov. Nicolls, the boundaries of the towns were settled, new patents required and a code of laws promulgated (known as the Duke's Laws); Staten Island and the west end of Long Island were organized into the West Riding of Yorkshire. Under the laws thus established the Court of Assize, consisting of the governor and his appointees, was the unlimited head of the government. Upon the arrival of Gov. Andros in 1683, the first Colonial Assembly was called and a bill of rights adopted, courts of justice established and many of the Duke's Laws amended, the ridings were abolished and counties organized. In 1691, after the Leisler Rebellion, the Colonial government was reorganized and no further change of any importance took place until the Revolution; the government consisted of the governor, who could dissolve the assembly and negate its acts and who appointed all officers and disbursed the public funds and lands, the council appointed by the king, and the assembly of delegates chosen by the freeholders; their rule was subject to revision by the king. Colonial Long Island was the richest part of the Province of New York; even in 1787 more than one-fifth of the tax was levied here.

The Dutch at the time of the Revolution were opposed as ever to the encroachments of the crown but were averse to rebellion and wished to remain neutral; due to circumstances on Long Island many were or pretended to be Loyalists. After the Battle of Long Island in 1776, the Island was occupied by the British. Howe proclaimed security of person and property for those who remained peacefully on their farms. Nevertheless Long Island was under rigorous military rule, soldiers and American prisoners on parole were billetted on the inhabitants, cattle and wood were sequestered for the use of the British, and robbery by marauding gangs was unavoidable.

The first houses of the Dutch settlers on Long Island were of the rudest kind, frames of saplings covered with bark or mere excavations in the hillsides lined with bark and thatched with reeds. The earliest sawmills furnished timbers for the first permanent houses which were small, one story buildings with thatched roofs, stone fireplaces and ovens, and chimneys of boards plastered inside with mortar or mud. Houses built a little later were modelled after those in the fatherland, of good size, substantial and comfortable: the stone Vechte house, built at Gowanus in 1699, was a good example of this type. The later Dutch dwellings on Long Island, almost without exception, consisted of frames of lathwork filled with clay and straw mortar and sheathed with clapboarding and shingles, as there was very little stone available. The gable roof was extremely popular even for the large houses. Deep

53

overhanging eaves with a slight curve were characteristic, especially at the front of the house. Additions were generally built along the same lines as the original unit but on a larger scale.

In this section on King's County no attempt has been made to include houses which disappeared some time ago, partly because the limited space precludes accounts of all the houses in this thickly settled part of the country, and partly because the descriptions and information available are already in print. Many have been reproduced in *Historic Homesteads of Kings County*, by Charles A. Ditmas, *Keskachauge*, by Frederick Van Wyck, and *Rambles About Historic Brooklyn* (printed 1916 for the Brooklyn Trust Company). The survey of Kings County for this volume was made in 1925. Many of the houses photographed at that time have since been torn down. The text is based largely on the early land records, which have been assembled with great care by Dr. Frank L. Van Cleef, to whom the author is very indebted.

Queens County

The land in Queens County was a part of New Netherland although mainly settled by Englishmen from New England. The greater part of the territory is west of Kings County but a small section, later organized into the township of Newtown, borders on the East River north of Kings County from which it is separated by Newtown Creek (in early days known as Mespat or English Kills). In 1642 Rev. Francis Doughty and his associates were granted the Mespat Patent for over 13,000 acres, at which date there were only three settlers near the creek. A settlement was organized immediately along Mespat Kill but was wiped out the following year in the Indian war. It rose slowly from the ashes. Trouble was created by Doughty who considered himself the patroon; the rights of the other patentees were upheld and he departed for Flushing. Vlissingen or Flushing was founded in 1645 by the Dutch, the only Dutch town in Queens County; it soon acquired a large English population. Hempstead had been founded further east in 1643; Rusdorp or Jamaica was settled in 1655. In 1652 an English colony from New England located at Middleburg, midway between the English Kills and Flushing; this embraced the present Elmhurst, Corona, Woodside and Winfield, and was called the town of Hastings in 1662. The lands to the northeast along the bays of the East River were settled by Dutch farmers; they never organized a separate community but remained dependent on Flatbush or New Amsterdam for civil and religious advantages.

The Dutch allowed Englishmen to form colonies on taking the oath of allegiance to the States General and the Dutch West India Company; their towns were largely independent in town affairs while the Dutch settlements were subject

54

to the absolute rule of the Dutch government. The Middleburg colony was allowed to hold its lands without rent or tax for ten years, after which a tithe of the produce was to be rendered; town officers were appointed by the governor. The new charter of Connecticut, granted in 1662, greatly enlarged its boundaries, and the English towns in Queens County took the opportunity to forswear their Dutch allegiance and join their English neighbors across the Sound. At this time the settlement of Middleburg adopted the name of Hastings. After the English conquest of New Netherland in 1664, Queens County was considered to be a part of the Province of New York. The town of Hastings, including the various out-plantations at the Poor Bouwery (on Bowery Bay), Hell Gate Neck, English Kills and vicinity, was organized into the township of Newtown and included in the West Riding of Yorkshire. It formed the northeast corner of Queens County, organized in 1683. Although the Dutch had purchased the land in Queens County from the Indians in 1638-39, the English thought it best to extinguish all Indian rights in 1666, and the government then granted a patent to Newtown in 1667. It is in this township that the few old houses remain which are of Dutch architecture. Unfortunately these do not include a homestead of the prominent Riker family. The settlers here were all engaged in farming, and a few ran sawmills and grist mills.

Of the three houses in Newtown treated here, the two on Bowery Bay were built by Dutchmen and the other one was owned and probably erected by an Englishman. However, all three are typical of the architectural styles developed by the Dutch in America, and are very similar to the houses in Kings County. The photographs were taken in 1925.

HOUSES IN KINGS AND QUEENS COUNTIES

Kings County

Cornell—Schenck House
in Highland Park, Jamaica Avenue, East New York
PLATE 7

This house was inherited by Judge Teunis Schenk from his father-in-law Isaac Cornell in the first ten years of the nineteenth century. It stands on Cornell land and is said to have been built about 1760, presumably by Isaac Cornell or his father. They were not members of the English Cornell family, but of the Continental family which finally adopted the patronymic Cornele or Cornell.

Guillaume Cornelise[1] was probably a Huguenot but became identified with the Dutch colony. In 1658 he obtained a patent for a plantation at Flatbush, where he settled and where he and his wife died in 1666. He was survived by two sons, Peter and William, both of Flatbush, and possibly others. The latter, known as William Guilliamse,[2] married Margrietje Polhemus, and died about 1701; his name is mentioned in the 1677 patent of the New Lots of Flatbush and in the 1685 patent of the Town. He had six children, Johannes of New Lots, Peter of Jamaica, Cornelis of Flatbush, and three daughters. The eldest son, Johannes Williamse,[3] born several years before 1671, is supposed to have lived in New Lots on the farm conveyed him on March 4, 1701/2 by the heirs of his father according to the terms of his will. He is said to have married Aeltje Gerritse Voorhees, bap. Oct. 4, 1685 at Flatlands; their issue is not known but they are presumed to be the ancestors of the Cornell family of New Lots. The Cornell family owned a great deal of property in New Lots (now East New York), and the old homestead, which no longer exists, stood back in the present Evergreen Cemetery near the Queens Borough line.

Southeast of this former house stands the later Cornell house on the northerly of the two highways from Brooklyn to Jamaica, sometimes called the Road to the Ferry. The property, known as the northerly half of lots No. 17 and No. 18, was in the possession of Isaac Cornell about 1770 according to deeds to neighboring land, the south half then being owned by Frederick Simonsen. These two lots had been granted originally in 1680 to Jan Stryker. Isaac was probably a son of Johannes Cornell, who in 1768 and 1772 bought lands nearby, between the two highways, known as lots No. 23 and No. 24, which were later part of the clearland of Isaac Cornell, deceased, according to the transfer of adjoining property to Nicholas Williamson on March 1, 1808. Isaac was still living on June 20, 1804 when the Snedeker property east of his house changed hands.

The home land of Isaac Cornell in the New Lots (the north half of Lots No. 17 and No. 18), was deeded on Sept. 2, 1808 by Teunis Schenk and his wife Gitty Cornell to Coert Van Brunt and reconveyed to them the next day, the transfer stating that this farm of 34 acres on the Brooklyn-Jamaica road belonged to Isaac Cornell, who failed to make a will in favor of his sole heir Gitty.

Judge Teunis' Schenk, b. Feb. 15, 1767, was the son of Teunis' Schenk of Bushwick, who was the grandson of Johannis' Schenk, the progenitor of the family in Bushwick (see plate 16). On December 18, 1794 he married Gertrude or Gitty Cornell, b. March 5, 1778, d. Nov. 20, 1860, and had many children: John of Flatbush, Catharine, Ann, Isaac of New Lots, Peter, a bachelor, Maria, Alletta Jane, Eliza, Gilliam of New Lots, and Cornelia. The judge lived in his father-in-law's house at New Lots from the time of his marriage until his death on Dec. 29, 1842. On the death of his father-in-law 1804-1808, the judge inherited a great deal of Cornell property in New Lots, including various scattered lots and a large tract on the north side of the road from Jamaica to the Brooklyn Ferry extending into Queens County. He sold some of this property but deeded the major part to his sons Isaac and Peter in 1837. Peter never married. Isaac C.' Schenck, b. Jan. 17, 1802, married Catharine, daughter of Peter Meserole, and had several children including John C.' Schenck, who lived in this family homestead at East New York (formerly New Lots), and finally sold it in 1906 to the City of Brooklyn for a park.

The main house was probably built about 1760 by Isaac Cornell or his father. It was partially rebuilt and remodelled in 1792 by Isaac Cornell and in 1812 by Judge Teunis Schenk. It is of stone, covered with a thick coat of whitewash, and has a steep gambrel roof unmarred by dormers. It is two rooms deep and has four chimneys. The small frame wing is of later date, probably built in 1812. The house stands opposite Ashford Street on the north side of Jamaica Avenue in Highland Park. It nestles below the hills, which protect it from northerly winds.

House of John Covert
1410 Flushing Avenue, Bushwick
PLATE 8

It is possible that this house was not built until immediately after the Revolution, when the Coverts obtained possession of the land. On April 22, 1709 Paulus Van Ende bought a one hundred acre plantation in the new lots of Bushwick, which eventually came into the possession of his granddaughter Jannetje Van Ende and her husband Moses Beegel. Their house is mentioned in the Bushwick-Newtown boundary settlement of 1769, and stands to this day adjoining the Covert house to the north (plate 22). On April 29, 1786 (deed recorded Nov. 3, 1866) Moses Beadel and his wife Jenny sold to Johannis Cuvert 48 acres in Bushwick and Newtown, bounded on the northwest by the highway, on the northeast by Moses Beadel, on the southeast and southwest by Nicholas Wyckoff.

Johannis or John Covert (probably a descendant of Teunis Janse who emigrated in 1651) settled here on his purchase and died about 1842. This and other property on the north side of the highway, bought by John Covert in 1801, passed to William Covert, undoubtedly his son. William Covert died intestate Sept. 20, 1858. Surviving him were his widow Helena, Rebecca, widow of William D. Ballagh, Abraham D. Covert and his wife Mary, Cornelia, Sarah, Michael S. Covert and wife Catharine, Francis M. Covert and his wife Emma, who were no doubt his children. These heirs partitioned his property in 1864, the homestead falling to Michael Covert. He disposed of it outside the family in 1866 to John G. Jenkins. The latter sold the house and tract in two parcels, in 1867 and 1886, to Peter Wyckoff, who lived in the Schenk—Wyckoff homestead across the highway (plate 16).

The house is two full rooms in depth and two rooms and a hall in width. It is covered with long rounded shingles and is surmounted by a gable roof overhanging both front and rear. The frame annex is recent. The house faces Purdy Place, the only opened portion of a projected road between Cypress and Onderdonk Avenues. It is on the southeast side of old Newtown-Bushwick Road, now called Flushing Avenue.

House of Lady Moody (?); the Van Siclen House
Gravesend Neck Road, Gravesend
PLATE 9

Lady Deborah Moody was the widow of Sir Henry Moody of Garsden in Wiltshire, who had been created a baronet of the realm in 1622 and died about 1632. She was the daughter of Walter Dunch, M.P., a champion of liberty and constitutional rights. True to her inheritance, she was a woman of education, refinement and great force of character, and prominent in Colonial councils and public matters. She emigrated in 1640 to Massachusetts with her son Sir Henry, was excommunicated for her religious views and retired in 1643 to New Netherland.

That same year Lady Moody obtained a patent for lands at Gravesend on Long Island, and was joined by fellow countrymen in forming a new settlement dedicated to the free enjoyment of religion. Gravesend was laid out according to a definite plan; a 16-acre square, bisected by two roads, was sufficient for the forty house plots of the patentees, and was surrounded radially by the same number of planters' lots or farms outside the palisades, each farm being easily accessible from the house of its owner. In this manner, it was hoped there would be adequate protection from the Indians, who had almost wiped out the little settlement in the early days of its existence.

On Nov. 18, 1646 Lady Moody was allotted a double plantation (No. 9 and No. 10), and presumably at the same time the corresponding house lot, which was on the north side of Gravesend Neck Road in the northwest of the four village squares. Lady Moody was living in Gravesend as late as Nov. 4, 1658, and had died before May 11, 1659 when her son sold the house lot inherited from his deceased mother. Her son Sir Henry soon removed to Virginia. He had disposed of his mother's house lot to Jan Jansen Verryn, who in 1663 sold it to Ralph Cardell. The latter died 1684-89, leaving his real estate to his widow Elizabeth. She was married two more times, to Thomas Bayles, d. 1689, and thirdly on March 17, 1689/90 to Isaac Haselbery, b. 1649, who deeded the house and two garden spots in 1701 to Nicholas Stillwell, Jr. The latter sold it the following year to Ferdinandus Van Sickelen, Jr.

Ferdinandus' Van Sycklin emigrated in 1652 and settled at Flatlands. When he took the oath of allegiance in 1687 he stated he had been in the country for thirty-five years. He later settled at Gravesend where he died about 1712. Among his children by his wife Eva Antonis Van Salee was Ferdinandus² Van Sickelen, Jr., who married Gertruy, daughter of Minne Johannes and Rensje Feddans. They had two sons, Ferdinandus and Minne, and six daughters, Eve, Remge, Elizabeth, Margaret, Annie and Jannette. Ferdinandus² Van Sickelen, Jr. was still living in Flatlands in 1698; in 1702 he bought from Stillwell the house plot and half the bouwery in Gravesend and settled here. He willed this property in 1737 to his son Ferdinandus³ Van Siclen. The latter married Maria Van Nuys; he was living as late as 1798 and eventually left his property to his three children, John, Abraham, and Maria Antonides. These two sons divided the double house plot in half, and it came down thus in these two branches of the family until the middle 1800s when both halves passed into the ownership of Thomas Hicks. The west half of the lot was released by John and Maria to their brother Abraham⁴ Van Siclen in 1809; in 1841 John Van Siclen and his wife Maria conveyed it to Cornelia, wife of Thomas Hicks, Sarah Hicks, and Maria, wife of Epenetus Smith, all of whom sold their interests in 1842 to Thomas Hicks. The east half of the lot was released in 1841 by Abraham's heirs to their uncle John⁴ Van Siclen, who willed it to his two sons Court J. and Ferdinand. The latter willed his share to John C. Van Siclen. In 1851 Court J. and John C. Van Siclen sold it to Thomas Hicks. The double house lot belonged to the estate of Mrs. Hicks in 1890. In the partition of 1904 it was sold to William E. Platt who in 1912 sold it to Bert Cole. The present owner is Miss Anna Anderson.

There is a strong and persistent tradition that this house was occupied by Lady

Moody, the founder of Gravesend. It was at her house in Gravesend that Director Stuyvesant and other officials dined and discussed with her the problems of the province. The title to the property shows that Lady Moody did indeed have her home here, but it was undoubtedly in an earlier house than the present one, which, although of great age, belongs to a later period. The present house may have been built by Ferdinandus Van Sickelen about 1702 or more probably in the second half of the seventeenth century by one of the three husbands of Elizabeth ————. It is probably this house which was mentioned in the deed drawn when the third husband sold the property in 1701. The house stands on the north side of Gravesend Neck Road opposite the cemetery and between Van Sicklen Street and Gravesend Avenue.

House of Pieter Lefferts
in Prospect Park, Flatbush Avenue, Flatbush
PLATE 10

The old Lefferts house was burned in 1776 and the present house was built on its foundations along the old lines. Pieter Janse[1] emigrated with his wife, Femmetje Hermans, and children about 1660, settling at Flatbush; he died soon after his arrival and guardians were appointed for his two minor sons by the Court of Flatbush on Oct. 15, 1662. The orphan child Leffert Pietersen[2] (also called Leffert Pietersen Haughwout) lived in Flatbush, where he was assessed in 1675, named in the patent of 1685, and took the oath of allegiance in 1687 stating he had been in the country for twenty-seven years. On Feb. 29, 1687/8 he bought of Anna, widow of Egbert Van Borsom, 58 acres in Flatbush between the main road to the village and the road from Bedford; this tract had been originally patented to Cornelius Van Ruyven in 1664. On Jan. 19, 1692/3 he enlarged his farm by purchasing from Gerrit Stryker a tract adjoining it on the south, which had been patented to Cornelius Janse in 1661.

Leffert Pietersen married about 1675 Abigail, daughter of Auke Janse Van Nuyse, b. about 1654, d. July 19, 1748, and had eight sons and five daughters. After his death on Dec. 8, 1704, his farm was inherited by his son Pieter[3] Leffertze, b. May 18, 1680, d. March 13, 1774 in his 94th year, who served as county treasurer for thirty-five years. He married Ida, daughter of Hendrick Suydam, and had three sons and five daughters. On Aug. 24, 1767, shortly after his son's second marriage, Pieter deeded the homestead farm to his son Jan. Jan or John[4] Lefferts, b. March 16, 1719, died on Oct. 20, 1776 two months after his ancestral home had burned. He was a very wealthy farmer, county judge, and delegate to the Provincial Congress. On April 29, 1746 he married Sarah Martense, b. Nov. 23, 1727, d. Dec. 30, 1762, and had five children; on April 17, 1765 he married secondly Lemmetje Vanderbilt,

b. May 25, 1720, d. April 17, 1782 and had two more daughters. The homestead farm passed to John's son, Pieter[5] Lefferts. Pieter, b. Dec. 27, 1753, d. Oct. 7, 1791, married May 13, 1775 Jannetie, daughter of Jacobus Lefferts, b. May 13, 1753, d. Feb. 21, 1783, having borne one son who died in infancy and two daughters; he married secondly June 17, 1784 Femmetje, daughter of Evert Hegeman, b. May 3, 1753, d. Aug. 5, 1847, and had one son and one daughter.

Pieter Lefferts was an important member of the colony, a delegate to the Constitutional Convention, lieutenant in the army, and a senator. On Aug. 22, 1776 his home was accidentally set on fire by the Americans, who were burning the grain in the nearby fields to prevent supplies falling into the hands of the approaching British. This was just before the disastrous Battle of Long Island. Pieter Lefferts rebuilt his house on the old foundations and followed the old design as closely as possible. On May 8, 1785 he enlarged the farm by purchasing 100 acres adjoining him on the south from the other heirs of his father-in-law Evert Hegeman.

Pieter's only son, Senator John[6] Lefferts, b. Dec. 14, 1785 in the new house, d. Sept. 18, 1829, married June 3, 1823 Maria Lott Lefferts, daughter of Jacobus Lefferts, b. Aug. 20, 1786, d. Sept. 23, 1865. Like his father, he was a member of the Constitutional Convention and a senator. His only son was John[7] Lefferts, b. Aug. 12, 1826, d. April 18, 1893. He continued the family custom of marrying a cousin and of marrying twice; on June 17, 1851 he wed Eliza, daughter of James Lefferts, b. April 18, 1831, d. Nov. 13, 1867, having borne three sons and three daughters; on Feb. 1, 1871 he married secondly Helen Evans, b. July 30, 1840, and had three more sons. James[8] Lefferts, b. March 27, 1855, was a son by the first wife; he owned the homestead and was occupying it with his family in 1909.

Another version of the destruction of the old family home is that the Americans deliberately burned it in their war maneuvres because the British were taking advantage of its cover and firing from behind it. This account seems less credible than the other, considering that it was the home of an important family and of ardent patriots.

It is generally believed that the house was rebuilt immediately after the old one was burned in 1776. However, it is questionable if such a display of wealth would be indulged in while the British occupied Long Island. It was more probably erected at the end of the war. The house is a well built, commodious structure of clapboard and shingle. Its gambrel roof has a more deeply curved slope than was customary. The doorway with its sunburst carving and flanking narrow windows is typically post-revolutionary. The house formerly stood at No. 563 Flatbush Avenue in the vicinity of Lincoln Road. The large farm was bounded on the west by the Flatbush Road and on the north by the no longer existing Road to Bedford, also called the

Clove Road. The Flatbush Road led from Flatlands and forked a short distance north of the Lefferts farm, one branch going to the port and the other to the ferry to Manhattan. The house has been moved a short distance to Prospect Park, and now stands on the west side of Flatbush Avenue, north of the park entrance from Empire Boulevard. It is maintained by the Daughters of the American Revolution.

House of Johannes Lott
1940 East 36th Street, Flatlands
PLATE 11

This pre-revolutionary house in Kings County is still in the possession and occupancy of descendants of the builder, Johannes Lott. His grandfather, Pieter[1] Lott, emigrated to America in 1652 from Ruinerwold and settled in Flatbush. His son, Hendrick[2] Lott of Flatlands and Jamaica, married Katrena De Witt and had among others a son, Johannes[3] Lott, b. May 11, 1692, d. April 8, 1775, married Antie, daughter of Claes Folkert, bap. Oct. 7, 1703. Johannes was a colonel of a Kings County regiment, a member of the Assembly and the largest slaveowner in Flatlands. On Dec. 12, 1719 he bought a farm in the southern part of Flatlands from Coert Voorhies (who had purchased it June 10, 1711 from Roeloff and Albert Terhuynen), and later bought more land, until he had a large farm extending to the bay. He built and died on this tract. His house, part of which is now the east wing, stood a short distance northeast of the present house. Among his eight sons and five daughters was Johannes[4] Lott, Jr., b. Dec. 31, 1721, d. Jan. 25, 1782, married April 6, 1745 Jannetje Probasco, d. Oct. 28, 1802, and had four sons and four daughters. He died only a few years after receiving his father's house, and it passed to his son Hendrick. In 1796 the house was recorded as 50 x 34 feet, condition old, value $600 (which was high), the barn 48 x 52 feet, farm of 124 acres, value of barn and farm $3600.

Hendrick I.[5] Lott, b. Oct. 3, 1760, d. Feb. 24, 1840, married July 15, 1792 Mary Brownjohn, d. Sept. 7, 1853 in her 83rd year. Hendrick Lott had only three children and so his father's house was adequate. However, he no doubt felt that an imposing mansion was better suited to his position as a large landowner. He built the present main house and west wing in 1800 on another portion of his ancestral farm, and moved part of his forefathers' house from its old site to become the east wing of his house.

On Hendrick's death the property was inherited by his only son Johannes H.[6] Lott, b. Aug. 20, 1793, d. Feb. 26, 1874, married Dec. 28, 1817 Gashé Bergen, b. July 24, 1797, d. Jan. 21, 1883. The house came into the possession of one of their seven children, Henry De Witt[7] Lott, b. June 21, 1821, d. Jan. 25, 1889, married

Oct. 28, 1863 Annie Bennett, died Sept. 1, 1882. At the time of Henry D. Lott's death, the farm consisted of 100 acres of upland and 100 acres of meadows. Three of his children were living in the house in 1909: John B.[8] Lott and his family and George[8] Lott in one part, and Mrs. Jennie Suydam in another part. Mrs. Suydam (nee Jennie Lott) still owns it and resides here. The farm recently dwindled to a truck farm of 17 acres, and now consists of but a few acres around the house.

A road was opened at an early date from the center of Flatlands village southwards to the bay and was called the Road to Lott's Landing; the name was shortened to Lott's Lane and for a short time was called Kimball's Road. It has been recently obliterated by the development of the neighborhood. The house was some distance to the west of it, reached by its private farm lane which curved around the side and back of the house to the immense Dutch frame barns, which stood until recently. Early in 1926 (after the photograph was taken) 36th Street was cut through the property, so near the house that the stone slave kitchen (seen in the photograph behind the tree) had to be torn down; 35th Street runs near the west end of the house.

The neighborhood has been developed with small modern houses, and one comes upon the Lott homestead (now painted a glistening white) with considerable surprise, pleased by its spaciousness and its graceful, peaceful lines. The wing is a part of the old house built about 1720; its gable roof is steep, its window openings are small, and in the rear of the house the original windows are still in use, their width of four tiny panes, thick moldings, and narrow lower sash being typical. Although the wing seems so small, at one time there were two bedrooms under its roof. The main house has on the ground floor two rooms and an ample hall, which connects with the room in the west wing. The gambrel roof over the main house has a beautiful curving sweep in front, forming an overhang now supported by columns; the straight slant of the roof in the rear is now marred by the gable window. A view in Ditmas, p. 37, shows the front of the house, the slave kitchen, and part of the farm.

House of Adrian Martense
formerly at 21 Church Avenue, Flatbush
PLATE 12

This house was built by Adrian Martense on property inherited from his father and grandfather. Adrian Ryerse[1] emigrated from Amsterdam about 1646 and settled at Flatbush, where he died Nov. 24, 1710. On July 29, 1659 he married Annetje, daughter of Martin Roelofse Schenck of Flatlands; her uncle built the Schenck house on Mill Island (plate 13). Between 1661 and Feb. 1, 1670 when his ownership was recorded, Adrian bought a plantation in Flatbush, patented in 1655 to Isaak Foreest; in 1693 he bought a double plantation to the north of it from Margaret Verschuur.

His son, Martin Adriance,[2] b. March 9, 1668, d. Oct. 30, 1754, was called Martin de Boer because he had one of the largest farms in Flatbush. He had inherited his father's three plantations; his homestead formerly stood on the Parade Grounds. He married Sarah Remsen Vanderbeek, b. Dec. 1670, d. April 30, 1724, and had five children, Rem, Gerret, Adrian and two daughters.

Martin's son, Adrian[3] Martense, b. Oct. 24, 1707, d. Sept. 17, 1784, received his father's west farm and built his home thereon. His descendants adopted his patronymic of Martense for their family name whereas some of their cousins had taken the name Ryerson, the patronymic of their emigrant ancestor. By his wife Neeltje, Adrian Martense had four sons and five daughters. His farm was divided between his three surviving sons: Jores (1737-1804), a bachelor, Garret (1740-1826), a bachelor, and Adrian (1742-1817), who built a house after the Revolution, reproduced in Ditmas, page 67. The youngest son, Isaac[4] Martense, b. Jan. 9, 1748, d. Nov. 12, 1778, married Nov. 5, 1775 Maria Meserole, b. Oct. 22, 1758, d. June 18, 1846; he predeceased his father, leaving an only child, Adrian, who continued to reside in his grandfather's house. In a partition of 1819 Adrian was allotted 65 acres together with his uncle Garret, and when the latter died in 1826 he willed his nephew the balance of his share in the farm of his father Adrian.

Thus Adrian I.[5] Martense, b. Oct. 3, 1776, d. Sept. 13, 1826, indirectly inherited the house and part of the farm of his grandfather, after whom he had been named. He lived in his grandfather's house and farmed his and his uncle Garret's farms. He married Deborah Berry, b. Sept. 23, 1780, d. March 1, 1865, and had four daughters: Maria, Rachel (1801-1906), a spinster lady who lived to the age of 105 years, Jane (1803-28), also unmarried, and Elizabeth (1806-1871), wife of Henry Crabb. On Feb. 1, 1865 Maria, Rachel and Elizabeth divided their father's and great uncle Garret's lands. The eldest daughter, Maria[6] Martense, born about 1799, married first in March, 1825, Stephen Schenck, who died immediately after on Dec. 25, 1825; she married secondly Jan. 25, 1831 Capt. William Story, d. March 10, 1875, aged 77 years. They resided in the Adrian Martense home, which became known as the Story homestead, and had three sons: William who married but had no issue, Martense, and Joseph, a bachelor who lived with his aunt Rachel. The property was sold out of the family about 1908 to settle the estate.

The house was built at two different times. The wing was erected by Adrian Martense about the middle of the century or earlier. The main unit may have been built by him shortly before he died in 1784, but was probably built by his grandson Adrian Martense about 1800. The house was torn down to make room for a row of modern buildings since the photograph was taken in 1925. It formerly stood on the northeast corner of Church and Chester Avenues, south of Greenwood Cemetery.

The Old New Utrecht Road until recently wound northwards from that settlement to the Martense farm, where it joined Church Avenue (originally called Cow Lane), which led to the church and the center of Flatbush village. Nearby, Martense Lane ran in the direction of the present Greenwood Cemetery to Gowanus. It was followed by the British and Hessian soldiers in their attack upon the right wing of the American Army commanded by Lord Stirling, which was holding the ground on the hills of the present cemetery.

House of Jan Martense Schenck on Mill Island
East 63rd Street near Mill Avenue, Flatlands
PLATE 13

There is much controversy about the age of this and other old houses in Kings County to determine which was the earliest erected. Regardless of its actual date, the house of Jan Martense Schenck is without doubt the oldest house from the point of view of its style of architecture, and is also the oldest house still standing as originally erected.

When Jan Martense Schenck took the oath of allegiance in Flatlands in 1687, he stated he had been here 37 years, and therefore was brought to this country in 1650 as a child. He is supposed to be a grandson (or greatgrandson?) of a Martin Schenck of Doesburg, Gelderland, b. Aug. 7, 1584. Jan Martense' Schenck, probably born at Amersfoort in Holland, died in 1689 at Flatlands, married about 1672 Jannetje, daughter of Stephen Van Voorhees, who, after his death, married secondly at Flatlands Oct. 12, 1690 Alexander Simson. On Aug. 20, 1660 Jan Martense was granted by Stuyvesant two parcels of land near Mill Lane in the village of Flatlands, one of which he immediately sold to his neighbor Pieter Claesen (Wyckoff). He resided in the village until he sold his house, lot, and 12 morgens of land on Feb. 15, 1676/7.

The year previous, on Dec. 29, 1675, Jan Martense had bought from Capt. Elbert Elbertse (Stoothoff) one half of a mill at Mill Island with the island, and no doubt built his house on the island the following year before disposing of his home in the village. The island had been included in the Indian deed of May 13, 1664 for Equandito or the broken lands by John Tilton, Sr. and Samuel Spicer of Gravesend. They may have been acting as agents for Elbert Elbertse, for the latter appears to have been in possession long before the Indian deed was officially assigned to him on May 3, 1681. A map made on July 3, 1666 by James Hubbard shows that the mill already existed at this time, and had no doubt been built by Elbert Elbertse in the two years since the execution of the Indian deed.

As stated above, Jan Martense Schenck who bought the mill and half the island from Elbert Elbertse on Dec. 29, 1675, doubtless immediately built his house and moved in when it was completed the following year. Before 1700 vessels from Holland entered the inlet here (now called Mill Basin) and discharged and received cargoes. By tradition the two brothers Jan and Roelof were interested in trading with Holland by these vessels. Jan may very well have been interested in shipping, as his house is constructed like the hull of a ship with curved timbers and archlike inverted frame, a method of construction not found in any other old Long Island house. Jan was not a large landowner and was not primarily a farmer; judging by his legacies he owned more readily convertible assets than any contemporary in Flatlands. He died between Jan. 28 and April 2, 1689, the dates of execution and probate of his will, in which he mentioned his wife, his two sons Martin and Stephen, and his daughters Jannetie, Willemtie, and Neeltie.

The elder son Martin Janse[2] Schenck, b. 1675, inherited from his father the "old land with the small island and mill and dependencies," and continued to reside here. On Dec. 2, 1703 he married Cornelia Van Wesselen, widow of Dominie Gulielmus Lupardus. The house passed to their only known son, Capt. John[3] Schenck, b. Dec. 13, 1705, d. between 1775 and 1784, married Femmetje Hegeman on Nov. 15, 1728. Capt. Schenck is also said to have been interested in shipping to New Netherlands, his boats docking at his wharf on Mill Island. The will of John Schenck, miller of Flatlands, provided that his estate should be sold and divided between his son Martin, the heirs of his daughter Cornelia deceased (Ulpianus and Femmetje Van Sinderen), the heir of his daughter Maria deceased (Femmetie Hooglant), and his daughters Margrieta and Femmetie. The mill property consisting of 66 acres of upland, 6 acres of woodland, and salt meadows, was sold by the heirs to Joris Martense of Flatbush on April 15, 1784.

From this time it is probable that the owners of the house on Mill Island did not dwell here, although they continued to operate the mill. For a while at least the Schencks continued to live here. In 1796 the house is recorded as occupied by John Schenck but owned by Jane Martense (widow of Joris) of Flatbush, house in good condition, size 41 x 22, value $650., barn 44 x 42, mill 28 x 28, farm of 121 acres, value $5600.

The purchaser, Joris[4] Martense, son of Rem, was a member of the landholding family of Flatbush. He lived there on his father's farm, which had once formed the east portion of the large farm of his grandfather Martin Adriance[2]; the west portion had been inherited by Rem's brother Adrian[3] Martense who built thereon (plate 12). Joris was a leading citizen of Flatbush and a large landowner. He advanced $5500. in specie to the American cause while the British supposed he was favoring them.

It was in his house at Flatbush that Major Moncrief of the British army was captured in a midnight raid by Capt. William Marriner, who discovered him hiding in the garret behind the large Dutch chimney.

Joris Martense, bap. May 29, 1724, d. May 23, 1791, married and had two sons who died in infancy, another son who was a bachelor, and a married daughter who inherited the mill property. The daughter Susan⁵ Martense, b. Jan. 15, 1777, married Feb. 11, 1802 John H. Cowenhoven of New Utrecht (1769-1806) and had two daughters who remained in New Utrecht; she married secondly Patrick Caton and had one daughter before he died April 13, 1818. This daughter, Margaret Caton, b. May 31, 1815, d. March 8, 1858, married Nov. 26, 1837 Gen. Philip S. Crooke; they lived in the old Martense home in Flatbush. Mrs. Caton devised the mill and other property in trust for her daughter Margaret, wife of Philip S. Crooke, and she in turn willed the property in trust for her children. After eleven conveyances between various members of the Crooke family, the first dated July 5, 1870 from Philip to Robert for 500 acres of meadows and 5 acres on Mill Island with grist mill and mill dam and 66 acres of upland, the title to the Mill Island part of the property became vested in Robert L. Crooke. He and his wife Elizabeth sold it Jan. 12, 1906 to Florence C. Smith. The property changed hands, was dredged, filled in and developed, creating 332 acres of upland, by the Atlantic, Gulf and Pacific Co., who on Jan. 14, 1909 was deeded the property in payment for its work.

The Jan Martense Schenck house is one of the most interesting of the early houses. Its method of construction is most unusual, resembling the hull of a ship. Its proportions are pleasing and its lines graceful. The very steep slant of the roof is evidence of the extreme age of the house and may be favorably compared with the earliest houses in New Amsterdam. During the early eighteenth century the size of the house was doubled by the addition of a similar unit at right angles. The photograph in Eberlein, p. 246, emphasizes this wing and shows the old round-edged shingles with which it was covered.

The house stood on the north shore of Mill Island, close to the mill and the inlet, and Mill Lane wandered down to it from Flatlands village. Since the property has been filled in, Mill Island is now part of the mainland and the end of Mill Lane has become Mill Avenue. The house can be seen from the end of Mill Avenue, and stands on a lane called East 63rd Street behind a public school. The house presents the same appearance as of old, painted a glistening white, its old windows still doing duty, and spic and span as a shipper's home would be; it is still somewhat secluded from the modern developments of the neighborhood.

House of Nicholas Schenck at Canarsie
now in the Museum of the Brooklyn Institute of Arts and Sciences

PLATE 14

Great Neck or Canarsie was the name given at an early date to a point of land in eastern Jamaica Bay, within the Town of Flatlands and northeast of the village. A petition was presented in 1661 to the government of New Netherlands for the opening of plantations at Canarsie. It was evidently granted as six existed there in 1663. These were soon given up (except for one) and the point was allowed to return to undeveloped woodlands. The claim of one plantation owner must have been purchased by Stephen Janse or his father Jan Martense Schenck; this 23 acre tract is omitted from the Woodland Division of 1719. Jan Martense[1] Schenck, builder of the house on Mill Island in Jamaica Bay (plate 13), willed his younger son Stephen in 1689 "the lott land in the neck with the middow, to hoggs neck with all ye dependences." It is not known whether this is a reference to the Canarsie land.

Stephen Janse[2] Schenck was probably the first permanent settler at Canarsie, where he built his home. He was born Jan. 2, 1685, on his father's mill farm, d. Nov. 6, 1767, married Sept. 26, 1713 Antje, daughter of Nicholas Wyckoff of Flatlands, b. Aug. 29, 1693, d. July 15, 1766. In his will of 1758 Stephen mentioned his wife Antje, left his farm at Oyster Bay on which John was living to his elder son John, left his lands and buildings at Canarsie in Flatlands to his son Nicholas, and mentioned his seven daughters: Jannetie wife of Folkert Sprong, Sara wife of Abraham Emans, Antie wife of Abraham Duryee, Willemtje wife of Petrus Amerman, Neeltje, Margarite and Maria. The younger son Nicholas[3] Schenck b. Sept. 4, 1732, d. April 3, 1810, married Oct. 11, 1757 Willemtje Wyckoff of Newtown, b. Dec. 23, 1736, d. Sept. 12, 1779.

Nicholas Schenck, Sr. was a farmer at Canarsie Point and built the present house in 1772. He was a captain of the provincial militia. During the Revolutionary War Kings County was in the hands of the British and they established a guard at his house in 1776. In June 1781 the house of Capt. Nicholas Schenck, at Canarsie about three miles from Flatbush, was surprised by the crews of two rebel whaleboats under Hyler. The family were at supper and of course not prepared to make any resistance. Arms and silver were seized, and a sergeant's guard quartered in the house was sent to report to Col. Axtell. In 1796 the house was recorded as 42 x 33 feet, 25 years old, in good condition, value $850. (which was high), barns 40 x 56 and 36 x 46 feet, value of barns and farm $3390.

Nicholas Schenck, Sr. had four sons of whom only John and Nicholas survived him, and also four daughters most of whom died in infancy. On his death he willed his homestead to his younger son Nicholas[4] Schenck, Jr., b. Feb. 23, 1765, d. Sept.

10, 1836, married April 20, 1788 Alletta Remsen, b. Dec. 3, 1768, d. May 6, 1855. In his will of 1832 Nicholas mentioned his wife Aletti, left the homestead or neck to his two sons James and Stephen, and mentioned his other children: Anthony Remsen, Abraham, Jane wife of Ralph Malbone, Anna wife of Hezekiah Dans, Adriana wife of Cornelius Stryker, and his grandson Nicholas Schenck. Although Stephen N.[5] Schenck owned one half interest in the homestead farm, which he willed to Stephen R. Schenck in 1842, it is probable that a partition was made, as his brother James seems to have been in possession of the house itself. James[5] Schenck of Canarsie, b. April 19, 1800 on the old farm, died in the last twenty years of the nineteenth century. He was a farmer, surveyor, and town supervisor. He was one of the last of his family and never married. After his death what remained of his ancestral farm was divided into small lots and sold at public sale. The present Canarsie Beach Park was bought by the Brooklyn Commissioner of Parks, from the buyers at this sale and their successors, about 1897.

The Schenck house remained standing south of Rockaway Avenue in Canarsie Park until after this photograph was taken in 1925. It has been demolished since, but a very large part of the exterior and interior has been rebuilt within the Museum of the Brooklyn Institute of Arts and Sciences, and set up in a permanent exhibit of colonial architecture. Thus are preserved for all time the beautiful curved sloping roof, the large old shingles, the old window sashes, doors and interior panelling, and the built-in cupboard bed. It is greatly to be desired that other localities follow this museum's example and set up historic or architecturally interesting houses which would otherwise disappear.

There formerly stood nearby, north of Rockaway Avenue, a much older Schenck house, shingled and covered by a very steep gable roof. A painting of this house is reproduced in *Keskachauge*. In the middle of the nineteenth century it was owned by Jeremiah Schenck, a distant cousin of the Schencks nearby. The house was torn down in 1912.

Schenck—Williamson House
East 53rd Street north of Avenue N, Flatlands
PLATE 15

This house was undoubtedly built in the third quarter of the eighteenth century by Martin Schenck, the owner of the land at this time. On Nov. 29, 1660 Cornelius Dircksen Hoogland sold to Steven Koerten 7 morgens of woodland (on which the house was later erected) and 9 morgens of maizeland. These tracts were bought by Jan Martense Schenck, who purchased the land adjoining to the north in 1676. He never occupied this property, but built and settled on Mill Island nearby (plate 13). In his will of 1689 he left his son Martin Janse the old land (meaning this property) as well as the island; the same lands passed to the latter's son Capt. John' Schenck. At his death his heirs sold most of the property to Joris Martense on April 15, 1784, but this particular woodland plottage was not included in the sale; the land of Martin Schenck is mentioned in the deed of sale as the west boundary of the upland.

Martin' Schenck was the only son of Capt. John Schenck and his wife Femmetje Hegeman, whom he had married in 1728, and was born after this date in the Mill Island home. Martin's wife Sarah is named in the deed of 1784. They undoubtedly built this house about the time of their marriage. We next find mention of it in a sale of Feb. 22, 1809, when the 15 acre property was sold by several members of the Van Sinderen family (Catalina, John, Hotso, and Jane). As other members of this family had joined with the heirs of Capt. John Schenck in selling the Mill Island property, it is probable that these Van Sinderens were related to Martin Schenck (possibly they were grandchildren of his sister?). Hendrick J. Lott bought the house in 1809 and conveyed it in 1814 to his young son Johannes H. Lott, who sold it in 1829. It is improbable that the Lotts ever resided here, as Hendrick had built his mansion in southern Flatlands only a few years before (plate 11).

On April 28, 1829 Johannes Lott sold to John Williamson the house and 7 acres which adjoined his lands. On May 1, 1883 the executors of John Williamson and Maria Williamson deeded the house and 14 acres to Garret Williamson, who was no doubt their son. Whether or not John Williamson dwelt here, we know it was occupied for many years by Garret Williamson, who was about eighty years of age when he died without issue about 1915.

The house is in Flatlands, east of the old village. The property was bounded on the west and on the south by the old Road to the Mill (Jan Martense Schenck's mill and house on Mill Island). It is said that the house does not stand on its original site; it was probably moved a short distance when the streets were cut through in the 1890s. It is now on East 53rd Street between Avenues M and N, nearer the latter. Since the photograph was taken in 1925, the house has been painted a violet brown which rather subdues its character, but otherwise it is unchanged.

Schenk—Wyckoff House
1325 Flushing Avenue, Bushwick
PLATE 16

Mespat Kills (now Newtown Creek) empties into the East River and from early times has been the division line between the Dutch settlement of Bushwick in Kings County and the English settlement of Mespat, later called Newtown, in Queens County. John Scudder emigrated in 1635 to Salem and removed to Mespat Kills; by 1661 he owned the mill pond at the head of the kills in Bushwick, which was called

Scudder's Pond in the 1687 Patent. His grandsons John and Richard B. Scudder are said to have sold property in 1700 and removed to New Jersey. Presumably this land was included in the 350 acres among the headwaters of the kill sold in 1709 by John Stevenson to Teunis Titus. A large part of this tract was sold by Titus to Johannes Schenk in 1711.

Mynheer Johannes' Schenk, b. Sept. 19, 1656 in Holland, was a son of Martin Schenck (1633-1704), bailiff of Nydeck. He married Maria Magdalena de Haes, b. Oct. 7, 1660 at Middleburg, d. April 10, 1729, daughter of Hendrick de Haes. They emigrated from Middleburg in 1683, locating successively at New York City, Esopus, Flatbush, and Bushwick. On Sept. 17, 1711 Johannes Schenk, late of Flatbush and now of Bushwick, bought from Teunis Titus and his wife Mary, 83 acres of land with a water mill and stream in Bushwick and other smaller parcels including 7 acres in Newtown, in all 115 acres. He settled here near the stream. He undoubtedly became a miller, and was also schoolmaster, town clerk, and supervisor of Kings County. He died here Feb. 5, 1748, aged 92 years, and was buried on the place. In his will he ordered that his estate be divided between the heirs of his five deceased children. Five of his children matured but all predeceased him. They were: Johannes Schenk (1691-1729) of Bushwick, Peter Schanck (d. 1736) of Newtown, Susanna wife of Johannes Janse, Margrietie wife of John Stryker, and Cornelia wife of Capt. Charles Durje. The mill property with 45 acres was sold in 1770 by Abraham Schenk (son of Johannes, Jr.) to his cousin Teunis Schenk (son of Peter). The old family homestead burned down 1840-45; its foundations were for many years visible near the stream and north of the present Metropolitan Avenue.

It is not known which member of the Schenk family built the old house (now the wing) immediately to the south, on the Road to Newtown (now Flushing Avenue), but its construction suggests the probable date to be about 1719. Johannes Schenk, Jr. (1691-1729) of Bushwick married Maria Lott of Flatbush and had six sons and one daughter: Judge Abraham Schenk (1720-1790) lived on the Millstone River in New Jersey but returned to live in Bushwick in 1748 and at a later date settled at Fishkill; John (1715-1777) lived on the Raritan River in New Jersey; Hendrick (b. 1717) settled at Weston, New Jersey, as did his brother Peter (b. 1722); Cornelius (1724-1744) remained at Bushwick, but died before his grandfather leaving an infant daughter; Isaac the youngest (b. 1725) was still living in 1755. The other son of the pioneer was Peter Schanck of Newtown, who died Sept. 14, 1736, leaving sons, John and Teunis Schenk b. Feb. 9, 1723, d. July 31, 1806. On Sept. 16, 1749 Teunis married his first cousin Catharine, only daughter of Johannes Schenk, Jr., and had eight sons and four daughters. Teunis lived at Bushwick, where he inherited property from his father and grandfather, and purchased the mill property from his cousin Abraham in 1770. It is possible that he or his wife had previously inherited the house on the Road to Newtown, and that they sold this home about this time to the Wyckoffs and removed to their grandfather's mill home, where we know that Teunis' and Catharine's eldest son Peter (1752-1808) lived.

The exact date of transfer of the property on the Road to Newtown is not known; it is said that Nicholas Wyckoff purchased it in 1765 (but no deed is on record nor among the family papers), and that he lived here during the Revolution when not engaged in vidette duty with a troop of horse for the patriot cause. He probably settled in Bushwick about the time of his marriage, but the first mention of him on this particular farm is in the sale of adjoining property to John Covert (plate 8) on April 29, 1786. He undoubtedly built the main portion of the house as well as the big barn at the rear, with its date 1788 chiselled into an oak beam over the big front doors. The smaller portion of the house is much older, dating from about 1719, and must have belonged originally to the Schenk family, many of whom lie buried in the family graveyard at the rear of the hovel (the name applied to a very early type of barn which is still standing and greatly antedates the 1788 barn). The lot on which the house stands (on the northwest side of the road) is only a few acres in size, surrounded by property purchased in 1801 by his neighbor John Covert from Isaac Schenk. Most of the 200 acre farm of Nicholas Wyckoff stretched to the southward on the opposite side of the Road to Newtown and was bought in part from the Schenk family and the balance in 1797 from the executors of Charles Duryee.

The purchaser, Nicholas⁶ Wyckoff, was born March 23, 1743, in the family homestead on Canarsie Lane in Flatlands (plate 23), the ninth son of Pieter Wyckoff, Jr., and died May 19, 1813 in Bushwick. On May 23, 1767 he married Antie, daughter of Folkert Rapalye and Matilda Polhemus, b. Oct. 28, 1745, d. March 30, 1813 only two months before her husband. They had nine sons and one daughter, but only three children matured, Folkert who was a bachelor, Peter and Nicholas, Jr. In his will of 1813, Nicholas Wyckoff, Sr. of Bushwick left his wife Anne the use of $4490. and either of his dwelling houses which she should choose, devised to his son Peter two acres of woodland bought from Benjamin Coe, left the residue of his lands to his sons Folkert and Nicholas, and mentioned that his three sons and their descendants were to have the use of the burial ground. Various deeds and releases passed between the three sons in 1814. Nicholas N.⁶ Wyckoff received 100 acres, the southwest half of his father's farm, a part of which extended north of the Newtown Road to the headwaters of the creek; he lived in a house (destroyed in 1890) facing the present Johnson Avenue in the small triangle on the north side of the Newtown Road. His brother Peter⁶ Wyckoff received 103 acres, the northeast half of his father's farm, on which stands the Schenk—Wyckoff home.

As Nicholas devised his son Peter Schenk very little property, it is probable that Peter had already received a large portion of his inheritance; as a young man he had bought the Mansion House on Woodpoint Road north of the village of Bushwick, and it was there that his son Nicholas was born in 1799; he returned to the homestead on the Newtown Road in 1814 after his father's death. Peter⁶ Wyckoff, b. March 13, 1768, d. Sept. 20, 1842, married Dec. 2, 1790 Gertrude, daughter of Capt. Lambert Suydam of Bedford, b. March 23, 1771, d. Aug. 9, 1864; they had four sons and two daughters. Nicholas⁷ Wyckoff, b. Oct. 30, 1799, d. June 24, 1883, was the only member of this branch of the family to carry on the name; two of his brothers had died in infancy and a third brother Lambert married but had no children, his uncle Folkert was a bachelor, and the sons of his uncle Nicholas never married. He inherited his father's and grandfather's farm and home in Bushwick; he was a prominent citizen and kindly man, and for twenty-two years was president of the bank now called the First National Bank of Brooklyn. On Dec. 20, 1826 he married Sarah Ann, daughter of Gen. Jeremiah Johnson, b. Dec. 26, 1805, d. April 9, 1888. Their only son who grew to maturity was Peter⁸ Wyckoff, b. Feb. 27, 1828, d. Feb. 9, 1910, in his 82nd year, married Jan. 2, 1851 Catharine Maria Rapelye, b. May 20, 1825, d. March 24, 1900. They lived and died in the old Wyckoff farmhouse. After they passed away, the farm was sold in 1911 and laid out in building lots. The acreage about the house is still undeveloped and remains the only rural section on Flushing Avenue.

The house, 1325 Flushing Avenue, is on the northeast side of this road, north of Cypress Avenue, and south of the projected Seneca Avenue. Flushing Avenue was the old road from the Ferry to the outskirts of Bushwick and on to Newtown in Queens County. The old village of Bushwick was toward the north above Metropolitan Avenue, and reached from the Newtown Road by Bushwick Avenue. The Nicholas Wyckoff farm extended from above Flushing Avenue southward beyond Myrtle Avenue, and is now intersected by Wyckoff, St. Nicholas, and Cypress Avenues. A view of the house from the front can be seen in Streeter's *Wyckoff Family Genealogy;* this view shows the characteristic overhang of the roof on both parts of the house. The exposure in the present photograph was taken to emphasize the very long roof line of the pre-revolutionary wing.

Stoothoff—Bergen House on Bergen Island
formerly on East 72nd Street, Bergen Beach, Flatlands
PLATE 17

There is a great deal of controversy concerning the early history of this house and the possible builder of its earliest unit, which some claim to antedate the house of Jan Martense Schenck on Mill Island. No definite proof of its age has yet been found, but the possibilities have been exhaustively set forth in *Keskachauge*. Until the inlet was filled recently, Bergen Beach was an island in western Jamaica Bay north of Mill Island; it was known as Bergen Island, and in very early days as Mentelaer's Island. On Jan. 27, 1643 was recorded the deposition of Geertjen Manninex, wife of Claes Mentelaer, told at her house in the bay, concerning some corn hills in Brooklyn. If the present house was in part this 1643 house, it must have been erected prior to 1633, for the houses built by the West India Company in Van Twiller's time (1633-39) are known by a deposition of Gillis Pietersen made March 22, 1639; we also know that it was not built 1636-43 by Wolfert Gerritsen van Kouwenhoven, who on June 16, 1636 had with another obtained the original Indian deed or Dutch ground brief to a large tract in this vicinity. Gov. Kieft evidently considered that the West India Company had a claim to the land, as on May 14, 1646 he patented Mentelaer's Island to Capt. John Underhill for his services in the Indian wars; he might have built the house then to strengthen his title. Underhill sold his patent to Thomas Spicer who extinguished the Indian claim on July 2, 1652; this deed mentioned that it was called by the Dutch Metler's Island and by the Indians Wimbaccoe. The house was probably not built in Stuyvesant's time after 1652, as this would call the governor's attention to a new purchase, and he had just cancelled the unnecessary large grants in Flatlands. Elbert Elbertse Stoothoff proceeded to buy up the various claims to the island; on April 27, 1662 he purchased the rights of the heirs of Wolphert Gerritsen to the western flat, and on Nov. 25, 1665 he obtained an assignment from Machtel, widow of Thomas Spicer, for Mentelaer's Island containing 90 acres of upland. Elbert Elbertse continued to live in the village of Flatlands, where he ran a store, as late as 1680, and may never have occupied the island. Claes Mentelaer (Mitaler), who had been living on the island as early as 1643, was still there in 1671, probably as the tenant of Elbert Elbertse.

Elbert Elbertse Stoothoff van de Vrede, to give his full name, emigrated from Nieuwkerken in North Brabant and eventually settled at Flatlands. There are conflicting statements concerning his age and arrival: Van Tienhoven, in his Remonstrance in which he attempted to deprecate the leaders of the people, stated that Elbert Elbertse emigrated in 1633 at the age of 10 or 11 as a farmer's boy in the service of Van Twiller; Elbert himself affirmed in 1644 that he was about 24 years old, and in 1687 that he had been in the country for fifty years. He was one of the Nine Men of 1649-50, a magistrate of Flatlands for many years, and its representative at various conventions and assemblies. On Aug. 24, 1645 he married Altie Cornelis, daughter of Cornelis Lambertse Cool of Gowanus, and widow of Gerrit Wolphertse Van Couwenhoven; she was the mother of his children, one son and two daughters. He

75

married secondly July 21, 1683 Sara Roeloffs, widow of Cornelius Van Borsum. He died about 1688, leaving the island in entail to his son Gerrit and then to the latter's children in succession, and if he had no issue then to the testator's two daughters.

Gerrit Elbertse[2] Stoothoff of Flatlands married first Willemetie Pieters Monfoort, and secondly on Aug. 10, 1684 Johanna Nevius of Brooklyn Ferry. He died March 30, 1730, the father of six sons and five daughters. Gerrit lived on the island and probably built the house under discussion. Thinking he had a legal right, he bequeathed the island to his youngest son Wilhelmus[3] Stoothoff (1705-1783). However, on Gerrit's death, his eldest son Elbert[3] Stoothoff of Somerset Co., N. J. and of Flatlands, placed his elder son Garret in possession. Garret[4] Stoothoff, b. Aug. 13, 1715, married in 1739 Lammetje Stryker and had three daughters; he was drowned in Flatlands Bay Aug. 1, 1746. His father Elbert next placed his younger son Wilhelmus[4] Stoothoff (b. ca 1716, d. ca 1782) in possession. On Elbert's death Sept. 19, 1756, his son Wilhelmus for some reason delivered up possession to his uncle Wilhelmus[3] (1705-1783), and on his death the island went to the latter's son Peter.

About 1764 a suit was commenced by Eitie Nallison, Annatie Bergen and Saartie Stephens, the three daughters of Garret[4] Stoothoff (the one who had drowned), and their three husbands, against their great-uncle Wilhelmus[3] Stoothoff for the recovery of the island. The suit dragged on until Sept. 3, 1791, when the entailment in the first Elbert Elbertse's will was declared lawful and therefore the three sisters the rightful owners. The eldest had meanwhile died without issue, and on May 10, 1792 Teunis Bergen, husband of the second sister, bought out the third sister, and placed his son John Bergen in possession. In 1796 the house of Johannes Bergen was recorded as 34 x 34, in good condition, value $350., barn 36 x 48 feet, farm of 82 acres, value of barn and farm $2,460.

The ancestor of the Bergen family, Hans Hansen,[1] emigrated in 1633, settling later at the Wallaboght on Long Island. His grandson Hans Machielse[3] Bergen of Brooklyn had among others a son, Teunis[4] Bergen of Gowanus, b. Oct. 15, 1730, d. May 2, 1807, married in April 1760 Annatie or Johanna[5] Stoothoff, b. Feb. 21, 1743, d. July 23, 1819. In 1763 Teunis bought the Bennet farm at Gowanus, and lived and died there. In his will he bequeathed to his son John the island in the town of Flatlands, on which his son already resided. John[6] Bergen, b. Sept. 23, 1764, d. Aug. 12, 1824, married April 23, 1793 Rebecca Stryker of Gravesend, b. Jan. 8, 1774, d. Jan. 28, 1854. The island was later owned and lived on by their son Cornelius[6] Bergen, b. Feb. 26, 1798, d. March 31, 1865, married March 10, 1825 Fanny Baldwin of Flatlands. Their only son John C.[7] Bergen, b. Jan. 19, 1826, resided at home and was the last of the family to own the homestead. In 1893 John C. Bergen sold the house and the island to speculators, who opened an amusement park and cut it up into building lots under the name of Bergen Beach.

Bergen, in his genealogy of his own family, stated that the house on the island built and occupied by the Stoothoffs forms part of the present (recent) building; that in 1801 the wing on the east side was added by John Bergen, and afterwards in 1819 he enlarged the main building on the westerly side; and that after his death the west wing was built by his son Cornelius Bergen. Varying views of this interesting house are shown in *Keskachauge, Bergen Family* p. 299, Ditmas p. 31, and Eberlein p. 194. The plate reproduced here shows the small west wing, built after 1824 according to the early style. The kitchen wing on the east was slightly larger and had a chimney. The house formerly stood in the center of Bergen Island, on East 72nd Street south of Island Avenue. It has been demolished since this photograph was taken in 1925.

Stoothoff—Baxter—Kouwenhoven House
1640 48th Street, Flatlands
PLATE 18

Mrs. Remsen, the owner (in 1925), is a descendant of the builders of this house, and states that the wing was erected in 1747 and the main house along the same lines in 1811. The property is on the south side of the old Mill Lane which led from Flatlands Village to Mill Island (the home and mill of Jan Martense Schenck—plate 13).

On May 13, 1653 Jacob Couwenhoven sold a tract here to Thomas Spicer, which his widow transferred to Coert Stevense (Van Voorhees). On Oct. 9, 1699 he sold to his son Gerret Coerte 90 acres bounded all along by the Mill Path to the Kings Highway. It was probably sold by his heirs. The next known owners of this property were Cornelius Nevius in 1731 and Johannes Nevius in 1741 when the road was changed; they were probably brothers, sons of Pieter Nevius of Flatlands. At some date in the middle of the eighteenth century, the land came into the possession of Wilhelmus Stoothoff, who deeded this, the west portion of his tract, to his son Garret, the east portion to his son Wilhelmus, and the north portion to his son Johannes.

This Wilhelmus' Stoothoff, b. 1705, d. Feb. 14, 1783, was a son of Gerrit Stoothoff, probable builder of the house on Bergen Island (plate 17). Wilhelmus married Nov. 9, 1728 Aeltje Van Voorhees, b. May 3, 1709, d. June 1788, daughter of Albert Van Voorhees; he willed that most of his property should be divided equally between their five sons, Johannes, Albert, Wilhelmus, Abraham and Peter, and their granddaughters Aeltje and Deborah, daughters of their son Garret, deceased. It is very

77

possible that Wilhelmus Stoothoff bought and lived here on Mill Lane until he settled in 1756 in the family homestead on Bergen Island (plate 17). On Oct. 21, 1772 he sold to his son Garret 95 acres south of Mill Road, bounded east by Wilhelmus Stoothoff, Jr. and north by Johannes Stoothoff. This Garret' Stoothoff, b. Oct. 1, 1730, d. Sept. 22, 1780, married in May 1762 Maria Voorhees, and was survived by two children, Aeltie wife of John Baxter and Deborah wife of Abraham Wyckoff. On July 2, 1796 the latter released their interest in the property to the former couple.

In 1796 the house of John Baxter was recorded as 18 x 28 feet in size, condition middling, value $400., barn 44 x 36 feet, farm of 91 acres, value of barn and farm $2400. John Baxter is remembered mainly for his Journal; he was a schoolmaster of Flatlands village. He and Aeltie (Aletta) Stoothoff had a son Garret Stoothoff Baxter, bap. Sept. 9, 1792 at Flatlands. Garret evidently was married twice, first to Abigail Wyckoff, by whom he had a daughter Abigail, b. April 18, 1817 in this house, and secondly to Sara ——, who survived him. Garret S. Baxter of Flatlands died about 1836, and his widow Sara released the property on May 1, 1838 to her step-daughter Abigail Baxter. She married on March 22, 1843 William I. Kouwenhoven, b. April 5, 1818, d. Dec. 17, 1904, son of John and Susan Kouwenhoven. They lived here throughout the nineteenth century and had many children, of whom the ninth is Kitty Kouwenhoven, b. March 19, 1861 in this house, and married John Marshall Remsen. Mrs. Remsen is the owner (in 1925) of her family's homestead.

The old portion of the house (the wing) is now the dining room. Mrs. Remsen remembers when it was still the kitchen, with a very large fireplace, at the right of which was the mouth of the Dutch oven. The oven extended back into a shed attached to the wing, and known as the oven shed; it was taken down in 1880 when the new kitchen was built. Mrs. Remsen also remembers the windows in the old portion of the house as they were when she was a child, with their many small panes of glass. She states that the old house was built in 1747 by Garret Stoothoff. It is very probable that it (the present wing) was built at this early date but, if so, it must have been erected by Johannes Nevius or by Wilhelmus Stoothoff, the owners shortly before and after this date respectively, as Garret Stoothoff was a minor at this time. The steep roofline of the wing, characteristic of a very early period, is better emphasized in the vignette. The roof does not overhang the rear wall of the wing and the windows are smaller in back. The main house was built in 1811 by one of the Baxters, undoubtedly the father John Baxter. Although of such a late date, it follows the lines of the original house, thus achieving a harmonious composition. The house is on the east side of East 48th Street, south of Avenue M. It is now vacant.

Stryker—Schenck House
formerly on Church Avenue and East 53rd Street, Flatbush
PLATE 19

The property on which this house stands is in the Third Division of the New Lots of Flatbush; how it came into the Stryker family is not clear, but it was owned by John Stryker as early as 1729, when adjoining property was sold by Jeremiah Vanderbilt. Church Lane in very early times turned abruptly northeastward between the present 51st and 52nd Streets; other names were the King's Road and the Road to New Lots. At an early date the road was extended to continue directly westward, and called the Road to New Lots or Flatbush Lane, and the diagonal road was discontinued. The property in the gore between these two roads, and extending from 52nd Street west to 56th Street, was the tract owned in 1729 by John Stryker, in 1786 by his son Michael Stryker, and in 1818 by his son Cornelius Stryker, according to the bounds mentioned in the deeds to adjoining property. The lands on the northwest and east were in the possession of the Lott family. Johannes Lott willed them to his son Peter, and on his death they passed to his only surviving children, three daughters: Lammetie, wife of Petrus Wyckoff, Jannetje, wife of Johannes Stryker (eldest son of Michael), and Annetie, wife of William Williamson. These were the neighbors of the Strykers.

The ancestor of the family in this country was Jan[1] Strycker, b. 1615, d. about 1697, emigrated from Ruinen in the Province of Drenthe in 1652 with his wife and six children. In 1654 he was a leader in the founding of Midwout, later called Flatbush, on Long Island. He was immediately selected as chief magistrate and held this office for the greater part of twenty years; he was named by the towns for the embassy to the Lord Mayors in Holland concerning the annoyance caused by the Indians and English; in 1664 he was a representative to the assembly called to consider the grave situation of the country, and the following year was a representative at the Hempstead Convention, and in 1674 he was a deputy to the conference with Gov. Colve on the state of the country; he was a patentee of the town and captain of a company of the town militia; in 1654 he was a member of the commission to build the Dutch church at Flatbush and was an active supporter of Dominie Polhemus. He married three times, but his first wife Lambetje Seubering was the mother of all his eight children.

Jan's youngest son Pieter[2] Strycker, b. Nov. 1, 1653 at Flatbush, d. June 11, 1741, married May 29, 1681 Annetje Barends, d. June 17, 1717. Pieter was a patentee of Flatbush, high sheriff of Kings County, and a captain in the militia. His residence in Flatbush was built of brick with the lettering "P.S. 1696" over the doorway; it was torn down about 1845. His eldest son Jan or John[3] Stryker, b. Aug. 6, 1684,

d. Aug. 17, 1770, married first in 1704 Margrietje Schenk, daughter of Johannes Schenk, founder of the branch of this family at Bushwick (see plate 16); she bore him nine children, most of whom settled in New Jersey, and died in August, 1721. John Stryker was remarried Feb. 17, 1722 to Sara, daughter of Michael Hansen Bergen of Brooklyn, bap. June 2, 1678, d. July 15, 1760, and had five more children. John Stryker was a member of Vanderveer's company of Kings County militia. He lived in Flatbush, where he owned considerable property, including the tract in which we are interested in Church Lane.

It is not known who built the house on Church Lane, but as the tract went in its entirety to John Stryker's son Michael it is probable that the latter built the house. Michael[4] Stryker, b. March 4, 1723, d. Sept. 26, 1807, was the eldest child by John's second wife; he married Hanna, daughter of his cousin Cornelius Stryker, b. Feb. 13, 1733, d. Oct. 1, 1807, a few days after her husband. They had four sons and four daughters, including John Stryker of Flatbush who married Jannetje Lott and received from his wife's family several tracts of property northwest and east of his father. The only other son who reached maturity was Cornelius[5] Stryker, b. April 26, 1760, d. March 12, 1841, married Jan. 16, 1789 Adrianna Schenck, b. Aug. 22, 1768, d. Sept. 1, 1830, a descendant of Jan Martense Schenck of Mill Island. In 1818, shortly after his father's death, Cornelius Stryker was in possession of his father's homestead in the gore and of other property of his father adjoining it on the south. Of his six children, many died in infancy and only Ann and Michael married. On May 1, 1843 the executors of Cornelius Stryker deeded the property south of Church Lane to Michael Stryker. Twenty years before, on April 25, 1823 (deed recorded June 18, 1832), Cornelius and Adriantje Stryker had deeded the house and land in the gore to their daughter Ann, wife of Johannes Schenck, describing it as ten acres of land and woodland in Flatbush by the highway from Flatbush to New Lots, and by the land of Cornelius Stryker.

John[5] Schenck of Flatbush, b. Oct. 18, 1795, d. Feb. 18, 1873, was the eldest son of Judge Teunis Schenk and Gertrude Cornell of New Lots, and was undoubtedly born in his grandfather Cornell's house at New Lots (plate 7), which his parents later inherited. On Dec. 21, 1819 he married Ann, daughter of Cornelius Stryker of Flatbush, and made his home in his father-in-law's house, which in 1823 was deeded (as above) to his wife. She died Aug. 5, 1834, and her heirs released the 10 acre property by various deeds (1847-50-54) to her husband John Schenck. On July 15, 1837 he bought some land adjoining this to the northwest from his father Teunis Schenk, who had purchased it May 1, 1818 from John Stryker, who had inherited it from his wife's family, the Lotts. John Schenck married secondly Nov. 28, 1838 Catharine Van Dorn, b. July 26, 1808, d. Dec. 31, 1870, daughter of John

Ryder, and widow of his neighbor William Williamson, son of William Williamson (1755-1830) and Antje Lott (d. 1850). John Schenck had five children by each marriage, his eldest child Wilhelmina marrying her neighbor, still another William Williamson.

After John Schenck's death, the property was divided between his only two sons who remained in Flatbush: John T. Schenck (a son by the first wife) obtained the eastern portion; the balance of the property, including the old house and his father's purchase of 1837, was released Sept. 29, 1884 to George Schenck (a son by the second wife). George⁶ Schenck, b. May 26, 1845, married Feb. 17, 1869 Annie Blanche Kilgour. He was still living in his father's home in 1890, and his children were the third generation of Schencks to occupy it.

Until the end of the nineteenth century, the house was in rural surroundings. It stood in the east end of the town of Flatbush, at the end of the road to the church and village. It has been torn down since 1925 to make room for a row of modern buildings. The house was on the north side of Church Avenue on East 53rd Street.

House of Jacob Swaert; the Van Brunt Homestead
formerly at 1752 84th Street, New Utrecht
PLATE 20

On Nov. 22, 1652 Cornelius Van Werckhoven bought of the Indians the so-called Nyack tract on the end of Long Island along the Narrows and Lower Bay. On Jan. 16, 1657, shortly after his death, Jacques Cortelyou, private tutor to his children and manager of his properties, laid out the village of New Utrecht, consisting of twenty village plots in a square surrounded by the same number of 50 acre farms. The first house here was a small, square one of clapboards, removed from Gravesend by Jacob Hellakers (or Swaert), a carpenter. In 1657-58 he built at New Utrecht three houses contracted for by Nicasius De Sille, Rutger Joosten (Van Brunt) and Pieter Buy, respectively. De Sille sold his house in 1674 to Rutger Joosten, and it passed down in one branch of the Van Brunt family until finally torn down in 1850. It is reproduced in Stiles' *Kings County*, v. 1, p. 259. Its construction is very interesting, built of roughly cut stone covered with a roof of rounded tiles. In 1660, three years after New Utrecht had been laid out, there were eleven houses standing in the village. In the spring of 1675 the home of Jacques Cortelyou and most houses in the village were destroyed by fire.

Jacob Hellakers, alias Swaert, may have emigrated as early as 1634. He probably came from Amsterdam where a daughter of his was living in 1679. He was a master carpenter in New Amsterdam in 1652. He had a farm in Gravesend in 1657 and removed that year to the new village of New Utrecht, where his activity as a carpenter has been mentioned. He was one of the original commissaries of 1661 and a patentee of New Utrecht in 1668. He was living in New York in 1679. By his first wife (name unknown), he is said to have had two daughters and a son. He married secondly Tryntje Jacobs or Teunis, who later (in 1687) married Jan Stryker. Their only child was undoubtedly William Helleker of Smiths Valley on Manhattan, who was a ship carpenter; on April 2, 1682 at New York he married Katherine, daughter of Boelle Roeloffsen, and both died between 1691 and 1702, leaving an adult son Jacob and three minor daughters. The unnamed son of Jacob Swaert and his first wife was a carpenter in the East Indies in 1679. He was probably the Johannes Swaert or Swart who was on the assessment rolls of New Utrecht in 1693, 1698 and 1706, was a constable in 1700, church officer in 1711, and a witness in 1713 to the will of Nicholas Van Brunt of New Utrecht. He and his wife Femmetje had four children, Jan, Barent, Jacobus, and Lysbet, whose descendants are said to have resided in Monmouth County. It is not known when the house (that part later the wing) was erected which Johannes Swaert sold in 1714 to Cornelis Van Brunt, but it was of very great age and was probably built in 1675 after the disastrous fire which destroyed most of New Utrecht, or possibly even earlier by Jacob Swaert, the village carpenter.

Rutger Joosten[1] Van Brunt emigrated to this country as a young man in 1653. He was one of the original settlers of New Utrecht in 1657, receiving 100 acres of farmland and a double village plot east of De Sille and west of Cornelius Beekman; he contracted with Jacob Swaert to build thereon a house, which was one of the first four in the village. He became a large landowner and was very influential in the new village, its schepen and overseer. In 1657 he married the widow of Stoffel Harmensen, Tryntje Claes, b. about 1618, living in 1688, and had three sons: Nicholas, Cornelis and Joost, all of whom resided in New Utrecht. Rutger's second wife Gretian was living as late as 1721. In 1698 his household consisted of himself, his wife, and five slaves. He died about 1713 in New Utrecht intestate, leaving his grandson Nicholas (son of Nicholas deceased) his heir-at-law. His lands were divided among his heirs in 1717.

Rutger's second son Cornelis Rutgersz[2] Van Brunt of New Utrecht also became a large landowner and made many purchases, including the extensive Pennoyer Patent in Gravesend and in 1714 the house and lot of Johannes Swaert in the village. He was an elder of the Dutch Church, a justice of the peace, and member of the N. Y. Colonial Assembly. On Dec. 18, 1685 he married Tryntje Adriaense Bennet of Gowanus, who died about 1738. In 1698 his household consisted of himself and his wife, six children and six slaves. In his will executed in 1748 and probated in 1754, he bequeathed to his son Rutgert the Pennoyer Patent in Gravesend, a farm adjoining the old Bath Road, and various village plots in New Utrecht, and to his other son Nicholas a farm in New Utrecht west of the tract given to Rutgert with a house and plot, a tract adjoining the hills, and his undivided right in the New Utrecht Patent.

Cornelis' son Rutgert[3] Van Brunt bought of his brother Nicholas on Jan. 8, 1752 all his lands in Kings County, when Nicholas planned to remove to Monmouth County, New Jersey. Rutgert was a farmer, a deacon and elder of the Church, and a colonel in the militia. He married Elizabeth Alberts Van Voorhees of Flatlands, bap. Dec. 10, 1695, d. July 17, 1748, and had eleven children. He died April 7, 1760. His youngest son Adrian[4] Van Brunt of New Utrecht, b. Nov. 17, 1735, d. Sept. 18, 1785, married Jan. 12, 1760 Engeltie Rapalje, b. Jan. 17, 1741, d. Aug. 23, 1826. He cultivated and lived on his inheritance, a very large farm on the south side of the village, extending from Main Street to the bay. It was on this farm that the British landed their forces in 1776. Adrian's only surviving son Rutgert A.[5] Van Brunt, b. Aug. 10, 1761, d. March 7, 1818, owned and occupied that part of his father's home farm within the village later cultivated by his son Jeremiah. On June 15, 1782 Rutgert married Abigail, daughter of Jeremiah Vanderbilt, b. Feb. 15, 1767, d. Oct. 9, 1828, and had five children only one of whom married. Jeremiah[6] Van Brunt, b. Jan 22, 1791, d. about 1868, married first Jan. 12, 1815 Jane Maria, daughter of George Van Brunt, b. Sept. 15, 1795, d. Dec. 5, 1818, and had one daughter Aletta. On April 20, 1835 he married secondly Catharine, daughter of Abraham Berre, widow of George Van Brunt and stepmother of his (Jeremiah's) first wife, and had two sons Jeremiah and Abraham, both farmers of New Utrecht.

In 1869 the two brothers and their half-sister released to each other various properties of their father Jeremiah Van Brunt, with the exception of the 17 acre homestead which they were to continue to own in common in equal shares. Evidently this plan did not succeed as the 17 acre Van Brunt homestead was divided in 1879 into many plots, of which the three northern ones lay on the south side of the village road: No. 1 was allotted to A. Van Brunt, No. 2 adjoining to A. G. Cropsey (originally sold in 1718 by Smack to Rutgert Van Brunt), No. 3 adjoining No. 2 to T. E. Bergen (previously sold in 1714 by Swaert to Cornelis Van Brunt). The old house, which has been torn down since 1925, is supposed to have stood on plot No. 3, and to have been the house deeded in the sale of 1714.

The oldest unit of the house, emphasized in the photograph, has the very steep roof characteristic of the earliest houses in New Netherlands, built under inspiration of the houses in the old country. This was probably one of the first houses built in the village. The main unit of the house was erected at an early date by a member of the Van Brunt family. It is of stone covered with whitewash. A reproduction in

83

Rambles about Historic Brooklyn, p. 21, shows the house from a different view and when it was in better condition; the roof and gable end of the main house were then shingled. It stood on the south side of what is now 84th Street, which was the south side of the village square.

House of Jan Van Cleef (?)—the Van Pelt Homestead
in the Park at 18th Avenue and 82nd Street, New Utrecht
PLATE 21

The Van Pelt house, incorrectly known as the Van Pelt Manor House, is erroneously said to have been built in 1664 by Teunis Van Pelt, the emigrant ancestor of the family, and to have been inherited by his son Anthony. The records disclose that neither Teunis nor Anthony ever owned this property, and that the house could not have been built before 1672 and may not have been erected until some twenty years later.

A land dispute between Jacques Cortelyou and Jan Van Cleef over property on Gravesend Bay in New Utrecht was settled in favor of Cortelyou Dec. 5, 1671, and in compensation therefor Van Cleef was about this time awarded a plot east of the Road to Flatbush (now 18th Avenue) and north of the Road to Gravesend (later the King's Highway). Van Cleef probably forfeited the plot under mortgage to Nicolaes De Mayer, whose heirs conveyed it July 16, 1694 to Hendrick Mathyse Smack (Smock). The latter sold it to Aert Teunisse Van Pelt on April 20, 1697. Van Pelt had occupied the land before this date under a ten year lease from Nicolaes De Mayer, dated Dec. 12, 1689 and calling for 215 guilders rental per year. It is thus possible that the old stone section of the house was erected by Aert Van Pelt about 1690, although it was probably built in the early 1670s by Jan Van Cleef with the money obtained by the mortgage.

Jan[1] Van Cleef was born about 1628 and emigrated in 1653, probably from Cleef in the Netherlands. He was a farmer in Gravesend in 1656 and settled in New Utrecht by 1659, where he became a patentee and a member of the Church, and where he took the oath of allegiance in 1687. By 1662 he married Engeltje, daughter of Laurens Pietersen, and had several children.

The ancestor of the Van Pelt family was Teunis Jansen[1] Lanen Van Pelt, who emigrated on the *Rosetree* in 1663 with his family from the Province of Liege in North Belgium. He eventually settled in New Utrecht, where he bought lands in 1675-78 and was a patentee in 1686. He was known as Tunis the fisher. By his wife Grietje Jans, he had six sons and two daughters, and by his second wife Gertrude Jans Otter, a widow, whom he married Aug. 2, 1696, he had three more daughters. Aert Teunise[2] Van Pelt, one of the younger sons, was born in this country. On

Sept. 10, 1686 at New York he married Nieltje Jansen Van Tuyl and had eight children: Petrus and Jan, both of New Utrecht, Aert of Flatlands, and five daughters. He was a magistrate in 1698 and a captain of the militia in 1715. Shortly after his marriage, as detailed above, he leased the plot in the village of New Utrecht which has become associated with his family's name, and purchased it in 1697. He also bought plantations No. 11 and No. 10 nearby on the west side of the road (now 18th Avenue), but had disposed of some of his property before 1706 when he was assessed for only 80 acres. His house passed to his eldest son, Petrus Aertse[3] Van Pelt, who married Oct. 19, 1734 Antje Dorland and had five sons and four daughters.

Petrus Van Pelt was a captain of the colonial militia in 1758 and was an old man at the time of the Revolution. On the night of June 13, 1778 Capt. William Marriner led a raid to capture some British officers. He called on "Old Man Van Pelt" for advice, knocking softly on his window, and he sent them to his son Rem's house, where they made their plans resulting in a successful raid. The brothers Rem and Aert Van Pelt and two Van Brunts were arrested on suspicion by the British authorities, but released as nothing could be proved against them. Upon one of the panes of the Van Pelt homestead are scratched the names of the prisoners confined here under Howe's orders.

Petrus[3] Van Pelt died Sept. 6, 1781 at New Utrecht, leaving his home to his son Aert. Aert[4] Van Pelt, b. Oct. 20, 1748, died about 1830, married Femmetje Stellenwerf but left no issue; on his death he willed the paternal homestead, subject to payments, to his grandnephew John L. Van Pelt, son of Jacob, the son of Rem, who had both predeceased the testator. Aert's older brother Rem[4] Van Pelt, b. April 17, 1738 at New Utrecht, d. March 8, 1829 at Brooklyn, married Nov. 24, 1767 Ida, daughter of Jacobus Lefferts, b. Jan. 26, 1745, d. July 2, 1828. His only son Jacob[5] Van Pelt, b. March 10, 1774 at New Utrecht, d. Oct. 16, 1827 before his father, married Maritie Lott. Jacob's only son John Lott[6] Van Pelt, b. Aug. 1, 1806 at New Utrecht, d. 1885, married Dec. 17, 1834 Anna Maria, daughter of Timothy Cortelyou. John L. Van Pelt inherited from his greatuncle the family homestead on the King's Highway in New Utrecht but did not reside here. He was born and lived in a house on 86th Street and 20th Avenue in New Utrecht, where his father Jacob had been born and lived before him, and where his son Townsend was born. John's son Townsend Cortelyou[7] Van Pelt, b. Nov. 13, 1837 in New Utrecht, married Oct. 24, 1866 Maria Elizabeth, daughter of John Ditmars, b. Sept. 24, 1843. After their marriage Townsend and Maria Van Pelt moved into the old family homestead on the King's Highway, put in heat and improved the second story, and were still residing here in the beginning of the twentieth century. The property has been bought by the city and converted into a small park.

85

The house was erected in sections at three separate times. The earliest part is built of undressed stone, covered with whitewash. This unit is very narrow, only about two-thirds of the depth of the present house. Some time before the Revolution, the house was deepened and the ridgepole raised and carried back, in order that the front and rear slopes of the new gable roof should be equal in length and have the same slant. A view from the road on the west shows this addition plainly, as the newer part is covered with shingles. The wing was added at some later date. The lie-on-your-stomach windows may have been added by Townsend Van Pelt, when he added the bay window and dormers, and the gingerbread supports for the roof overhang.

The house stands on the east side of the old village square. To the south is the Dutch church of New Utrecht, used during the Revolution by the British as a hospital. Between the Van Pelt house and the church ran the King's Highway, which went eastward to Gravesend and Flatlands and then northward to the New Lots of Flatbush, where it connected with the Road to the Ferry and so reached Manhattan. On the west side of the house was the Flatbush or New Utrecht Road, which ran northeastward from the village to the Martense farm in the western part of Flatbush, and connected with the rough road over the hills to Manhattan. An old milestone by the house records that it was 6 or 10 miles from New York (by the two different routes), 15 miles to Jamaica, and 2½ miles to Denys's Ferry to Staten Island. Along the King's Highway passed the traffic of the day from New York City to Philadelphia. The Van Pelt house stands on the east side of 18th Avenue between 81st and 82nd Streets, facing the latter.

House of Paulus Van Enden, later Beegel's and Onderdonk's
1416 Flushing Avenue, Bushwick
PLATE 22

This is one of the very few stone houses in Kings County. Long Island is a wooded rather than a stony land, and most of its early houses were built of wood, unlike the houses on the west shore of the Hudson River which were built of sandstone from the local quarries. Bernardus Smith, who about 1690 inherited the tract to the south, later Wyckoff's, came into the possession of this adjoining tract. An early undated Queens County deed records the transfer of land here from Bernardus Smith to Edward Stevenson; in 1709 John Stevenson sold to Tunis Titus a tract of 350 acres which extended to the Maspeth Kills, and much of which came into the hands of the Schenk and Wyckoff families (see plate 16). On April 22, 1709 Teunis Titus and his wife Mary sold to Paulus Vander Ende a plantation in Bushwick of 100 acres, laid out by Peter Cotilleou, surveyor, bounded northwest by the

86

highway (from Bushwick to Newtown), northeast by Peter Lott, southeast and southwest by Teunis Titus. This plantation was later adjudged to lie partly in Newtown, Queens County.

Paulus Van Enden, as he wrote his name in his will, lived in Bushwick, and undoubtedly spent his later years in the stone house which still stands here. He was baptized Dec. 28, 1679 in Utrecht, son of Bastiaen Van den Ende of Amsterdam and Sophia Van Cortlandt. His mother was a first cousin of Stephanus Van Cortlandt, first Lord of the Manor, of Catharina the wife of Frederick Philipse, and of Jacobus Van Cortlandt. Catharina and Jacobus, just mentioned, acted as sponsors in 1706 for Paulus' child Catryna. Jannetie, the wife of Paulus Van Enden, was probably Jannetie Hendricks, bap. at Flatbush June 23, 1685, daughter of Hendrick Ryke (she is generally credited with a different marriage). Her father had emigrated in 1663 and settled in Flatbush; his three sons (Jacob, Hendrick and Ryck) took the name of Van Suydam and are the ancestors of the Suydam family. In Paulus Van Enden's will, executed in 1732 and probated in 1737, he mentioned his wife Jannetie, his children Catryna (bap. 1706 in Brooklyn), Hendrick, Adrian, Jacob, Abraham, and Ryck, named as executors his wife, the three Van Suydams (his brothers-in-law, although not so stated) and his son-in-law Jan Vanderbilt. The son Hendrick Van Ende lived in the stone house on the plantation in the New Bushwick Lots. He died early in life between Jan. 8 and March 2 of 1750, the dates of execution and probate of his will, in which he mentioned his wife Antie, daughter of John Colyer, his brother Abraham Van Ende, brothers-in-law John Colyer and Abraham Duryea, all of Bushwick, and his four minor children, Hendrick, Jannetie, Sarah and Antie. The plantation eventually came into the hands of his daughter Jannetie, wife of Moses Beegel (Beigle, Beadel). His identity is not known; possibly he was a grandson of Robert Beedle of Hempstead who died intestate in 1702.

The boundary settlement of 1769 between Newtown and Bushwick reads: up along the branch of Maspeth Creek to the pond near the head of Mr. Schenk's mill pond, and thence east to Arbitration Rock, which lies west of the house of Joseph Woodward and northwest of the house formerly of "Frederick Van Nanda" and now in the possession of "Moses Beigle," and from said rock southerly up the hills to the Flatbush line. The name in this agreement has been published as Frederick Van Nanda, and is no doubt a misreading of the manuscript for Hendrick Van Nanda (Van Ende).

Moses Beadel and his wife Jenny sold April 29, 1786 to Johannis Covert (deed recorded Nov. 3, 1866) 48 acres in Bushwick and Newtown. This was the south half of the plantation bought by Paulus Van Ende in 1709, and was occupied by the

Covert family until about 1866 (plate 8). How much longer Moses and Jannetje Beegel lived, we do not know, nor whether they had any children. Wilhelmus Van Nuys appears in possession of the north half of the plantation twenty years later, but it is probable that he purchased rather than inherited the house as his father-in-law was Elias Hubbard. Wilhelmus Van Nuys of Bushwick died in 1805, and his executors sold to John Corzine on Sept. 1, 1806 a house and 50 acre farm in Bushwick and Newtown, which ran northeast along the highway, southeast along Woodward's land, southwest along the land of Philip Edsal, northwest along the land of John Covert to the road. In 1812 John Couzine sold the tract to George Ryerson, whose executors sold it in 1821 to Adrian Onderdonk.

Adrian[5] Onderdonk, b. Jan. 20, 1795 at Cow Neck, d. July 2, 1831 at Bushwick, was a son of Jacob, and a member of the branch of the Onderdonk family which settled in the town of Hempstead at the beginning of the eighteenth century. On March 4, 1819 he married Ann Wyckoff, b. Dec. 17, 1793, d. Nov. 16, 1863. She was a daughter of Peter Wyckoff and granddaughter of Nicholas Wyckoff, who had bought and improved the Schenk farm (plate 16) on the Newtown Road in Bushwick. In 1821, shortly after his marriage, Adrian Onderdonk bought the Van Ende farm near his father-in-law's. He had two daughters before he died at the youthful age of 36 years. In 1848 Andrew Hegeman, husband of Adrian's daughter Dorothy Ann, released their interest in the property to the widow Ann Onderdonk. It remained the home of the other daughter Gertrude Onderdonk, b. July 31, 1825, married Dec. 24, 1845 Nicholas II. Schoonmaker, and here were born their three children, Anna Gertrude, Mary, and Adrian Onderdonk Schoonmaker. The house of late has been known as either the Onderdonk or Schoonmaker house.

The house is said to have been built about 1731. If correct, it was probably built by Paulus Van Ende shortly before he died. The house can be compared with the stone houses of the early eighteenth century in Bergen County. It is built of roughly cut stone, thickly coated with whitewash and covered with a gambrel roof; the door and windows are in uneven alignment. The frame wing belongs to the early nineteenth century. The house stands on the southeast side of Flushing Avenue (the old road to Newtown), southwest of Onderdonk Avenue.

The Wyckoff Homestead
Canarsie Lane near Ralph Avenue, Flatlands
PLATE 23

There is great controversy about the age and early history of this house. The chain of title is clear from the time that Pieter Wyckoff, Jr. bought the property on Feb. 28, 1737, but it has been claimed that the house was built 1639-41, and that it was occupied after 1652 by his great grandfather Pieter Claesen (Wyckoff). The arguments have been exhaustively set forth in *Keskachauge* and in the *Wyckoff Family Genealogy*, of which a brief summary is as follows. On July 16, 1636 Director Wouter Van Twiller bought of the Indians a large tract of land in eastern Flatlands. On April 11, 1641 he reported to the Amsterdam Chamber of the West India Company that he had caused houses (presumably including the Wyckoff homestead) to be erected on his land purchases from the Indians after his departure (in 1639) from New Netherland.

The property came under the control of Stuyvesant as Director, since the original deed to Van Twiller had not been confirmed nor a patent issued to him, and he kept the farm for his personal use while governor. Van Twiller's and his heirs' rights were formally annulled on July 1, 1652 by Stuyvesant, who placed Pieter Claesen (Wyckoff) as his representative to farm and live on the property. Their formal agreement is dated July 10, 1655, but it is thought that Pieter Claesen may have moved directly into Van Twiller's house when he settled in Flatlands (which was by 1653 and possibly as early as 1649). Since it was government property, the title automatically passed to the Duke of York on the English conquest of 1664, and it became the property of the town of Flatlands under the new Indian deed of 1665 and the new charter. There is no deed known to Pieter Claesen, but his title may have been derived or strengthened by the Act of Settlement of Oct. 26, 1683:—Whereas wars and other causes have deprived several inhabitants of their deeds to prove their respective rights to their lands, whoever has actually possessed and improved his land for four years previously, if no legal demand is made in fifteen months from now, shall be accounted the lawful owner. Pieter Claesen died in 1694 and his widow between 1699 and 1703. There follows a period of obscurity in the title. In the Woodlands Division of 1719 the land was left undivided, probably because the title to it was disputed at the time of the division. In some manner it came into the possession of the Van Voorhees family, who sold it to Pieter Wyckoff, Jr. in 1737.

Pieter Claesen[1] Van Norden was a native of Norden, a town near Ems in East Friesland; he emigrated in 1637 on the *Rensselaerswyck* in the employ of Simon Walichsz, and lived at Rensselaerswyck until 1649. He removed to New Amsterdam, and had settled at Flatlands by 1653, when he described himself as a farmer of Amersfoort (the old name of Flatlands). In 1655, he contracted to cultivate the bouwery and keep the cattle of Director Stuyvesant in Flatlands. He was a patentee of the town in 1666 and 1685 and a magistrate for many years. He took the oath of allegiance in 1687, stating he had been in the country for 51 years. He died on or about June 30, 1694 intestate. About 1645 he had married Grietje, daughter of

Cornelis Hendricks Van Ness, who survived him and died between 1699 and 1703. They had six sons and four daughters. Their sons Claes, Hendrick, and Gerrit lived in Flatlands village on lands adjoining Mill Lane; Jan later settled in New Jersey; Cornelis lived in Flatbush, and Martin in Gravesend.

The son in whom we are interested is Nicholas or Claes[2] Wyckoff, b. about 1646 at Beverwyck (Albany), died after April 27, 1719 at Flatlands, married about 1672 Sara, daughter of Pieter Monfoort, bap. April 2, 1656, died a few days before Dec. 31, 1704. They resided on a townplot in Flatlands village given him by his father, who had bought it Feb. 15, 1676/7. On May 21, 1703 he took title to various of his father's lands from other heirs of his father. On Feb. 24, 1714/15 Claes deeded 48 acres in Flatlands to his son Pieter of Middletown; this is supposed to be a deed of partition from Claes to his son Pieter, the balance to go to his other son Cornelius; all parcels are described and divided between the two, but the property on Canarsie Lane is not mentioned, inferring that he did not own it. This son Pieter[3] Wyckoff, b. about 1675, d. 1759 at Flatlands, married first Willemtje Janse Schenck, daughter of Jan Martense Schenck of Mill Island (plate 13) who had been a friend of his grandfather. His second wife Anne Elizabeth survived him. Pieter removed to New Jersey, living in or near Middletown. He returned to Flatlands about the time of his father's deed to him in 1715, and died here. His son Pieter[4] Wyckoff, Jr., b. March 28, 1704, d. Nov. 14, 1776, married Aug. 5, 1727 Sarah, daughter of Jan Amerman, b. May 5, 1705, d. June 20, 1792, and had nine children.

On Feb. 28, 1737 Pieter Wyckoff, Jr. bought of Koert and Petronella Voorhees the house and 42 acres on Canarsie Lane, which remained in the hands of his descendants until 1901 and is known as the Wyckoff homestead. Undoubtedly a part of the present house was standing at this time and they moved in immediately; the first child probably born here was the one who eventually inherited it. He was Peter A.[5] Wyckoff, b. May 8, 1737, d. Oct. 22, 1823, married Dec. 17, 1768 Heyltie Remsen, b. April 25, 1747, d. Feb. 1, 1830. It is stated that in 1776 a British guard was established at Mr. Wyckoff's on Flatlands Neck. The record of 1796 reads that the house was occupied by Heyltje Wyckoff, that the house was in middling condition, size 29 x 37, value $480., barn 44 x 30, farm of 100 acres, value of farm and barn $2500. After Heyltie's death, the children conveyed the house and 42 acres on Canarsie Lane Oct. 18, 1830 to their brother Abraham. After Abraham's death in 1846, there were various deeds between the widow Ida (his second wife) and sons, until it was finally released to their son John in 1849. The last of the family to own and occupy the house was John A.[7] Wyckoff (1817-1891), a son of Abraham and his second wife Ida. John's widow and five children conveyed the homestead farm May 24, 1901 to Francis Gross, who sold it to the Brooklyn Realty Trading Co.

A close inspection of the house shows that different sections have been built at various times. The original house was about three-fifths of the depth of the present one, and might be the house built for Van Twiller between 1639 and 1641. The original cellar, attic beams and floor partitions all extend to only three-fifths the depth of the present house. At some later date, the building was deepened, changing the line of the east chimney and the roofline. The oldest shingles are on the southeast front of the main house, of cypress 42 inches long, of which 14 inches are exposed. Probably at one time these rounded shingles covered the whole house, but they have been partly replaced with square cut, shorter cedar shingles of a later make. The typical double Dutch door on the north front is panelled like the old shutters. At some later period, the wing was added, its front is of clapboard and the gable end of the newer cedar shingles. Van Wyck does not consider that this wing was built before 1784, but the steep pitch of its roof extending to a low level suggests an earlier date, and was certainly built according to an earlier style. The house has been for many years quite dilapidated. Before 1867 Canarsie Lane was straightened, causing it to run in the rear instead of in front of the house. Canarsie Lane more or less parallels the present Clarendon Road for most of its distance, and led from the Flatbush Road in Flatbush across the King's Highway to the Canarsie settlement in Flatlands. The Wyckoff house stands on the south side of Canarsie Lane, west of the modern Ralph Avenue. Several views of the house, showing it in various conditions and from different angles, are reproduced in *Keskachauge*.

Houses in Queens County
House of Abraham Lent, later Rapelye's
Bowery Bay Road, North Beach
PLATE 24

The settlement in which this house stands, the bay and its adjoining shorelands, took their names from the nearby Poor Bouwery, the farm owned by the Dutch Church of New Amsterdam and cultivated for the benefit of the poor. Harck Siboutsen from Langendyck married at New Amsterdam Nov. 16, 1642 Wyntje Theunis from Naerden and had fifteen children. He was a ship carpenter. He settled near the Poor Bouwery about 1650 and received a patent for his land here July 2, 1654. He was a freeholder of Newtown in 1666 and died here 1681-84. He was succeeded on the farm by his son Jacobus Krankheyt, bap. Sept. 7, 1659, d. Feb. 18, 1729 without issue, leaving the farm to his nephew Abraham Lent. Catrina, daughter of Harck Siboutsen, had married about 1671 Ryck Abrahamsen[2] Lent, b. 1637 in New Amsterdam, one of the purchasers and settlers of Ryck's Patent on the Hudson River, near the present Peekskill. Their eldest son, Abraham[3] Lent, b. March 10, 1674, d. Feb. 5, 1746, lived the first fifty odd years of his life in Westchester County, and in 1729 took possession of his uncle's and grandfather's farm at the Poor Bouwery in Newtown. Here he built his home, the center room of the present house, no doubt on the site of his grandfather's dwelling. He was a leading member of the Dutch Church at Tarrytown and at Newtown. On Dec. 24, 1698 he married Anna Catharine Meyer, bap. March 21, 1677, d. July 2, 1762, daughter of Adolph Meyer from Westphalia. They had eleven children, born before they removed to Newtown: Ryck, Jacob, Adolph, Isaac, Abraham, Catrina, Jacobus, Elizabeth, Maria, Wyntie and Ann. The youngest son succeeded to the farm: Jacobus[4] Lent, b. July 3, 1714, d. Dec. 13, 1779, married Margaret, daughter of Daniel Rapalje, d. Sept. 11, 1794 in her 74th year. The farm passed to one of their sons, Daniel[5] Lent, b. May 31, 1754, d. April 20, 1797 in his 43rd year, married Dec. 9, 1792 Rensie, daughter of Martin Rapelye, b. Jan. 17, 1774, who married secondly Bernard Rapelye. Shortly before his untimely death, Daniel Lent sold the farm. Isaac Rapelye became the owner about this time, making it his home until he died. This Isaac[6] Rapelye, b. Dec. 23, 1782, d. Oct. 20, 1850, was a son of Daniel Rapelye; he married Margaret Polhemus and left a son Jacob and two daughters. The house was still in the possession of his family in 1923. It is a long, low shingled structure, with its west wall of rough stone. The wing, which has a very steep gable roof, has an earlier appearance than the main house. It stands on the north side of Bowery Bay Road on a hill overlooking Bowery Bay, and on the opposite side of the bay from the North Beach development.

Luyster—Kouwenhoven House
formerly on the Bowery Bay Road, North Beach
PLATE 25

Pieter Cornelisz[1] Luyster emigrated in 1656. He was a carpenter and lived in King's County until he removed to Newtown, where he was a freeholder in 1666. Here he bought the Poor Bouwery from the Dutch Church of New Amsterdam, a farm which had been granted to the Church for the benefit of its poor; it extended from Fish's Point westward one mile along the bay to the Riker homestead. Peter married Jannetie, daughter of Jan Snediker. After his death in 1695, his farm on the bay in Newtown was bought from the other heirs by his youngest son Cornelius[2] Luyster, b. 1662, d. 1721. Cornelius lived at Flatbush until the time of this purchase. He became prominent in Newtown, a magistrate and captain. He married Sarah Catharine Nevius and had four sons and six daughters, willing his farm to his sons. The eldest, Peter[3] Luyster, b. March 10, 1687, d. Dec. 17, 1759, inherited that part of his father's farm which later came into the hands of his Kouwenhoven descendants. On April 30, 1713 he married Sarah, daughter of Daniel Rapalje, d. Jan. 23, 1773 aged 85 years, and had four sons and four daughters. The second son succeeded to his father's farm: Daniel[4] Luyster, b. Sept. 26, 1722, d. May 31, 1788 aged 65 years, married Nov. 29, 1744 Anna Van Nostrand, d. June 20, 1811 in her 89th year, having survived her husband twenty-three years. They had three daughters and no sons; Rensie and Anna never married, Sarah[5] Luyster married George Wyckoff of Flatlands. Their daughter Anna Wyckoff married Luke Kouwenhoven, b. June 3, 1766, d. Oct. 22, 1853, son of Gerret Kouwenhoven of Flatlands. Luke resided on the Bowery Bay farm until his death. It was later owned by George Kouwenhoven or Conover, presumably his son. It recently formed a part of a road-house called the German Castle and has been demolished since the photograph was taken in 1925. It is not known who built the house. The steep roofline and small windows are suggestive of great age. It was probably erected by Peter[3] Luyster on a portion of his father's farm about the time of his marriage in 1713. The house stood on the southeast corner of the Bowery Bay Road and the old Trains Meadow Road, near the shore of Bowery Bay. Trains Meadow was the name of the common pasturage inland.

House of Joseph Woodward
Flushing and Woodward Avenues, Maspeth

Maspeth or Newtown Creek, which flows into the East River, divided the Dutch settlements in Kings County to the south from the English settlements in Queens County to the north. Rev. Francis Doughty and his associates received a patent for land at Maspeth Kill in 1642 and commenced a settlement there, which, however, was destroyed by the Indians the following year. The later settlement in this section was often called the English Kills to distinguish it from the settlement of the Dutch Kills on the south side of the creek, parts of Newtown and Bushwick respectively. The boundary settlement of 1769 between Newtown and Bushwick ran in part as follows: up along a branch of the Maspeth Creek to the pond near the head of Mr. Schenck's mill pond (see plate 16) and thence east to Arbitration Rock, a little west of the house of Joseph Woodward, and northwest of the house formerly of Hendrick Van Nanda and now in the possession of Moses Beigle (plate 22), and from this rock southeast up the hills to the Flatbush line. This house of Joseph Woodward thus immediately adjoins the Dutch settlement, where still stand the Schenk—Wyckoff, Van Ende—Beegel, and Covert houses (plates 16, 22 and 8). Woodward's house is typically Dutch in style, a good-sized, one and a half story, shingled structure, covered by a high gambrel roof extending to form an overhang. It is not known when or by whom it was built. If erected by Woodward, he was greatly influenced by the style of his Dutch neighbors. Joseph Woodward was probably descended from Lambert Woodward, freeholder of Newtown in 1666. A Woodward owned the property in 1806, according to the deed to adjoining land. In 1873 the owner was H. Diehl. The house is still in good preservation, although slightly altered by porch and dormers. As it is hidden by porch, vines and trees a satisfactory photograph is not possible. It stands on the northeast side of Flushing Avenue, near the corner of Woodward Avenue.

PLATE 7

Cornell—Schenck House
in Highland Park, East New York

This house is believed to have been built about 1760 by Isaac Cornell or his father; it passed by inheritance into the Schenck family and was inhabited by descendants until sold to the city in 1906. Stone houses were seldom erected in Kings County; this is the only existing example of the late eighteenth century on Long Island. The stonework has been plastered and whitewashed; the gable is clap-boarded. Note the four chimneys, more typical of the Bergen County stone houses than of the Kings County shingled houses. The beautiful sweep of the roofline has not been broken by the addition of modern dormers. The photograph shows the house in the rural surroundings of the mid-nineteenth century. It is reproduced by courtesy of Mrs. Sarah Woodson.

PLATE 8

House of John Covert
1410 Flushing Avenue, Bushwick

This house is pre-revolutionary in character, but as the land on which it stands was a part of the Van Ende plantation until purchased by John Covert in 1786, the house may not have been erected until this later date. It is similar in style to the Schenck-Williamson house in Flatlands (plate 15). The use of the gable roof to cover a house two full rooms in depth is typical of Kings County houses until far into the nineteenth century. The narrow window in the rear is unusual. Note the double Dutch door.

PLATE 9

House of Lady Moody (?); the Van Siclen House
Gravesend Neck Road, Gravesend

Persistent tradition calls this the house of Lady Moody. She was the founder of the Gravesend colony in 1643 and died 1658-59. It is true that Lady Moody's home stood on this plot of ground, but the house, in its present condition at least, belongs to the last half of the seventeenth century. Compare the Sip house in Bergen (plate 107) built in 1664; similar in style and in depth, it nevertheless has the early steep roofline which the so-called Lady Moody house does not have. The house has a great deal of character; the low ceilings and the long sweeping lines of the roof result in its seeming almost a part of the earth; its charm lies in its conformity with the surroundings. The large dormers are of course modern.

PLATE 10

House of Pieter Lefferts
now in Prospect Park, Flatbush

The old Lefferts homestead on the Flatbush Road was burned during the Battle of Long Island in 1776 and the present house was erected on the site by Pieter Lefferts along the old lines. The deep curve of the roofline is unusual. It is not to be seen in any other Dutch house still existing but can be noted in the sketch of the Second Church of Breuckelen, built 1766 (Stiles, p. 332). The sunburst decoration over the doorway is typically post-revolutionary.

PLATE 11

House of Johannes and Hendrick Lott
1940 East 36th Street, Flatlands

The left wing of the present structure is a part of the house built by Johannes Lott shortly after he purchased the farm in 1719. Typical of the early period are the small window openings, the old windows with twelve-paned upper sash, narrow lower sashes, and thick moldings, and also the steep gable roofline with no overhang. The Dutch were masters of the art of compact building and the spaciousness they achieved in small houses is often surprising. Two bedrooms were to be found under the roof of this small wing until the partition was knocked out recently. Hendrick I. Lott built the main house and west (right) wing in 1810 on another part of the farm and moved a part of his grandfather's house to form his east wing. The difference in the size of windows and window panes between the old and newer sections is as notable as it is typical. The rear view is shown here. The house is still owned and inhabited by descendants of the builders.

PLATE 12

*House of Adrian Martense
formerly at 21 Church Avenue, Flatbush*

The wing of this house was the home of Adrian Martense (1707-1784) and was built by him about the middle of the eighteenth century. The main house belongs to the last quarter of the century. The combination of gable and gambrel rooflines is more often seen in the Dutch houses of Bergen County. The roof of the wing is not extended over the rear wall to balance the overhang in front. Notice the small size of the attic windows.

PLATE 13

House of Jan Martense Schenck
on the former Mill Island, East 63rd Street, Flatlands

This house was built by Jan Martense Schenck immediately after he purchased the mill and half the island in 1675. A much earlier date has sometimes been attributed to the house due to its very steep roofline, which is comparable to those on the earliest houses in New Amsterdam. The construction of the house is very unusual; it resembles the hull of a ship with its curved timbers and archlike inverted frame. An addition, doubling the size of the house, was made in the early eighteenth century and was formerly covered with long round-edged shingles. Dormer windows of the early slanting variety were added at some period, and the overhang of the roof was extended and pillars built to form a porch. The early type fanlight over the door is to be noted. One chimney for each unit of the house is a smaller number than was customary, especially in view of the fact that the house was situated on a bleak island.

PLATE 14

House of Nicholas Schenck at Canarsie
now in the Museum of the Brooklyn Institute of Arts and Sciences

This house was built by Nicholas Schenck in 1772 on his father's farm at Canarsie Point in Flatlands. In the closing years of the nineteenth century the Schenck homestead farm became a city park; recently the house has been removed and rebuilt within the Museum as an example of Dutch colonial architecture. It is one of the few remaining pre-revolutionary houses with a gambrel roof in Kings County. The double Dutch door and the small windows are to be noted. Windows of this size were more common in the early eighteenth century.

PLATE 15

Schenck—Williamson House
East 53rd Street, Flatlands

This house was probably built in the third quarter of the eighteenth century by Martin Schenck on land near the house and mill of his father, Capt. John Schenck. Later it was owned for almost one hundred years by the Williamson family. The house is characteristic of a type greatly in favor in Kings County, used with variations well into the nineteenth century. Note the small size of the windows. The dormers are of course modern additions.

PLATE 16

Schenk—Wyckoff House
1325 Flushing Avenue, Bushwick

The wing of the present house was the pre-revolutionary home of members of the Schenk family, and was probably built about 1719 by one of the sons of Johannes Schenk, the miller. Nicholas Wyckoff purchased the property and erected the main house probably in 1788, the year he built the new barn. His descendants lived here until 1911. The long, sloping roofline on the rear of the wing is a typical variation sometimes seen in the Dutch houses. The overhang of the roof in front is balanced asymmetrically by the long roofline extending almost to the ground, and thus including and covering a lean-to behind the house. The main house is similar in style to many of the pre-revolutionary houses.

PLATE 17

Stoothoff—Bergen House
formerly on Bergen Island, Flatlands

It has been claimed that a part of the present house was built before 1633 as a trading post with the Indians. The original unit was more probably erected in the third quarter of the seventeenth century by Gerrit Elbertse Stoothoff. The house passed by marriage from the Stoothoffs to the Bergens and was occupied by their descendants until sold for a development in 1893. Many changes and additions have been made, all in the style of the original unit. The main house was enlarged on the west side in 1819. It is probable that the roof was raised about this time, for the two and a half story height under the long roofline is to be seen in several Kings County houses of the early nineteenth century; certainly the original seventeenth century unit was not this high and probably not this deep. The east wing was added for a kitchen in 1801 and the smaller west wing, shown in the photograph, was not added until after 1824, but they harmonize in style with the main building.

PLATE 18

Stoothoff—Baxter—Kouwenhoven House
1640 48th Street, Flatlands

The wing of the present house is believed to have been built in 1747 but its very steep roofline (emphasized in the vignette) suggests an earlier date. It may have been erected by the Stoothoffs; certainly it came into their possession shortly afterwards and has remained in the possession of their descendants ever since, passing by marriage to the Baxters, Kouwenhovens and Remsens. The early wing has a steep roofline with an overhang only in the front, very small windows and also dormers in the rear. The main house, built in 1811, is a successful adaptation of the earlier house on larger lines. The rather ingenuous windows under the overhang are a modern effort to give more ventilation to the second story without breaking up the roofline.

PLATE 19

Stryker—Schenck House
formerly on Church Avenue, Flatbush

This house was built by a member of the Stryker family, passed by marriage into the Schenck family, and continued to be a Schenck homestead until recently. The photograph shows the Schenck farm as it was in the mid-nineteenth century. It is reproduced by courtesy of Mrs. P. L. Schenck. The repetition of roofline forms a pleasing harmony. The winter door is of course modern.

PLATE 20

*House of Jacob Swaert; the Van Brunt Homestead
formerly at 1752 84th Street, New Utrecht*

The small wing was undoubtedly one of the earliest houses on Long Island surviving until recently. It was probably erected about the time New Utrecht was settled in 1657, although it may date no further back than the fire of 1675 which destroyed most of the village. It was built by Jacob Swaert or his son Johannes and sold by the latter in 1714 to Cornelis Van Brunt, in whose family it remained until 1879. The very steep roofline of the wing is characteristic of the very earliest houses of New Netherland. The main house was probably built by Cornelis Van Brunt shortly after he purchased the property in 1714. Although larger, it resembles the Schenk wing of the Schenk-Wyckoff house in Bushwick (plate 16). The long roofline at the rear probably originally covered an open lean-to; the curve of the roofline in front suggests that it once overhung the wall. Roof and gable end were formerly shingled, thus giving the house a more respectable appearance. The dormers and door porch of course are later additions. This was one of the few stone houses on Long Island.

PLATE 21

House of Jan Van Cleef (?)—the Van Pelt Homestead
18th Avenue and 82nd Street, New Utrecht

The original unit of this house is the stone section; it was probably erected about 1672 by Jan Van Cleef, although possibly not until about 1690 by Aert Teunisse Van Pelt under a leasehold. The latter purchased the property and it has remained the family homestead until recent years. The stone unit is only two-thirds the depth of the main house. This increase in depth is plainly seen from the west (street end) as the newer part is shingled. The roofline had to be changed at the same time. The present lines resemble the Stryker-Schenck house in Flatbush (plate 19). The wing belongs to a later period but is undoubtedly also pre-revolutionary. The heavy gutter on the wing, the bay window, dormers, and gingerbread supports to the roof are all modern changes.

PLATE 22

House of Paulus Van Enden, later Beegel's and Onderdonk's
1416 Flushing Avenue, Bushwick

This stone house was built by Paulus Van Enden or his son Hendrick about 1731. It closely resembles the Bergen County stone houses and can be compared with the Demarest House at Old Bridge (plate 83), built before 1720. Notice the uneven alignment of door and window openings. The old twelve-pane window sashes have been replaced by six-pane sashes. The door and dormers are modern. This is the earliest example of a gambrel roof still existing in Kings County; the gable roof was more often used here rather than the gambrel roof prevalent in Bergen County.

PLATE 23

The Wyckoff Homestead
Canarsie Lane, Flatlands

The original unit, about three-fifths the depth of the main house, is claimed to have been built for Director Van Twiller between 1639 and 1641, and to have been occupied from 1652 to 1694 by Pieter Claessen Wyckoff. It came again into the possession of the Wyckoff family in 1737 and remained the family homestead until 1901. Beams, partitions and cellar indicate the size of the original unit. It is said that the wing was not added until 1784 but the steep pitch of the roof extending to a low level is characteristic of an earlier period. Notice the very deep overhang of the roof on the main house and the early type round-edged shingles, which are of cypress 42 inches long.

PLATE 24

House of Abraham Lent, later Rapelye's
Bowery Bay Road, North Beach

The original unit of this house is the center room, erected about 1729 by Abraham Lent. It is built of roughly cut stone, still to be seen in the west wall. At some early period the east half of the house was added and the whole building was shingled. The fanlight over the door is very large. The very steep roofline of the wing is evidence of its age. All units were undoubtedly built by members of the Lent family. The house was purchased by Isaac Rapelye about 1800 and has since been in the hands of his descendants. The magnificent box-tree by the door is a reminder of the better days the house has seen. In the distance is Bowery Bay, an inlet of Long Island Sound.

PLATE 25

Luyster—Kouwenhoven House
formerly on Bowery Bay Road, North Beach

This house stood until recently on the old Luyster bouwery and may have been built by Peter Luyster about the time of his marriage, 1713. It passed by inheritance into the Kouwenhoven family. The slope of the roofline is at a very pleasing angle. Recent use as a roadhouse has rather marred the appearance of the house and is probably the cause of the cheap porch and railing and of the boarding up of the stone Dutch oven back. Dormers also are modern.

RICHMOND COUNTY

CRUSER—WINANT—PERO HOUSE

RICHMOND COUNTY (Staten Island)

STATEN ISLAND, the large island at the mouth of New York Bay separated from the New Jersey mainland by the Arthur Kill and the Kill Van Kull, attracted the Dutch in early years but had no permanent settlement until some thirty years after Long Island. Staten Island, with other territory on the New Jersey shore, was granted by the Dutch West India Company to Michael Pauw in 1630. As he made no settlement and hence did not comply with the conditions of the grant, he gave up his rights in 1634. There followed three unsuccessful attempts at colonization. David Pietersen De Vries received a grant and started a colony in 1639 at the Watering Place (Tompkinsville), in the northeastern part facing the Upper Bay, but it was wiped out by the Indians in 1641. Before the rights of De Vries had been extinguished, Cornelis Melyn tried to establish a patroonship on Staten Island; he commenced a settlement in 1640 which was wiped out by the Indians in 1643. He placed another settlement at the Watering Place in 1650, but this also was destroyed by the Indians in 1655, and Melyn gave up his patroonship in 1659. The various wars with the Indians had proved disastrous to the farms and plantations but were ended by treaty in 1660.

In 1661 nineteen Dutchmen and Frenchmen from the Palatinate (to use Stuyvesant's term) petitioned for permission to settle on Staten Island. The petition was granted and the first permanent settlement was formed by them at Oude Dorp (Old Town), the site now occupied by St. Mary's Cemetery, inland from Arrochar and Fort Wadsworth. Pierre Billeau, a Walloon, was one of the petitioners and the leader of the colony. A small garrison was established here for its protection. Dominie Drisius, who could preach in English, French and Dutch, ministered to them every two months.

The English conquest of New Netherland in 1664 caused little change. The colonists were allowed to retain their property, local government and religion, but were required to take the oath of allegiance. Staten Island was organized with western Long Island into the West Riding of Yorkshire. In 1670 Gov. Lovelace made the final purchase of the Island from the Indians, requiring the young Indian lads to sign the deed so that it would not be quickly forgotten. The court for Staten Island continued to be held in the nearby settlement of Gravesend on Long Island until 1675. Gov. Dongan called the first Provincial Assembly in 1683 and Staten Island was then organized into Richmond County. The early county seat was at Richmond, formerly called Cuckold's Town, southwest of New Dorp. In 1688 were established the four townships of Northfield, Southfield, Westfield and Castletown, corresponding to the earlier precincts and Castleton Manour.

The settlement at Old Dorp soon spread to the fertile valley nearby, which was laid out and called the New Lots of the Old Town, now Dongan Hills. In 1671 the village of New Dorp was settled on the shore east of the present village of that name. After the Dutch capture of 1673 and subsequent recapture by the English, the surveying of Staten Island continued apace and many settlers and speculators were granted patents, generally for 80 acres or multiples of that figure. Gov. Dongan also granted several manorial estates, of which the two most important were the west end of the Island (Tottenville) to Christopher Billop and central Staten Island to John Palmer, who in 1685 sold out to Dongan. A large part of the west side of the Island was formerly covered by the Great Swamp, which drained into the Fresh Kills. Scattered plantations were cleared at the edge of the swamp but mainly on the high lands and meadows south of the Kills. The Labadists estimated that in 1670 there were about one hundred families on the Island, mainly Dutch and French.

It is believed that by 1668 the Waldensians had established a Church at Stony Brook and the Huguenots another at Fresh Kill (now Green Ridge); both combined with the Reformed Church at Richmond village in 1717. The Dutch depended for many years upon the monthly visit of the Dominie from New Amsterdam; a Dutch Church on the north side of the Island was organized about 1680. Cornelis Van Santvoord was called by these two Reformed Churches in 1718 and was the first Dutch minister established on Staten Island. The English worshipped in the Dutch church at Richmond until 1713. A Moravian congregation was established in 1742 and their church built at New Dorp in 1763.

The original habitations of most families on Staten Island (according to Clute) were cabins of squared logs, built for durability. In the course of time these were supplanted by more substantial houses, generally of stone, with long, low, massive lines. The stone, timber and shingles were procured on the farms, lime was obtained from the oyster shells along the shore, and nails were made by a nearby blacksmith. As the stones for the houses were gathered together in clearing the fields, their shapes were very irregular and often no attempt was made to lay the walls in courses. The steep gable roof was very popular but was seldom combined with the graceful overhanging eaves characteristic elsewhere. The houses were generally long and narrow, only one room in depth, and without a hallway. The windows and doorway were seldom symmetrically placed and their arrangement varied greatly, for most of the houses were built before the balanced style became popular. Unlike the houses in the other counties, the original unit was generally the largest section.

Peter Kalm, the Swedish naturalist, travelled through North America in

1748-49 and recorded that: ". . . (We spent the night at Elizabeth Town Point near the ferry and crossed over it to Staten Island.) . . . Most of the people settled here were Dutchmen, or such as came hither whilst the Dutch were yet in possession of this place. But at present they were scattered among the English and other European inhabitants, and spoke English for the greatest part. The prospect of the country here is extremely pleasing, as it is not so much intercepted by woods, but offers more cultivated fields to view. Hills and vallies still continue as usual to change alternately. The farms were near each other. Most of the houses were wooden; however some were built of stone. Near every farmhouse was an orchard with apple trees . . . (and) a press for cyder . . . cherry trees stood along the enclosures round cornfields. The cornfields were excellently situated and either sown with wheat or rye. They had no ditches on their sides, but only furrows . . ."

The early houses and the identity of their owners were found partly by the study of a series of maps, the most important of which was the "Plan (No. 31) du Camp Anglo-Hessois dans Staten Island de 1780 a 1783" in the Archives of the French War Department. The text is based largely on a study of the original land and probate records, in which the author was ably assisted by Rev. Lefferd Haughwout, Alexander S. Rowland and Loring McMillen. The latter's architectural criticisms were of great aid. With the exception of six photographs, made about 1900 and reproduced through the courtesy of William T. Davis, the plates in this section were taken in 1925. A great many of the old houses remained standing until very recently, with the result that enough photographs of them are available to devote an entire book to Staten Island. The account here has been limited largely to houses still existing. A few no longer extant have been included which were old family homesteads and others where their supposed history has been found radically wrong. Many of the houses which have disappeared are reproduced in *Staten Island and Its People*, by Charles W. Leng and William T. Davis.

HOUSES IN RICHMOND COUNTY (Staten Island)

House of Nathaniel Britton, later Walton's and Cubberly's
New Dorp Lane, New Dorp
PLATE 26

The father of the builder of this house (the main stone section) was William Britton. Mention is made of him in 1661 as an Englishman living at Maspeth, the early English colony at Newtown on Long Island. Nathaniel Britton, probably a brother, settled on Staten Island by 1670 when he was appointed to treat with the Indians for the purchase of the Island. William came to Staten Island before 1678 when he was appointed constable. He died intestate in 1683, and his widow Mary conveyed land on Staten Island to their son Nathaniel in 1686. The wife, Mary Britton of Staten Island, had been baptized in the Flatbush Church at the age of 30 in 1678 with her seven children, including Nathaniel aged 13 years.

This Nathaniel[2] Britton, b. 1665, d. about 1708, and his wife Mary sold 400 acres at Old Dorp on Staten Island in 1694. The following year, on Oct. 28, 1695, he bought a 96 acre tract at New Dorp from Obadiah Holmes, to whom it had been patented by Gov. Andros in 1677. Nathaniel and Mary probably built and settled here immediately; they were termed residents of New Dorp in a sale of 1699. Nathaniel died 1707-08, in which latter year letters of administration on his estate were granted April 10, 1708 to his widow Mary, then wife of Mr. Duchan. She married thirdly Lambert Garrison of Staten Island, d. 1725, and was still living in 1754 at an advanced age. Her son Nathaniel[3] Britton (Jr.) and his wife Elizabeth (Lake?) sold his parents' home at New Dorp on April 9, 1714 to Thomas Walton; they removed to Bybury, Pa., where he made his will in 1754, mentioning his mother Mary Garrison, his wife Elizabeth, and their children.

The purchaser of the New Dorp house was Capt. Thomas[2] Walton 2nd, b. 1672, d. 1728, son of Thomas Walton of Staten Island, an Englishman. He married Mary Stillwell and secondly Martha ———; at his death he left the farm where he lived to his wife during her widowhood and all his property to his six children, Thomas, Richard, Matthew, William, Martha and John. By various releases, the New Dorp house came into the possession of the eldest son Thomas[3] Walton 3rd, b. Jan. 23, 1699 on Staten Island, d. 1780 in Monmouth County. He married Rebecca Lawrence. They settled in Upper Freehold about 1750, and on June 20, 1761 sold the New Dorp property to Isaac Cubberly. The wing had undoubtedly been built previous to this time by one of the Waltons.

Isaac Cubberly and his wife Anne (Journeay?) made their home here. He died in 1786 leaving a widow, five sons and two daughters. He willed to his son James the south part of the farm where he (the testator) then lived with the buildings thereon, but left to his widow Anne the right to live in his house during her widowhood with their son James. Another son Stephen received the west part of the farm. Adria Cubberly, spinster, daughter of Stephen and granddaughter of Isaac and niece of James deceased, granted to Isaac Cubberly 2nd on July 18, 1833 all her interest in the New Dorp estate devised by Isaac to James. Isaac Cubberly 2nd, b. March 17, 1761, d. here Aug. 22, 1841, was a brother of James and Stephen and another son of Isaac Cubberly who had purchased the house in 1761. The place was called *The Cedars* by this family.

The property was sold by Isaac Cubberly 2nd's executors on June 26, 1847 to David J. Tysen, who resold it two days later to Harriet Lord. She later married Mr. Britton, a descendant of the original builder of the house. Their son, Dr. Nathaniel Lord Britton, a botanist, and his wife Elizabeth Gertrude Knight, later lived here. In January, 1915, they deeded it to the Staten Island Association of Arts and Sciences for its home and for preservation as an example of old colonial architecture.

The house is in four units. The oldest section is the central unit, built about 1695 with rough fieldstones, very heavy beams, and a huge open fireplace with a beam across the top. Its moderately sloped roof may be a later change. The wing has very low stone walls and a very steep gable roof; its more careful joining is proof that it was built later than the main house. The lean-to at the rear of the wing formed the third addition; its roof slopes down almost to the ground. The frame section on the road end dates from about 1800. There are no overhanging eaves in front or rear. A photograph of the front view of the house, when it was still a private residence and well kept up though completely hidden by vines, can be seen in Leng and Davis, p. 866, and other views in the *Proceedings of the Staten Island Institute of Arts and Sciences*, V, plates 6 and 7. The house is on the south side of New Dorp Lane, corner of Cedar Grove Avenue, near the beach. This locality was the site of the original New Dorp settlement and was lately known as Elm Tree. The property has been put in better condition since the accompanying photograph was taken in 1925.

Cozine—Bodine—Martling House
40 Wachogue Road, Myer's Corners
PLATE 27

This house is erroneously known as the "home of Daniel Corsen." The latter lived in the 1780s on the bend of the Willow Brook Road, not far from the Christopher house, and later bought property on the Clove Road, where he died in 1801.

The house was probably not erected before 1760 and the builder may have been Garrit Cozine, but unfortunately there are no early records for the property. It formed a part of the large tract in the center of the Island granted to John Palmer and sold by him in 1685 to Gov. Thomas Dongan, who became the Earl of Limerick. A deed of 1769 to adjoining land states that the property in question was then in the possession of Garrit Cozine. On April 8, 1784 Wilhelmus Cozine mortgaged his half of this house, stating that the house and land formerly belonged to James Cozine, deceased.

On June 1, 1789 Wilhelmus Cozine of Staten Island, yeoman, and his wife Phebe, sold to Vincent Bodine of the same place, blacksmith, for £394.12s, land and lot of salt meadows with buildings and improvements, being a part of the plantation formerly belonging to Cornelius Cozine, deceased, situated on the main road that leads from the New Blazing Star Ferry to the Narrows, beginning by a wild cherry tree by the road, then northwest by the land of Jacobus Cozine, southwest by John Tison, Jr., east by John Simonsen and John Wright, then west by Benjamin Seaman, deceased, then northeast to a hickory tree, northeast "to the middle or center of the dwelling house, 5 feet to the westward of the west doorpost of the door that leads into the entry of the said house, from thence through the middle of said house along by the partition of the west side of the entry through the said house," northeast to the road, bounded by Jacobus Cozine to the beginning, 43 7/10 acres; "Excepting therefrom and always forever hereafter that Privilege unmolested for the use of Jacobus Cozine, his heirs and assigns, the use of one half of all the cellar room under the said house, the use of the kitchen and oven, for doing all kinds of drudgery work, washing, baking, etc., and that the said Jacobus Cozine . . . shall and may from time to time and at all times hereafter have free Privilege to pass and repass from his premises to the Cellar and Kitchen as often as necessity requires, and further the said Vincent Bodine, his heirs and assigns, shall have and may by virtue of these presents have the liberty of going in the entry to go up the stairway on his part of the garrett."

Thus one half of the house with the grounds on that side were sold to Vincent Bodine and the other half kept by Jacobus Cozine, who was presumably a son of Cornelius Cozine, deceased. These are the only recorded land transactions on Staten Island to or from a Cozine; neither is there any mention of the family in the early church records of Staten Island. There was a Cornelius Cosine of New York, cordwainer, who died 1762-65, bequeathing his farm in Bloomingdale (Manhattan) to his five children, but there was neither a Jacobus nor a Wilhelmus among them; the eldest of them was Garret, also of New York City, who died between 1759 and 1773. The house is marked G. Cozine on the map of 1783. Jacobus Cozine, who retained one half the house in 1789, seems to have disposed of it to James Bodine who at some period sold it to his brother Vincent Bodine, but these deeds are not on record.

The will of John Bodine of Richmond County, dated and probated in 1778, mentioned his wife Dorcas, and his seven children: Rachel, John the oldest son, Mary Egberts, James, Martha (bap. 1762), Vincent (bap. 1766) and Ann (bap. 1769). They were probably descendants of Vincent Boden of New York, mariner, who in 1735 willed his estate to his wife Elsje. John's son Vincent Bodine, bap. Nov. 26, 1766 on Staten Island, died between 1814 and 1824 (according to the marriage records of his sons), married June 7, 1789 Jane Blake, and had at least three children: Martha, bap. 1789, John and Vincent, Jr. Vincent Bodine conducted a tavern in another house further down the road; it was evidently well known, for it was referred to in deeds even after his death. In 1829 the adjoining property of John Tysen, deceased, was partitioned, and the land was then described as on the south side of the road leading from the Tavern, formerly of Vincent Bodine, deceased, to Mersereau's Ferry, bounded east by Garret Martling (then the owner), etc. On Jan. 18, 1805 (recorded 1836) Vincent Bodine of Castleton, Richmond Co., and his wife Jane sold the former Cozine property for £1400 to Garret Martling, using the same description almost word for word as in his deed of purchase from Cozine; this conveyance transferred, besides the 43 7/10 acres in the above deed, "one other small lot including part of the dwelling house that the said Vincent Bodine bought from James Bodine my brother . . .", 2 7/10 acres.

Martling resided here for almost half a century. His father John Martling lived in a house he built on the Manor Road, and there the son Garret was born Dec. 9, 1778, and died in another house on Manor Road Aug. 15, 1852. Garret married first Jan. 29, 1799 Mary Wood and secondly Oct. 6, 1818 Catharine Marston, widow of J. H. Jones. At the time of their occupancy, Watchogue Road was an important thoroughfare—it was a part of the highway from New York City to Philadelphia, via Long Island, the ferry over the Narrows, and Staten Island. The road at this point was quite narrow and had a dangerous curve, so that the coach drivers always blew their horns loudly here in foggy weather and proceeded only if they heard no response. On Oct. 2, 1848 Garret Martling sold this property for $5488. to Alvin C. Bradley of Brooklyn, being the house and two tracts he had purchased from Bodine in 1805 and an adjoining 21 8/10 acres which he had purchased from John Tysen in 1815. The property has since changed hands several times. It is now owned by Ernest Voges.

The house is a small one; with the kitchen wing on the end it measured 68 feet. The house is built mainly of unhewn fieldstone, but the front wall is of carefully cut and jointed sandstone blocks. The stones were formerly whitewashed. As there was little or no sandstone on Staten Island of a quality for masonry, it is possible that the blocks for this house were brought from nearby Bergen County, New Jersey. The wing was moved in 1920 and set behind the main house, thus destroying the typical Dutch arrangement. A small hallway runs the depth of the house and has typical double Dutch doors. On the east is a narrow room, used as parlor and best bedroom. On the west of the hall is a large, square living room in which the chimney breast is panelled and the mantel shelf is narrow. The small kitchen wing connects with this room and formerly had the old type of casement windows. The house is covered with a steep gable roof, which has a very slight "flip" or curve at the ends although there are no overhanging eaves. The house is on the south side of Watchogue Road just west of the junction with Victory Boulevard and Jewett Avenue. A more familiar view of the house is in Leng and Davis, p. 880.

De Hart House
3373 Richmond Terrace, Holland Hook
PLATE 28

This house stands on a tract granted to John Taylor in 1680. It is not known how or when it came into the possession of the De Hart family, but it seems possible that it was part of the estate inherited by Daniel De Hart and his wife Catharine Van Pelt from her father Jan Teunissen (Van Pelt), who died 1720-34. It remained a De Hart homestead until recent years.

Daniel's father, Balthasar De Haert, emigrated about 1660 from the Province of Guelderland, in which there is a village of Hart; he or his ancestors were probably French and his will was partly written in that language. He settled in New York City where he became a merchant and a shipper, and died in 1671. He had two natural sons, Matthias the ancestor of the Elizabeth, New Jersey, branch, and Daniel, the ancestor of the Staten Island branch. Daniel[2] De Hart, bap. Sept. 1, 1671, son of Balthasar De Haert and Margaret Stuyvesant, widow Backer, married Catharine, daughter of Jan Teunissen Van Pelt. He sold property in Elizabethtown in 1704 and shortly after that date removed to Staten Island where he lived and died in 1753, in his 84th year, and was buried at Port Richmond. Daniel had six children, all baptized on Staten Island: Daniel (1707-1753) of Canada, Baltus, Sarah, Elizabeth, Matthys, and Samuel.

On the map of 1783 the house is marked "S. D. Hart". Samuel De Hart, Sr., son of Daniel, is presumably the owner referred to. Samuel De Hart, Sr., bap. Aug. 1717, d. May 17, 1798 and buried in Port Richmond, married Abigail Jones, d. April 24, 1804 in her 83rd year. In his will of 1785, Samuel left his wife Abigail half of his farm with the furniture; he ordered that his estate should be sold and divided between his six children, but that the share of his daughter Catharine, should remain with the executors during the life of her husband Garret Post. Samuel, Sr.'s six children were: Samuel, Jr. (bap. 1750), Edward of Staten Island (1753-1791) who left two sons, Edward and Abram, both of the Town of Northfield, Catharine (b. about 1755) who married Garret Post and was living in a house on her father's property in 1783, Matthias (1758-1849) of Northfield, Staten Island, who had ten children but was only survived by Samuel and Edward and two daughters, Daniel (1760-1842) who was a sea captain buried in Canada, and Moses (1763-1831) of Morris County, New Jersey. The homestead in which we are interested seems to have become the property of Samuel, the eldest child. Samuel[4] De Hart, Jr., bap. May 20, 1750 on Staten Island, married Eleanor Van Tine, and died between 1811 and 1819, the dates of execution and probate of his will. He bequeathed his entire estate to his wife (unnamed) for life and then to his sons William, Mathias and John, provided they paid to Samuel Dehart's children $250. (the latter Samuel was evidently a son who had predeceased him); he also left legacies to his four daughters, Eleanor, Catharine, Magdalen and Abigail, left his wearing apparel to his son Jacob (who settled in Michigan), and mentioned among his executors his son-in-law William Degroot. One of the sons, Matthias[5] De Hart (1783-1820), built a house about 1818 nearby on the west corner of Holland Avenue.

The old home on the water front evidently fell to the lot of Matthias' brother John[5] De Hart (1790-1872), who lived here for so many years that it has become known as the John De Hart Homestead. He married Elizabeth Lipscomb and had nine children, including Henry[6] De Hart, who was the last of the family to occupy and own the old homestead.

The house stands between the shore of the Kill van Kull and Richmond Terrace, a short distance east of Holland Avenue, in the northwestern tip of the Island. In its present condition, it only dates back to about 1735-40. Construction shows that a part of a former building was used in the present one in a rather unusual manner. The original house faced westerly. Its north end was preserved (possibly the south end had been burned in a fire) and incorporated as the west end of the main unit of the present house, which was built to face southerly; a new east end completed the main unit and a wing was added on the west end. This unusual remodelling may have been done by Samuel De Hart, Sr. or his father. The very steep roofline of the wing and the small sized windows are characteristic of an early period. The so-called German hood over the windows and door of the front wall of the main house has been cut in two recently for the second story window; its sawn timbers show that it was not a part of the house originally.

Dissosway House

formerly near the Outerbridge Crossing, Richmond Valley

PLATE 29

This house stood until recently on land granted to Mark Dusochay; it was built by him or by his son and remained the home of the family until the third quarter of the nineteenth century. The ancestor of the family was Marc¹ du Sauchoy, a Huguenot. Our first record of him in New Netherland is on May 31, 1655 when he appeared in court as a plaintiff concerning the clearing of 3 morgens of land in Midwout (Flatbush), Long Island; he had probably arrived at least a year previously. He returned to Holland where he married Elizabeth Rossignol, and set sail again for New Netherland April 2, 1657 on the *Draatvat*. He leased a tide mill on the Mespath Kill from Burger Jorisen, and in the following years leased farms successively at Cripplebush (in Brooklyn), Harlem and Fordham. He is first mentioned on Staten Island in 1681 when he was a defendant with Capt. Billop concerning the branding of some pigs. The Staten Island references could equally apply to him or his son, Mark, who was of age by this time. In 1683 he transferred his allegiance from the Dutch Church to the French Church. In 1684 he petitioned successfully for a land grant of 255 acres on the west side of Staten Island, and it was surveyed that same year. In 1695 more land was granted to him and Lockerman, and that same year he purchased from Obadiah Holmes 160 acres and a house. In 1702 a warrant of survey was granted him and new letters patent issued for his various holdings. He or his son appears on the records as assessor, surveyor and constable. He was recorded as 80 years of age in the Staten Island census of 1706; his wife is not listed and had probably died by this time. Their children were: Magdelene, bap. 1658, married Martyn Hardewyn, Marcus or Mark, bap. 1659, Jannetie, bap. 1662, married Conradus Boeg, Jean, bap. 1665, probably died in infancy, and Maria, bap. 1669.

The son Marcus or Mark² Dusochay (Dusachoy, Dusochany, Dusway, etc.) is said to have been born at Mespath, Long Island; he was baptized March 21, 1659, and died on Staten Island between Dec. 23, 1713 and Jan. 27, 1713/14, the dates of execution and probate of his will. His first wife Susanna is mentioned in a deed of sale June 3, 1703. She had probably died before 1706, as she is not listed in the census of that date. This census, however, does not appear to give a complete list of this family; it mentions three of the daughters, but none of the three sons who were all born before this date; possibly the mother and sons were living elsewhere temporarily. Mark's second wife Jane is mentioned in his will; he married her in or before 1712, when they sold property together. Mark Dusochay probably inherited or bought the lands mentioned above, he purchased more land in 1708 and 1710, and on June 24, 1712 he successfully petitioned for two lots of vacant land on Staten Island of about 80 acres each, contiguous to the land on which he resided, bounded north by the water side. In his will of 1713 he left the farm on which his dwelling house stood, containing 85 acres of upland and 10 acres of salt meadow, to his eldest son Job, left the north lot on the water side, containing 85 acres of upland and 10 acres of meadow, to his son Israel (b. 1700), left the south lot on the water side, of similar size and adjoining John Rue, to his son Gabriel (bap. 1703), left tracts of approximately the same size, situated inland on and near a brook, to his four daughters: Elizabeth (wife of Pieter Barberie), Susanna Hendricks, Dinah (wife of Hendrick Bries), and Sarah (Mary, still another daughter, had evidently died between 1706 and 1713 as she is not mentioned in the will); the father stated in this will that none of these tracts were to be sold, but to be inherited by his children's issue; the negroes Jack and Betty were to be sold; "my wife Jane is to live with any of my children she chooses, but if she cannot agree with them a convenient house is to be built for her at their charge."

It has been always understood that the house we are interested in was the one erected in the 1690s by Mark, Sr. or Jr. That home was bequeathed to the eldest son Job.[3] Little is known of Job other than that he married Sarah Denis and had a son Johannis, bap. on Staten Island in 1723. He sold some property adjoining his family's to Lewis DuBois in 1723, which may or may not have been his father's home.

As the house in question stood on the water side and was at a later date occupied by Israel Dissosway's descendants, it seems possible that Israel Dissosway built it on the north water lot which he inherited from his father Mark, to whom it had been granted as a vacant lot of land in 1712. Israel[3] Dissosway (as he spelled his name in his will) was born in or about 1700 and died 1753-54. He was appointed a major of the militia in 1738. He married Gertruy Van Deventer before 1723 and had five children: Israel the eldest (died in 1769 in Middlesex Co., N. J.), Cornelius, Gabriel, Mark (died 1766), and Annetie, wife of John Bedel; Israel bequeathed his real estate to his four sons equally. It seems probable that the son Cornelius obtained the homestead: he lies buried near the old house and on a map of 1783 three adjoining houses by the water here are marked C. Dusaway. Cornelius[4] Dissosway, b. 1731, d. Dec. 19, 1785 in his 54th year, married first Dec. 16, 1756 Catharine Corsell, and secondly Aug. 13, 1765 Mary Baldwin who died Sept. 10, 1808; he had two sons and five daughters: Ann, wife of Joseph Guyon, Charity, wife of Israel Prall, Cornelius, Israel (1777-1825), Catharine, wife of William Van Brunt, Mary, and Violetta, wife of James Britton. In his will Cornelius bequeathed the residue of his estate to his two sons Cornelius and Israel when they should attain the age of 21 years, including the plantation on which he (the testator) resided nearly opposite Perth Amboy, except for 450 acres which were to go to Israel and Mark, the sons of his brother Mark deceased, thus leaving a balance of 600 acres for his own sons, together with houses, barns, millhouses, etc.

On May 12, 1801 (recorded 1813) Israel R. Disosway of Staten Island, cabinet maker, conveyed property on the north side of the mill race (including the old house) to his brother Cornelius Disosway, farmer, in a division of the farm bequeathed to them equally by their father Cornelius, deceased. The son Cornelius[5] Dissosway, Jr. lived in the homestead in Old Creicherville; he bought a mill several hundred yards from the house at the mouth of Mill Creek, which he ran and rebuilt about 1803. In 1801 he married Ann, daughter of Peter Winant, and had five sons and four daughters. He had died by 1828 when his widow sold some property. In the 1853 map the house is marked Mrs. Dissosway and in the 1859 map, D. Dissoway. The latter might be Cornelius, Jr.'s son Daniel W. The last of the family to occupy this old homestead was Cornelius, Jr.'s daughter Ann M.[6] Dissosway, b. August 1812, married Abraham Cole, Jr. (1810-1876); they had four sons and one daughter. On the 1874 map the house is marked Mrs. Totten's; she was Susanna, another daughter of Cornelius Dissosway, Jr.

The family homestead was a stone house built in the closing years of the seventeenth century by Mark Dusachoy or in the opening years of the eighteenth century by Israel Dissosway. It was covered by a gable roof with deep overhanging eaves both front and back. In the rear was a later frame addition. The accompanying photograph was taken about 1900. The house was torn down in 1926. It stood in the fields on the bank of the Arthur Kill off the Arthur Kill Road, near Richmond Valley and south of Charleston (or Creischerville). This region was known as Sandy Ground at the time of the Revolution.

Dongan—Christopher House
Willow Brook Road, Willow Brook
PLATE 30

This house is known as the home of Joseph Christopher, who lived here during the Revolution. It is erroneously believed to have been built by an earlier Christopher about the middle of the eighteenth century. Actually it was one of the many farmhouses erected on Dongan's lands. A very large part of central Staten Island was granted to John Palmer in 1684 and came into the possession of Thomas Dongan, who was commissioned Governor of the Province of New York in 1682. He lived on Staten Island for some years, and his immense tract of lands here became known as the Manour. He later returned to Ireland where he became the

Earl of Limerick, and died Dec. 14, 1715, aged 81 years. Shortly before, on May 9, 1715 he conveyed to his nephews, Thomas, John and Walter Dongan, all his Manour of Castleton on Staten Island. Walter Dongan married twice and died in 1749. The Staten Island estates were inherited by his eldest son Thomas Dongan, who married first Rachel, daughter of Nicholas Britton of New Lots (plate 26), and secondly Magdalena, daughter of Rev. Richard Charlton of Staten Island. This last named Thomas was evidently a colonel. He made his will in 1765.

The first mention of this particular house and property is found in an advertisement in the New York Gazette Post Boy of Dec. 24, 1760: Nicholas Haughwout here announced for sale an 80 acre farm belonging to Col. Duncan (that is, formerly belonging to Col. Dongan), with a good dwelling house about 4 years old, a saw mill about 3 years old and a barn about 5 months old. A mortgage of June 7, 1768 by Daniel Simonson and his wife Mary states that this was part of a tract of approximately 175 acres in the Manour of Castle Town bought from Thomas Dongan by Peter and Nicholas Haughwout and their mother. The latter was Nelly, widow of Peter² Hagewout, whose home stands a short distance to the northwest (plate 33). No further mention is made of Nicholas who probably died. That part of the tract advertised by him is next found in the possession of his mother, who in her will of 1761 bequeathed "the house and land I bought of Thomas Dongan, lying in the Manour" to her four daughters, Catrina, widow of John Brestead, Dirckje, later wife of Matthias Smith, Nelly, wife of Antony Brat, and Maritie, probably later the wife of Daniel Simonson. Later surveys show that the widow's portion was divided into four lots, each of 21 and a fraction acres stretching north and south, and that the house in question stands on Lot No. 1.

Lot No. 1, the westernmost of the four lots, came into the possession of Joseph Christopher after the above will of 1761 and in or by 1764. On May 24, 1764 Joseph Christopher and his wife Heirtry mortgaged these premises, being 21¼ acres bounded on the north by Abraham Krusen (then owner of the Pieter Pietersen Hagewout house), west by Peter² Hagewout and east by Derickey's land. The 1770 road survey of the present Willow Brook Road read: by the partition line of Jacob Mercereau (plate 36) and Abraham Kruse (plate 32), across the lands of Peter Haughwout, Joseph Christopher, Matthias Smith, Daniel Simonson and John Wright, to the land of the said Peter Haughwout (formerly part of the share of his brother Nicholas); thus the road crossed the family's lots. Some time after 1783 Christopher also acquired the adjoining property of Derickey (Hagewout) Smith, on which she was living in 1783; the map of this date shows that Christopher was then occupying his portion as was also Peter² Hagewout on the west.

The ancestor of the family was Hans[1] Christophel, who was one of the original group of permanent settlers on Staten Island in 1661. In 1678-79 he purchased land and a house from Pieter Pietersen Hagewout in the New Lots of Old Dorp, adjoining and immediately west of the Stillwell—Perine house (plate 38); it is probable that he lived there until he died (before 1703); his widow Tryntie Barents died 1703-06. They had at least four children: Stoffel, b. 1676, d. 1727 intestate; Barent, bap. 1680; Hans, b. 1683, d. 1719 without issue leaving half his lands to Nicholas and Hans, sons of his brother Barent; a daughter, probably named Wyntie, who married Aert Simonsen. The son Barent[2] Christopher, bap. June 6, 1680 at Flatbush, married Anna Catharine, daughter of Nicholas Stillwell, Jr.; they had eight children and were living on Staten Island as late as 1732. The father Barent Christopher and his brother Stoffel purchased a tract on the Fresh Kills Jan. 30, 1701/2; it has heretofore been presumed that the Christopher house in which we are interested stood on that tract, but its detailed division between the two brothers in 1717 and also the road survey of 1705 locate it as the southern half of the Isaac See patent on the present Richmond Avenue in New Springville. It is probable that Barent Christopher's house stood there; that tract passed to Abraham Jones about 1760. Barent's son John[3] (Hans or Johannes) Christopher, b. about 1706, married Jane Arrowsmith, probably daughter of Joseph Arrowsmith who owned land in the vicinity, and had four sons.

The third son was Joseph[4] Christopher, bap. Aug. 8, 1736 on Staten Island; he married Charity (Heirtry, Geertruy) Hagewout, whose relationship to the Hagewout family is undetermined. Between 1761 and 1764 (as stated above) Joseph Christopher and his wife acquired the Dongan property on Willow Brook, which has been known since as the Christopher place. They mortgaged it in 1764, probably to build the large addition, and undoubtedly resided here the rest of their lives.

Willow Brook is one of the many streams which empty into the Fresh Kills, draining a large territory in the west end of Staten Island, which was formerly known as the Great Swamp, and which extended many miles into the interior. Joseph Christopher was a member of the Committee of Safety during the Revolution and it was at his house on the edge of the swamp that the Committee met. Staten Island was occupied by the British during the greater part of the war and the patriots were forced to meet secretly. Their knowledge of the paths through the swamp enabled them to escape from Christopher's house at a moment's notice when warned of the approach of an enemy.

The house is believed to have been inherited by the son Joseph[5] Christopher, Jr., who was a cordwainer and removed to a farm on the Manor Road early in the nineteenth century. On Sept. 4, 1827, this property, described as fifty acres on either side of the road and adjoining the mill, being the estate of Joseph Christopher, deceased, was sold by the Master of Chancery to David Decker, who probably held a mortgage on the property, as he was the defendant in the suit. The house was later purchased by Mr. Standring and is now owned by his descendant, Mrs. Adelaide Egans, nee Sykes, of Brooklyn, who leases it.

The house is of unusual length; the division of its two units is shown by the chimney. The early portion, which was evidently a farmhouse on the Dongan Manour and built about 1756, is the small one room unit farthest from the road. A similar addition, almost twice its size, and with two front doors, was presumably built by Joseph Christopher when he mortgaged the property in 1764. The house is of rough, whitewashed stone and is covered by a gable roof without overhanging eaves. Porch and dormers are later changes. The house stands on the north bank of the headwaters of Willow Brook. It is reached by a private lane from the north side of Willow Brook Road, a short distance east of the point where this road makes a sharp turn northward to the Victory Boulevard.

House of Jacques Guyon
formerly at Guyon Avenue, Oakwood

Among the earliest settlers on Staten Island were the Guyons. Jacques Guyon, a French merchant, emigrated from St. Martin en L'Isle de Re, and settled on Staten Island by 1670 as a planter and as the agent of Jean Collyn. A tract of land at New Dorp was confirmed to him in 1675. On April 18, 1692 he mortgaged his plantation to Paulus Richards, doubtless using the proceeds to build his house. He died in 1694, and his widow Sarah, daughter of Phillipe Casier of Harlem, paid off the mortgage in 1699. Their house was a part of the beautiful homestead, which remained in the family until sold and torn down in 1924. The elder son Jacques or James[2] Guyon, b. about 1682, d. 1742, married Mary, daughter of Joseph Holmes, and had nine children. His father's patent was confirmed to him in 1708. One of his sons, Capt. James[3] Guyon (1714-1761), inherited the homestead, and it passed to his son James,[4] b. 1749, to the latter's son Major James,[5] b. 1778, then to his only child Ann Bedell[6] Guyon, wife of Dr. Ephraim Clark. Their granddaughter Miss Gertrude Clark sold the homestead in 1924 to real estate developers, who demolished it. A fuller account and various views of this beautiful and typical Dutch home are in the *Proceedings of the Staten Island Institute of Arts and Sciences*, VI, p. 113. Another view is reproduced in Leng and Davis, p. 902. The house stood on Guyon Avenue between Hylan Boulevard and Mill Road in Oakwood.

Guyon—Lake—Tysen House
Tysen's Lane near Hylan Boulevard, New Dorp
PLATE 31

This house is known as the Lake—Tysen homestead, but it was not until 1812 that the Lake family came into possession of it. An 80 acre tract adjoining the Guyon patent on the northeast was granted in 1677 to Hans Laurence, and later was in the possession of James Hanse Dye, probably his son. The next definite record of the property is its possession by Joseph Guyon 2nd, in 1772 according to a mortgage deed to adjoining property and in 1773 according to the relocation of Mill Road. It is probably the unidentified land which Joseph³ Guyon, the bachelor, willed in 1758 to his nephew Joseph, son of Capt. James³ Guyon; the latter had inherited and dwelt in the family homestead adjoining it on the southwest (see supra). As construction of the house shows that it was erected about 1720-1740, it is possible that it was built by Joseph³ Guyon, the bachelor. His nephew Joseph⁴ Guyon 2nd, b. July 20, 1751, married Jan. 27, 1773 Ann Dissosway. Martinew Swaim came into the possession of the property and sold it in 1790 to Peter Cortelyou, who in 1772 had married Addra Guyon.

The ancestor of the Lake family was John Lake, who was an associate of Lady Moody in the Gravesend Patent of 1645. His son Daniel² Lake was living in Gravesend as late as 1694. He removed to Staten Island 1694-96 and was still living here in 1710. In 1696 he purchased the Billiou patent for land immediately southwest of the Guyon patent at the Great Kills, and on this property he or his son Daniel built the first story of the stone house standing until recently near the Hylan Boulevard, south of Oakwood. Daniel² Lake, Sr. married secondly in 1683 Alice Stillwell, widow of William Osborne, and had by her a son Daniel, Jr., who died in 1727, leaving a widow Sarah, and among others a minor son Daniel. This Daniel⁴ Lake (b. 1719, d. Aug. 30, 1792, aged 73 years, 1 mo. and 4 days) added a second story of stone to his family homestead in 1786. By his wife Sarah, Daniel had three sons, William (1750-1783), who predeceased him, Daniel and Joseph. The son Daniel may be the Daniel Lake, Jr. who lived during the Revolution in a small house by the mill in the midst of the Great Kills; the house was surrounded by a swamp from which it was protected by a dyke built around it; it stood at the end of Mill Lane to the southwest of both the old Lake homestead and the Guyon—Lake—Tysen house; the small pre-revolutionary unit was enlarged by the addition of a two-story frame building about 1808; this house has since disappeared but the property is still owned by the Lake family. To return to the old Lake homestead, the aged Daniel⁴ Lake bequeathed it to his grandson Daniel, son of William, deceased, and this Daniel W.[6] Lake sold it in or about 1812; it was later owned by the Lockman and Moore families and no longer stands.

The house which had once been Joseph Guyon's, and which is located to the northeast of the above two Lake houses and of the Guyon homestead, was purchased about 1812 by Daniel W.[6] Lake, b. Sept. 9, 1780, d. Oct. 6, 1835. He married March 31, 1803 Mary Gifford and had several children. After his death there was a partition of the property and that portion on which stands the old house fell to his son-in-law D. J. Tysen. The daughter Elizabeth P.[7] Lake, born in this house in 1814, married here July 29, 1831 David Jacques Tysen, b. Aug. 28, 1807, d. March 27, 1885, whose ancestor is believed to have built the Tysen house on the west side of the island (plate 39). The mother of many children, Elizabeth Lake Tysen, died here Jan. 25, 1898. The house was occupied until a few years ago by her son Daniel Tysen and her daughters. It is now owned by the widow of another son, Mrs. David J. Tysen of Dongan Hills, and is leased to Jack Porter.

Unlike the majority of the Staten Island homes, and probably because it belongs to a later period than many of them, this house is built of wood and shingled. It is larger than the stone houses. Construction details place its erection about 1720-1740. Its size, gambrel roof and curved overhanging eaves can be compared with the stone houses in Bergen County. The overhang of the roof beyond the front wall is, however, not original; a study of its timbers shows that it was added at a later date. The small porch at the rear of the house belongs to the early nineteenth century. The kitchen wing is also an addition. The house stands on the south side of Tysen's Lane, west of Mill Road and east of Hylan Boulevard; the Britton house (plate 26) is nearby on the east. A view of the front of the house can be seen in Morris, v. 1, p. 335, although the caption there is incorrect.

House of Pieter Pieterse Hagawout, later Krusen's and Vreeland's
formerly on Watchogue and Willow Brook Roads, Graniteville
PLATE 32

Watchogue Road from an early period was an important highway linking New York and Philadelphia, via the Ferry over the Narrows and the Ferry over the Arthur Kill to New Jersey. On Dec. 30, 1680 three lots of 80 acres each, in the rear of the land of Cornelius Corsen and associates, were granted respectively to David Thomas, John Taylor and John Fitzgaret. These lots were on the south side of Watchogue Road and were known throughout the eighteenth century as the "Soldiers' Lots" (so presumably these three were soldiers). Fitzgaret sold his lot and probably the other two did likewise, or else the grants were declared invalid for non-occupation or some other reason. On Dec. 9, 1697 Peter Petersen and Co.

owners of the lots near Capt. Cornelius Corsen's land, petitioned to be confirmed in their possession of the same and also of 15 acres of meadow adjoining. Patents were issued on this very day for these same lots to Peter Petersen, Jan Harmensz and Yellis Inyard respectively. These men figure in various documents together and therefore it is probable that all three built and settled on their tracts. The Willow Brook Road ran along the division line between the patents of Petersen and Harmensz (the well-known Mersereau house stood on the latter's property—see plate 36).

The ancestor of the Haughwout family (as the name became standardized) was Pieter Janse, who emigrated to New Netherland about 1660. He died shortly after his arrival, leaving a widow Femmetje Hermans and two minor sons, Leffert and Pieter, for whom guardians were appointed by the court at Midwout (Flatbush) on Oct. 15, 1662. The son Leffert² Pietersen was the ancestor of the Lefferts family of Flatbush, whose homestead there still stands (plate 10).

The other son was Pieter² Pieterse, also called Peter Petersen and Peter Hagawout. He was born in Dykhuizen in Overyssel, in the Province of Drenthe, and settled on Staten Island before 1677. On Feb. 22, 1678/9 he sold one-half the plantation in the New Lots of the Old Town which he had previously bought from Pierre Billou, together with a dwelling house, to Hans Christoffelsz; this adjoined the Stillwell—Perine house (plate 38) on the west. On Dec. 9, 1697, as stated above, he was granted the middle of the three Soldiers' Lots. The house standing on this tract until recently dates from his time and was probably erected by him for his home until his death. In 1701 he signed the petition of loyalty to King William together with his neighbor John Harmenson, and he witnessed the will of his other neighbor Yelis Ingart; in 1702 the three leased neighboring land, which they owned in partnership, to James Fitchett, a blacksmith, possibly with the idea of a smithy being conveniently erected near their little settlement. On Dec. 4, 1683 at Bergen he had married Dirickje Egberts of Midwout, and they had eleven children: Egbert (died before his father, leaving two daughters), Altie, Peter, John, Geertie, Hermettie, Abraham (died young), Isaac, Jacob, Leffert of Middlesex Co., N. J., and Leah. In his will, dated Feb. 13, 1715/16 and probated Oct. 29, 1716, Pieter Hagawout of Richmond Co., yeoman, directed his executors to dispose of all his estate at public vendue. Thus the house did not remain in the family of the builder. Indeed it never became a family homestead in the strict sense, as none of the families identified with it owned it for more than half a century.

On May 2, 1726 Frederick Berge sold to Garret Kroosen for £253 a farm or plantation at the Soldiers' Lots, which had been conveyed to Berge by the executors of "Peter Hagoute," the patentee. Garret Krusen (Kroosen, Crusen), b. May 20,

1703 on Staten Island, d. May 11, 1760 aged 57 years and 11 months, was the elder son of Hendrick[2] Kroesen whose homestead stood on the north shore of Staten Island (see infra), where he had a burying ground in which various members of the family, including Garret and his wife, were buried. As the Hagawout house is a large one, Garret undoubtedly purchased it with the intention of making it his home. He married twice, first about 1722 to Gertrude Van Tuyl, by whom he had three children, of whom only Abraham (b. 1732) lived to maturity. He married secondly Closha (Claasje, Clausia) Brinckerhof and had six children, of whom four survived: Maria, b. 1743, Clausia, b. 1748, Henry, b. 1752, and Charity. It is possible that the house was occupied by some tenant rather than by the family, for Garret's widow Closha was undoubtedly the Widow Krusen who occupied one of the family homes on the Kill van Kull during the Revolution (plate 40); she may, of course, have left home for her brother-in-law's at the time of her husband's death, and turned over the house to her stepson Abraham. Garret's son by his first wife, Abraham[4] Crusen (1732-1771), mentioned in his will his wife Lena, his two fathers-in-law Johannes Simonson and Anthony Stoutenburgh, his two sons John and Garret, and three daughters, and left to his brother Henry land to the rear of the widow Kruse. His executors immediately sold the property. The elder son John[5] Cruser remained in the vicinity as he lived in a house (see vignette) still standing on the northwest corner of the same road crossing; that house, erroneously known as the Pero—Christopher house, was in his possession when it was deeded to him on May 1, 1784 by his uncle, Henry[4] Crusen of Southfield, and may have been built by him at that time, as it is not shown on a map of 1780-83; John's greatgrandfather Hendrick Kroesen had originally purchased the property, then a wood lot, in 1729.

On Sept. 19, 1771 the executors of Abraham Kruse sold the house and tract of 80 acres, in which we are interested, to Isaac Cubberly for £800. He was probably the Isaac Cubberly, who owned and lived in the Britton house at New Dorp (plate 26) and died in 1786, leaving among others a son Joseph. On Feb. 19, 1784 Joseph and Addra Cubberly sold that part of the farm lying north of Richmond Turnpike to Peter Prall. The will of Peter Prall, Sr. of Castleton, dated 1820 and probated 1823, mentioned various children and grandchildren, and also his wife Elizabeth, late Elizabeth Mercereau. On May 1, 1823 Peter Prall's executors sold to Harmanus Garretsen an 80 acre tract at the place formerly called the Soldiers' Lots, separated by a road from Jacob Mercereau's farm (plate 36) and partly bounded on the south by Joseph Christopher (plate 30). A suit between a large number of people resulted in the sale of the property by the Master in Chancery in 1831. It was purchased in 1832 by David J. Tysen. It was again sold at a sheriff's sale to Jeremiah Rowland, to satisfy a mortgage. It was purchased between 1853 and 1859 by Eder Vreeland, and is generally known as his home.

The main section of the house was undoubtedly built by Pieter Hagawout about 1697 when he received the patent. It was a good-sized house of stone with a very steep gable roof. The photograph, taken about 1900, shows the end and south wall, the latter sheathed with clapboarding. The north wall was extensively altered in later days. The house was torn down about 1912. It stood on the southeast corner of Watchogue and Willow Brook roads in the extreme northwestern part of the Town of Castleton.

House of Peter Hagewout (Haughwout)
1424 Richmond Avenue, south of Graniteville
PLATE 33

This house was built by Peter Hagewout 2nd (or his widow), the son of Pieter Pietersen Hagawout, builder of the house on Watchogue Road (plate 32), and remained the home of his Haughwout and Lisk descendants for about a century. It stands on a 540 acre tract patented on Dec. 31, 1680 to John West, who disposed of it to Cornelius Corsen and John Palmer. Cornelius Corsen conveyed 135 acres of the upland in 1687 to Ephraim Taylor, who in turn sold it to Peter Hagewout, the latter transaction being shown in a deed to adjoining property, mentioned below. Cornelius Corsen sold an adjoining tract on the south to John Shotwell, which was later conveyed by Daniel Shotwell to Abraham Brouwer of Brooklyn, who on May 5, 1734 sold his 135 acre holding here to Peter Hagewout. That same day Hagewout sold his original parcel to Richard Merrell; the highway known as Lambert's Lane divides these two tracts.

Peter^3 Hagewout 2nd, son of Pieter Pietersen Hagawout, was born in 1689 on Staten Island and died 1745-46, presumably in his Richmond Avenue house. He married Neeltje or Nelly Bakker, who died in 1761, and had many children. The will of Peter Hagewout of Staten Island, dated Nov. 27, 1745 and probated April 8, 1746, discloses that it was written because he was very sick; in it he bequeathed all his lands and tenements to his wife Neeltie during her widowhood and then to his sons Peter and Nicholas, he left £100 legacies to his younger sons Egbert and Jacob, and named his five daughters, Catrina, Derrickje, Neeltje, Geertryd and Margreta; the executors were to be his wife and Daniel Corsen; the witnesses were Gerritt and Klaes Kroese and John Roll, Jr. The will of his widow Nelly Haughwout, dated March 22, 1761 and probated April 15, 1761, was also made because she was sick; in it she bequeathed "to my son Egbert the plantation and house where I now dwell with salt meadows and buildings in lieu of £100 left him by his father"; she mentioned two other sons Peter and Nicholas, and left "the house and land I bought of Thomas Dongan, lying in the Manour" (plate 30) to my four daughters, Catrina, widow of John Brested, Derrickje, Nelly, wife of Antony Brat, and Maritie (called Margreta by her father); the executors were the son Egbert and John Merrill; for some reason the daughter Geertryd or Charity, wife of John Christopher, was not mentioned although living, presumably having already received her share.

Since Peter Hagewout left his tenements to his wife during her widowhood and since she later bequeathed the house where she lived to their son Egbert, it is probable that Peter Hagewout built the house in question a few years before he died. Construction of the house indicates that it was erected in the period 1740-1750. Evidently there was a family settlement whereby the house went after the death of the widow to the third son Egbert rather than to the older sons; Peter, the eldest, lived in (and presumably built) a house in the bend of the Willow Brook Road on the west end of a tract he had purchased with his widowed mother and brother, and his house stood immediately west of the home of Geertyd or Charity Hagewout, wife of Joseph Christopher (plate 30), whose home was west of his sister Derrickje Hagewout, wife of Matthias Smith.

The son Egbert[4] Haughwout, bap. Sept. 16, 1726, d. 1773, married Eleanor Garrebrants. In his will, dated Jan. 28, 1773 and probated March 11, 1773, he left all his estate (therefore including the homestead) to his wife Nelly during her widowhood, and eventually to his five children "now born and the child as my dear wife is like to have"; the executors were his wife, Joseph Christopher and Daniel Gerbrantz. The six children were: Peter, Francis, Egbert, Eleanor, Elizabeth, wife of John Merrill, and Ann, wife of Thomas Lisk. The Widow Eleanor resided in the homestead at the time of the Revolution. She deeded 50 acres of the homestead farm to her son Peter Haughwout on April 7, 1806; this included the old house, as it was bounded on the north by the nearby Merrell tract. It was bounded on the south by the land of Francis Haughwout, who had therefore received that 50 acre tract from his mother, and who in 1813 sold his portion to John Merrill, presumably his brother-in-law. Egbert's widow confirmed these conveyances in her will, dated Oct. 5, 1818 and probated Feb. 13, 1821, in which she devised to the children of her son Peter Haughwout the farm whereon she then resided, and to her son Francis the house and premises whereon he then resided. The elder son, Peter E.[5] Haughwout, b. May 1, 1762, d. July 3, 1815 before his mother, married Hannah Bogert and had six children. In his will, Peter ordered that after his mother's death the homestead farm should be sold at public vendue. From a deed given by his son Egbert P. Haughwout for an adjoining parcel, we find that the farm had been purchased from the estate of Peter E. Haughwout, deceased, by Thomas Lisk.

Thomas Lisk, who purchased the Haughwout homestead after 1821, was a brother-in-law of Peter E. Haughwout, the last owner of this name. On Sept. 14, 1794 Thomas married Ann Haughwout, daughter of Egbert and granddaughter of Peter Hagewout, who had built the house. On March 14, 1837 Egbert Lisk and Phebe, his wife, and Nathan Crocheron and his wife Eleanor Lisk, children of Thomas Lisk, deceased, sold the farm, described as the "late residence of Peter E. Haughwout," to their brother John Lisk, sometimes known as John T. Lisk. On an unknown date the heirs and grantees of John T. Lisk conveyed the property to Sarah R. Decker, wife of David D. Decker, who disposed of it in 1877. It is not known whether Sarah R. Decker was a relative of the family.

On May 1, 1884 Samuel P. White and Sophia, his wife, sold to Charles W. Hunt a farm, "being the same premises conveyed March 4, 1837 by Nathan Crocheron and wife to John, sometimes called John T. Lisk, and by his heirs and grantees ... to Sarah R. Decker, and by said Sarah R. Decker and David Decker, her husband, by deed dated March 20, 1877, conveyed to Samuel P. White." The Hunt family have been in possession since 1884; the present owner is Charles Hunt.

The house is a small, one story building, covered with clapboarding and with a gable roof. The overhanging eaves in front were probably added at a later date; their sheathed cornice extends down to the windows with a resultant top-heavy feeling. The extension of the roof in the center, to form a porch over the front door, the slatted blinds and the composition roof detract from the original character of the house; an earlier view is reproduced here before these changes were made. Its appearance suggests that of a modern bungalow in many respects. Inside there are examples of early woodwork and panelling. The house is on the west side of Richmond Avenue south of Lamberts Lane, and some distance north of the Victory Boulevard.

Hendrickson (?)—Winants House
formerly on Arthur Kill Road, south of Rossville
PLATE 34

The stone unit of this house was one of the oldest buildings standing until recently on Long Island; although not erected by the Winants, it was their family homestead for over a century and a half. One stone is marked "1696 I. H.," showing that it was built in 1696, probably by John Hendrickson. Little is known of him other than that he received a grant of land on the west end of Staten Island in this vicinity, the exact location of which has not been definitely determined but presumably it was here.

It is not known when the Winants family came into the possession of the property. Our first record of them in this vicinity is in a deed of 1725/26 (recorded 1752), wherein Israel and Gabriel Dusosway sold to John Andreuvet land inherited from their mother in Sandy Brook at the rear of the land of Cornelius and Peter Winants. Sandy Brook was the old name for the stream which emptied into the Arthur Kill south of the Winants property and north of Kreischerville (or Charleston). This reference may not apply to the particular property in question. Nothing is known of Cornelius and Peter, neither of whom is mentioned in their father's will of 1754. They were brothers of Winant Winants who is the first of the family known to have owned the house.

The ancestor of the family was Wynant Pieterse, who emigrated from Betuwe in Gelderland about 1655-60. He settled in Breuckelen, living first at Wallabout and then at Gowanus, and became a wealthy landowner and a member of the government. On Dec. 4, 1661 he married Anneken Aukes (Van Nuyse) and he died between Dec. 13, 1679, when a complaint was lodged against him, and November 1695, when Pieter sold property as his only son and heir. This Pieter² Winant (Wynants or Wynantse), bap. Sept. 9, 1663, d. Aug. 6, 1758, aged 94 years, was buried on Staten Island. He lived first in Breuckelen, where he took the oath of allegiance in 1687 as a native, and later at Rossville (some distance north of the Winants homestead) on Staten Island, where he was recorded in the 1706 census as 40 years of age. He married Anna Maria ———— and had many children: Winant, Daniel, Manuel, Cornelius, Peter (bap. 1707), and Jacob are listed in the 1706 census. In Peter's will of 1754, he left legacies to his eldest son Winant, Margaret (relationship unstated), the wife of John Sleight, his grandson Peter, son of John Winants, deceased, his son Daniel and his daughter Catharine, the wife of Hendrick Sleight; the balance of his estate was to be divided equally between his grandchildren (unnamed); the original executor had died by 1760 so the court appointed Peter's grandson Daniel Winant as executor.

The eldest son was Winant³ Winants; he was a cornetist of the troop of Richmond County militia and saw service in 1739. In his will, dated Sept. 28, 1773 and probated Nov. 23, 1773, he left to his (second) wife Rhoda £100, the best bed and its furniture, the use of household goods, and the privilege of living in the house with his grandson Winant Winants, who was to furnish her with food and firewood while she was a widow; he bequeathed half of all his lands and also all his horses and cattle and a negro boy to his grandson Winant Winants, son of Abraham Winants, deceased, and the other half of his lands to his grandson Jacob, son of Winant Winants, deceased; he left legacies to his eldest son Peter (bap. 1720) and to his son Daniel, the latter to get three houses in Perth Amboy, mentioned his granddaughter Catharine, daughter of Abraham, his grandchildren Winant,

Peter and Lidda, children of Peter, the seven children of his daughter Elizabeth deceased, his grandson Winant and the other five children of his son John. Rhoda was the second wife of the above testator, Winant Winants; he had previously married Ann Cole, who was the mother of Pieter and Abraham and possibly others. Abraham[4] Winants, bap. March 14, 1724/5 on Staten Island, d. between 1762 and 1773, married Mary————, who died between 1805 and 1809, willing her goods to her three daughters Ann, Mary and Elizabeth.

Abraham's eldest child Winant[5] Winants (b. Nov. 25, 1744, d. between July 5 and Aug. 11, 1804) inherited that half of his grandfather's property on which stood the old homestead; it is marked W. Wynant on the map of 1783. The name of his first wife is unknown; he married secondly Dec. 15, 1785 Mary Garretson, b. July 5, 1764. In his will Winant Winants left his wife Mary £300, a bed and its furniture, and the best room in the house while she was a widow; bequeathed all the lands in the farm where he then lived adjoining the sound at Sunken Marsh to his son Winant, other lands to his other sons and legacies to his daughters. Winant[6] Winant, Jr., b. Feb. 1, 1799, d. April 30, 1871, married Christina Mary Johnson, d. Dec. 1866, aged 68 years; she may have been a neighbor as the Johnsons owned the adjoining property. At Winant Winant's death, the property was divided between his two children: Wynant[7] Winant obtained the southern 40 acres of the farm and Mary Jane[7] Winant, wife of James Johnson, obtained the northern 51½ acres on which stood the old house.

The small stone unit was erected in 1696; the stones were laid in mud and lime made from oyster shells, and there was no cellar beneath this part. It had one of the rare early primitive fireplaces built out into the room, with a hole in the garret floor for the smoke to escape through and a short chimney to conduct the smoke from the garret outside. The frame unit was built after the Revolution along similar lines. A steep gable roof covered both sections. Study of the timbers show that the deep overhanging eaves were an afterthought and added many years later when they became popular. The house was torn down about 1929. A Standard Oil plant now stands on the site.

House of Hendrick Kroesen (Cruser)
formerly on Richmond Terrace, West New Brighton

Until 1831 there existed a stone house on the north shore of Staten Island which was the homestead of the Cruser (Croesen, Crusen, Kroesen, Kruser) family. Garret Dircksen[1] Croesen emigrated from Weinschoten in Groningen about 1660 and settled at Gowanus in Breukelen on Long Island, where he died March 7, 1680. About 1661 he married Neeltie Jans, daughter of Jan Pieterse[1] Staats of Gowanus, and had at least four children: Dirck, bap. 1662, who eventually settled in Pennsylvania, Elsje, wife of William Clasz, Hendrick, and Annetje, bap. 1677. On Oct. 31, 1680 his widow married secondly Volckert Hendricksz. She sold the Gowanus farm to pay her deceased husband's debts and the children removed to Staten Island, where their father Garret had obtained a patent to 160 acres on the north shore on Sept. 29, 1677. The father's will was lost in a fire and the whole estate claimed by the elder son Dirck as the heir under the English law. On Feb. 2, 1698/9 the younger son Hendrick petitioned to be protected in his rights, left him by his father's will which had been burned, as he had been settled on the property bequeathed him for twelve years, since he came of age. A family settlement and conveyances in 1709 released to Hendrick that part of the patent on which his house stood for over a century.

This Hendrick² Kroesen was born about 1665, as he was 40 years of age in 1706-07, and died in 1760-61. He was a man of education, as the entries in the records of the new Dutch Church at Port Richmond nearby were made by him in a beautiful hand and good spelling. He married Cornelia Corsen, bap. July 24, 1681 at Flatbush, daughter of Capt. Cornelius Corsen of Staten Island. They had five children: Marretje, bap. 1698, married Jacob Bergen; Garret, bap. 1703, d. 1760, who undoubtedly lived in the Hagewout house on Watchogue Road (plate 32); Cornelius; Neeltje, bap. 1713, married Denys Van Tuyl, and secondly between 1739-43 Joseph Rolph; Cornelia, bap. 1716, married Jacob Corsen. In his will of 1760, Hendrick Kroesen bequeathed his homestead and other property to his son Cornelius, other land to his daughter Neeltje, and legacies to his children, grandchildren, and his son Garret's widow.

The surviving son Cornelius³ Krusen, bap. Oct. 19, 1708, d. 1784-86, married about 1730 Helena, daughter of Abraham Van Tuyl, bap. Sept. 22, 1709, and had three sons. He became a large landowner, among his purchases being the adjoining farm which had once been Dominie Van Santvoord's (plate 40). The map of 1783 shows that he made his home there while his son Cornelius, Jr. lived in the old family homestead. The will of Cornelius Krusen of Richmond County, yeoman, left to his son Henry (b. 1731) the plantation on the Raritan River where Henry lived, to his son Abraham (b. 1735) part of the Vincent patent on Staten Island, and the residue of his properties to his son Cornelius (b. 1736), including the farm the testator lived on and the farm Cornelius lived on. In his will of 1807 Cornelius, Jr. left the two adjoining farms in a life estate for his son John⁴ Cruser (d. 1829) with vested remainder to his six grandchildren. This resulted in the partition suit of 1830 and the sale of the property in various parcels. Parcel No. 4, containing 52½ acres with the "dwelling house" (that is, the homestead of Hendrick Kroesen) and the family cemetery, was allotted to the grandson Morris Hatfield[e] Cruser, who sold it immediately to John King Vanderbilt. The latter tore down the old stone house and erected a Victorian, two story, frame building.

The survey of the property, filed for the partition suit of 1830, shows the old stone house to have been a one and a half story building with a steep roof, having a central doorway on the north front with two windows on either side. The house stood on the south side of Richmond Terrace, facing the Kill Van Kull, immediately west of the Van Santvoord—Krusen—Pelton house (plate 40).

Lakeman—Cortelyou—Taylor House
Richmond Road opposite the Moravian Cemetery, New Dorp
PLATE 35

The land on which this house stands was granted in 1675 by Gov. Andros to Lewis Lakeman. This name appears on the early records in many forms: Lackerman, Lockman, Lalman, Larrman. On March 18, 1683/4 Peter Lockerman of Staten Island made an agreement with George Cumins and Abraham Lockerman, both of Staten Island, stating that whereas Lewis Lakeman, late of Staten Island, deceased, father of the parties to the present indenture, had in his lifetime desired his property to be divided equally between them, said Peter Lockerman agreed to divide the estate in three equal parts. It is believed that Abraham Lakeman thus became the next owner and built the main part of the present house. He was born about 1661, as he was 45 years of age in 1706. The will of Abraham Lakermans of Richmond Co., gentleman, was probated in 1734; in it he left his farm whereon he then dwelt to his three married daughters, Hester, Catharine and Elizabeth, directed that other properties should be sold, and mentioned his wife Anje, his son Jacob and another married daughter Mary. It is possible that he was also the father of Abraham, Jr. and Isaac, who were listed in the 1706 census as 23 and 21 years of age respectively.

It is not known when or how the family disposed of the house at New Dorp; Peter Cortelyou came into the possession of it but probably owned it for a short time only, as there is no record of his ever living on Staten Island. On Feb. 27, 1714 (recorded 1724) Peter Cortelyou of Kings County, deeded to Rem Van der Beeck of Staten Island, yeoman, and Dorthea, his wife, for £300, a 40 acre tract on the south side of Staten Island bounded by the land of George Commons, beginning at the highway and including the house, orchard, barn and fencing, and also a 60 acre tract of uplands on the hills. Thus we know that the house was in existence by this date. Rem Van der Beek married Dorothea Coteleau (Cortelyou) and had four children baptized on Staten Island between 1719 and 1736. He only owned the house a few years and was living in New York in 1734. Isaac Van Tuyl was the owner in 1719. Isaac, recorded as aged 25 years in 1706, married Sara Lakerman, probably a daughter of Abraham Lakeman, builder of the house, as he stood sponsor to two of her children and his daughter Esther to a third. Augustine Creed came into possession of the property. On Feb. 19, 1751 (recorded 1764) Augustine Creed and his wife Mary sold to Aaron Cortilieu, all of Staten Island, for £500, a 40 acre tract of upland, being one-half the breadth of the patent lot, running the length of the land of George Commons, beginning at the highway and including the house, etc., also a lot of meadow in the Great Kills adjoining Joseph Guyon, and woodland adjoining Gozen Adrianse.

Aaron Cortelyou was descended from Jacques Cortelyou, a Huguenot, who emigrated in 1652 as tutor to the children of Cornelis Van Werckhoven. On the death of his patron Jacques succeeded to a large share of his property and laid out the village of New Utrecht on Long Island. He was surveyor general of the colony in 1657 and is believed to have made the first map of New York City. By his wife Neeltje Van Duyn he had four sons and two daughters. One of them, Pieter Jacquez' Corteljou, b. about 1664, d. April 10, 1757, married Dieuvertje De Wit. He was a surveyor and owned and cultivated his father's tract at New Utrecht. At least three of his children settled on Staten Island: Dorothea who married Rem Van der Beek (see above), Cornelis, b. 1701, and Jacques, b. about 1698. The latter married Jacomintie Van Pelt and had three children baptized on Staten Island: Deborah 1720, Peter 1722, and Nieltje 1726. He is believed to have returned to New Utrecht and was considered one of the most active members of the Moravian Society of New York in 1747.

Aaron' Cortelyou, supposedly b. 1726, d. Aug. 22, 1789, is believed to be a son of Jacques, but as the latter's family seems to be accounted for, he may be a son of Cornelis. Col. Aaron' Cortelyou bought the house in New Dorp in 1751 and made his home here. He and Cornelius Cortelyou were among those who in 1762 petitioned to the Moravian Church at Bethlehem, Pa., that a church be established on Staten Island. The petition was granted, and Aaron was one of the original members of the Moravian Church at New Dorp opposite his home. Aaron was a patriot and a delegate to the Provincial Congress; he managed a store both before and after the war. He married Elizabeth, daughter of Peter Androvet of Staten Island, who mentioned them in his will of 1761. In 1789 Aaron Cortelyou of Southfield bequeathed to his wife Elizabeth £500, the furnishings of one room and one horse, the use of one room in the house while she was a widow and a negro girl; to his son Peter he left lands, negroes and a legacy (Peter was a farmer at Green Ridge on Staten Island); to his daughter Elizabeth, wife of Richard Seamons, he willed the land bought of Creed, which he (the testator) then lived on; he also left legacies to his Bedell, Seamons and Cortelyou grandchildren.

On April 13, 1794 (recorded 1801) Richard Seaman of New York City and Elizabeth his wife sold to Joseph Taylor of Richmond Co., for £1000, the farm and buildings in the Town of Southfield formerly belonging to Aaron Cortelyou, deceased, situated on the public road leading from Richmond to Yan Duersens Ferry. The Taylor family owned it for many years. In 1874 the house was owned by Mrs. S. Barton and in 1916 by David J. Tysen. It was sold in 1928 by William Miles to the present owner, Xavier Kirchhoffer.

Both units of the house are built of fieldstone, of various shapes fitted together as well as possible but with no attempt at courses. Construction shows that the main house was the original unit. It is covered by a gambrel roof of which the lower slope is about the same length as the upper. Both sections of the house have very small windows. Another and earlier view of the house, when the stone was white-washed and there was a cellar trap door by the main entrance, and before the dormers and hoods over the doors were added, can be seen in Leng and Davis, p. 918. The back of the house is shown in the photograph in the present volume, taken in 1925. The house has been greatly altered recently. A greenhouse has been built to connect the house with the florist's office by the roadside. The house stands on Richmond Road, east of Otis Avenue and opposite the Moravian cemetery.

House of John Roll, later Mersereau's
formerly at Watchogue and Willow Brook Roads, Graniteville
PLATE 36

This house was erected about 1740 probably by John Roll. It was purchased by his Mersereau son-in-law in 1762 and was until lately the Mersereau homestead. The land on which it stands was granted in 1680 to John Taylor, and was the westernmost of the three lots known throughout the eighteenth century as the Soldiers' Lots. It was granted a second time on Dec. 6, 1697 to Jan Harmensz, the two adjoining Soldiers' Lots being then also repatented to Pieter Pieterse (Haga-wout) and Yellis Inyard; they were 80 acres each. It is probable that Jan Harmensz (John Harminsone) lived here in an earlier house. Harmensz is a patronymic and his last name is unknown. By inference from deeds and wills, John Roll (Jan Ral) was in possession of the property by 1740 and the house dates from this period.

The name appears as Ral and occasionally as Rol on the Dutch Church records and as Roll on the real estate transactions. Jan Mangels Ral (Rol), also called Hans Ral (Rol), acted as a sponsor to children of various families at the Dutch church on Staten Island in 1719, 1726, 1728, 1732 and 1736; he purchased land on the south side of Staten Island in 1722. He was evidently the father of Jan Ral, Jr. (John Roll), who married Fytje Van Boskerk and had a daughter Fytje, bap. May 26, 1740. She is their only known child. Her father was in possession of the property in question about the time of her birth and probably built his home here then. In 1745 John Roll, Jr. witnessed the will of Peter Hagewout, who lived a short distance to the southwest (plate 33). His daughter Fytje Ral, whose name was anglicized to Sophia Roll, married on Oct. 17, 1755 Jacob Mersereau. On June 7, 1762 John Roll conveyed the farm whereon he then lived to this son-in-law.

The first of this family in America was the Widow Mercereau, who came to New York about 1698 with a family of children, two sons and two daughters. Her son Joshua² Mercereau, b. 1667, d. May 23, 1756, aged 98 years and 5 mos., married at the French church in New York June 16, 1693 Maria Chadrayne, and had at least four children. Joshua and Maria settled on Staten Island. Their son Joshua³ Mersearau, Jr., b. May 18, 1696 at New York, d. Aug. 9, 1769* on Staten Island, married Oct. 21, 1727 Mary Corsen, b. Oct. 21, 1704, d. July 8, 1763,* daughter of Jacob Corsen of Staten Island, who mentioned his daughter and son-in-law in his will of 1742. Joshua "Musshrow" (he or his father) of Richmond Co., ship carpenter, purchased on May 22, 1732 a tract of 32½ acres at Holland Hook on the north shore of Staten Island; it was there that he kept his shipyard. Joshua Mersereau, Jr., ship carpenter, purchased on May 1, 1758 a 25½ acre tract near the north shore and adjoining the Widow Arrowsmith's land.

The second son of Joshua Mersereau, Jr.'s ten children was Jacob,⁴ b. April 25, 1730* on Staten Island, bap. May 29th, d. Sept. 7, 1804. This Jacob Mersereau purchased his father-in-law Roll's homestead in 1762 and is shown in possession on a map of 1783; when he had the deed recorded in 1792 he was a colonel. He was an outspoken patriot during the Revolution and fled for safety to New Jersey. On one of his occasional stealthy visits to his family, he was recognized by a Tory and had a narrow escape from capture, jumping from the window and fleeing into the nearby swamp. On Oct. 17, 1755 he married Sophia Roll, and had one son, John (1758-1826) of Staten Island, and three daughters, Mary wife of Thomas Cubberly, Elizabeth wife of Daniel De Hart and Sophia wife of John Crocheron. Col. Jacob married secondly March 29, 1779 Charity De Groot and had three sons, Jacob of Staten Island, David of New Brunswick, and Peter. The homestead was inherited by the youngest child, Peter⁵ Mersereau, b. July 6, 1788, d. June 2, 1879, married Eliza Thatcher, b. March 6, 1796, d. May 25, 1874. He was a member of the State Legislature. After the death of his wife, Peter deeded the homestead on Sept. 10, 1874 to the youngest of his six children, Theodore⁶ Mersereau, b. Oct. 22, 1834, d. Dec. 18, 1875. He married Ann Messier; one of their two daughters was Emma⁷

146

---

* Taken from family Bible.

Mersereau, wife of Mr. Ettlinger. She sold the property on May 13, 1896 to Peter Clarius.

The house was a long, low building of whitewashed stone, covered with a gable roof. It had very few windows. It was built about 1740 and torn down in 1913. The house stood on the southwest corner of Watchogue and Willow Brook Roads, in the district formerly called Butcherville and more lately known as Graniteville. Watchogue Road was a part of the old road running across the Island, from the ferry over the Narrows at the east end to the Blazing Star Ferry over the Arthur Kill at Linoleumville on the west end.

Simonson—Blake House
2329 Richmond Avenue, New Springville
PLATE 37

This house stands on the northern half of the tract at the Fresh Kills granted to Isaac See on Sept. 29, 1677. The southern half came into the possession of Christian Corsen who sold it Jan. 30, 1701/2 (recorded 1717) to Barent and Stoffel Christopher, mentioning the bounds on the north as the land of Wyntie Simerse; in the division of 1717 between these brothers, their tract is stated to be 80 acres or the southwest half of the Isaac See patent. Thus we know that the Simonsen homestead land had come into the possession of the family between 1677 and 1702. The end of this tract lies on the east side of Richmond Avenue, immediately below the crossing of the Springville Creek, in the region formerly known as Karle's Neck.

The ancestor of the Simonsen family was Barent Simonsen. His widow Tryntje Claes married about 1644 Juriaen Blanck, Sr., goldsmith of New Amsterdam. In 1662 they made their joint will, in which she mentioned her son Symon Barentszen, son by her former husband Barent Simonsen; she again mentioned this son in her will of 1698. This Symon Barentszen, a young man from Amsterdam, married in the Dutch church at New Amsterdam Nov. 18, 1661 Wyntie Arents, a young girl of New Amsterdam, and had three sons and six daughters.

The youngest son was Aert (Arent) Simonsen or Symonsen, bap. May 19, 1679 at New York. He settled on Staten Island as a young man: "Aert Blank" (using his step-father's surname), freeholder here, signed the petition to King William in 1701. It is believed that his home stood south of the creek, on the tract at the Fresh Kills which was owned in 1702 by Wyntie Simerse, who was presumably his mother or his wife; he later purchased more land nearby. The old stone house here was torn down in 1895 and replaced with a brick house by David Simonson, a descendant. Aert Simonsen married twice; judging by the first names of his elder children (baptized 1708 to 1717), his first wife, possibly named Wyntie, belonged to the Christophel family, who probably lived on the adjoining tract and whose descendants owned the house at Willow Brook (plate 30); he was married secondly by 1721 to Margaret Daniels. The will of Aert Simonsen of Staten Island, husbandman, dated 1747 and probated 1753, mentioned his wife Margaret, left legacies to his two married daughters, Catharine Housman and Anna Crocheron (bap. 1722), and left his lands to his eight sons: Simon (bap. 1708), Hans, Arthur, Christophel (bap. 1717), Daniel (bap. 1724), Barent, Cornelius, and his minor son Isaac (bap. 1734).

On the map of 1783 two houses are marked on the tract, "Simeson" and "B.S." Presumably the tract was divided between two of Aert's sons and the southern half fell to Barent, who may have built upon it the house in which we are interested. Barent (Barnt) Simonson (Simonsen), bap. July 14, 1728 on Staten Island, died by 1801, married March 8, 1755 Abigail, daughter of John Crocheron, who mentioned her in his will of 1761. The will of Abigail, widow of Barnt Simonson, mentioned her daughter Abigail wife of Walter Dongan, her sons Barent, Rheuben and Jacob, and left to Rheuben the part of the homestead which she bought of her son Isaac. She evidently referred to a 40 acre tract adjoining the house on the southwest, which had come into the family in the latter part of the eighteenth century, and seems to have been part of the land purchased by the Christophers in 1702. Possibly Isaac was the eldest son and inherited all his father's lands on his death, intestate, and hence the necessity for the purchase of part of it by the widow. The son Isaac Simonsen predeceased his mother by many years, dying in 1787; he mentioned in his will his wife Helethay (the widow Hetty was still living in 1808), and his sons Isaac and Jeremiah (who died in 1808 at Southfield). The son Esaac or Isaac Simonson, Jr., was probably the Isaac who married Elizabeth Barnes Sept. 25, 1794. He died in 1842, leaving a widow Elizabeth and three daughters; he gave a legacy to his daughter Abigail wife of Stephen Egbert (he was a carman of New York when she married him in 1839), and bequeathed his lands equally to his other daughters Dorothy, and Anne wife of Daniel Blake.

Dorothy Simonson of Northfield (bap. 1797 as Dorothy Barnes Simonson) conveyed Dec. 27, 1842 to Daniel Blake of Northfield for $2,000. one undivided half of the farm late of Esaac Simonsen, deceased, bounded on the southwest by Reuben Simonson, on the northwest by Henry Crocheron, on the northeast by the heirs of Joseph Simonson and John Vallenburgh, and on the southeast by John B. Hillyn, also another small tract by the Neck Creek, 40 plus 5 acres. Thus Daniel Blake purchased forty acres of the original homestead of his wife's family. In 1874 he was bounded on the southwest by M. Simonson (probably Matthias, b. 1806, son of Reuben), and on the northeast by D. Simonson, undoubtedly the David Simonson

(d. about 1897) who built the present brick house and probably a son of Joseph Simonson whose heirs owned it in 1842. Daniel Blake had died by 1897. The house has been owned for the last forty years by William Eith.

It is a one and a half story house built of stone, now covered with shingles for protection from the weather. It stands in the fields off the east side of Richmond Avenue, south of Travis Avenue and the Springville Creek crossing.

House of Capt. Thomas Stillwell, later Britton's and Perine's
1476 Richmond Road, Dongan Hills
PLATE 36

In 1661 Pierre Billeau (father-in-law of the builder of this house), a Walloon, and others petitioned to be allowed to live on Staten Island. Their petition was granted and the first permanent settlement was made at Old Dorp, the site now occupied by St. Mary's Cemetery inland from Arrochar. A survey of the property in the New Lots of the Old Town (later Garretsons and now Dongan Hills) was made April 4, 1685 for Capt. Thomas Stillwell under order of Gov. Thomas Dongan: 145 acres of land in the New Lots at the Old Town in the County of Richmond, a part of which was formerly granted to Peter Belew (Billeau) by the Dutch and confirmed Sept. 20, 1677 to Thomas Stillwell by Gov. Andros, beginning on the west side of a run in the valley by the side of Iron Hill, bounded by land of Hans Christophel on the southwest and by the highway on the northwest.

Thomas' father, Lt. Nicholas' Stillwell, came from an old English family; he emigrated from County Surrey in England to Virginia before 1639, when he was made a tobacco viewer of a district on the Charles River. Having engaged in a land controversy between Virginia and Maryland, he fled northwards in 1645 and settled at Deutil Bay in New Amsterdam. In 1648 he bought a house, lot and farm in Gravesend on Long Island, where he lived and became a magistrate. In 1660 all were ordered to live within the village for greater safety from the Indians, but he obtained permission to remain on his bouwery between Gravesend and New Utrecht, as he had so many sons he could defend it. At the time of the English conquest of 1664, he upheld the Dutch; at odds with his English neighbors, he sold his plantation and removed to New Amsterdam, but by 1670 had settled at Old Dorp on Staten Island, where he was an important member of the community and died Dec. 28, 1671.

Capt. Thomas' Stillwell, bap. July 9, 1651 at New Amsterdam, d. 1704-05, married at Gravesend Jan. 8, 1670 Martha Billeau, bap. Feb. 8, 1652 at Leyden, daughter of Pierre Billeau and Françoise Du Bois. They settled on her father's land in the New Lots of the Old Town and probably built the oldest part of the present house

149

about 1680. Thomas Stillwell was an important man on the Island, constable, sheriff, magistrate, captain of the militia, and member of the Colonial Assembly. As his only son had predeceased him, Thomas Stillwell in 1704 bequeathed the property on which he then lived to his daughters, Frances wife of Nicholas Britton, Ann (married first Samuel Van Pelt and secondly Jacobus Billeau), and Rachel (married William, son of William and Mary Britton). Thomas' widow Martha Billeau married secondly Rev. David de Bonrepos, minister to the French congregation on Staten Island; she died in 1735 at New Rochelle. In 1709 the widow Martha released the house in the New Lots to her daughters, reserving for herself "the room over the cellar in the little house before the great house" (indicating a different arrangement of buildings than at present). That same year Ann, one of the daughters, conveyed her portion to Nicholas Britton, reserving the "old dwelling house" and garden, which eventually also became his; in 1713 Rachel, another daughter, sold her share to Nicholas Britton without any reservation.

Thus the son-in-law Nicholas Britton came into possession of Capt. Thomas Stillwell's house. Col. Nicholas[2] Britton, b. 1679, d. 1740, was a son of William and Mary Britton, and a brother of Nathaniel Britton, builder of the house at New Dorp on Staten Island (plate 26). He married Frances[3] Stillwell, b. 1682, and probably built the newer stone part of the house shortly after 1713. Nicholas and Frances had an only son Nathaniel, who married and had children but who died before his parents, and also two daughters. Nicholas Britton willed the Stillwell house to his two daughters, Martha, wife of Samuel Moore, and Rachel (later wife of Thomas Dongan). On Aug. 13, 1746, the widow Frances and her two daughters sold the property to Walter Dongan, nephew of Sir Thomas Dongan. He died in 1749, and his eldest son and heir, Thomas Dongan (husband of Rachel Britton), sold the 60 acre tract on which the house stood to Joseph Holmes, Innkeeper, on Nov. 12, 1749.

Presumably Joseph Holmes continued his vocation and kept an inn here until he died Sept. 22, 1759 aged 63 years. His widow Sarah died Aug. 17, 1775 aged 75 years. Previously, in 1764, she had released her interest in the house in the New Lots to their only surviving child, Ann Holmes wife of Edward Perine. His greatgrandfather Daniel Perrin emigrated in 1665 from the Isle of Jersey with Philip Cartaret; in 1666 he married Maria Thorell, and they settled on an 80 acre tract in southern Staten Island at the present Rossville. Edward[4] Perine, b. 1729, d. 1777, married Ann Holmes in 1758, and had six children. He was a weaver. They made their home in her parents' stone house, where Ann was still living as late as 1800. During the Revolution so many British soldiers were quartered here, that the widow and six children were allowed only one room. Capt. Coghlan was among the British stationed here.

Two of the children, Joseph and Henry Perine, who were born, lived and died in this house, were each left an undivided half of the house and property. For over one hundred years, two families lived in the two sections of the house, operating as independent households. The older or rear portion was occupied by the younger son, Henry[5] Perine, b. Nov. 29, 1768, d. Dec. 3, 1860, married 1795 Mary Winant. Henry was a sheriff and supervisor of Southfield and a member of the New York Legislature. He served in the War of 1812. His half of the house was inherited by his daughter Elizabeth Winant[6] Perine, b. Jan. 19, 1804, d. Dec. 6, 1883, married May 19, 1830 Richard Tysen of Northfield. In September 1870, some years before her death, she sold her interest to Charles B. Waring, who on Feb. 27, 1886 deeded it to Cornelius L. Perine, occupant of the other half. The front portion of the house was inherited by Edward and Ann (Holmes) Perine's elder son Joseph[5] Perine, b. 1759, d. April 16, 1814, married Sept. 25, 1782 Catharine Swaime. He was a clerk of the Court of Common Pleas, delegate to the Constitutional Convention of 1801, and Lt. Colonel of the militia. His portion of the house was inherited by his son Simon Swaime[6] Perine, b. Nov. 10, 1783, d. Feb. 20, 1860, married 1810 Sarah Ann Lake. The front half of the house passed to Simon's son Cornelius Lake[7] Perine, b. May 2, 1821, d. March 19, 1896, married Eliza Britton. It was he who bought the rear half of the house. The house was inherited by his son Hamilton Britton[8] Perine, b. Aug. 14, 1854, who sold it Feb. 13, 1913 to Donald C. Craig. It was bought Feb. 15, 1915 by the Staten Island Antiquarian Society, now the Staten Island Institute of Arts and Sciences.

As suggested by its history, the house really consists of two connecting buildings. The rear stone house (partly shown at the right of the photograph) is believed to be the dwelling erected by Capt. Thomas Stillwell about 1680. One tradition states that the original house burned, but this may refer to the old dwelling mentioned in the releases of 1709. The stone house nearer the road is later but also belongs to an early period, and was probably erected by Stillwell's son-in-law Nathaniel Britton about 1713. These units are built of undressed fieldstone; the small windows are of the early period. The huge beams are still to be seen overhead in the main room of the rear house. Attached to it (just off the photograph) is the old frame kitchen, believed to have been built about 1749 by Joseph Holmes. It has a huge fireplace and plastered walls. The front stone house lies several steps higher; here in the parlor is some fine Jacobean paneling. The front door opens directly into the dining room, and off this (partially seen in the photograph) is a frame addition, similar in lines to the stone house but smaller, which is said to have been built as early as 1758, and was used as another kitchen. The dormers are modern. Various views of the house can be seen in *The Story and Documentary History of the*

Perine House by C. G. Hine, and elsewhere. The house stands on a turn in the old Richmond Road, on its east side north of Cromwell Street. A stream on the east side of the house was a branch of the stream (now dried up) which was mentioned in the various deeds as the boundary on the west.

House of Barnt Tysen
Richmond Avenue, south of New Springville
PLATE 39

This house is erroneously stated to have been built in 1680 by Barne Tysen; it does indeed stand on a grant of land to him, but the house itself belongs to a much later period and was probably built by his grandson Barnt Tysen.

The ancestor of the Tysen and Swaim families was Thys Barentsen, who emigrated from Leerdam with his wife and three children on the *St. John the Baptist* in 1661. He was one of those who formed the first permanent settlement on Staten Island, at Old Dorp in 1661, and was a schepen here in 1673. He was recorded as 60 years of age in 1681 and probably died in that year, leaving a widow Scytie; letters of administration were granted on his estate Feb. 1, 1682. His son Barne² Tys or Tysen received a grant of land at the Fresh Kills in southwestern Staten Island in 1677; if he settled on this grant it must have been in an earlier house than the present one. He took part in the expedition against Canada in 1711. He is said to have been married in 1672 to Maria Kroesen, and to have had three sons, David, Cornelis and Abraham. He married secondly Magdalena Jans and had a son Johannes, bap. 1680 at Flatbush, one of the sponsors being the grandfather Tys Barandz. The son David³ Tysen married (supposedly in 1698) Magdalena Morgan and had but two children, Barent and Sarah, before he died in 1710 at an early age.

David's son Barnt⁴ Tysen, b. Feb. 4, 1699, married Oct. 20, 1723 Elizabeth Swaim, and had three children, Elizabeth wife of John Staats, David who died fairly young leaving an infant son Barnt, and John. As the present house dates from the second quarter or the middle of the eighteenth century, it is probable that Barnt⁴ Tysen built this house; it is marked "Pyson" on the map of 1783. Barnt's surviving son was John⁵ Tysen, b. Oct. 30, 1731, d. March 7, 1808 in his 77th year. He lived in the house on his ancestral grant, and was the last of the family buried on the property.

John Tysen headed the Committee that addressed the Provincial Congress in 1775, praying for a reconciliation with England, but when all hope of this was past he became a member of the local Committee of Safety and a strong supporter of the patriot cause. He was a supervisor of Northfield 1789-98 and made the first official survey and map of Staten Island. He was a trustee and elder of the Dutch Church. On May 1, 1757 he married Cordelia Bergen and had two sons. In his will, dated 1796 and probated 1808, John Tysen of Northfield bequeathed to his wife Cordelia "my best bed and the furniture for same, my best cupboard desk and table, and six of my best chairs, and my oldest negro wench Teen and two cows, and furniture for one room"; he left to his son John all his land and salt meadow which he (the testator) had bought from John De Groot and all the land he had bought of Daniel Simonsen now in Castletown; he left to his son Jacob all the lands and salt meadow which he (the testator) bought of the executors of Moses Dupuy, deceased, at Karle's Neck and all the lands which he (the testator) heired of his "father Barnt Tysen, alias Swaim" at Karle's Neck. The son Jacob who thus inherited the house was probably the Jacob Tysen of Castleton who, in his will dated 1846 and probated 1848, mentioned his wife Mary and many children, grandchildren and greatgrandchildren, and directed that his real estate in Northfield was to be sold and the proceeds divided between his four sons, Jacob, John, Richard, and Raymond M. Tysen. Thus if Jacob Tysen had not sold the property during his lifetime it was sold by his executors. The map of 1853 shows no Tysen house on this road.

Capt. John[6] Tysen (1758-1827), the elder son of John, the patriot, lived in the Town of Castleton on a farm adjoining the Bodines and Martlings (plate 27), probably on the farm he eventually inherited from his father. By his wife Elizabeth Jacques, he had ten children including David Jacques[7] Tysen (1807-1885) who married Elizabeth Lake and lived in the Lake home (formerly Guyon's—plate 31) at New Dorp and also at Port Richmond. Their son David Jacques[8] Tysen was born in the Lake home; he built a home on the high point of Staten Island near Dongan Hills and died Aug. 8, 1928 in his 87th year. He was a lawyer, large tomato grower and realty owner. He purchased many of the homes with which his ancestors had been connected, including the house on Karle's Neck at the Fresh Kills which stands on the grant of his ancestor. It is now owned by his family and occupied by tenants.

The roughly tooled stone with which this house was built was not used during the early period on Staten Island. The house probably dates from the second quarter or middle of the eighteenth century. The roofline is not so steep as in the early houses. The present roof, extending slightly beyond all four walls, is a modern type, and possibly replaces an earlier one with curved overhanging eaves, since the ends of the beams have been sawn off. The house is on the west side of Richmond Avenue, a short distance south of the Simonson-Blake house (plate 37) and twice that distance north of the Arthur Kill Road. This section was formerly known as Karle's Neck and the old road here ran along the edge of the lowland west of the house, rather than along the crest of the upland as at present.

House of Cornelius Van Santvoord, later Krusen's and Pelton's

1262 Richmond Terrace, West New Brighton

PLATE 40

Garret Dircksen[1] Croesen and Pieter Jansen[2] Staats, brothers-in-law and residents of Gowanus in Breukelen, received on Sept. 29, 1677 grants for 160 acre tracts adjoining each other along the Kill van Kull on the north shore of Staten Island. The Kroesen homestead, which no longer stands, was erected on the former (see supra) and the Van Santvoord house on the latter near the division line. Pieter Jansen Staats, generally called Peter Johnson, was a son of Jan Pieters[1] who had emigrated from Huysen and settled at Gowanus on Long Island. In 1689 and 1709 Pieter deeded portions of his grant on Staten Island to his son John, who had with his brother Peter obtained a patent to land on Staten Island opposite Amboy in 1674. It is not known where on Staten Island John Staats settled. John or Jan Pietersen[2] Staats married Catrina Corsen; they had five daughters, Mary, bap. 1689 at Flatbush, Jannetje, Cornelia, bap. 1696, Annetje, bap. 1700, and Rebecca, bap. 1707 (the last three baptized on Staten Island).

The daughter Annetje[4] Staats, bap. June 20, 1700, d. before 1748 in Schenectady, married Dominie Cornelius Van Santvoord, b. 1697, d. Jan. 6, 1752 in Schenectady aged 55 years. He had emigrated from Leyden and was dominie of the Dutch Church at Port Richmond, Staten Island, until about 1740, when he was given charge of the Dutch Church at Schenectady. The Dominie and Annetje had six children: Maria Catharine, Anna, Cornelius, Staats, Jacoba and Zeger, all of whom were born on Staten Island (presumably in this house) between 1720 and 1733, and later lived at Schenectady or Albany.

It is stated in Morris, v. 2, p. 175, that the so-called Kruzen-Pelton house was built in 1722 by Joseph Rolph and that it later passed into the Kruzen family; on a plaque recently placed on the wall of the house, it is stated that it was built in 1730 by Johannes De Groot, and in Leng and Davis, p. 887, it is called the early De Groot homestead. These statements are all incorrect; these families were neighbors and connections. On a map of 1783 the houses along the shore from west to east were those of J. D. Groot, C. Kruse, C. Kruse, Jr., and J. Rolph. The house in question was built and occupied by Dominie Van Santvoord, according to Clute, p. 460, which statement is undoubtedly correct as he was the son-in-law of John Staats, owner of the property.

On June 3, 1689 Pieter Jansen deeded 300 feet of his patent to his son John, who was the owner at the time of the road survey of 1705 but seems to have later disposed of it. On Aug. 13, 1709 Hendrick Kroesen sold John Staats a tract 188 feet wide on the west side of the partition line. On March 21, 1709 (evidently Old

Style, 1709/10) Pieter Jansen sold his son John a tract 300 feet wide, bounded east by land he had formerly conveyed to John and on the west by land John had bought from Hendrick Croesen. On Feb. 4, 1730 (recorded 1743) John Staats conveyed this double property, 488 feet in width and about one mile in length, to his son-in-law Cornelius Van Santvoord. The Dominie may have built his home here (the present stone wing) at this time, although he probably built it about the time of his marriage, a few years before his father-in-law actually turned the property over to him. The statement in Morris may be reconciled with this if Joseph Rolph was a carpenter by trade, for he might then have erected it for the Dominie. On July 3, 1745 (recorded 1763) Dominie Van Santvoord sold the property to Jacob Bergen, Jr., grandson of Hendrick Kroesen, and he sold it April 24, 1751 (recorded 1760) to Cornelius Krusen, son of Hendrick, describing the property as the 188 feet west of the partition fence and the 300 feet adjoining on the east, which John Staats had purchased in 1709 from Hendrick Kroesen and Pieter Jansen respectively.

The main section of the house is said to have been erected about 1776, and was undoubtedly built by Cornelius Krusen, Sr. in the years following his purchase of the farm in 1751. Cornelius' Krusen (b. 1708, d. 1784-86) continued to make his home here even after he inherited his father's homestead on the west (see supra). The map of 1783 shows him here and his son Cornelius, Jr. at the old homestead.

The British occupied Staten Island during most of the Revolution and Gen. Cortlandt Skinner, Commander of the "American Loyalists," occupied this house for his headquarters, and entertained here Prince George, who later became George IV. There is a strong tradition that the Widow Kruzen lived here at the time of the Revolution. By process of elimination, she was Clausia Brinckerhof, d. March 21, 1787 in her 77th year, the second wife of Cornelius' brother Garret Crusen, who is believed to have lived on Watchogue Road (plate 32). Why she should live on her brother-in-law's property rather than with her step-son is not known; of course the house was larger.

Cornelius Krusen, Sr. in 1786 bequeathed to his son Cornelius, Jr. the farm on which he (the testator) lived and the adjoining farm on which the son lived, as well as other property. Cornelius' Krusen, Jr., bap. Aug. 8, 1736, d. Dec. 25, 1807, married 1757 (marriage bond of April 5) Beletje, daughter of Johannes De Groot, the owner of the adjoining farm on the east, and of his wife Elizabeth Sickels, whose brother William Sickels built the first of the Sickels houses in Rockland County (see infra). On his death, Cornelius, Jr. willed the two homestead farms to his son John for life with vested remainder to his six grandsons. However, after the death of John' Cruser Aug. 31, 1829 intestate, a partition suit was filed in 1830, and the farm was sold in various parcels.

Lot No. 1, consisting of 57½ acres and the "Mansion House" (that is, the Van Santvoord-Krusen house), was bought May 31, 1830 by Joshua Sutton, who became insane and whose guardian sold the farm he occupied on Sept. 28, 1835 to Daniel Pelton. The following year (not 1832 nor 1839 as sometimes stated) Daniel Pelton replaced the old east wing, originally similar to the west wing, by a two story brick building. The Pelton family who made their home here consisted of Daniel Pelton, Sr., formerly of New York City (son of Philip of Hempstead), b. June 21, 1788, d. July 10, 1867, who was married on May 1, 1813 in New York City to Catharine Cortelyou Van Arsdale, b. Feb. 17, 1788, d. Dec., 1862, and their two unmarried daughters, Cordelia and Angeline, all of whom died in the Van Santvoord house. Here also dwelt their youngest daughter Mary Ann (1828-1910), who in 1860 married Alfred Napoleon Duffié, son of Count Auguste Duffié. He taught cavalry tactics during the Civil War and served in the Union army, becoming a Brigadier General; he died Nov. 8, 1880 in Cadiz, Spain, while United States Consul there. The house remained in the Pelton estate until about 1918. It has been owned for some years by Mrs. F. W. James.

The photograph emphasizes the small house, built 1720-30 of roughly cut stone, and with a steep gable roof. The main unit of the present house (only half of which is shown in the photograph), is built of stone with a covering of clapboards, and also has a steep gable roof. Notice the characteristic difference in size of the 1720-30 and 1751-76 units. The roof brackets and dormers are modern. A photograph of the entire house, taken in 1933, is reproduced in the *Proceedings of the Staten Island Institute of Arts and Sciences*, opp. p. 57, in connection with an article on the house, from which the present account has been freely drawn. The house stands on a bluff overlooking the Kill Van Kull. It is on the southeast side of Richmond Terrace adjoining Pelton Avenue, and is not far west of Sailors' Snug Harbor.

PLATE 26

House of Nathaniel Britton, later Walton's and Cubberly's
New Dorp Lane, New Dorp

The stone section of the main house is the original unit and was erected by Nathaniel Britton between 1695 and 1699. In the interior is a huge open fireplace with a beam across the top. The moderately sloped roof is not characteristic of this early period and may be a later alteration. The property was sold to Thomas Walton in 1714 and was conveyed by his family to Isaac Cubberly in 1761. The wing was probably erected by the Waltons after their purchase. Its very steep roof is characteristic of an early date. The lean-to, sloping almost to the ground, is a later addition. The frame section of the house by the road was not built until about 1800. The house has no overhanging eaves in front or rear. The small entry porch is of a later date than the house but is a type frequently found on Staten Island.

PLATE 27

Cozine—Bodine—Martling House
40 Watchogue Road, Myer's Corners

This is the rear view of the house as it was about 1900, before the wing was moved to the back. It is erroneously known as the home of Daniel Corsen, who lived on another road. The house was erected about 1760, probably by a Cozine. Two members of the Cozine family inherited it before 1784, one-half of the house going to each, so that later deeds transfer each half of the house separately. The house is only 68 feet long, including the kitchen wing. It is built of unhewn fieldstone except for the north front which is of finished sandstone blocks. The steep gable roof has a slight curve at the eaves. The windows are small and few in number. Those in the wing were formerly of the old casement type. The house was sold by the Cozines in and about 1789 to Vincent Bodine; in 1805 he disposed of it to Garret Martling who owned it until 1848.

PLATE 28

De Hart House
3373 Richmond Terrace, Holland Hook

It is not known when or by whom this house was built. It first appears in the possession of Samuel De Hart in 1783, but may have been his father's homestead before him. It remained the home of the family until recent years. The house in its present condition was built about 1735-40 and incorporates a part of an earlier building in an unusual manner. The original house on the site evidently faced the west; its south end was destroyed; its north end was enlarged on the east and a wing added on the west to form the present house which faces south. The steep pitch of the roof and small size of the windows are characteristic of an early date. The so-called German hood on the main unit is a later addition which has been marred recently by cutting a window through it.

PLATE 29

Dissosway House
formerly near Outerbridge Crossing, Richmond Valley

This is understood to be the house built by Mark Dusochay in the 1690s but it is possible that it was erected by his son Israel Dissosway in the early eighteenth century. It is of stone, whitewashed, and covered by a steep gable roof, with deep overhanging eaves both front and rear. It has a greater depth than many of the Staten Island houses. This view was taken from the fields about 1900. The house has since been torn down. It remained the home of the Dissosway family until the end of the nineteenth century.

PLATE 30

Dongan—Christopher House
Willow Brook Road, Willow Brook

This is erroneously known as the Christopher homestead. The original unit was one of the numerous houses built on Gov. Dongan's Manor. It was purchased in or shortly before 1760 by the Widow Nelly Hagewout and her two sons; by 1764 it had been acquired by Charity Hagewout and her husband Joseph Christopher, in whose family it remained until 1827. The original unit consists of only one room and was built about 1756. Joseph Christopher and his wife mortgaged the property in 1764, presumably in order to obtain the money to build an addition. This is twice the size of the other unit, the division line being marked by the chimney. The house is built of roughly cut stone and covered by a steep gable roof without overhanging eaves. There is an outside door opening into each of the three rooms. The porch is later.

PLATE 31

Guyon—Lake—Tysen House
Tysen's Lane, New Dorp

Contrary to popular belief, this is not an early Lake homestead; the property was not bought by the Lake family until 1812. Joseph Guyon was in possession in 1771, and his family probably built the house about 1720-40. It is a larger house than the average on Staten Island. It differs in other respects, being built of shingles and covered by a gambrel roof. The graceful overhanging eaves on the south front of the house were added at a later date, as was the kitchen wing. In the main house there are two rooms on either side of a wide central hallway; the three chimneys are characteristic of this type. The house passed by marriage from the Lakes into the Tysen family, who still own it.

PLATE 32

House of Pieter Pieterse Hagawout, later Krusen's and Vreeland's
formerly on Watchogue Road, Graniteville

Pieter Pieterse Hagawout received a confirmatory patent for this property in 1697 and undoubtedly built the west (left) unit of the house about this time. The house was 22 by 60 feet in size; it was built of stone, 18 to 24 iches thick, carried up the gable end to the roofline; the masonry of the long walls was sheathed with clapboarding. The gable roof was very steep; at some early period deep overhanging eaves were added, but were taken off the north wall when the front was remodelled at the end of the nineteenth century. The original unit consisted of only two rooms: the best chamber was small and had a small fireplace; the outside door led into the kitchen which had a large fireplace with built-in crane and a stairway to the attic opposite the chimney, a location usual at this very early date. There was a seventeenth century casement window in the gable end. The smaller unit, probably added after 1726 by the Krusens, consisted of a hallway, nine feet wide, and another room with fireplace. The sloping dormers belong to an early type. This photograph was taken about 1900.

163

PLATE 33

House of Peter Hagewout (Haughwout)
1424 Richmond Avenue, south of Graniteville

Peter Hagewout, son of Pieter Pieterse Hagawout, the builder of the house in plate 32, purchased in 1734 the tract on which stands this house, which he or his widow erected shortly after this date. It remained the home of descendants until its sale between 1837 and 1877. It is a small house consisting of one room on either side of a central hallway; the parlor may have been built at an earlier date than the other room. The house is sheathed with clapboarding and is covered by a steep gable roof with overhanging eaves in front. There are good examples of early panelling in the interior. Slight alterations and a large addition at the rear have been made since this photograph was taken about 1900.

PLATE 34

Hendrickson (?)—Winants House
formerly on Arthur Kill Road, south of Rossville

This was the Winant Winants homestead for over a century and a half. The family obtained possession of it in the second quarter of the eighteenth century. Its history previous to this is unknown. The stone section of the house was very old. A stone marked "1696 I.H." suggests that the builder was John Hendrickson who received a grant of land in this vicinity. The stones were laid in mud and oyster shell lime. There was a primitive fireplace built out into the room with a huge beam over it; the smoke escaped through a hole in the garret floor and up a short chimney. This older section had no cellar beneath it, and no windows on the gable end. The frame unit was built along similar lines after the Revolution. A steep gable roof covered the whole house. The early type sloping dormers may have been built at the same time as the addition. The deep overhanging eaves were also an early alteration. This photograph was taken in 1907.

PLATE 35

Lakeman—Cortelyou—Taylor House
Richmond Road, New Dorp

Abraham Lakeman is believed to have come into possession of this tract at the division of his father's estate in 1684, and he is understood to be the builder of the house. The house and other improvements are mentioned in a deed of 1714. Among its many owners was Aaron Cortelyou who purchased it in 1751 and whose son-in-law sold it to Joseph Taylor in 1794. The house is built of very irregular fieldstone and practically no attempt has been made to lay it in courses. The small size and number of the windows is characteristic of an early period. The large section is the original unit; it is covered by a gambrel roof of the New England type. The house was formerly whitewashed in the manner popular on Staten Island. It has been restored and has since undergone considerable alteration.

PLATE 36

*House of John Roll, later Mersereau's
formerly on Watchogue Road, Graniteville*

Some of the early deeds to this property are missing but from various records it is inferred that John Roll was in possession about 1740. The house was probably built by him as it dates from this period. In 1762 he sold it to his son-in-law Col. Jacob Mesereau and it remained the home of the family until 1896. The house was built in the style common on Staten Island, of stone, with long, low, massive lines and a steep gable roof. The small number of windows is characteristic, as is their unbalanced arrangement.

PLATE 37

Simonson—Blake House
2329 Richmond Avenue, New Springville

This is one of the later Simonson houses built on their homestead tract, which they had acquired by 1702. It is probable that this house was erected by Barent Simonson after his marriage in 1755. In the middle of the nineteenth century it passed by marriage into the Blake family. It is a stone house covered with modern shingles, and has a steep gable roof with overhanging eaves in front.

PLATE 38

*House of Thomas Stillwell, later Britton's and Perine's
1476 Richmond Road, Dongan Hills*

This house is in reality two separate dwellings, and two families lived here as independent households for over one hundred years. It is believed that the rear stone dwelling was built by Thomas Stillwell about 1680 and the front stone dwelling by his son-in-law Nicholas Britton about 1713. The property was purchased in 1749 by Joseph Holmes, innkeeper, who probably added one of the frame kitchens, built on similar lines. His daughter married Edward Perine and the house remained the home of two branches of their descendants until 1913. Both sections are built of irregular fieldstone, carried all the way up the gable end. The whitewashing adds greatly to the picturesque quality of the house. The gable roofs are not so steep as in many of the early houses. The windows are small and are not grouped in a balanced design. The front door is near one end of the house and opens directly into one of the main rooms, since there is no hallway. There is some fine Jacobean panelling in the best room.

169

PLATE 39

House of Barnt Tysen
Richmond Avenue, south of New Springville

It has always been stated that this house was built by Barnt Tysen about 1680, shortly after he received the land grant. However, construction shows that the present house was not erected until about the middle of the eighteenth century, and was therefore undoubtedly built by the grandson Barnt Tysen. The house is built of roughly tooled stone and is covered by a gable roof of moderate slope, neither of which are characteristics found in the early houses on Staten Island. The beam ends have been sawed off, suggesting that the present modern roof replaces an earlier one with overhanging eaves. The low lands of the Fresh Kills are seen in the background of the photograph.

PLATE 40

*House of Cornelius Van Santvoord, later Krusen's and Pelton's
1262 Richmond Terrace, West New Brighton*

This house stands on a grant of 1677 to Pieter Jansen Staats. The original stone unit was erected by his granddaughter's husband, Dominie Cornelius Van Santvoord, presumably shortly after their marriage (about 1719). Van Santvoord was the first minister established on Staten Island. The property was purchased in 1751 by Cornelius Krusen, in whose family it remained until 1830. The main section was erected by the Krusens before the Revolution. The small unit is built of roughly cut stone and is covered by a steep gable roof without overhanging eaves. The main house is similarly built of stone and with a steep roof, but it has been sheathed with modern clapboarding and has a row of roof brackets. Less than half the main unit is shown in the photograph because of the unfortunate effect of the large enclosed doorway. The De Groots and Rolphs have been incorrectly connected with this house; they were near neighbors.

ROCKLAND COUNTY

HOUSE OF GERRET BLAUVELT

ROCKLAND COUNTY

THE southern portion of New York State which borders on the west bank of the Hudson River was a part of Orange County, and was known as Orange County under the Mountains until it was organized into Rockland County in 1798. A ridge of mountains separated it from the larger part of Orange County whereas a mathematical and artificial line was its only demarcation from Bergen County in the Province of New Jersey. Therefore except in its political life it was connected with the other province, with which communication was so much easier. Many of the same families settled Bergen County and the future Rockland County; the two groups intermarried, developed the same habits of thought and mode of living, and built similar houses. In great contrast to this, the two portions of Orange County on either side of the mountains were settled by different families, developed different types of homes and had only a political connection with each other. Therefore the territory that became Rockland County has been included in this volume rather than in the previous work on the Hudson River counties by Miss Reynolds.

The Rockland County territory was opened up and settled under a few large patents. The lands at the southern end around Tappan were purchased from the Indians on March 17, 1681/2 by a group of eight white men and three free negroes from the Bouwery Village on Manhattan together with five men from New Jersey. The deed was acknowledged before Gov. Carteret of New Jersey on July 1, 1682. When the boundary between the provinces was determined in 1687 the tract was found to lie largely in New York and a patent was issued by Gov. Dongan of New York on March 24, 1686/7. Unlike most of the patents of the period, this land was obtained not by rich speculators but by farmers who were prospective settlers. Lambert Adriaense Smidt and Adriaen Lambertse Smidt, patentees, and Hendrick Gerritse Blauvelt, brother of two of the patentees, came here in the summer of 1683 and were soon followed by others. The early settlements fell into three groups: at Jan Claus' land or Greenbush, now Blauvelt and Orangetown, at Tappan, and at Old Tappan over the border in New Jersey. The lands were for many years owned in common, the first division was not made until 1704 and the second in 1721. A Dutch Church was organized here as early as 1694 and a house of worship erected in 1716.

A large part of the county was included in the Kakiat Patent, granted June 25, 1696 to Daniel Honan and Michael Hawdon, speculators. The Tappan Patent ran as far west as the Hackensack River and the Kakiat Patent extended from this river as far west as Tallman's and as far north as the mountains below Haverstraw. Hawdon's executors in 1712 sold the North Moiety of the patent to a group of Englishmen from Hempstead, Long Island, who caused the patent to be divided Nov. 5, 1713. Benjamin Osborn became the first known settler in this northern moiety in 1714. This region was known as Kakiat or New Hempstead, the English settling in the more westerly portion and selling the easterly lands to men of Dutch descent, who opened up farms around the present New City. The South Moiety was sold by Honan in 1716 to John McEvers who disposed of a one-half share to Lancaster Symes. They also were speculators and it was not until 1727 that their moiety was surveyed and laid out in lots. Settlement was made about this time, probably by Dutchmen from the adjoining Tappan Patent, and a Reformed Church was organized at Clarkstown in 1749. The expense of the 1713 division and survey was paid by the sale of an expense lot of 1000 acres in Orangetown on the Hackensack River, and this land was settled on shortly after this date by Tunise Cuyper and in 1736 by William Sickels.

The patents along the Hudson River were smaller in size. Claes Jansen (Kuyper) van Purmarent obtained New Jersey patents for two tracts at Nyack in 1671 and his son Cornelius Cuyper later settled here and became a leader of the county. The former sold part of his tract to Douwe Harmanszen Tallman who came here between 1678 and 1686 and whose son Harman was the first settler here in 1675. The lands to the south of him along the Hudson River as far as Piermont were taken up by Theunis Roelofse Van Houten who settled here about 1686. A tract at Palisades was granted in 1687 to George Lockhart and was occupied by William Merritt in 1701; among the settlers here were the Snedens. Further north, the territory around Rockland Lake from Nyack to Haverstraw was granted by the Pond or Quaspeck Patent on Sept. 27, 1694 to Jarvis Marshall and William Welch, both speculators. The tract changed hands several times before portions were purchased by farmers. Most of the south half around the Lake was settled by a group of Germans about 1711. The extreme northern portion of the patent was sold by Capt. John Sands of Cow Neck on Oct. 23, 1707 to Tunis Snedeker of Hempstead, who settled here with his sons and daughters in or by 1731. Two tracts at Haverstraw were granted in 1671 under New Jersey patents, one to Balthazar De Hart of New York and the other to Nicholas Depew and Hendrick Van Bommel. Depew sold his interest in 1685 to Florus Willemse Crom, who had already settled on it in 1681. Part of Van Bommel's share came into the possession of Reyn Van Ditmarsen, who located here between 1683 and 1687. Minne Johannes (Minnelay) was one of the earliest settlers of Haverstraw in or by 1681.

The western point of the Rockland County territory was only sparsely settled and there were few recognized titles here before 1775. A group of farms were cleared around Suffern after 1709. John Zabriskie purchased a tract near Tallman's in 1724 from a New Jersey Proprietor and succeeded in having his claim recognized. Isaac Van Duser was probably the first settler in the Clove, on the Ramapo River north of Suffern, where he had located by 1735. Peter Wanamaker settled east of Suffern about 1740. The Dutch did not locate in the northern point of the county above Haverstraw.

The Rockland County territory remained a part of Orange County until 1798, but the mountain barrier was recognized in the formation of townships. Orangetown was organized as early as 1686. Haverstraw Precinct was set off in 1719 and comprised the territory from the north bounds of Tappan to the north bounds of Haverstraw, including the Kakiat Patent. Semi-annual county courts were established in 1703.

The first homes of the settlers were of two kinds, either an excavation in the side of a hill, lined with bark, faced with upright posts and furnished with shelves, or a hut of woven saplings covered with bark. These were followed by hand-hewn frame buildings with shingled walls and thatched roofs. The abundant sandstone was soon quarried and the great majority of houses built before the Revolution were constructed with the indigenous red sandstone blocks, cut and roughly shaped by the settlers or their slaves, and often quarried on the property. Clapboarding was rarely used before the Revolution.

The similarity between the houses of Bergen and Rockland Counties is remarkable. In both territories we find a predominant use of sandstone blocks, of a gable roof for a narrow house and a gambrel roof for a wide house, and the same interior arrangement. The curved overhanging eaves are a characteristic feature especially in Bergen County. There are a greater number of small, narrow farmhouses in Rockland County, possibly because living conditions were more primitive since it was sparsely settled.

The houses in the Rockland County territory were discovered through an intensive search of the roads shown on Erskine's Revolutionary maps. The early owners were determined with the aid of local residents and historians and the perusal of maps, and the genealogy of the families compiled from the church records. The author is indebted to Wilfred Blanch Talman for notes on the Smidt and Tallman families, to J. Elting Sloat for his Sneden family researches, to Louis L. Blauvelt for his extensive card index of the Blauvelt family, to M. Montgomery Maze for his study of the land records of lower Rockland County, and to George H. Budke for his generous and exact advice on numerous families and houses, also to Stanley V. Blauvelt, James V. Clarke, Frederick Demarest, P. L. Huested and Miss Emma J. Quidor for information concerning various regions. There was no published material available except for a few articles in the *Rockland Record*. Most of the photographs were taken in 1933 and a few in 1925.

HOUSES IN ROCKLAND COUNTY

House of Benjamin Benson
Old King's Highway, West Haverstraw
PLATE 41

The house stands on a large tract at the mouth of the Minisceongo Creek bought from the Indians by Balthazar De Harte; he sold a part to Nicholas Du Poins of New York City, who sold it Oct. 17, 1685 to Florus Willemse Crom. The latter immediately obtained a patent for 730 acres north of the creek, settled here and died in 1706. Although he ordered the farm at Haverstraw to be sold and the proceeds divided among his children, it passed intact to his son Willem Florus Crom, who left it to his six children. They divided it. The farm adjoining the creek on the north fell to Willem's eldest son Dirck Crom, who sold it Oct. 20, 1737 to Matthew Benson; he sold it April 26, 1742 to John Allison, in whose family it remained. The 94 acre farm next but one north of the creek fell to Willem Crom's daughter Tryntie, wife of Paulus Yorkse. Thomas Mapes bought it, and sold the north half to John Alsop, who sold to Matthew Benson before 1757; the south half was sold by the heirs to John James, who sold to Benjamin Benson in 1757. The farm again became a unit, as Benjamin Benson inherited the north half from his father.

The ancestor of the family, Dirck[1] Bensingh, was a native of Groningen and emigrated via Amsterdam to New Amsterdam, where he bought a house in 1649; he soon removed to Ft. Orange (Albany), where he died Feb. 12, 1659. A son, Capt. Johannes[2] Benssing or Benson, removed to a farm in the village of Harlem in 1696; by his wife Elizabeth Van Deusen, he had Matthew and nine other children. Matthew[3] Benson, b. Jan. 5, 1693, died 1757-58, married Dec. 12, 1716 Elizabeth Bussing, married secondly Dec. 9, 1727 Hannah Edsall, widow of Gerrit De Groot, and had three sons and one daughter by his second wife. He was a cooper by trade. He sold his Harlem lands in 1730, removed to Bergen County and became a member of the Hackensack Church in 1731. It is possible he lived for a time on one of his purchases at Haverstraw (mentioned above); he became a vintner in New York City, and died in his house there on Dey Street. Matthew's son Benjamin[4] Benson, b. Feb. 13, 1732 at Hackensack, d. Aug. 5, 1779, married April 30, 1756 Catharine Deronda, and had six sons and four daughters: Joanna, Catherine, Charity, Matthew (1764-1843), Henry, Benjamin (1768-1823), Jacob, Maria, William and Abraham, who were probably born on the Haverstraw farm, or possibly in the Dey Street home.

Benjamin[4] Benson was a Revolutionary soldier, a signer of the Articles of Association and a member of the Committee on Correspondence. He was shot and killed by some British spies here at his Haverstraw farm.

Benjamin Benson probably built the present stone house about the time of his purchase of the property in 1757; he is the first known owner of the house. The farm was in the possession of the Benson family at the time of the Revolution and in 1790, when a map was made of the Crom Patent. Lossing probably refers to this house when he mentions stopping overnight in 1848 at the tavern of Mr. Benson near Sampsonville, about three miles below Stony Point and two miles from Haverstraw.

The old King's Highway went north from Tappan, crossed the mountains at the Long Clove, and followed a tortuous course through the lowlands of Haverstraw and West Haverstraw; a quarter of a mile above the Minisceongo Creek it turned sharply west for a short distance, and then progressed northwards toward Stony Point. The house stands on the old King's Highway in the southwest corner formed by this westward turn; to the west is the present West Haverstraw railway station.

House of Hendrick Gerritsen Blauvelt
Blauvelt
PLATE 42

A stone in the front wall of the house bears the date 1710; it is the oldest of the existing Blauvelt houses, and has been gutted by fire since the photograph was taken in 1925. For many years the lands of the Tappan Patent were held in common by the patentees. Early settlements were made at three centers, the most northerly being known as Jan Claus' land (after an Indian of the vicinity), later called Greenbush, now Blauvelt and Orangeburg. The lines of allotment in the division of the patent are not clear at this point, but it is probable that this was the location of Hendrick Blauvelt's 50 acre purchase in 1709; it is considered that he was the builder of this house at Clausland in 1710.

His father Gerrit Hendricksen[1] was born at Deventer in Overyssel and worked as a shoemaker in Nykerk. At the age of fifteen, he emigrated in 1637 on the *Key of Kalmar*, under a six year contract with Kilian Van Rensselaer as a tobacco raiser or farm hand. He soon removed to New Amsterdam, where on May 7, 1646 he married Marretje Lamberts Moll, whose father owned a shipyard there. On Dec. 6, 1646 he obtained a grant of 25 morgens, a tract on the east side of the Bouwery Road extending to the East River, and settled here. He married secondly on Oct. 22, 1679 Josyntie Thomas, widow of Pieter Wesselszen, and died 1683-84. Seven of his fourteen children by his first marriage survived him, and all removed to Tappan. His widow and their daughter Elizabeth remained in New York City. The eldest surviving son was Hendrick Gerritsen' Blauvelt, b. Sept. 30, 1654, married Sept. 20, 1673 Marretje Josephs Waldron, and had ten children: Marretje, Marretje, John, Harman, Gerrit, Annatje, Joseph, Abraham, Isaac and Daniel. Although not a patentee, he was one of the first to remove from Bouwery Village to the Tappan Patent, and settled here late in 1683. His first habitation was probably a rude temporary structure; it was not until he was fifty-six years of age that he built the present stone house in 1710. He joined the newly organized Tappan Church in 1695, served on the first grand jury of Orange County, was a tax collector, and head of a family in Orangetown in the Census of 1702. The later ownership of the house is not known. It may have been inherited by Hendrick's eldest (surviving?) son Harman' Blauvelt of Tappan, b. April 3, 1681, married April 1704 Sarah De Pew, daughter of François Du Puy of Flatbush, and had eight children. A resident of Tappan, Harman married secondly at Tarrytown Oct. 10, 1730, Catharina Ecker(son), widow of Nicholas de Vouw. The house is marked but unnamed on Erskine's Revolutionary map. In 1876 the owner was T. Dinan, and its present owner is a Mr. Dinan of Brooklyn.

The house overlooks the Sparkill (creek), the King's Highway beyond and the new state highway. It stands east of the railway on the north side of a crossroad, which formed part of the Revolutionary road northward to Clarksville. It is south of the village of Blauvelt, nearer Orangeburg, in the region formerly known as Clausland.

House of Johannes Blauvelt, later Smith's
Blauvelt
PLATE 43

This house was built in three units, each of about the same size. A stone on the front wall of the central portion is marked 1741. A stone on the western unit bears the inscription:

I.I.B.	M.B.
M.I.	24
ANO	1752.

These two units are similar, and are covered by one roof. The smaller east wing belongs to a slightly later period.

Hendrick Blauvelt, builder of the house to the southward (plate 42), had a younger son named Joseph Hendrickse' Blauvelt, bap. Nov. 20, 1687, d. 1733-39, married at Tappan Jan. 11, 1711 Elizabeth Van Dalsen. Joseph mentioned eight of their children in his will: Hannes the eldest, Hendrick, Frederick, Garret, Abraham,

Martha, Annatie and Altha. The eldest son was Johannes Joseph[4] Blauvelt, b. Nov. 19, 1714, d. Oct. 2, 1789, married Sept. 28, 1739 Margrietje Smidt, b. July 6, 1720, d. July 18, 1784, daughter of Cornelius Lambertsen Smidt, and granddaughter of Lambert Adrianse[2] Smidt, one of the Tappan patentees and settlers (plate 58).

Johannes Joseph and Margrietje (Smidt) Blauvelt undoubtedly built the first unit of the house, which was erected two years after their marriage; the inscription on the second unit states they were the builders of the west portion in 1752. He was First Major of the Orangetown Regiment of Orange Co. Militia, but appears to have lost his rank after that regiment was consolidated with the Haverstraw regiment; he served in the Revolution although over sixty years of age. He and his wife lie buried in the Clausland cemetery. Their children were: Joseph, Catharina, Elizabeth, Maria, Cornelius, Anatye, Margrietje, Johannes and Vrowtye. The eldest daughter Catharina, b. 1743, was the second wife of Harmanus Tallman, whose father Douwe was bayonetted by the Tories at Closter. They lived with his father-in-law, and thither came their son Major Peter Tallman to recover from a wound received on a Jersey battlefield. Johannes' and Margrietje's youngest son was Johannes J.[5] Blauvelt, b. May 13, 1758, d. March 28, 1811; married Clausha Blanch, b. Jan. 21, 1763, d. Dec. 6, 1842, and buried with her husband at Sickeltown (Nauraushaun); her father was Col. Thomas Blanch, an active member of the militia during the Revolution, whose house formerly stood on the creek north of Closter village and west of the railway. The Blauvelt house was inherited jointly by Johannes' and Clausha's two daughters, Margrietje[6] Blauvelt, wife of Honshy Haring, and Aefie[6] Blauvelt, b. July 21, 1785, d. Nov. 29, 1848, wife of John J. Smith, b. June 22, 1777, d. Nov. 13, 1848. He was the son of Major John Smith of Germonds (plate 60). The last in the family to own the house was their son John De Windt Smith, b. Feb. 23, 1806, d. Sept. 29, 1871, married May 2, 1832 Eleanor Cornelison Blauvelt, b. Dec. 14, 1808, d. Feb. 5, 1850, married secondly Martha Griffith, who survived and died in 1892. John De Windt Smith removed to Nyack shortly before his death, and the house was probably sold at this time. The owner in 1876 was John W. Moison, from whom it descended to his son Courtney, and then to his son Emmett Moison of Blauvelt; he is the present owner and rents it.

The house is north and west of the village of Blauvelt; it is near the Erie Railroad, on the north side of a crossroad, between Gerret Blauvelt's house (plate 44) on the West Nyack Road and Nauraushaun. The photograph was taken in 1925. The house is fast falling into ruin, and may not last many more winters.

House of Johannes Blauvelt
Blauvelt Road, Blauvelt

The builder of this house was a second cousin of the Johannes Blauvelt who built the house north of the village (plate 43), and must not be confused with him. Abraham Gerritsen² Blauvelt, b. June 17, 1663, was a younger brother of Hendrick Blauvelt of Clausland (plate 42). Their two eldest brothers, Johannes and Huybert, were among the sixteen original patentees of Tappan; Abraham also became a patentee later in life, by purchasing a half-right of Adriaen Lambertsen Smidt in 1700, and another half-right from the heirs of Cornelius Adriaensen Smidt in 1714; these and other land purchases amounted to about 1,000 acres, situated partly at Old Tappan and Harrington Park. He lived at Tappan, was chosen assessor, and a deacon and elder of the Tappan Church, and died between 1731 and 1751. By his wife Margrietje Minnelay, whom he married April 8, 1691, he had five sons and five daughters. She had married as her first husband, Harmen Douwesen Tallman, patentee of Nyack (see plate 64). One of the elder sons was Jacob³ Blauvelt of Orangetown, b. about 1693, d. 1774-79, married Jan. 12, 1715 Pieterje Haring, bap. April 15, 1696, daughter of Pieter Haring and Margrietje Bogart. Jacob settled on the farm of 50 morgens bought by his father in 1714 from Hendrick Van Campen and his wife Derricke Smidt, which she had inherited from her father Cornelius Smidt. In his will Jacob mentioned his sons Johannes and Peter, his daughter Elizabeth wife of Peter Perrie (brother of Isaac Perry—see infra), and the children of his three deceased sons, Abraham, Jacob and Isaac.

The youngest son was Johannes J.⁴ Blauvelt, b. March 20, 1735, d. March 26, 1815, married Antje Blanch, d. June 1, 1810. He built the south unit of the present house on his father's farm about 1755. He was probably the Johannes Jac. Blauvelt who was Captain of the Orangetown Company of Minute Men in 1776. In his will dated 1806, he divided his 296 acres between his two sons: Jacob J., b. Mar. 31, 1757, married Rachel Demarest, and Richard, b. May 5, 1759, d. Sept. 20, 1827. This Richard⁵ Blauvelt was a Judge of Public Affairs; on April 16, 1781 he married Sarah Van Dolsen, d. Feb. 16, 1857 aged 96 years, 8 months, 14 days. Of their three children, John, Gitty and Richard, the youngest was Richard R.⁶ Blauvelt, b. May 18, 1787, d. May 26, 1837, married April 12, 1809 Margaret Clark, d. Sept. 1, 1873 aged 85 years, 6 months, 30 days; they lie buried at Orangeburg with his parents and grandparents. Their daughter Maria Ann⁷ Blauvelt, b. Dec. 19, 1814, d. Feb. 2, 1903, received the ancestral homestead. On April 25, 1837 she married a distant cousin, Isaac Blauvelt of Piermont, b. Sept. 10, 1810, d. 1885, son of James and Letty Blauvelt, and a descendant of Isaac, another son of the above Abraham Gerrits² Blauvelt. Their son James⁸ Blauvelt, b. May 3, 1840, d.

Aug. 20, 1898, married Sept. 26, 1861 Catharine Ferdon, and had two daughters: Mary Adelaide, whose marriage took place in this house in 1886, and Effie, who placed her family record at the author's disposal. James Blauvelt built the frame north wing about 1862, shortly after his marriage, and remodelled the house shortly after his father's death in 1885; James ran a stock farm and raised horses here. In 1892-93 he sold the house and farm of about 130 acres to Mr. Larkins of New York City. It was occupied by Mr. Larkins' daughter Mrs. Cunningham, and later inherited by a daughter Mrs. Daley. It was finally sold to the Broadacres Estate, and purchased a few years ago by John Derfuss, the present owner.

The house is in three units. The south wing is small, it is built of dressed red sandstone with a gable roof; it was erected about 1755, and is shown on the Revolutionary map. The main house, of stone and frame, was built at some period after this war; at that time or shortly later, the roof on the small wing was raised and a frame half-story added. The frame north wing was built about 1862. The first house on the property was the home of Jacob and Pieterje; it was a log cabin located between the present house and barn, and was built about the trunk of a huge tree, this trunk serving as a table. The house stands on the west side of the main road in the village of Blauvelt, south of the railway and north of the Convent.

House of Gerret Blauvelt
Road to West Nyack, Blauvelt
PLATE 44

On Feb. 24, 1763 Elizabeth Blauvelt of Orange Township, County of Orange, widow of Joseph Blauvelt, deceased, and their son Abraham Blauvelt, yeoman, for a consideration of £8, deeded four acres to her son Gerret Joseph Blauvelt, weaver, to be laid so as to include "the house which the said Gerret Joseph is yet going to build," and also the existing house, barn, well, orchard, and other buildings already in his possession. Thus we know that the present stone house was built in or about 1763; it was preceded by a log cabin located about 300 feet north on the corner, which was the first home of Gerret Blauvelt. The builder of the house was the youngest son of Joseph Blauvelt and Elizabeth Van Dalsen; in his will of 1733, Joseph named all his family and specifically left half of his farm on the Demarest Kill (*i.e.*, Hackensack River) to his son Abraham. The eldest son was Johannes Blauvelt, builder of the house on the lane nearby (plate 43). It is interesting to compare the houses of the two brothers. As Gerret did not build his permanent home until nine years after his marriage, he planned a house large enough to contain all his children, while Johannes built his in two separate units as his family grew in numbers; the two houses are quite similar in size, but that of Johannes is more primitive.

Gerret Joseph[4] Blauvelt, b. Jan. 4, 1731, d. July 28, 1810 aged 79 years, 6 months, 24 days, married Sept. 8, 1754 Elizabeth Mabie, d. Feb. 5, 1826 aged 92 years, 10 months, 5 days, probably the daughter of Johannes and Susanna Mabie. Gerret and Elizabeth are only known to have had four children: Elizabeth, Johannes, Joseph and Abraham. The youngest was but a child at the time of the Revolution; his grandson (John Calvin Blauvelt 1823-1921) used to relate how he was placed in front of the closed stairway when the British invaded the house on a raid, that they vented their spleen in smashing a mirror, and did not bother to disturb the child, behind whom the family treasures were hidden. This child, Abraham G.[5] Blauvelt, b. Dec. 26, 1769, d. Feb. 24, 1850 aged 81 years, married June 8, 1792 Elizabeth, daughter of John I. Blauvelt, d. Jan. 27, 1860 aged 85 years; they remained in the family home. Their son John A.[6] Blauvelt, b. Feb. 28, 1797, d. Jan. 14, 1875 aged 78 years, 10 months, 14 days, was a scholar and teacher of Greenbush (the general name for this locality). He married Catharine (1797-1881), daughter of David J. Blauvelt. Their son John Calvin[7] Blauvelt (1823-1921) was born here but at the age of one year moved to a stone house one mile northward (built 1799) which was later given him by his parents. Another son Abraham Thompson[7] Blauvelt, b. about 1818, d. Nov. 13, 1886 aged 68 years, made his home in the ancestral Gerret Blauvelt homestead. He married Mary Ann Blauvelt, d. Aug. 10, 1879 aged 59 years. The family papers of their daughter Catharine Elizabeth were placed at the author's disposal by her son P. L. Huested, who owns the original deed quoted above. Abraham's son John Melancthon[8] Blauvelt, d. March 20, 1887 aged 32 years, 6 months, 16 days, was the last member of the family to own and reside in the homestead. His widow, Nettie Burr, sold the house July 23, 1900, to David F. Moody. On Oct. 24, 1919 he sold it to I. Spencer Graham, the present owner, who is a descendant of the Lent family and a former owner of the Lent house (plate 53). The builders of the house lie buried at Orangeburg, while the later owners are all interred at Blauvelt.

This house is a good example of the eighteenth century Dutch house in its original condition; it is in good preservation, yet has never been remodelled, nor altered with porches and dormers. Thus its proportions and unbroken roofline stand forth. Remains of whitewash on the house-end suggest that there may once have been a small wing. Another view is shown in the vignette. The house is north of the village of Blauvelt, on the east side of the road to West Nyack. It stands on a hill at a jog of the old road, which has recently been straightened so the house is no longer on the main highway.

Blauvelt—Secor House
Phillips Hill Road, New City
PLATE 45

This house probably dates from the second quarter of the eighteenth century. It stands on Lot No. 1 of the North Moiety of the Kakiat Patent. This moiety had been sold to a group of men from Hempstead, Long Island, who took steps for its division and survey in 1713. The region became known as Kakiat or New Hempstead. The western part of the moiety was settled by these men of English descent; the eastern part was also apportioned to them but soon passed into the hands of Dutch settlers. The earliest owner of this house, known to an old resident of the locality, was Peter Blauvelt, b. Oct. 28, 1774, d. April 8, 1850 aged 75 years, 5 months, 11 days, and his wife Maria Van Houten. He was the son of Johannes Blauvelt, b. July 30, 1745, d. Jan. 15, 1830 aged 84 years, 5 months, 16 days, and his wife Catharine Tallman. Both generations lie interred at New City, so it is probable that Johannes owned the house before Peter. In all likelihood the house was built by the father of Johannes Blauvelt, but his parentage is undetermined. He came of the same stock as the Blauvelts of Tappan Patent. Peter and Maria Blauvelt had a daughter Trina, b. March 13, 1796, who lived here with her husband. The 106 acre farm passed into the hands of the Wood family, and then to George D. and Edward Secor, who were the owners in 1876. George inherited his brother's share, but willed the farm to Edward's daughter, Mrs. Brownsell; it is now owned by Walter Brownsell.

The house stands on the north side of the Phillips Hill Road near the Road to Haverstraw. It is one and a half miles north of New City.

Blauvelt—Lane House
Haverstraw Road, New City
PLATE 46

This house was undoubtedly built by a member of the Blauvelt family in the third quarter of the eighteenth century. It stands on Lot No. 5 of the North Moiety of the Kakiat Patent, a tract of 300 acres which was allotted to William Campbell of Haverstraw. He sold the tract on May 9, 1741 for £100 to Jacob A. Blauvelt of Tappan. This Jacob[3] Blauvelt and his wife Pieterje Haring lived on a farm in the present village of Blauvelt in Tappan Patent, in a house later superseded by the existing stone house built by their son Johannes (see supra). In May 1753 Jacob sold the north half of his 300 acre purchase to his eldest son Jacob J.[4] Blauvelt; his descendants still reside here in a red brick house built in 1830. The south half of the tract (on which the house in question stands) was presumably deeded or willed to another of Jacob's numerous sons. The earliest owners, remembered by an old resident, were a brother and two sisters: Jacob Blauvelt, b. June 19, 1789, married Ann, daughter of Jacob Wood; Maria Blauvelt, b. Sept. 4, 1799, married in 1817 Jabez, son of Jacob Wood; Elizabeth Van Orden Blauvelt, b. May 23, 1809, married in 1824 John, son of Samuel De Baan. It is logical to presume that they were joint inheritors of their father's farm. They were the children of Isaac Blauvelt and Annetje Hennion, both residents of New Hempstead (the early name of this region) at the time of their marriage Dec. 18, 1788. The house was probably built by Isaac Blauvelt's father; his name is unknown, but he was undoubtedly a grandson of Jacob Blauvelt, the purchaser of the tract.

The house was later owned by the Lane family, father and son, and the brother-in-law John Schroeder. It passed through several hands, and is now owned by W. C. Christie. It stands in the fields one and a half miles north of New City, on the road to Haverstraw locally called The Street. The use of lintels over the door and windows suggests that the house was built later in the eighteenth century than the other stone houses in the vicinity.

Blauvelt—Hogencamp House
Old Brewery Road, near New City
PLATE 47

Little is known of the history of this house. According to an old resident, it was owned by a Jacobus Blauvelt about the end of the eighteenth or beginning of the nineteenth century; he willed it to his daughter, wife of John Everett Hogencamp (J. E. Hogenkamp was the owner in 1876), and she willed it to her son-in-law Everett Fowler, and it is now owned by his son John Fowler. Jacobus Blauvelt was of course descended from the Blauvelt family of Tappan, but his lineage is undetermined. The house is now rented to a family named Goetschius. It stands on the east side of the Old Brewery Road, about one mile southeast of New City as the crow flies. At some early period in its history the house was considerably deepened, thus altering the line of the chimney, and a wide gable roof placed over the whole. Originally it probably resembled the narrow houses of the neighborhood.

House of Michael Cornelison
Cornelison Point, South Nyack

The house stands on the shore of the Hudson River at Cornelison Point. Built in 1770, it was a large, recently erected stone house at the time of the Revolution, and was often the target for the enemy's fire as the British ships sailed up the Hudson. Early in the war the enemy occupied it for a short time.

A tract of 640 acres in this locality was patented in 1671 to Claes Jansen[1] (Kuyper) van Purmarent; he was a resident of Ahasymus (part of Jersey City). As he died intestate, all his property devolved upon his eldest son, Cornelius Claesen[2] Kuyper, in accordance with the English law. In the settlement of his father's estate, he deeded the South Nyack portion of the patent to his younger brother John Claesen[2] Kuyper, who settled on Cornelison Point and built the first house here, near the present one. His son Claes Jansen[3] Kuyper married Lena Westervelt, and their daughter Catharine[4] Kuyper, b. March 3, 1731, married Michael Cornelison, Sr. on March 21, 1751. In 1765 Michael Cornelison bought out the other heirs of his father-in-law, and in 1770 built the present stone house. His daughter Eleanor Cornelison married Teunis Smith; their daughter Mary Louise Smith married John Laurence Salisbury, whose ancestors came from Blenheim in Austria. Although there have been sons in each generation, the house has passed down in the female line. The present owners are John Salisbury's two daughters, the Misses Jennie Smith and Louisa Dean Salisbury.

The house is a large two story stone building. Its proportions are marred by its present heavy gambrel roof. The house is situated on a bluff and commands a beautiful view of that part of the Hudson known as the Tappan Zee. The shore road curves around and behind it to Piermont Avenue in South Nyack.

House of Tunis Cuyper, later Van Houten's
Sickeltown Road, Nauruashaun, Orangetown

This house stands on the Expense Lot of the Kakiat Patent, which was set off and sold to pay the expenses of the division in 1713. It was a 1000 acre tract, two-thirds of which was bought by Capt. Cornelius Claesen[2] Kuyper on March 6, 1714. He was a large landowner and prominent personage in Rockland County. He lived at Upper Nyack where he died in 1731 (see plate 80). At his death he willed to his eldest son Tunise 330 acres at Fiuken, the name evidently then applied to this southern portion of the Kakiat Patent in the interior back of Tappan. Tunise or Tunis[3] Cuyper, born at the Wallabout, Long Island, bap. April 8, 1685, settled on the tract inherited from his father and in 1732 built here a typical one and a half story stone house. On April 26, 1718 he married Marritje, daughter of Abraham Blauvelt, and had many children. In his will, executed in 1757 and probated in 1767, he styled himself a resident of Naringshaw, and mentioned his wife, his sons Cornelius, Abraham, and Tunis, his daughters Altje and Maritje Terneur, and his granddaughter Grietie the daughter of Grietie. The son Cornelius lived in this vicinity at Sickeltown and was the father-in-law of William Sickels, Revolutionary owner of a house nearby (plate 57). The son Tunis built a short distance west of his father's at the foot of the road to Pearl River. It is a stone house now disfigured by a heavy mansard roof, and is known as the MacKenzie house. The remaining son inherited the father's house. He was Abraham[4] Cooper, b. June 6, 1725, d. July 14, 1797 and lies buried at Sickeltown. On April 7, 1750 he married Sarah, daughter of Abraham Blauvelt, b. July 27, 1729, d. Sept. 24, 1820, and buried with her husband. They had two daughters and two sons. The house was sold to the Van Houten family early in the nineteenth century.

Claus R.[5] Van Houten lived in a stone house on the bank of the Hackensack River near New City (see infra). Among his children was Rulef C.[6] Van Houten, b. April 23, 1779 in his father's home, d. Aug. 13, 1866 aged 87 years, and lies buried at Sickeltown. On Nov. 14, 1800 he married Sarah Sickels, b. Dec. 22, 1780, d. July 11, 1857 and was buried with her husband. She was one of the daughters of Squire William Sickels of Sickeltown (plate 57). They settled in New York City in 1800 where he pursued the trade of wheelwright. In 1812 they moved to Orangeville not far from her father's, and purchased 13 acres, a saw mill and a grist mill, later becoming the owners of 250 acres in the township. The place came to be called Van Houten's Mills and is now again known as Nauraushaun. They bought the Cooper house here and considerably remodelled it, adding a second story in 1832. They had three children: John R., b. 1803 in New York City, lived at Orangeville until 1865, d. 1881 at Nyack; William S., b. 1806, d. 1828; and George, b. June 9, 1814, d. Aug. 15, 1895, buried at Sickeltown. George succeeded to his father's mill business. The house is still owned by the family and is now in the possession of Morris Van Houten.

The house has marked pictorial quality and beauty of line but it is not typical of the pre-revolutionary Dutch houses. Little of the rough stonework of 1732 remains. The walls have been relaid in tooled blocks and carried up a second story. The gambrel roof has curved overhanging eaves. A dated stone on the south wall records the date of the rebuilding. The house stands on the south side of the Sickeltown Road at the bend of the road near the foot of the hill. The Sickeltown Road led from the old Dutch church at Clarkstown south through West Nyack and Sickeltown to Nauraushaun, up the hill, and southward again towards the Old Tappan settlement. Klaes[3] Van Houten, great-grandfather of Rulef C.[6] Van Houten, may have been the builder of the old Van Houten home on the hill here. It was a stone house no longer existing.

House of Daniel De Clark
De Wint House; Washington's Headquarters
Tappan
PLATE 48

Although built by Daniel De Clark, the house soon passed out of his family's possession and is generally known as the house of John De Wint, who was Washington's host, and whose descendants occupied it for over a century. Daniel De Clark (De Klerck) was born about 1654, as he stated in 1692 that he was about 38 years old. His early home was at Oostberg in the Netherlands. There his young son Jacobus was born and his wife Marie de Moll probably died. He emigrated to New York City, settling in the Bouwery Village, north of Wall Street, and joined the Dutch Church in December of 1684. He married his neighbor Grietje Cozyns, widow of Jan Pietersen Haring, on March 4, 1685. Haring had been the leader of the Bouwery villagers in purchasing a large tract on the Hudson River from the Tappan Indians, but died before the patent was obtained. Daniel De Clark took the place of his predecessor and became the leading man of the Tappan community, whither he removed in 1686-87. He was a brewer, captain of the militia, and a justice of the peace. He was a Leislerian adherent and was chosen a justice and a member of the Committee of Safety acting for Orange County in 1689.

Daniel De Clark's first home at Tappan no longer exists; it may have been the low west wing of the present house, which was still standing in 1850. As the leader of the young settlement he no doubt felt a more handsome house befitted him. The present house was built in 1700, of stone brought across the swamp from an outcrop on the Palisades, and of brick which is said to have been brought from Holland as ballast on the ships. The date 1700 is worked in brickwork in large lettering across the front of the house (the second "0" can be seen in the photograph near the window). The very steep pitch of the roof is characteristic of this early period, and the ceilings are so low that special headroom had to be cut out for the grandfather's clock. Note the "Indian hole" high up in the east gable end, a reconnoitering point in case of attack by savages. This is the only early brick house known to exist on the western shore; the widespread and generally false tradition that the bricks were brought from Holland is probably true in this instance; there would be no local brick kilns on the frontier at such an early date, and the leader of a settlement would probably go to the trouble and expense of building a more pretentious house than his neighbors, who used the local sandstone exclusively. The younger of his wife's seven children were probably raised here; his own two children by the second marriage may have been born and died here, as they died in infancy. His son by his first marriage was Jacobus, b. at Oostberg, married at Tappan Oct. 16, 1706 Annetje

Van Houten of Ahasimus. Daniel De Clark died intestate shortly before Nov. 16, 1731, when his son Jacobus was appointed administrator. Jacobus evidently sold the house to settle his father's estate.

The house and farm of 200 acres were sold by Rem Remsen of Kings County for £675 on May 1, 1746, to John De Wint of New York City. John De Wint was a wealthy man, owning a sugar plantation on the Island of St. Thomas in the West Indies, where he was born. He married Anna Kermer, and had eight children, the three eldest born in New York City, and the five others born in his new residence at Tappan. He was George Washington's host here on four separate occasions: Aug. 8-23, 1780, Sept. 28 to Oct. 7, 1780, May 5-8, 1783, Nov. 12-13, 1783. His second stay was the occasion of Major André's trial and execution; Washington ordered the shutters closed on October 2nd so as to be spared the sight of the gallows on a nearby hill. In May, 1783 Washington held an interview here with Sir Guy Carleton, British Commander in Chief, after the signing of the Treaty of Paris, and he gave a dinner here for Carleton, the dinner being served by Sam Fraunces, the famous chef of the time, who was brought up from New York for the occasion.

John De Wint died Nov. 7, 1795, willing his home to his eldest child Anna Maria, who lived with her father. Anna Maria De Wint, b. April 16, 1737 in New York City, married at Tappan Nov. 29, 1753 Major Fredericus Blauvelt, d. May 9, 1809 aged 81 years, 5 months, 6 days; at her death on June 22, 1805, the property passed by will to their only child Elizabeth Blauvelt, b. Jan. 14, 1755, d. June 4, 1827. Jacobus De Clark and his wife Marretje, grandson and granddaughter-in-law of the builder of the house, acted as Elizabeth's sponsors at her baptism in the Tappan Church. Elizabeth Blauvelt married Cornelius C. Mabie, b. March 17, 1754, d. March 6, 1843, son of Casparus Mabie, owner of the "1776 House" in Tappan at the time of the Revolution. Cornelius and Elizabeth Mabie sold the homestead and 35 acres on Aug. 27, 1818 to Arthur and Ann Johnson of Paterson; the house came again into possession of the family when Ann Johnson, widow, sold the house to Samuel S. Verbryck on Aug. 14, 1850. Cornelius and Elizabeth Mabie's daughter Anna Maria Mabie, b. Feb. 2, 1788, died at the age of 94 years, 1 month, 5 days, married first on Oct. 15, 1808 David J. Haring, and secondly on Dec. 24, 1814 Samuel S. Verbryck, Jr., d. June 23, 1860 aged 72 years, 8 months, 23 days, a grandson of the Rev. Samuel Verbryck of Tappan. After his purchase of his wife's ancestral homestead in 1850, Verbryck demolished the kitchen stone wing (which may have been the original house), and built a two-story frame addition. They did not live here long, as they sold the house and 5 acres to Dr. T. Blanch Smith on Aug. 30, 1858. The house has passed through various hands. William Rogers was the owner when the photograph was taken in 1925.

It has been purchased recently by a Masonic lodge, restored and opened to the public. The house has been painted white with the date brought out in black. The old windows have been removed. Crenellated woodwork along the edge of the overhanging roof, which is typically Victorian in style and was no doubt added by the Johnsons, has been restored! The atmosphere of a private home has been completely destroyed by a large parking space near the building. Two sketches of the house made by Lossing can be seen in his *1776 or the War of Independence*, p. 326, and in his *Pictorial Field Book of the Revolution*, v. 1, p. 764. This account has been freely drawn from Budke's article in the *Rockland Record* for 1930.

The house stands on a fifty morgen lot confirmed to Daniel De Clark in the 1704 division of the Tappan Patent. It was a short distance east of the King's Highway which wound through the village of Tappan, and at the time of the Revolution was reached by a private lane across the Sparkill (creek). It stands in the south end of the village.

De Pew House
Haverstraw Road, New City
PLATE 49

This house stands on Lot No. 5 of the North Moiety of the Kakiat Patent, allotted to William Campbell in 1713. It was a 300 acre tract which was sold May 9, 1741 by William Campbell of Haverstraw to Jacob A. Blauvelt of Tappan; he sold the north half of the tract to his son Jacob J. Blauvelt in May, 1753, describing the bounds as the headwaters of the Hackensack River and the lands of the De Pews and Van Houtens. The house in question stands on the south part of Lot No. 5. It was built at two separate times. The east unit is of a very early type of construction and may have been built by William Campbell between 1713 and 1741, since he was living at this time in Haverstraw Precinct, which in early days included the Kakiat Patent. Some time between 1741 and 1753 Jacob A. Blauvelt must have sold the property to his brother-in-law Peter Du Puw, although we have no record of the transaction, and it is probable that Peter Du Puw built the house at this time according to an early style.

His grandfather, François Dupuis of Calais in France, emigrated to this country and married at Brooklyn Sept. 26, 1661 Geertje Williams of Amsterdam. He was one of the original inhabitants of Bushwick in 1661, later removed to Haverstraw where he took the oath of allegiance in 1687, and settled in Westchester County by 1702. He had eight children by his first wife; in 1687-89 he married secondly Annie Elsten, mother of his youngest child. His eldest son Willem² Dupuis or Du Puw, b. about 1663 at Bushwick, removed as a young man to VerPlanck's Point in Van

Cortlandt Manor, where he resided at the time of his marriage on Aug. 10, 1688 to Elizabeth White of Barbadoes. Among their seven children was Peter³ Du Puw, bap. March 28, 1703 at Tarrytown Church, married Elizabeth Blauvelt and had three sons, all baptized at Tappan Church, Abraham in 1729, Peter in 1732 and Isaac in 1740. Elizabeth Blauvelt, b. April 11, 1705 at Tappan, was the daughter of Abraham Gerritsen² Blauvelt; she had previously married on Oct. 5, 1723 Johannes Pietersen Haring, nephew of Cozyn Haring of Old Tappan (plate 89). Elizabeth's brother Jacob A. Blauvelt lived on a farm in the present village of Blauvelt; he undoubtedly sold part of his Kakiat tract to his brother-in-law, who probably built and settled here in the 1740's. The eldest son Abraham⁴ Du Puw, b. Jan. 6, 1729, is known to have owned the house. On Nov. 23, 1750 he married Rachel Blauvelt, both being recorded as residents of New Hempstead (i.e., Kakiat, now New City), and had several children, including Petrus, Elizabeth and Cornelis. Cornelis⁵ Depew, b. July 27, 1761, married Annatje Gerretse, and had two sons Garret and Abraham, and other children. Abraham⁴ Du Puw (b. 1729) willed the house to his grandson Abraham C.⁶ De Pew (b. 1780). The latter's brother Garret and wife Mary lived on the south side of the road in a stone house no longer standing. Since Abraham C. De Pew's time, the house has changed hands frequently. In 1876 it was owned by Samuel De Baun Paul, then by his son Cornelius Paul, a journeyman. The present owner is Will B. Blauvelt, a florist.

The east unit of the house, consisting of one room, door and chimney, was doubtless built in the 1740's or earlier; the west unit (shown in the photograph) was built during the Revolution about 1780, probably by Abraham Du Puw at the time of his son's marriage. Examples of very early woodwork are to be seen in the interior; the enclosed stairway in the hall (part of the second unit) is interesting. The house is two miles north of New City; it stands on the north side of the road to Haverstraw, a half mile beyond the sharp turn eastward. The Blauvelt-Lane and Blauvelt-Secor houses (plates 45 and 46) are less than one mile nearer New City.

House of Peter De Pew
near the Hackensack River, Orangeburg
PLATE 50

In 1778 Peter De Pew signed the petition of inhabitants in the vicinity of Tappan, asking for protection against the British marauders. The house is marked on Erskine's Revolutionary map, and had been built a few years previously. Peter⁴ De Pew, the owner, was undoubtedly the one who was baptized Dec. 17, 1732, son of Peter Du Puw and Elizabeth Blauvelt of Kakiat (plate 49). About 1758 he married Annetje Van Dalsen, d. Aug. 13, 1805, aged 72 years, 3 months, 21 days,

daughter of Johannes Van Dalsen and Dirckje Theunis Tallman, and had at least
four children: Peter, Johannes, Bregje, and Theunis. As the three younger ones
were baptized at the Clarkstown Church to the north, it is logical to presume that
Pieter and Annetje continued to reside with his parents until after 1768, when they
removed southwards and built east of Tappan. The eldest son Peter P.[5] De Pew,
bap. Feb. 2, 1759 at Tappan, is said to have fought in the Revolution from Dutchess
Co. Another Peter P.[6] De Pew, b. Oct. 12, 1782, d. Nov. 8, 1856, was undoubtedly
his son and was the last of the family to reside here; a Peter P. De Pew (father or
son?) sold some of the outlying property about 1810, describing it as a part of his
father's homestead land. The last Peter De Pew married at Tappan Nov. 23, 1800
Margrietje De Pew, both being recorded as residents of Tappan. She was born
Jan. 3, 1784, died March 24, 1856, and was buried with her husband in Tappan
Cemetery. Their daughter Rachel De Pew, b. Oct. 13, 1802, married at Tappan
April 1, 1820 Abram Lent Blanch and removed elsewhere. The house and farm
was recently a part of the large Broadacres Estate.

The property is now owned by the State of New York and is occupied by the
Mitchells who work at the Rockland State Hospital nearby. They are interested in
the history of the house and are attempting to restore it along the old lines (it was a
mere shell when bought by the state). The house is a scant mile north of the state
line, on the northeast side of the road to Old Tappan, on which the two Haring
houses also stand (plates 90 and 91) south of the border. The road at this point is an
unimportant lane, joining the Orangeburg Road north of the house and near the
bridge over the Hackensack River. The house is over two miles west of the village
of Orangeburg.

De Pew—Holdrum House
south of the Orangeburg Road, Orangeburg

Like the one above, this house is also owned by the State of New York and
inhabited by employees of the nearby State Hospital. It is very similar in style,
although the stones on the end are more irregular in size; the roofline is unchanged,
the lintels are of stone, and the old twelve-pane window sashes still remain. As it
was occupied by the family until the present century, its original character is less
changed than in the case of the former house, but it is in an unkempt condition and
a satisfactory photograph could not be taken. The house is about one half mile east
of the other De Pew house, on a branch of the road to Old Tappan (now the more
important highway of the two), and also immediately south of the Orangeburg
Road. Erskine did not survey this road, but the house was probably built about the
time of the Revolution by Isaac De Pew.

Isaac⁴ De Pew, b. March 25, 1740 at Tappan, d. April 30, 1823 aged 83 years, 1 month, 5 days,* was the youngest son of Peter Du Puw and Elizabeth Blauvelt of Kakiat (plate 49), and the youngest brother of Pieter De Pew, who built the house nearby (plate 50). As their grandfather, Abraham Gerritsen² Blauvelt, owned a great deal of land in the vicinity of Old Tappan, the two brothers may have settled on land received from their mother. Isaac De Pew married Brechje or Bridget Smith, b. Dec. 22, 1746,* died Aug. 5, 1826,* daughter of Abraham Smidt and Maria Tallman, and sister of Major John Smith, owner of the house at Germonds (plate 60). Their only son Abraham⁵ De Pew, b. July 3, 1768,* d. Aug. 1, 1833,* married Marritje or Martha Cooper, b. Sept. 18, 1774,* d. April 24, 1835.* These two generations of De Pews lie buried at Orangeburg Cemetery. Their only child Elizabeth⁶ De Pew, b. Dec. 16, 1809,* d. April 26, 1881,* married June 16, 1831* Cornelius J. Holdrum, b. June 6, 1806,* d. Dec. 10, 1871,* and had one daughter and three sons. Elizabeth De Pew inherited the house and continued to reside here as a widow. Her estate sold the property about 1900. Her husband was born at Old Tappan, son of James C. Holdrum, the grandson of William Holdrum of Pascack (plate 93).

Eckerson House
Old Post Road, Spring Valley

The builder of this house is unknown. It stands on the large Vanderlinda tract, which was portioned off and sold at various times. When the present owners reroofed the house, they discovered a small book bound between boards, and published in 1752. The house was probably built in the third quarter of the eighteenth century. The region was in early times known as Upper Pascack. There were members of the Eckerson family here and in adjoining localities in the late eighteenth century. The first known owner of the house is David D. Eckerson; his son Christian D. Eckerson died over thirty years ago at the age of 84; as he was born in the house the Eckerson family owned it at least as early as 1815. Whether David D. Eckerson bought or inherited the property is not known; but since two of his brothers owned adjoining houses (still standing and owned by Mrs. Catharine Hirsch, one to the south, and one on the hill to the west), it is probable that the whole tract once belonged to their father, and that the houses were built rather than bought by the Eckersons. The family lineage is undetermined; it is possible that David D. Eckerson was the David baptized Aug. 12, 1783 at Clarkstown Church, son of David Eckeson and Rachel Conkling. Christian D. Eckerson sold the house towards the end of the nineteenth century. The present owner is Leo Glasel.

The curved roofline of this house has a beautiful sweep, but the character of

195

---

* Taken from family Bible.

the house is marred by a porch on either side, built up of cobblestones. The Eckerson house further south on the road is also altered and is in poor condition; the Eckerson house on the hill has had a low frame story added. All three are of stone. The Eckerson-Glasel house is about three miles south of Spring Valley; it is on the east side of the old Post Road, which becomes the Chestnut Ridge Road across the state border, half a mile to the south.

Haner—Ryder House
at the south end of Rockland Lake
PLATE 51

This is considered to be the second oldest house standing in Rockland County; it is only surpassed in age by the De Clark—De Wint house at Tappan, built in 1700. Unfortunately the first century of its ownership is lost in obscurity. It stands on the Ponds Patent granted to Marshall and Welch Sept. 2, 1694. Welch sold his share to John Hutchins, who obtained the south half of 2500 acres in the division of 1700. The house was built shortly after this date. John Hutchins almost lost his life in the Leisler Rebellion in New York City; he may have built the house and retired here for safety. In 1711 he sold 200 acres of the land on the west side of the lake to John Slawter, and some time afterward sold most if not all of his remaining land to a company of German settlers. The house is shown on a map of 1713, made by James Townsend, surveyor of the Kakiat Patent; it is illegibly marked "Haner hous" (?). Haner is a German family name, found among the Palatines who settled on Livingston Manor in 1710; so it is possible that the Haners were the first German occupants of this house.

When and how it came into the possession of the Ryder family is not known. Our first definite conveyance of this plot is by deed of May 3, 1800 from John Ryder to his son John Ryder, Jr., in which the bounds are described as the lands of John Smith on the southwest and of William Hoffman on the southeast, while on the northeast lie the lands John Ryder bought from Abner Brush. The latter parcel was bought by John Ryder in 1775; the previous owner Abner Brush had purchased it Aug. 3, 1772 from David, son of Jurry Hoffman; it was 39 acres of the seller's share, bounded west by the Pond, south by Ephraim Terrell, north by John Ryder, and southwest by William Dobbs. Thus possibly William Dobbs was the owner of the house at the time of the Revolution; he may have acquired it from the Hoffmans, who lived in this vicinity. Hermanus Hoffman was one of the early German settlers and owned a plantation or farm on the east side of Quaspeck Pond near the south end; in his will of 1752 he left his son Jurry the north 106 acres of his farm and his eldest son Hermanus the south 106 acres of his farm. As the above deed showed that Jurry Hoffman owned northeast of the house, the farm willed to Hermanus Hoffman, Jr., may have included the old house, but this is conjecture. John Ryder was a large landholder: on June 8, 1753 he bought 225 acres, the original share of Peter Geslar, the owners of adjoining lands including John Ryder; the village of Valley Cottage is on this tract and an old house called the Green House (because of its color) stands here on the King's Highway by the river; it is much later in date and remodelled.

The small whitewashed stone house is little more than a hut. It consists of three rooms, one downstairs and two upstairs, to which access is had by means of a ladder. The window casings and walls are over twenty inches thick. The house is at the southeast end of Rockland Lake (formerly Quaspeck Pond), and sets low in the bank (a short distance east of the new state highway) off the east side of the road to Valley Cottage. There is a beautiful spring of water near at hand. The present owner is Mrs. Francis X. Deering of New York City and Rockland Lake; the house is unoccupied.

Haring House
King's Highway, Tappan
PLATE 52

Little is known of the early history of this house. It is marked on Erskine's Revolutionary map, and was undoubtedly built a few years before the war. An old resident states that it was owned in the early 1870's by a John Haring, who had three sons: Samuel, John and Isaac; they lost it, and it was sold by foreclosure to Roger Haddock, a successful Piermont grocer; then it was bought by a land promotion company, a Mr. Barnwell and Mr. Austin, the latter now President of the First National Bank of Sparkill; they sold it to John Collier, a lecturer, who finally sold it to the Standard Oil Co. of New York, who rent it to Italian tenants. The King's Highway was rather circuitous in this locality; it came north across the state border to Tappan, then wound northeastward between the two branches of the Sparkill (creek) to Sparkill village, and finally took a northwesterly direction skirting the mountains to Orangeburg. The house is between Tappan and Sparkill, and stands off the King's Highway on a knoll surrounded by low ground. It is on the northwest corner of the King's Highway and the new state highway. The house is a beautiful example of the gambrel type of Dutch architecture with the early type of sloping dormer windows. Interest is added to the house by the brick lintels.

House of Abram Lent
Road to Tappan, Orangeburg
PLATE 53

A stone records the erection of the house in 1752. It was built by or for Abram Lent. The ancestor of the family, Abraham de Ryck, was one of the earliest settlers in New Amsterdam. His son Ryck Abrahamsen[2] van Lent obtained (with his brothers) a patent to land on the Hudson River in Westchester Co., which became known as Ryck's Patent. His grandson Adolph[4] van Lent, b. 1703 in Westchester Co., removed to Rockland County and married Claasje Haring, bap. June 3, 1711, daughter of Peter Janse Haring and Grietje Bogart; they had nine children baptized at Tappan from 1728 to 1753, including Peter who was a patriot of Dutchess Co., Jacobus (or James) and Abram who were loyalists. Adolph, the father, was evidently also a loyalist, as his property is said to have been confiscated.

The eldest son Abram[5] Lent, b. May 27, 1732, d. Oct. 29, 1813, aged 81 years and 5 months, built the house (or his father built it for him) the year before he was married. He and his wife were both residents of Tappan at the time of their marriage July 7, 1753; she was Sarah Haring, d. Aug. 30, 1807, aged 76 years and 8 months; both lie buried at Orangeburg. On Dec. 22, 1775 the Colony of New York issued a commission to Abram Lent of Orangetown as Colonel of the First Regiment of Militia of Foot of Orangetown; on March 23, 1776 he resigned, due to the blame and slander of some officers in the regiment. A descendant states he was captured in Clinton by the British and made no effort to return, so he is presumed to have changed his allegiance. After the war he settled on the Tusket River in Nova Scotia with his brother, but returned to Rockland County. His son Peter[6] Lent was the father of James[7] Lent, who married at Tappan Aug. 21, 1808 Sarah Gisner, and had at least four children: Peter, Adolph, Maria and Ann. Ann[8] Lent married Philip Graham who was of Scotch descent, and their son John William Graham was the father of I. Spencer Graham. The latter sold the house about 1916 to some cousins who did not keep it, and he sold the house out of the family about 1918 to the present owner, Morgan Stinemetz.

The house stands on a hill in the village of Orangeburg, on the east side of the road between the two railroad crossings. An unusual feature is the steep, gable roof used to cover a house of this depth.

House of Jeremias Mabie
Orangeburg Road, Nauraushaun, Orangetown
PLATE 54

This house stands on Lot No. 10 of the South Moiety of the Kakiat Patent, which was allotted to Lancaster Symes in the division of 1727. In some manner, this 380 acre tract passed into the possession of Jeremias Mabie, who mentioned it in his will dated 1780. The house, which is shown on Erskine's Revolutionary map, was undoubtedly built by him, possibly about the time of his marriage in 1752. His ancestor Sergeant Caspar[1] Mabille had emigrated to New Amsterdam before 1650; he came of a Huguenot family of Anjou, which had fled to Naarden in Holland where his son Pieter was born. Pieter Casparszen[2] Mabille became a small burgher of New Amsterdam, and married Aechtje Jans, also from Naarden, widow of Abraham Willemszen. Their youngest son, Caspar Pietszen[3] Mabie, bap. Feb. 15, 1660, settled at Harlem and later at Closter, New Jersey. His son Peter[4] Mabie, bap. Dec. 26, 1689 at New York, d. 1769-72 in Orangetown, married at Hackensack June 19, 1715 Katalintie Bogart; they removed to Tappan and became the ancestors of the Mabies of Rockland County.

Their sixth child was Jeremias[5] Mabie, b. Dec. 13, 1727 at Tappan, married there Feb. 9, 1752 Sara Blauvelt, b. Sept. 5, 1728, daughter of Johannes A. Blauvelt; two of her uncles were Jacob A. Blauvelt of the farm in Blauvelt and Peter Du Puw of Kakiat (plate 49). Jeremias and Sara had at least three daughters, Rachel, Catalyntie and Elizabeth; about 1783 their son-in-law Michael Salyer acquired the property. Elizabeth[6] Mabie, b. April 23, 1761, married Michael Salyer, b. March 8, 1757, d. April 9, 1810, son of Edward Salyer and Sara Turneur. Elizabeth had by him at least four daughters, Elizabeth, Mary, Sara, and Rachel; after his death, she married secondly Feb. 8, 1811, Teunis A. Cuyper, widower. Only the south half of Lot No. 10 was owned by Michael Salyer at the time of his decease; this property was divided in 1811; the house stood on Lot No. 1 of the partition and was allotted to the daughter Mary Salyer, b. Jan. 1, 1791, married July 30, 1808 David Bogert. Mary Bogert later deeded the property to James Aymir, who in 1854 devised it to the children of Mary, wife of Tunis Blauvelt. In 1876 the house was owned by T. J. Blauvelt. The property has since changed hands frequently; the house is now owned by A. W. Hopper, and occupied by his son D. L. Hopper.

The house stands on the west side of the Orangeburg Road, south of Convent Road, and is three miles west of the village of Orangeburg. It has recently been restored with good taste, although the addition of French windows and the very white repointing detract slightly from the original character.

House of Cornelius Meyers (?); Tavern of Casparus Mabie; The 1776 House; André's Prison
King's Highway, Tappan

In the heart of Tappan still stands a stone house known far and wide as the "1776 House," for what reason is not known, unless the date is symbolical for its Revolutionary history. The house was probably built by Cornelius Meyers, who sold it to Casparus Mabie in 1753 (Tompkins' History). Casparus' Mabie, b. April 10, 1716 at Tappan, d. 1782-84, was the oldest child of Peter and Katalintie Mabie, and an older brother of Jeremias Mabie of Orangeville (plate 54). He kept the first tavern in Tappan village which became known as the Yost Mabie Tavern. On July 17, 1775 was held the most important meeting of the locality (doubtless at this house), at which every man was called upon to declare allegiance to the cause of liberty. When Major André was captured later on in the war, he was sent to Tappan and lodged here at the house of Mr. Mabie; he was treated with the attention suitable to his noble character and rank, and supplied with refreshment daily from General Washington's table at his headquarters in the De Wint house nearby (plate 48). As the courthouse had been burned recently, André's trial took place in the Dutch church opposite; he was executed at noon on Oct. 2, 1780, and buried on a hillside back of the village. Casparus Mabie later sold his tavern to Frederick Blauvelt, who resold it in 1800. The tavern was kept by a Dupuy in 1821, when the British stopped here to obtain André's remains for reburial in Westminster Abbey. At a later date it was kept for a time by Abraham Snedeker (b. 1793) of Congers. The house stands on the west side of the main street of Tappan, almost opposite the church, and is now run as a cheap refreshment stand. It is built of stone with a wide gable roof; it has been altered and is covered with billboards, so that its character is lost.

Mann Houses
Palisades

There were three houses built by the Mann family at Rockland, now Palisades, but the two still existing were not erected until 1784 and 1793. Since the former is generally known as a pre-revolutionary house, a short account is given here to correct this impression. George' Mann was one of the six children of David Mann, a mason, who lived in Seitzen, Wurtemburg, and died there in 1752. George came to America in 1753 with his widowed mother, Anne Margaret, and probably settled at Rockland immediately or shortly thereafter, as he was termed George Mann of Rockland in a deed of 1767. The land in this vicinity was a part of the Lockhart

Patent of Feb. 20, 1685. It eventually passed into the possession of Mary Corbett and her husband Henry Ludlow, who sold it in parcels from time to time. 196 acres were purchased on Nov. 14, 1752 by Jonathan Hazard of New York, who in 1759 disposed of the tract to James Lawrence of New York City, and he sold 98 acres in May, 1767 to George Mann of Rockland. The latter built a house on this tract and here all his six children were born. On May 9, 1772 he bought 32 acres more on his south border, being the hill land. It is on this hill property that he built the present house in 1784, according to Serviss' map of 1874. The house is not on Erskine's Revolutionary map. George Mann, b. 1735, d. 1806, had married Maria Cook Vincent, b. 1733, d. 1808.

The 1784 house passed to their second son George [2] Mann, b. May 29, 1770, d. April 24, 1856. He married Helen Alvord and had eight children. The house was inherited by the son David G.[3] Mann, b. May, 1801, d. May, 1873, married in 1834 Margaret Riker, b. Sept., 1812, d. July, 1891. One of their six children was George W.[4] Mann, b. 1835, married Sarah Line and had four children. Their son Charles[5] Mann continued to reside in the old homestead. By his wife Alice he had two sons David and Lindley. The house was sold by the family about 1870 to a land company and leased until it was purchased by the present owner, Dr. Henry Smith.

This 1784 house is built along the pre-war lines but by a later method. The main unit is of dressed stone, carefully cut and laid, and is covered by a gable roof having an overhang. The early interior arrangement is followed, of two main rooms adjoining each other, each with its separate outside door. A wing on the south end is similarly built but is smaller and lower; its east front has but one door and two windows. Early in the nineteenth century this wing was lengthened to half again its size with a frame unit carefully built to follow the original lines, and to this was added another small, very low wing. The house has been successfully restored recently. It faces east and stands on the south side of the Road to Sneden's Landing, not far from the main highway.

The 1793 house was built by the eldest son of the emigrant, David[2] Mann, b. Feb. 1768, d. 1852, married Catharine Lawrence and had seven children. He built the house in 1793 near the cow path. The members of his family were called the "Manns in the field" to distinguish them from the Manns in the village. Their first son George D.[3] Mann, b. 1801, d. 1886, never married. Their second son David D.[3] Mann, b. March 10, 1805, d. March 24, 1897, married Eliza Powles. The house was inherited by the latter's son David[4] Mann, b. 1842, married Alester Mabie. Their only son George[5] Mann married Margretta Wahrenberger but had no children. This George Mann sold the 1793 homestead in 1929, and moved to Tappan with his wife and mother. The house is now empty.

Oblenis House
Sickeltown Road, West Nyack
PLATE 54

This house and two adjoining it on the south are shown on Erskine's Revolutionary map, but the owners are not named; they stand on the Oblenis tract and were doubtless built by various Oblenis sons. Joost[1] Van Oblenis emigrated and purchased land in Harlem in 1663, but soon returned to the old country. His son Joost[2] Van Oblenis, b. 1640 in Holland, d. 1706, settled at Harlem where he was a patentee; he married Maria Sammis in 1661 and had six children. Their son Hendrick[3] Oblenis, bap. Feb. 18, 1672, d. 1745, married Aug. 28, 1692 Jannetie, daughter of John Tibout; they removed to his purchase in the Kakiat Patent. By deed dated Dec. 11, 1732 Hendrick Oblenis, yeoman of Harlem in New York, bought from Thomas Clark, merchant of New York City, 800 acres of land in the Kakiat Patent, known as Lots No. 11 and No. 12, extending from the north boundary of the Expense Lot to the south boundary of Emil Kline's farm 1¼ miles to the north, and extending one mile west from Demarest Kill. In more modern parlance, this tract extended from Nauraushaun (Sickeltown, or the Expense Lot) northward beyond West Nyack Four Corners (formerly Oblenis Corners), and lay west of the Hackensack River (Demarest Kill). Hendrick Oblenis settled on this tract with some of his seven children. He was succeeded by his son Peter[4] Oblenis, d. 1763-64, married on April 10, 1731 Sarah, daughter of Barent Nagel, the patentee of Closter, and sister of John Nagel of Closter (plate 97). Peter willed the north part of his property at New Hempstead (i.e., Kakiat) with house and barn to his son Hendrick, already in possession, and the south part with house and barn to his unmarried son John.

The elder son Hendrick[5] Oblenis, b. April 5, 1732, d. Dec. 14, 1815, married Jan. 1, 1757 Antie Lydecker and had seven children, married secondly Dec. 10, 1792 Catrina Blauvelt, and thirdly Bridget De Clark. At least three of Hendrick's children lived on the Oblenis tract: Peter[6] Oblenis (1757-1831) occupied a farmhouse adjoining the original one, which is (or was recently) standing although modernized; Garret[6] Oblenis (1760-1839) had a house on the tract still (or recently) in good preservation; Maria Oblenis (b. 1762) married Philip Demarest, and was probably the mother of the J. J. Demarest who owned two houses on the tract (south of the one in question) in 1876. John Van Houten (who may or may not have been a relative) removed the original stone house of Hendrick[5] Oblenis in 1838, and built the present brick building (south of the Demarest houses, and owned by the M. Van Houten estate in 1876). Three houses stood at the time of the Revolution within a distance of a quarter of a mile, and four houses in 1876. The above description of the houses is taken from Tompkins' History of Rockland Co.; it is difficult at this late date to assign each house to its owner, without a thorough search of the land records. It is scarcely likely that Garret (b. 1760) would have erected such a spacious house by 1778, when he was only eighteen years old, but his home may have been built by his father Hendrick and eventually inherited by him. As the house in question has been altered to such a small extent, and only recently, Tompkins' description of the conditions of the houses points to its being Garret's house " in good preservation" rather than Peter's house "modernized." It is possible that the house stood on the southern tract inherited by their uncle John⁵ Oblenis, who later removed to Pennsylvania, but Tompkins makes no mention of the fact. The house inherited by John was probably the original Oblenis house.

Lile and Otto were the owners of the property in 1876. The present owner, Mrs. Grace Welton Mallery, bought it about 1914; her husband's great-uncle, Judge William Otto of Delaware, purchased it about sixty years ago (1870) from Mr. Nickerson; before then it was part of the Van Houten estate.

This is one of the few frame houses in Rockland County known to have been built before the Revolution (or possibly in the first years of the war); in both Rockland and Bergen counties the native sandstone was used exclusively as it was near at hand, indeed it was often quarried from a pit on the property. Frame houses came into fashion after the war, and the large gambrel-roofed houses of the next fifty years were built of frame as often as stone. The construction of this house points to its being one of the earliest frame houses erected: the chimney foundation in the cellar is of an early eighteenth century type, the ceilings are low, the mantels simply decorated, and there is no architectural trim over the windows which was so characteristic of the post-war frame houses. The dormers are of course recent, and the roof of the south front has been raised and extended to cover the present large porch. The house is south of West Nyack Four Corners, and stands on the west side of the Sickeltown Road north of its junction with the road from Blauvelt.

House of Isaac Perry, later Blauvelt's
Blue Hill Road, Nauraushaun, Orangetown
PLATE 56

This house was undoubtedly built by Isaac Perry to supersede an earlier house of his father's. It stands on Lot No. 9 of the South Moiety of the Kakiat Patent, which was allotted to John MacEvers in the Division of 1727; he sold the tract March 13, 1728 to John Perry, who immediately settled here, building a house nearer the road than the present one. On March 17, 1686 in New York City, his father John

Perry, widower of Marie Thomas, married Saratie Jans, born in Gowanus, daughter of Jan Staats; they removed to Rockland County where he was high sheriff in 1703. Their family in 1702 consisted of their son John and three daughters; the widow Saratie Staats acted as sponsor to her grandson Peter in 1726 at the Tappan Church. The only son was John Perry, b. about 1695 in New York City, d. Sept. 18, 1767 at Tappan; on March 10, 1723 he married Catrina Styper, widow of Philip Serven, b. about 1689 at Wittsenlingen in Germany, d. Aug. 9, 1768; although the marriage took place in New York City, the banns were published at Tappan where they both resided. Shortly afterward he bought the above tract west of Tappan and settled here, raising a family of five sons: John, Peter, Isaac, Jacobus, and Daniel. He willed his property to these children, who released various portions to each other; Jacobus (or James) settled to the south on the state border, Peter lived at Harrington in New Jersey, and Isaac obtained the homestead.

Isaac Perry, b. July 23, 1729 at Tappan, d. Dec. 27, 1811, aged 82 years, 5 months, 3 days, married Nov. 18, 1752 Margaret Haring; he built part of the present house, and at his death left the property to his daughter Catharine, a widow. Catharine Perry, b. Aug. 22, 1753, died shortly after her father on Feb. 23, 1813, and lies buried at Tappan Cemetery with her father and his mother. By her husband David Blauvelt she had a son David D. Blauvelt, b. 1777, married at Tappan Oct. 7, 1795 Lenah Fowler, and had an only son Gilbert D. Blauvelt, b. April 28, 1807, d. 1877, married Nov. 11, 1828 Marya Mabie. After his son's marriage, David built the main house in 1830. The property eventually passed to Gilbert's two daughters, the house standing on the portion which was allotted to the daughter Margaret, wife of Edward Lydecker. She sold the house about 1906-09 to Montgomery Maze, the present owner.

A descendant, Mr. Lydecker, informs me that the original house on the premises (that of John Perry) stood near the road. He also states that the west wing of the present house was the first unit erected in the early days before the Revolution, as well as the stone wing on the east (shown in the photograph) which was built somewhat later but before the war. The middle portion of the house was torn down about 1830, and the present frame structure connecting the two wings was erected at that time by David D. Blauvelt. Thus the first unit was probably built by Isaac Perry about the time of his marriage (1752), and the balance of the house at the time of his daughter's marriage (about 1776). The house stands on the north side of the present Blue Hill Road, a short distance from the Hackensack River and the same distance from the state border; it is three miles west of the village of Orangeburg. This road connected the Sickeltown settlement with the settlements on the Middletown Road.

House of Jacob Perry
Convent Road, Nauraushaun, Orangetown

Peter Perry (1726-1796), older brother of Isaac Perry (plate 56), bought the north half of Lot No. 10 from their neighbor Michael Salyer between 1783 and 1796 (see plate 54), and may have built the west unit of the house at this time, although he may never have lived here as he died at Harrington. No house is shown here on the Revolutionary map. Peter married Elizabeth Blauvelt, b. 1729, daughter of Jacob and sister of Johannes Blauvelt, who built and lived nearby in Blauvelt village (see supra). Peter Perry willed this property to his son Jacob P. Perry, who built the east unit in 1801 (a stone is marked J. P. 1801) and died in 1839, leaving it to his son Jacob J. Perry (1802-1849). Although evidently built after the war, the house belongs to the pre-revolutionary period in its style; the east unit and the earlier west unit are identical, they are built of roughly dressed stone and covered by a steep gambrel roof with an overhang in front. The house has been lately carefully restored and modernized by its owner Mrs. C. H. Chester. It stands on the brow of the hill on Convent Road, north of the Isaac Perry and Jeremias Mabie houses.

Perry—Horne House
Middletown Road, Pearl River

This house stands on Lot No. 42 of the South Moiety of the Kakiat Patent. The builder of the house is not known. An early undated sheepskin map, made after 1713, shows a house over the state border at about this location; it is marked Waldron. The present house may have been built by this family but it belongs to a later period; it is similar in style to the Lent house built in 1752 (plate 53). At some later date it passed into the possession of the Perry family. The house, which was on the middle third of a homestead farm, was inherited by Margaret Perry, wife of Abraham Horne. Little more is known than this. It is said to have been in the Horne family for 150 years. J. Horne was the owner in 1876. Harold Dutcher of Newark, son-in-law of the last Horne owner, sold the place about 1908 to George Lange, who sold it in 1923 to Frederick Guterl, the present owner. The house is of stone with a wide gable roof. An unusual feature is the overhang of the roof, which extends around the north end as well as the two sides. The addition of windows, dormers, sun parlor and trellises completely mar the appearance of the exterior, and the interior has been entirely torn out. The house stands north of the state border, on a hill west of Middletown Road.

Sickels Houses
Sickeltown Road, Nauraushaun, Orangetown

Several houses of the Sickels family stand near each other on the Expense Lot of the Kakiat Patent. This patent was granted in 1696 to Honan and Hawdon; in 1713 they had the tract surveyed and divided between them. To pay the expenses of this division, they laid aside 1000 acres, known as the Expense Lot, which they sold, two-thirds to Capt. Cornelius Claesen Kuyper and one-third to Jonathan Seaman, on March 6, 1714. Cornelius Kuyper was an extensive landowner in Bergen and Rockland Counties, and lived at Upper Nyack (see plate 80). Elizabeth Kuyper, wife of William Sickels, is believed to have inherited 100 acres at the north end of the Expense Lot; her son Robert Sickels eventually acquired most of the 1000 acres through various purchases.

The family ancestor, Zacharias[1] Sickels, came from Vienna in Austria; he went to Curaçao as an adelborst (cadet) in the employ of the West India Company, and left there in 1655 with Stuyvesant, who stationed him at Ft. Orange (Albany) as a corporal; while there he was town herder, porter, crier and a carpenter; he followed his son Robert to New York in 1693. By his wife Anna Van Valkenberg, he had nine children, who settled in New York City, Harlem, Brooklyn and Bergen. His eldest son was Robert[2] Sickels of Bergen, b. 1664 at Albany, d. Dec. 27, 1729 at Bergen, married Gertruy Rettenhaus and had eleven children. Their ninth son William[3] Sickels, b. Oct. 26, 1704 at Bergen, married there Aug. 10, 1732 Elizabeth Kuyper, bap. Dec. 6, 1713 at New York, daughter of Hendrick Claesen Kuyper of Ahasymus (part of Jersey City).

After the birth of their two eldest sons in 1734 and 1736, William and Elizabeth removed to Rockland County, and their third son was baptized at the Tappan Church here in 1737. Their first habitation was a log cabin on the west bank of the Hackensack River, the remains of which were visible within recent years. Its site was the field north of the Erie Railroad on the Sickeltown Road. He later built a stone house, which still stands immediately south of this railroad and east of the road; it is a narrow house originally of the same type as the two Blauvelt houses nearby (plates 43 and 44), but has had a half-story of frame added during the early nineteenth century. It passed into the Lydecker family and is now owned by the Hackensack Water Co. Here William and Elizabeth Sickels raised their many children: Robert, Nicholas, Hendrick, Johannes, William, Sara, Gertrude, Roelof, Jannetje, Jacob, and Elizabeth. The eldest son Robert[4] Sickels, b. July 16, 1734, bap. Aug. 4th at New York, d. Oct. 17, 1809 at Sickeltown, was a bachelor. He inherited and purchased most of the 1000 acre tract, divided the land between his brothers and also gave them the money to build their houses.

The four Sickel houses shown on Erskine's Revolutionary map are still standing; one was built by William, as stated above, and the other three belonged to three of his sons. The Sickels' lands stretched to the Hackensack River, which flows nearby. A short distance south is the cemetery, where three of the brothers (Robert, Johannes and William) and later members of the Sickels family lie buried. This section is locally known as Sickeltown; once called Orangeville, it has recently been named Nauraushaun after the Indian tribe of the region, and is three miles northwest of Orangeburg village. The Sickeltown Road led from the settlement at Old Tappan northward to the church at Clarkstown in the Kakiat Patent.

William's second son Nicholas⁴ Sickels, b. March 15, 1736, is said to have built the stone house on the east side of the Sickeltown Road, north of his father's log cabin. He raised and equipped a company for service and fought in the Revolution, according to a descendant, but probably died early in the war, as his house is marked on the 1778 map as William Sickel's. Nicholas had married Annatje De Clark and had several children including a son William, b. Feb. 17, 1769. The latter married Dec. 24, 1789 his cousin Elizabeth Sickels and the house passed to their son Nicholas⁶ Sickels, b. Jan. 24, 1798. It is still in the family and is now owned by Mrs. John E. Sickels. It is a stone house greatly altered both inside and out. The early fanlight over the door is an interesting feature.

Across the road stands the stone house built by William's fourth son Johannes⁴ Sickels, b. Feb. 13, 1740, d. Oct. 13, 1813, married Elizabeth De Clark, d. Jan. 6, 1844, aged 98 years, 19 days. He kept a "bloson shop" here during the Revolution. His daughter Sarah Sickels married Johannes Tallman and lived in the Tallman house at Germond's (plate 64) until he died; she then returned to her father's home, married Andrew Tinkey, and died Nov. 17, 1857, aged 91 years and 9 months. After her death, her father's home was owned by her son John J. Tallman who married June 1, 1819 Margaret Demarest, and had an only child Sarah Tallman, b. Feb. 18, 1829, married April 18, 1850 Dr. Isaac C. Haring. The Harings probably sold the house, which has since passed through several hands, and is now owned by E. C. M. Rand. This house is of stone with a gambrel roof; it has been altered and enlarged.

William's youngest son Roelof⁴ Sickels, b. April 1, 1749, is said to have built the stone house north of his brother Nicholas. He probably erected it shortly after the Revolution, as it is not shown on the map. It passed into the Remsen family. This house burned down and was rebuilt. The present house is now owned by Dr. Ivan Sickels, a descendant of Nicholas.

William's eldest son Robert⁴ Sickels, the bachelor, is said to have lived with his brother Nicholas, but at the time of the Revolution evidently lived in his father's stone house, which is marked Robert Sickel on Erskine's map. Nothing is known of the third son Hendrick, who probably died in infancy; as Roelof is said by a descendant to have been the youngest son, his brother Jacob (b. 1755) probably also died in childhood. Thus all the sons of William and Elizabeth Sickels have been accounted for except the fifth son William⁴ Sickels. By process of elimination, confirmed by a descendant, William must be the Squire Sickel, who is marked on Erskine's map as the owner of the house on the Sickeltown Road near the cemetery. An account of this house is given below.

Sickels—Vanderbilt House
Sickeltown Road, Nauraushaun, Orangetown
PLATE 57

William⁴ Sickels, b. July 2, 1742 and bap. at Tappan, d. Sept. 6, 1819, was the fifth son of William and Elizabeth Sickels of Sickeltown (see supra). He married Marretje Cuyper, b. July 15, 1750, d. March 10, 1805, only surviving child of Cornelius Cuyper of Sickeltown. Squire William Sickels' house still stands on the east side of the Sickeltown Road, a short distance north of the cemetery and about half a mile south of the group of Sickels houses built by his father and brothers. It is believed that his older brother Robert Sickels distributed his property among all his brothers for them to build upon, and therefore presumably this house was built by Squire Sickel about 1768 when he married. However, the appearance of the house suggests a greater age and so it is possible that prior to this date it was built and owned by his father-in-law Cornelius Cuyper, who lived here in Sickeltown. The fact that the house is some distance from the other Sickels houses, between them and the Cuyper houses, strengthens the suggestion of separate ownership of the lands. This Cornelius⁴ Cuyper, b. April 17, 1722 at Tappan, d. Dec. 27, 1776, married Annetje, daughter of Jan Cozyn Haring, b. Aug. 9, 1722, d. Nov. 14, 1803; both lie buried at Sickeltown. It will be noted that Cornelius Cuyper died two years before Erskine made his survey, on which the house is marked as owned by Squire Sickel. Cornelius was a son of Tunis Cuyper who built the original part of the two story house on the Sickeltown Road, a short distance south of the Squire Sickel house (see supra).

William Sickels was given the title of Squire because he was a justice of the peace. He and his wife Marretje had nine children baptized at the Tappan and Clarkstown Churches: Elizabeth, b. 1769 (probably married 1786 Abraham J. Haring); Aeltje, b. 1772, married 1791 Martinus Hogenkamp; Marretje or Martha, b. 1774 (probably married 1793 Gerrit J. Blauvelt); Antje, b. 1778, married 1796 David Blauvelt; Sarah, b. 1780, married 1800 Rulef C. Van Houten who eventually purchased the Cuyper house to the south; Cornelius, b. 1786, married at Hackensack 1803-05 Lea Blanch, and lived in the post-revolutionary stone house on the west side of the Sickeltown Road between his father's and his brother-in-law Van Houten's houses; William W., b. 1789, married 1808 Fanny Fowler; and Jannetje or Jane, b. 1792, d. 1870, married 1810 Hendrick Banta of Pascack and Hackensack, son of Hendrick Banta of Pascack (plate 77).

It is said that Squire Sickels' house passed by marriage into the Vanderbilt family, that the last to inherit it was James Vanderbilt, and that it was sold out of the family about 1850. The only Vanderbilt connection that the author has discovered is as follows: Aeltje or Aletta[5] Sickels, b. March 8, 1772, second daughter of the Squire, married at Tappan Oct. 28, 1791 Martinus Hogenkamp; their daughter Aeltje Hogenkamp, b. Aug. 27, 1793, married at Tappan May 10, 1809 Cornelius Vanderbilt, both being residents of Clarkstown, and had at least two children, Johannes Hogenkamp, b. 1810, and Richard, b. 1811. It is possible that they had another son James Vanderbilt who might have been the last of the family to own the old homestead. By 1876 the house had passed to the ownership of J. Parsels. The present owner is the Corwick Realty Co. of Haverstraw.

This is the only one of the Sickels houses whose pre-revolutionary appearance has not been marred by extensive alterations. Dormers and a frame wing on the road end are the only changes. The photograph shows the rear view of the house.

House of Stephen Sloat
Sloatsburg

The house stands on a tract bought from the Indians March 7, 1738 by Wynant Van Gelder and given by him to his father-in-law (not son-in-law) Isaac Van Duser by assignment of June 13, 1747 on the reverse of the original deed. Isaac Van Deuse or Van Dusen was born in New York where he was baptized Feb. 6, 1698, son of Isaac Van Deurse and Metje Christianse. He was living at Tappan when he married at Hackensack May 24, 1718 Angenitie Laroe of Hackensack. In an affidavit of 1769 he stated that he was then 71 years of age and moved to New Jersey when he was 22 or 23 years old. It is probable that he settled along the Ramapo River as early as 1719, as his daughter Lea who married in 1735 was born at Ramapo. He had two sons baptized at Hackensack in 1720 and 1721. On Dec. 14, 1723 at Hackensack, Isaac married secondly Elizabeth Rooseboom, who was born in New York and living at Ramapo. They had a son baptized in 1726 at Hackensack and two daughters baptized in 1740 and 1741 at the new church in Paramus. Any children born between these dates were probably baptized at the Ponds Church in the Ramapo valley, whose records were lost by fire. The upper Ramapo valley, in which Sloatsburg is situated, was known as the Clove. Isaac Van Dusen bought a tract from the Indians adjoining the Van Gelder tract and was probably the first white settler in the New York part of the valley. He was living here by 1735, for the marriage record of his daughter Lea Van Deusen states that she was born at Ramapo, living at the Clove, married Dec. 12, 1735 (entered at Paramus and recorded at Hackensack) Wynant Van Gelderen, who was born at Paramus and was living at Ramapo. Clinton lodged with Isaac Van Dusen the night of Sept. 21, 1739 when on a surveying tour. Another daughter of Isaac's was Marritje Van Dusen who married Stephen Slot or Sloat of Hackensack. In 1755 Stephen built his home (the rear wing of the present house) on the tract his father-in-law had bought from Van Gelder, and on June 3, 1763 the property was turned over to him by endorsement on the original deed. The house is marked Slott on Erskine's map.

The ancestor of the family, Jan Pietersen[1] Slot, emigrated before 1662 from Holstein with two children born and reared in Amsterdam; their mother was his first wife Aeltje Jans. The son Pieter Jansen[2] Slot, b. in Amsterdam, was living in Harlem when he married at New Amsterdam Jan. 2, 1663 Marritje Jacobse Van Winkle. Their grandson Johannes[4] Slot, bap. May 14, 1699 at Hackensack, married first Sept. 17, 1720 Willemete Van Voorhees, widow of Cornelius Bogart. Their son Stephen[5] Slot or Sloat, b. March 25, 1726 (old style), bap. April 2, 1727 at Hackensack, d. Dec. 11, 1806, married about 1753 Marretje Van Dusen, b. Feb. 23, 1729, d. July 28, 1807. Stephen built and settled on his father-in-law's tract in the upper Ramapo River valley. Of his four children, all baptized at Paramus, John, b. 1754, was killed in the Revolution, Isaac inherited the house, Elizabeth, b. 1761, married James Westervelt, and Maria, b. 1767, married Peter Christie. The son Isaac[6] Slot or Sloat, b. July 1, 1758, was baptized Aug. 20th at Paramus, with his grandparents Isaac and Elizabeth Van Deuse acting as his sponsors. About 1779 he married Lea Zabriskie, bap. July 29, 1752 at Paramus. He died Nov. 12, 1821 and she died Dec. 10, 1832. Isaac probably built the main house in 1814. It served as a public house on the old post road and was the meeting place of Supervisors and Judges of Orange and Rockland Counties for twenty-three years. At his death the property was inherited jointly by his two sons Stephen and Jacob. Stephen[7] Sloat, b. Dec. 28, 1789, d. March 2, 1851, married Dec. 25, 1809 Catharine Mead Ward, b. July 2, 1790, d. May 1, 1876; he was a prominent farmer and widely known manufacturer; in his youth he conducted a woolen mill at Paramus and later a cotton twine factory at Sloatsburg. His son William Lafayette[8] Sloat, b. June 23, 1824 in the old homestead, married twice and had two children; he bought out the other heirs and lived in the homestead. It was sold out of the family about 1910 to the present owner, Benjamin Moffat, Sr.

The original unit, now the rear wing, is typical of a pioneer house. It is small and is built of rough whitewashed stone with a gable roof. This was erected in 1755 by Stephen Sloat. His son Isaac or grandson Stephen Sloat built the main part of the present house in 1814. It is in the Georgian style, of two stories, with a flat roof. The house stands on the west side of the main road in the village of Sloatsburg, in the upper Ramapo River valley.

House of Lambert Adriaensen Smidt (?)
Road to Orangeburg, Blauvelt
PLATE 58

This house stands on a tract in the Tappan Patent which was allotted to Lambert Adriaensen Smidt in the Division of 1721, and therefore may have been built by him. Born Dec. 30, 1655 at Tiel in Gelderland, he emigrated with his father Adriaen and his brother Cornelius in the *Rosetree* in 1663, settled at Flatbush and later removed to Stuyvesant's Bouwery Village outside the wall in Manhattan. They joined their neighbors as patentees of Tappan, and were among the first to settle here in 1683. Lambert became an important member of the little community, was an organizer of the Tappan Church and its elder. The lands of the patent were held in common in the early years; in the first division of 1704 Lambert was allotted 248 acres at Clausland in the Sparkill valley near the cemetery and the fair grounds (later called Greenbush, now part of Orangeburg and Blauvelt); probably before this date Lambert built a stone house here near the cemetery which was torn down after the Revolution. In the division of 1721 he obtained a large tract of 648 acres on the high lands extending from the Blauvelt-Orangeburg road westward to the Hackensack River. It is on this tract that the present house stands. As head of the influential and wealthy Smidt family, it is logical to presume that he immediately erected thereon this large substantial house, the interior of which was very elegantly finished. On April 9, 1682 at New York City he had married Margrietje Blauvelt, b. Sept. 25, 1661, d. before 1729, daughter of Gerrit Hendricksen and sister of the Blauvelt brothers who also settled at Tappan (plate 42). They had ten children: Marretje wife of Johannes Meyer, Gerrit, Arie, Cornelius died young, Cornelius, Maria wife of Henry Leroe, Dirckje wife of Cornelius Cuyper, Catharine wife of Samuel Leroe, Abraham and Lena. The home of Gerrit, the eldest son, was in the hollow near the Clausland Cemetery. Arie settled at Tappan Slote (Piermont) and later at Upper Nyack. Cornelius built a house on the ridge, across the road from his father's mansion; this is still standing but is greatly remodelled. Abraham, the youngest son, lived in his father's old home. Lambert Adriaensen Smidt, the father, was still living in 1731.

This house is of a very old type of construction and was undoubtedly built shortly after the Division of 1721. Although it is probable that Lambert erected it, it is possible that he sold the land shortly after it was allotted to him; there is no deed to this effect on record. In the middle of the nineteenth century it was owned by the Westervelt family, who sold it about 1860. In 1876 the owner was I. S. Hosman. In December 1878 Joseph Eustace sold the house and 30 acres of ground to the Order of St. Dominic of New York City for a juvenile asylum. This Order still owns it and has erected large modern buildings nearby. The house stands on the west side of the Orangeburg Road at the head of the lane to Hendrick Blauvelt's house (plate 42).

Smidt House (?)
Greenbush Road, Blauvelt
PLATE 59

Very little is known of the history of this house. It is in the Tappan Patent. The land on which the house stands was allotted in the division of the patent to Lambert Adriansen Smidt (see plate 58). As his home and those of his sons have been located, this house was probably built by a grandson or son-in-law, unless the family sold the tract unimproved. This road was not surveyed by Erskine during the Revolution, but the house was undoubtedly built early in the eighteenth century. It is not known how long it was owned by descendants of the builder. In 1876 the owner was J. W. Campbell; it is now owned by Mrs. W. D. Atkinson. This region was formerly known as Greenbush. The house stands on the west side of the Greenbush Road, a short distance north of its intersection with the new state highway.

House of Major John Smith
Germond Road, Germonds
PLATE 60

The first known owner of this house is Major John Smith; he built or purchased it. The youngest son of Lambert Adriaensen Smidt, the patentee (see plate 58), was Abraham³ Smidt, bap. Oct. 13, 1703 at Tappan, d. Oct. 27, 1755, married May 7, 1726 Maria Tallman and had ten children. They lived in Lambert's house in Greenbush near the cemetery. One of their youngest children was Major John⁴ Smith, b. Oct. 30, 1743 at Greenbush, d. Jan. 12, 1833 at Clarkstown, now Germonds. He anglicized his name. On May 15, 1767 he married Jemima De Wint, b. Sept. 4, 1740, d. May 25, 1811, daughter of Johannes De Wint and Antye Kermer, Washington's hosts at Tappan (plate 48). They had many children: Pieter Dewint, Abraham, Antje, Maria, Elizabeth, John, Christina, Guert Sprewer, and David.

On May 28, 1778 John Smith was appointed Major of the First Regiment of Orange Co. Militia, and was so honored by the commission that he spent his rainy afternoons practising the unfamiliar military tactics in the garret of his house; the story goes that he once fell through the open trapdoor down the steep garret stairway, after giving the order "Backward March"; on hearing the clatter, his wife came running and called out in Dutch, "Hans, Hans, what's the matter?" and he replied "It's nothing at all. Go in the house, woman. What do you know about war?" This major is not to be confused with his cousin, Major John L. Smith of Nyack, also a Revolutionary figure.

Missing deeds make it impossible to trace the history of the house; a receipt proves that Major John Smith divided his lands between his many children, but the deeds are not on record. The present owner of the house is Karl H. Gerlach; his father purchased it in 1865 from Henry Schrever.

The house stands in the North Moiety of the Kakiat Patent, which was granted in 1696 and divided in half in 1713. The road northward from the Old Tappan and Sickeltown settlements branched a short distance north of the present West Nyack Four Corners; one fork led east to the King's Highway, and the other road followed an Indian trail in a northwesterly direction past the old Clarkstown Church (where the settlers of the Kakiat Patent were baptized and married) to the division line. The greater part of the present Germond Road runs westward along this division line. The Major John Smith house stands on the south side of a curve in the latter road; the Tallman house (plate 64) stands at the head of the Indian trail; midway a road was laid along the 400 acre lots which led to the settlement at the north end of the patent, around New City. The construction of the house is interesting: the beams in the cellar are of great size, there is an inside smoke house and also a double chimney, the flues of which curve and join in the attic.

Barn of Major John Smith
Germond Road, Germonds
PLATE 61

This barn was originally on the property of Major John Smith of Revolutionary fame; his house now stands across the road (plate 60). The barn had been disposed of to other people before the stone house was sold in 1865. The present owner is C. E. Fessenden. It is notable as the only stone barn in the county. The style and proportions are very interesting and differ radically from those of the stone barn of the Zabriskies at Paramus (see text for plate 112). The date 1735 is said to have been visible at one time; it was undoubtedly built in the early eighteenth century.

House of Cornelius Smith
Cherry Lane, Tallman
PLATE 62

This house stands in a part of the Zabriskie Patent bought by Cornelius Smith from the heirs of John Zabriskie (who died in 1765). He was the fourth of the name in a direct line. His great-grandfather Cornelius Adriaensen[2] Smidt, b. about 1652 in the Netherlands, emigrated to this country in 1663 with his father Adriaen and younger brother Lambert (see plate 58). The three became patentees of Tappan and settled there, but Cornelius died soon afterwards, about 1686. He had married Aug. 8, 1680 at New York City Jannetie François, who died about 1693. Their son Cornelius[3] Smidt, born on the farm in Manhattan, married at Tappan Oct. 15, 1707 Seytie Minnelay, born at the Bay on Long Island. Among their children was Cornelius C.[4] Smith, b. Dec. 19, 1714 at Tappan, d. 1785; he and his wife Maria Haring had nine children born in the Tappan Patent from 1738 to 1759: Cornelius, Jan, Aeltye, Jan, Gerrit, Albert, Rachel, Abraham and Petrus. Shortly after the birth of this brood, Cornelius Smith bought a farm many miles to the west on the Zabriskie Patent; here he built a stone house and a grist mill on the headwaters of the Saddle River. Before his decease he conveyed his mill property to his son Garret C.[5] Smith, b. Nov. 23, 1746 at Tappan, d. 1829. The farm then passed to one of his sons Garret G.[6] Smith (1800-1892). During his lifetime he gave it to his son Garret G.[7] Smith, Jr. (b. 1824), and the latter's heirs sold the property about 1910. The house has since passed through several hands, and is now owned by John Britt.

The central unit is the stone house built by Cornelius Smith, the purchaser of the farm; the old door and fanlight have been removed since the photograph was taken in 1925. The frame units on either side are of later date, built by his descendants. In Revolutionary days two roads led across the county from Suffern; they were called the North Road to Nyack and the South Road to Nyack; their courses were very devious and winding, and formed the basis for most of the country roads of today. The Smith house stands on the north side of the South Road to Nyack, on the east corner of its intersection with Cherry Lane. This lane leads from the West Saddle River Road in Bergen County north to the present village of Tallman.

House of Arie Smith, later Onderdonk's
Upper Landing, Piermont

This locality early acquired importance as the shipping point for the produce of the region around Tappan. Ships could anchor in the mouth of the Sparkill (creek) which empties into the Hudson River at Piermont, in early days known as Tappan Slote. The second son of Lambert Adriaensen Smidt, patentee of Tappan (plate 58), was Arie or Aurie[3] Smith, b. September 25, 1687 at Clausland in Tappan Patent. He married about 1711 Jannetje, bap. May 23, 1687 at Bergen, daughter of Theunis Roelofse Van Houten, who had a house and store at Tappan Slote (see infra). Arie and Jannetje settled near Tappan Slote, and probably built the present stone house. On March 26, 1736 (recorded 1755) they sold to Garret and Abraham Onderdonk of Hempstead, Long Island, a farm on the North River in Tappan, bounded north by Tunis Douwe Tallman and south by the slote, consisting of 320 acres with houses and barns. Arie and Jannetje proceeded to buy a farm of 320 acres at Upper Nyack, on which they settled; this farm was inherited by their son Lambert[4] Smith, d. in March 1764 at the age of 52 years, and then passed to his sons Arie[5] and John L.[5] Smith; both sons served in the Revolution, and the latter is not to be confused with his cousin Major John Smith of Clarkstown (plate 60).

The ancestor of the Onderdonk family, Andries Adrianse[1] Onderdonk, was a native of New Castle on the Delaware; he removed to Flatbush and married there Nov. 11, 1683 Maria Dircks Van der Vliet, and died in Jamaica, Long Island, before Aug. 13, 1687, when his widow married Jacob Janse Vanderbilt. The elder of their two sons was Adrian[2] Onderdonk, bap. Aug. 24, 1684 at New Utrecht, married Sara Snedeker, and removed to Rockland County shortly before 1745, settling near the quarries in the vicinity of Nyack, where he died at the age of 80 years. Two of his sons, Garret and Abraham, purchased the farm at Tappan Slote in which we are interested. Abraham[3] Onderdonk, b. 1711, d. about 1758, lived further north at Rockland Lake; at his death his share in the farm passed to his brother who resided on it. Garret[3] Onderdonk, b. Oct. 11, 1709 at Jamaica, removed with his father to Hempstead as a boy. On Nov. 6, 1736 he married Sara Hegeman, and had eight sons and one daughter born between 1738 and 1758. They removed to his purchase at Tappan Slote before 1750, when they became members of the Tappan Church. He died here in 1768. The farm undoubtedly passed to his sons. It is marked Onderdonks on Erskine's Revolutionary map, and lies on the shore road a scant mile north of the dock at the Slote. His eldest son Adrian (1738-1818) may have lived here, and also his unmarried son Garret (1742-1818), who had a large quarry business south of Nyack as early as 1785. Another son Daniel[4] Onderdonk (1747-1828) was an ensign in the Revolution; he lived in his father's house or nearby, and many of his eight children lived and died at Piermont.

The house was often under fire during the Revolution from the British ships on the Hudson River. The settlers along the shore were also harassed by marauding parties from the ships, guided by Tories, and their dwellings were only saved from utter annihilation by the vigilance of the Shore Guard formed by the citizens in self-defense. The house stands on the west side of the shore road at the Upper Landing in Piermont. It is an unusually long house built of red sandstone. It is in good condition, but its many dormers detract from the original appearance of the house.

House of Johannes Snedeker
formerly at Congers

The house stood on the Ponds Patent granted to Marshall and Welch in 1694. Capt. John Sands of Long Island bought the north quarter of the patent, and on Oct. 23, 1707 sold a large fertile tract to Tunis Snedeker of Hempstead, Long Island, extending between the Hackensack and Hudson Rivers, and from the mountains south to the Rockland Lake Road. Due to opposing claims of ownership, his eldest son Garret Snedeker obtained a confirmatory deed from John Sands on Oct. 23, 1770, and gave new deeds for various sections to his brothers.

The ancestor of the family was Jan[1] Snedeger, who was a shoemaker, and emigrated to this country before 1642. He located at New Amsterdam where he kept a taphouse, and later became one of the early settlers of Flatbush, where he was a magistrate in 1654 and died in 1679. He and his second wife Egberttie Jansen made their joint will in 1677, naming a son Gerrit and mentioning other children (all girls). The son Gerrit[2] Snedeker, bap. March 25, 1640, d. 1693, also lived at Flatbush. He married Willemtje Vocks, and secondly in December 1669 Elsye Teunise, bap. May 10, 1648, daughter of Tunis Nyssen. Gerrit is believed to have had six sons and two daughters, the three eldest by his first wife: Jan, Margaret and Christiaen; Tunis, Garret, Elsje, Abraham, Isaac and Sara. The will of Gerrit of Flatbush, dated 1692 and probated 1693, named the oldest son Jan, another son Christiaen, and mentioned other children.

Tunis[3] Snedeker was named for his maternal grandfather. Judging by the names of his children, he probably married a girl of the Polhemus family. He was living in Hempstead, Long Island in 1707 and removed to his tract in the Ponds Patent as early as 1731, dying Aug. 3, 1750, probably without leaving a will as several Snedekers (presumably his sons) released various parcels of his tract to each other. The various brothers and sisters who were undoubtedly the children of Tunis[3] Snedeker were: Garret, the eldest, married Altie and died 1776-87 without issue; Theodorus, b. 1706, d. 1767 (see below); Abraham, d. 1771 without issue and probably unmarried; Johannes, b. 1721, d. 1779 (see below); Altye or Elsie married first Jan Thew and secondly Harmanus (?) Coerter; Rebecca married Harmanus Tallman; Sarah married Peter van de Woort; Elizabeth married John Smith of the Hook.

The youngest brother, Johannes⁴ Snedeker, b. 1721, married about 1747 Affie, daughter of Daniel Martyne. He obtained the portion of his father's tract west of the King's Highway, extending to the Demarest Kill or Hackensack River, and built a stone house here standing until recently. He was appointed Captain of a company of the colonial militia in 1746. He was a patriot during the Revolution and was captured with his son Garret and imprisoned in the Sugar House in New York City. Johannes caught the smallpox and died Sept. 28, 1779 in prison. He had three sons, Theunis b. 1748, d. about 1809, John who was living in 1776 but probably died shortly afterwards, and Garret, and many daughters. Garret⁵ Snedeker, b. April 1, 1764, bap. at Clarkstown, d. April 13, 1843, married Elsie Thew. (One account calls her Elsie Brower. This may have been her maiden name since her son was named Abraham Brower; if so, she was a widow, for she was called Elsie Thew on her son's baptismal record.) Garret was taken prisoner by the British during the war but was exchanged. In 1793 he enlarged his father's house, in which Washington is supposed to have dined on the way to West Point. His son Abraham Brower⁶ Snedeker, b. March 15, 1792, bap. at Clarkstown, still living in 1884, married Mary Ann Bell. He served in the War of 1812. At one period he kept a tavern at the "1776 house" in Tappan and later built a hotel on the Haverstraw Road which was kept by his son Daniel after 1868. Abraham's other son Garret⁷ Snedeker, b. Jan. 3, 1824, bap. at Clarkstown, was still living in the homestead in 1902. Most of Johannes Snedeker's estate had been sold many years before, in 1840, to Abraham B. Conger, after whom the village is now named. The site of the house is 40 rods west of the King's Highway, a quarter mile northwest of the old Waldberg Church in Congers.

Snedeker—Swartwout House
Road to Rockland Lake, Congers

Tunis³ Snedeker of Hempstead purchased a large tract here in 1707 and died in 1750 (see above). One of his probable sons was Theodorus⁴ Snedeker, b. March 10, 1706, d. April 29, 1767, married Nov. 16, 1729 Derricke Vliet; they raised three sons, Tunis, Richard, b. 1735, living 1776, and Theodorus, and several daughters. Tunis⁵ Snedeker, his eldest son and heir, b. June 29, 1732, bap. at Tappan, was deeded his father's portion by his uncle Garret in 1770; it was a 388 acre tract bounded south by Rem Remsen, west by Garret Snedeker, north by the mountain, and east by Abraham Snedeker and the Pond. Tunis sold 185 acres to his youngest brother Theodorus, who inherited all his lands on Tunis' death in 1773. This Theodorus⁵ Snedeker, b. May 1, 1742, bap. at Tappan, d. Oct. 1, 1816, married Dec. 6, 1768 his first cousin Aefie, daughter of Johannes Snedeker, b. Oct. 22, 1750, and had three daughters. He was a sheriff of Orange County and a member of the Colonial Legislature. When the war broke out he remained loyal to the king, and sold supplies from his farm to the British on the Hudson River, doubtless conveying them in wagons to the nearby Slaughter's Landing (now Rockland Lake). He was apprehended, his property confiscated and sold Aug. 18, 1782 to Jacobus Swartwout.

His ancestor Tomys Roelofse[1] Swartwout was a tobacco merchant at Amsterdam in Holland; he emigrated to this country with his family in 1652 and settled at Midwout on Long Island; in 1661 he removed to Esopus where his family became very prominent. His descendant Jacobus[5] Swartwout, b. Nov. 5, 1734 at Wiccopee, d. Feb. 16, 1827, was a resident of Swartwoutville in Dutchess County; he was an important officer in the state militia in the Revolution, later becoming a General, and was for many years an assemblyman and senator. His 384 acre purchase at Rockland Lake was immediately occupied by his son Derrick, and willed to him in 1823. This Derick[6] Swartwout, b. Aug. 21, 1762 in Fishkill, d. April 24, 1852 at Rockland Lake in his 99th year; was married twice, to Lucretia and Elizabeth Polhemus, and had five sons and three daughters. In 1786 he was appointed paymaster of a regiment of Orange Co. militia, and later served in the War of 1812; he was a large slave owner but liberated his slaves before his death. His eldest son Jacobus or James[7] Swartwout (1791-1874) was the father of George[8] Swartwout, who was the owner in 1876 and still occupied the house in 1902.

The stone house of Theodorus Snedeker is said to be the house south of Congers near the railway. Some other Snedeker erected the main part of the Swartwout house, which was standing at the time of the Revolution; it is built of whitewashed stone; its roof has a very steep pitch characteristic of the early part of the eighteenth century. The side of the house has been refaced, window openings cut down to form long French windows, and a porch has been added. It is closed and very dilapidated. The house stands on the north side of the road to Rockland Lake, east of Congers railway station and west of the new state highway.

Sneden Houses
Sneden's Landing, Palisades
PLATE 63

A tract of 3410 acres on the west side of the Hudson River at the state line had been patented to George Lockhart of New York City on June 27, 1687; at his death in 1698 the property was taken over and occupied by William Merritt, mortgagee, principal creditor and administrator; on May 14, 1705 various members of the Lockhart and Merritt families deeded the tract to Capt. John Corbett, who had taken a mortgage two years previously. John Corbett was an English sea captain, who retired here and died in 1717;"Corbett's old house" is mentioned in Alexander's survey of the state line in 1719. This is supposed to be the house photographed in plate 63, although the appearance of the house does not suggest such great age. Corbett willed the property to his daughter Mary, wife of Henry Ludlow; they had a survey made in 1745 by Philip Verplanck, on whose map is marked "Sneden-ing house the Ferry" by the river's edge. Robert, or some other member of the Sneden family, had probably crossed the Hudson River and bought from the Ludlows shortly before 1745. In 1752 Jonathan Hazard bought land from Henry Ludlow, commencing at Robert Sneden's west line by the road that comes from the Ferry. On Oct. 9, 1769 the Commissioners appointed to settle the state boundary line placed it 79 chains and 27 links south of Sneydon's house, formerly Corbet's.

The Sneden family is probably descended from Jan Snedick, who emigrated in 1657 with his wife Grietje Jans and two children, Carsten and Grietje, and obtained a patent to property at Harlem in 1660; the family is found in Queens County towards the end of the century, about 1700 at Eastchester in Westchester County, and in 1745 in Rockland County. The name had many various spellings: Sneeding, Sneydon, Snyden, Snyder, Sneder. Robert Sneden owned property at the landing in 1752 and probably in 1745. On Sept. 26, 1766 letters of administration on the estate of Robert Sneden of Orange Co., farmer, deceased, were granted to his son Dennis of Orange Co. Robert's wife was Mary or Molly Sneden, b. 1709, d. Jan. 31, 1810, at the advanced age of 101 years and 18 days, and lies buried at Palisades Cemetery. She supplemented her husband's calling of farmer as ferry mistress and she may have run the ferry as early as 1745; the place was called Sneden's Landing by 1759.

Molly Sneden and all her children (except her son John) were Tories. An interesting Revolutionary order of the Committee of Orange Co. reads: "Whereas Dennis Snyden, James Snyden, William Snyden, and Samuel Snyden, all living at or near a place commonly called Snyden's or Dobbs Ferry on the west side of Hudson's River in the County of Orange and State of New York, have refused to sign any or either of the Associations that have been put forth or recommended by our honorable convention; and as the above said persons are greatly suspected of carrying on a treasonable correspondence with our natural enemies, or ships of war belonging to the King of Great Britain, lying in aforesaid river, by the great opportunity afforded them in the privilege they have by keeping the ferry: knowing the aforesaid persons to be inveterate enemies to the common States of America, Therefore Resolved, that the above Dennis Snyden, Jesse (sic) Snyden, William Snyden and Samuel Snyden are hereby forewarned not to keep ferry, or employ any other person to ferry in their room, or employ a craft on the aforesaid river, upon any pretence whatsoever, and all other persons are hereby forewarned against having any correspondence with the above said Snydens, or any other person or persons whatsoever that are in any degree enemies to the liberties of America. And whereas John Snyder is advertised in the public Gazette as pilot of the ships of war on the above said river, greatly to the damage of the said John Snyder, it is hereby requested that the said Printer shall insert Robert Snyden instead of John Snyder, who has always appeared to be a warm friend to the common cause of America". Per Order of the Orange Co. Committee, Clarkstown, July 29, 1776. During the Revolution, Molly Sneden lived in a white frame house on the road by the river (still standing but rebuilt); with her lived her son Dennis, a bachelor (1735-1824). The story goes that a British soldier was pursued down the gully by some patriots; she hid him in her house in a large chest on which she set pans of cream to rise, and when the patriots arrived she misinformed them; they were tired and asked for refreshment, and she offered them all the milk she had, but told them not to disturb the pans of cream which she had just set out; in the evening she is said to have ferried the soldier across the river. Some of her sons settled in Nova Scotia after the war and received grants of land there.

The patriot son was John Sneden, Sr., b. about 1738, d. April 1, 1822 aged 84 years, and lies buried at Palisades. At his death he owned the 100 acres previously owned by his father Robert, so it is probable that his Loyalist brothers (Dennis, James, Samuel and William) were deprived of their lands. John Sneder's house is shown on Erskine's map part way up the hill from the landing; it is a frame house still standing, known as the Watson house. By license of Oct. 5, 1762 he married Ellison Lawrence and had two sons; he had eight more children by his second wife Margaret Riker, d. Nov. 18, 1828 aged 75 years, 1 month and 24 days. After his death his farm was surveyed by James Demarest on June 7, 1822 and divided between his widow and eight surviving children, his house being allotted to the widow. John Sneden's children were: Lawrence Sneden, married Leah ———— and lived in the humble whitewashed stone house near the top of the hill, later owned by Joshua Martin and Jacob Gesner and now owned by Harry Brearley; John Sneden, Jr. of Tappan Slote, b. 1770; George Washington Sneden, b. 1781, married Rachel Bogert, and probably predeceased his father as he is not mentioned in the division of the farm; Elizabeth, b. 1783, married Capt. L. B. Rice; Richard Sneden, b. 1785, married Elizabeth Wood of Northport, L. I., and lived in New York City; Mary, b. 1787, married Stephen Hagen; Robert Sneden, b. 1788, married Jane Crum, and lived in a house above his father's, later called the Doughty house and no longer standing; Rachel, b. 1790, married Benjamin Grovestein; Abraham,

1792-1829; William, b. 1795, probably predeceased his father as he is not mentioned in the division of the farm.

John Sneden, Jr., b. Aug. 10, 1770, d. Sept. 18, 1829, married at Tappan Feb. 28, 1796 Phebe Gesner of Nyack, b. March 15, 1779, d. July 14, 1857. He had a shipyard at Tappan Slote (now Piermont); his frame house stands on the creek in the section called Bogerttown. He probably inherited his father's house from his mother, as it was sold by the executors of John Sneden, Jr. in 1859 to Mary E. Watson. Mrs. Watson, nee Mary Carter, settled here and built the main part of the present house. It was later the first home of the Palisades Library.

In some fashion the two other pre-revolutionary Sneden houses came into the possession of the children of John Sneden, Jr., or Boss Sneden as he was called. His daughter Ellison Sneden, b. 1798, married Sept. 7, 1816 Peter Westervelt, lived in Molly Sneden's frame house in the 1860s and 1870s and possibly for a longer period. It was later sold to Dan Conklin who rebuilt it; it is now disfigured by a mansard roof almost the size of the house itself.

The stone house nearby, which may have been Corbett's, is known in the family as William Sneden's house. Boss Sneden's son, Capt. Lawrence J. Sneden (1800-1871) was living here in 1826 when his daughter Mary was born; in 1834 he bought the Storms house on the south side of the Landing road at the river (a stone house built after the Revolution in pre-war style), where his daughter Clara was born in 1837; he was an important member of the family, ferryman, shipbuilder, and assemblyman. To return to the stone house which may have been Corbett's, it appears to have been owned in the nineteenth century by Boss Sneden's youngest son William, whose heirs owned it in 1876 and sold it about 1890 to Joseph Lawrence. The three pre-revolutionary Sneden houses and the Storms-Sneden house are now owned and leased out by Mrs. Mary Tonnetti, nee Lawrence.

This locality was for many years known as Rockland or Sneden's Landing; it is now a part of Palisades. The old road went straight down the valley, or dingle as it was called. The William Sneden house, which may have been Corbett's, is a good-sized stone house with steep gambrel roof. Built on a hillside, its river front is of two stories, at present covered by porches. The view taken in plate 63 is from the northwest. It stands on the river a short distance north of the Landing road. The Molly Sneden house in its rebuilt condition is a small white frame house with a large mansard roof; it stands on the north side of the Landing Road near the river and the former house. The house of the patriot John Sneden is a small white house built of wide clapboards with a gable roof. Built on the hillside, its river front is also of two stories, the basement walls being of rough stone. The north wing is smaller and is similarly built, although the roof has no overhang; it is probably pre-revolutionary. The south portion of the house is a large two story frame structure added by Mrs. Watson. This house stands part way up the hill on the river side of the road by the bend. Railings, pillars, dormers and trellises tend to hide the lines of the original house.

Tallman House
formerly on Upper Broadway, Nyack

Douwe Harmanszen[1] (Talama or Tallman) was the first of the family in America. He emigrated from Friesland in 1658 on the ship *The Porpoise* with his wife Dirckje Theunis and three children. They settled at Bergen, where they made their joint will on March 25, 1678. Claes Jansen (Kuyper) van Purmarent obtained a patent for a large tract at Nyack on Nov. 20, 1671, and sold 100 acres to Douwe, the sale being confirmed by the heirs of both on June 18, 1694. Some time between 1678 and 1686 Douwe may have removed to his Nyack lands, as he was appointed Justice of the Peace of Orange County Oct. 4, 1686. He died June 19, 1687 and lies buried at Bergen. His widow was still living at Tappan with their son Theunis in 1702; she probably died shortly after this as Theunis sold his parents' property at Bergen in 1703. Only two of Douwe's and Dirckje's children grew to maturity. Harman Douwesen[2] Tallman, born about 1655 in Friesland, was the first white settler of Nyack, removing here as a young man in 1675. In 1687 he petitioned (successfully) to be allowed to buy from the Indians 200 acres back of Nyack, extending to the Hackensack River, stating that he had been living at Nyack for twelve years. On June 21, 1686 he married Margrietje Minnelay and had two children: Dirckje, who married Abraham Janse Haring and is believed to have lived on the Pascack Road north of the state border, and Douwe Tallman, who lived at Closter and was bayonetted during a Tory raid for the wealth he is supposed to have had in his chest. Harman was less than thirty-five years of age when he died; his widow married in 1691 Abraham Gerritsen Blauvelt of Tappan, and had ten more children, of whom Jacob settled on a farm at Blauvelt and Elizabeth Du Pew at Kakiat (see supra). On Harman's death, his father's lands and seemingly also his own property reverted to his younger brother Theunis.

Theunis Douwensen[2] Tallman, bap. Feb. 8, 1665 at Bergen, died July 17, 1739 and lies buried on the Bight at South Nyack, where stands or stood a tombstone inscribed: "T.D.T.; July 17, 1739". He was living at Nyack by 1688, when he took the oath of allegiance. In 1690 he was commissioned ensign in the Orange Co. militia and in 1700 he was appointed high sheriff of the county for the first time. He was married twice: first in 1694 to Brechje Jans Haring, b. 1675 in New York, daughter of Jan Pietersen Haring and sister of Cosyn Haring, builder of the house at Old Tappan (plate 89); by her he had four sons and four daughters. He married secondly at Tappan Jan. 11, 1710 Margrietje Hogenkamp, and had two sons and three daughters.

Theunis Tallman is said to have built the stone house standing until 1910 on Upper Broadway near Tallman Place, Nyack. This house is claimed to have been erected in 1678; if the date is correct it must have been built by Theunis' elder brother Harman, as Theunis was then but thirteen years old. Such an early date could only apply to a small portion of the house, which is eighteenth century in style; at different times a second story of stone and a porch were added. It was owned by a descendant, Miss Clara Tallman, when demolished. Her line of ancestry is recited in Tompkins' History.

House of Harmanus Tallman
Germond Road, Germonds
PLATE 64

The eldest surviving son of Theunis Douwensen[2] Tallman of Nyack (see supra) was Douwe[3] Tallman, b. Feb. 13, 1703, married Annetje Blauvelt about 1731 and had four sons and six daughters; it is not known exactly where in Rockland County they resided, but presumably they lived at Nyack or Clarkstown. Their second son was Harmanus or Harme[4] Tallman, b. Jan. 30, 1737, d. July 19, 1819 and buried at Clarkstown; he is the first known owner of the house at Clarkstown, now Germonds. About 1761 he married Elizabeth Blauvelt, b. July 11, 1744, daughter of Johannes Isaac Blauvelt and Helena Pullen; their children were Douwe, Johannes, Harme, Isaac, Jannetje and Helena. After his wife's death Harmanus married secondly on Sept. 29, 1786 Maria Onderdonk, by whom he had no issue. The house passed to his second son, Johannes[5] Tallman, b. Sept. 13, 1765, married at Tappan Nov. 24, 1785 Sarah Sickels, daughter of Johannes Sickels of Sickeltown; after his death she married secondly at Kakiat Feb. 17, 1806 Andrew Tinkey, and died Nov. 17, 1857 aged 91 years and 9 months. On the death of her first husband she removed to her father's house in Sickeltown (see supra) with her son John, and lies buried in the Nauraushaun Cemetery near there. The Tallman house was inherited by her daughter Elizabeth[6] Tallman, b. Oct. 2, 1787 at Clarkstown, married at Tappan Feb. 26, 1805 Aarie Demarest of Clarkstown, and had at least ten children baptized in the nearby church. The house passed out of the family ownership. In 1876 it was owned by J. Popp, and is spoken of locally as the Popp house, and the corner on which it stands as Popp corner. The present owner is John M. Torr.

The house stands on the north side of the present Germond Road, which was laid along the division line of the North and Suth Moieties of the Kakiat Patent, and at the head of the road leading to the old Clarkstown Church and eventually to the Sickeltown settlement. The settlements in the North Moiety were in early days referred to as Kakiat or New Hempstead; Clarkstown later became the name for the township, in which stood the old church. Before this Church was organized in 1750, settlers of the North Moiety had to travel along the Indian trail through the unbroken forests of the South Moiety, and through the farmlands of the Tappan Patent, to the church at Tappan some distance to the south.

It has been stated that this house was built in 1737 by Harmanus Tallman. This is probably a misstatement of the fact that the first known owner was Harmanus Tallman, b. 1737. But it is possible that part of it was built by his uncle, Harmanus' Tallman, b. Jan. 12, 1709, who was one of a set of triplet children of Theunis Tallman. He married Catrina Ecker and had a son Abraham born in 1734, who probably died in infancy. In 1737 he acted as sponsor for his nephew Harmanus, son of his brother Douwe, and future owner of the house. It is logical to presume that if he were alive, he would have acted as sponsor in 1750 for his nephew Harmanus, son of his half-brother Harme. It may be that he died shortly after 1737, leaving his house to his nephew and namesake, but this is conjecture. Such an early date could only apply to the wing. The main house was undoubtedly built by Harmanus Tallman (b. 1737) about the time of the Revolution. The high and steep gable roof of the main house is more characteristic of the post-war houses in Kings County. It is built along lines similar to the wing; the panelling and sunburst decoration on the doorway belong to the post-revolutionary era in style; the dormers are of course modern. The house has been restored.

Tallman House
Road to Valley Cottage, West Nyack
PLATE 65

The builder and early occupants of this house are unknown, other than that they belonged to the Tallman family. The house stands on the bank of the Hackensack River, on the west end of the tract of 200 acres granted Oct. 27, 1687 to Harmen Douwesen' Tallman of Nyack. The land is believed to have passed, together with his father's patent nearby, to his younger brother Theunis, rather than to his children (see supra). By his second wife Margrietje Hogenkamp, Theunis Douwensen' Tallman had five children including a son Harme, who inherited the Nyack lands (probably both tracts). This Harme' Tallman, b. 1719, married Rebecca Snedeker, and had four children: Neeltje, Abraham, Theunis and Harmanus. The Nyack lands were divided between the three sons. If Harme Tall-

224

man inherited the tract in the interior as well as the one along the shore, it is probable that he or one of his three sons built this house, which was undoubtedly erected about the time of the Revolution. Unfortunately the deeds to the property are missing. The first known owner of the house is Peter Tallman, who was in possession in 1876. His daughter married a Fisher, and it was until lately occupied by Mrs. Gesner, one of her daughters. Mrs. Gesner or her estate sold it about four years ago to Jean Guerrin, the present owner.

At the time of the Revolution, there were many houses along the stretch of road near the Hackensack River; unfortunately Erskine's map does not name any of the owners. A short distance north of West Nyack Four Corners a road branches eastward over the Hackensack River and then branches again; one road passes under the railway culvert and continues eastward to the King's Highway south of Valley Cottage; the other road goes northward but eventually reaches the King's Highway north of Valley Cottage. The Tallman house is beyond the fork on the east side of the second-mentioned road; in Revolutionary times it was probably reached by a private lane, as the other road is the old one.

Terneur—Hutton House
Sickeltown Road, West Nyack
PLATE 66

This house stands on Lot No. 11 of the South Moiety of the Kakiat Patent. On Dec. 11, 1732 Hendrick Oblenis, yeoman of Harlem in New York, bought from Thomas Clark, merchant of New York City, 800 acres of land in the Kakiat Patent, known as Lots No. 11 and No. 12, extending from the north boundary of the Expense Lot to the south boundary of Emil Kline's farm one and one-quarter miles to the north, and extending one mile west from Demarest Kill or Hackensack River. A stone in the front of the west unit of the house is inscribed: "1731 M.P.:S.T." It was the custom to record thus the date of erection and the initials of the builder and his wife; they were probably tenants of Thomas Clark. Hendrick Oblenis built and settled a stone's throw to the north (see plate 55). He undoubtedly gave this house to his daughter Jacomina, bap. May 4, 1698, married May 26, 1720 Jacobus Tourneur, also of Harlem.

Jacobus[3] Tourneur, bap. Nov. 20, 1695, was a son of Jacques,[2] and grandson of Daniel[1] Tourneur, b. at Amiens in Picardy, fled to Leyden where he married Sept. 5, 1650 Jacqueline de Parisis, and emigrated to this country in 1651, settling at Harlem where he died in 1673. Jacobus[3] Tourneur is said to have settled at Haverstraw, a misleading statement; in very early days the Kakiat Patent, extending south of West Nyack, was a part of the Haverstraw Precinct. Jacobus' children were baptized at Tappan, and he undoubtedly lived nearby on the Kakiat Patent in the house later occupied by his son Hendrick. Jacobus and Jacomina had six children: Jacobus, Jr., Hendrick, John, Aefie, Sarah, and Jannetie; they married their neighbors in Tappan and south Kakiat. Hendrick⁴ or Henry Terneur, as he often spelled his name, came into possession of the house on the tract of his grandfather, Hendrick Oblenis. In 1787 he was assessed for 158 acres in Clarkstown, and his first cousin Capt. Hendrick Terneur for 180 acres. These two are not to be confused. They were doubly related, as the latter was a son of Michael Tourneur and Maria, daughter of Hendrick Oblenis; Capt. Terneur married Margrietje Blauvelt and unlike his cousin had childen; he lived opposite, on the south side of the road. The Henry Terneur in whom we are interested married at Tappan Sept. 23, 1753 Marritie Kuyper of Tappan; as they had no children, they adopted John Hutton and bequeathed him the property. Henry Terneur died Dec. 9, 1819 at the age of 85 years, and lies buried at Nauraushaun.

John Hutton, b. Feb. 1, 1759, d. Sept. 15, 1841, married Elizabeth Sickels, b. May 12, 1757, d. Jan. 12, 1850, daughter of William Sickels and sister of the various Sickels brothers who built their homes nearby (see supra). Their elder son Henry Hutton, b. Aug. 10, 1789, d. Aug. 19, 1812 at 23 years of age, the sponsors at his baptism being his father's adopted parents, Henry and Marritje Terneur. Their younger son William Hutton, b. May 28, 1792, d. April 28, 1831 at the age of 38 years and 11 months, married at Tappan April 14, 1814 Agnes Blanch, b. Oct. 26, 1796, d. June 13, 1877. These two generations of the Hutton family also lie buried at Sickeltown (now Nauraushaun). William and Agnes had five sons and one daughter: John, Richard, Henry, Isaac, William and Anna. Isaac was drowned at the burning of the steamboat *Swallow;* the others married and had children and removed elsewhere to live. The house was sold to Mr. Nickerson about 1847. In 1876 Lile and Otto were joint owners of this and adjoining property. Dr. Harry Baker, the present owner, purchased the house about 25 years ago from Mr. Goldberg.

The house is built in two similar sections. The west unit is dated 1731. The east unit was undoubtedly erected some time before the Revolution, probably by Henry Terneur at the time of his marriage in 1753. The house is built of roughly cut stone and is covered by a gable roof, the back slope of which is longer and extends nearer the ground. The small windows with the narrow lower sashes are typical of an early period. Each unit consists of a square room with fireplace and a small rear room. Dormers and slim Corinthian columns have slightly changed the aspect of the house. A wing has been added on the west side. The house is south of West Nyack Four Corners, on the north side of the Sickeltown Road, which runs westward at this point. It is south of the Oblenis house and north of the various Sickels houses.

House of Jacob Vanderbilt
Road to Clarkstown, Germonds
PLATE 67

The house stands in the South Moiety of the Kakiat Patent, which was subdivided between McEvers and Symes in 1727. The patentees did not settle here, but were active in selling portions after this division. The house was undoubtedly built shortly after 1727; its irregular stonework, mud plastering, split laths, wooden locks, handwrought nails, small windows, crude glass, all point to construction at an early date. Unrecorded deeds make its early history uncertain; the first known owner of the house is the Jacob Vanderbilt born 1768, but it is probable that he inherited it from his grandfather Jacob.

The first of the family in this country was Jan Aertsen, who emigrated before 1650, settled at Flatbush and later at Bergen where he died Feb. 2, 1705. His son Jacob Janse² Van Der Bilt of Flatbush married Aug. 13, 1687 Maria Dircks Van der Vliet, widow of Andries Adriaensen Onderdonk. Their son Jacob³ Van Der Bilt married Hilletie or Hillegont Hardenbergh about 1724, and settled in Rockland County shortly before the baptism of their third child Jacobus in 1731 at Tappan Church. It is probable that they built the present house at Clarkstown when they arrived here about 1730. They had many children: Maria wife of Johannes Meyer, Johannes, Jacobus, Margrietje wife of Abraham Meyer, Sara wife of Joris Van Nostrand, Dirck, Annetje wife of Teunis Tallman, and Gertruyd wife of Jan Eckeson (the six youngest were baptized from 1731 to 1744 at Tappan, the only church of the vicinity at that early period). An added point in favor of the father's home being at Clarkstown rather than at Tappan, is that his children's children were baptized at Clarkstown as soon as that Church was organized, so that they had probably been born and raised here. The third son Jacobus⁴ Van Der Bilt, b. June 15, 1731, d. 1774, married Brechje Tallman, b. May 27, 1739, d. 1798, daughter of Douwe Tallman and sister of Harmanus Tallman, probable builder of the house nearby (plate 64). They had seven children, all baptized at Clarkstown between 1757 and 1770: Hilletje, Douwe, Annetje, Brechje, Jacob, and twins Johannes and Sarah. The house is known to have been owned by their son Jacob⁵ Vanderbilt, b. Jan. 28, 1768 at Clarkstown, married at Tappan Oct. 22, 1791 Jannetje Blauvelt, both residents of Clarkstown. They had a son Jacob, b. 1798, who probably died in infancy, and a daughter Annatje⁶ Vanderbilt, b. March 1, 1803, married at Tappan Dec. 23, 1820 Isaac H. Tallman, bap. Nov. 17, 1799, son of Harmanus Tallman and Jannetje Vanderbilt. In a will probated July 16, 1853, the property is mentioned

227

as land inherited from her father Jacob Vanderbilt. Ann, widow of Isaac Tallman, sold the house to Henry Schriver; he sold it about 1860 to George H. Budke, whose son of the same name disposed of it in 1934.

The house stands on the west side of the old Indian trail connecting the Clarkstown settlement with the settlements to the south. It is a half mile south of the head of the road, where stands the Harmanus Tallman house in Germonds, and a short distance north of the old churchyard.

House of Roelof Van Houten
on the Hackensack River east of New City

Roeloff Cornelissen[1] Van Houten was the first of several brothers to come to America. He emigrated in 1638 to Rensselaerswyck, where he married Gerritje, daughter of Cornelis Van Nes, and later settled at Amersfoort (Flatlands) on Long Island. A son Theunis Roelofse[2] (Van Houten), born at Amersfoort, settled as a young man at Bergen where he married Jan. 8, 1678 Tryntje Klaesen Kuyper. They probably removed to Rockland County about 1686; he took the oath of allegiance here in 1688. His house and general store was at Tappan Slote (now Piermont) on the Hudson River front by the Landing, his lands extending along the river halfway to Nyack. Like Daniel De Clark of Tappan (plate 48), he was a Leislerian adherent; in 1689 both were appointed justices of the peace for Orange County and represented the county on Leisler's Committee of Safety. He was a justice of the peace for the greater part of the period between 1703 and 1717. He died here July 27, 1737, his wife predeceasing him on Aug. 20, 1734. Of their thirteen children, Klaes[3] Van Houten, bap. July 12, 1685 in New York, may have been the member of the family who built the stone house of the Van Houten family, on the hill at Orangeville near the Hackensack River. He married at Tappan Oct. 13, 1708 Grietje Haring and had seven children. Their youngest was Roelof[4] Van Houten, b. March 11, 1721 at Tappan, married Catharine, daughter of Resolvert Nagel of nearby Closter, and had three sons and three daughters, baptized at Tappan. The three sons, Resolvert, b. 1743, Claus, b. 1749, and Jan, b. 1761, all married into the Blauvelt family.

The house on the headwaters of the Hackensack River is said to have been built in 1761 by the son Claus[5] Van Houten, but as he was barely twelve years old at this time, the house must have been erected by the father Roelof. Additional proofs of this are that Roelof's youngest son is said to have been born near New City and that Roelof lies buried in the Martinus Cemetery near New City. The house evidently passed to the son Claus R.[5] Van Houten, b. Nov. 14, 1749, d. Oct. 1818 and buried at Nauraushaun, married Caty Blauvelt, b. Aug. 11, 1753, d. Feb.

17, 1837, daughter of Isaac Jacobse Blauvelt. Claus Van Houten was a farmer and miller; his house is marked Van Houten's on Erskine's Revolutionary map. His son Isaac B.[6] Van Houten (1776-1850) settled on a farm nearby (which had been purchased in 1760 from William Lupton and placed in the name of Claus R. Van Houten). In 1807 he built the stone house on the east side of the river still standing. The older homestead therefore probably passed to another son or daughter of Claus. His children were Caty and Mary, twins, Isaac B., Rulef C. of Orangeville, Jacob, John and Margaret. An old resident states that about 1860 the house was owned by John Hardwick, then by Jacob Stark and later by Jacob Goebel.

In the sale of the north half of lot No. 5 by Jacob A. Blauvelt to his son Jacob Blauvelt in May 1753, the bounds are described as the headwaters of the Hackensack River, the De Pews (plate 49) and Van Houtens. Therefore Roelof had bought this tract as early as 1753; he may have settled here immediately in a temporary structure, or he may not have removed here until he built the present house in 1761. The Roelof Van Houten house stands on the west bank of the Hackensack River, on the north side of the road leading to the De Pew house. The old house is the present wing, and is built of stone rubble, whitewashed green. The Isaac Van Houten house (a typical stone structure with gambrel roof) stands a short distance south on the east bank of the river. The road continues southeastward to the Snedeker houses at Congers.

Zabriskie (?)—Goetschius—Tallman House
Cherry Lane, Tallman
PLATE 68

On Nov. 6, 1724 John Zabriskie bought a tract of 630 acres near the present village of Tallman from Peter Fauconier and associates, which they had purchased in 1709 from one of the East Jersey Proprietors. This is one of the very few small grants which was not cancelled and swallowed up in the network of large patents. It was occupied at a very early date: on May 18, 1739 Clinton, the surveyor, noted in passing the Zabriskie tract: "Entered a cleared field. Here a negro house, belonging to Samuel Francisco, a free negro who settled the place for John Sabrisco, who holds it under a Jersey title."

John's father Albrecht[1] Zaborowsky was a Pole; he emigrated by way of Prussia to New Netherland in 1662, settling at Old Hackensack (Ridgefield Park) in Bergen Co., New Jersey, where he died Sept. 1, 1711. His second son John[2] Zabriskie was married twice, to Elizabeth Romeyn and to Margrita Durie, and had thirteen children; he made various land purchases including this tract which was later found to be in the province of New York, but continued to reside at Old

Hackensack, where he died in 1765. In his will John divided his lands between his children, leaving to his daughter Rachel 200 acres at "Messanekes." Presumably this is the tract in question, for "Masonicus" is a name applied to the region south of Tallman village. It is possible that John had previously given a part of the tract to Rachel for her marriage portion, as her husband appears to have been in possession of 300 acres here.

Rachel[2] Zabriskie, bap. Sept. 7, 1729, was a daughter of John by the second wife; on Aug. 26, 1750 she married Dominie Johannes Hendrikus Goetschius, and had ten sons and two daughters. His father Maurice[1] Goetschi was a powerful preacher at Bernegg and Salez in Switzerland. He left Zurich for America with four hundred followers; after a trip of eight months which was accomplished with a great deal of suffering and hardship, the company reached Philadelphia in 1735, but they were left leaderless within two months of arrival, as his son writes of the preacher's death in a letter of July 21, 1735. By his wife Esther Werndtlin he had eight children, of whom the eldest was Dominie Hendrikus[2] Goetschius, as he was called. Dominie Goetschius, b. 1717 in Switzerland, preached in his youth to his father's flock near Philadelphia; he served the churches of Queens Co. on Long Island (Newtown, Jamaica, Hempstead and Oyster Bay) as assistant to Antonides (1741-48); for the remainder of his life (1748-74) he had pastoral charge of the Reformed Churches at Hackensack and Schraalenburg in Bergen Co., New Jersey. Like his father, he was a learned, powerful and independent preacher, and the head of a strong faction during the schism of the church; he died Nov. 14, 1774. The Dominie's second son Stephanus followed in his footsteps and became an important minister of the churches in Ulster Co. and later of northern Bergen Co., where he owned the old Hopper house (plate 94). The Dominie's eldest son was John Goetschius, b. July 1, 1751 and baptized at Schraalenberg; he probably married Maria Decker. It is undoubtedly this John Goetschius who came into possession of the Rockland Co. tract of his grandfather John Zabriskie, Sr., and sold it in 1797 to John Tallman.

The identity of the builder of the house is a puzzle. It is built of a slaty rubble covered with whitewash on the front side; the gable roof has a fairly steep slope; the typically early interior arrangement is followed, of two main rooms each with its separate outside door; the windows have the small lower sash and they are not in true alignment with the doors. Thus its construction places it in the early eighteenth century. Yet the first owner of the tract remained at Old Hackensack, and Dominie Goetschius, the second owner, could scarcely have lived here and tended his churches at such a distance. John Goetschius, the next owner, came of age only shortly before the Revolution, and the house antedates the war by many years. Possibly it was the house of Francisco mentioned by Clinton in 1739; or it may have been built shortly after this date by some other tenant of John Zabriskie, who undoubtedly placed farmers here in order to retain possession of the tract.

Jan³ Tallman, b. Jan. 12, 1709, was one of triplet children of Theunis Douwensen² Tallman of Nyack and his first wife Brechje Jans Haring, and uncle of Harmanus Tallman who lived in the house at Clarkstown (plate 64). On Sept. 19, 1735 at Hackensack he married Helena Blauvelt; both were residents of Tappan, where he was a farmer. His son John⁴ Tallman, b. Sept. 3, 1751 at Tappan, d. 1839 at Tallman village, married about 1777 Fanny Mabie. He was a farmer and lived at Greenbush (now Blauvelt). He was commissioned ensign on Nov. 1, 1786 for his services during the Revolution. On March 23, 1797 he bought from John Goetschius for £1525 a farm of 157 acres in the Zabriskie patent near the present village of Tallman, and settled here. He is said to have built the house still standing but, as the house is pre-revolutionary in construction, he probably merely enlarged it by adding the frame east wing. This farm was inherited by his son Abraham I.⁵ Tallman, b. July 14, 1793 and baptized at Clarkstown, married Sept. 14, 1814 Maria De Ronde. It passed to their son John A.⁶ Tallman, b. May 16, 1815, married Dec. 8, 1842 Caroline Conklin. In 1902 it was occupied by their son John Cornell⁷ Tallman, and is now owned by James C. Tallman.

The house stands on the east side of Cherry Lane, midway between the Cornelius Smith house (plate 62) on the old South Road to Nyack and the present main highway passing through the village of Tallman. The property lies on the headwaters of the Saddle River.

Unidentified House
Pomona Road, New City
PLATE 69

Very little is known of the history of this house. It stands on one of the so-called Dry Swamp Lots in the Division of the North Moiety of the Kakiat Patent. The North Moiety was purchased in 1713 by a group of men from Hempstead, Long Island. These men of English descent formed a settlement in the western part of their tract, selling the east portion from time to time to Dutch settlers. This house stands in the extreme northern end of the patent south of the mountains (seen in the photograph) and the headwaters of the Hackensack River. It stands alone, part of neither the English nor the Dutch settlements, although nearer the Dutch farms. Built of roughly cut stone and covered by a gable roof with a curving overhang, it is a typically Dutch house, but shows an English influence in its depth and in the long low slope of the rear roofline. It was undoubtedly erected before the Revolution, but its builder is unknown. The Blauvelt family is in some manner connected with its ownership in the minds of several old residents. It is also said to have been owned by Richard Coe about 75 years ago (1855). In 1876 Richard Coe owned property to the north, while the owner of this house was W. Roberts. The present owner is Tom Roberts. The house stands south of the mountains on the east side of Pomona Road, which is the next road west of the road from New City to Haverstraw, and is connected with it by the Phillips Hill Road on which stand the Blauvelt—Secor house (plate 45) and other old stone houses.

PLATE 41

House of Benjamin Benson
Old King's Highway, West Haverstraw

The first known occupant of the house is Benjamin Benson. He probably erected it shortly after he purchased the land in 1757. Haverstraw was the northern outpost of the Dutch settlements in Rockland County and this is the only pre-revolutionary Dutch house remaining in this vicinity. The broad gable roof is seldom found on those Rockland County houses which are two full rooms deep. In comparison with the Lent house at Orangeburg (plate 53), built in 1752, it is much flatter and has no curving overhang. The slight extension of the roof beyond all four walls is a modern change. The three chimneys are unusual.

PLATE 42

House of Hendrick Gerritse Blauvelt
Blauvelt

This house was built in 1710 by Hendrick Gerritse Blauvelt, one of the pioneers in this neighborhood. It belongs to an early type of architecture popular with the Dutch. Two main rooms adjoin and each has its separate outside door. At the rear two very narrow bedrooms open directly into the main rooms. The gable roof is customary for these narrow houses. The foundations of the chimney in the cellar are in the form of a very large arch, giving the impression of a bricked-up fireplace; this is to be seen in many of the early houses.

234

PLATE 43

House of Johannes Blauvelt, later Smith's
Blauvelt

This is the house of Johannes Blauvelt, grandson of Hendrick Gerritse Blauvelt, builder of the house nearby (plate 42). The central unit was erected by Johannes in 1741 and the west (left) unit was added by him in 1752. The east wing belongs to a slightly later period. The twelve-paned upper sash and the narrow lower sash are more frequently found in seventeenth century houses but continued to be used at this late date in the less pretentious farmhouses. The overhang of the roof adds to the appearance of the house. The dormers are of course modern. Notice the old Dutch double door and solid shutters. The house passed by marriage into the Smith family in which it remained until it was sold about 1890.

235

PLATE 44

House of Gerret Blauvelt
Road to West Nyack, Blauvelt

This house was built in or about 1763 by Gerret Blauvelt, younger brother of Johannes Blauvelt, builder of the house nearby (plate 43). It is interesting to compare the houses of the two brothers. Johannes started in a modest stone house and added to it as his family grew; Gerret set up housekeeping in a humble log cabin and built his permanent home after the birth of his children. The result is that although Gerret's house is no larger than Johannes' and has the same proportions, its construction is not so primitive and the larger size windows indicate a desire for greater comfort. The curving overhang of the roof has been omitted. The two-paned window sashes and the shutters are modern. Otherwise the house is in its original condition. It was occupied by the family until sold by a descendant in 1900.

PLATE 45

Blauvelt—Secor House
Phillips Hill Road, New City

The earliest remembered occupant of this house is Peter Blauvelt, son of Johannes Blauvelt (1745-1830) and Catharine Tallman. As both generations lie buried in this vicinity it is probable that Peter's parents owned the house before him. They undoubtedly bought or inherited it as the house belongs to the second quarter of the eighteenth century. Its length is less than the usual house of this type. It nestles close to the ground and is surrounded by an orchard, probably as in the early days. The rear view is shown here.

PLATE 46

Blauvelt—Lane House
Haverstraw Road, New City

The stone lintels and the dressed stonework of the front of the house are evidences that this is not so old as the other Blauvelt houses, although otherwise it is similar in style. It was probably erected in the third quarter of the eighteenth century. The land was purchased by Jacob A. Blauvelt of Tappan in 1741; the first known occupant of the house was Jacob Blauvelt, born 1789, and his sisters. Notice the panelling of the deep door jamb. Its simple type is similar to the old solid shutters.

PLATE 47

Blauvelt—Hogencamp House
Old Brewery Road, New City

This house was built at two different times. The line in the masonry shows that the first unit was less than three-fourths the present depth. The original house undoubtedly resembled the other narrow houses of the vicinity. At some period it was deepened, the line of the chimney changed, and the steep gable roof enlarged to cover the entire house. As it is very similar to the Lent house at Orangeburg (plate 53), built in 1752, the alteration may have been made about this time, but unlike the Lent house the roof has no overhang. The small porch is later. The rear view is shown here.

PLATE 48

House of Daniel De Clark; the De Wint House
Tappan

The house is generally known as the house of Johannes De Wint, probably because he was Washington's host on several occasions. It is the oldest house still standing in Rockland County and was built by Daniel De Clark, leader of the Tappan settlement. The date of its erection, 1700, is worked in brickwork in large lettering across the front (the "0" can be seen in the plate). It is built of sandstone cut in a local quarry and of brick brought from Holland. The gable roof is even steeper than that on the Mill Island Schenck house (plate 13) and resembles the earliest houses in New Netherland. Daniel De Clark probably drew his inspiration directly from the old country where he was born but the curving overhang shows the influence of his neighbors in this country. Notice the spy hole high up in the east gable end; it was of use when Indians were lurking around.

240

PLATE 49

De Pew House
Haverstraw Road, New City

This house was built at two different times. The west unit, consisting of one room, was the original house. As William Campbell of Haverstraw was the owner from 1713 to 1741 and as the house is of an early type of construction, it is possible that he erected it; otherwise it was built in the 1740s by Peter Du Puw according to an early style. The west unit (shown in the photograph) is similar but later in period and includes the hallway down the center of the house. It is said to have been built about 1780, probably by the son Abraham De Pew. The photograph shows the character of the undressed stonework used so extensively for the rear and side walls even at a late period. Notice the careful cornering with the use of dressed stones. The slope of the roof is more moderate than was customary. The curving overhang of the roof is seen on this type of house in Rockland County but is more common in Bergen County.

PLATE 50

House of Peter De Pew
near the Hackensack River, Orangeburg

This house was built between 1768 and 1778 by Peter De Pew, son of the Peter Du Puw who may have erected the house at New City (plate 49); it remained in the family until about 1856. Notice the character of the lintels and the fact that the chimneys are on different sides of the ridge pole. The house has recently undergone substantial restoration: the extension of the gambrel roof over the gable end, the two-paned window sashes, double door and porch are not original items.

PLATE 51

Haner—Ryder House
at the South End of Rockland Lake

This is considered the second oldest house in Rockland County. It was built shortly after 1700 and before 1713 when it was called the Haner house. It had passed into the possession of the Ryder family before 1800. There was an early German settlement in this vicinity and both the Haners and Ryders were of this nationality. The house is very primitive. Its stone walls are over twenty inches thick. The attic is reached by a ladder from the one room on the ground floor. The site for this early house was no doubt chosen because of the spring nearby and the protection afforded by the surrounding hills.

PLATE 52

Haring House
King's Highway, Tappan

This is a very beautiful example of the type of house built in the settled communities of Rockland County a few years before the Revolutionary War. Unfortunately its builder is unknown; the first known owner was John Haring in the 1870s. The front and rear walls of this house were built of dressed stone and the sides are of roughly cut stone. The high gambrel roof has a curving overhang of good proportions. The sloping dormers, although not original, are the early type; commencing at the break in the roofline, they form a continuation of the slope of the upper roof and thus they seem less like an excrescence and more like an integral part of the house. The Dutch are known for their successful mixture of architectural materials; to the stone of the walls and the wood of gable end and roof is added in this case the contrast of the brick lintels. The rear view is shown.

244

PLATE 53

House of Abram Lent
Road to Tappan, Orangeburg

This house was built in 1752 by or for Abram Lent and remained the home of his descendants until about 1918. It is an outstanding example of the steep, equilateral, gable roof over a house two full rooms in depth. The resulting proportions are effective, especially in combination with the curving overhang. The sloping dormers blend well, although of course they are modern additions. The house is not so wide as the average. In the case of the wing, variation is seen in the use of stone lintels and the absence of overhang. This is the rear view; there is a modern enclosed porch in front.

245

PLATE 54

House of Jeremias Mabie
Orangeburg Road, Nauraushaun

This house was built in the third quarter of the eighteenth century by Jeremias Mabie, who was of Huguenot descent, and it passed down in the female line. Notice the close-to-the-ground feeling of the house and the use of several different architectural materials. The stonework is carried very far up the gable end. Recent restoration has been very successful although the whiteness of the repointing and the French windows are slight detractions. The modern benches by the front door are suggestive of the old Dutch "stoep" where the family gathered in good weather

PLATE 55

Oblenis House
Sickeltown Road, West Nyack

Although the name suggests an Irish origin, the Oblenis family was Dutch and came to this country in the middle of the seventeenth century. This is a later family homestead, built only a few years before the Revolution, on a tract purchased in 1732. It is one of the very few frame houses built by the Dutch in Rockland County before the Revolution. Heavy chimney foundations, low ceilings, simple mantels, and the lack of architectural trim over the windows are points of difference from the otherwise similar, large, frame houses of the post-war era. Notice the unusual spaciousness of the house and the characteristic three chimneys. The various types of dormers are all modern alterations as well as the large enclosed porch in front.

PLATE 56

House of Isaac Perry, later Blauvelt's
Blue Hill Road, Nauraushaun

Isaac Perry built his house on his father's homestead shortly before the Revolution, first the present west frame wing, and then the present stone wing shown in the photograph. The middle section was torn down by his grandson David D. Blauvelt and rebuilt about 1830. The house remained in the family until 1906-09. This stone wing is typical of the pre-war period in its stonework and contrasting lintels. The heavy roof is of course modern; the original roof undoubtedly resembled that on the Goetschius-Tallman house at Tallman (plate 68) except that there is an overhang in both front and rear. The main house is built along pre-revolutionary lines although larger in size, but notice the dentil cornice; such details are characteristic minor differences of the late period in which it was erected.

248

PLATE 57

Sickels—Vanderbilt House
Sickeltown Road, Nauraushaun

William Sickels was the first known owner of the house and may have built it about 1768. As the house has the appearance of greater age it may have been erected earlier by his father-in-law Cornelius Cuyper. The house is built for the most part of very roughly cut stone of varying shapes and sizes, but notice the careful cornering. The wing had a gable roof probably without an overhang. The gambrel roof over the main house has a very deep overhang. A sparsity of windows is characteristic of early houses and of the rear rooms of later houses: in this instance there is only one window on either side of the rear door of the main house and no window next to the door in the wing. The frame wing on the road end belongs to a later period and the dormers are of course modern.

PLATE 58

House of Lambert Adriaensen Smidt (?)
Road to Orangeburg, Blauvelt

This house stands on that part of the Tappan Patent allotted to Lambert Adriaensen Smidt in the Division of 1721. Construction indicates that the house belongs to this early period. This, together with the fact that the house is an unusually large and well finished one such as only a prominent and wealthy member of the community would erect, leads to the belief that it was built by Lambert Adriaensen Smidt. The house is unusually spacious in both length and breadth for this early period in Rockland County. It is built of roughly cut stone and is covered by a gambrel roof of ample proportions with an overhang only in front. It is probable that originally the ground did not slope away so sharply in front; certainly the piazza running the length of the house is a modern addition and probably replaces a Dutch "stoep." The sun has unduly emphasized the modern gutter along the roof edge. Note the chimneys, one at the front and one at the rear. Later houses of this size have three or four.

PLATE 59

Smidt House (?)
Greenbush Road, Blauvelt

The land on which this house stands was allotted in the division of the Tappan Patent to Lambert Adriaensen Smidt, who is believed to have built a home on other property of his (plate 58). The house must have been erected shortly after the division as it belongs to the early eighteenth century. It is the average size house of the type covered by a gambrel roof. Notice the old windows with the twelve-paned upper sash and narrow lower sash. The square cornice along the front of the house is a later alteration and undoubtedly replaces the original curved overhang of the roof. Dormers, porch, and diamond-paned window sashes are also changes. This house and the one attributed to Lambert Adriaensen Smidt both depart from the almost invariable rule of early Rockland County Dutch houses in facing the south to get the maximum sunlight regardless of the direction of the road; both these houses face in an easterly direction toward the road.

PLATE 60

House of Major John Smith
Germond Road, Germonds

This is known as the house of Major John Smith, a Revolutionary figure and grandson of Lambert Adriaensen Smidt, reputed builder of a house further south (plate 58). It is probable that Major John purchased rather than erected the house, which may have been built as early as 1735, the date attributed to the barn on the property. The rear view is shown. It will be noticed that the doorway is not centrally placed; in later years houses invariably had a balanced composition. Interesting details are the double chimney and the inside smoke house.

PLATE 61

Barn of Major John Smith
Germond Road, Germonds

This barn was on the property of Major John Smith and stands a short distance back of his house (plate 60). It is said that the date 1735 could once be deciphered. It is the only old stone barn in the county still in existence. The marked difference in the proportions of its gambrel roof with those on the houses is no doubt due to the desire for more storage space for hay. Notice how comparatively close to the ground the roof extends.

PLATE 62

House of Cornelius Smith
Cherry Lane, Tallman

This stone house was built by Cornelius Smith on a farm purchased by him shortly after 1765, and remained in the family until about 1910. The house is more characteristic of an earlier period. It is built of very irregularly cut stones and has the old windows with twelve-paned upper sashes and narrow lower sashes. Houses of this late date generally have a balanced composition with the door flanked on either side by the same number of windows. The panelled double Dutch door and the early simple fanlight were removed after this photograph was taken. Originally there must have been a "stoep" in front. The sloping cellar hatch is as usual under the window by the front door. The wooden additions on either side of the stone house belong to the early nineteenth century.

PLATE 63

Sneden House
Sneden's Landing, Palisades

A group of Sneden houses still stand by the Landing on the Hudson River. To distinguish it from the others, this is known as the house of William Sneden, as he was the owner in the mid-nineteenth century. This is believed by some to be the mansion erected by William Merritt about 1700 and known as *Cheer Hall,* shown as a two story house and mentioned as "Corbett's old house" in Alexander's survey of 1719, bought by the Snedens before 1745, and in the state line survey of 1769 called "Sneydon's house, formerly Corbet's." The house has not the appearance of such great age and it is possible that it was rebuilt at some time. It is typically Dutch and does not suggest an English builder. Due to an abrupt slope of the land the river front is two stories in height. The stone lintels are characteristic of the pre-revolutionary period. The steep gambrel roof has no overhang. The exterior brickwork of the chimney, dormers and large porch are alterations.

PLATE 64

House of Harmanus Tallman
Germond Road, Germonds

The first known owner of this house was Harmanus Tallman, born 1737. It is probable that the wing was built before his occupancy but the earlier owners of the land are unknown. It is built of roughly cut stone and has a steep gable roof. The overhang in front has been recently greatly extended and propped by simple square supports, forming a deep porch which blends unusually well with the original architecture and emphasizes the close-to-the-earth feeling of the house. The main house was probably built by Harmanus Tallman about the time of the Revolution. The roof is carried up to an unusual height, the equivalent of almost three stories, thus following and emphasizing the lines of the original unit. The large window sashes, four small panes in breadth, the stone lintels and panelled door jamb are all characteristic of this period. The sunburst decoration over the front door was especially in vogue in the years following the war. Dormers and shutters are of course modern. The house has undergone a very successful restoration.

PLATE 65

Tallman House
Road to Valley Cottage, West Nyack

It is believed that this house was built a few years before the Revolution by a member of the Tallman family, on property bought from the Indians by Harman Tallman in 1687. It has been occupied by descendants until very recent years. Notice the difference in type of lintels in the wing and main part, the panelled jamb of the front door, and the small size of the windows in both units. It is probable that the main house once had overhanging eaves. The alternation of long and very short stones in the courses of the main house adds life to the masonry and is characteristic especially in Bergen County.

257

PLATE 66

Terneur—Hutton House
Sickeltown Road, West Nyack

This house was erected in two similar units. A stone records that the west section was built in 1731 by M. P. and S. T. They were probably tenants of Thomas Clark who sold the tract in 1732 to Hendrick Oblenis. The first known occupant was Hendrick Terneur (1734-1819), who bequeathed the property to his adopted son John Hutton. This Hendrick Terneur was a grandson of Hendrick Oblenis so it is probable that his parents, Jacobus Terneur and Jacomina Oblenis, lived here before him and built the east unit of the house shown in the photograph. The house is built of roughly dressed stone covered by a gable roof, having an overhang in front and extending in a long slope closer to the ground in the rear. Notice the old windows with twelve-paned upper sashes and narrow lower sashes. The main room of each unit has its separate outside door, thus eliminating any need of a hall, and the small rooms at the rear, originally bedrooms, open directly into the main rooms.

PLATE 67

*House of Jacob Vanderbilt
Road to Clarkstown, Germonds*

The first known owner of the house was Jacob Vanderbilt, born 1768, and it remained in his family until the 1850s. He probably inherited it from his grandfather Jacob Vanderbilt who came to this region about 1730. Construction of the house shows that it was built at about this date. Notice how far up the gable end the rough stonework is carried, the carefully laid stones at the corners, the small windows, and the steepness of the gambrel roof. Mud plastering, split laths and handwrought nails are other evidences of its early age. The lean-to and door porch are of course later alterations. The view shows the rear and west end.

PLATE 68

Zabriskie (?)—Goetschius—Tallman House
Cherry Lane, Tallman

The tract on which this house stands was bought by John Zabriskie in 1724 and sold by his grandson John Goetschius in 1797 to John Tallman, whose descendants are still in possession. None of the early owners seem to have lived here, so it is probable that the house was erected by some tenant of the Zabriskies in the second quarter of the eighteenth century. The house was built in an early style and consists of two main rooms each with its separate outside door. It is built of a slaty rubble and the front wall is plastered; the moderately steep roof overhangs in front; the small-sized window openings with the narrow lower sash and an early form of fanlight are to be noted. The row of dormers is of course modern. Like the majority of Dutch houses, especially in Rockland County, it was built to face the south in order to get the maximum of sunlight, regardless of the direction of the road, which in this case is at the end.

PLATE 69

Unidentified House
Pomona Road, New City

Built of undressed stone and covered by a gable roof having a curving overhang in front and a long low slope in the rear, it greatly resembles the Terneur-Hutton house at West Nyack (plate 66), the first unit of which was built in 1731. This house was probably erected in the middle of the eighteenth century but its builder is unknown.

BERGEN AND HUDSON COUNTIES

WESTERVELT HOUSE, TENAFLY

BERGEN (INCLUDING HUDSON) COUNTY

THE west shore of the Hudson River opposite Manhattan Island soon attracted the attention of the Dutch. In 1630 Michael Pauw acquired two large tracts at Hoboken and Ahasimus with the intention of erecting the patroonship of Pavonia, but he was obliged to give them up in three years as he did not comply with the conditions of settlement. The first buildings on the west shore were erected in 1633 by the West India Company at Paulus Hook, Communipaw and Ahasimus; various grants and leases were made, but the small settlements were wiped out by the Indian massacre of 1643, brought on by Director Kieft's stupidity. This continued to be the fate of the venturesome settlers until the land east of the Hackensack River was purchased from the Indians for a second time in 1658 and the inhabitants were required by Stuyvesant's order to concentrate within the palisaded villages of Communipaw and Bergen. The latter village, founded in 1660, was located in the heart of the present Jersey City and became the township and county seat. A Reformed Church was organized here in 1662 and was the first Dutch church in the Province of New Jersey. No pre-revolutionary houses remain in the present Hudson County, in which these settlements were situated.

New Netherland had become English territory before any building was commenced in the present Bergen County. Various tracts were granted by Carteret and the later Proprietors to speculators and prospective settlers, as individuals or in groups, the earliest in 1668 and 1669. William Sandford of Barbadoes was granted in 1668 the neck on which Rutherford stands and divided it with Nathaniel Kingsland, also of Barbadoes, who settled here. Hackensack stands on the tract granted in 1668 to Capt. John Berry, who soon sold parcels to many settlers including the Westervelts, Ackermans, Terheuns and Kipps. In 1677 David Demarest purchased a large tract from the Indians near River Edge and Schraalenburg, where he immediately started a French colony, which the Duries and Loziers joined. The region south to the juncture of the Overpeck and the Hackensack was sold by the Indians in 1676 and confirmed by the Proprietors in 1682 to a group of Dutchmen, including Laurence Andriessen Van Buskirk and Hendrick Jorisse Brinkerhof, both of whom removed here. The land near the state border was settled under the Tappan grant of 1682 and the Lockhart patent of 1687 by the Harings and others. A tract east of Paterson was granted in 1687 to a group including several of the Garretsons, who located here later. Roeloff Lubberts Westervelt in 1695 purchased two tracts near Tenafly, where he made his home. Albert Zabriskie obtained two large grants near Paramus, and in 1708 sold a large part at Saddle River to Thomas

Van Buskirk who settled here, and the Zabriskie sons made their homes on other portions. After passing through several hands, the lands around Closter were purchased in 1710 by Resolvert and Barent Nagel, who immediately located here. A large part of the Kinderkamack lands, patented to the Demarests, was purchased by the Cooper family who removed here. Among the early settlers in the western part of the county were the Garretsons, Van Alens, Van Houtens, Hoppers, Ackermans and Van Voorhees.

Thus the county was gradually opened up. It is probable that the earliest settlement of any size was located at the present Ridgefield Park, between Overpeck Creek and Hackensack River. This was the site of Old Hackensack, the home of the Brinkerhofs and other Dutch families. A Dutch Church was organized at Hackensack in 1686 and at Schraalenburgh to the north in 1724. The Ponds Church at the western end of the county was in existence as early as 1710 and the Paramus Church in 1725.

The Province of East Jersey was divided into counties in 1682. The original Bergen County comprised the strip of land along the Hudson River from the end of the peninsula near Staten Island north to the New York border and west only as far as the Hackensack River, which was then the division line with Essex County. In 1709/10 Bergen County was greatly enlarged to include all the territory west as far as the Passaic and Pequannock Rivers. A large part of this was eventually taken from it in 1837 for the formation of Passaic County, and in 1840 the original Town of Bergen with other land at the south end was organized into Hudson County. The northern part of the county was claimed by the Province of New York and the boundary line was not definitely settled until 1772.

The so-called Dutch Colonial style reached the height of its development in Bergen County. Until after the Revolution the great majority of houses were built of red sandstone blocks, often quarried on the property, cut, roughly dressed and laid by the slaves. The 75 acre bounty offered by the Proprietors for each slave brought into the county resulted in abundant cheap labor and the consequent extensive use of the local sandstone quarries in the construction of the houses. The gambrel roof with a short, shallow upper slope and a very long, sweeping lower slope was developed in Bergen County where it became very popular. Eaves overhanging the front and rear walls by several feet added to the sweeping quality of the roofline, whether gable or gambrel, and their curved slope contributed to the beautiful effect. The roofline is the dominating feature in these houses. The next point of interest is the variety of building materials in each house—stone, shingle and clapboarding, also sometimes brick and iron.

In Bergen County we find a balanced architectural composition more frequently than elsewhere. In early days this was an unplanned development, a natural result of the growth of the family in numbers and wealth: the original home became too small or too humble, a larger one was added adjoining it and the former became the kitchen and slave wing; later a wing was added on the other side for the grandparents' home. This balanced three unit composition was only popular in Bergen County. There are very few examples of these houses in which all three units were built before the Revolution; in the majority of cases the newer wing was built in the style popular around the opening of the nineteenth century.

An intensive field survey of Bergen County was made with the help of Erskine's Revolutionary surveys, the old roads were located and a surprisingly large number of old houses found. The discussion of early land grants in Harvey's *Genealogical History of Hudson and Bergen Counties* proved very useful. The ownership of the houses was determined with the aid of old residents and local historians, county histories and maps. The genealogical sketches were compiled from family Bibles and church records where no satisfactory publications were available. The author is especially indebted to Miss Saretta Demarest and Miss Mary A. Demarest for information concerning the Demarest family genealogy and landholdings. A few of the photographs in this section were taken in 1925 but the great majority in 1933. The various short articles on the Dutch architecture of Bergen County have been consulted, the most important being: *Colonial Building in New Jersey* by William N. Black, in the Architectural Record for January 1894, *Some Early Dutch Houses in New Jersey* by John T. Boyd, Jr., in the July, Aug., Sept., 1914 issues of the same periodical, *Farm Houses of New Netherland* by Aymar Embury II, in the White Pine Series of Architectural Monographs for December 1915, and *Early Dutch Houses of New Jersey* by Clifford C. Wendehack, in the same series, Vol. XI. Many differing views of the houses are reproduced in these articles, and also in the *250th Anniversary of the Founding of Bergen, 1910.*

HOUSES IN BERGEN (INCLUDING HUDSON) COUNTY

Achenbach House
Chestnut Ridge Road, Saddle River
PLATE 70

Hans Georg Achenbach emigrated from Saxony and settled on Zabriskie's New Paramus patent, locating on the eastern hill overlooking the Saddle River valley. Romance is connected with his name, for tradition states that he was a shepherd boy who eloped with his employer's daughter, and was therefore compelled to leave Germany. They are buried on a promontory on their hill farm overlooking the river. He was elected an elder of the Lutheran Church of Ramapo in 1770 and retired as senior elder in 1774. He or his son probably built the house; the high ceilings and carved woodwork of the main house testify to a date around 1790, but the wing may be older and pre-revolutionary. In 1876 the house was owned by a Mrs. Achenbach, and the property adjoining on the north was owned by Thomas Achenbach, undoubtedly descendants of the builder. About 1835 Mary Ann Achenbach married Thomas Terhune. They later inherited the house, which came to be known as the Terhune house. The present owner, E. Percy Smith, bought the property about twenty years ago from a land company.

Although the Achenbachs were of German origin, they settled in a Dutch locality and adopted their neighbors' style of building. The stones of the house are dressed and well cut and laid. The house has a neat and methodical feeling, a slightly different atmosphere from other similar houses, which may be attributed to the builder's German origin.

The house stands on the east side of the Chestnut Ridge Road, north of the road which climbs the hill from Saddle River village.

House of Abraham Ackerman, later Brinkerhoff's
184 Essex Street, Hackensack
PLATE 71

An interesting stone in the east end of this house (from which the ivy has been carefully trained away) bears the inscription: "A.A.M.: G.A.M.: D.A.M.: 1704"; followed by several symbols of husbandry and hieroglyphics, which may be good luck signs. Thus we know that the house was built by Abraham Ackerman (Acker Man) and his two eldest sons David and Gerrit, in the year 1704. The plan of the house conforms to the usual Dutch arrangement, a central hall flanked by rooms on either side. One of these rooms, the present dining room, is separated from the hall by a very thick wall; it is probable that the original house consisted of this dining room and the old west wing (which was torn down in 1865 and replaced then by the present frame wing). This part of the house may have been built as early as 1696: one of Abraham's children was baptized at Bergen in 1694 and the next child baptized at Hackensack in 1696, showing that he removed to Hackensack at this time. The house stands on property bought by Abraham Ackerman from Capt. John Berry, to whom it had been granted in 1668.

David[1] Akkerman emigrated from the Mayory in the Bosch (s'Hertogenbosch) in North Brabant with his wife Lysbet de Villiers, four sons and two daughters, and arrived in the ship *Fox* at New Amsterdam Aug. 31, 1662. He died within a year of his arrival, and the Orphanmasters soon called upon the widow to settle his small estate. She opened a little shop in her home in the Marketfield, New Amsterdam, where she sold provisions, shoes and beer, to support her young family. Their youngest child, Abraham[2] Ackerman, was born May 15, 1659 according to the legend on an old painting in the house, although recorded as aged six years on the passenger list of 1662. In 1682 he was living in Midwout, but soon removed to Bergen. On May 28, 1683 Abraham, born in Berlicum (five miles east of s'Hertogenbosch), living in Bergen, married Aeltye Van Laer, who was living in Bellfort; she was born April 15, 1666 at Kingston, daughter of Adrian Van Laer and Abigail Ver Planken. They lived in Bergen until about 1696, when they removed to their new lands in Hackensack. They had eight sons, David, Gerrit, Johannes (died young), Adrian, Johannes, Gellyn, Abraham, and Lawrens, and six daughters. The house was evidently inherited by the youngest son, Lawrence A.[3] Ackerman, born about 1706, married Oct. 27, 1727 Geesje Paulusse, bap. Dec. 2, 1709. In his will of 1770 he left his estate including his residence at New Barbadoes (the name given to the neck between the Hackensack and Saddle Rivers) to the two children of his only son Abraham, deceased, willing the old farm where he lived to the grandson Laurens. Laurens A.[5] Ackerman, bap. Sept. 2, 1759 at Schraalenburg, died in 1822, married about 1781 Sophie Lozier and had four sons and one daughter. On May 6, 1822, shortly after the death of their father, Laurens and Nicholas Ackerman gave a quit-claim deed to John L. and Henry L. Ackerman (all four being sons of Laurens A. Ackerman) for 90 acres along the public road to Saddle River including the old house. On Nov. 10, 1825 they sold this land and house to Albert Brinkerhoff.

Albert[5] Brinkerhoff (1763-1844), son of Jacob[4] Brinkerhoff, inherited the ancestral house and homestead at Old Hackensack (now Ridgefield Park) and eventually left it to his son Jacob (see plate 79). He bought the Ackerman house in Hackensack for his other son Albert, Jr., shortly after the latter's marriage. Albert⁶ Brinkerhoff, Jr. married Altia Hopper (1802-1885), whose grandmother, Cornelia Ackerman, was a descendant of the builder of the house. One of their children, Harriet B.⁷ Brinkerhoff (1841-1913), sold the house in 1899. Another of their children, Catharine Jane⁷ Brinkerhoff, b. 1831, married Gerret Cortelyou and lived in Flatbush. Their daughter Garetta Vanderveer Cortelyou married John S. Mabon, and they bought back the ancestral place July 31, 1906 from a Mrs. Montgomery. The present owners are their daughters, Miss Elizabeth Mabon and her sister Mrs. A. J. L'Heureaux.

The house is well known as a beautiful example of Dutch architecture. Note the long, sweeping curve of the gambrel roof. Over the doorway is a fanlight of the sunrise type. The old west wing of the house, now gone, was the old stone kitchen with stone floor, huge fireplace and Dutch oven, and slave quarters in the attic above. When Mrs. Cortelyou (born 1831) lived here as a child, the entire upstairs of the main house was open attic, where the big wool wheels and looms for weaving blankets were stored. The stairs were enclosed, with a door at the foot, to prevent any of the heat from ascending into the attic and being wasted. The family slept downstairs, the parents in the room behind the dining room. The present library was two bedrooms. The upstairs bedrooms were partitioned off one by one from the attic (their ceilings are of different heights), and dormers added one at a time. The road was much nearer the house in those days. During the seven years it was out of the family, the stoop was shortened, and the unsuitable heavy pillars were added. The house stands in a lawn a short distance from the street, and has an air of seclusion and quiet dignity, although in the heart of Hackensack near the railway station. Other views of the house may be seen in Black's article, p. 259, and in Boyd's article, pp. 34 and 42.

House of Johannes Ackerman, later Brinkerhoff's
formerly at 651 Polifly Road, Hasbrouck Heights
PLATE 72

The pre-revolutionary part of this house is the picturesque wing (torn down since this photograph was taken in 1925). A stone near the door of the wing was inscribed "H. x B. ACKn"; these initials have been ascribed to Hannes and Betje Ackerman. Johannes⁹ (or Hannes) Ackerman, bap. Nov. 15, 1696 at Hackensack, was the ninth child of Abraham Ackerman, the builder of the Hackensack house (plate 71). On May 5, 1720 he married Maria, daughter of Thomas Weeckvelt, and had four children: Maria, Abraham, Thomas, who died before his father, and Aeltje.

271

He married secondly on Feb. 28, 1728 Elizabeth, daughter of William Stegge (or Stagg), and had seven sons: William, David, Johannes, Gerrit, Petrus, Laurens, who died before his father, and Cornelis. Johannes Ackerman undoubtedly built this house about the time of his second marriage in 1728 and brought up his second family here. About the middle of the century he and most of his children removed to Paramus, where he was a resident at the time he made his will in 1759. Petrus is the only one of his children known to have remained in Hackensack, where he died in 1813.

The main part of the house, although of a pre-revolutionary character, was built shortly after 1800 by Jacob Brinkerhoff. This Jacob is not positively identified, but he may belong to the following line: George Brinkerhoff bought a farm of 200 acres in the borough of Woodridge, formerly Polifly. Henry and Jacob, two of his four sons, divided the farm equally. The latter, Jacob G. Brinkerhoff, b. 1772, married Margaret Bartholf, and had issue.

The house is south of Hackensack in a section formerly called Polifly. It stands on the west side of the Polifly Road, immediately north of its intersection with the new state highway. Since 1925 the old wing has been taken down, and the main house has been so completely altered and modernized with a solid row of dormers and other changes that it has lost all character. It is now the Stagg Produce Farm. The wing, although actually not built until about 1728, was a well-known example of the Dutch stone house of the early type: the straight slopes of its gable roof extended only to the line of the walls, and did not curve and overhang the walls as in the later development of Dutch houses. Another view can be seen in Wendehack's article, plate 22.

Ackerman—Naugle House
415 East Saddle River Road, Paramus, Ridgewood
PLATE 73

This house is supposed to have been built by an Ackerman, the dates 1692, 1701 and 1760 being variously ascribed to it. The first two dates should be considered in connection with the early half of the house. According to the Terhune family, it was built in 1692 by David T. Ackerman, but there was no member of the family with this name at this early period. Three of the sons of Abraham Ackerman, builder of the house in Hackensack (plate 71), settled at Paramus: David A.' was living here in 1742 and died here in 1760, Adrian A.' came between 1720 and 1723, and Johannes A.' about 1722 and died here in 1760. Many of their sons remained here at Paramus. The above David A.' Ackerman was born in 1684 and was therefore but eight years old in 1692 and seventeen years of age in 1701; he helped to build his father's house at Hackensack in 1704 and was still living there when he married

272

in 1707. He had removed to Paramus before his son David, Jr. married in 1742. In 1760 David A.[5] Ackerman willed his farm at Paramus to his son Gerrit; the latter in 1773 willed the old plantation whereon he dwelt to his son David (born about 1745), except for three acres on the old place to his son Cobus (or Jacobus) on the south side of the lot near the King's Road; Gerrit also willed land to his son Hannes on the west side of the Saddle River. It is probable that this is the branch of the Ackerman family who built and dwelt in this house. It stands on a tract which was granted to Jacob Albertse Zabriskie, and divided among his children, including his son-in-law John Ackerman. The latter was a son of the above David A.[5] Ackerman; at his death in 1751 without issue, he left his estate to his brothers and sisters. The property may have been acquired by the family in that manner. There is a tradition in the Naugle family that the house was built in 1760 by an Abram Ackerman. Presumably this refers to the later half of the house, but it was probably erected by some other member of the Ackerman family. The above three brothers all had sons named Abraham, but David's son Abraham lived at Tappan, Adrian's son Abraham lived at Schraalenburg, and Johannes' son Abraham lived at Paramus on the west side of the river.

The house is sometimes called the Carlock—Naugle house. It may have been owned by the Carlocks in the early nineteenth century. David Barent[6] Naugle, b. Aug. 24, 1803 at Closter, was a member of the extensive Naugle family around Closter; his grandfather John was the eldest son of Hendrick[5] Nagel (1718-1806) and his first wife Catharine Blauvelt (see plate 98). This David B. Naugle married Harriet Carlough (or Carlock) on Dec. 6, 1828 at Paramus. He made many land purchases in this locality over a period of years after 1835 and may have bought the house from his wife's relatives. At all events he was living in this house by 1861. "Old Dave" Naugle, as he was called, kept a hotel for many years in a house further south on the Paramus Road, a famous place for musters on "training days" and for political conventions; the social leaders of the day were frequent patrons at the dances in the ballroom; the hotel was still standing in 1896 but no longer exists. Sometime before David died in 1883 he moved his family down to this hotel to live but continued to own the house farther north. David and Harriet had eleven children, among them John D. Naugle, whose heirs sold the property in question out of the family about 1914. It is now owned by John Woodward and leased out.

The house has only two main rooms. The east half is said to have been built as early as 1692 and 1701. It belongs to this very early period, but if built by an Ackerman it was probably not in existence until some time after 1707. The architectural style, low ceiling, exposed beams, and simple mantel shelf in the east room are all characteristic of the very early eighteenth century. The date 1760 has been ascribed to the house and undoubtedly applies to the later west half. The west room has an early mantel, cupboard, and panelled walls typical of the middle of the century. The age of the house is not brought out by the photograph, due to the abundance and whiteness of the wood trim which the camera has overemphasized. This is a good example of the early one room type of house with neither hall nor stairway.

The house stands on the east side of the Saddle River Road, a few hundred feet north of the Paramus Road, which turns here and crosses the Saddle River to Paramus Church. This locality is the old settlement of Paramus, now included in the eastern part of the City of Ridgewood.

Ackerman—Van Emburgh House
Head of Paramus Road, Paramus, Ridgewood
PLATE 74

This house is also supposed to have been built by an Ackerman and its early history is likewise obscure. The above discussion of early Ackermans at Paramus can be considered here; the two houses are only a few hundred feet apart, and were probably both on the same tract originally. This house may stand on the three acres on the south side of David Ackerman's property near the King's Road, willed by him to his son Cobus in 1773. Here also there is a tradition that an Abraham Ackerman probably erected it. Albert Terhune, recently deceased, a former owner and local historian, believed it to have been built in 1701, and painted this date over the door. Paramus was being settled at about this time and the curve of the roofline does resemble that on the Ackerman house at Hackensack, built in 1704 (plate 71). But if it was erected by an Ackerman, the house probably dates from the second quarter of the eighteenth century. Another view of the house can be seen in Albee's article, p. 285. Here the house is stated to have been built about 1710 by Abram Hopper and to have been occupied by the Hoppers during the Revolution. The latter statement, at least, is incorrect for the house is marked illegibly on Watkins' map of 1778 as "Van dirkin . . . s" (?).

An Ackerman is believed to have sold the house to John Van Emburgh, who married Mary Terhune in 1811 at Paramus Church. He later sold the property to his brother Henry[6] Van Emburgh, b. July 13, 1801 at Paramus, son of Henry[5] Van Emburgh of Paramus and Polly Voorhees, a descendant of Dr. Gysbert[1] Van Imbroch, who had emigrated to this country by 1653 and married Rachel De La Montagne. Henry Van Emburgh, Jr., married Margaret Demarest. The house was inherited by their son Jacob Demarest[7] Van Emburgh, b. July 12, 1822 at Paramus. He married Maria Jane Bogert and they conveyed the property Aug. 7, 1781 to

Albert D. Terhune who had married their daughter Sarah Jane. Mr. Terhune sold it June 2, 1924 to the present owner Peter Zigmunt.

The house stands on the north side of the Paramus Road, at the turn, and at the head of the road's descent to Saddle River and the church. This locality was known as Paramus, and is now a part of the City of Ridgewood.

House of Abram Ackerman; Washington's Headquarters
East Saddle River Road, Saddle River
PLATE 75

This house was built by Abraham Ackerman, the wing in 1750 or 1760 and the main part in 1781, according to descendants. Gerrit³ Ackerman, born in Bergen and baptized May 3, 1685 in New York City, was the second son of Abraham Ackerman, builder of the house at Hackensack in 1704 (plate 71). On Oct. 4, 1712 at Hackensack he married Jannetje Alberts Van Voorhis, and had six children all baptized at Hackensack. He later removed to Saddle River, where he died in 1758. He willed the farm on which he lived to his son Albert (their house has been torn down within the memory of people living), and 100 acres on the east side of the Saddle River to his elder son Abram.

Abram⁴ Ackerman, bap. Jan. 22, 1716 at Hackensack, was a bachelor of 40 odd at the time of his father's death, and probably built this small house for himself at about this date (1758). On Oct. 26, 1764* he rather unexpectedly married. His wife Marytye Hopper* had first married Nov. 23, 1755* Andries Hopper, who died Aug. 22, 1760* after they had had three children.* (A family record, quoted in Viele's *Ackerman Genealogy MS*, states her maiden name to have been Zabriskie, but she is called Marytye Hopper in the Bible records from which the above dates are taken). By her second marriage to Abram Ackerman, she also had three children, Antye (1765-1788*), Weentje (1773-1799*), and Gerrit. Marytye died March 5, 1781,* and was followed by her husband Oct. 25, 1789.* Having married, and acquired a family of his wife's as well as one of his own, the house became too small, so Abram built the main part of the house in 1781 as soon as war disturbances were over.

During the Revolution the patriot army encamped on the grounds by the river, and bread for the soldiers was baked in the old Dutch oven connected with a detached building, which was the servants' (slaves?) quarters. The house (which consisted then of the present small wing only) held six children, but had room for Washington also! It was his headquarters for a time, and is marked thus on a map of 1876. Abram was a miller as well as a farmer (Erskine's map marks the place Abram Ackerman and Watkins' map Ackerman's Mills). The mill was operated until recently.

275

---

* Taken from family Bible.

Abram's only son Gerrit A.[5] Ackerman, b. May 25, 1769* in the old house, d. Nov. 1, 1855,* married June 27, 1790* Charity Hopper, b. April 1, 1763.* Of their five sons and four daughters, all born in the homestead, Charity Ann[6] Ackerman, b. Jan. 12, 1819, inherited the house. She married Henry Achenbach and died in the 1890's. The house was sold in 1921 by the Achenbach estate to Charles Scott, whose family owned it until about 1935.

The Scotts were very interested in the house, and carefully restored without marring it. The pre-revolutionary wing is now a modern kitchen; the main part of the house contains unusually beautiful examples of woodwork of a post-revolutionary character. The wing is built of roughly cut stone covered by a fairly steep, gable roof. The main house is conservatively built in typical eighteenth century style; it is of dressed stone covered by a gambrel roof with an overhang. The road formerly ran between the house and the river, as is shown in the photograph (taken in 1925), but now takes a wide turn around the south and east sides of the house. It stands a short distance north of the village of Saddle River.

Alyea—Outwater House
445 River Road, Fairlawn
PLATE 76

The early ownership of this house is not known. It is shown (but the owner not named) on Erskine's Revolutionary map. A marker has been erected by the Daughters of the Revolution to the effect that the house (only the wing then existed) was the headquarters of Major Henry Lee, better known as Light Horse Harry, in the fall of 1780 when guarding the approach to Lafayette's camp at the Goffle. Lee's occupancy must have been for a very short period, as he was ordered south to join the Southern Army in October of that year.

Early in the nineteenth century the house was owned by Albert Alyea. He and his wife Sophia Bush had a daughter Eliza Alyea, born Aug. 30, 1821,* married Sept. 14, 1842 Peter R.[6] Outwater of Rutherford, b. July 12, 1814 at Moonachie, son of Richard[5] Outwater, who built the stone house in Rutherford still standing, and a descendant of Thomas Fransen[2] (Oudewater), who in 1717 built the stone house at Moonachie (now destroyed), a son of Franz Jacobsen[1] who emigrated from Oudewater and settled at Albany by 1657. After his marriage to Eliza Alyea, Peter Outwater bought the house at Wagaraw from his father-in-law, and settled here. He died Dec. 4, 1871; his widow survived him many years and died Aug. 25, 1906. They had three children, Albert, Richard and Catharine. The two sons inherited the property jointly, Albert receiving the portion on which the house stands. Albert

276

---

* Taken from family Bible.

Alyea[7] Outwater, b. June 29, 1845, d. Feb. 26, 1909, left the house to his widow, Sarah Elizabeth Oldis, for life. In 1927 it was sold by the A. A. Outwater estate. The present owner is Stanley Mortlock.

The primitive stonework, gable roof, and small windows of the wing are very early eighteenth century in style. The main house is post-revolutionary. The character of the house has been spoiled unfortunately, the wing by the modern glass door, and the main house by the large screened porch; the interior has been completely altered.

The house faces south toward the extreme northern bend of the Passaic River above Paterson. The locality was formerly known as the Wagaraw, and until recently the present River Road was called the Wagaraw Road. The house stands on the north side of the River Road, between Paterson and Lincoln Avenues, in the southwestern corner of Bergen County.

House of Hendrick Banta
Pascack Road, Woodcliff Lake
PLATE 77

Hendrick's ancestor, Epke Jacobse[1] Banta, emigrated in 1659 in the ship *De Trouw* from Harlingen in Friesland, with his wife and children; he settled at Flushing where he was an innkeeper, then at Bergen and later near Hackensack. His grandson Hendrick[3] Banta lived at Paramus and later on a farm in the English Neighborhood (now Ridgefield); his or his brother's stone farmhouse is still standing here (but greatly altered into a garage) at 1184 Edgewater Avenue, on the bank of the Overpeck Creek; in his will of 1766 he stated he had already provided for his son John. John[4] Banta, b. Oct. 6, 1723 at Paramus, bap. Dec. 1st at Hackensack, married at Schraalenburgh Dec. 18, 1747 Margrietje, b. Feb. 11, 1729, daughter of John Durie of Schraalenburgh (see plate 86), and had four children, Henry, John, Agnes and Jacob. After the birth of his eldest son, he removed from the English Neighborhood to Pascack. He was a very religious man, deacon of the nearby Paramus Church in 1756, elder, and delegate to the Classis in 1790; he died Dec. 10, 1806. It is possible that John Banta built the house when he removed to Pascack in 1750, but it is unlikely that he had given his house to his young son before the Revolution (Erskine's map marks the house Henry Banta's).

Hendrick J.[5] Banta, b. May 27, 1749 and bap. June 18th at Hackensack, d. Feb. 15, 1803, leaving 500 acres to his sons; he married Margaret Demarest, b. July 8, 1748, d. March 24, 1802, and had three daughters and five sons: John and Garret of Washington Twp., Jacob, Henry H. and Theunis of Hackensack. The third son, Jacob Banta, b. July 6, 1781, d. Oct. 7, 1859, married Margaret Eckerson, and lived on his father's homestead. His daughter Rachel, b. July 19, 1822, married James I. Demarest, and lived on the Pascack homestead all her life (the house is marked James I. Demarest on a map of 1876). It passed through several hands, and has been owned since about 1920 by Mrs. Robert Muirhead.

This locality was formerly known as Pascack; the old Pascack Church is on the same road a short distance northwards. The countryside has been greatly changed by the damming up of the Pascack River to form a considerable lake, and the historic name of the place has been changed to Woodcliff Lake and Park Ridge. The house stands on the east side of Pascack Road, half-way between Werimus Lane and Woodcliff Avenue.

The roughly dressed stone of the south front, the fairly low ceilings and steep gambrel roof are pre-revolutionary in style, although the feeling of age has been destroyed by the long new windows and the very heavy roof.

House of Jan Berdan; the Vanderbeck Tavern
formerly on Camden Street, Hackensack

On June 9, 1708 Jan Berdan purchased all the tract between Isaac Van Giesen's north line and the King's road (Passaic Street), extending from the Hackensack River to the Saddle River. His father Jan[1] Baerdan was a Huguenot, who fled to this country with his wife and only son Jan. He settled at Flatlands on Long Island, where he plied his trade as a weaver. After the death of his first wife, he married again and had two daughters. His only son Jan[2] Berdan, Jr. married at Flatbush May 20, 1693 Eva Van Siclen and had eleven or twelve children. After the birth of their eldest child Marretje in 1694, they removed to Hackensack where their second child Jan was born in 1695. It was not until 1717 (according to the cornerstone) that he built his permanent home in Hackensack on his purchase of 1708. The house was surrounded by its fields, and approached from the main road by a private lane, now Camden Street. After the death of his first wife, Jan married secondly at Hackensack Nov. 6, 1733 Vrouwtjen Van Dien, widow, nee Verway. He was Justice of the Peace for Bergen County for many years. It is not known who inherited his house; it may have been his eldest son Jan, b. 1695, who married his neighbor Christyntjen Van Giesen in 1738.

After enlarging the property about 1822-33, Isaac Vanderbeck established here the Hackensack Tavern, noted far and wide, and a popular resort for forty years. At a still later date the house was used as a private classical and mathematical school. It was destroyed in 1921. This house is not to be confused with the Vanderbeek homestead, which stood nearby until recently (see infra).

A Berdan house built in 1762 is photographed in Boyd's article, page 45. It was a large two story house built of dressed stone, with a shingled side, and had a gambrel roof with no overhang. It stood on Main Street in Hackensack. Further than this nothing is known of the house. It is not mentioned (by this name) in either Ackerman's or Bird's *Recollections*.

House of Isaac Bogert
Darlington Road, north of Campgaw, Hohokus Township

Erskine did not survey this road during the Revolution, but the house was probably built shortly before the war; it is known as the Isaac Bogert homestead. On July 24, 1733 John Bogert bought some land in northwestern Bergen County which he divided equally between his brothers Stephen and Isaac Bogert. Before 1736 the latter exchanged the property for Peter Van Alen's lands at Campgaw. The land in northwestern Bergen County was subject to many land disputes and conflicting claims. Franconier, one of the original proprietors, sold to Valleau and Stout in 1742, and 1752 they sold to Magdelene Valleau, nee Franconier; she released her interest in the 42,000 acre tract for a deed from the New Jersey Proprietors for 900 acres at Campgaw, which she later sold to several settlers including Isaac Bogert. He came to this region in the Yaupough Valley about 1760, and built (probably on one of these tracts) the house later owned by Henry Vandenhoff in 1876. The last Bogert owner was an Isaac Bogert, probably a son or grandson of the builder. The present owner, H. B. Hand, has remodelled the house into an attractive residence; the lines have not been altered but no clearly defined pre-revolutionary or post-revolutionary character remains. The house is in three sections; the oldest unit is in the center and is built of rough stone, has fairly low ceilings and old windows; the east wing is built of whitewashed stone; the west wing is modern; all sections are covered by broad gable roofs. The house stands on the south end of Darlington Road on its east side, near the intersection with Pulis Avenue, which leads to Campgaw village over a mile to the south.

Brickman (?)—Ackerson House
Island Road, north of Ramsey
PLATE 78

The old Island Road wandered by many indirect byways from Paramus to Suffern; its course has been straightened and altered so radically that it is impossible to compare the Revolutionary and late nineteenth century roads with any degree of accuracy. A map made in 1778 by Watkins, a surveyor under Erskine, shows a house marked Brickman's on the east side of a turn of the road in this general locality. The apostrophe suggests that Brickman's was a tavern. As the existing house stands on the east side of a turn in the present Island Road and, by tradition, was used as a tavern during the Revolution, this house may very well have been Brickman's. In the second half of the eighteenth century, a German family named Brueckman attended the nearby Lutheran Church of Ramapo: Heinrich Brueckman resigned as elder of the church in 1770 but continued to act as clerk and assistant overseer of the accounts and church book. He and Jacob Brueckman with their wives (both named Catharine) acted as sponsors for the children of Ludwig and Coa Brueckman, and of Reinhard and Wilhelmina Brueckman.

The first known owners of the house are Abraham Van Horn and wife who sold the property in 1855. As several Van Horns came to this locality in the mid-nineteenth century, the house may not have been a Van Horn residence for any length of time. David P. Ackerson bought the property from the Van Horns on Mar. 23, 1855, and settled here with his wife Margaret and infant baby Charles. Shortly before his death he deeded the property to his young son Charles on Oct. 15, 1866 (recorded 1874), excepting therefrom the west half of his dwelling house for his wife's use as long as she should live or until she remarried. On May 20, 1893 Charles D. Ackerson deeded the property to his son-in-law Walter Vanderbeek, who sold it out of the family to Albert B. Hague on July 19, 1897. After changing hands numerous times, the present owner, Rudolph Schweizer, Jr., bought it about 1925.

The house is undoubtedly of early date. It is built of undressed and very irregular stone, almost a rubble, laid with a combination of clay, chopped straw and hogs' hair (still to be seen and analyzed in the cellar). The ceilings are low, with very large exposed beams; one of these is cracked, and the story goes that it gave way under the weight of the grain stored in the attic, so that a blacksmith had to be sent for to rivet an iron plate to the beam. There was formerly a barn across the road with the date 1747 on a beam; it is probable that the house was built about this time, although the plan of the house is typical of the very early part of the century. There is no hall; two large rooms adjoin each other, each with its outside door, and a small room opens out from each room at the rear. The worn stone sill bears mute evidence to the use of the west room as inn and taproom. It is here that Aaron Burr is supposed to have stopped for liquid courage on his way from Sufferns to Hohokus to see Theodosia. The east rooms and a large wing (torn down by the Ackersons) formed the family residence. At the end of the nineteenth century the upper floor under the gambrel roof was still attic, reached by a ladder and trap door; there are as yet no dormers to break the roofline. The photograph unfortunately seems to emphasize the good condition in which the house is kept rather than its age. The house is over one mile north of Ramsey, on the east side of a turn in the Island Road to Mahwah, and south of its intersection with the new state highway.

House of Hendrick Brinkerhof, later Demarest's

493 Teaneck Road, Teaneck

PLATE 79

The ancestor of the family, Joris Dircksen[1] Brinkerhof, emigrated from the Province of Drenthe about 1638, settling at Staten Island and later in Brooklyn. One of his sons was Hendrick Jorisse[2] Brinkerhof, who founded the New Jersey branch of the family. He built at Old Hackensack (now Ridgefield Park) a house which was lived in by five generations of the family (Hendrick Jorisse,[2] Jacobus,[3] b. 1685, Jacob,[4] b. 1721, Albert,[5] b. 1763, and Jacob A.,[6] b. 1802), until finally sold by his descendant Jacob A.[6] Brinkerhoff in 1861. Part of it was demolished for the construction of the railway and the remainder burned down; a sketch of it can be seen in *The History of the Brinkerhoff Family*, p. 106.

Another Hendrick[4] Brinkerhof, son of Jacobus and grandson of the above Hendrick, was born Nov. 1, 1710, and married Elizabeth Kip on Nov. 19, 1731. He built this house at Teaneck about 1728-35 on property bought in 1682 by his grandfather and others. Hendrick and Elizabeth had five children baptized at Hackensack between 1733 and 1755: Jacobus H., Nickasi, Joris, Antje wife of Henry Verbryck, and Henry H., all of whom married and had issue. After the death of the youngest son Henry H.[5] Brinkerhof in 1826, a survey was made of the farm Oct. 10, 1827 and it was divided between the latter's child James H. Brinkerhof (born 1799, married 1820 Rachel Romeyn) and Jacob J. Brinkerhof (probably the Jacob born 1771, son of Henry's brother Joris). James H.[6] Brinkerhof received the parcel on which the house stood, and sold it Feb. 18, 1829 to Jasper Demarest.

Casparus or Jasper[5] Demarest lived in his grandfather's house on the Hackensack River opposite River Edge (plate 83). He bought the Brinkerhof house and gave it to his third son George as a wedding present. Joost or George C.[6] Demarest, b. May 17, 1808,* d. April 26, 1899,* married first April 18, 1830* Sarah Brinkerhoff, b. May 2, 1809,* d. Dec. 7, 1860,* married secondly Nov. 1, 1862 Margaret Holdrum, b. April 25, 1817, died without issue April 8, 1884. His son James Brinkerhoff[7] Demarest, b. Sept. 7, 1834, d. Oct. 18, 1913, married Dec. 21, 1865 Mary Elizabeth Vreeland, b. Sept. 17, 1839. His widow is the present owner. Thus the house was owned by the Brinkerhof family for one hundred years and has been owned by the Demarest family for another hundred years.

The house is a good example of Dutch architecture. Construction shows the main house and wing to have been erected at the same time. The inside walls are built of stone with no lathwork. A second story was added under the roof of the main house about 1800, with the use of rough machined lath. An unusual feature is the overhang of the roof, which extends around the gable end. The photograph was

---

* Taken from family Bible.

taken to emphasize this point and therefore does not do justice to the house as a whole. Other views may be seen in Boyd's article, pp. 36 and 37, and in Wendehack's article, plate 23. The rural surroundings of former days are shown in Albee's article, p. 291. Teaneck Road has always had a northerly direction, but the house faces the south with its end to the road, showing the persistence of the Dutch in orienting their homes to get the maximum of sunlight, regardless of the position of the road. The house stands on the east side of Teaneck Road, about midway between Cedar Lane and Fort Lee Pike.

House of Cornelis Cuyper (Cooper)
Kinderkamack Road, Oradell
PLATE 80

The great-grandfather of the builder was Claes Jansen[1] (Kuyper) van Purmarent, who emigrated to this country about 1655 and settled in 1664 at Ahasymus (part of Jersey City); he was a cooper and wheelwright. On Nov. 11, 1656 he married Annetje, daughter of Cornelis Van Vorst. She died a widow on Jan. 12, 1725. He had died Nov. 30, 1688, intestate, and all his lands were inherited by his eldest son Cornelius. Cornelius Clausen[2] Cuyper, bap. March 21, 1659, d. March 5, 1731 at Upper Nyack, was apprenticed as a waterman, and by the age of 21 was a captain freighting on the Hudson River. He settled at Upper Nyack on lands inherited from his father, became one of the leading men of Orange County, and a large landowner. By his wife Altie, daughter of Theunis Gysbertsen Bogaert of Wallabout, he had fifteen children. On Oct. 31, 1716 he bought from Jean Demarest, Sr. and Jr., a large tract at southern Kinderkamack, which he willed to his son Derick,[3] bap. Oct. 13, 1696 at Tappan, d. Oct. 2, 1753, who settled here near the Hackensack Water Co. works.

The latter's son Cornelis[4] Cuyper or Cooper, b. Sept. 27, 1724 at southern Kinderkamack, died about 1794, married March 7, 1751 Marritie, daughter of John Van Dien, and had nine children, of whom the sons were: Richard, Cornelius, John, Garret, Thomas and Peter. He was a tanner by trade, and his 70 acre farm and tannery were at Kinderkamack, on the main road north from Hackensack, three-quarters of a mile north of his parents' home. He built his home (the present wing) about the time of his marriage on land purchased by his father. During the Revolution the elevation at the rear of his home was often occupied by American soldiers (it is now called Soldier's Hill), and Washington is supposed to have been a welcome and frequent guest of the Coopers. Of his nine children, Cornelius C.[5] Cooper, b. April 8, 1756 at Kinderkamack, d. Oct. 3, 1832, married May 9, 1784 Neiltje Stoutenburgh of Rockland County; he was a saddle and harness maker at New Hempstead, Rockland Co. until 1806, when he returned and settled on part of the lands inherited by his father at southern Kinderkamack. Of his two sons, Cornelius C.[6] Cooper, Jr., b. March 17, 1788 at New Hempstead, married Ellen Mowerson and had five children; he was a cabinet maker and house carpenter by trade. He bought from his relatives his father's farm near New Milford (southern Kinderkamack) and later his grandfather's homestead at Kinderkamack, where he also resided. On retiring from business, he sold his New Jersey lands Feb. 10, 1847, and removed to New York City, where he died in 1850, and was buried at Schraalenburg with his father, grandfather, and great-grandfather. The house was bought by Isaac Zabriskie, and later by Isaac Mabie, who built the main part of the house. It has been owned since about 1931 by Upson Van Varick. The old house (the wing) has been altered with modern clapboarding, window sashes and dormers, but the rough stonework of the gable end, steep roof and overhang preserve the atmosphere of early days.

Thunise Cuyper (1737-1791), a younger brother of the builder of this house, built and lived farther south opposite New Milford, also on lands inherited from their father. This house (still standing at No. 610 Brookside Ave., Oradell) was sold about 1870 by his grandson Rev. John Cooper (1827-1887), son of Richard, after he had forsaken his blacksmith trade, and taken up the calling of minister at Nanuet. It is a frame house similar in type, but its proportions are ruined by a screened porch the size of the house.

Cornelius Cuyper's house is in the locality formerly called Kinderkamack, and stands on the west side of Kinderkamack Road above the present village of Oradell, and immediately south of Soldiers Hill Road. His brother Thunise Cuyper's house stands off the east side of Kinderkamack Road south of Oradell, on the north side of a brook, and across the river from New Milford.

House of William De Clark
Piermont Road, Closter
PLATE 81

This house was not built until about 1800-1805 by William De Clark, but it is included in this volume as an example of the persistence of eighteenth century styles for over a generation after the Revolution.

It stands on the northern part of the 1030 acre purchase of April 25, 1710 by Barent and Resolvert Nagel from the patentee Symes. The Naugles settled and built on this tract. Sarah[5] Naugle, daughter of William J. and granddaughter of John J. Nagel, was born April 4, 1749, possibly in the latter's house built by her great-grandfather Barent[2] Nagel (see plate 97). On Sept. 26, 1766 she married Daniel De Clark (or De Klerck), b. May 3, 1748, d. Dec. 27, 1834; she had died before him

(Jan. 28, 1810) and both are buried in the family cemetery on the Naugle tract. The De Clarks came from Tappan (plate 48), and Sarah removed to her husband's home in Rockland County where their children were born.

Their son William (or Billy) De Clark, b. April 11, 1781 at Clarkstown, probably received some of the Naugle tract from his mother or her relatives, as he returned to New Jersey and built here. He married Eliza Haring, b. Nov. 17, 1780, d. March 27, 1829. They had a son Daniel W. (1807-1849) and an older daughter who married Jacob Outwater about 1819. The Outwaters lived with her father, had a son born here about 1820, and built the frame kitchen wing about this time; they later sold the place. In 1867 the farm was bought by Capt. Elisha Ruckman, a retired ship-builder; he removed to Tappan in 1875. It became a part of the W. W. Phelps stock farm, and for the last thirty years has been owned by Mrs. Marie Breisacher.

The house stands on the east side of the Piermont Road (the old road to Tappan) south of a small brook, one mile north and east of Closter village.

House of David des Marest (Demarest)
at the French Cemetery, north of New Bridge
PLATE 82

This is the oldest house but one of the existing Bergen Co. houses. Built within twenty years after the first permanent settlement of New Jersey, it can be considered typical of the home of a well-to-do pioneer of this period. The roughly cut stone and the very steep slant of the roof are characteristic, also the plan of the interior, which consists of two adjoining rooms, each with its outside door. The west room has an early panelled mantel and over-mantel of unusual beauty.

David des Marest (De Maree) was born about 1620 at Beauchamp in Picardy, son of Jean. The members of his family were French Protestants, and removed for greater freedom in religion to Middleburg, Walcheren, on the Island of Zeeland. There he married July 24, 1643 at the Walloon Church, Marie, daughter of François Sohier of Nieppe in Hainault. In 1663 David emigrated with his wife and four children in the ship *Bontecoe*, and soon settled at Harlem in New Netherland. In 1677 he refused to support the Dutch Church there as he was a member of the French Church at New Amsterdam, and contributed to the funds of the latter. This was the immediate cause of his removal to New Jersey. On June 8, 1677 he bought of the Tappan Indians a tract two miles wide and six long on the Hackensack River. For some reason he did not patent this and other purchases immediately (and some lands not at all) with the result that others made claims and he eventually had to pay for it three times. He and his family immediately removed here in the spring of 1678 and lived in a temporary shelter, while they leveled off and built retaining walls for a plot of ground on which to erect their permanent stone home, built 1678-80. David's wife died here of smallpox shortly after Oct. 3, 1681. Other Huguenots soon settled in this region. They left the Dutch Church at Bergen which they had helped to build and organized a French Church here, which was occasionally supplied by a pastor from New York City; the foundation of the church building was to be seen until very recently in the cemetery adjoining the Demarest house; they gave up this church in 1696 in favor of the recently organized Dutch Church at Hackensack, and also generously contributed to the building of the latter church. In 1681, his house completed, David Des Marest built a mill and dam nearby on what came to be called French Kill. Between 1686 and 1689 he removed to his lands on the west side of the Hackensack River (then in Essex Co.), and built another mill there. On Aug. 26, 1689 he made his will, in which he declared himself as a yeoman and miller of the County of Essex, dividing his estate equally between his three surviving sons, except for a 100 acre legacy to his maid Anna Counk (free servants were very unusual). He died shortly before Oct. 16, 1693, when his heirs made a division of the property.

The eldest son Jean² des Marest, b. April 14, 1645 at Middleburg, d. 1719, received the land around New Bridge, but resided on a farm on the west side of the river (in his father's house?), probably on land bought by him and his father jointly. Jean married three times and had five sons and six daughters. He left his farm on the west side to his grandson David, son of David deceased, and his property on the east side at New Bridge to his son Peter. Peter's son by his first wife, Peter, Jr., b. 1715, later inherited it; he married Altie Van Horn in 1740, and they kept a tavern at New Bridge in 1768; the property was inherited by their only child Maria, b. 1741, who married Abraham Eli in 1764. This house has long since disappeared. By his second wife, Peter had a son called Squire Jacobus Demarest, b. 1735, who married Maria Smith in 1758, and built a house (now much modernized) inland from River Edge, near the Schraalenburgh Church.

The second son David² des Marest, Jr. (1652-1691) died before his father, and his young children were represented at the agreement of 1693 by their "cousin" Jean Durie, who (at that time or by 1696) married David's widow; David, Jr.'s heirs received the lands at "The Flats," near Oradell. The eldest son David settled near the present Dumont; so did Daniel, who built a house there in 1724, still standing but rebuilt on the old lines after a fire. Peter built a house at The Flats, later rebuilt in 1819 by a descendant, and recently removed to a new site nearby. Jacobus lived at Old Bridge (plate 83). David, Jr.'s youngest son Benjamin may have inherited the old house near the cemetery.

The third son Samuel³ des Marest, b. 1656 at Manheim on the Rhine, d. 1728, married 1678 Maria Dreuyn and had five sons and six daughters. In the division he received lands near Closter.

In the division of 1693, the great mill at Old Bridge (now River Edge) with the land adjoining was left jointly to David's heirs and to Samuel, and it was decided that two houses should be built for them equal in size to Jean's. Whether these were ever built or not, we do not know.

We have little further knowledge of David des Marest, Sr.'s house behind the French cemetery. It may have been considered a part of Jean's New Bridge tract, although the latter lived on the west side of the river, and probably inherited his father's house over there. It may have been on David, Jr.'s property which was north of Jean's, but if so, why should provision be made for a new house for his children? At all events, it was owned during the Revolution by a grandson of David, Jr.'s (Erskine's map).

David des Marest, Jr., born 1652 at Manheim on the Rhine, married at New York April 4, 1675 Rachel Cresson, born at Delft, whither her father Pierre Cresson had fled from Picardy. David died about 1691, and Rachel married secondly by 1696 Jean Durie, a widower and her neighbor (see plate 86); she married thirdly April 25, 1702 Roelof Vanderlinde, a widower, who died about 1708. David and Rachel had six sons and six daughters. Their youngest son, Benjamin³ De Maree, born about 1691, married Nov. 7, 1713 Elizabeth Pieterse De Groot, and had numerous children, including Beletje, born about 1718, married Oct. 12, 1739 Nicholas (or Claes) Romeyn, bap. Dec. 16, 1711 at Hackensack. They resided in the Demarest house by the cemetery and had nine children. The house has since passed through various hands: in 1876 it was owned by C. G. F. Heina, in 1912 by Mrs. E. Riemann; it is now owned by Henry Riemann, and rented to the Pochard Club, a group of artists.

The house stands on the east bank of the Hackensack River behind the old French Cemetery, some distance from the River Road, and is between Old Bridge (now River Edge) and New Bridge (now North Hackensack). Another view can be seen in Boyd's article, p. 33.

House of Jacobus Demarest
River Road, opposite River Edge
PLATE 83

Jacobus Demarest is the first known inhabitant of this house. A son of David² des Marest, Jr. (see plate 82), he was born at Hackensack, bap. Oct. 30, 1681 at Flatbush, died 1763. He married first March 8, 1707 Leah, born at the Bowery on the

Bay, a daughter of Peter De Groot, and had six children: David, Pieter, Rachel, Beletie, Maria and Benjamin. He married secondly Sept. 26, 1719 Margrietje Haring, bap. April 17, 1700, daughter of Cozine Haring of Old Tappan (plate 89), and had by her four children: Johannes, Lea, Gerret and Samuel. His eldest son by his second matrimonial venture was Johannes or John[4] Demarest, b. Aug. 2, 1720,* d. Feb. 5, 1783, married March 7, 1744 Rachel Zabriskie, who married secondly Aug. 1, 1788 Arent Schuyler; she died April 16, 1812. John and Rachel lived in this house and had four sons and one daughter, all of whom lived to great age, dying between the ages of 78 and 96 years.* The youngest child Casparus[5] or Jasper Demarest, b. April 6, 1766,* d. July 6, 1844,* married April 12, 1789* Rachel Vorhase, b. April 7, 1766,* d. Nov. 14, 1860.* They lived in this house, in which all their eight children were born. The property was bought about 1850 by John H. Zabriskie (who lived in the frame house opposite), and inhabited for a while by his father Henry Zabriskie. It was sold by the Zabriskie family about 1908. John A. Gurd bought the property about 1910 from a land company, and it is now owned by his widow.

The time of erection of this house is uncertain. The small wing (remodelled by the present owners with a modern bay window) is very similar in construction to the Demarest house by the cemetery. Possibly it was built for David des Marest, Jr.'s heirs under the agreement of 1693 (see above). If not, it was built by Jacobus[3] Demarest about the time of his first marriage (1707). The main part of the house is also of very early date, and was undoubtedly built by Jacobus[3] Demarest about the time of his second marriage (1719); it was in existence by 1720, as his son Johannes was born here in this year. This son lived here all his life.

Judging by their houses, the Demarest family possessed instinctive taste and a love of beauty. Although totally different in style from the house by the cemetery, this house also possesses great charm. It is built of roughly cut stone, plastered and whitewashed, and is covered by a curving gambrel roof. Below the overhang, the old windows are in uneven alignment with the door. Unfortunately the interior has been greatly changed; only the hall is untouched: a low chair rail is still to be seen, and also the steep enclosed stairway, with a door at its foot. The wing of the house has been marred by the addition of a large bay window, where formerly were a door and a small window. An outside Dutch oven has been demolished. A view of the house in rural surroundings, before the alteration of the wing, can be seen in Boyd's article, p. 39, and in Black's article, p. 254. The house stands on the west side of the River Road, at the head of the turn to the bridge over the Hackensack River at River Edge (formerly Old Bridge).

287

---

* Taken from family Bible.

House of Abram Demaree (Demarest)

Schraalenburgh Road, Closter

PLATE 84

Abram Demaree resided here at the time of the Revolution (Erskine's map), and probably built the house (the old wing) only a few years before. A son of David J. Demarest, and grandson of Jacobus Demarest, the builder of the house at Old Bridge (plate 83), Abram[5] was born Sept. 21, 1738 and baptized at Tappan; about 1763 he married Margrietje Demarest, probably his cousin, b. Dec. 9, 1744,* d. June 13, 1834,* daughter of Johannes Demarest and Rachel Zabriskie, of Old Bridge (plate 83). Abram lived at Old Bridge for many years, and later at Hackensack. Shortly before the Revolution he bought a large farm on the Schraalenburgh Road, on both sides of the Old Hook Road. Here, until his death July 9, 1824, he kept a general store of groceries, hardware and miscellaneous wares for farmers, and until 1809 he also kept a tavern. He was a man of note and held many town offices. Most of his five children may have died in infancy as he left all his property to his son David. David A.[6] Demaree, b. Aug. 28, 1764 at Old Bridge, d. Feb. 1, 1860 at the home of his daughter in Nyack, married in 1787 Charity Haring, and had an only child Margrietje who married John Perry. In 1809 David superintended the building of his father's new stone house, after demolishing the old one. This statement in Harvey undoubtedly applies to the main part of the house only, as the existing wing is probably pre-revolutionary. Old Fordie Demarce (in the country districts all old men were called Fordie and old women Otie—spelling approximate) owned all the land in the vicinity, including the farm opposite (bought by his father) on which a stone house still stands, which has been altered since it was owned by Cornelius Van Horn during the Revolution. In 1868 James Henry Stephens, from Colt's Neck in Monmouth Co., bought the house from David Demarest's estate, and commenced remodelling but died the same year. The Victorian fretwork was undoubtedly added by him. It descended to his two children. The present owner, F. M. Curtis, bought the property about 1922, and runs an antique shop here.

Notice the old fanlight over the door of the wing and the difference in stonework between the wing and the main house. Two doors lead from the main house into the wing; cut in the panelling of each door is a small square spy-light, through which the owner could survey his slaves. The stairs, mantels and other woodwork of the main house are beautifully carved.

The house stands on the west side of the Schraalenburgh Road immediately south of the present Oradell Reservoir, and over one mile west of Closter village. The country road adjoining the house on the south is the Old Hook Road, formerly an important thoroughfare leading to the Pascack settlements.

288

---

* Taken from family Bible.

Doremus House
formerly on Saddle River Road, west of Arcola
PLATE 85

This is known as the house of George Doremus for the reason that he lived here for many years in recent times. When it was built and by whom is not known. As the Doremus family from an early date owned a large tract in Saddle River Township in the vicinity of Red Mills (now Arcola), it seems probable that this was the original Doremus homestead. John Doremus, son of Joris, and grandson of Cornelis, b. Sept. 1, 1720, d. July 22, 1784, bought several hundred acres at Red Mills in 1740. On March 31, 1748 he married Maria Lutkins, whose home stood farther south on the Paramus Road towards Hackensack. During the Revolution he was taken prisoner by the British, and confined in the Sugar House in New York City. He contracted a disease there, of which he died soon after his return home. He had but two children, a daughter Marretje, and a son George. George Doremus, b. Aug. 28, 1754, occupied the homestead farm until he died in 1830; in 1805 he built nearby the present large stone house, with a gambrel roof, in the style of the period. In 1777 he married Anna, daughter of John Berdan, and left six children: Richard who settled at Lower Preakness and at Old Bridge, Albert who ran a stage from Hackensack, George, Jr., John B. who succeeded to the homestead and lived in his father's house until he retired from business in 1869 (later occupied by his son Jacob W., born 1835), Peter, and Maria wife of Gen. Andrew Hopper. The third son, George Doremus, Jr., might have been the occupant of the old house: he was born in 1794, married Harriet Zabriskie, was a blacksmith, tavernkeeper and farmer at Red Mills. His youngest brother, Peter Doremus, born 1801, married Jane Brinkerhoff, was a blacksmith at Red Mills until he removed to Jersey City late in life; of his six children one was George Doremus. The latter was probably the owner of the old house, rather than his Uncle George who could hardly have kept a tavern in such small quarters. The house has been demolished since the photograph was taken in 1925. It stood on the west bank of the Saddle River, between Arcola and Rochelle Park.

House of John Durie
Schraalenburgh Road, Haworth
PLATE 86

By tradition the house was in process of erection at the time of the Revolution. Jean Durie (Jan Du Rie or Durji) was a French Huguenot, supposed to have been born in Picardy and to have fled to Manheim with his parents, as did his cousin David des Marest (see plate 82). He was a blacksmith by trade, and tradition states that he worked for his passage to this country at the tender age of 15 years. Shortly after 1682 he joined the Demarest colony on the Hackensack River, and in 1686 with other Frenchmen he obtained a patent to lands on the west bank at Kinderkamack. In 1694 he is said to have received 233 acres west of Closter between the Tenakill and Hackensack Rivers (possibly from the heirs of David Demarest, Sr.?), and to have built his home here on the site of the present Durie house owned by Riker Turnure (or farther south, see below). He was a very prominent early settler. By his first wife, probably a French girl, he had four children: Jannetje, Margrite, Pieter, and Jan, all born and living at Hackensack according to their marriage records (this locality was a part of the jurisdiction of the Hackensack Church). In 1696 the French Church was abandoned, and the French colonists, including Jean and his wife Rachel Cresson (he had married secondly the widow of David des Marest, Jr., a few years previously), joined the newly organized Dutch Church at Hackensack. A stone marked "J. D. R. 1696" records his contribution to the building of this church. Jean appointed Samuel Demarest guardian of his minor children and died in or shortly after 1698.

His son Jan[2] Durie inherited his father's Closter lands, and married Aug. 30, 1718 Angenitie Jansen Bogart. There is said to be a date 1718 in the stone foundations of the present Durie house, now owned by Riker Turnure, so it is possible that Jan built the first house on this site at the time of his marriage, rather than his father. (This property was bought in 1870 by John L. Turnure from the Nicholas Durie estate; the present house was built by a member of the Durie family, and is a beautiful example of the development of the eighteenth century style in the early nineteenth century.) By 1752 he had married a second wife named Margaret. In his will of 1773 he divided his lands on the east side of the Schraalenburgh Road, stretching from Cornelius Van Horn on the north to Henry Herring on the south, between his two sons John and David and his grandson John, only son of his deceased son Peter. On Erskine's Revolutionary map are marked three houses, no doubt owned by these three heirs. The eldest son John,[3] bap. March 26, 1722, inherited the middle third of his father's lands; he married Wyntie Lydecker and had two sons Garret and John; the latter had many children, including John born 1778 and Garret born 1784. This Garret J.[5] Durie (1784-1837*) built the present house in 1812, near his grandfather's; it is now owned by Garret's great-grandson J. Westervelt Mount. Jan's second son Peter,[3] bap. Aug. 29, 1731, married Maria Post and died as a young man, leaving a young son John P.[4] Durie (1754-1819) who inherited the south third of his grandfather's lands; he married Maria Demarest about 1774 and had many sons, including a John born 1796. Jan's third son David[3], bap. Jan. 14, 1739, inherited the north third of his father's lands, on which stood

290

---

* Taken from family Bible.

the old home; on Nov. 16, 1762 he married Margrietje, daughter of his neighbor Cornelius Van Horn (who lived opposite the Abram Demaree house, plate 84), and had nine daughters and two sons, John born 1767, and Cornelius born 1784.

John D.[4] Durie, b. Sept. 8, 1767, died in 1842, married May 27, 1790 Beeletje Demarest. He is the first known owner of the house, and probably built it about the time of his marriage. Tradition states that the house was in course of erection during the Revolution to supersede the house of the emigrant Jean[1] Durie, which stood in a field nearby; that John was a fifteen-year-old boy living on the present Turnure property, and amused himself with a bean sling picking off the patriot army as it marched by, until he was found hidden in a tree and sent home. There seems no reason for David[3] Durie (who had inherited his father's home) to have built this one while his children were still young; and he probably did not own this property, unless he exchanged some of his lands at the settlement of their father's estate with his brother John P. Durie. The latter died in 1819 and so could not have built the house; for the John Durie who first owned it brought up his grandson and died shortly after his grandson's marriage in 1841, leaving all his property to him.

John D.[4] Durie had several children, of whom only one is said to have matured: Cornelia Durie, born about 1801, died in 1859. She had a son John Ackerman, Jr., b. Oct. 20, 1819,* and left him with her father when she married April 30, 1823 her neighbor Christian Van Horn (1801-1885), by whom she had thirteen children. John D. Durie brought up his grandson and heir, John Ackerman, Jr., b. Oct. 20, 1819*, d. Feb. 18, 1905,* m. June 3, 1841* Gertrude Westervelt, b. Oct. 12, 1819,* d. Oct. 9, 1904,* daughter of Daniel and Mary Westervelt of Tenafly (plate 110). They had one son who died in infancy and three daughters, including Sarah Louisa Ackerman, b. March 1, 1854,* d. May 7, 1884,* m. Jan. 13, 1876* John J. Bell of Oradell. Their daughter Cora Bell married J. Carlton Oren; she inherited the house from her grandfather John Ackerman, and is the present owner.

The exterior of the stone house is little changed, although the modern windows give it a vacant expression. The interior is completely altered. John Ackerman built the frame wing at the east end about 1854. The house stands on the east side of the Schraalenburgh Road, a short distance above the crossroad at Haworth village.

House of Peter Garretson
River Road, Fairlawn
PLATE 87

The house stands on a tract granted to nine proprietors in 1687, divided in 1692 and sold from time to time to various settlers, including four members of the Van Wagoner family. Gerrit Gerritse[1] emigrated from Wageningen on the Rhine

---

* Taken from family Bible.

on the *Faith* in 1660, and settled at Communipaw on New York Bay, where he became a minor official and died April 6, 1703. His son Gerrit[2] of Pembrepogh, a Judge of Bergen court, was the father of Peter Garritse[3] (Garretson, Garrison), b. Oct. 4, 1684, who married March 26, 1709 Vrowtje Hessels, and was probably married a second time to Antje Aeltse June 22, 1733. Peter bought (as above) a large tract of land on the Passaic River at Slooterdam, a portion of which is still in the hands of his descendants, and undoubtedly built this house (the old wing) which is mentioned in a deed of 1708. Some of the family adopted the name Van Wagoner to denote their place of origin, but Peter's descendants on this property retained the patronymic Garretson. He had four sons and six daughters: Gerrit of Iapogh, Elizabeth, Hessel of the Goffle, Peter, Johannes, Neesje, Frowtje, Lea, Helena, and Gerretje. One of his sons, Johannes or John P.[4] Garretson, b. Nov. 14, 1721, married Geertje Ryerse, lived and died on the homestead, and was succeeded by his youngest son Garret[5] Garretson, b. Feb. 18, 1780. By his wife Mary Romaine, he had three sons, of whom Ralph and Abram remained on the homestead (R. Garrison the owner in 1876). The house is now (1925) lived in by Mrs. F. Brocker, a descendant in the sixth generation from Peter, the builder.

The old part of the house is built of rubble and undressed stone. Originally it was probably covered by a steep gable roof. The present gambrel roof is too heavy for the house and its proportions are unusual for Bergen County. The main house is of stone and of later construction, and is completely hidden behind a large pillared porch. The house stands on the east bank of the Passaic River, above the main road (Broadway) into Paterson.

Garrison (?) House
Ramapo Valley Road, Hohokus Township
PLATE 88

The Ramapo valley was settled early in the eighteenth century in the vicinity of Ponds Church (south of the present Oakland), and farms were gradually cleared to the northwards. It is not known who built this house; Erskine's Revolutionary map marks a house on the west side of the road in this locality as Garret Garrison's. Possibly the course of the road has been changed and this is the house; it is certainly of an early type of construction, it is built of whitewashed rubble, with fairly small windows and a gable roof, and has been slightly altered. The house stands on the east side of a curve in the Valley Road at the foot of a hill, near the so-called Cleveland Bridge, and is three miles north of Yaw-paw (now Oakland). The present owner, Carl E. Koch, leases it to F. Crawford.

House of Cosyn Haring, later De Wolf's

near the state border, Old Tappan

PLATE 89

Pieter Jansen[1] emigrated early in the seventeenth century with his son Jan Pieterse[2] Haring, b. Dec. 26, 1633 at Hoorn in North Holland. On Whitsuntide 1662 at the Church in the Bouwery, Jan married Margrietje Cosyns, daughter of Cosyn Gerritszen and Vrouwtie. She was baptized May 5, 1641 at New Amsterdam, and at the age of thirteen years married April 19, 1654 Herman Theuniszen of Zell in Munsterlant and had a daughter bap. 1658. Jan and Margrietje lived on a 100 acre farm in the settlement called the Bouwery (which grew up around Gov. Stuyvesant's bouwery beyond the wall in New Amsterdam) and had four sons and three daughters. Under the leadership of Jan Pieterse Haring, a group of Bouwery villagers and a few others obtained a deed from the Tappan Indians March 17, 1681/2 for a large tract of land on the west side of the Hudson River, and obtained a patent from Governor Dongan of New York March 24, 1686/7. Settlement was commenced immediately, but without their leader, who died in December of 1683. He was succeeded in the leadership of the Tappan community by Daniel De Clark, who soon married the widow, Grietje Cosyns, and built the brick house at Tappan (plate 48). Two of the sons, Pieter and Cornelius Haring, later represented the county in the Provincial Legislature.

Although only a lad, Cosyn Janse[3] Haring, the second son, was mentioned as one of the Tappan patentees. In addition to his many purchases he eventually received over 900 acres in the various divisions of the patent, of which one-half was located at Old Tappan. Cosyn Haring, bap. March 31, 1669 at New York, died 1743 at Old Tappan, married Maria Gerrits Blauvelt, b. Jan. 28, 1668 at New York, a sister of two of the Tappan patentees (see plate 42); they had three sons and five daughters, of whom only John, Marretje (wife of Johannes Bogert), Margrietje (wife of Jacobus Demarest—plate 83), and Maria (wife of Cornelius Eckerson) survived their father and are mentioned in his will of 1733. Cosyn was an important member of the community, an organizer of the Tappan Church, assessor, and Captain of the militia. He built a large house befitting his station; the date of erection has been set as 1704, immediately after the first division of the patent.

This house, which is shown on a map of about 1713, was inherited by his only surviving son Jan Cosyn[4] Haring, b. Nov. 24, 1693 at Tappan, d. June 16, 1771, m. Jan. 15, 1718 Aeltye Van Dalsen, born at Haarlem in Holland. They had three sons who inherited or built the three adjoining Haring houses (plates 89, 90 and 91), and several daughters: Annetje, Elizabeth, Sarah and Rachel. The eldest son Johannes J.[5] Haring, b. July 1, 1720, d. March 17, 1798, lies buried at Tappan with his parents and his widow, Margaret Blauvelt, b. March 6, 1725, d. Dec. 13, 1800. Their son Abraham I.[6] Haring, b. Dec. 7, 1759, d. March 13, 1810,* m. Feb. 15, 1793 Maria Blauvelt, b. Dec. 22, 1772,* d. Feb. 5, 1838 aged 65 years.* Their son John A.[7] Haring, b. May 7, 1794,* d. March 18, 1874,* was the last of the name to own the old home, as he had but two daughters. On Nov. 29, 1813* he married his cousin Mariah Van Orden, b. Jan. 31, 1795,* d. March 5, 1875,* daughter of Peter S. Van Orden 1763-1846* and Margrietje Haring 1770-1812,* and granddaughter of neighbor Frederick Haring (plate 91). Their elder daughter Margaret died unmarried Sept. 30, 1848 at the age of 31*; their other child Catharine Haring, b. Jan. 28, 1829,* d. Dec. 28, 1886,* married Sept. 23, 1852* Martin De Wolfe, b. Dec. 29, 1829,* d. May 5, 1906.* Of their five children, the old homestead was inherited by the eldest: John Haring De Wolfe, b. Oct. 7, 1853,* d. July 6, 1927,* married Nov. 24, 1875* Maggie Cleveland, who survives and lives in the old house with her two children and her grandchildren. The present owner is her son, Charles De Wolf, b. June 9, 1880,* a direct descendant of the builder.

This is a good example of an early eighteenth century house of a well-to-do farmer; it consists of two large rooms each with its separate outside door (and no hall), the small rear rooms opening directly from the main rooms. The chimney breast is panelled, the overhead beams remain uncovered and one may still see the original double Dutch doors and hardware. The large garret remains undivided. The frame wing is mid-nineteenth century in style, and is ample enough to house the present large family. Since the photograph was taken in 1925, the roof has been repaired, and square pillar supports added, which blend in well with the house. The house presents the same rural aspect as it has from the time of its erection: set in the middle of a farm on a back country road, with geese in the front yard and an old well sweep nearby. It stands just south of the state border, on the east side of a former main road, leading from Old Tappan to the settlements at Sickeltown (now Nauraushaun) and Clarkstown (now West Nyack).

House of Gerrit Haring
Old Tappan Lane, Old Tappan
PLATE 90

Gerrit J.[5] Haring, second son of Jan Cosyn Haring (plate 89), undoubtedly felt the need of a house of his own when he married about 1751. He built on a part of his grandfather Cosyn's lands, but erected a less pretentious house, consisting of only two rooms, each with its separate outside door, and very little attic space for storage purposes. Gerrit J. Haring, b. April 25, 1725 in the old house (plate 89), married Cornelia Lent about 1751 and raised many children in his new home: Jan,

294

---

* Taken from family Bible.

Abraham, Aeltje, Petrus, Frederick, Kobus, Catherine and Elizabeth. The house was inherited by his son Frederick G.[6] Haring, b. Aug. 8, 1762, married April 6, 1786 Maria Smith. At his death in 1834, his large farm was divided into five portions, each with hill and meadowland, for his five daughters: Letty Zabriskie, Mrs. Gardenier, Margaret wife of Joost Demarest, Mary Eckerson, and Cornelia wife of Albert Bogart. The house stood on portion No. 1 allotted to Lettie Zabriskie and was probably sold by her. In 1876 it was owned by Mrs. Myers, and in 1912 by the W. W. Phelps estate. The present owner, Charles Angela of Greenwich, Conn., rents it to Oliver Pearson. The house nestles under a hill on the north side of Old Tappan Lane, about one mile south and west of the Haring-De Wolf house (plate 89) towards Rivervale.

House of Frederick Haring
Old Tappan Lane, Old Tappan
PLATE 91

Frederick[5] Haring, youngest son of Jan Cosyn Haring (plate 89), also branched out for himself. It is possible that he did not build until he had become a prominent man of the community, for his house is more spacious and larger than his brother's (plate 90). It was erected on his grandfather's lands before the Revolution, in which he served as First Lieutenant of Capt. Eckor's Company of Foot in the Orange Regiment of Militia. Frederick, b. Dec. 7, 1729, d. March 16, 1807, m. May 30, 1752 his cousin Rachel Haring, b. July 18, 1732, d. Aug. 27, 1795, daughter of Abraham Haring and Dirckje Tallman. They had ten children: Aaltye, Abram, Dirckie, Jan F. (1760-1836), Gerret (1762-1840), Harmanus, Rachel, Margrietje, Maria and Abraham. The house passed to the youngest child, Abraham F.[6] Haring, b. April 7, 1775, d. Aug. 14, 1858,* married March 17, 1797* Margaret Haring. Their son Frederick A.[7] Haring, b. Nov. 4, 1804,* married Nov. 13, 1824* Mary Ann Bogert of Closter, b. Jan. 6, 1808,* daughter of Albert Bogart and his first wife. The youngest son of their thirteen children was Garret F. Haring, b. March 10, 1854. He was the last Haring owner and gradually sold most of his acreage. The house was sold by his widow Elizabeth Eckerson about 1930 and has been recently bought by Mrs. Evelyn Wiseman of New York City for a summer home.

The photograph shows the house as it was in 1925. If examined, marks will be seen where a low wing formerly stood on the road end. In this wing and the room adjoining it in the main house lived the grandparents of the last Haring owner, leaving the remainder of the house to their son and his brood of thirteen children. The grandfather's clock by the door was too high for the ceiling, so a section of the

295

---

* Taken from family Bible.

floor was lowered beneath it. Three windows with old sashes now give light on the road end and dormers have also been added. The barn, now gone, stood west of the house, and a descendant informs me that it is the one described in Whittier's "Snowbound." The house stands on the north side of Old Tappan Lane, at the corner of the country road to Nauraushaun, midway between the homes of his brother (plate 90) and his father (plate 89).

House of Abraham Haring, later Moses Taylor's
Piermont Road, Rockleigh Borough
PLATE 92

This house was built about 1758 by Capt. Abraham A.[5] Haring. He was the third of this name, as he was the son of Abraham A. Haring (1709-1791) and Maria Demarest (1709-1786), and grandson of Abraham Haring (1681-1772). The latter is said to have lived on Pascack Road in Rockland Co. and was the youngest brother of Cosyn J. Haring of Old Tappan (plate 89); his (Abraham, Sr.'s) daughter married Frederick Haring of Old Tappan (plate 91). The land is a part of the Lockhart Patent of June 27, 1687, and was sold to the builder or his father. Capt. Abraham A. Haring, b. Oct. 22, 1734, bap. at Tappan, married three times. By his first wife Catharine Lent, he had a son Abraham, b. March 4, 1758, died in infancy. He married secondly June 25, 1760 Jannetje Verbryck, and had two sons: David A., b. Dec. 15, 1760, who was married twice, to Elizabeth Blauvelt and to Maria Alyea; and Abraham B., b. Jan. 2, 1766, who settled at Parsippany. He married thirdly March 20, 1770 Margrietje Blauvelt, b. Feb. 26, 1749, and had by her two children: Maria, b. June 17, 1774, married Roeloff Verbryck; and John A. Haring, b. April 6, 1780, d. Feb. 22, 1854, who built nearby. Capt. Abraham Haring was absent collecting taxes when the British came for him; the next time they were more successful and carried him away prisoner before his youngest child was born. He was never heard from again, and the widow later married her neighbor John Riker, who lived across the way in a house still standing but greatly altered. It is not known what happened to the homestead in the next few years. The youngest son, John A.[6] Haring, received only the southern part of his father's land, and built a stone house here 1805-08; his son Nicholas J.[7] Haring rebuilt his father's house in 1838; it is still standing, and a good example of the same style as rendered by a later period.

Moses Taylor, Jr., was a child during the Revolution and fled with his parents from New York City to this region during the war. On retiring from active life, he returned here and bought the Abraham Haring house. His young wife Margaret died here April 27, 1813 aged 32 years, and was buried with her still-born daughter in the cemetery at Palisades. He married secondly a daughter of Joshua Martin of

Sneden's Landing, and had children by her. His son Moses Taylor, Jr., had a daughter Mary who married John Vervalen, and sold the house early in the twentieth century. The present owner is H. S. Kniffin.

This is one of the few examples extant in Bergen County of a gable roof covering a deep house. Its lines and proportions are good. The contemporary Lent house, built 1752, has a similar roof (plate 53). The frame kitchen wing in the rear was built in 1812 by Moses Taylor. The house is in Rockleigh Borough, on the west side of Piermont Road, which formerly turned northeast at this point and wound toward Palisades (this end of the road is now known as Rockleigh Avenue).

Holdrum—Wanamaker House
Pascack Road, Upper Montvale
PLATE 93

This house was built about the time of the Revolution, possibly shortly after, by a Holdrum; the date 1778 is said to be cut in an attic beam. William[1] Haldron was a blacksmith; he emigrated and settled at Flushing and later at Harlem, and was drowned on or about Dec. 6, 1687. His son John[2] married May 18, 1707 Cornelia Van Tienhoven, widow of Andries Holst and granddaughter of Cornelis Van Tienhoven, the Secretary of New Netherland. They removed to Tappan about 1713. Their son William[3] Holdrum, bap. May 16, 1708 at New York City, married 1734 Margrietje Peters, daughter of Claes Peters of Rockland Co., on Dec. 18, 1760. William bought 258 acres west of the Hackensack River and south of the State line, from Rev. Benjamin Vanderlinde, and resided here the balance of his life. William had nine children, including Claes, William, Jan, Abraham, and Cornelius. It is not known who built this house, but it may have been Cornelius, as he is known to have lived in this vicinity. Cornelius[4] Holdrum, b. Oct. 22, 1749 at Tappan, d. May 31, 1831, married Elizabeth Haring, and had three children: James C. born 1785, William C., and Cornelius C. The house was eventually inherited by Catherine Holdrum, b. Dec. 2, 1827, d. Oct. 8, 1866, married May 14, 1846 (as his first wife) John Wanamaker, b. April 4, 1827, d. March 30, 1904; they had two daughters Elizabeth and Sarah. (John Wanamaker's daughter by his second wife believes Catherine's father to have been a Cornelius Holdrum.) About 1850 John and Catharine Wanamaker exchanged houses with James Van Houten. His son Garret had a son Edmund Van Houten, who sold the house about 1925. It is now owned by C. C. Cook and rented; it is run as the Pascack Poultry Farm. Modern alterations and neglect detract from the character of the house. It stands a short distance south of the state line, just below Upper Montvale four corners, on a hill on the east side of the Pascack Road (or Spring Valley Road), which goes north to Spring Valley.

Hopper—Goetschius House
East Saddle River Road, Upper Saddle River
PLATE 94

This house is of an early type of construction and was undoubtedly built in the beginning of the eighteenth century, but its early history is lost in obscurity. On an undated sheepskin map made about 1713 the house is marked Gerrit Hoppa; on Erskine's Revolutionary map it is marked John Hopper. So it is safe to presume that it was built and owned by members of the Hopper family for about one hundred years. There are several distinct Hopper families whose histories are not clear. The only Gerrit Hopper known at such an early date lived at Polifly near Hackensack, and did not die until 1786 (see infra). It is possible that he built on the Upper Saddle River as a young man before settling at Polifly; the names of his children are not known, but he may have had a son John and given the northerly farm to him during his own lifetime; this is pure conjecture. There was also a John Hoppe, born and living at Paramus, married at Hackensack 1736 Elizabeth Kip, who was a widow by 1799, but this John appears to be the son of Andries, a brother of the above Gerrit. Whatever his connections, the house was probably built by a Gerrit Hopper, who owned it about 1713.

The house has been in the possession of the Goetschius family for the last hundred years. Dominie Stephanus' Goetschius, bap. Nov. 5, 1752 at Schraalenburgh, d. 1837, came of a family of powerful preachers: his father Hendricus was a minister on Long Island and later at Hackensack and Schraalenburgh; his grandfather Maurice' Goetschi was a pastor in Switzerland, from which country he brought four hundred followers to America (see plate 68). Dominie Stephanus Goetschius was a strong Calvinist and the organizer of no less than nine churches in Ulster Co.; he was a powerful preacher, sharp and fearless in his denunciation of sin. He preached at New Paltz and New Hurley and at Marbletown and Shokan, all in Ulster County; it was not until he was 62 years of age that he was appointed to the Saddle River and Pascack Churches, which he served from 1814 until he retired in 1835. He doubtless bought the Hopper house when he came to this region. By his wife Elizabeth Du Bois, he had six children baptized at New Paltz. One son John Henry Goetschius, b. March 18, 1795, was probably the father of the Dominie's grandson Stephen J.' Goetschius, who was the father of the present owner, George E. Goetschius.

The careful cornering but otherwise rough stonework of the house is typical of the early period. The front of the house has been refaced. Age has blended the heavy roof, absurdly small posts, and large dormers so that they scarcely detract from the appearance of the house. The house stands on the East Saddle River Road, on the northwest corner of the crossroads at Upper Saddle River.

Hopper House
formerly at Polifly Road, Hackensack

Andries[1] Hoppe or Hoppen emigrated to New Amsterdam in 1652 and was an extensive freighter and trader until he died in 1658. He was survived by his widow Geertje Hendricks, three sons and one daughter, all of whom settled at Hackensack. One son Hendrick,[2] b. Jan. 9, 1656 at New Amsterdam, bought from John Berry May 17, 1694, a tract of 300 acres east of the Saddle River, in the section which became known as the Polifly, now the south part of Hackensack. His eighth child Gerrit (1696-1786) left his father's farm to his son Jacob, who in turn willed it to his son John, stating that it had been in the family for three generations. John I.[5] Hopper, b. Nov. 1774, d. 1883, married Maria, daughter of Albert Terhune, and had several children including Cornelia who married and removed to the Terhuen homestead in Hackensack by the river (plate 100). Descendants inform me that John I. Hopper tore down the home of his forefathers, which stood on the east side of the Polifly Road, and built the present stone house opposite on the west side of the Polifly Road in 1818. This house is standing today, and is a good example of the early nineteenth century development of the typical stone house of the Dutch settlers.

Hopper Houses
formerly at Hohokus

Settlers cleared farms at an early period by the crossroads of the highways from Wagaraw (north of Paterson) and Paramus (eastern Ridgewood); the place was called Hoppertown after its early inhabitants. This was the nucleus of the present Hohokus. On Erskine's Revolutionary map, a house on the northeast corner of the crossroads by a stream was marked Abram Hopper, and another on the southwest corner was marked G. Hopper. Neither of these stands today. The first mentioned house was probably torn down early in the nineteenth century for the present two story stone structure, owned by John J. Zabriskie in 1876, and now run as the Hohokus Inn. Obscurity also rests with the early Hopper history of these houses. Casual reference can be found to two buildings at Hohokus (presumably these) known as the Henry Hopper house and the Captain John Hopper house. The author has been unable to determine the identity of either a John Hopper or a G. Hopper living in this region about the time of the Revolution.

Abraham[5] Hopper, born about 1741, son of Hendrick and grandson of Hendrick[2] Hoppe of Polifly, bought and settled on a tract at Hohokus before the Revolution.

By his wife Antje he had several children baptized at Paramus Church, including three sons, Henry, Jacob and Andries. The son Henry⁶ Hopper, bap. June 4, 1770, married Feb. 8, 1795 Charity Conklin, and had many children born at Hohokus. It is possible that this branch owned the house on the northeast corner of the crossroads.

House of Isaac Housman
525 Terrace Avenue, Hasbrouck Heights
PLATE 95

Iron ends on the beam supports of this house are to be seen high in the front wall; they read 1773, the date of erection of the house. It is said that the Revolution interrupted the building, and that the house was not finished until 1783. The father of the builder, Abraham Housman (Huysman), settled in this locality as a young man in 1695. He was born in Bushwick on Long Island, and married at Hackensack Nov. 29, 1701 Gerrebreght Terhune, born on the Bay. They had ten children, of whom Isaac was the ninth. Isaac Housman, bap. March 22, 1724 at Hackensack, married there Nov. 3, 1748 Grietje Ackerman, bap. March 9, 1729 at Acquackanonk, daughter of Lauwrens A. Ackerman; they had at least two children, Abraham and Geesie, who were baptized in 1756 at Schraalenburgh. Isaac was a member of the Church at Hackensack, an overseer of the poor, and a member of the consistory of the Hackensack Church. He built this house at the age of fifty years. It was inherited about 1885 by Housman De Baun who married Josephine Wiser, nee Griffith. In 1890 her sister Mrs. Ida Myers, nee Griffith, bought the house from the estate, and it is now owned by her son John G. Myers.

The house varies in style from most stone houses of the time. It has the feeling of a town residence rather than of a farmhouse; the builder may have been influenced by the two story houses being erected in the nearby village of Hackensack, for although the Housman house is but the usual one and a half stories, its height has the suggestion of more space. The house is in the region formerly known as the Polifly, south of Hackensack. The grade of the road has been changed, with the result that the house now stands on an eminence overlooking Terrace Avenue (the continuation of Polifly Road) and the valley, immediately southwest of the intersection of the new highway.

House of Nicasius Kip
formerly at Polifly Road, Hackensack

The ancestor of this family in America was Hendrick Hendricksen¹ Kip, b. 1600 at Niewenhuys, married there April 20, 1624 Tryntje Lubberts from Swoll. They emigrated about 1637 by way of Amsterdam to New Amsterdam, where they settled. He became one of the leading men of New Netherland, and was satirically called "Hendrick Kip of the haughty lip" because he was strong and fearless. He died after 1665 on his estate *Kippenburg* at Manhattan. His son Hendrick, Jr., had a son Nicasius' Kip, b. about 1666 in the vicinity of Flatlands on Long Island, d. 1712 at Polifly south of Hackensack. As a boy he was apprenticed in New York to the trade of cooper. On Dec. 20, 1691 he married Antie, daughter of Pieter Breyant. He soon settled in the vicinity of Hackensack, joined the Church there in 1694, and became active in town and church affairs. In 1705 he bought from Garret Lydecker a tract of 220 acres at Polifly, where he settled. His house is said to have been built in 1696, on what authority is not known; it is possible that the deed was not given to him until several years later, after all payments had been made. (We know that the Hendricksen land at Middletown was bought on the partial payment plan.) The original house was the stone wing; at a later date the main house was built of stone with a gambrel roof and a very small number of windows; during the nineteenth century the roof of the wing was raised for a half-story of frame, and various changes were made in the main house. A photograph of the house taken in 1905 is reproduced in the *Kip Genealogy*, p. 138. It was burned in 1910-12.

Nicasius Kip had five sons and three daughters. He divided his homestead farm between his sons Henry and Peter. Peter⁴ Kip (1696-1787) obtained the north half of the farm on which stood the house; he married Elsie Van der Beek, and at his death left his Polifly plantation to his son Abraham (1726-1812). Abraham's son Peter was the father of Judge Henry⁷ Kip (1811-1882), who retired in 1846 to the Polifly home of his forefathers.

House of Hendrick Kip
formerly at Meadow Road, Rutherford

Hendrick⁵ Kip, b. Sept. 1, 1720 at Polifly, d. Dec. 10, 1796, was a son of Peter, and grandson of Nicasius' Kip, builder of the house at Polifly (supra). On Dec. 4, 1741 he married Jannetje Banta, b. Aug. 8, 1721, d. Sept. 24, 1797. He bought a large tract at Boiling Spring (now Rutherford) and built a stone house here shortly after his marriage, which was still standing on Meadow Road in 1928. The original house was probably the wing with a gable roof. He undoubtedly built the main house after his family grew larger: it was of fine cut stone with quoins, covered by a gambrel roof, and was later marred by the addition of a porch and Victorian gable. Hendrick had six children, but at his death willed all his lands to his only son Peter, except for 50 acres to his grandson Henry, son of Peter. Peter H.⁶ Kip, b. Dec. 2, 1743 and bap. at Hackensack, d. March 8, 1813 and lies buried at Passaic, married Willemyntje Van Winkle. At his death he willed the farm where he lived on the north side of the Boiling Spring Road to his two daughters and the farm on the south side of Boiling Spring Road with remainder to his only son Henry. Henry P.[7] Kip (1770-1840) inherited the homestead farm and willed it in 1828 to his only son Peter (1791-1845). Peter[8] Kip's eldest son Henry was the father of Peter H.[9] Kip (1840-1920), a bachelor. This Peter H. Kip was the fourth generation to be born in the old Kip homestead on Meadow Road, but he lived and died in the later Kip house on the north side of Boiling Spring Road (now 138 Union Avenue), which is still standing, a post-revolutionary house of similar style.

House of Cornelis Lozier
Goffle Road, Midland Park
PLATE 96

The date of erection of this house is uncertain. It is marked Cornelis Lozier on Erskine's Revolutionary map, but it was undoubtedly built some time previous to the war. The ancestor of this family was Francois[1] Le Sueur, born 1625 at Challe Mesnil near Dieppe, in Normandy, who emigrated to this country about 1657 and soon settled at Esopus; he was a civil engineer by profession; on July 12, 1659 at New Amsterdam he married Jannetie Hildebrand, daughter of Hildebrand Pietersen, and had five children before he died about 1670. His son Nicholas[2] Lozier, bap. June 10, 1668, died 1745, removed from Kingston to the vicinity of Hackensack (probably Demarest's French colony) about 1697, and had at least seventeen children by his two wives. Johannes[3] Lozier, bap. Feb. 26, 1699 at Hackensack, a son by the first wife, married Sept. 8, 1727 Lea Cornelisse Banta of Hackensack. This Johannes inherited land west of the Hackensack River. Among his children was Cornelis[4] Lozier, bap. Aug. 29, 1731 at Schraalenburgh; he was probably the Revolutionary owner of this house. In his will probated in 1815, "Cornelis Lezere" of Franklin devised the farm on which he then lived to his son John, mentioned his son David and his two youngest children, Jane and Abraham Whitten Lozier, also his wife Catharine, who had a daughter Catharine by her previous husband Abraham Whitten; one of the executors named was Garret A. Lydecker.

At the time of the Revolution, a mill stood on the south side of the road. The house is said to have been always a part of the mill property. The later history of the mill is as follows: Early in the nineteenth century it was a flour mill owned by a Lydecker (probably Garret A. Lydecker, a landowner in this locality), and the region was then called Lydecker's Mills. Later it came into the possession of Abraham Van Riper, and the place came to be called Van Riper's Mills; he built the present stone mill north of the house in 1826. About 1829 the firm of Van Winkle and Park, cotton manufacturers, bought both mills; then the owners were Munn &

Whitehead. Later the mill was purchased by two brothers John B. and Isaac Wortendyke, sons of Abraham Wortendyke of the adjoining village of Newtown (later called Wortendyke); then their brother Cornelius A. Wortendyke owned and ran the mill for some time as President of the Wortendyke Manufacturing Co.; Cornelius was the owner in 1876. The stone mill is still in operation. The stone house is now owned by Henry J. Wostbrock.

In early days the owner of a mill was an important man, as his mill was often the *raison d'etre* for the settlement which grew up around it, and which was given his name by the neighboring farmers who journeyed there to have their corn ground. Thus we can expect a mill owner to have a well-built house such as we find in this instance. The stone lintels suggest that the main house was built no earlier than the third quarter of the eighteenth century. The graceful lines of the simple fanlight are to be noted. The half story of frame added above the wing is typical of the early nineteenth century, when more bedroom space was desired but no need of height was felt in a room used only for sleeping.

The house is in Midland Park near Ridgewood. It stands on the northwest side of Goffle Road (which led from the settlements at the Goffle, Wagaraw, and Totowa near Paterson), on the corner of Paterson Avenue on which the mill stands, and about one block southwest of Godwin Avenue (which wandered east toward the Paramus settlement).

House of Barent and John Nagel (Naugle)
Harvard Street, near Piermont Road, Closter
PLATE 97

Two houses were built on Barent Nagel's tract before 1745; the later of the two still stands and is generally known as the John Naugle house since two of that name occupied it. Jan[1] Nagel emigrated from Holland as a soldier in the employ of the West India Company. He retired to Harlem in 1664 after the English conquest, and on Aug. 27, 1670 married Rebecca Waldron; after his death she married May 12, 1690 Jan Dyckman of Spuyten Duyvil. Three of Jan and Rebecca's sons grew to manhood: Jan of Harlem, Barent and Resolvert. On April 25, 1710 Barent and Resolvert bought from Lancaster Symes, merchant and land speculator, the north 1030 acres of his tract in the King's Woods (deed recorded May 2, 1750 in Orange Co.), which was divided in 1748, the north portion to Barent's heirs and the south portion to Resolvert (the latter had seven daughters and no sons). The land near the Hudson River from the Lockhart Patent on the north extending down to the Closter Dock Road (which was at one time thought to be the state border) was

303

known as The King's Woods, and had been patented in 1701 to Bernardus Vervelen of New Rochelle, who sold to Symes in 1709.

Barent[2] Nagel (bap. Dec. 18, 1678, died before 1745) immediately settled on his purchase and built a stone house standing near the main road until burned a few years ago. It was in two units covered by very steep, gable roofs; the smaller part had very small windows and no overhang, and the larger part had an overshot roof. (A photograph taken in 1901 can be seen in Gilman's *Story of the Ferry*, plate 59). Barent was a justice of the peace and kept order in the little community. He married Sarah Kiersen in 1708 and had seven children: John, Rebecca, William, Hendrick who built to the southward (see plate 98), Sarah, Johanna and Jacob. The eldest son, John[3] Nagel, born about 1709, had inherited his father's home by 1745 (Verplank's map), and he or his eldest son John was the owner at the time of the Revolution (Erskine's map). John[3] Nagel married Elizabeth Blauvelt about 1730 and had eleven children: Sarah, John J., Barent, Catharine, Maria, Elizabeth, Henry (died young), Rebecca, David (died young), Elizabeth and David; in 1754 John married secondly his cousin Magdalena, daughter of Jan Nagel of Harlem.

The present stone house, built in the fields behind the old Barent Nagel house, was erected about 1740 according to a descendant. It is shown on Verplank's map of 1745, but the owner is not marked. Evidently Barent Nagel built a second house behind his own for one of his children—possibly for William who was of age and married shortly after this date, or for a daughter. The new house came into the hands of Barent's grandson David, youngest son of John. David[4] Nagel, b. Sept. 2, 1750, d. May 29, 1831 and buried in the family cemetery, married in 1775 Dirkie Haring, b. Dec. 24, 1757, d. Oct. 1, 1821 and buried beside her husband. She was the daughter of Frederick Haring of Old Tappan (plate 91). They had four children, Jan, Frederick of Tappan (who had no issue), and two daughters. Jan or John D.[5] Nagel, b. May 7, 1776, d. Oct. 22, 1841, married Oct. 12, 1796 Sarah Mabie, d. June 2, 1876 at the age of 99 years and 4 months; they lie buried with his parents. He had a grist mill near the house and was called "Jan, the honest miller." His only son was John J.[6] Naugle, b. July 1, 1818, died in 1882, married Hannah Maria Eckerson and had eight children. He built the large frame house on the hill on the main road in the 1870's and lost the whole property shortly afterward. The stone house is often referred to as the John Naugle house because of its ownership by two Johns for a large part of the eighteenth century. In 1912 it was a part of the Bingham estate. It was inhabited recently (and at the time the photograph was taken in 1925) by some Civil War squatters. The present owner, Mrs. Nannette Mehlin, purchased the property in 1930, and has completely renovated and remodelled it for her residence.

The existing house was at one time used as a church and as a school, probably during the lifetime of Jan, the honest miller. Views of the house in different conditions are shown in plate 5 in this volume and in Gilman, plate 62. The house stands at the end of a short lane called Harvard Street, which starts on the east side of Piermont Road, over one mile north and east of Closter village.

House of Isaac Nagel (Naugle)
Hickory Lane, near Piermont Road, Closter
PLATE 98

This house also stands on the tract purchased by Barent Nagel in 1710. His third son, Hendrick[3] Nagel, bap. March 10, 1718, d. Jan. 7, 1806, owned all the property south of Hickory Lane, and built his house here on the corner of Piermont Road. In 1745 he married Catharine Blauvelt, and had four daughters and three sons: John, the ancestor of the Paramus Naugles (plate 73), Isaac and Barent; he married secondly Nov. 22, 1764 Mary De Clark. He divided his lands between his twin sons: Barent received the old homestead (since gone), he served in the Revolution and lived to the age of 81 years; Isaac received the inland portion, on which he had already built his house about 1775.

Isaac[4] Nagel, b. April 26, 1753, married about 1775 his cousin Maria Auryansen and had three daughters, including Cornelia, bap. Feb. 13, 1785, who married Henry Vervalen. Isaac Nagel, widower, married secondly at Tappan March 28, 1793 Lea Poulousse (Powles) and had an only child Henry. Lea was born May 2, 1763 at Tappan, daughter of Marte Paulusse; by her first husband Jan Ferdon, she had a daughter Lea, bap. 1785, m. 1810 Jacob Ryker of Tappan; on March 17, 1809 Lea Poulouse, widow of Isaac Nagel, married Benjamin Blackledge, Jr., widower, both of Tappan, and on Jan. 4, 1817 at Hackensack she was married a fourth time to Benjamin Westervelt of Cresskill (plate 111); she survived all her four husbands, and died Feb. 11, 1848 at the age of 86 years. Tradition states that the house was sacked three times during the Revolution by Tories and was used as a smallpox hospital while the army was camped in the vicinity during André's trial. The house was inherited by Isaac's only son Henry I.[5] Naugle, b. March 9, 1794 in this house and bap. at Tappan, d. Jan. 13, 1830, buried in the family cemetery; on Aug. 10, 1816 he married Hester Westerfield, who died aged 69 years (no dates given) and was buried with her husband. During her widowhood, she ran the farm, carting produce to Sneden's Landing (in southern Rockland Co.), from where it was shipped to New York City. Henry and Hester had three children: Leah (1817-1886) married Jacob Mabie, James Westerfield Naugle (1824-1856) of Bergenfield married Maria Christie, and Eliza (born 1828) married Hildebrand Naugle. The farm was divided when the children came of age; the house fell to the son James who lived here a short while, and then conveyed it to his sister Leah. Leah sold the house out of the family in the 1850's, and it has changed hands frequently. It was owned in 1912 by Louis Hagen; the present owner is August Bentkamp of Alpine, who leases it to Hugh MacBein.

Issac Nagel was a very conservative man, judging by his house, which is early eighteenth century in character. It consists of two large rooms each with its separate outside door, and two fair-sized rooms in the rear (larger than the average rear rooms); the front windows with the lower short sash are typical of an early period, as are the very small rear windows; the ceilings are low and the exposed beams are very strong and heavy. There is an unusually large and complicated iron lock on the inside of one of the doors; the hinges are hand-wrought. Isaac built for permanence and for comfort. A smoke house stands nearby, but it is of recent construction, built of old stones by the Hagens.

Hickory Lane branches east from Piermont Road, a scant mile from Closter Dock Road or from Closter village, and the house stands on the south side of Hickory Road near its end. Hickory Lane is a short distance south of the houses of John Nagel (plate 97) and William De Clark (plate 81).

Newkirk House at Bergen
formerly on Newkirk Street, Jersey City

Until recently this house stood in the village of Bergen near the present Bergen Square in the heart of Jersey City. On July 20, 1669 Philip Carteret, Governor of New Jersey, gave a patent to John Berry for several tracts: the lot known as No. 162 within the east corner of the village of Bergen, the tract known as No. 70 consisting of 6 lots of woodland and 6 adjoining lots of meadow, running west from the village to the Hackensack River, and also the tract known as No. 125, consisting of two adjoining plantations, running from the south side of Hans Diderick's Out-Garden Plot northwards along the fence by the road that led from the village to the English Neighborhood. This latter tract was a large plantation surrounding the east corner of the village square, and it was here that the Newkirk house was eventually built on Newkirk Street, facing the head of Tuers Avenue. This plantation (No. 125) and the adjoining lot within the village square (No. 162) were sold by Berry to Samuel Edsall on July 12, 1670. A century later, in 1764, they were partitioned between two Newkirk brothers; it is not known when the property came into this family's possession.

The ancestor of the family was Mattheus Cornelissen' Van Niewkercke, who emigrated as a boy of twelve years in 1659 with his older brother Gerrit on the ship

De Moesman. He was born about 1647 at Slechtenhorst in the Province of Gelder-land, near Niewkercke. He settled at Flatbush on Long Island and sold his farm there in 1665 when he removed to Bergen village. On Dec. 14, 1670 at Bergen he married Anna, daughter of Jacob Luby, an official of the West India Company. She bore five children and died Dec. 20, 1685. On Aug. 15, 1687 Mattheus married secondly Catrina, daughter of Poulus Pietersen, who bore him seven more children. He died at Bergen May 12, 1705 and she survived him many years, dying between 1731 and 1764. Matheus probably purchased the plantation as it was later divided between two of his younger sons, Gerrit and Poulus. The latter's home was on a two acre plot willed to him by his mother in 1731. Gerrit also lived in Bergen but the exact location of his house is unknown; it may have been on the tract in question. Gerrit[2] Niewkerk, b. Nov. 17, 1696 at Bergen, d. April 23, 1785, married at Bergen Sept. 5, 1730 Catrina, daughter of Hendrick Kuyper, b. at Ahasymus, d. Sept. 12, 1751, and had two unmarried daughters and two sons. In 1764, the year after the death of Poulus and the year of probate of their mother Catrina's will, the plantation (No. 125) and adjoining lot (No. 162) in Bergen were surveyed and partitioned between Gerrit and the heirs of his deceased brother, the south half being allotted to Gerrit. On July 7, 1795 the south half of this tract and also the woodland and meadow lots to the west (No. 70) were subdivided between Gerrit's two sons, Mattevis and the heirs of his deceased brother Hendrick, the north half falling to the former. Mattevis[3] Nieukerk, b. about 1739, d. July 10, 1811, married Catlyntje, daughter of Arent Toers, and had three sons: Garret, Aaron, and Henry. On Aug. 1, 1810, a year before he died, Mattevis deeded to his son Garret the land he had received in the division of 1795. Garret[4] Nieukerk, b. April 9, 1766, d. Aug. 28, 1832, married Polly Ackerman and had two sons and four daughters. In his will Garret divided the property between his sons Garret G. and Henry, the division line being Niewkirk Street. The younger son Garret G.[5] Nieukerk, b. Oct. 17, 1808, was occupying the family homestead in the north half of the property in 1841 and 1882. He was married three times, first on Oct. 25, 1828 to Rachel Van Houten, d. Dec. 1, 1835, secondly about 1837 to Jane Fowler, widow of Abraham Tise, d. Oct. 6, 1849, and thirdly on Sept. 6, 1851 to Eliza Ann Beaty. He had nine sons and eight daughters by the three marriages, but many of the children died in infancy. In 1915 the house was still occupied by members of the family.

The house stood until recently on the north side of Niewkirk Street and at the head of Tuers Avenue. These two thoroughfares once formed the boundaries of Bergen village, which is now in the heart of Jersey City. The house was a long, narrow, one and a half story building, of well dressed stones, covered with a gable roof. In the Holland Society Yearbook for 1915 is the statement that this house was built by the Newkirks in 1810. Mattevis deeded the property this year to his son Garret[5] Nieukerk, so it is possible that the latter erected it then. However, the lines of this house are more typical of the first half of the eighteenth century. In the later period the more usual type of building was a deeper house covered by a gambrel roof. As the house has been torn down its methods of construction cannot be examined to determine its age. A photograph of it may be seen in the *250th Anniversary of the Founding of Bergen* (1910), p. 54.

Packer House
Ewing Avenue, Franklin Lakes Borough
PLATE 99

The early history of this house is lost in obscurity. Erskine did not survey this road during the Revolution, so we do not know the owner at this time; but its method of construction shows that the house belongs to an earlier period than the war. The early titles to a large part of northwestern Bergen County were involved and dubious; possibly in an attempt to rectify this, Stevens and Company obtained a grant in 1789 for 5000 acres, consisting of tracts in various localities in western Bergen Co.; they sold to many settlers, including a Packer. The sale may refer to this property, as the first Packer arrived about this time.

The progenitor of the Packer family in this region came to Wyckoff from a place unknown; he died when still a young man and lies buried at Wyckoff; his first name is unknown but may have been John, since his son William's eldest son was named John. He is supposed to have had but one child, William J. Packer, b. Jan. 10, 1795,* d. Jan. 26, 1863,* married Sept. 27, 1817* Peggy Micklor, b. March 13, 1799,* died about 1875, issue six sons and five daughters. William Packer must have been well-to-do and have had his full complement of land, for he gave farms to every one of his six sons. The homestead was inherited by the son Henry W. Packer, b. Jan. 29, 1837,* died in 1918, married Jane Cole. He sold the place about 1910 to the Newmans of New York City, and they sold to Henry Barrett Crosby, the present owner.

The house was probably built at three different periods. The first story of the old wing is built of stone laid with a clay and straw mortar and has hand-hewn laths; its construction places its erection in the early eighteenth century; the diminutive size of the window opening was also typical of the early period. The main house may have been built by the first Packer shortly after the Revolution: the stone quoins and the stone lintels left in their natural color in patterned contrast to the whitewashed stone front of the building are characteristic of the late eighteenth century, although the size of the windows is more typical of the pre-revolutionary era. The

308

---

* Taken from family Bible.

frame half-story was doubtless added to the wing by William Packer. Dormers and porch are of course modern. The house is west of Wyckoff in Franklin Lakes borough; it stands on the west side of Ewing Avenue, between Franklin Lakes Road and Franklin Avenue, nearer the latter.

Terheun Homestead
450 River Street, Hackensack
PLATE 100

This house is still in the possession and occupancy of a direct descendant of the probable builder. The Terheun family is said to be of French Huguenot extraction and to have come to America possibly by way of Huynen in Holland. Albert Albertse,[1] known as Albert the lintweaver, was in New Netherland as early as 1650; he settled on Long Island and was a member of the Dutch Church of Flatlands in 1677; he died in 1685 and his widow Geertje in 1693. A son Albert Albertse[2] Terhuyne (Terheun), bap. Aug. 13, 1651 at New Amsterdam, died 1708-09 at Hackensack, married first Hendrickje Stevense Van Voorhees, secondly between 1691-94 Weyntie Brickers, and thirdly Sept. 8, 1705 at Hackensack, Maritie De Graves, widow of Andries Tibout. He was a member of the Church at Flatlands in 1677, and was assessed for his farmlands there in 1676 and 1683. He (or his father) and Jacques Cortelyou obtained a patent for 5000 acres on the Passaic River, which was confirmed to them May 27, 1685; he also bought a large farm from Capt. John Berry, extending from the Hackensack to the Saddle Rivers. He settled at Hackensack between 1683 and 1689 (when he joined the church here), and probably after 1686 when a daughter was baptized at Flatbush. He became an important member of the little community, and was chosen a member of the New Jersey legislature in 1696. He may be the builder of this house. In his will, "done at my common dwelling house in Hackensack in the cellar chamber at nine of the clock in the evening" on Feb. 16, 1707/8, he left his wife Mary the northwest chamber of the house and firewood, a piece of ground for a garden, and 10 schepples of corn and 6 schepples of wheat yearly, and named his thirteen children (by his two former wives).

A son by Albert's second wife was Dirck[3] Terheun, bap. July 26, 1702 at Hackensack, d. 1766, married Oct. 13, 1727 Catharina Kip of Hackensack, the mother of his children, and was remarried by 1760 to Elizabeth. In his will of 1766 Dirck mentioned his wife and five daughters and divided the lands he had purchased between his four sons (to Johannes went land bought from the Van Giesens and Romeyn). Dirck made no mention of any inherited property; he may never have received his father's house or he may have previously deeded it; neither did he specify his own home farm, so we do not know if he built a house or remained all his life at his father's.

The present house seems to have been the home of Dirck's youngest son, Johannes or John[4] Terheun, b. Aug. 3, 1742,* bap. Aug. 8 following at Hackensack, married December, 1766* Catharine Bogert, b. Aug. 19, 1748,* daughter of Peter Bogert. They had eight children: Catharine, Peter, Jane, Richard, Elizabeth, Ann, Matilda and John. The youngest was John J.[5] Terheun, b. July 10, 1793,* died before 1876 (when his heirs owned the house) and was buried on the Green at Hackensack, his body being later removed to Fairmont. In 1816 he married Cornelia Hopper, b. April 23, 1800, daughter of John I. Hopper and Maria Terheun of Polifly; she was born in the old Hopper homestead on the east side of Polifly Road (see supra). John J. and Cornelia Terheun had a son Albert H.[6] Terheun who married Elizabeth J. Townsend of Wilmington, Delaware. Their daughter, Miss Cornelia Hopper[7] Terheun, is the present owner of the homestead, which has been always owned and occupied by her family.

Every word of the statement that the house was built in 1670 by the emigrant John Terheun seems to be erroneous although frequently quoted. The first of the family in Hackensack was Albert Terheun, who was still living in Flatlands as late as 1683, so the house could not have been built by this family before 1683-89 at the earliest. As it is said to have superseded a temporary habitation, its erection can safely be placed even later; it may have been the house built by Albert Terheun shortly before his death in 1709 (the description in his will shows he had a good sized house with four rooms), or it may not have been erected until about 1727 by the son Dirck. Although the ownership has not been traced further back than John Terheun, construction of the house places its erection before his time. The name John Terheun probably became connected with it because of its ownership for a period of one hundred years by two John Terheuns. The house is built of roughly cut, whitewashed stone, the walls are over a foot thick and the ceilings are low. The gambrel roof is very high. The large frame kitchen and dining room wing were built about 1800. Frame entrance way, dormers and pillared porch are nineteenth century changes. Varying views of the house may be seen in Boyd's article, p. 40, and in Wendehack's article, plate 24. The house is a veritable museum of French, Dutch and English heirlooms brought by the brides from their childhood homes. There is still in use a Franklin stove, which is believed to have been installed shortly after Benjamin Franklin invented it in 1740. Beside it are an iron shovel and tongs, the property of John Terheun, said to have been brought over by the family from Holland.

Until late in the nineteenth century the house faced south over a large, waving

310

---

* Taken from family Bible.

field of rye which extended down to Ward Street. The house stands on the bank of the Hackensack River, secluded from the busy Anderson Street bridge by an elm many centuries old. Since the photograph was taken in 1925, some of the elms on the property were ruthlessly cut down for the continuation of River Street, which immediately adjoins the house on the west.

Another Terheun house still stands a block farther north. The original unit, now completely encompassed by the later units, is said to have been built by an uncle of the above John Terheun in 1773. It is also known as the Knapp or Lincoln house. A view of it may be seen in Wendehack's article, plate 33.

Terhune House
East Saddle River Road, Hohokus
PLATE 101

The early history of this house is unknown; it is a short distance north of Paramus and stands on the Saddle River Road which was not surveyed by Erskine during the Revolution. It is said to have been the home of Abraham Terhune, whose wife may have been a Westervelt; he had a cannon on his property which he shot off to celebrate the Northern victories in the Civil War, and was killed by this cannon when honoring Grant's election to the Presidency in 1868. His nephew was Albert D. Terhune of the Ackerman-Van Emburgh house (plate 74). His (Abraham's) daughter Polly Terhune married about 1820 John Van Emburgh, son of Henricus, and lived in her father's house for a short period before building a house a little to the north. Abraham Terhune sold the house before 1860 when the Randalls owned it. The above information was given me by a neighbor and old resident, a descendant of the daughter Polly.

The ancestor of this Abraham Terhune is unknown. It is probable that he was the Abraham, bap. Aug. 29, 1773 at Paramus, son of Abraham and Marytie Terheun. This Marytie or Maria was a member of the Paramus Church in 1790. The son Abraham married about 1796 Tryntje Westervelt, b. Aug. 8, 1781 at Paramus, d. 1852, daughter of the Hon. Abraham Westervelt, and had at least two children, Maria or Polly, b. March 31, 1797 at Paramus, married here in 1811 John Van Emburgh, and also Abraham, Jr., b. Nov. 16, 1801 at Paramus. Both the Terheun and Westervelt families settled at Paramus at an early date. The house may have been inherited by Abraham Terhune from his or his wife's family (her grandfather Roelof Westervelt came here between 1740-50).

The house is better known as the Joseph Jefferson house. This famous actor was the owner in 1876. More recently it has been a part of the Jacquelin estate, and it is now owned by H. Ruegg.

The house is built in two uniform sections, the west half of stone plastered over and whitewashed and the east half of clapboards, with a gambrel roof over all. The stone half belongs to the Revolutionary period. The Victorian dormers were probably added by Jefferson. The whole interior of the stone part was ripped out at some period, to form one large room extending to the roof in timbered English hall effect! The house is not elevated from the ground and gives the impression of being a part of the soil, an effect very much in keeping with its early history, which must have been that of a farmhouse. The house is one and a half miles north of Paramus, on the east side of a turn in the East Saddle River Road; the village of Hohokus is to the westward and reached by a bridge over the river at this point.

House of Henry Van Alen
Oakland Avenue, Oakland

At Yaw-pough (now Oakland) a stream flows into the Ramapo River. The house and grist mill of Henry Vanalen are shown on Erskine's Revolutionary map at the point where the Ramapo Valley Road (here called Oakland Avenue) crosses the stream. His father Pieter Gerritse[1] Van Alen emigrated from Rotterdam and settled along the Saddle River in New Jersey; on Aug. 11, 1706 at Hackensack he married Trintje, daughter of Hendrick Hoppe and Maria Janse, had twelve children and died in 1759. The eldest child was Henry[2] Van Alen (or Hendrick Van Ale), bap. June 2, 1707 at Hackensack, died shortly before July, 1783. He married Elizabeth Doremus, b. Feb. 3, 1717, daughter of Henry Doremus, and had ten children, some of whom were baptized between 1739-48 at Pompton Plains Church, of which he had become a member in 1738. It is probable that he first settled in that region, and removed to the neighborhood of Yaw-pough in 1748, for in this year he became deacon of the nearby Ponds Church. On Jan. 20, 1761 he married secondly Thomasina Earle, widow of Gerrit Hallenbeck. In his will of 1778 he mentioned his wife, stated that his eldest son Peter and another son William had already received their portions, mentioned three other sons Hessel, Gerret and John, and his deceased son Doctor Andrew Van Alen. On Aug. 2, 1783 John H., Garret and Hessel Van Allen and the heirs of Doctor Andrew Van Allen, deceased, deeded property to Cornelius Vanderhoof, the instrument commencing as follows: "Whereas Henry Van Allen, late of Yapough, by his last will did direct the sale and division of his property among the said John H., Garret, Hassel, Elizabeth Mead, now wife of said Cornelius Vanderhoof, and the heirs of Doctor Van Allen deceased . . ."

It has not been determined who next owned Henry Van Alen's house and mill. In 1876 it was in the possession of Aaron G. Garrison. In 1932 Mr. Waldron sold it to the Sherwood Forest Friar Tuck Club, the present owners. The house is built of stone rubble now whitewashed green, and is covered by a gambrel roof; it is in several units and has suffered many alterations.

Van Alen (?)—Hopper—Van Horn House
Ramapo Valley Road, Mahwah
PLATE 102

The earliest knowledge we have is from Erskine's Revolutionary map: a house on the Ramapo River bank in this locality (and undoubtedly this house) is marked John Vanalen. His identity is not determined, but it is probable that he was the youngest brother of Hendrick Van Alen of Yaw-pough (supra). This John Van Alen was baptized Jan. 14, 1728 at Hackensack and died shortly before Oct. 26, 1807 (when the inventory of his estate was taken). It is not known when he settled in this vicinity. He was already a resident of Ramapough when he bought 139 acres here Dec. 12, 1769; and still lived in the valley when he sold these same 139 acres, at over ten times his purchase price, to Andrew W. Hopper on Sept. 13, 1779. He probably removed that year to Wagaraw on the Passaic River, where he had purchased in 1779 a considerable tract confiscated from John Ryerson, Tory; in 1797 he and his wife Wyntie sold some of this property. He was a resident of New York City when he bought lands in 1797 at Cedar Swamp in Franklin Township. In his will of 1807, John Van Alen of Franklin Township devised his farm in Saddle River Township (probably the Ryerson tract) to his son Peter, and his homestead lot in Franklin Township to the heirs of his son Henry; his executors later sold his lands at Cedar Swamp. The first wife of this son Henry Van Alen was Jannetje Lozier, daughter of Cornelis Lozier, owner of the house now in Midland Park (plate 96).

The house and farm on the Ramapo River, which was probably John Van Alen's during the Revolution, came into the possession of the Hopper family shortly thereafter. As in the case of the other Hopper houses mentioned earlier, the ramifications of this branch of the Hopper family are also obscure. Dr. John B. Hopper of Ridgewood writes that his great-grandfather (unnamed) owned the house, and sold it to his son Garret I. Hopper, who sold to Abraham Van Horn; Garret I. Hopper then removed to New York City where he first bought property in 1824, and where he lived until he settled at Ridgewood; Garret's son (John B.'s father) spent his boyhood days on the Ramapo Valley farm.

Abraham Van Horn, formerly of New York City, settled here upon the Ramapo Road, and was a freeholder of Hohokus Township in 1850. He married one of the Hopper girls (a sister of Garret?), and had numerous offspring, including Hopper and William Van Horn of Hohokus. Doubtless the latter was the William Van Horn, owner of the house in 1876. Later the house is stated to have formed a part of the large Havemeyer estate. For many years the owner has been Stephen Birch, and his herdsman occupies it.

The house was probably built during the Revolutionary era. Both units are of roughly cut whitewashed stone. The gambrel roof of the main house is unusually high and has a very straight slope. The house stands on the east bank of the Ramapo River, a short distance south of the crossroad to Mahwah village. It is in Hohokus Township, part of the old Franklin Township.

House of Thomas Van Boskerk (Van Buskirk)

East Saddle River Road, Saddle River

PLATE 103

The house stands on the Wearimus tract, purchased from the Indians in 1702 by Albert Zabriskie. He conveyed one-half of this land March 29, 1708 to Thomas Van Buskirk (Boskerk) on the reverse of the Indian deed, which is owned by a descendant, J. Hosey Osborn of Passaic. Laurens Andriessen[1] Van Boskerk was a native of Holstein in Denmark (now part of Germany), and emigrated to New Netherland about 1654. He lived in New Amsterdam until 1662, when he purchased 170 acres on the west shore of the bay at Mingackwa (later Greenville, now a part of Jersey City) and built a house there. He was a turner by trade, and soon became one of the most important members of colonial New Jersey—justice of the peace, judge of the Bergen Co. court and later its president, and a member of the Council under several Governors. On Dec. 12, 1658 he married Jannetie Jans, widow of Christian Barentsen Van Hoorn; by their joint will of 1679 they divided their property between their four sons and her three sons by her first husband. The homestead at Mingackwa was left to their two youngest sons, Peter (1666-1738) and Thomas; the latter probably released to his brother, as Peter became the sole owner and willed the property to two sons.

Thomas Van Boskerk removed to his purchase on the Saddle River, mentioned above. He married Margrietje Hendricks Van der Linden, and had seven sons and three daughters: Johannis, bap. 1694, Abraham, Peter, Laurens, Andries, Isaac, Michael, Fitje, Geertruy, and Margrietje. The original unit of the house at Saddle River was undoubtedly built by Thomas Van Boskerk, or possibly by a son. It descended in the Van Buskirk family to another Thomas Van Buskirk, who married at Paramus Aug. 29, 1807 Rachel Hopper, and had three daughters but no sons. Thomas willed the property to his daughter Catharine, wife of William Osborn of New York City. It was sold out of the family to William Bond (the present owner) in 1922, to settle the estate of Catharine's son. The latter was the father of J. Hosey Osborn, who states he is the ninth generation of the family to be born in this house.

314

The present stone house was built in many sections. The first unit was erected in the beginning of the eighteenth century of stone quarried from the hill on the farm; it consisted of one large room with a large open fireplace and a gable roof; it forms the northeast corner of the present house. There is no cellar under this section; a nearby cave was used for winter vegetables. De Witt Clinton mentioned the "stone house" standing here in his survey of this section in 1734. In later years the stone house was enlarged to form the usual two rooms on either side of a wide hall. It probably had a wide gable roof, which was raised early in the nineteenth century for the addition of the frame story. The porch was undoubtedly also added at this time; it has simple square wooden columns of different lengths, resting on uneven stone flagging.

Prior to the Revolution, the family ran it as an inn, and the large garret above was used for public meetings. The first church service of the valley was held in this garret, and the Lutherans held their services here until the Lutheran Church was erected nearby in 1820 on land donated by Thomas Van Buskirk. During the Revolution soldiers were billeted here. Thomas Van Buskirk, the last owner in the male line, was a large slaveowner and the last to own a slave in the vicinity; his remaining slave was incited to run away by William Osborn, the son-in-law.

The house stands in Saddle River village, at the southeast corner of the main village street and the East Saddle River Road, and nestles at the foot of Chestnut Ridge.

House of Paulus Vanderbeek
formerly at Salem Street, Hackensack

In 1717 Jan and Eva Berdan sold half of a tract in Hackensack, bought by them in 1708, to Paulus Vanderbeek who in 1717-21 built thereon a house standing until 1922. His grandfather Paulus[1] Van der Beek emigrated from Bremen in Germany as a surgeon in the employ of the Dutch West India Company, shortly before Oct. 9, 1644 when he married Mary Thomas Badie, widow successively of Jacob Verdon and William Adriaense Bennet. He was farmer of the revenue and ferry-master between Manhattan and Brooklyn, to which place he removed about 1655. He died in 1680, survived by his widow who was still living in 1690. His eldest son Coenradt[2] Van der Beek (1647-1706) was a measurer by trade; he lived in the Gowanus section of Brooklyn and later in New York City. His eldest son, by his first wife Elsje Jans, was Paulus[3] Vanderbeek, b. about 1676, d. in or before 1762, married at New York Dec. 18, 1695 Jannetje, daughter of Johannes Springsteen and widow of Jacob Colve. Their eldest five children were born in New York City.

Between 1706 and 1708 Paulus Vanderbeek removed to Hackensack, where were born his two youngest sons Abraham and Isaac. In 1717 Paulus bought the above tract at Hackensack and built a stone house on it. In his will proved in 1762, he devised to his eldest son Conradus the land at Werimus he had bought of Thomas Van Buskirk, to his son Isaac the lands he had bought of John Berdan and Nicholas Romeyn, and after his death it was to go to Isaac's sons Barent and Isaac; he also mentioned his daughter Elsie Kip and the children of his deceased son Jacob. Paulus' youngest son Isaac⁴ Vanderbeek, bap. March 30, 1712 at Hackensack, married there June 25, 1736 Annatje De Boog, bap. May 26, 1717 at New York, daughter of Barent de Boog and Rachel Hoppe. They had nine children (including Salomon, bap. 1749) and were living as late as 1774 at Hackensack. Two of their sons, Barent and Isaac eventually inherited the house from their grandfather Paulus; one of them was probably the father of Solomon Vanderbeek, who was the owner of the property about 1840-50. It was noted as the home of Aunt Sally Hering, according to Bird's *Rambling Reminiscences* which go back to the period of 1858. The house was used for several years as a store house of the New York Telephone Company before it was demolished in 1922.

The original house was built of stone covered with white plaster; it was a very narrow house with a gable roof. In front was a wide Dutch stoop with railings and benches. At some later date the depth of the house was increased by a frame unit, the gable end shingled, and a gambrel roof with curving overhang built over the whole. A frame wing was also added, it was clapboarded, had a gable roof, a lean-to, and one door and two windows in front. It is from this wing that Washington is said to have watched the retreat. The house stood in its fields off the east side of the main road, and was reached by a private lane (now Salem Street). It fronted on the present Moore Street and stood at the rear of the Telephone Exchange. Various aspects of the house can be seen in the photograph in Boyd's article, page 34, and in two earlier lithographs in Black's article, pp. 250 and 255.

Vanderbilt House
Middletown Road, Rivervale
PLATE 104

The history of this house is unknown. Erskine's Revolutionary map shows a house at this location, but does not state the owner. An old resident and neighbor, speaking of his earliest recollections, states that an old couple named Vanderbilt resided here until about seventy years ago (i.e., about 1860), and that they had no children. The owner in 1876 was Howard Cole. Mrs. E. Garnier has owned it for the last forty years, and leases it. The house is on the old Middletown Road which leads northwards to the early settlements over the border (to the present Pearl River in Rockland Co.). The house stands on the northwest corner of this road, sometimes called the Rivervale Road, and the modern Glen Eyre Road, in the section west of the Hackensack River now known as Rivervale. It was probably built shortly before the Revolution. It may have been originally a Blauvelt or Haring home, as many members of these families settled in this neighborhood at an early period.

Van Horn House
Wyckoff Avenue, Wyckoff Township
PLATE 105

This house is a beautiful example of successive growth, carried out in the spirit of the original unit, yet embodying the later ideas of architecture. Christian Barent-sen[1] emigrated before 1653 to New Amsterdam, and soon settled at None Such Creek (near the present Wilmington, Delaware) in the South River Colony, where he died just prior to June 26, 1658; he was a carpenter and builder by trade. His widow Jannetie Jans soon consoled herself, and married Dec. 12, 1658 Laurens Andrieesen Van Buskirk, ancestor of that family in America; she had three sons by her first husband, and four sons by her second, including Thomas Van Buskirk of Saddle River (plate 103). Her eldest son Barent Christiansen[2] Van Horn (Van Hoorn) bought and settled at Pembrepogh (now Bayonne); by his wife Geertje Dircks Claussen, he had many children, most of whom removed to Bucks Co., Pennsylvania. One son, Dirck[3] Van Horn of Pembrepogh and later of Saddle River near Hackensack, willed to his son Barent land on the northeast side of the Great Pond (i.e., Franklin Lake) in 1733.

Barent[4] Van Horn, b. Sept. 8, 1705 and baptized at Acquackanonk (now Passaic), married Rachel Aeltse and lived at Wezel on the Passaic River (now part of Paterson). They removed to the vicinity of Wyckoff before 1742 when they acted as sponsors at the nearby Paramus Church; Barent became a member of this Church before 1748 when he signed the call for a minister. He had at least three children, Aeltje, Elizabeth, and Dirck. Barent was probably the builder and owner of this house. It was still owned by the Van Horn family at the time of the Revolution (Erskine marked it merely Van hoorn). It later passed into the hands of the Ackerman family and was owned for many years by Gerrit Ackerman, bap. June 2, 1800, died about 1890, a great-grandson of Johannes Ackerman and Elizabeth Stagg of Polifly (plate 72); it is then said to have been owned for a year by Gerrit's brother-in-law John De Baan (husband of Rachel Ackerman), who sold it about 1870 to Robert Branford, the father of the present owner, John E. Branford. Since the house was owned by both a brother and a brother-in-law, it may have been inherited by them from their father Johannes G. Ackerman, bap. Aug. 28, 1768, died 1828-29, married Nov. 18, 1791 Mary Daniel Haring, and had four children baptized at Paramus Church.

The two small sections of the house belong to an early period in the eighteenth century, the smallest being the original unit. There is an old, low, double Dutch door in the small section; at present the middle section has only a small window on either side, but the stonework shows that formerly there was a door or another window on the front side. The front walls of these two units are built of undressed stone, almost as irregular as the stonework of the back of the house; the steep pitch of the roofs can be compared with other early houses. The age of the large section of the house is uncertain; the front wall is built of well-dressed stone while the rear wall is of irregular stone, the door has an early fanlight and the windows are fairly small in size, so this part of the house may also have been built before the Revolution. Its extra height is partly due to a high cellar underneath. The house stands on a hillside, so that from the rear view (shown in the photograph) it seems to nestle, almost burrow, into the ground. The broad gable roof (rather than the more usual gambrel of the late eighteenth century), the lack of dormers, the single chimney, and the added height of the large unit carry out and continue the style and feeling of the earlier units, and give us a beautiful creation of several generations of builders.

The house stands in the southwestern part of Wyckoff Township on the south side of Wyckoff Avenue, which ends one-half a mile beyond in the Goffle Road, south of the Lozier house in Midland Park (plate 96). It is about three miles southeast of the village of Wyckoff.

Van Houten House
Franklin Lakes Road, Franklin Lakes Borough
PLATE 106

This region was in early days known as Sicomac. On Erskine's Revolutionary map the road he surveyed ran directly from the lake, now called Franklin Lake, northeastward towards Wyckoff village. The present road, on which the Van Houten house stands, turns southeast in the general direction of the Goffle settlements, and this portion of it may or may not have existed at the time of the Revolution. The date of this house is uncertain. John Van Houten was living here when he helped to build the Wyckoff Church in 1806, and the house had then been in existence for some time. He came to this region between 1794, when a son was baptized at Kakiat in Rockland County, and 1799, when another son was baptized at the Paramus Church. It is probable that John Van Houten built the house between these dates, although it may have been standing when he bought the property. His descendants, the present owners, believe it is about 160 years old, which would place its erection in the vicinity of 1775. The lines of the gambrel roof are similar to that of the Van Alen—Hopper house in the Ramapo Valley (plate 102), which belongs to this same 1770-1790 period.

The first known owner of the house is John Van Houten, d. April 29, 1832, aged 71 years and 20 days. He and his wife Anna, d. August 8, 1838, aged 69 years, 6 mos., 15 days, both lie buried in the family cemetery north of the house, which he set aside for his descendants. This John (Johannes or Jan) Van Houten, b. April 9, 1761, bap. at Tappan, is believed to have been born in the house near New City (then called Kakiat or New Hempstead) in Rockland County which had recently been erected by his father Roelof⁴ Van Houten (see supra). In Tappan Church on Oct. 13, 1785 Johannes married Antje Blauvelt, b. Jan. 25, 1769, bap. at Clarkstown, daughter of Jacob Blauvelt and Maria Talama, the marriage record stating that they were both then living at New Hempstead. John⁵ (Johannes or Jan) and Anna (Antje) Van Houten had eleven children: Roelof or Ralph, b. 1787, d. Jan. 5, 1860, aged 72 years, 11 mos., 22 days, buried in the Van Houten plot with his wife Rachel and three sons John, Ralph and Isaac; Jacob, b. 1789 at New Hempstead, bap. at Clarkstown Church, lived at Paterson, d. May 2, 1856, aged 66 years, 8 mos., 18 days, buried in the Van Houten plot with his wife Elizabeth and a son James; Maria, b. Oct. 5, 1791, bap. at Clarkstown Church, d. April 29, 1866, m. Feb. 24, 1810 Isaac Stagg of Paterson; James, b. 1794, bap. at Kakiat; Isaac I., b. 1799, bap. at Paramus, d. March 24, 1851, aged 51 years, 5 mos., 7 days, buried in the Van Houten plot, married Margaret Westervelt; Margaret, b. Jan. 1, 1803, bap. at Paramus, d. April 9, 1881, buried in the Van Houten plot, married Nicholas Romaine; Abraham, lived at Preakness and was drowned, married Bridget Garrison; Douwagh, a bachelor; Levi, married Ann Van Gelder; Catharine, married about 1824 John Ryerson (1791-1835) of Totowa and Paramus; Ann, married Cornelius Van Horn and went west to Illinois.

The house was later occupied by the son James⁶ Van Houten, b. May 11, 1794,* bap. June 5, 1794 at the Kakiat Church, d. Aug. 24, 1877,* aged 83 years, and buried in the Van Houten family plot nearby. He married Nov. 19, 1814* Cornelia Ackerman, b. July 12, 1794,* d. May 7, 1877* in her 83rd year, daughter of Jacobus A. Ackerman. They had two daughters, Maria and Cornelia Jane, and an only son who inherited the farm. He was John Ryerson⁷ Van Houten, b. Feb. 6, 1822,* d. Aug. 5, 1872 at the early age of 50 years, married Jan. 4, 1843* Ann Youmans or Yeomen, b. April 20, 1825,* d. May 3, 1900,* daughter of Daniel Yeomans, b. May 7, 1768* and his second wife Mary Vanblercom, b. Jan. 16, 1784,* whom he had married June 3, 1820.* John and Ann had four children who died in infancy and then four more who lived to maturity: Daniel, Jesse, Isaac and James. Isaac⁸ Van

319

---

* Taken from family Bible.

Houten, b. Sept. 14, 1857, still lives in the old homestead; on Nov. 8, 1879* he married Eliza Ellen Courter, b. Sept. 20, 1856,* d. Oct. 16, 1928, daughter of William Marten Courter. The present owner of the old house is their son John Ryerson⁹ Van Houten, b. May 20, 1880.*

The house is built on a hillside overlooking a small brook. It stands on the south side of Franklin Lakes Road, which makes a sharp curve up the hill at this point, and is east of the intersection of Ewing Avenue. Franklin Lakes Road is called Sicomac Road in nearby Wyckoff Township.

House of William Van Voorhees
Franklin Avenue, Wyckoff

The house stands on a 550 acre tract bought Aug. 17, 1720 from John Barbetie and associates, merchants of New York City, by John and William Van Voor Haze, yeoman of Bergen Co. and repurchased by them April 2, 1745 from John Hamilton and associates to setle their claim. Steven Coerte¹ Van Voorhees, born 1600 at Hees in the Province of Drenthe, married, and emigrated with wife and children to this country in 1660 on the *Bontekoe*. He settled on a farm at Flatlands, conducted a brewery and was a magistrate there. He remarried late in life, and died Feb. 16, 1684 at Flatlands. One of his sons, Albert Stevense² Van Voorhees, removed after his father's death to a large tract he had purchased on the west side of the Hackensack River, between Kinderkamack and Hackensack; he was married three times, first to Barrentje Willemse by whom he had no children, secondly on April 24, 1681 to Tilletje Reiniers Wizzel-pennig, and thirdly by 1693 to Helena Van der Schure. The eldest son by the third wife was William Albertse³ Van Voorhees, b. 1694, d. July 19, 1745, married first April 19, 1718 Susanna Laroe, and secondly Jan. 6, 1728 Maria Van Gelden.

This William Van Voorhees and his youngest brother Jan bought the 550 acre tract at Wyckoff, which was divided between their heirs May 7, 1767. William settled here and undoubtedly built the oldest part of the present house. He had seven sons and four daughters, but only Jan and Albert (both by the second wife) carried on the name. Albert⁴ Van Voorhees, b. Feb. 1, 1738, d. Aug. 25, 1825, aged 87 years, married Jannetje Van Houten, b. 1735, d. May 31, 1810. The doorknocker on the main house is inscribed "A.V.V.H. 1824," so Albert probably built the main house at the advanced age of 86 years, no doubt to house his numerous grandchildren with their wives and children. His only child, John A.⁵ Van Voorhis, b. 1763, d. May 25, 1833, married Christina Bogert, b. 1763, d. Jan. 30, 1847; they had nine children: Albert, James, William, Abraham, John, Ralph, Jane, Ann, and Corines Van Voorhis.

320

---

* Taken from family Bible.

Corines Quackenbush, b. July 11, 1800, died at the age of 89, bought the stone house nearby on the main corner of Wyckoff, supposedly from a John Van Voorhis (this house is not marked on Erskine's map, and was probably built shortly after the Revolution), and left it to his eldest son John (1820-95). Corines' seventh son, Uriah Quackenbush, b. May 20, 1836, bought the Van Voorhis house on the hill. He married Kaziah ——, and willed the property to his granddaughter Grace (daughter of John), wife of Judge John B. Zabriskie, the present occupants. There may have been an intermediate owner between the Van Voorhis and Uriah Quackenbush. Before the latter bought it, a woman, known as Aunt Jennie to the neighborhood, had a candy store in the basement. The house at various times in its history has been used for a grocery store, candy store, hotel and ballroom.

The house was erected at three separate times. The oldest part, built by William Van Voorhees, is now in the center and almost completely hidden; it is very small, has very low ceilings, and a gable roof sloping almost to the ground; it faces east, which is unusual for that early period. The main house was added on the road side, and faces south; it is of whitewashed stone, with gambrel roof and high ceilings. A late nineteenth century kitchen wing of no architectural style has been added at the rear. The house stands on a knoll overlooking a brook in the west end of Wyckoff village. It is on the north side of Franklin Avenue, called Wyckoff Road further west.

House of Nicholas Varleth; the Sip Homestead at Bergen
formerly in Jersey City, now at Westfield.
PLATE 107

This is the oldest Bergen County house still in existence, although, as it has been altered, removed, and rebuilt, the Demarest house by the French Cemetery (plate 82) may be considered the truest example of the early house in this county (Hudson was originally part of Bergen County). Both houses have the very steep pitched roof, which was typical of the houses in the old country and of the earliest houses in New Netherland.

Several attempts to settle the western shore of the Hudson River were made at an early date, but the farms were burned and the inhabitants massacred by the Indians. In an effort to give some degree of protection to the settlers, Gov. Stuyvesant decreed in 1660 that all should dwell within a palisaded village and go to their outlying farms by day. Thus in 1660 was established the village of Bergen, around the present Bergen Square in the heart of Jersey City.

The Sip homestead stood until recently on the southeast corner of Bergen

Avenue and Newkirk Street. The latter was one of the boundaries of the original village and the former was the road which led from the green in the center of the village northeastward to the English Neighborhood (the Ridgefield section). The corner plot on which the house stood was a double town lot, known as No. 160, east of the plain or green, which was granted together with two out-garden plots and two tracts of upland and meadow near the village by Stuyvesant to Nicholas Varleth and Balthazar Bayard on Jan. 3, 1662. The same lots, plots and tracts were confirmed to them by Gov. Carteret on Aug. 10, 1671. Therefore, considering the dated stone 1664, it is probable that the house was erected by one of these patentees, probably the former as Bayard's house is believed to have been near the Newkirk house.

Nicholas Varleth emigrated to New Netherland by 1652 and became an important member of the Colony, appointed commissary, ambassador to Virginia, peace commissioner, Captain of the militia of Bergen, Communipaw, Ahasymus and Hobocken (the early Dutch settlements on the Jersey side of the Hudson River), member of the court of Bergen, and member of Gov. Carteret's Council. These last three appointments were made in 1665, showing that he had settled in New Jersey by that date. As well as the above and other land purchases at Bergen, he was granted the Hobocken tract before 1656 and the Secaucus tract in 1658. In the patent of 1667 to the latter tract he was described as a resident of the Town of Bergen and Balthazar Bayard as of New York. Varleth died in 1675. By his wife Anna Stuyvesant, widow of Samuel Bayard, he had a daughter Susanna and a son Abraham who left the province in 1675. Balthazar Bayard, a stepson of Varleth and his partner in many land purchases, lived in Bergen as early as 1663 when he was appointed schepen of the town, and returned to New York about 1667, where he later became an alderman. On the death of Varleth before division had been made of their joint properties, Bayard took the land (including the double lot No. 160 at Bergen in which we are primarily interested) by right of survivorship. On Dec. 11, 1686 he sold several meadow lots and the double house lot (No. 160) in the village to Tadeus Michielsen, who sold to Jacob Luby. He died in 1697 and his heirs sold the property to Jan A. Sip on Oct. 25, 1699. Sip also obtained a quit claim from Bayard's heirs on April 30, 1713.

There seems to be no full nor reliable account of the early generations of the Sip family. Adriaen (or Arie) Hendricksen[1] Sip emigrated from Breda in North Brabant and married at New Amsterdam Feb. 4, 1656 Grietje Warnaerts of Schonevelt. They had four children, baptized at New Amsterdam 1657 to 1662: Annetje, Marritje, and twins Jan and Jacob. Adriaen died about 1663; it is possible he settled in Bergen shortly before this date, since his two eldest children were recorded as young daughters of New York whereas his son Jan was recorded as a young man of Bergen at the time of their respective marriages. Adriaen Sip's widow married at New Amsterdam Aug. 9, 1664 Hans Diederick of Isleven. Hans and Grietje (and presumably her young children by her first husband) were living at Bergen in 1665, when Hans took the oath of allegiance here. He kept a house of entertainment at Bergen, was a town deputy to the legislature and a judge; he died Sept. 30, 1698 at Bergen.

Jan Arianse[2] Sip (or Johannes Adriaenszen Sip) was the only son of Adriaen who lived to maturity. He was born May 24, 1662, probably in New Amsterdam where he was baptized, although it is possible that he was born in Bergen where he was undoubtedly living with his mother and stepfather by the time he was three years of age. Recorded as a young man of Bergen, his marriage banns were published here and his actual marriage took place in New York City. On April 23, 1684 he married Johanna (or Anna) Van de Voorst, bap. April 16, 1666, daughter of Iden Van Vorst of Ahasymus. They had eleven children, all born at Bergen, although the eldest five were baptized at New York: Adriaen or Arie of Acquackanonk (see plate 149), Hillegond married Johannes Walings Van Winkle, Iden died young, Margaret married Johannes Gerritse Van Wagening, Annetje married Gerrit Hermanisse Van Wagening, Edee or Ide of Bergen, Johannes, Cornelius, Abraham, Hendrick (the last four died young), and Helena or Lena married John Van Horn. It was the father of these children who in 1699 purchased the double house plot (No. 160) in Bergen which is known as the Sip homestead. He was a Captain of the militia. He died Aug. 12, 1729, leaving all his Bergen lands and rights to Edee, his younger son. Ide[3] (Edee or Eida) Sip. b. Sept. 3, 1695 at Bergen, d. Feb. 26, 1762 at Bergen, married first Ariantje Cornelissen Cadmus, and married secondly at New York June 9, 1725 Antje Gerrits Van Wagening of Bergen, who died here Jan. 25, 1750. He was a lieutenant of the town militia. On his death, Ide divided his property between his three sons and four daughters, leaving the homestead where he lived to his son Cornelius, who died March 9, 1793 without surviving issue. Another son of Ide was Garret[4] Sip, b. Aug. 21, 1739 at Bergen, d. here Oct. 1, 1775, married by 1763 Jenneke Marselus, b. Oct. 26, 1740, younger sister of Edo Marselis, builder of the house at Upper Preakness (plate 146). Their only son Peter[5] Sip, b. Aug. 18, 1767 at Bergen, d. May 1, 1852, probably came into the possession of the family homestead on the death of his uncle Cornelius without surviving issue. Peter was a prominent jurist and Judge of the Bergen Co. Court of Common Pleas. By his wife Elizabeth Vreeland, whom he married Nov. 1, 1789, he had three children, the youngest of whom, Richard, lived in and eventually owned the old homestead. Richard[6] Sip, b. Aug. 31, 1800, d. April 10, 1865, married Sept. 15, 1856 Sarah E. Wayland, and they had a son Richard Garret[7] Sip, b. July 2, 1860, who in

1910 was still occupying the homestead where six generations of his forebears had lived and died.

In recent years the house was sold and removed to the Wychwood development outside of Westfield in Union County, and now stands in an orchard on the north side of Woodland Avenue, west of East Broad Street. Much that is typical of a seventeenth century house is now lacking, and except for the steep roof line it has more the feeling of an eighteenth century house; this is partly due to its modernization by the Sips while it still stood at Bergen. The house is now owned by the Wychwood Corporation. A photograph in *the 250th Anniversary of the Founding of Bergen* (1910), p. 54, shows its condition at that date.

Vreeland House
125 Lake View Avenue, Leonia Borough, near Englewood
PLATE 108

There is some question as to whether the stone wing of this house was built before the Revolution. A descendant, Isaac Vreeland, considers that the whole house was built at the same time (1818), as it was the third Vreeland house on the property, the first further east and the second just south, and he sees no reason for the third house to have been built while the second was still standing. The wing, however, is Revolutionary in style; it may have been built about the time of the son's marriage in 1786.

Michael Jansen[1] van Broeckhuysen (a village on the river Maes in the Duchy of Limburg) emigrated in 1636 on the *Rensselaerswyck* with his wife Fitje Hartmans and two children. He was engaged as a farm servant for the patroon; he left in 1646 to strike out for himself, and died in 1663; his wife survived him, dying Sept. 21, 1697. Their eighth child, Cornelis Michaelsen,[2] b. June 3, 1660, d. May 1727, married May 12, 1681 Metje Dircks Braecke, and lived on his tract at Pembrepogh (now Bayonne). His only son, Michael[3] Vreeland, b. Sept. 18, 1694, married Oct. 23, 1718 Janneke Van Houten; they lived on the Wesel Road (now part of Paterson) and had ten children.

Their son Derrick or Dirck[4] Vreeland, b. March 1, 1736* (old style) bap. March 11, 1737 at Bergen, married and removed to a large farm he had bought in the English Neighborhood, a part of the Berry patent of 1669. He undoubtedly built the first two houses here, a temporary structure and later his permanent stone home. In 1777 he was imprisoned at Morristown for British sympathies. He had only two children, Michael and Elizabeth, and died in his 86th year on Nov. 5, 1821.* Michael D.[5] Vreeland, b. March 12, 1760,* d. May 13, 1832,* married Margaret Terhune, b. Feb. 28, 1770,* d. March 22, 1837.* Their son Richard M.[6] Vreeland, b. Oct. 5,

324

---

* Taken from family Bible.

1787,* d. Feb. 2, 1849,* married Dec. 1, 1810.* Mary Sipp, b. March 26, 1793,* d. July 10, 1880.* Richard built the main frame house about 1818 (or his father built it for him); it is noted for its beautiful lines, proportions and carvings. Richard and Mary's children were: Isaac who married and lived just south; Margaret wife of Henry Westervelt, who lived in a stone house further north in south Englewood; and Michael. Michael R.[7] Vreeland, b. April 27, 1812,* d. Oct. 12, 1893 aged 83 years,* married Sept. 24, 1840 Lavina Brinkerhoff. The last of the family to own and occupy the old home was their son Richard M.[8] Vreeland, who died about 1928 when almost ninety years of age; he had four daughters, two by his wife Helen Harris. Mrs. Natalie T. Corbett, the present owner, bought the property in 1930 from the Richard M. Vreeland estate.

The house is in the northern part of the locality originally called the English Neighborhood. It stands on a hill, overlooking a brook to the north and the old road (now Grand Avenue) to the west. It is in the former Nordhoff, now the borough of Leonia, south of Englewood.

Westervelt—Bogert House
393 Main Street, Hackensack
PLATE 109

This house was built at three different times, but none of the builders are known. It is occasionally called the General Poor House. Gen. Enoch Poor was a New Hampshire man and a prominent leader in the Revolution; he is supposed to have been stationed in this house at one time, and to have fought a duel while here; he died Sept. 8, 1780 of putrid fever, while stationed at Kinderkamack to the north, and was buried at Hackensack. According to George Ackerman's *Recollections of Sixty Years Ago* (pub. 1902), the house was occupied around 1840 by "Long John" Westervelt; he was given this name because he was so very tall. It is called the Bogert house by Eugene Bird, in his *Rambling Reminiscences* (pub. 1922), which go back to the period of 1858. On a map of 1876 John Demarest was the owner. Standing in the heart of Hackensack, it has been conservatively remodelled into stores, but still preserves its character.

There were many John Westervelts, and the identity of "Long John" is undeterminable. He may have been a son of Lucas and Belinda (Demarest) Westervelt: John L.[6] Westervelt, b. Aug. 2, 1809, d. Nov. 4, 1860, married Catharine Larmour, and had three daughters, the eldest of whom was Ann who married Henry Bogert; this would account for a Bogert occupancy immediately after "Long John's". Lubbert Lubbertsen[1] Van Westervelt, a native of Meppel in the Province of Drenthe, emigrated to this country 1662 on the *Hoop* with wife, children, and

325

---

* Taken from family Bible.

brother, and settled at Flatbush. In the early 1670s he removed to Hackensack, transferred his membership to the Bergen Church in 1676, and to the Hackensack Church when it was organized in 1686; he died within a short time, his wife Geesie surviving until after 1696. Of their six children, the youngest was Jurrien Lubbertse[2] Westervelt, born on Long Island and still living in 1738; he married four times at the Hackensack Church, and had eleven children by his first three wives. He lived at Hackensack, and in 1687 made many extensive purchases of land here from the patentee Capt. John Berry, of which he sold 1500 acres in 1734. The south wing of this house is said to have been built in 1688 and, if so, may have been built by Jurrien Westervelt on one of his purchases of 1687 at Hackensack. A son by his third wife, Roelof,[3] remained at Hackensack, but the latter's son Johannes[4] Westervelt (grandfather of John L.) lived at Wagaraw, so it is probable that John L. Westervelt, if he owned the house, did not inherit it in a direct line from his forebears.

The south wing is the oldest unit. The central portion is said to have been built in 1800; its high ceilings and high steep gambrel are post-revolutionary in character. Early in the nineteenth century the half stories of frame were added to the two wings, possibly by "Long John" Westervelt; they are higher and have larger windows than the usual half stories with their "lie-on-your-stomach" windows. The rough stonework of the house is whitewashed in red, and the whole is covered by a red tin roof, which harmonizes and therefore does not destroy the character of the house by its modern composition. The house stands on the southwest corner of Ward and Main Streets, one block south of Anderson Street, in the heart of Hackensack.

House of Roelof Westervelt
Tenafly Road, Tenafly
PLATE 110

Roelof[2] Westervelt, grandfather of the builder of this house, was baptized March 10, 1659 at Meppel in the Province of Drenthe, and came to America with his parents, Lubbert and Geesie (see plate 109); on March 25, 1688 he married Orsolena or Wesselena, daughter of Caspar Stynmets of Bergen, and had three sons and six daughters. In 1695 he and nine others bought from the Proprietors for £100 some thousands of acres between the Hudson and Overpeck, extending from the present Englewood northwards nearly to Tenafly; to Roelof fell the northern section, on which he is said to have settled. On Sept. 17, 1695 he also bought from the patentee a triangular tract of land between the branches of the Overpeck Creek northwards to the head of the Tenakill (brook), for which he had to obtain an added release from the Indians in 1705; it was on this tract that his grandson later built. Roelof Westervelt was a religious man, a member of the Church of Hackensack, deacon and church master. On May 15, 1731 he married secondly Lea, widow of Abram Brouwer, and daughter of Jean Demarest of the French colony (see plate 82), when he was 73 years of age and she was 50. His son Johannes' married Oct. 11, 1718 Efie De Groot and had ten children, of whom we are interested in Roelof.

Roelof[4] Westervelt, b. Dec. 4, 1723, died 1800, married about 1745 Dirkjin Taelman, and had two sons, Douwe and Johannes, and five daughters; he probably built the old wing of the house at Tenafly. His elder son Douwe[5] Westervelt, b. Jan. 9, 1753, d. May 16, 1822, aged 69 yrs., 4 mos., 17 days,* married first Oct. 28, 1773* Rebecca Demarest, and secondly June 12, 1802* Margrietje Banta, b. Aug. 16, 1759,* widow of Renis Kuyper; by his first wife he had four children: Roelof, b. Sept. 9, 1774,* d. March 7, 1837,* unmarried, Daniel, and two daughters. Daniel[6] Westervelt, b. Oct. 4, 1779,* d. April 13, 1877* at the advanced age of 97 yrs., 6 mos., and 9 days,* was married on Jan. 31, 1801* to Polly Cole, b. Dec. 8, 1785,* d. Sept. 8, 1867, aged 81 yrs., 9 mos.* He was the builder of the main stone house about 1798. He had an only surviving son Peter and five daughters, including Gertrude who married John Ackerman, Jr. and removed to the Durie house on the Schraalenburgh Road (plate 86). Peter D.[7] Westervelt, b. March 9, 1806,* d. June 4, 1885, aged 79 yrs., 2 mos., 26 days,* married Nov. 19, 1825* Rachel Westervelt, b. Oct. 25, 1809,* d. Feb. 22, 1874, aged 64 yrs., 3 mos., 25 days,* daughter of his cousin Johannes' Westervelt, Jr. (son of Douwe's brother Johannes) and Rachel Brinkerhoff; they had six children. Peter D. Westervelt added the frame wing on the north end of the house when he married in 1825. He had six children. His youngest son, Charles P.[8] Westervelt, b. April 17, 1857,* now lives nearby, having sold the homestead about 1923 to Mr. Sulzer, who sold it to The Tenafly Weavers, the present owner.

The pre-revolutionary wing is built of roughly dressed stone; its roof has a steep pitch and no overhang, characteristics of an early eighteenth century house; it was undoubtedly built by Roelof about the time of his marriage in 1745. The very irregular stonework in a part of the end shows the location of the old Dutch oven, which was formerly built out here. A ladder behind the large fireplace leads up to the old slave quarters above. The fanlight over the door with its panes of peep-hole size is very unusual; a similar one is also found over the rear door of the main house; they are probably of post-revolutionary date. Charles Westervelt states that the main stone house was built by his grandfather Daniel[6] Westervelt (who married in 1801); therefore it is likely that it was erected a few years later than 1798, the date attributed to it. A beautiful example of the post-revolutionary style, it is built of dressed stone, with lintels over door and windows, a gambrel roof still unmarred by dormers, and interesting woodwork in the interior. Unusual features are the outside entrances to the cellar at either side, built to repeat the style of the wing. Its capacious

327

* Taken from family Bible.

garret is open except for one very small, windowless closet bedroom. The north wing, built by Peter D. Westervelt in 1825, is characteristic of this period: of frame, with small "lie on your stomach" windows in the second half-story, and a gable roof which balances the early wing; its stone cellar is known as the harvest kitchen, for the extra harvest hands were fed here. A view of the entire house is to be seen in the vignette.

The house is now the Exhibition House and retail salesroom of the Tenafly Weavers; some of the weaving is done in the capacious garret above, and meals are served inside and on the attractive stone terrace behind. The house stands on the northeast corner of the present Westervelt Road and the old Tenafly Road, south of Clinton Avenue in Tenafly.

Westervelt House
County Road, Cresskill
PLATE 111

The house stands on a tract patented to Isaac Bedlow in 1669, and sold by him in 1728 to Colonel Jacobus Van Cortlandt. Johannes Roelofse[3] Westervelt, bap. July 11, 1696, son of Roelof, and grandson of Lubbert Lubbertse,[1] the emigrant, is supposed to have bought and settled on this tract; if so, his house no longer exists. On Oct. 11, 1718 he married Efie, daughter of Pieter De Groot and Belitje Van Schaick, and had five sons and five daughters; his second son Roelof built the house at Tenafly (plate 110). His eldest son Petrus[4] Westervelt, bap. Feb. 18, 1722, lived here at Cresskill; about 1745 he married Catelyntje Taelman, and had nine children.

Petrus' son Benjamin P.[5] Westervelt (b. Aug. 1, 1763, d. 1845) built the main unit of the house in 1808. He fought in the Revolution, serving in the militia, as a minute man, and in the county and state regiments; he was imprisoned twice by the British and thrown into the Sugar House; he was captured a third time by some Tory neighbors but recaptured by his friend Col. Blanch of the patriot militia. In September, 1784 he married Sarah Durie, probably a daughter of Jan Durie, Jr. of the Schraalenburgh Road (see plate 86), and had six children; in 1817 he married secondly Leah, widow of Benjamin Blackledge, as her fourth husband; her second husband was Isaac Nagel, builder of a house at Closter (plate 98). His son Petrus[6] Westervelt, b. Oct. 15, 1796, d. Nov. 28, 1863, married March 29, 1817 Sally Nagel, b. March 19, 1799, d. Dec. 28, 1870, daughter of Jan D. Nagel, the honest miller (plate 97). Their only son John P. B.[7] Westervelt, b. April 13, 1831, married Nov. 7, 1849 Elizabeth Van Voorhis, and was still the owner in 1912. Their son Peter[8] Westervelt is the present owner.

328

On Erskine's Revolutionary map a house here is marked Westerfell's. Unfortunately no first name is given, so we cannot tell whether Johannes Westervelt's home stood here then. It is possible that the old house (if it stood here) was torn down, and the present house built all at one time by Benjamin P. Westervelt in 1808. The present stone wing does not date so far back as Johannes Westervelt's time and may not even be pre-revolutionary. The low wide pitch of the roof, the stone lintels, and the carefully laid stones of the side wall are characteristic of the late eighteenth century. Lacking any proof that Johannes ever settled on this particular spot, we must presume that his son Petrus Westervelt built the wing shortly before the Revolution, unless the present structure is not the one shown on Erskine's map. An unusual feature is the position of the chimney, which is not at the end of the wing. The south front has two doors and one window instead of the usual one door and two windows. The main house is built of well-dressed stone with a wide gambrel roof, unmarred by dormers. The typical, large windows and the door have stone lintels, each with a raised stone decoration in the center, an early nineteenth century style. The overhang of the roof may have been extended; it is supported by square wooden columns. A view of the main house may be seen in Embury. The house stands on the west side of the County Road, north of the village of Cresskill. This road is the eighteenth century continuation of the Tenafly Road, and led northwards to Sneden's Landing in Rockland County.

The two Zabriskie—Board Houses
formerly on Paramus Road, north of Arcola
PLATE 112

At an early date many members of the Zabriskie family settled and built on their extensive land tracts along the Paramus Road (and adjoining side roads), from Red Mills (now Arcola) northward to Paramus Church (now in the east part of Ridgewood). Many Zabriskie houses stand to this day but, unfortunately for the purposes of this volume, the existing houses were built in the half century following the Revolution. The Zabriskie house reproduced here was the only pre-revolutionary house to survive and it was completely burned down shortly after the photograph was taken in 1925.

Albrecht[1] Zaborowsky was born at Enghstburgh in Poland about 1638, emigrated by way of Prussia and came to this country in 1662 on *The Fox*. He settled at Old Hackensack (now Ridgefield Park) and died there Sept. 1, 1711, aged about 73 years. He was the first Justice of the Peace for upper Bergen County. He was a large land speculator, and by several purchases came to own more than 4000 acres in the county; he was the patentee of the Paramus and New Paramus tracts and of a tract at Cherry Hill. On Nov. 17, 1676 at Bergen he married Machteld Van der Linde, born 1656 at New York, died 1725, daughter of Joost Van der Linde, and had five sons. Three of these, Jacob, Hendrick and Christian, settled on the Paramus tracts.

The south portion of the patent was allotted to Christian Zabriskie; here stood the two Zabriskie—Board houses, the more northern of which is the famous one built in 1790 and occasionally called the Wessels house. Christian is said to have settled on what became known as the Wessels or Board property, so it is possible that his home was an earlier one on the site of the 1790 house. As both Zabriskie—Board houses were originally on the same property, it may be that Christian's home was the old house reproduced here; certainly it belongs to this early period. This Christian[2] Zabriskie, bap. July 3, 1694 at Hackensack, d. 1774, married May 28, 1715 Lea Hendrickse Hopper. They settled at Lower Paramus and raised four sons, Albert, Hendrick, Jacob and Andries, all of whom remained in this locality. Andries or Andrew[3] Zabriskie, the youngest, bap. Jan. 15, 1729 at Schraalenburgh, married Elizabeth ———, and is only known to have had two children, a son Christian, b. 1751 and a daughter Jane, b. 1761. Andries may have inherited his father's home as it was later owned by his descendants.

Andries Zabriskie built a beautiful house nearby at the age of 69 years, judging by the stone lintel inscribed "A. C. Z. 1790." It is probably on the site of an earlier house of his own (or his father's?), since the barn antedates the 1790 period by many years. His only son Christian[4] Zabriskie, bap. Feb. 24, 1751 at Paramus, married Martyntje ———, and had several children: Cornelius, Andrew, who married Mary Ryerson; Abraham, who married Maria Zabriskie and lived in Saddle River Township; Catharine, wife of John Anderson, and possibly James. The son Cornelius C.[5] Zabriskie married at Paramus May 21, 1803 Maria Hopper and had four children: Christian Andrew, bap. 1804, Mary, wife of Isaac Zabriskie, Catharine, wife of Wessel Wessels, and Matilda, wife of Peter Board. The 1790 homestead came into the possession of the above Catharine L.[6] Zabriskie, b. Nov. 22, 1814, living in 1882, who married Wessel Wessels. She probably had no children as the place was later owned by her nephew, Cornelius Z. Board, whose son Frederick Board disposed of it.

The very early house came into the hands of the above Matilda B.[6] Zabriskie, d. 1870, and her husband Peter Board, whom she had married at Paramus May 30, 1833. Peter Board, b. Aug. 19, 1809 in Pompton Township, Passaic Co., died 1891, was a son of Nathaniel Board, who was a leading farmer of Passaic County and a member of the New Jersey Legislature. Peter and Matilda doubtless built the modern two story brick house which lately surrounded the old unit on two sides. After their death, it went to their son Cornelius Z. Board, and then probably to the latter's son Frederick Board.

The old Zabriskie house is a small house built of irregular stone and shingled on the gable end; its roof has a steep slope characteristic of the early eighteenth century; the windows are in uneven alignment, the original sashes were replaced some time ago by large modern ones. Until recently, it stood over a mile north of Arcola, on the east side of the Paramus Road, near Sprout Brook Road.

The 1790 homestead of Andrew Zabriskie stands just north on the same side of the road, and almost opposite the intersection of the Dunkerhook Road from Fairlawn. Rather it may be said that its ruins are here, for a recent explosion or fire has partly demolished it. The house was of stone with a gambrel roof, and with a frame wing on the road end. Its proportions and detail work were exquisite; it was one of the finest and best known of the post-revolutionary Dutch houses. A view may be seen in Boyd, p. 37. It was used recently as the clubhouse of the Saddle River Golf Club. Instead of rebuilding the roof to preserve it the barn has been remodelled for the clubhouse.

The barn behind the 1790 home was much older than the house, a typical and interesting example of an early Dutch barn. The low sides were of stone. The ridge-pole was very high, so that the roof could cover a broad spread and yet slant very steeply almost to the ground; it was undoubtedly thatched originally. Unfortunately Miss Brown arrived too late in the spring of 1933 to photograph the barn; its beautiful lines are now completely hidden and changed.

House of John Zabriskie; Baron Steuben House
New Bridge, North Hackensack
PLATE 113

Two or more John Zabriskies are believed to have erected various parts of this house during the eighteenth century; the two dates most generally ascribed are 1737 and 1752. John Zabriskie of New Bridge was a colonial magistrate. He had a grist mill here and a large trading station, and schooners plying to New York tied at his dock. One of these schooners was burned at its moorings by the Americans so it would not be captured by the British. John was ordered arrested in 1777 for British sympathies, and his property was later confiscated.

On Dec. 23, 1783 the New Jersey State Legislature gave the estate, formerly belonging to John Zabriskie, to Baron Steuben for his personal use. But as he did not want to settle on it, the state legislature on Dec. 24, 1784 ordered the estate to be sold to the highest bidder, and the proceeds given to Steuben for life. It was therefore sold on April 1, 1785, and bought by Captain Walker (Steuben's aide), who could not meet the payments. On Sept. 5, 1788 the state legislature gave Steuben full title to the estate outright, as an act of gratitude for his services during the Revolution. But Baron Steuben had no use for it, as he lived on his large farm near the modern Utica, presented to him by New York State. Shortly before his death at Utica on Nov. 27, 1795, he conveyed the New Jersey estate back to John Zabriskie for £1200.

The next owner is said to have been Andrew Zabriskie, a brickmaker; on July 21, 1793 at Schraalenburgh he married Elizabeth Anderson; they brought up a family of eleven children and adopted two more, one of whom may have been Jane Anderson who later married their son David A. Zabriskie. David A. Zabriskie is said to have moved into the house in 1812; he was still the owner in 1876; he was a miller, and had a mill on the river here, which burned many years ago. The house was sold by a Mrs. Outwater (nee Zabriskie) to William R. Hearst, who sold it to the State of New Jersey. It is now kept as a Memorial to Baron Steuben.

The house probably stands on the tract at Cherry Hill patented to Albert Zabriskie in 1682. He had emigrated to this country in 1662 and settled at Old Hackensack (see plate 112). John was a name in frequent use in the Zabriskie family, and to identify a particular John is rather impossible; but the probable dates of erection and the numerous John Zabriskie owners seem to point to the following line for this house: Albert's son Jan A. or John[2] Zabriskie, Sr. remained at Old Hackensack (Ridgefield Park) and died in 1765; he married Sept. 20, 1706 Elizabeth Claes Romeyn and had four children; he married secondly Dec. 6, 1712 Margrita, daughter of Jean[1] Durie of the French Colony (see plate 86), and had nine children. His son John[3] Zabriskie, Jr., bap. Aug. 5, 1716, married June 15, 1739 Annaetjen Ackerman, bap. Aug. 14, 1720, daughter of Egbert and Elizabeth. Their son John[4] Zabriskie, Jr., bap. Sept. 3, 1741 at Hackensack, married Nov. 21, 1764 Jane Goelett, and had at least two children, Annatje, b. 1765, and John, b. 1767. When John and Jane acted together as sponsors in 1774 he was not called "Jr.," suggesting that his father had died by this time. It would seem probable that John[3] Zabriskie, Jr. built the original unit of the house about the time of his marriage (1739), and that his son John[4] Zabriskie, Jr. made additions before he lost and after he recovered the property, and that the latter was the magistrate and Tory; the latter's wife might have been a relation of the Tory, Peter Goelet of Hackensack, whose land was also confiscated. What relation Andrew Zabriskie was to John Zabriskie is undetermined.

The original unit (now in the center) was a small stone structure put together with old clay mortar and rat-tail nails of a type manufactured about 1726; it has hand-split laths and hinges of a type made before 1776 which are not to be seen in the later ends. The approximate date of 1737 for the original unit is therefore a correct one. The south end was added next. Some time before 1800 the north unit was added and the depth of the house was increased by an addition along the rear. Access to the new rooms was at the landing of the stairs. The result is a variation in floor level which gives the appearance of a low, two story house from the rear view (seen in the photograph). The original gable roof was replaced by a long gambrel roof over the entire building. The house thus does not conform to the usual style of main building with two wings, but is a uniform structure of double the average length. Part of the rear view was photographed to preserve its unusual appearance; the front view, marred by porch and dormers, may be seen in Boyd's article, p. 41, and the end view is reproduced in *Historic Roadsides of New Jersey*, p. 110.

The house stands on the curve of the road at the west end of the bridge over the Hackensack River. The first bridge here was built shortly before the Revolution and the locality became known as New Bridge to distinguish it from Old Bridge to the north (now River Edge). New Bridge is now a part of North Hackensack.

House of Peter Zabriskie; the Mansion House
on the Green, Hackensack

This house was built in 1751 by Peter Zabriskie for his private residence. The only member of the family of that name was Peter³ Zabriskie, bap. Nov. 5, 1721, d. 1800, a son of John Zabriskie, Sr. of Old Hackensack and his second wife Margrietje Durie and a brother of John Zabriskie, Jr., who probably built the house at New Bridge (plate 113). On Oct. 25, 1747 Peter married Martina Varick, bap. April 22, 1722, daughter of Abraham Varick, and had three children, Marretje, Annetje, and Abram.

The American army retreated through Hackensack in the fall of 1776. When Washington arrived, he occupied the private home of Peter Zabriskie until all the troops had passed through. His meals were served from the tavern of Archibald Campbell which stood on the Green nearby. This would seem to infer that Peter, his host, was absent, otherwise the meals would have been prepared in the house by his slaves.

The house was probably sold about the time of Peter Zabriskie's death, and became a tavern. The Weehawk bank, established at Weehawken, removed here in 1825 and became Hackensack's first bank. It was housed in the barroom of the tavern until a brick building was later erected for it nearby and it then became known as the Washington Bank. It was the home of the post office in 1834 when David D. Demarest was postmaster. He was the tavern keeper, and placed the mail in a box nailed to the wall, at the disposal of those concerned to help themselves.

333

During the time of the stage coaches it was called the Albany Stage Coach Tavern. About 1858 it became known as the Washington Mansion House, a name it still bears. Elections were often held in its ballroom. On June 25, 1863 it was the scene of a great collation on the return of the 22nd Regiment from the Civil War. At this period it was owned by John Lovett. The old Company C of the National Guard was organized in 1872 and held its drills here.

The house is of dressed sandstone, with walls nearly three feet thick. At the time of the Revolution it was two stories high, and was probably covered by a gambrel roof. At some later date a third story with a brick front and clapboard end was added. A two story pillared porch was built the length of the house. It has since been greatly enlarged at the rear and is now in bad repair. Dutch tiles with Biblical scenes still adorn two of the rooms, one of which was occupied by Washington. The house stands on the northeast corner of Main Street and Washington Place, and faces the Green and the Church. A view of the Mansion House can be seen in Black's article, p. 251.

Zabriskie—Van Dien Smoke House
Paramus Road, south of Paramus, Ridgewood
PLATE 114

The house in this plate is of too late a period for the purposes of this book, but the smoke house in the rear is much older. The farm is located in one of the Paramus tracts granted to Albert Zabriskie. It has been said that the smoke house is the original Van Horn house built in 1731; the date may be correct, but the large size of the chimney suggests that the building was always used as a smoke house and never as a home. It is not known who was the supposed Van Horn builder, and it is possible (in fact probable) that no member of this family owned it.

The farm was in the possession of the Zabriskie family at the time of the Revolution, when an earlier house stood on the site of the present one. Shortly after the war, Harmen Van Dien married Aeltie Zabriskie, bap. Sept. 30, 1770, daughter of Jan. J. Zabriskie and his wife Lea. It is probable that Harmen purchased or inherited the farm from his wife's family. He settled here and undoubtedly built the present stone house about 1800. His house (although larger) is very similar in style to the eighteenth century houses, but lacks their spontaneity of feeling; it is typical of a mature, finished style, in which the original spirit has disappeared and only the form remains; the result is a well-proportioned, but cold and lifeless structure. Harmen and Aeltje Van Dien had a son John H. Van Dien, b. July 15, 1796 and baptized at Paramus; after his death in 1878 his widow Hannah occupied the place. Since this time there have been many owners; the present owner is John Truwer.

Since the photograph was taken in 1925, the old smoke house has been repaired and its chimney taken down, thus destroying its character. The front of the house has been refaced. It stands on the west side of Paramus Road, on the brow of a hill, less than two miles south of Paramus Church in eastern Ridgewood, and a short distance south of the intersection of Ridgewood Avenue with Paramus Road.

Unidentified House
Fairlawn Avenue, Fairlawn
PLATE 115

The house stands on a tract granted in 1687 to nine proprietors, divided and partly sold in 1692 to the Van Wagoners, Van Ripers, etc. The house is marked but unnamed on Erskine's Revolutionary map. The builders and early owners have not been determined. The house is said to have had only three sets of owners, the second family being the Strehls. Henry Strehl bought the place about 1867 and was the owner in 1876; his son John S. Strehl inherited the property, and sold it to the Radburn City Housing Corp. This Corporation leases it at present, but plans to tear it down to make room for a wide boulevard. The two stone sections of the house are both typically pre-revolutionary; the two story frame addition is of ugly modern vintage. The house stands on the north side of Fairlawn Avenue, east of the railway and of the overhead bridge, and opposite the telephone exchange.

PLATE 70

Achenbach House
Chestnut Ridge Road, Saddle River

The wing of this house may have been built a few years before the Revolution by Hans George Achenbach, a Saxon shepherd boy. The main house is definitely post-revolutionary. The house is Dutch in style, but a different atmosphere, a neat and methodical feeling which pervades, may be due to the builder's German origin.

PLATE 71

House of Abraham Ackerman, later Brinkerhoff's
184 Essex Street, Hackensack

The large stone in the center of the east gable, from which the ivy is carefully trained away, has a date, initials and hieroglyphs, which show that this house was built in 1704 by Abraham Ackerman with the aid of two of his sons. This is one of the best known early Dutch houses of the gambrel roof type. Notice the very beautiful curving sweep of the roof and overhang, and the depth of the house. The gradual improvement of the open attic in the mid-nineteenth century is indicated by the different height of the upstairs bedrooms. The heavy pillars flanking the front door are not suitable and were not added until about 1900. One room in the west end of the house has very thick interior walls. It is believed that this, together with an old stone kitchen wing no longer existing, was the original family house, probably built by Abraham Ackerman about 1696. The house has been in the continuous possession of the Ackerman and Brinkerhoff families with the exception of six years.

PLATE 72

*House of Johannes Ackerman, later Brinkerhoff's
formerly at 651 Polifly Road, Hasbrouck Heights*

The wing of this house was built by Johannes Ackerman about 1728. Although erected at such a comparatively late date, it has been known for many years as a good example of one of the earliest types of Dutch houses in Bergen County. Before the overhang was developed and extensively adopted, the roofs were built only to the face of the wall as in this instance. The main house was erected by James Brinkerhoff in 1800 along pre-revolutionary lines.

339

PLATE 73

Ackerman—Naugle House
415 East Saddle River Road, Paramus

This house consists of two similar units. The east half is said to have been built as early as 1692 and
1701 by a member of the Ackerman family and the west half (near the road) by another Ackerman in
1761. Interior woodwork affords proof that both dates are approximately correct. The recently painted
white trim of the house is over-emphasized in the photograph; in reality the house has the appearance
of very great age. The gable roof has the steep pitch characteristic of the early houses; the overhang
in front is asymmetrically balanced by the long low slope in the rear. There is no hall and each main
room has its outside door. Except for the improvement of the second floor and addition of dormers,
this house remains practically unchanged.

PLATE 74

Ackerman—Van Emburgh House
Paramus Road, Paramus

It is believed that this house was erected in 1701 by an Ackerman. It was still in the possession of this family at the time of the Revolution and was later owned by Henry Van Emburgh's family for about a century. It seems scarcely so old as the Ackerman house nearby (plate 73), but it is similar in lines to the Ackerman house in Hackensack (plate 71), which was built in 1704. It is one of the few houses of the gambrel roof type with a hall at the side of the house. The position of the chimney in the center of the house is also unusual. The existence and contrast of the modern twenty-paned window sashes with the modern two-paned sashes in the dormers is unfortunate.

PLATE 75

House of Abram Ackerman
East Saddle River Road, Saddle River

The original unit of the house is the wing, which was built in 1750 or 1760 by Abram Ackerman, who was Washington's host during the Revolution. At this time there was also a detached slave kitchen. The main house was added by the builder at the close of the war, 1781. He faithfully followed the architectural lines developed in the eighteenth century, but the beautifully carved woodwork in the interior is characteristic of the post-war era. The house has undergone a very successful restoration. Among the nineteenth century and recent changes are the dormers, the extension of the roof overhang and addition of square supports to form a porch, the projection of the roof of both units beyond the gable ends, and probably the second chimney between the main house and the wing. The Dutch roofs did not extend beyond the gable ends (plates 71 through 74)

PLATE 76

Alyea—Outwater House
445 River Road, Fairlawn

Only the wing of this house is pre-revolutionary. This original unit was probably erected in the beginning of the eighteenth century. The very rough stonework of the front wall and the small size of the window openings are characteristic of this early period. Unfortunately the modern glass door and the adjoining window mar the effect of the house. The owners are unknown until the nineteenth century.

PLATE 77

House of Hendrick Banta
Pascack Road, Woodcliff Lake

This house was built by Hendrick Banta in the years immediately preceding the Revolution. Notice the unusual height of the roof and the consequent steep pitch of the gambrel. The long four-paned windows and dormers, the extension of the overhang in both front and rear supported by pillars, and the roof continued beyond the gable ends result in a very heavy and overladen feeling which was not originally characteristic of the house.

344

PLATE 78

Brickman (?)—Ackerson House
Island Road, north of Ramsey

This may have been Brickman's Revolutionary tavern; Aaron Burr is believed to have been a frequent patron here. The house is early eighteenth century in style and was probably erected at the same time as a nearby barn, which was dated 1747. It is built of stone of very irregular sizes, much of it not more than rubble, laid in a binding material of clay, chopped straw and hogs' hair. The small window at the side and the larger windows at the rear with their narrow lower sashes are types still in use at this period. The gambrel roof has a very straight lower slope. The early interior arrangement is followed, of two main rooms each with its separate door and a small room opening directly from each room at the rear. At the end of the nineteenth century the upper floor was still open attic reached by a ladder and trap door. The photograph emphasizes the well-kept condition rather than the great age of the house.

PLATE 79

House of Hendrick Brinkerhof, later Demarest's
493 Teaneck Road, Teaneck

This house was built about 1735 by Hendrick Brinkerhof. It has been the home of only two families, the Brinkerhofs and Demarests, for one hundred years each, with the result that the house remains unchanged to this day, and is a well-known example of the Dutch style. This view is reproduced here because of the unusual feature of the roof overhang extended around the gable end. The overhang, such a characteristic and beautiful feature of the Dutch houses, was developed to prevent the clay mortar from being washed out by the rains, so it is strange that the end walls were generally left unprotected. The varying colors of the sandstone blocks and the occasional use of very small stones, not much more than chips, add life and variety to the building. Notice the careful jointing of the corner. The main house and small wing were built at the same time and are an earlier type from which the Ackerman house at Saddle River (plate 75) was adapted. The second story was improved about 1800

PLATE 80

House of Cornelis Cuyper (Cooper)
Kinderkamack Road, Oradell

This house (or rather the wing) was built about 1751 by Cornelis Cuyper. It is an example of the unpretentious home of a farmer and tanner. Notice its narrowness and length, the small sized window openings, and the steep pitch of the roof. It was more usual to carry up the stonework of the gable end at least to the line of the eaves. The modern narrow clapboarding, four-paned windows, door and dormers do not materially alter the original aspect of the house.

PLATE 81

House of William De Clark
Piermont Road, Closter

This house was built by William De Clark about 1800-1805 on his wife's (Sarah Naugle's) ancestral tract. It is included in this volume as an example of the persistence of pre-revolutionary styles for over a generation after the Revolution, even until about 1837. In the case of some of the later houses the very smooth, tooled finish of the stonework is evidence of the later period, as well as the greater use of carving in the interior woodwork. In this instance the architectural lines and roughly dressed stonework are undistinguishable from the pre-revolutionary examples. The view shows the rear and end walls.

PLATE 82

House of David Des Marest (Demarest)
at the French Cemetery, north of New Bridge

This is deservedly one of the best known of the very early houses still in existence. It was built in 1679-80 by David Des Marest, a Huguenot who became identified with the Dutch settlements. This type of house was very prevalent in the late seventeenth century. It consisted of only two rooms, each with its outside door. The irregular stonework was originally laid in a clay mortar the color of the stones. The very steep pitch of the roof is characteristic of the earliest houses and the beautiful curving overhang was developed about the middle of the seventeenth century. The dormers of course are a later alteration.

PLATE 83

House of Jacobus Demarest
River Road, opposite River Edge

The small wing, now unfortunately marred by the large brick bay window, is similar in style to the David Des Marest house nearby (plate 82) and may have been built as early as 1693 by the Demarest family. The main house was built by David's grandson Jacobus Demarest before 1720, and was occupied by the family until the middle of the nineteenth century. In style it resembles the more skillfully built Ackerman house at Hackensack (plate 71), erected in 1704. There is an undefinable charm about this house which is not merely the quaintness inherent in the crooked set of the old windows and in the plastered stonework. It is felt in the totally different David Des Marest house nearby (plate 82) and presumably must be attributed to the French blood of the builders. Except for the slanting bottle glass eyes which were more generally inserted in doors in the interior of the house, this double Dutch door is typical, with its outside panelling forming a cross in the upper half, and with its massiveness increased on the inside by narrow strips of wood laid obliquely side by side. It will be noted that the roofline is still unbroken by dormers.

PLATE 84

House of Abram Demaree
Schraalenburgh Road, Closter

Abram Demaree settled here shortly before the Revolution and probably built the present wing for his home (or a part of it) at that time. It has been stated that he demolished his old home when he built his new one in 1809; it is possible that he used the old rough stones in building a wing for his new house, but wings built at the same time as the main house were generally very small in contrast with this particular wing which has the appearance of having once been an independent unit. Compare it with the Alyea and Cuyper houses (plates 76 and 80). Notice the contrast with the very smooth tooling and finish of the stones of the main house, built 1809. The fanlight over the door is an early type but the door is later.

PLATE 85

Doremus House
formerly on Saddle River Road, west of Arcola

This is a good example of an unpretentious home which remained substantially unchanged by later occupants. It is very similar in lines to the Alyea house on the Passaic River (plate 76) but a comparison of the stonework will show that the Doremus house belongs to a later period. The roughly dressed stonework at the side and the dressed stonework on the front wall are more finished specimens of masonry, typical of the middle of the eighteenth century. This agrees with the suggestion that it may be the original Doremus house, erected by John Doremus on land he purchased in this vicinity in 1740. Notice the slight overhang of the roof in front and the characteristic total lack of continuation of the roof over the gable end. The vestibule before the door is of course modern.

PLATE 86

House of John Durie
Schraalenburgh Road, Haworth

It is believed that this house was in course of erection during the Revolutionary War; it is still the home of descendants of the builder, John Durie. It has the close-to-the-ground feeling of many of the Dutch houses. A comparison of the slopes of various gambrel roofs demonstrates that the Dutch did not build in stereotyped fashion. In this instance the pitch is not very steep and the curve does not commence until the line of the stone wall has been reached. Dormers and porch are of course later alterations and the modern single-paned window sashes unfortunately give the house a rather vacant expression.

353

PLATE 87

House of Peter Garretson
River Road, Fairlawn

The wing of the present house was built by Peter Garretson shortly before 1708, and is mentioned in a deed of that year. It is still the home of his descendants. The original unit is built of irregular stones of many shapes and sizes. It is now covered by a heavy gambrel roof. Its proportions are those of the early New England gambrel but as this style was not used in Bergen County, it probably replaces a steep gable roof. The main house belongs to a much later date. It is of stone, covered by a gambrel roof, the overhanging eaves of which have been extended for a porch and supported by heavy columns not in keeping with the style of the house.

PLATE 88

Ramapo Valley Road, Hohokus Township
Garrison (?) House

The history of this house is not known, but it is possible that it was owned by the Garrison family at the time of the Revolution. The primitive construction of the house suggests that it was built when this part of the valley was first opened up for settlement, in the second quarter of the eighteenth century. Notice the small size of the windows and the very rough stonework even of the south front. The roof is modern both in its material and in its continuation beyond the gable end.

PLATE 89

House of Cosyn Haring, later De Wolf's
near the State Border, Old Tappan

This house is believed by descendants to have been erected in 1704 after the first division of the Tappan Patent. It was built by Cosyn Haring, a patentee, and is still owned by his descendants, having passed by marriage into the De Wolf family. The plan of the house, that of two main rooms adjoining each other, each with its separate door, thereby eliminating any hall, is a modification of one of the earliest types in vogue but differs from the Demarest house by the French cemetery (plate 82) and others in greater length and considerably greater depth. The gambrel roof is much steeper than that on the Ackerman house at Hackensack (plate 71), which was built at the same time, and there is an overhang only in front. The upper floor is still open garret and is thus one of the very few large houses which can be said not to have been improved. The fanlights over the doors are an early type. Notice the old well sweep, so seldom seen any more. The frame wing belongs to the early nineteenth century.

PLATE 90

House of Gerrit Haring
Old Tappan Lane, Old Tappan

This house was probably erected about 1751 by Gerrit Haring, grandson of Cosyn Haring, builder of the house nearby (plate 89). Although of such a late date, it follows the early plan of two main rooms adjoining each other, each with its separate door, and no hall. The position of the second chimney in the center rather than at the opposite end is unusual. Notice the smoother finish and better jointing of the front wall, characteristic of the later date.

357

PLATE 91

House of Frederick Haring
Old Tappan Lane, Old Tappan

This house was erected prior to the Revolution by Frederick Haring, another grandson of Cosyn Haring, builder of the house nearby (plate 89). The different color and texture of the stones, the continuation of the masonry in the gable to a point above rather than below the upper floor windows, and the more moderate slope of the gambrel roof are features contributing to the dissimilarity of Frederick's house and his grandfather's. The vague outline of the former wing on the road end may still be discerned. The supports to the roof overhang in front are later alterations.

PLATE 92

House of Abraham Haring, later Moses Taylor's
Piermont Road, Rockleigh Borough

This house was built about 1758 by Captain Abraham A. Haring, who was carried away by the British during the Revolution. It was later owned for about one hundred years by the Moses Taylor family. This is an example of the gable roof used occasionally over a house two full rooms in depth. It may be compared with the Lent house at Orangetown (plate 53), built in 1752. The varying hues of the stones add life to the carefully cut and jointed stonework. It is probable that the overhang of the roof in front was extended when the pillars were added. Frame additions and different sized dormers are also later.

359

PLATE 93

Holdrum—Wanamaker House
Pascack Road, Upper Montvale

This house was built about the time of the Revolution by a member of the Holdrum family, and passed by marriage into the Wanamaker family. It is said to have been built in 1778 but its appearance suggests a slightly later date. Even at this period the Dutch seldom used dressed stones for the sides and back of their houses, reserving the careful jointing and finish for the south front. This house shows that the well dressed stone was not even carried up to the actual roofline, as the wooden boxing under the overhang has been dismantled, exposing the rough stonework beneath. The large four-paned modern windows and glass door give the house a vacant expression. The poorly designed dormer, entry porch, and wing are modern alterations. Notice the old panelling of the door jamb.

PLATE 94

Hopper—Goetschius House
East Saddle River Road, Upper Saddle River

This house is shown on a map of 1713 as **Gerrit Hoppa's**. It was probably built shortly before this as it greatly resembles the Ackerman house at Hackensack (plate 71) and the Haring house at Old Tappan (plate 89), both of which were built in 1704. The variety of masonry is characteristic of the early Dutch houses: very irregular stonework in the rear, at the sides roughly dressed stones interspersed with rows of stone chips, for the front wall similar or more carefully finished stonework (the front of the Hopper house has been refaced recently), and always carefully jointed corners. The old windows with the narrow lower sashes and the old irregular glass panes are still in use at the rear of the house. Supports to the roof overhang, both front and rear, and the long dormers were alterations made at different times. Although the heavy roof continued beyond the gable end is not the original one it blends with the house and is less noticeable than a similar one in better condition. The length of the house is less than average, the house being almost square; it is also unusual to find three windows at the rear with no door.

PLATE 95

House of Isaac Housman
525 Terrace Avenue, Hasbrouck Heights

This house was erected in 1773 by Isaac Housman in the section known as the Polifly, south of Hacken-sack. Houseman was probably influenced by the two story town residences being built at this time in Hackensack, as his house has not the feeling of a farmhouse and, although it is the usual one and a half stories in height, it has the suggestion of more space. As a rule the upper section of the gable end was clapboarded or shingled, but in this case the stonework was carried up almost to the apex and finished with a few rows of brick. Even in the earliest houses there was a tendency to use both long and short stones to add variety and life to the masonry; this became developed in some of the later houses, such as this one, into a definite pattern of alternation of sizes.

PLATE 96

House of Cornelis Lozier
Goffle Road, Midland Park

This house was owned at the time of the Revolution by Cornelis Lozier and had probably been built by him in the previous quarter century. Lozier owned a mill on the stream nearby, and ever since there has been a mill connected with the property. The two units of the house were probably built at separate times. The trapezoidal stone lintels are generally seen in houses built in the period of 1770-90. Only occasionally are windows with the narrow lower sash found at this late date. The fanlight is the simple sunburst type; it resembles the one on the Ackerman house at Hackensack. The frame half-story on the wing belongs to the early nineteenth century. Both the doors and the cellar opening have been changed.

363

PLATE 97

House of Barent and John Nagel (Naugle)
Harvard Street, near Piermont Road, Closter

The stone unit of this house was built before 1745, presumably by Barent Nagel for one of his children. It descended in succession to several John Nagels and remained in the family until the late nineteenth century. This photograph was taken before its recent modernization and is reproduced partly because the patch of garden truck suggests its original rural surroundings. The east unit of stone is the original house; at a shortly later period the frame unit was added along similar lines. This is an example of the asymmetrical balance often used by the Dutch: the curving overhang of the roof in front is balanced by the long, low slope of the roof at the rear. Other views are shown in plate 5.

PLATE 98

House of Isaac Nagel (Naugle)
Hickory Lane, near Piermont Road, Closter

This house was erected about 1775 by Isaac Nagel, grandson of Barent Nagel who built the house nearby (plate 97). It is very similar in lines and interior arrangement to the Cosyn Haring house at Old Tappan (plate 89), built in 1704. It is unusual to find a house at this late date without a central hallway. The windows also are early types; those in front have the narrow lower sash and those in the rear are very small in size. The stones are unusually light in coloring. Dormers and large porch are modern additions.

365

PLATE 99

Packer House
Ewing Avenue, Franklin Lakes Borough

The original unit of this house is the stone part of the wing, built in the early eighteenth century. Hand-hewn laths were used and the stone was laid in a straw and clay binding. The main house may have been built about 1789 by the first Packer in the vicinity. The stone quoins and the trapezoidal stone lintels, in patterned contrast to the plastered stone of the walls, are characteristic of the late eighteenth century. However, the small size of the windows and the lack of any hallway are more typical of an earlier date. The row of modern dormers and the porch have been added in such a way as not to materially alter the lines of the house. The half story of frame over the wing belongs to the early nineteenth century.

PLATE 100

Terheun Homestead
450 River Street, Hackensack

This is known erroneously as the house built in 1670 by John Terheun. The first John of the family was not born until 1734; the house was probably erected by his grandfather Albert Terheun, who did not come to Hackensack until about 1686 and probably did not build his permanent home until a few years before 1709. The juxtaposition of roughly cut white painted stone and white clapboarding shows the Dutch eye for delicate contrast. It will be noted that the door is not in the center of the house and is not flanked on both sides by two windows as was usual at a later period. The deep door jamb is panelled. The steep gambrel roof has a very straight slope and the curve of the overhang does not commence until the stonework has been almost reached. Pillars now support it to form a simple porch. Dormers and frame additions belong to the nineteenth century. The house is still the home of a member of the Terheun family. It overlooks the Hackensack River.

367

PLATE 101

Terhune House
East Saddle River Road, Hohokus Borough

The stone unit of this house belongs to the Revolutionary era and was probably built a few years before the war. The prominent quoins and trapezoidal lintels are characteristic of this period; they give the needed contrast to the smoothly plastered stone walls. The frame unit was built at a later date along similar lines. The close-to-the-soil feeling is stronger than in many of the houses. The simple pillared supports do not detract from the original house in the way that the Victorian dormers do. These were probably added by Joseph Jefferson, the actor, who owned the house for a time.

PLATE 102

Van Alen (?)—Hopper—Van Horn House
Ramapo Valley Road, Mahwah

This is probably the house designated as John Van Alen's on Erskine's Revolutionary map. Its known history commences a generation later with the ownership of the Hopper family. The main house belongs to the Revolutionary era and it is possible that it was not erected until a few years after the war, although the use of such very irregular stonework for the side wall would be unusual at this late date. The upper slope of the gambrel roof is more moderate than was customary and the lower slope is very long and straight; it is probable that there was never any overhang. The simple porch belongs to a slightly later period. The very irregular stonework of all walls of the wing is to be noted; generally the front wall was better finished, as is the case with the main house.

PLATE 103

House of Thomas Van Boskerk (Van Buskirk)
East Saddle River Road, Saddle River

The northeast room of the house was the original unit and was built by Thomas Van Boskerk between 1708 and 1734; it consisted of one large room with a gable roof and no cellar; a nearby cave was then used for storage of the winter vegetables. The house was enlarged by a descendant to form the usual two rooms on either side of a wide central hallway, with a cellar beneath the new part. It was probably covered by a gable roof which was raised early in the nineteenth century for the addition of a half story of frame. The simple porch may have been added then; its square supports are of different lengths and rest on uneven stone flagging. The shutters are modern.

PLATE 104

Vanderbilt House
Middletown Road, Rivervale

This house was probably erected a few years before the Revolution, but the builder and early owners are unknown. The Vanderbilt family lived here in the middle of the nineteenth century. The old twelve-paned window sashes still remain in the southwest corner. Various minor changes have been made. It is unusual to find two cellar doors.

PLATE 105

Van Horn House
Wyckoff Avenue, Wyckoff Township

The three units of this house were all erected at different times. The house was owned by the Van Horn family during the Revolution and it is possible that Barent Van Horn, who settled in this vicinity, built the smallest unit shortly before 1742. The largest and latest unit was probably built about the time of the Revolution. The progressive sizes of the sections of this house are an unusual form of the gradual growth customary in Bergen County, where the central unit generally became the main section. The gradual increase in length, depth, and height, in breadth of roof and overhang, in size of windows and doors results in an unusual and beautiful composition, in which a sense of balance is given by the single chimney of the large unit placed at its far end. Since the house burrows into the side of a hill the front walls are higher than this view from the rear would indicate.

372

PLATE 106

Van Houten House
Franklin Lakes Road, Franklin Lakes Borough

This house is still the home of descendants of John Van Houten, the owner in 1806. It belongs to the Revolutionary era and may have been built or bought by him when he settled in this section between 1794 and 1799. The main feature to be noted is the gambrel roof with its long, straight lower slope and the absence of any overhang; it can be compared with that on the Hopper house (plate 102) of the same period. The roofline has never been broken by the addition of dormers. Marks in the stonework point to the former existence of a door in the center of the rear wall. The low second story of frame is a characteristic nineteenth century addition to the wing.

PLATE 107

*House of Nicholas Varleth; the Sip Homestead at Bergen
formerly in Jersey City, now in Westfield*

This house was built in 1664 presumably by Nicholas Varleth, one of the patentees of the property. It was purchased by Jan Adriaensen Sip in 1699 and remained the homestead of his descendants until very recent years, when it was removed from Bergen Square, Jersey City (the former village of Bergen) to Westfield. The very steep pitch of the roof is characteristic of the very early houses. It is probably one of the earliest examples of the curving overhang which became so characteristic a feature. This building shows that the large windows with twelve panes in each sash were in use even at this early period in well-built houses in the settled communities. The house is photographed as it now stands rebuilt in its new location, appropriately behind an apple orchard. The wing on the east end is smaller but is flush with the south front. Dormers, trellis work, chimneys and shutters have been changed or added.

374

PLATE 108

Vreeland House
125 Lake View Avenue, Leonia Borough

The main house of frame is the well known Vreeland house south of Englewood, built about 1818 by or for Richard Vreeland; it is noted for its beautiful lines, proportions, and carvings. The small stone wing is said to be pre-revolutionary but it is possible that it was not erected until about the time of Michael Vreeland's marriage in 1786. It remained the home of the family until 1930. The wing is pre-revolutionary in style but its character is considerably marred by the modern dormer, four-paned windows, door and stoop. The characteristic sloping cellar hatch under the window has been altered.

375

PLATE 109

Westervelt—Bogert House
393 Main Street, Hackensack

This is a typical example of the gradual balanced growth of Bergen County houses. The original unit is the stone part of the south wing; this is believed to have been built in 1688, possibly by Jurrien Westervelt on his purchase of 1687. The central unit is said to date only from 1800; notice its steep gambrel roof with the straight lower slope and absence of any overhang. The gable roofs of the wings were later raised for frame half stories which have the small windows typical of the early nineteenth century. The rough stonework of all units has been painted red with which the red tin roofs harmonize in color so that their modern composition is scarcely noticeable. Standing in the heart of the business section, the house has been conservatively remodelled into stores.

PLATE 110

House of Roelof Westervelt
Tenafly Road, Tenafly

The original unit of this house is the wing, which was probably built by Roelof Westervelt about the time of his marriage in 1745. The property remained in the family from 1695 until about 1923. The steep pitch of the roof is reminiscent of the very early houses. Notice the difference in finish of the stones in the early wing and in the main house, which was erected about or shortly after 1798 by the grandson Daniel Westervelt. This main house is a beautiful example of its period, built along pre-revolutionary lines with well dressed stones, stone lintels, and a sweeping gambrel roof still unbroken by dormers, and with interesting woodwork in the interior. Over the door of the wing and over the back door of the main house is an unusual fanlight consisting of a row of minute panes of glass, which was probably an individual conception of the Westervelts, as no other like it has been found. The original unit consists of one large room with an immense fireplace, behind which a ladder leads to the old slave quarters in the garret.

377

PLATE 111

Westervelt House
County Road, Cresskill

A house on this site was marked Westerfell's on Erskine's Revolutionary map. Presumably this was the wing of the present house. Johannes R. Westervelt is said to have settled in this vicinity after 1728; it was his grandson Benjamin P. Westervelt who built the main house in 1808, which is still the home of his descendants. The date of the wing is uncertain. It belongs to the Revolutionary era and may have been erected a few years before the war by Petrus Westervelt. There are many unusual features in the construction of the wing: the cutting and laying of stone in the side wall in as finished a manner as in the front, the use of stone lintels in such a small unit, the two doors and one window rather than one door and two windows in the south front, and the position of the one chimney near the center rather than at the end. The first two features mentioned and also the moderate slope of the roof are characteristic of the late eighteenth century, thereby tending to disprove the supposition that the house was built by Johannes Westervelt about 1730 or by his son Petrus when he married about 1745.

378

PLATE 112

Zabriskie—Board House
formerly on Paramus Road, north of Arcola

This is not to be confused with the more famous Zabriskie—Board house built nearby in 1790 and owned by the same families. The stone wing of the house here reproduced was the original unit and may have been built by Christian Zabriskie shortly after his marriage in 1715. The steep slope of the roof is characteristic of this early period. The south front of the house is built of roughly cut stones, some of which are rounder and more irregular than usual. Unfortunately the four-paned windows, shutters, decayed porch, dormers and lean-to, all of which are alterations, change and hide a large part of the original house, but the shingled gable end is impregnated with the feeling of the period. The house has a greater length than the average similar small unit, having four rather than two windows in the front wall.

PLATE 113

House of John Zabriskie
New Bridge, North Hackensack

This is better known as the Baron Steuben house; it was awarded to him out of gratitude by the State, which had confiscated it from its Tory owner. Various dates have been ascribed to this house, presumably applying to its different sections. The original unit in the center was built about 1737-39 by John Zabriskie, Jr. with hand-split laths, clay mortar, early rat-tail nails and gable roof. Similar additions were later made at both ends, the depth of the house was increased by an addition along the rear and a gambrel roof placed over the entire building. The result is an unusually long house under one roof rather than the more general main house with two wings. When the depth of the house was increased about the end of the eighteenth century, access to the new rooms was arranged for at the landing of the stairs with a resulting variation in floor level. The photograph shows part of the house from the back. This view gives the suggestion of a low two story house. The front view shows it to be the usual one and a half story house with deep overhanging eaves. The Hackensack River flows by the end of the house.

PLATE 114

Zabriskie—Van Dien Smoke House
Paramus Road, south of Paramus, Ridgewood

The house in this plate belongs to a period not covered by this volume as it was erected about 1800 or even later. A comparison with earlier houses will show that it was built along pre-revolutionary lines but the style had become stereotyped and the result is cold, insipid, and lifeless. It stands on the site of an earlier house which was owned by the Zabriskies during the Revolution. The smoke house was built about the middle of the eighteenth century. Notice the characteristic broadening chimney, which occupies all of the end wall in the interior. In the same manner as the houses of the period, the stones in the front wall are more smoothly cut than those in the side walls, and the gable end is clapboarded.

PLATE 115

Unidentified House
Fairlawn Avenue, Fairlawn

The stone units of the house are typical of the eighteenth century in which they were built. The wing is practically unchanged. The main house has the early arrangement of rooms without a hallway. The slight extension of the roofline beyond the front walls and the gable end is a change which alters the feeling of the house. The addition of the porch caused the elimination of the characteristic sloping cellar hatch.

MONMOUTH AND MIDDLESEX COUNTIES

**HOUSE OF
CORNELIUS COUWENHOVEN**

MIDDLESEX AND MONMOUTH COUNTIES

Middlesex County

MIDDLESEX COUNTY was predominantly Scotch and English. A few Dutch families also settled here, mainly along the Raritan River and the Somerset County line in old Piscataway Township.

A large tract, extending south to the Raritan River, was granted by Gov. Nicoll in 1664 to some Englishmen from Long Island, and Elizabethtown was started by them the following year. In the meantime the Duke of York had sold the Province of New Jersey to Berkeley and Carteret. In 1666 Gov. Carteret and the Elizabethtown Point Associates sold the southern portion of their 1664 purchase to Joshua Pierce and others. In 1667 Piscataway was sold to Daniel Pierce and his associates. None of these early owners were Dutch.

Piscataway originally included an immense tract across the Raritan River as well as on the northeast side. The Somerset—Middlesex County line was changed seven times, thus affecting its bounds considerably. Piscataway Township was organized as early as 1675. Thomas Lawrence purchased a 1300 acre tract on the south side of the Raritan River in 1678; the house of his step-son Cornelius Longfield at the mouth of Lawrence Brook was mentioned in 1679 by the Labadist travellers. In 1681 John Inians and associates purchased from the Indians the land along the southwest side of the Raritan River from Bound Brook to Lawrence Brook. Inians bought for himself a 1280 acre tract on which now stands the City of New Brunswick. In 1686 the Highway Commissioners approved of Inian's Road, running between his house here and Claswick's Bridge, as the best road to Burlington. The village was first called Brunswick in 1724 and was given a city charter in 1730. Its population was both Dutch and English; in 1774 John Adams estimated that it had from three to four hundred houses and about one hundred and fifty families. Among the early Dutch settlers of New Brunswick were the families of Van Voorhees, Van Aersdalen, Schuyler, Van Deursen, Van Veghten, Ten Broeck, Van Dyk and Van Alen. Among the Dutch who purchased land in Piscataway before 1725 were the Clausons, Garretsons, Hendricks, Sutphens, Bibouts, Smocks and Van Horns. The First Reformed Church of New Brunswick was organized about 1703. Another Dutch Church was organized in 1717 at the settlement of Six Mile Run, now Franklin Park, along the county line halfway to Kingston.

As Middlesex County was largely settled by the English, it is not surprising to find the influence of their styles in the Dutch houses. Both the stone two story mansions included in this group are Georgian although very different from each

385

other. On the other hand the more modest frame farmhouses are typically Dutch; they are covered with gable roofs without overhanging eaves.

The photographs were taken in 1933 after the field survey was completed. A series of maps of the Middlesex—Somerset County line, together with Judge Ralph Voorhees' *Recollections* (1874), were of great aid in determining the age of the houses and the identity of the owners. The author is indebted to Miss Marian Cushman and Charles Deshler for information concerning the Raritan River valley, and to Cornelius C. Vermeule for notes on the land titles of the valley.

Monmouth County

The first land purchase in Monmouth County was in 1663, when about twenty Englishmen from Gravesend on Long Island bought from the Indians the three necks separated by the Navesink and Shrewsbury Rivers, the tract extending inland to include the site of old Middletown. Gov. Nicoll issued the Monmouth Patent on April 17, 1665 to the Long Island men for all of the present Monmouth County and parts of Middlesex and Ocean Counties, on condition that they settle thereon at least one hundred families; they were to be tax free for seven years, have their own forts and town government, and enjoy liberty of conscience. This patent was issued before news had been received that the Province had been transferred in 1664 to Berkeley and Carteret; under its authority General Assemblies of the Patentees were held, the deputies ignoring the Proprietors' claim to the soil and government. The title was in litigation for many years; the patentees eventually lost and had to take out new patents for their lands from the government of the Proprietors.

The first settlement of the county was made in 1664-65 under the Monmouth Patent in the vicinity of Middletown and Shrewsbury by John Bowne, Richard Stout and other Englishmen from Long Island and Rhode Island. They were mainly Baptists and Quakers. The second settlement was made in 1682-83 by the Scotch in the vicinity of Freehold, and a Presbyterian Church was built at Tennant in 1692. The third settlement was started between 1690 and 1695 by the Dutch from New York City and Long Island. Among these were the Couwenhovens, Schencks and Hendricksons. The Dutch occupied only a small territory around Holmdel, a land of rolling valleys and streams, part of which is appropriately known as Pleasant Valley. The Reformed Church of Freehold and Middletown, occasionally called the Navesink Church, was organized in 1709 and a brick house of worship erected in 1719 on the Road to Middletown one mile from Holmdel. It was the only Dutch church in the county until 1826 and is known as the Old Brick Church of Marlborough.

Monmouth was one of the four original counties organized in 1683. The first townships, Middletown, Shrewsbury and Freehold, were formed in 1693. The county court house was built in 1714 at Monmouth Court House, the present Freehold. This is still the county seat.

The Monmouth County houses are shingled and covered by gable roofs, generally with a steep slope. In other respects the houses vary greatly, and there seems to be no predominant type among the small number extant.

The photographs in this section were taken in 1925 and 1934. The field survey was undertaken with the aid of Judge and Mrs. Henry E. Ackerson, Jr. The text has been drawn largely from private family Bible records, Beekman's *Early Dutch Settlers of Monmouth County* and Stillwell's *Historical and Genealogical Miscellany.*

HOUSES IN MIDDLESEX AND MONMOUTH COUNTIES

Houses in Middlesex County

Field Houses

River Road, Piscataway Township

The Fields were an English family, but became almost Dutch by adoption after settling in the Raritan River valley—they spoke Dutch, attended the Dutch church and married Dutch wives—so it is fitting that some mention of their homes should be made in this volume. Robert[1] Field is supposed to have come to Rhode Island with Roger Williams. We find him in Newport in 1638. He removed to Flushing, Long Island, an English settlement, where he was one of the patentees in 1645. His son Anthony had a son John[3] Field, b. May 15, 1659 on Long Island. John's early home was at Flushing, where he was a patentee in 1685.

On Dec. 14, 1695 John Field bought a tract of 1,055 acres, extending for two and a half miles along the northeast bank of the Raritan River, commencing one mile below Bound Brook and running in the direction of Raritan Landing. He purchased it from Benjamin Clarke who had inherited it from his father Benjamin Clarke, Sr. John Field settled on the bank of the Raritan in the middle of his tract, and built a stone house here, which had a cornerstone dated 1710. This same year, 1710, he was chosen Justice of the Peace for Middlesex and Somerset Counties. His will, dated in 1725, was probated in 1729. His wife Margaret also died before 1729. Judge Jeremiah[4] Field, b. May 17, 1689, d. Nov. 10, 1746, was his only son and inherited the Raritan tract. He was a lieutenant in the colonial militia and a Judge of the Court of Common Pleas. On Feb. 19, 1712 he married Mary, b. Oct. 8, 1687, d. Aug. 28, 1742, daughter of Michael Van Vechten, widow of Albert Teneicke, and sister of Derrick Ven Vechten, the builder of the present house on the Raritan at Finderne (plate 139).

Judge Field's twelve children included: Jeremiah, b. 1713, who lived in a stone house which was the home of Stephen Voorhees shortly before 1901; John, b. 1714, who lived in a stone house which had a dated stone marked "1743 J. F." and which was known as the Oliver farmhouse in 1901; Margaret, b. 1717, who married Jacob Van Deventer, and built a frame house on the extreme north end of the Field tract (plate 119); Sarah, b. 1728, who married John Pool, and whose son John Pool, Jr., purchased and lived in the Cornelius Low Mansion at Raritan Landing (plate 116); Michael, b. 1723, who owned the mill property east of the village of Bound Brook and was a member of the Committee of Correspondence during the Revolution;

Benjamin, b. 1725, who lived in a frame house, the newer portion of which was dated "1761 B. F.," and which was owned in 1901 by Benjamin M. Field.

Still another son of Judge Field was Richard[5] (or Dirck) Field, b. Oct. 31, 1726, bap. at the Dutch church of Raritan, d. Sept. 21, 1800. He was known as "Pine Tree Richard" to distinguish him from the other Richards in the family and no doubt also because his place had many pine trees. His house was standing in 1901, when it was owned by John D. Field, son of Dennis, and was torn down a few years ago. It had a cornerstone marked "1710 F." which was taken from his grandfather's house, the foundations of which were recently visible a few hundred yards distant. The houses of these brothers all stood on the River Road. On Nov. 23, 1749 Pine Tree Richard married Elizabeth Smock, b. Jan. 28, 1728, d. Sept. 2, 1808, probably the daughter of Henry and granddaughter of Matthias Smock, who had built the house a few miles down the road at the ford (plate 117). They had five sons, four of whom served in the Revolution. The father set apart the north portion of the homestead tract near Bound Brook for one of these sons, Richard R.[6] Field, b. 1755, d. 1840, who built the main part of the house still standing here and now owned by J. A. Smith. This Richard married Dinah Vermeule of the Blue Hills (part of present Plainfield) but had no children and eventually gave his home to his nephew Capt. Richard J.[7] Field. The latter, b. Sept. 12, 1785 at Lamington, d. May 6, 1871, was a son of Jeremiah Field who lived near North Branch and a grandson of Pine Tree Richard. On Dec. 22, 1808 he married Mary Kline, and in 1826 they moved into his uncle's house on the north end of the Field tract. It was inherited by their son John K.[8] Field, and is now or was recently owned by J. A. Smith.

The Field—Smith house is a shingled structure in several units, of which the main section is the pre-revolutionary part. A photograph of it may be seen in the *Field Genealogy*, p. 575. It stands on a bend of the River Road, between the road and the river, south of the Van Deventer place (plate 119), and about one and a half miles from Bound Brook. The sites of the houses of John Field and of Pine Tree Richard are also between the road and the river, a short distance to the southeast. The homes of Pine Tree Richard's brothers Benjamin and Jeremiah were further southeast on the Field tract. There are many other houses on this tract built by later members of the Field family.

House of Cornelius Low
River Road, Raritan Landing, Piscataway Township
PLATE 116

The grandfather of the builder of this house was Pieter Cornellessen[1] Lowe, who emigrated from Holstein in 1659 on the *Faith*, and settled at Esopus. His son

Cornelis' removed to New York City, where Cornelius' Lowe or Low was born and baptized March 31, 1700 in the Dutch church there. On May 21, 1729 Cornelius Low, Jr., married Johanna, daughter of Isaac Gouverneur, bap. April 15, 1705, d. Oct. 17, 1763. They came to Raritan Landing in New Jersey in 1730 and lived in a house on the flats near the river.

Raritan Landing, one mile above the village of New Brunswick, was a very important shipping point for the produce of western New Jersey and a part of Pennsylvania. A great flood covered the flats in 1739, and caused Cornelius Low to build for greater safety on the bluff overlooking the Landing, on a 2 acre plot of land he had bought in 1738 from William Williamson. The house was finished late in 1741 and the family moved in. In his family Bible he records that his child William was born "at the new house on the mountain, Raritan Landing" on Jan. 24, 1742. Cornelius was a prominent surveyor, attorney, and landowner. He lived in his new home until he died early in April, 1777.

At the time of Cornelius' death the village of New Brunswick was in the possession of the British, and his residence was the headquarters of the Post Commander. Mute evidence of the British occupancy are the musket marks on floors, balustrades and wainscotting. Some of the family continued to reside here for a few years. Cornelius' granddaughter Mary Margaret⁵ Lowe (1768-1841) lived here with her widowed mother (Catharine Hude, widow of Cornelius⁴ Low, Jr.) at the time of her marriage in 1789 to Jacob Rutsen Hardenbergh. Nicholas⁴ Low was the executor of the estate of his father (Cornelius, the builder of the house), but due to adverse business conditions he could not dispose of the property until 1793, when he sold it to John Pool.

John Pool, Sr., married Sarah, one of the daughters of Jeremiah Field, who owned and lived on the 1,055 acre field tract further up the Raritan River toward Bound Brook, and a sister of Margaret Field, wife of Jacob Van Deventer, who built on the Field tract (plate 119). It was their son John Pool, Jr., who later purchased the Low house at Raritan Landing in 1793. John Pool, Jr., married Mary, daughter of Lucas Voorhees. They resided in the Low Mansion, and here ir 1797 was born their son, the future Dr. John Adams Pool, who continued to live here until he died in 1866. Dr. Pool married Harriet Lawrence, daughter of Isaac Lawrence and Cornelia Beach. Her grandfather, Rev. Abraham Beach, was a noted clergyman of New Brunswick and owned the stone house a few miles up the Raritan River on the other side (plate 141). Shortly after the doctor's death, the place was sold in the summer of 1871 to George W. Metlar. He tore down the wing of the house which had become dilapidated. Mr. Metlar's wife was Catharine, daughter of John Van Doren. Her home was the Van Doren family homestead at Millstone (plate

137). The Metlars lived here at Raritan Landing. Their daughter, Miss Mary Metlar, sold the Low Mansion about 1914 to Mrs. E. B. Voorhees, the present owner.

The Low Mansion is considered one of the finest houses in the province. It is interesting to compare it with the Dey Mansion at Preakness (plate 144), built at the same time by a member of another Dutch family. The Low house is unusually deep, almost square, being 50 feet by 40 feet. It is two stories high, built of yellow sandstone, and covered with a hipped roof. The arch heads of the windows are a feature common to houses in West Jersey. The rear view of the house is shown in the photograph, as the roofline in front is broken by modern dormers. The front has a balanced composition, with windows on either side of the central doorway. The irregularly placed door and window in the center of the rear wall are out of alignment due to the stairway. The interior of the house is Georgian rather than Dutch, a variation typical of the wealthy who rarely build true to style in any country. A wide hall traverses the house with mahogany wainscotting on the first floor and pine trim on the second. Two rooms open off either side of the hall; they are large square rooms with high ceilings, very wide hand-hewn doors, beautiful panelling and mantels, and shell-top carved corner cupboards. Dutch, blue, scenic tiles still line the fireplaces of two of the second floor bedrooms. A few of the old twelve-pane window sashes remain in the rear of the house. There was formerly a kitchen wing on the west end, also of two stories but with lower ceilings.

The house stands on a bluff or high embankment overlooking the north bank of the Raritan River, and directly opposite the bridge and causeway. It is over a mile from the Lincoln Highway and the Albany Street Bridge, New Brunswick. The house is surrounded by beautiful trees, and in summer is hidden from the road by their foliage. The first bridge over the Raritan at the Landing was erected while Cornelius Low, the builder of the house, was still alive, in 1772; it was a covered wooden bridge. It might be worthwhile to state here that the name Low is pronounced similarly to cow.

House of Matthias Smock
River Road, Piscataway Township
PLATE 117

This house was built by Matthias Smock about 1718-21. His father, Hendrick Matthyse[1] Smock or Smack emigrated about 1654 and settled at New Utrecht, where he bought land in 1665, was a magistrate and patentee. He was probably of Dutch origin. He married Geertje Harmens, niece of Guert Coerten from Voorthuizen, Guelderland. She died in 1708 and he survived her. They had three sons

392

and four daughters, one son removing to Monmouth County and the other two to Piscataway Township in Middlesex County.

Matthyse Hendrickse[2] Smock, otherwise Matthias Smock, born in New Utrecht, married in the Dutch church in New York on Sept. 12, 1701 Elizabeth Stevens, widow. The name of her first husband is unknown. She was baptized in New York on Oct. 11, 1676, daughter of Jan Stephenszen and Lysbeth Lucas. In 1700 Matthias was an officer in the foot company of New Utrecht militia. He sold his farm in New Utrecht and removed about 1718 to Piscataway Township and settled on the Raritan River in New Jersey. He built his house here before he made his will in 1721. In it he named his wife Elizabeth and his children, Hendrick, John, Lucas, Matthias, Jacobus, Elizabeth (bap. 1704 in N. Y. C.), Geertie (died 1738 unmarried), and Mary. Of these children, Hendrick[3] was a freeholder of Piscataway in 1726; he died in or before 1754, leaving a widow Antie, daughter Elizabeth, and minor children, Henry, Denys, and Ann; in his will he mentioned his home farm of 130 acres at Bound Brook. The son Lucas[3] or Luke lived in Piscataway Township. The son Jacobus[3] is possibly the James Smock who died intestate in Hunterdon County in 1772, leaving a widow Margaret.

John[3] Smock (1712-1791), who was probably the second son of Matthias, seems to have received his father's homestead on the Raritan River in Piscataway Township. He was surveyor of the highways in 1749 and town clerk in 1767. He married Lea, daughter of Charles Fontine of Somerset, who mentioned his daughter in his will of 1743. They had eight children baptized in the Dutch churches at Raritan and New Brunswick between 1731 and 1757: Lena, John, Jr., Abraham, Jacob, Abraham, Maria, Lea and Jannetie. By their eldest son John, Jr., and his wife Saertie, they had four grandchildren, Maria, Annatie, Matthew and John, baptized between 1760 and 1767. The homestead farm next appears in the possession of Mary Smock, who on March 30, 1848 transferred it to her son Jonathan B. Smock and her son-in-law Martin Nevius. The latter released the south half to Smock whose son built upon it, and Smock released to Nevius the north half, on which stood the old house. As Martin Nevius named one of his children John Smock Nevius, it is probable that his father-in-law was John Smock. There was a John I. Smock who died in 1841, only a few years before Mary, presumably the widow, gave up the farm. There was a John Smock who married Mary Fall in Middlesex between 1795 and 1800. These are very suggestive clues in tracing the gap in ownership of the house in the early nineteenth century.

The next known owner was Martin David Nevius, b. July 13, 1822, living in 1900, son of David Nevius, farmer. On Dec. 14, 1847 he married Deborah Ann Smock, b. March 1822, probably a daughter of the above John and Mary Smock.

Martin Nevius was a farmer, and a collector of taxes in Piscataway Township. They had two children, John Smock Nevius, b. 1851, died young, and Maggie Peppard Nevius, b. 1849, d. about 1930. In 1868 she married William Blish, a merchant of New York City. She owned the homestead after her father, and moved away about 1910, probably selling it at this time. In 1923 we find the house in the possession of Marian S. Orten, who deeded it that year to Raymond Paterson, who sold it in 1927 to the present owner, Page L'Hommedieu.

The original section of the house was built by Matthias Smock about 1718-21, and added to probably by his son John Smock. Like most early houses, it faces south regardless of the position of the road, which in this case runs along the west end. The west unit, comprising more than half of the present house, includes the hallway; above the main floor is another story under the eaves, with "lie on your stomach windows" seen from the rear view. The east unit has not these additional low windows. The two sections of the house are clearly seen from the rear view, due to this difference in windows and also to the separate clapboarding of the two parts. The house is covered by a gable roof, unbroken in back by dormers. The fairly small size of the windows is characteristic of the early period. The front of the house, shown in the photograph, has been conservatively modernized and the grounds well planted. This is a good example of a pleasing residential treatment of an early house. The house is about three and a half miles from New Brunswick on the way to Bound Brook, on the northeast side of the River Road, which follows the shore of the Raritan River. It lies opposite the two Van Wickle houses (plates 140 and 141), and was once connected with them by an important ford.

Soulard (?)—Suydam House
County Line Road, Franklin Park
PLATE 118

The road from New Brunswick to Kingston and Princeton follows the line between Middlesex and Somerset Counties, and is crossed by various small brooks known as runs, One, Three, Six, Nine and Ten Mile Run respectively, because of their approximate distance from the village of New Brunswick. Settlements were formed at an early date along these runs of which the most important was Six Mile Run, now called Franklin Park.

The early history of this house is obscure. On John Dalley's map of 1745, only one house is shown on the Middlesex side of the road about here, and is marked Peter Solar. On Dunham's map of 1766, the house is marked John Sydam and a house just above it is Peter Sydam's. On Erskine's map of 1778, it is marked James

Suydam, and the house above it is unnamed. According to a map of 1860 J. Garretson was the owner.

This region is part of a large tract granted to Harrison and Willocks in 1700. Ryck Suydam bought 158 acres from the former and settled at Six Mile Run about 1728; he died in 1798 at the age of 95 years, and is said to be a grandson of Hendrick Ryken who emigrated in 1663 and settled in Flatbush. Ryck's son Peter Suydam (generally spelled Sedam) bought land of Peter Soulard at Six Mile Run about 1743, and built his house (shown on the above map of 1766) which was torn down in 1806. By his wife Femmetje, he had six children, Ryke bap. 1757, Jannetje bap. 1759, Peter, Abraham, Ann bap. 1762, and Lawrence.

The son Lawrence Suydam (or Sedam), bap. Oct. 30, 1765 at Six Mile Run, lived 300 yards farther along the road (southwest of his father), in the house marked John Sydam in 1766 and James Sydam in 1778. Nothing is known of John and James. It would be logical to presume that John, James and Lawrence were closely related. Lawrence Suydam married Abigail Fry, and had many children: Phebe bap. 1792, Ann (1793-1865) married Cornelius Van Liew, Peter M. (bap. 1795, d. 1876), John S. of New Brunswick, William of Middlebush, Abraham of New Brunswick, Isaac, Jacob who died in infancy, Catharine and Maria. Lawrence Suydam, the father of these ten children, was killed by a bolt of lightning while standing in the front door of this house on Aug. 11, 1838, and was buried on the 13th. We next find the house in the possession of Garret S. Van Liew. He and his wife Mary Ann of New Brunswick Twp. sold it with 36 acres to John Garretson, Sr., on Oct. 3, 1859.

John Garretson, Sr., son of Rem, left Jersey City about 1854, as his son was 19 years of age when they settled at Six Mile Run village. He died in 1883 aged 83 years. He lived in a large white frame house on the Somerset side of the road, opposite the field in which formerly stood the Peter Suydam house. He bought for his son John the small house and farm adjoining this vacant field to the southwest, on the Middlesex side of the road. John Henry Garretson, Jr., b. 1835, married in 1858, and started housekeeping in this small house, formerly Lawrence Suydam's. Here his son John Garretson III was born, and now lives across the road in the John Garretson, Sr., house. Matilda Garretson, daughter of John Garretson, Jr., married Abraham S. Voorhees. She bought the small house from her father in 1909, and sold it in 1925 to A. D. Kleinrock, who sold to the present owners, Irving Julius and Miss Rose Julius.

This house was standing by 1766 and owned then by John Suydam. It was probably built much earlier, and was undoubtedly the house owned by Peter Soulard in 1745, unless Soulard's house burned down and was rebuilt before 1766. There was at one time a large addition on the south end, but this was torn down when John Garretson, Jr., left the house. As it stands today, it is a small frame house, of unusual depth for its breadth, covered by a broad gable roof. The old long shingles, old solid shutters, and small-sized windows are evidence of its age. Nestling beneath a beautiful elm tree, it stands in a field one mile northeast of the Dutch church in Franklin Park, and south of Six Mile Run.

House of Jacob Van Deventer
River Road near Bound Brook, Piscataway Township
PLATE 119

This house stands in the extreme northern end of the 1055 acre Field tract bought in 1695 by John Field. It was inherited by his only son Judge Jeremiah Field, who married Mary Van Vechten and had many children. One of these was Margaret Field, b. Oct. 2, 1717, married Jacob Van Deventer. The house was built by or for them about 1738-40 on the north end of her father's tract. Jacob married secondly Elizabeth ———, and died in Somerset County between March 24 and April 12, 1756 (the dates of his will). His executors, Michael and Jeremiah Field (brothers of his first wife) refused the executorship which was then given to the widow. Jacob Van Deventer and Margaret had two children: Jacob, who removed elsewhere, and Jeremiah, bap. April 20, 1740 at Raritan, died 1806 aged 65 years, and buried in the Presbyterian Cemetery at Bound Brook. Jeremiah was a Captain of the militia during the Revolution. He was the next occupant of his parent's home. The house is supposed to have remained in this family until after the Civil War.

Shortly after the Civil War, Richard Field returned from Chicago and bought the Van Deventer house. He is believed to have been the Richard R.[8] Field, b. March 8, 1818, who was a son of Capt. Richard J. Field and great-greatgrandson of Judge Jeremiah Field. He was probably born in Lamington, New Jersey, the home of his grandfather and early home of his father. He was a prominent wholesale merchant in St. Louis for a while. He built a large Victorian-style mansion on the property south of the old Van Deventer home, but did not keep the place. He settled in Plainfield, where he was a prominent man and died March 18, 1892. An insurance company sold the property with the two houses about the beginning of this century to Mr. Bryan, and it descended to his son. Until recently the small house was used as a tenant house. Its present owner, Mrs. T. L. Lewis, has restored it into a pleasing residence.

The house is a small, one and a half story house covered with shingles, except for the rear which is now clapboarded. Across a corner of the main room is a large fireplace, five feet ten inches wide, faced with brick, and topped by a mantel of an early simple type. The enclosed staircase is in another corner opposite the entrance door, suggesting that there was a hallway originally and that the partition has been torn down. The two small rooms in the rear, formerly bedrooms, have the typical very small windows and very low ceilings, smaller and lower respectively than in the main rooms. The house is built of large hand-hewn oak beams, put together with wooden pegs. It stands on the east side of River Road, which runs along the north-east bank of the Raritan River from New Brunswick to Bound Brook, and is one mile south of the latter village. Nearby is one of the old Field houses (see supra), across the river is the old Staats house, built at the same time (plate 136), and a few miles to the southeast along the river are the Smock and Van Wickle houses.

House of Matthias Van Dyke
Lake Road, Mapleton, near Kingston
PLATE 120

Although on the Middlesex County side of the Millstone River, this plantation is only a few miles from Princeton, the home of many Revolutionary worthies such as Richard Stockton the signer, Witherspoon president of the College, Joseph Hewes the signer, and Jonathan Deare a member of the Provincial Congress. We thus expect, and find, English influences prevailing in the Van Dyke house.

The ancestor of the family was Jan Thomasse[1] Van Dyck, who emigrated from Amsterdam in 1652 with his wife and seven children, who was one of the founders of New Utrecht on Long Island and died there in 1672. His grandson Jan Van Dyck or John[3] Van Dyke, bap. Nov. 19, 1682, d. Dec. 18, 1764,* married June 5, 1706* Anna Verkerk, b. Jan. 13, 1684,* d. June 27, 1754.* They left New Utrecht and settled in Middlesex County, New Jersey, in the vicinity of New Brunswick. Jan was a member of the New Jersey militia in 1715 and an alderman of New Brunswick in 1730. The will of John Van Dyck of the Corporation of New Brunswick, yeoman, was dated 1757 and probated in 1765. He devised his homestead farm of 600 acres to his (second?) wife Ann, left legacies to his three daughters and farms of 200 to 300 acres to each of his six sons. One son, Matthias[4] Van Dyke (Van Dike), b. Aug. 28, 1714* at New Brunswick, d. 1784, was married June 12, 1746 to Eleanor or Nelly Lane of Middlesex County, daughter of Matthias Lane of Middletown. They had one son and six daughters.

In 1756 Matthias Van Dyke built the present two story stone house on the banks of the Millstone River at Mapleton, on a 200 acre tract later inherited from his father who had bought it from Thomas South. Just before the battle of Princeton it was occupied by several British officers, and a dinner, ordered by them to be served when

397

---

* Taken from family Bible.

they should return "after routing the rebels under Mr. Washington," was eaten by the Americans.

Matthias Van Dyke died intestate and John Van Dike was appointed administrator of the estate on Oct. 29, 1784. In the inventory of his personal estate, it was noted that three-fourths was the property of Matthias deceased and one-fourth of his son Matthias. The only son was Matthias[5] Van Dyke, Jr., b. Jan. 8, 1752, bap. Feb. 9 at Six Mile Run Church, d. Sept. 18, 1832. He was a patriot soldier in the Revolution. On Jan. 25, 1774 he married Lydia Longstreet and had six children. The homestead was inherited by his son William J.[6] Van Dyke, b. Sept. 27, 1795 in this house, d. Oct. 27, 1865, and lies buried in the nearby cemetery at Kingston. In 1823 he married Margaret Nevius, b. April 3, 1799, d. Sept. 7, 1862, and buried by her husband. They had five sons and three daughters, of whom Henry L. R.[7] Van Dyke (1842-1895) was the owner, according to a map of 1876. The house passed through several hands before it was purchased by the present owner, William Flemer. He conducts the Princeton Nurseries across the road.

The house is a two story stone structure of irregularly cut fieldstone, surmounted by an architectural cornice and a broad, low gable roof. The English influence predominates, in fact there is no evidence of Dutch traditions. The house has been improved recently, but the old feeling is still imparted to us, especially in the slope of the roof. It is covered with ivy and the grounds are well landscaped. The house stands near the Millstone River in the northerly part of the old Mapleton section. It is on the west side of Lake Road, one mile south of Kingston, and north of a Roman Catholic institution.

Houses in Monmouth County
House of Cornelius Couwenhoven
Pleasant Valley, Holmdel Township
PLATE 121

Cornelius Couwenhoven is said to have built this house in 1700. He was born Nov. 20, 1672 at Flatlands, the son of William Gerritse[2] Couwenhoven and his second wife Jannetje Pieters Monfoort, and the greatgrandson of Wolfert Gerritsz[1] who emigrated by 1625 from Couwenhoven, near Amersfoort, in the Province of Utrecht. Cornelius, as a young man, settled here in what was then Middletown Township; his ear mark (cattle brand) was recorded here in 1696. He and Garret Roelofse Schenck, Stephen Court Van Voorhees, and Peter Wyckoff jointly purchased a 500 acre tract in the township from John Bowne, merchant of Middletown. Van Voorhees and Wyckoff sold their rights to the Schenck brothers, Garret and Jan, and they released 125 acres of the tract to Cornelius Couwenhoven on Dec. 24,

1700. Cornelius had probably built his house here the previous summer and hence desired a release for his home farm. He and his wife Margaretta Roelofs Schenck lived here and were soon surrounded by the farms of their Schenck and Couwenhoven brothers. They continued to keep in touch with their old home as Cornelius owned the sloop *Carroway*, in which he made trips between Monmouth County, New York City, and Kings County. He died May 16, 1736 on his farm, aged 64 years, 5 mos., 17 days, and was buried here, being followed some years later by his wife, who died Dec. 6, 1751 aged 73 years, 9 mos., 27 days.

In his will of 1735 Cornelius Couwenhoven divided his many land purchases between his two sons William and Rulif, left the old negro woman Hannah to his wife and two negroes to each of his sons, and ordered legacies to be paid to each of his eleven daughters: Annetje, Jannetje (married Arie Vanderbilt), Altje (married William Van Dorn), Leah, Sarah, Neeltje (married Benjamin Van Cleaf), Mary, Rachel, Margaret, Jacometje (married Jan R. Schenck), and Caterina (married Daniel Hendrickson). The elder son William C.[5] Kouwenhoven, b. July 20, 1700, d. Nov. 10, 1755, made his home at Carroway, near Keyport, in Middletown Township. Cornelius left various tracts, including the 125 acre homestead (released to him Dec. 24, 1700) to his younger son, Rulif C.[5] Couwenhoven, b. Oct. 5, 1706, d. Aug. 20, 1786. Rulif married Sarah Voorheese, daughter of Cornelius Voorheese and Marytje Ditmars, b. April 12, 1710, d. Dec. 12, 1789. Both lie buried with his brother and parents in the nearby Couwenhoven—Schenck cemetery.

In the early nineteenth century the house is said to have been purchased by a foreigner, who ran a boat for a short time between Keyport and New York, and who married into a family of this section (possibly a Schenck girl) and wished to retire on a farm here. The widow is believed to have sold it to George Schenck.

George Schenck, b. 1822, d. March 6, 1892 aged 70 years, is the next known owner of the farm. He was the son of David[5] and grandson of Capt. John[4] Schenck, whose home was on a nearby hill (see infra), a descendant of Garret[2] Schenck who came to Monmouth County in 1696 and whose home farm adjoined Cornelius Couwenhoven's (see infra). About the middle of the nineteenth century George Schenck removed to and remodelled a house across the road from and immediately west of the Cornelius Couwenhoven house, which had been built in 1791 by his cousin John[3] Schenck on the farm of his father Jan[2] Schenck (see infra). These three adjoining farms were the homes of three of the pioneers in this region, Cornelius Couwenhoven, Garret Schenck and Jan Schenck, and together formed the 500 acre tract which had been purchased from John Bowne. By 1873 George Schenck owned the farms on both sides of the road, although continuing to reside on the west farm. He married Ellen or Eleanor Conover.

Among their children was Mary Ella Schenck, b. Jan. 14, 1864,* d. April 26, 1931.* On Nov. 10, 1887* she married Hendrick (or Henry) P. Conover, b. June 29, 1864,* d. Sept. 18, 1931,* son of Peter H. Conover, a member of the Covenhoven-Conover family who lived to the southwards, near Tennant, and a descendant of the builder of this house. (This Peter H. Conover, b. Dec. 8, 1827,* d. Sept. 22, 1900* in Freehold, buried in the Old Tennant Cemetery, married Dec. 12, 1855* Abbey E. Cottrell, was the son of Hendrick P. Conover, b. Jan. 17, 1800,* d. May 13, 1869,* buried in the Baptist Cemetery, Holmdel, and his first wife Mary Holmes whom he married Jan. 25, 1821.* He in turn was the son of Peter Covenhoven, b. April 18, 1778,* d. Aug. 14, 1817,* and his first wife Mary Rue, b. Sept. 5, 1779,* d. July 11, 1814,* whom he married Feb. 17, 1799.*) Hendrick and Mary Ella (Schenck) Conover acquired the Cornelius Couwenhoven farm from her father, and made it their home. The year before they died, they sold it to the present owner, Henry Butler. However, their son Wilson N. Conover continues to reside here.

The house stands on the main Matawan-Holmdel highway, three and a half miles south of Matawan, on the northeast corner of a crossroad at the center of Pleasant Valley. The old road to Holmdel formerly made a jog here, which has been eliminated in the construction of the new highway. Willow Brook runs nearby. This section is locally known as Pleasant Valley.

Probably only the small wing of the house was built by Cornelius Couwenhoven in 1700 although the main section also belongs to an early period. It is a good example, both inside and out, of the early Dutch house in Monmouth County. Early panelling, over-mantel and cupboards are still to be seen in the main room. A Dutch door was sold in 1927 for $1,200 to Robert Babcock of Long Island; it was painted on the inside with an Amsterdam scene on the upper panel and spreading tulips on the lower panel. When purchased a few years ago, the house was conservatively remodelled and restored, and the shingles stained a variety of hues. The main change is in the end of the wing. The old chimney at the gable end went up the interior of the house. A new brick chimney was built outside the wall and windows were cut on either side of it. The appearance of the house in 1925 is shown in the vignette, in which is emphasized the steep slant of the roofs of both units. In Beekman's *Dutch Settlers*, p. 24, is a view of the house at the beginning of the century.

House of Jan Covenhoven
formerly north of Hillsdale, near Wickatunk.
PLATE 122

Jan Covenhoven followed his brother Cornelius Couwenhoven from Flatlands to Monmouth County. He is said to have built this house as early as 1703 but the

400

---

* Taken from family Bible.

correct date is probably about 1706. He was termed a yeoman of Flatlands when, on Oct. 3, 1705, he purchased from John Bowne of Middletown Twp. two adjoining tracts of 94 and 215 acres in Freehold (now Marlborough) Township. He built and settled here in the next few years as he was termed a resident of Freehold Township on Oct. 15, 1709, when he enlarged the farm by buying 38½ adjoining acres from Jacob Van Dorn of Freehold Twp. Jan⁴ Covenhoven, b. April 9, 1681 in Flatlands, d. Dec. 1756, married Jacoba Van Derveer, and was survived by seven sons, William, Garret, Cornelius, Peter, John, Jacob and Domenicus. All the sons, except Garret, settled at Penns Neck.

Garret⁵ Covenhoven, born on the homestead April 27, 1726, was the only son to remain in Monmouth County. He resided on his father's farm until he died Nov. 1, 1812 aged 86 years. He married first Neeltje, daughter of Benjamin Van Mater, and secondly about 1770-75 Antje, daughter of Peter Janse Schenck; both wives predeceased him, each having borne him five children. The homestead passed to the youngest child, Peter G.⁶ Conover, b. Jan. 2, 1797, d. May 21, 1886, married Nov. 10, 1819 Charlotte, daughter of John Lyall. The eldest of their eleven children was John Lyall⁷ Conover. He married Abbie M. Bishop and was still occupying the homestead in 1901. In 1925, when the photograph was taken, it was owned by his granddaughter Mrs. Acker. The house burned down about 1929, and its site is now a part of the grounds of the State Insane Asylum.

The one and a half story wing was undoubtedly the original house, built about 1706. The steep pitch of the roof, small windows and low ceiling were characteristic of the early period. The main house of two stories, with dentil cornice and large windows, was probably built in the Revolutionary period, very likely by Garret Covenhoven at the time of his second marriage. The house formerly stood on the west side of the road running north from Hillsdale, less than one mile above this village, and about one mile as the crow flies east of the village of Wickatunk.

Conover House
Pleasant Valley, Marlborough Township
PLATE 123

The early history of this house lies in obscurity. It is an early type and may have been built by one of the pioneers in this neighborhood in the beginning of the eighteenth century. Our only knowledge comes from the family Bible in the possession of the present owner, who states that those mentioned in the Bible were all born here but that the house was built long before. William Conover and his wife Elizabeth had a son Garret Conover, b. Nov. 13, 1761,* d. June 13, 1817,* who married at the Dutch church June 26, 1794 Nelly Hire, d. May 19, 1814,* and had six

---

* Taken from family Bible.

children: John, Elizabeth, Ann, Margaret, William, and Allis. The daughter Ann Conover, b. Sept. 21, 1797,* d. Oct. 28, 1851,* married Jan. 31, 1828* Peter Johnson West, d. July 5, 1867 aged 67 years, 2 mos., 17 days,* and had one son and two daughters, Caroline and Alice. The son John Henry West, b. Dec. 20, 1837,* d. Nov. 16, 1915, married Elizabeth Bennett. Their daughter Elizabeth West married Jacob E. Applegate, and is the present owner and occupant of the old home. "Conover" is a form of the name Couwenhoven or Covenhoven adopted by many branches of this numerous family about the end of the eighteenth century. The known owners of this house (and possibly the builder) are undoubtedly related to the Couwenhovens who settled to the southward in Pleasant Valley.

The house is built in two sections. The original unit is the east half shown in the photograph; it is still covered with the original hand-hewn shingles. The house stands near the brow of the hill about two miles south of Matawan, off the east side of the main highway leading to Holmdel, in the northern part of the region locally known as Pleasant Valley.

House of Daniel Hendrickson
Holland, Middletown

Daniel Hendrickson is supposed to have built this house between 1700 and 1720; an even earlier date is possible unless it supersedes a temporary structure. On Sept. 23, 1693 he and another, both residents of Flatbush, agreed to make annual installment payments to William Whitlock, on the 104 acres leased from him the previous September, until March, 1697 when said Whitlock would convey these lands upon completion of the payments. The deed of conveyance of the property is dated May 16, 1698 and was given by John Whitlock, probably a son of William deceased, the deed stating that the land had been obtained originally by patent from the Proprietors on Jan. 20, 1676.

Daniel Hendrickson, son of Hendrick, came from Flatbush about 1693, and was the first permanent settler of this region which came to be known as Holland. He probably chose this location due to a mill already erected on the adjoining Mahoras Brook. He became a large landowner and a very important citizen of Middletown Township, its constable, sheriff, Captain of the militia, organizer and elder of the Dutch Church. He married Catharine, daughter of Jan Janse Van Dyke of New Utrecht, and died in January 1728, survived by his wife and eleven children: Geesie wife of Roelof Janse Schenck, Teuntje (bap. 1699 in Brooklyn) wife of Jonathan Holmes, Hendrick, John, Mayke who married Gysbert Van Mater, Fran-

402

---

* Taken from family Bible.

cyntie who married Teunis Cortelyou, William, Ann who married William Couwenhoven, Catharine who married Henry Dusenberry, Jannetje who married Roelof Couwenhoven, and Daniel.

The house has passed in direct succession to the present owner. It was inherited by the builder's youngest son, Daniel Hendrickson, b. Jan. 5, 1723 on the homestead, bap. May 5, 1723, d. June 24, 1788 intestate, married Dec. 22, 1743 Catharine Couwenhoven, b. June 2, 1720, d. May 5, 1810, daughter of Cornelius Couwenhoven, builder of the house in Pleasant Valley (plate 121). He was so active in church affairs that he was called Dominie Daniel; his descendants state that he was also an artist and a musician. He built a grist mill on his property. After Daniel's death, his four surviving children—Col. Daniel D., Cornelius, Catharine and Hendrick—released his various lands to each other on Aug. 6 and 26, 1789. To Catharine (b. 1753, d. unmarried on the homestead after 1835) was allotted the western part of the home tract whereon Daniel Hendrickson lived, 122 acres bounded on the south by Luyster (the line agreed on between Johannes Luyster, owner of the house in plate 125, and Daniel Hendrickson on April 11, 1745) and the Mahoras Brook, being lands purchased by Daniel Hendrickson the elder from John Whitlock on May 16, 1698 and from Garret Wall on Dec. 29, 1709. Catharine Hendrickson conveyed this property to her brother Hendrick on April 1, 1800 for $2,000. To this Hendrick Hendrickson had been allotted the eastern part of the home tract, consisting of 154 acres bounded south and east by Luyster and the Mahoras Brook. Hendrick Hendrickson, b. May 2, 1758, d. Dec. 1, 1840, always lived on the homestead. He served in the Revolution. On May 13, 1781 he married Francinke Covenhoven, b. Nov. 18, 1763, d. March 26, 1845, daughter of Cornelius R. and greatgranddaughter of Cornelius Couwenhoven of Pleasant Valley (plate 121). Hendrick had two daughters and one son William (1787-1831) who predeceased him, leaving a son William Henry Hendrickson, b. June 3, 1813, d. 1899. The latter was a member of the New Jersey Senate for many years and president of the Farmers' and Merchants' Bank of Matawan until his death. He inherited the 276 acre homestead tract from his grandfather Hendrick, and it is now owned by the Senator's son, James Patterson Hendrickson.

Originally a fine example of Dutch architecture of the period, its lines are now hidden under porches and a crenellated cornice added by the Senator in the nineteenth century. A photograph of it is reproduced in Beekman's *Dutch Settlers*, p. 122. The house stands in the former village of Holland, now the southwest part of Middletown, on the north side of Holland Road which runs westward to Hominy. The property borders upon Middletown Township but actually is within the present Holmdel Township.

403

House of Hendrick Hendrickson
Pleasant Valley, Holmdel Township
PLATE 124

It is believed that this house was erected by Hendrick Hendrickson, son of the above Daniel Hendrickson, between 1730 and 1750, but may have been built a few years earlier when Hendrick first settled on the property. In 1727 Daniel Hendrickson willed to his son Hendrick the plantation on which Hendrick then dwelt, formerly Benjamin Stout's, and one half of his lots of meadow at Conescunk. Hendrick Hendrickson is believed to have been born in 1700 although he died at the age of 50 years on Feb. 21, 1753 according to his tombstone (he gave his bond as the eldest brother of John Hendrickson, born about 1702, d. 1790). About 1725 he married Neeltje, daughter of Garret Schenck, pioneer and owner of the house in Pleasant Valley (see infra). After her husband's death, she married secondly in 1761 Elias Golden. Hendrick had ten children: Tryntje bap. 1726, Daniel, Neeltje, Garret, Hendrick, Mary wife of Cornelius W. Couwenhoven, Tryntje, Neeltje wife of Jacob Van Meter, Antje wife of David Van Nostrandt, and William bap. 1748.

Only one child carried on the name: Garret Hendrickson, b. Jan. 22, 1734, d. Dec. 2, 1801, lies buried in the family graveyard at Holland with his father and his first two wives. Garret lived and died in his father's house in Pleasant Valley and ran a well-stocked farm. He was a lieutenant in the militia in the Revolution, was wounded in 1780, and taken prisoner in the raid of 1782. He married first by license of Dec. 8, 1755 Catharine, daughter of Tunis Denise, b. May 8, 1732, d. Sept. 8, 1771, and had three sons and three daughters; he married secondly Helena or Lena, daughter of Denise Van Lieu, b. Sept. 26, 1753, d. Jan. 1, 1785, and had one son and four daughters; he married thirdly Nelly, daughter of Arie Van Doorn and widow of Hendrick Smock, d. Feb. 11, 1834 aged 91 years. A son by the first wife, Hendrick Hendrickson, b. July 19, 1764, d. June 6, 1837, married Jan. 20, 1791 Phebe, daughter of Cyrenius Van Mater, b. Dec. 21, 1773, d. March 12, 1836. Their son Cyrenius Hendrickson, b. March 30, 1802, d. May 17, 1870, lies buried in the family cemetery at Holland with his parents and forebears. He married Sept. 18, 1823 Ida Van Mater, and lived and died on the family farm. Their only son Henry Denise Hendrickson had a son Cyrenius Hendrickson, who is believed to have lost the farm about 1873 due to his father's extravagance.

It was sold by sheriff's sale about 1873 to John Herbert and was owned by the Herbert estate until about 1930, when it was sold to the Bell Laboratories, the present owner. An experimental station for trans-oceanic telephoning is now conducted on this and adjoining farms. It is known locally as the Charlie P. Conover farm; he was a tenant for many years, renting from the Herbert estate.

The house is in good condition, although at present unused. It resembles the houses of Kings County and Bergen County in style. It stands in the eastern section of Pleasant Valley, about two miles north of Holmdel. To reach it from the main Matawan-Holmdel highway, turn east on the crossroad in front of the Cornelius Couwenhoven house (plate 121), take next turn right, then left, then right to the Bell Laboratories. The house stands in a grove in the middle of the property, and is not visible from the road.

House of Johannes Luyster
Holland, Middletown
PLATE 125

Johannes Luyster built this house between 1727 and 1730. It has been in the continuous occupancy of the family ever since and is now owned and lived in by his descendant John P. Luyster. An old deed hanging framed on the wall of the house records the granting of 104 acres here to Peter Wyckoff on Jan. 1, 1716/17. Early in 1717 Johannes Luyster and John Brower, brothers-in-law, bought this and other lands. The latter transferred his interest to Luyster, who settled here shortly after the property was surveyed Oct. 18, 1727.

Johannes Luyster, the builder, was a grandson of Pieter Cornelisz[1] Luyster who emigrated to this country in 1656 and settled at Bouwery Bay on Long Island; it was probably Johannes' brother Peter[3] Luyster who built the house standing there until recently (plate 25). Johannes[3] Luyster, b. March 22, 1691,* d. Jan. 29, 1756,* married April 16, 1716* Lucretia Brower, b. Aug. 12, 1688,* d. April 12, 1771,* and had six children: Sarah, Peter, Cornelius, Johannes, Anna, and Lucretia. The eldest son Peter[4] Luyster, b. May 5, 1719,* d. Feb. 12, 1810 aged 91 years, married May 25, 1756 Anna[4] Luyster, b. Jan. 9, 1726,* d. Nov. 23, 1799, daughter of his uncle Peter[3] Luyster who lived at Bouwery Bay (plate 25). They had one son and two daughters. The son John P.[5] Luyster, b. Nov. 29, 1763,* d. Sept. 11, 1848* in his 85th year, married June 3, 1790* Anne Conover, b. Sept. 18, 1764,* d. Dec. 6, 1852* aged 88 years. At the age of 19 John served on shore duty in the Revolution. He had five daughters and one son. The son Peter[6] Luyster, b. March 30, 1806,* d. Dec. 1, 1875,* married Dec. 20, 1829* Miranda Suydam, b. April 3, 1808,* d. Oct. 24, 1855,* and had three daughters and three sons. Their youngest child Garret S.[7] Luyster, b. Sept. 20, 1843,* married Sarah Burrows. They were the parents of John P.[8] Luyster, the eldest son and present owner of the family homestead.

405

---

* Taken from family Bible.

Mr. Luyster is very interested in his family home, and keeps it intact and unchanged as a beautiful example of early Dutch architecture, and as a museum for the family heirlooms. He lives in the modern wing, not seen in the photograph. The house stands in the former village of Holland, on Holland Road in the southwest part of Middletown. It is on the north side of this road (which goes toward Hominy) and adjoins the Daniel Hendrickson house (see supra) on the east.

The Schenck Houses
Pleasant Valley, Holmdel and Marlborough Townships

The Schencks were among the original settlers and are among the present inhabitants of Pleasant Valley, several of their old homes yet remaining, although none in their pristine condition. Pleasant Valley is the local name for the country between Matawan and Holmdel villages.

House of Garret Schenck

Garret Roelofse Schenck, Stephen Court Van Voorhees, Cornelius Couwenhoven and Peter Wyckoff jointly purchased a 500 acre tract here, in what was then Middletown Township, from John Bowne, merchant of Middletown. Van Voorhees and Wyckoff sold their rights to the Schenck brothers, Garret and Jan, and they released 125 acres of it to Cornelius Couwenhoven Dec. 24, 1700 (plate 121), and divided the balance between themselves, Garret keeping about 200 acres. Garret Roelofse[2] Schenck, b. Oct. 27, 1671, d. Sept. 5, 1745 aged 73 years, was a son of Roelof Martense[1] Schenck of Flatlands and his first wife Neeltje Gerretse van Couwenhoven, and a nephew of Jan Martense[1] Schenck who built the house on Mill Island in Flatlands (plate 13). About 1693 Garret married Neeltje Koerten Van Voorheese, b. Oct. 1, 1675, bap. Dec. 5, 1680 at Flatlands, d. Aug. 4, 1750. He settled on his Pleasant Valley purchase in the spring of 1696; his ear mark (cattle brand) was recorded here in June 1696.

The original unit of the present house (the stone portion) may have been erected by Schenck at this time (1696), but tradition states that it was built in 1692 by a Van Voorhees. Garret's father-in-law, Coert Stevense Van Voorhees lived at Flatlands and is mentioned there in 1689 and 1699; it is probable that he never came to Monmouth County. Garret's brother-in-law Stephen Coert Van Voorhees was one of the joint purchasers of the tract on which the house stands, and it is possible that he built it, although his eldest child was baptized in Brooklyn in 1694 and he was definitely living in Flatlands in 1698. He sold his share of the tract to Garret Schenck, whose descendants still occupy it.

406

Garret Schenck was an original member and an elder of the Church of Freehold, organized in 1709, and a member of the Provincial Assembly of New Jersey. He was a prosperous farmer and owned many large tracts of land, including property and a wharf at the present Keyport, which he gave and willed to his children. In his will of 1739 he called himself a gentleman of Middletown, mentioned his wife Neeltje, his five sons, Roelof (of Marlborough Twp.), Garret (of Holmdel Twp.), Koert (of Marlborough Twp.), John (of Penns Neck) and Albert (of Penns Neck), his five daughters, Mary, Altie, Neeltie, Rachel, and Margaret, and his deceased daughter Anne. Among other property, he left to his son Garret his home plantation "on condition that he allows his Mother the use of the two westernmost rooms of the Dwelling house below, with convenient furniture to furnish the same as his Mother shall think fit." This son Garret G.[3] Schenck, b. Nov. 2, 1712, d. intestate Aug. 20, 1757 aged 44 years, married about 1737 Jannetje, daughter of William Van Couwenhoven of Flatlands, b. Oct. 6, 1714, d. on the homestead farm Feb. 14, 1792. They are said to have had four sons and six daughters. One of these was Garret G.[4] Schenck II, b. 1743, d. Sept. 29, 1797 aged 53 years, 11 mos., and 5 days, married Sarah Covenhoven, b. July 23, 1744, d. Nov. 16, 1805, daughter of Rulif C.[5] Covenhoven, who had inherited his father Cornelius' farm nearby (plate 121). Garret G. Schenck II may have come into possession of the homestead after the death of his mother in 1792.

The house passed by inheritance into the Rappleye family through Jane Schenck, b. March 24, 1767, d. March 23, 1850 aged 82 yrs., 11 mos., and 30 days. She was a granddaughter of Garret G.[3] Schenck and probably a daughter of Garret G. Schenck II. Jane married Garret[5] Smock, b. Aug. 4, 1765 on the Smock homestead farm southeast of Holmdel village, d. March 30, 1856 aged 90 yrs., 7 mos., and 26 days, whose greatgrandfather Johannes Hendrickse[2] Smock settled in Monmouth County in 1712. Garret and Jane (Schenck) Smock lived at Pleasant Valley, probably in her family homestead; they were buried with her ancestors in the family cemetery at Pleasant Valley, rather than with his ancestors on his paternal farm. Garret and Jane had two daughters, Sarah[6] Smock who married George Smock, and Elizabeth[6] Smock who married George Rappleye, b. 1794, d. April 25, 1869 aged 75 years, 3 mos., 18 days. Theodore Rappleye was the owner of the farm in 1873, Thomas Thorne in 1889, Theodore R. Thorne in 1901, and the present owner is J. M. Thorne.

The house today is the result of several successive builders. The original unit is the small, narrow, stone portion, built in 1692 by Stephen Court Van Voorhees or in 1696 by Garret R. Schenck. As Garret Schenck left the use of the two westernmost rooms to his wife in his will of 1739, it was undoubtedly he who deepened the house with a shingled unit so that it became two full rooms in depth. A shingled wing was also added at some period, flush with the stone front wall but not so deep as the main house. Both sections are covered by a gable roof, extending over front and rear in straight slopes, thus greatly resembling the houses in Kings County, the early home of the builders. Views of the house, taken in 1900, can be seen in Beekman's *Dutch Settlers*, p. 12. Since this time, the stone wall has been covered with shingles to make the house uniform in appearance, dormers have been added and other changes made. The house stands on the west side of the Matawan-Holmdel highway, over three miles south of Matawan and a short distance north of the cross-roads in Pleasant Valley. It is in Holmdel Township.

House of Capt. John Schenck

This house stands on the hill west of the Garret Schenck house and overlooks the valley. It was built in 1767 by Augustus Reed and sold by him shortly afterward to Capt. John Schenck, whose descendants still live in it. Capt. John[4] Schenck, b. 1745, d. Aug. 28, 1834 aged 89 years, was a son of Garret G.[3] Schenck and a grandson of Garret R.[2] Schenck, owners of the house in the valley (see supra). On July 31, 1767 he married Mary Denise, b. July 9, 1750, d. July 15, 1829, daughter of Teunis Denise and granddaughter of Daniel Hendrickson, builder of the house at Holland (see supra). They had at least four sons: William (1772-1844), Col. John (1774-1864) married Micha Van Nuyse, Daniel I. (1778-1858) married Elleanor Schenck, and David (1783-1872) married Sarah Smock (1799-1832). The house was inherited by Capt. John's son David and then by his son David, Jr. The latter's son Luther[7] Schenck sold it a few years ago to a Mr. Johnson, but he still makes his home here.

Capt. John Schenck was one of the most active and daring of the officers of the county militia in the Revolution. So troublesome was he that the British offered a reward of 50 guineas for his capture or death. He and William Marriner led a midnight raid against Flatbush on June 13, 1778 to capture the Tory mayor of New York City and others, travelling 50 miles between six o'clock in the evening and six o'clock the next morning. Several midnight raids were made by the Tories and British to capture him. He generally slept out in the woods for safety or, if he was in his house, he had scouts posted about the country. Mr. Luther Schenck owns a beautifully engraved set of pistols used by Capt. Schenck in the Revolution.

The house is a small one story building. The long, old shingles recently wore out and have been replaced by clapboarding. The house stands on a hill in Marlborough Township, on the east side of a country road paralleling the Matawan-Holmdel highway on the west. It is reproduced in the *Historical and Biographical Atlas of the New Jersey Coast*, pub. 1878.

Farm of Jan Schenck—House of John Schenck

This farm is a part of the 500 acre tract jointly purchased from John Bowne of Middletown and divided between Cornelius Couwenhoven and his brothers-in-law Garret Schenck and Jan Schenck (see supra). The latter had bought out the rights of one of the original purchasers. Jan² Schenck, b. Feb. 10, 1670 at Flatlands, d. Jan. 30, 1753, came to Monmouth County in 1697-98; his ear mark (cattle brand) was recorded here in April 1698. About 1691 he married Sarah Couwenhoven, b. Jan. 6, 1675, d. Jan. 31, 1761, daughter of William Garretse Couwenhoven. In his will of 1746 he left all his property to his wife Sarah for her maintenance and that of their son John, who was to inherit it after her decease, and he ordered his son John to give legacies of £450 each to his other children: Roelof the eldest, Peter, Sarah (who married Johannes and Henry Voorhees), Altye (wife of Christian Van Dooren), Rachel, Maria (wife of Jacob Van Dooren), Leah (wife of Peter Couwenhoven), Jannetje (wife of Bernardus Verbryke), and Antje (wife of Arie Van Dooren).

The son John³ Schenck, b. June 27, 1722, d. Dec. 24, 1808, married about 1751 Nellie Bennett, b. Nov. 29, 1728, d. June 1, 1810, daughter of Jan Bennett. They lived and died on his father's homestead farm and were buried with his parents and other relatives in the Schenck—Couwenhoven family cemetery nearby. The present house on the farm is a two story frame structure of a post-revolutionary type. The doorknocker (taken by the family when the house was sold) is marked "J. S. 1791," indicating that the house was probably built in 1791 by John Schenck. He had ten children: John and William who went to Ohio, Ida, Sarah, Chrineyonce, Peter, Nellie, Anne, Capt. Daniel, and Mary. Some of these resided on the farm.

The house was remodelled about 1850 by George Schenck (1822-1892), a cousin, who made his residence here. He also purchased the Cornelius Couwenhoven house across the road (plate 121) and a fuller account of him is given under that house. The John Schenck house was inherited by George's son Edgar, who owned it in 1901. Edgar married Lydia Craig and their son George Schenck sold the property in 1932 to the present owner, Morton Allen. The house is on the southwest corner of the Matawan-Holmdel highway and the cross-road at Pleasant Valley in Holmdel Township.

Stout (?)—Hendrickson House
Pleasant Valley, Holmdel Township
PLATE 126

The old wing of this house may have been built by David Stout in the first quarter of the eighteenth century. His mother is well-known in early Colonial annals. Penelope, said to be a Dutch girl née Van Princes, sailed for New Amsterdam with her first husband about 1620; the ship was wrecked off Sandy Hook and the party attacked and killed by the Indians. She was saved by one of the Indians who brought her to New Amsterdam, where she met and married Richard Stout. He was an Englishman, who joined Lady Moody's colony in Gravesend, where he was a patentee in 1645. He was a patentee of Monmouth County in 1665, receiving 480 acres each for himself, wife and two sons, and 300 acres for his younger children; he made many large purchases of land later. He settled in Middletown village about 1664 and he died there in 1705, survived by ten children and his wife.

In 1690 Richard Stout conveyed lands on the Hopp River to his youngest son David, and it is on this or adjoining property that David built and lived until he removed to Amwell about 1725. His home was on the later Denise Hendrickson farm near Hop Brook, so it is possible that it was David Stout who built the old wing of the present house. David[2] Stout, b. about 1668, married about 1688 Rebecca (Ashton?), and had eight children, all of whom removed to other parts of New Jersey. Penelope, his mother, probably lived with him here on Hop Brook (or with one of her other sons, as all the territory in the vicinity was owned by her husband). She died in 1732-33 and is buried somewhere on this farm within sight of the Hendrick Hendrickson house (plate 124).

In 1823 the property was owned by Denise Hendrickson, b. Nov. 12, 1761, d. March 7, 1839, a son of Garret and Catharine (Denise) Hendrickson, who lived in the Hendrickson house on the adjoining farm (plate 124). He married Dec. 28, 1786 Anne Schenck, b. Nov. 15, 1766, d. Aug. 6, 1858, daughter of John Schenck, builder of the 1790 house in Pleasant Valley (see supra). It is probable that Denise bought the place shortly after his marriage, as the main part of the house, probably built by him, belongs to the 1790 period. His son John Schenck Hendrickson, b. May 9, 1807, married Ellen Hyres, and was the father of Mrs. Robert Carson. She sold the property at the end of the nineteenth century to Patrick Kelly, whose estate sold it in 1932 to John Clausen, the present owner.

The house stands in the east end of Pleasant Valley on the northeast side of the road from Everett to Hominy, across the road from the Bell Laboratories Experimental Station.

House of Squire John Taylor
Middletown
PLATE 127

This house is supposed to have been built by Squire John Taylor (1716-1798), and if so could not have been built much before 1735, when he was 19 years of age. The opinion is generally held that the house is much older, dating from the very beginning of the century. *The Story of Middletown* contains the statement that it was built in 1684 but the builder is not named. Its very early and typically Dutch architecture suggests some other builder than Taylor, probably a Dutchman, since Middletown was an English settlement, and there would be no reason for an Englishman among the English to build in the style of the Dutch.

The first known owner is Squire John³ Taylor, son of George the merchant, and grandson of Edward¹ Taylor who emigrated from England and settled at Garret's Hill near Sandy Hook in Monmouth County by 1684. Squire John, b. 1715-16, d. Nov. 23, 1798, married about 1743 Phebe, sister of General Nathaniel Hurd, b. about 1708, d. July 10, 1791, and had four sons and two daughters. He was a sheriff of Monmouth County and Judge of Common Pleas. He was a Loyalist and was appointed by Admiral Howe, Peace Commissioner for the British government. About the middle of the eighteenth century he sold his house and tract in Middletown to Bernardus Rider of Long Island, reserving therefrom a building site of 14 acres. Here he built a handsome house in 1752 at the head of Main Street, known as Taylor's Folly, which he sold in 1792 to George Crawford (it was burned in 1891). A few years later he removed to Perth Amboy where he died.

In 1771 Edward Taylor (a brother of Squire John) bought the house in question and 210 acres from Bernardus Rider, and the property has been owned ever since by Edward's descendants. This Edward³ Taylor, b. Aug. 20, 1712, d. Jan. 18, 1783, was a member of the Assembly and an active patriot. He lived in a house on the south side of the King's Highway and east of the church in Middletown village (still standing and known as the Dr. Taylor house), which has been variously stated to have been built by his father in 1719 and 1729 and by himself in 1739; it is on property bought Jan. 10, 1716 by his father George, then of Garret's Hill, from William Wilkins, and conveyed to his son Edward May 1, 1739. Edward married Mary Ogbourn and had three sons, Col. George, John and Joseph. In 1773 the son Col. George (1733-1799) was living on his father's purchase from Rider, but during the revolution he removed to the Taylor house near the church, which is still occupied by his descendants. His brother John (1740-1819) lived in early life in a house on the north side of the street, burned in 1848, but after the Revolution he removed to the house just vacated by his brother George (Squire John's house, known as the "grandfather homestead").

This John[4] Taylor served in the Revolution in the patriot army. He married about 1770 Mary, daughter of Samuel Holmes, and had three sons, Joseph who built nearby, Samuel who died in 1843 unmarried, and Edward. Edward[5] Taylor (1779-1845) was a merchant of New York City. On the death of his brother Samuel he succeeded to the homestead farm, but soon died, leaving an only child, Mary Holmes[6] Taylor, b. 1814. She married her cousin Joseph Dorset Taylor, and built and resided in the Victorian mansion nearby on the property, using the old homestead as her farmer's house. The house and property are now owned by the estate of Miss Mary Holmes Taylor, her daughter.

The house contains unusually beautiful panelling, overmantels, and cupboards in all its rooms. Although the exterior has been repainted since the photograph was taken in 1925, it is rapidly falling into sad neglect and decay. It is occupied by negro tenants. The house stands on the east side of the main street of Middletown (the old King's Highway), near the railroad bridge, after the road has left the village proper and turned northwards toward Keyport.

PLATE 116

House of Cornelius Low
River Road, Raritan Landing, Piscataway Township

Cornelius Low in 1741 built his new house on the bluff overlooking the Raritan River. It is a Georgian mansion very unlike the average Dutch farmhouse. Its dimensions are almost square and it is two stories in height. The irregular sandstone walls are surmounted by a dentil wood cornice and a hipped roof sloping down to the four sides. The front facade is balanced, the central doorway flanked on either side by two windows. The photograph reproduces the rear view, the central window and door out of alignment due to the stairway. The shallow arches over the doors and windows are a variation of those in Hunterdon County. A few of the old sashes are still in use in the second story rear. The characteristic panelled treatment of the fireplace walls in the rooms results in the absence of windows on the end walls. The wainscoting, panelling and carving of the interior are more Georgian than Dutch. A low, two-story wing formerly stood on the west end.

PLATE 117

House of Matthias Smock
River Road, Piscataway Township

A part of this house was built by Matthias Smock when he settled in this region about 1718-21. It passed by marriage into the Nevius family, who owned it until about 1910. This house is built in two units, the east (right) section is the earlier and was Matthias Smock's home, and the west (left) section was probably added by his son John. The clapboarding at the rear shows their division; the west unit has lie-on-your-stomach windows under the roof. The low ceilings and small windows are characteristic of the early period. Various alterations and judicious planting have transformed the old farmhouse into a modern residence. The large elm tree in front emphasizes the modest dimensions of the house.

PLATE 118

Soulard (?)—Suydam House
Countyline Road, Franklin Park

This house was in existence by 1766 when it was owned by John Suydam and is probably the house owned by Peter Soulard in 1745. It remained in the Suydam family until after 1838 and was owned by the Garretson family from 1859 until 1925. It is a small, deep house covered with long shingles; the window openings are characteristically small and few in number. There was formerly a large addition at the south end.

PLATE 119

House of Jacob Van Deventer
River Road, near Bound Brook, Piscataway Township

This house was built 1738-40 by Jacob Van Deventer on his father-in-law Field's large tract. It is a typical Dutch farmhouse, with a steep gable roof and no overhanging eaves. The window openings are small. The large fireplaces in the main rooms are not centered but placed across the corners. The roofline has not been changed; it still ends flush with the gable wall.

PLATE 120

House of Matthias Van Dyke
Lake Road, Mapleton, near Kingston

This house was erected in 1756 by Matthias Van Dyke on land later inherited from his father, and remained in the family until the last quarter of the nineteenth century. It has none of the characteristics of a Dutch house. Erected on the southern end of the territory inhabited by the Dutch, the builder fell under the influence of the English styles prevalent in Princeton nearby. It is a two story house built of irregularly cut fieldstone, with a dentil cornice and a low gable roof. The eighteenth century character is predominant in the lines of the gable end.

417

PLATE 121

House of Cornelius Couwenhoven
Pleasant Valley, Holmdel Township

The wing at the east (right) end of the house was the home which Cornelius Couwenhoven built in 1700. The main house was added at an early date. Recent restoration has not materially altered the lines. The main house was built flush with the south front of the original unit but has a greater depth. Both sections have a steep gable roof characteristic of the early period, and also a very slight overhang. The window openings in the main house are considerably larger and the old window sashes here are still in use. The end wall of the wing was recently remodelled with the addition of four windows and an outside chimney; formerly there was one very small attic window and the chimney was on the inside of the wall as in all Dutch houses. The multi-colored staining of the shingles has an unfortunate effect.

418

PLATE 122

House of Jan Covenhoven
formerly north of Hillside, near Wickatunk

The original unit of this house is the wing. It was erected about 1706 by Jan Covenhoven, brother of Cornelius, the builder of the house in Pleasant Valley (plate 121). The steep pitch of the roof line can be discerned in spite of the later extension of the roof to form a large outside summer kitchen. The dimensions of the old window are unusual; in general when both sashes were two panes in height they were three panes in width, and when the width of four panes was desired the upper sash was larger than the lower and three panes in height, as are the second story windows of the main house. This two story addition was not made until about the time of the Revolution by Jan's son Garret. The dentil cornice is typical of this period. The house was inhabited by descendants of the builder until it burned a few years ago.

PLATE 123

Conover House
Pleasant Valley, Marlborough Township

It is probable that this house was built early in the eighteenth century by one of the pioneer settlers, but the first known owner was Garret Conover who was born in 1761 in this house. The long shingles still remain. The roof has a more moderate slope than those on the two houses of the family further south (plates 121 and 122). The frame addition on the west end belongs to a later period but has been built to conform with the original unit. The house has passed by marriage through several families and is still the home of descendants of Garret Conover.

PLATE 124

House of Hendrick Hendrickson
Pleasant Valley, Holmdel Township

Hendrick Hendrickson was living on this property in 1727 when his father bequeathed it to him. As the house is believed to have been built by him between 1730 and 1750, it may supersede a more temporary home. It was owned by his descendants until about 1873. The house is similar in style to the Dutch houses on Long Island. The roof of the wing extends in a straight slope to form an overhang, while the roof of the main section has a slight curve which lightens the lines of the building. The narrow clapboarding on the side of the main unit is modern.

PLATE 125

House of Johannes Luyster
Holland Road, Middletown

This house was built between 1727 and 1730 by Johannes Luyster and is still owned by his descendants. It has a very steep and high gable roof which extends to form an overhang both front and rear. The ridgepole is not in the center of the house so that the roof line in the rear has a longer slope and the overhang is lower and nearer the ground. The roof makes a slight curve above the front overhang. It will be noticed that the windows on the south front are not all the same size.

PLATE 126

Stout (?)—Hendrickson House
Pleasant Valley, Holmdel Township

The present wing of the house may have been the home of David Stout who lived on this farm from about 1690 to about 1725. His mother, Penelope Stout, was buried on the farm in 1732-33. The steep roofline is characteristic of the early houses. The narrow clapboarding in front is modern and undoubtedly supersedes a covering of long shingles such as are still on the gable end. The lean-to was probably added at an early date. The main house was built in the post-revolutionary period probably by Denise Hendrickson.

PLATE 127

House of Squire John Taylor
Middletown

The first known owner of this house was Squire John Taylor, born 1716. He sold it and it was later purchased in 1771 by his brother Edward Taylor, whose descendants have owned it ever since. It has been stated that the house was erected in 1684 (presumably by John Taylor, which is impossible); it is more probable that the house was built about 1710 by an unknown Dutchman who had settled in the English village of Middletown. The house is typically Dutch. Like the home of Johannes Luyster nearby (plate 125), built 1727-30, the ridgepole is not centralized so that the roof line in the rear is longer than in front, but unlike this other house it extends no nearer the ground so the slope is not so steep. There is a slight curve in the front roofline and the suggestion of an overhang. Notice the unusual panelling of the double door and the cornice over the doorway. In the interior are beautiful examples of early panelling, overmantels, and cupboards.

SOMERSET COUNTY

HOUSE OF
HENDRICK AND ABRAHAM STAATS

SOMERSET COUNTY

SOMERSET COUNTY embraces most of the Dutch population of central New Jersey. It is mainly rolling country, watered by the Raritan and Millstone Rivers. Near Somerville the first settlers found broad alluvial lands without trees, ready for cultivation.

The first settlements were made in 1681 along the Raritan on various Indian purchases of that year. The land on the north side of the river, later Bridgewater Township, was purchased in 1681 from the Indians in four immense tracts. Title became vested in the Twelve Proprietors when they acquired the Province of East Jersey in February 1681/2. The first Indian deed covered the site of Bound Brook; Thomas Codrington and John Royce were two of the first settlers here. The second Indian deed extended from Middlebrook to the bridge at Raritan village. This land was divided and sold in many tracts. Two lots of 877 acres each were surveyed Sept. 25, 1683 for John Palmer and associates, one of whom was Michael Van Vechten who settled here before his son was born in 1699. Van Vechten gave the land for the first Church of Raritan (org. 1699) which was built in 1721. Somerville stands on a tract of 1904 acres patented Feb. 3, 1683 to James Graham and associates. Part of it was sold to Hendrick Corsen Vroom who had settled here about 1680. Peter Van Nest purchased portions in 1687, 1693 and 1709 and settled here; Peter's Brook is named after him. Van Nest sold one of his purchases on May 1, 1709 to his son-in-law Derrick Middagh, who had located in the Raritan section about 1699. Another tract, on which stands part of the village of Raritan, came into the possession of Andries Coejeman who settled here before 1736. The fourth Indian deed of 1681 covered lands on both sides of the North Branch of Raritan River. This was also divided and sold. A 1650 acre tract was surveyed for Lord Neill Campbell on Jan. 9, 1685; among the early settlers here was Gisbert Lane about 1730. A 400 acre tract on the west side of the North Branch River in Branchburg Township was acquired in 1690 by John Johnston; he disposed of it on Nov. 12, 1700 to Mathias Ten Eyck whose son settled here. Bedminster Township in the north end of the county was settled by many nationalities, but there were enough Dutch inhabitants to warrant the organization of a Reformed Church in 1758.

Some of the early settlements were made in Franklin Township. In 1681 John Inians and associates purchased from the Indians for Lady Elizabeth Carteret, the land along the southwest side of the Raritan River from Lawrence Brook to Bound Brook. Title became vested in the Twelve Proprietors when they acquired the Province of East Jersey in February 1681/2. Inians settled on the east end of this tract on the site of New Brunswick, which later became part of Middlesex County. Among the early patentees of the township were the Cortelyous (1711 acres) and the Wyckoffs (1703 acres). Small settlements were made along the county line at each brook, the most important about 1710 at Six Mile Run, now Franklin Park. There was also a small village in the center of the township at Middlebush. Reformed Churches were organized at New Brunswick about 1703 and at Six Mile Run in 1717. The land on the west side of the Millstone River was incorporated in Hillsborough and Montgomery Townships. In 1685 and 1693 John Royce received a patent for the land along the river as far south as Peace Brook (in Millstone) and about 1690 Clement Plumstead obtained a grant for the land from Peace Brook down to Blackwell's Mills. Portions of these tracts were sold and settled on from time to time; in 1738 there were already fifty families living within three miles of Millstone village. In 1693 Peter Sonmans obtained a deed for 36 square miles, covering most of Montgomery Township. On June 10, 1710 Sonmans sold the Harlingen tract of 9000 acres to a Dutch company of seventeen who settled here. In 1690 Thomas Hart received a patent for a tract on the Millstone River nearby; in 1702 he sold 4000 acres to Gerardus and Adrian Beekman and associates, part of which was disposed of in 1727 to Christopher Hoagland. Three Reformed Churches were organized in this section, in 1727 Harlingen, originally called the Church over the Millstone, in 1766 Hillsboro, formerly called New Millstone, and in 1752 Neshanic.

The territory was originally a part of Middlesex County but the interests of the inhabitants of the two sections were found to vary sufficiently to warrant the separation of Somerset County as early as 1688, although it was dependent on the Middlesex courts until 1713. The division line between the counties was changed seven times; a part of New Brunswick was transferred to Middlesex County as late as 1850. The county seat was established at Six Mile Run (Franklin Park) in 1714. When the courthouse burned down in 1737, it was reerected at the present Millstone, then known as Somerset Court House. This was destroyed by the British during the Revolution. After the war the county seat was established at Somerville, then called Raritan. The Great Raritan Road was laid out in 1684 from Piscataway to Bound Brook and along the north bank of the Raritan River almost to Somerville, and was continued to the Raritan Branches two years later. A main highway was established from New Brunswick along the county line through the various hamlets in the direction of Kingston, Princeton and Trenton. A road was laid from New Brunswick through Middlebush to Millstone, then down the east bank of the Millstone River to Rocky Hill and the main highway near Kingston. A road from Somerset Court House (now Millstone) was opened through Neshanic to connect with the Amwell Road in Hunterdon County, which ran down to the Delaware River at Lambertville.

There is great variety of style in the Dutch houses of Somerset County. Most are of frame but several are of brick or stone. The gable roof is very prevalent. The few gambrel roofs are usually of the New England type, with the upper and lower slopes approximately equal in length. Only a few of the houses have overhanging eaves. On the prosperous farms or estates along the Raritan and Millstone Rivers a number of large, two story houses were built. These are in striking contrast to the more humble one and a half story farmhouses prevalent elsewhere. Their owners lived on a luxurious scale comparable to that of their fellow countrymen in New York City.

Erskine's Revolutionary surveys and a series of earlier and later maps were of invaluable aid in locating the early roads and houses and the names of their owners. The author is deeply grateful for contributions of land records and family history for the Staats and Lane—Brokaw houses by Lewis D. Cook, of land records of the Raritan River valley by Cornelius C. Vermeule, for information about the Raritan valley from Miss Marian Cushman and Charles Deshler, and about the Bedminster and Rocky Hill regions respectively from John Powelson and Thomas Barrowman. Extensive information drawn from the county histories and the *Somerset Historical Quarterly* has been supplemented by original research in the church and probate records. A few of the photographs were taken in 1925 but the majority in 1933 after the completion of the field survey.

HOUSES IN SOMERSET COUNTY

House of John Berrien; Washington's Headquarters
Rocky Hill
PLATE 128

The date of this house has always been taken from the fireback—1764, or when it has been misread—1734. It is possible that the house was erected at the earlier date, and the fireback added subsequently. On John Dalley's undated map made shortly after 1745 is shown John Berrien's house a short distance south of the road on the east side of the Millstone River. Thus if this house did not exist then, Berrien lived in another house on the site.

The builder's grandfather Cornelius Jansen[1] Berrien was a Huguenot, a native of Berrien in the Department of Finisterre, France. He fled to Holland, whence he came to America, settled by 1669 at Flatbush and in 1685 at Newtown on Long Island, and died in 1689. He married Jannetje, daughter of Jan Stryker, one of the early leaders of Flatbush; after his death she married Samuel Edsall, widower. The son Peter[2] Berrien, b. 1672, d. April 5, 1737, was a scholar, surveyor and large land-owner of Newtown; he married Aug. 10, 1706 his step-sister Elizabeth Edsall and had seven children. They were the parents of Judge John[3] Berrien, b. Nov. 19, 1711, d. April 22, 1772.

John Berrien came to Middlesex County, New Jersey, from Newtown, as a surveyor. He was taxed here in Franklin Township in 1735, and may have built the present house about this date. He was chosen Judge of Somerset County in 1739 and Justice of the Supreme Court in 1764; he also served as a trustee of Princeton University, which was situated not many miles from his home. His house, which he called *Rockingham*, stood on the east bank of the Millstone River, but was reached from the Princeton side across a ford and up a long private avenue of trees from the river. His first wife is believed to have been Mary, daughter of Samuel Leonard of Perth Amboy. He and his brother Judge Thomas Leonard of Princeton owned a great deal of property in and around Princeton, Kingston and Rocky Hill, and it is possible that John Berrien obtained his land from his father-in-law. Judge Berrien married secondly Aug. 16, 1759 Margaret Eaton of Eatontown, N. J., b. 1722, d. 1819; she was the mother of his children. He died shortly before the Revolution and lies buried in the Princeton University Cemetery.

Judge Berrien's widow was the hostess of General Washington at the end of the war. Congress leased the place from her for his stay, Aug. 24th to Nov. 10, 1783. Washington lived here with his staff so as to be near Congress, which was then meeting at Princeton five miles away. Although the worries of active warfare were over, he was anxious to get a bill passed for the relief of his soldiers and he was then doing his best to keep them from open mutiny. It was here that Washington wrote his famous Farewell Address to the Army, a week before he started home; he dated it "Rocky Hill near Princeton, Nov. 2, 1783" and first delivered it from the balcony of the house.

Judge Berrien and Margaret Eaton had four sons and two daughters. The eldest son was Major John⁴ Berrien, b. 1758, d. 1816; he fought at the battle of Monmouth and was an aide to Washington. After the war he settled at Savannah, Georgia. It was at the Georgia home of his son John Macpherson Berrien, Attorney General under Jackson, that Margaret Eaton Berrien died in 1819, aged 97 years. She is said to be buried in Burlington. She had previously advertised the property at Rocky Hill for sale in the newspapers, stating it contained 320 acres with outhouses and orchards.

Rockingham, the Berrien place at Rocky Hill, was bought from Mrs. Berrien by Frederick Cruser in April 1802. Frederick Cruser, b. 1766, was the son of Abraham and the grandson of Cornelius³ Krusen, who owned the well-known family home on the north shore of Staten Island (plate 40). Frederick married Catharine Van Dyke, and lived here at Rocky Hill until about 1830, when the place was sold to David H. Mount. He disposed of it Nov. 1, 1872 to Martin Howell, whose executors conveyed it to the Rocky Hill Quarry Co. It was then used for the quarters of Italian laborers, who blasted away the whole face of the hill below the house. Two acres of the Berrien tract were purchased from the quarry company by the Washington Rocky Hill Headquarters Association June 17, 1897, and the house moved back a few hundred yards up the hill for greater safety.

The house is a two story frame structure which is unusually well preserved. Beautiful specimens of old panelling, old cupboards and doors remain, especially in the dining room (the southeast room). The house is now filled with Revolutionary furniture, some of which originally belonged to the Berriens and were used by Washington. The dated iron fireback is in the drawing room (the southwest room). Washington is supposed to have written his address in the southeast chamber above the dining room. The house is now entered from the rear, into what formerly must have been a back bedroom, and it is not until we reach the front rooms that we get the feeling of well-being and comfort, which must have made it pleasant for Berrien's friends and Washington's officers to dine here.

A sketch made in 1848 is reproduced in Lossing's *Pictorial Field Book of the Revolution*, v. 2, p. 631. The house was then in very bad repair. The cut shows a two story house with a gable roof having straight overhanging eaves on both sides and with the porch on the south front as it is today. At the east end there was a long, low, one story wing with overshot roof and a chimney in the center. Possibly this wing was the Judge's home when he came to this region.

The small two story frame wing on the east end of the house was built in 1897 for the Association's caretaker; it blends very well with the old house. The slave kitchen, a detached stone building, was erected recently to replace an earlier one. The custodian, Thomas Barrowman, is very much interested in the house and its history and in local families. The village of Rocky Hill is on the west side of the Millstone River. The Berrien house is near the east bank, halfway up the hill, on the south side of the present road to New Brunswick. It connects with the main Kingston road near Ten Mile Run.

Berrien (?)—Pumyea House
Old Rocky Hill Road, Rocky Hill
PLATE 129

The early history of this house is lost in obscurity. It is probable that it stood on the berrien tract. Peter⁹ Berrien, Jr. (1714-1781), was a younger brother of Judge John Berrien of *Rockingham* (plate 128). Peter left Newtown, Long Island, and settled at Ten Mile Run, north of Kingston. He had a large tract, which ran down toward the Millstone River and is believed to extend beyond the Pumyea house. In 1738 he married Anna Emmons who survived him, and had six children: Elizabeth, Henry (1743-1806) married Cornelia Van Dyck, Cornelius, John (1751-1797) married Neeltje Van Dyck, Sarah, and Anna. It is probable that the house (the old wing) was built by one of his sons.

P. Pomyee is marked as the owner on a map of 1850. It is known as the Peter Pumyea house, and one of its bedrooms is referred to as Peter's bedroom. He is believed to be the Peter J. Pumyea, d. April 14, 1869, aged 68 years, 7 months, and 25 days (b. 1800), who lies buried in the Ten Mile Run Cemetery with his wife Ann Berrien, d. Dec. 11, 1858, aged 51 years, 10 months, 14 days (b. 1807). By 1873 the house had passed out of the family. These two dates coincide with the Peter J. Pumyea in consideration, as he had died in 1869. It is probable that he had received the place from his wife's family. Since this time, the house has had a large number of owners and tenants. Recently it was owned by the Snedekers and Condits, and is now in the possession of Alfred G. Moment.

Both sections of the house are old, but the east wing is the oldest and distinctly pre-revolutionary. Its Dutch oven, extending outside the house, is one of the few examples still existing. The house stands on the north side of the old Rocky Hill road, about as far toward the river as the road is now passable. This road, a dirt lane, leaves the present Rocky Hill road (which leads to Judge Berrien's house) a short distance west of its junction with the Kingston-New Brunswick highway, and runs more directly west than the present road. It formerly connected with the Millstone River, and by a branch road with the river further north at Griggstown.

The following item concerns the probable owner of this tract: among the damages in Somerset County done by the Continental troops, for which claims were proved and allowed in the fall of 1782, was the claim of Peter Berrian deceased, to the effect that in November 1776 Continental carters had taken 35 window lights, 61 panes of glass, and one broadcloth coat half worn; the account was brought in by his son John Berrian, and the value placed was £3.14.6.

House of Andries Coejeman
Raritan

Barent Pieterse (Coejeman), the miller, emigrated to this country in 1639 and was employed at Rennselaerswyck. He later bought a large tract at the present Coeymans, where he and many of his descendants lived. One of his sons was Andries' Coejeman, probable builder of the house at Raritan. On June 3, 1716 at the Dutch church in New York, Andries Coejeman married Geertruy, daughter of Dr. Samuel Staats, and widow of Peter Nagel, whom she had previously married on May 25, 1711. Andries and Geertruy had five children baptized at New York: Johanna, bap. 1718, d. 1786, married 1741 Dr. John Neilson of Raritan; Mayke, bap. 1720; Barent, bap. 1721; Samuel Staats, bap. 1724, and Geertruy, bap. 1726, married Abraham Lott.

It was probably shortly after the birth of the youngest child that Andries Coejeman removed to the wilds of the upper reaches of the Raritan River. The exact date of purchase of this property is unknown. Part of the Indian deed of 1681, covering a large tract along the north bank of the river, was granted in 1683 to Graham and associates; the fourth quarter of this tract was in the possession of Andries Coejeman as early as 1736, the survey of 1736 showing that he owned 442½ acres here. He has always been considered the builder of the brick house on this tract, although the two dated stones, "S.C. 1732" and "S.S. 1736," are not marked with his initials as was customary. He died not long after the house was erected; the will of Andries Coejmans, gentleman of Somerset Co., dated 1739 and probated 1741, named his wife, only son (the elder son Barent had evidently died) and three daughters, all under 21 years of age, and his brother-in-law Lewis Morris, Jr.

The only surviving son was Samuel Staats' Coejeman, bap. Jan. 29, 1724 at New York, d. 1785, married Aryantje Schuyler of New Brunswick. His estate along

434

the Raritan is mentioned in the relaying of the road in 1764. During the Revolution, a party of Hessians stopped here, took its owner from bed and tied him to a tree while they ransacked and plundered the house. This exposure is believed to have caused his death. His only son Andrew⁴ Coejeman, bap. Sept. 27, 1772, d. 1804, lived and died in the family homestead and was buried with his ancestors. He married Jane Van Doren and had three sons baptized at the Raritan Church: Samuel Staats, Jacob Van Doren and John Neilson Coejeman.

In 1800 Andrew Coejeman sold the east 104 acres of the property to Frelinghuysen, and in 1804 the house and west half of the estate were sold to Dominie John S. Vredenburgh. The Dominie resided here until 1821; he sold the property to John Gaston, who in 1837 sold it to Albert Camman. Mrs. John Bartolette was born here and owned the house for a large part of the nineteenth century.

On the south side near the door is a stone inscribed "S.C. 1732," and in the middle of the east side is a stone marked "S.S. 1736." These were undoubtedly the dates of erection of the house. The initials are an enigma. We know that Andries Coejeman owned the property in 1736 if not earlier, therefore it is possible that the initials stand for the actual builder employed by him to erect his home. The house is built of brick. It formerly had a gambrel roof of unusual proportions, the upper slope being very steep and longer than the lower one. The basement is divided into as many as ten rooms. The main floor has a wide-arched hall and four rooms. The interior was planned and finished with an ideal of magnificence. The brick, interior woodwork and furnishings are supposed to have been brought largely from Holland. There was formerly an old fashioned well and well sweep nearby. The lines of the house have been completely destroyed by the widening and enlarging of the upper half story to form a complete second story the size and proportions of the main floor. The old lines of the gambrel roof are discernible in the brickwork of the ends. It stands on the river bank in a poor section of Raritan, some distance west of the old Dutch Parsonage. Views of the house in its better days and before its remodelling can be seen in the *Somerset Co. Hist. Quarterly*, v. 3, p. 241, and in *Northwestern New Jersey*, v. 1, p. 16.

The Parsonage of the Reformed Dutch Church
now at Washington Place, Somerville

Somerville was in early times a part of the village of Raritan, and was one of the centers of settlement along the Raritan River. It was situated in lot No. 7 in the second Indian deed of 1681, which was patented in 1683 to Graham and associates; on its division the second quarter of this lot No. 7 was assigned to Graham's partner, John White, who sold to Tunison and he to Peter Van Nest. It later came into the hands of Cornelis Bogert, who on Jan. 25, 1752 deeded the parsonage lot to the consistory of the Dutch Church, and on May 16, 1768 deeded the 114 acres adjoining and extending west to the Wallace-Miller farm (Washington's Headquarters) to Rev. Jacob R. Hardenburgh. Before this, on May 18, 1749, the Raritan, Millstone and North Branch Churches called Rev. John Frelinghuysen to be their pastor, assuring him a salary and a suitable dwelling with 30 acres of land, which was later paid for by the consistories.

The Frelinghuysens belonged to one of the Dutch-Westphalian border families. Rev. Theodorus Jacobus[1] Frelinghuysen, b. 1691 at Wolfenbuttel, was a minister for a few years in the Dutch church of Embden in East Friesland, before he came to this country in 1720. He settled at Three Mile Run near New Brunswick and had charge of the Dutch Churches of Middlesex, Hunterdon and Somerset Counties in New Jersey. All his five sons became Dutch ministers and his two daughters married ministers. His son Rev. John[2] Frelinghuysen, b. 1720 at Three Mile Run, married Dinah Van Bergh, b. Feb. 10, 1725 at Amsterdam in Holland, daughter of Louis Van Bergh, a rich merchant. He was called to the ministry in 1749 and appointed to the Raritan, Millstone and North Branch Churches. A dwelling was promised him. The present parsonage was erected in 1751 (the dated cornerstone reads June 7, 1751), supposedly under the directions of Dinah Van Bergh and with her money. Rev. John Frelinghuysen and his wife Dinah moved into it and used it not only as their home but also as a Theological Seminary. Rev. John Frelinghuysen lived to the age of only 34 years, dying in September, 1754. Shortly afterwards his widow was persuaded to marry Rev. Jacob Rutzen Hardenburgh, a pupil of her former husband, and a man many years her junior. They returned to the Raritan parsonage in 1758, when her husband was called to fill the vacant pastorate. In 1763 they were joined by her widowed mother, Mrs. Van Bergh. They entertained General Washington frequently, and lived here until 1781, when Rev. Hardenburgh was called to Rosendale. He later served the church at New Brunswick, where he died in 1790, aged 51 years, and where his widow Dinah Van Bergh continued to live, and died March 26, 1807, aged 81 years. The next occupant of the parsonage was Rev. Theodore Frelinghuysen Romeyn, a nephew of Rev. John Frelinghuysen; he came here about two years after Rev. Hardenburgh's departure.

The parsonage was sold about the time that Rev. John S. Vredenburgh was called to the pastorate, as he owned a house of his own, the old Coejeman homestead nearby (see supra). Dr. Swan bought the parsonage and land, and sold it in 1810 to Dr. Peter I. Stryker, member of the Legislative Council, who died 1859. Joshua Doughty (1799-1881) came to Somerville and in 1836 bought the old parsonage of

Dr. Stryker. He and his son Joshua, Jr. lived here. It was finally sold by the Doughty estate in October, 1912, to the New Jersey Central Railroad. It is now owned by the Frederick Frelinghuysen Chapter of the Daughters of the American Revolution.

The Dutch parsonage originally stood in old Raritan village (now called Somerville) south of the present Main Street and near the center of the village. In 1912 it was purchased by the New Jersey Central Railroad with the intention of demolishing it for trackage space. Mainly through the efforts of Senator Joseph Frelinghuysen it was removed in 1913 to its present site, 1500 feet towards Raritan, and in 1932 donated by him to the Society. The house is at present a large two story brick structure, surmounted by a modern, heavy, gable roof. The windows of the first floor are unusually long, and were undoubtedly cut down at some date. The only Dutch characteristic of the exterior of the house in its present condition is the old double door with bottle glass eyes. Views of the house when it had a nineteenth century porch running the length of the front and before the low two story service wing was demolished can be seen in *Somerset Co. Hist. Quarterly*, v. 2, p. 161, and in *Northwestern New Jersey*, v. 1, p. 208. The wing was similar to that of the Frelinghuysen house nearby (plate 133), and originally the main house probably resembled the Van Vechten house, also nearby (plate 139). The house is now situated on Washington Place, a stone's throw from the Wallace-Miller house which was occupied by Gen. Washington during the Revolution.

House of Hendrick Fisher
Canal Road, South Bound Brook

John Inians and associates purchased from the Indians for Lady Elizabeth Carteret a tract along the south side of the Raritan River from Bound Brook southeast to Lawrence Brook; they laid out the Raritan lots in 1681, consisting of 500 acres each with a half mile of river frontage. Three of the lots at the north end had by 1685 come into the possession of William Dockwra, one of the East Jersey Proprietors. By birth a Scotchman, he was a merchant in London and an extensive landowner in New Jersey; he never came to America, performing his duties as Secretary of the Board of Proprietors by deputy. The statement that the Fisher house was built by him in 1688 is therefore erroneous. He is believed to have sold 300 acres here on the Raritan River to Hendrick Visscher about 1703, but this statement likewise seems to be incorrect. The property lies to the southwest of the adjoining Staats lands (plate 136), deeds to which show that the Fisher place was still owned in 1722 by William Dockwra, was owned in 1738 partly by Jacob Walton and the other part lately by Robert Lurting, and in 1769 by Hendrick Fisher. The first mention of the latter in Somerset County was his election to the Assembly in 1740; he probably owned the place by this time.

The father, Hendrick[1] Visscher, Sr., emigrated from the Lower Palatinate by way of Holland and is believed to have died Oct. 17, 1749, at his home on the Raritan River. Evidently he did not purchase the Dockwra property about 1703. It is possible that he lived across the river in Piscataway Township until a few years before his death, when he may have moved to his son Hendrick's home on the Somerset side of the river. The following three references probably apply to him although possibly to his son: In 1739 he was named an executor of a will, in which he was termed a resident of Piscataway. In 1748 he was listed as a freeholder of Piscataway, but absent. On July 11, 1748, an advertisement appeared in the New York Gazette for a 200 acre farm for sale on the east (*i.e.* Piscataway) side of the Raritan River, 6 miles above Brunswick, with a dwelling house having two fireplaces, and with barn and orchard; those interested were to apply to Hendrick Visser living near the premises. This may have been the homestead of the emigrant Hendrick.

The son Hendrick[2] Visscher or Fisher, b. 1697 in the Lower Palatinate, d. Aug. 16, 1779 in the 82nd year of his age, and lies buried on his farm on the Raritan River (this date on the tombstone is obviously an error in either month or year, as his will was probated May 15, 1779). The family name gradually became anglicized and in later years Hendrick used the form *Fisher*. The homestead was probably built by him in the second quarter of the eighteenth century; he did not own the land in 1738 and was in possession in 1769. The first reference to him in Somerset County is in 1740 when he was elected to the Assembly, but not considered eligible as he had been naturalized only the year before. By trade he was a farmer and mechanic. He became a member of the Dutch Church of New Brunswick in 1721 and was a faithful worker and leader in the church for fifty-eight years. He was Judge of the Court of Common Pleas, a member of the Colonial Assembly for thirty years and for some time its powerful leader, a representative of New Jersey at the Continental Congress of 1765, and president of the first Provincial Congress of New Jersey in 1775. When in 1776 Lord Howe offered full pardon to those who would give up their allegiance to the American cause, he excepted Hendrick Fisher, his neighbor Abraham Staats and one other, as being beyond pardoning. After the battle of Bound Brook early in 1777, the victorious British army marched to New Brunswick, and on their way raided Hendrick Fisher's house and drove away over twenty head of cattle. He died two years later and was greatly mourned. In his will of 1778 he distributed property and legacies to his family, naming his wife Elizabeth and his children; among his executors he named his friend Abraham Staats, owner of the house nearby (plate 136), who, however, renounced the executorship.

Hendrick Fisher's wife was Elizabeth (Lybete or Libshe) Bries, daughter of Volkert Hendrickse Bries of Breuckelen and later of Piscataway Township, Middlesex Co. (he died 1771-72). Hendrick and Elizabeth had eleven children, all baptized at the New Brunswick or Raritan churches, between 1723 and 1746: Hendrick, Jr. of Bound Brook, whose wife was Effie; Elizabeth, wife of John Field; Volkert, who married Elizabeth Smith; Mary, wife of Jacob Fulkerson, concerning whom Andrew Johnston, surveyor, wrote on April 25, 1753: "Jacob Folkerse, Mr. Fisher's son-in-law, spoake to me about the place he lives on and wants to have 50 acres of John Smyth's land joined to it, which I told him he could hardly expect; consented to let him stay this year but chuse not to leas to him; he has the carractor of an idle fellow"; Nellie, wife of Hendrick Suydam; John, who married Margaret McCrae; Minne, died in infancy; Minne; Abraham of Lamington; Margaret, wife of Dr. Austin Craig; and Jeremiah, who inherited the residue of his father's real and personal estate.

The homestead farm passed to the youngest son Jeremiah³ Fisher, bap. Sept. 1, 1746, d. Jan. 9, 1807. He married by license of Dec. 9, 1769, Catharine Brokaw, b. Oct. 28, 1749, d. Jan. 6, 1832 and both were buried on the family farm; they had four sons and five daughters. They doubtless lived on the homestead until Jeremiah sold it in 1796 to Creighton McCrae. Jeremiah owned and conducted the Middletown Hotel in Bound Brook at one time. The Fisher house was occupied about 1875 by Isaac A. Brokaw and was owned in 1914 by Claude Goodsell. The present owner is Frederick L. Rossman.

The house is a one and a half story structure of frame, covered by a wide gambrel roof with no overhang. Long old windows, stoop and three (later) dormers are details shown in the photograph in the *Somerset Co. Hist. Quarterly*, v. 2, p. 1. The house was remodelled recently with diamond-paned window groupings and other changes which alter its character sadly. The house is on the southwest side of the Canal Road about one mile south of the river crossing at South Bound Brook. The old Revolutionary road led along the banks of the Raritan River and was displaced by the canal in 1834. The present turnpike was cut through in 1823 and is variously called Main Street in South Bound Brook, Canal Road, Easton Turnpike, and Easton Avenue in New Brunswick. The Fisher house is a short distance south of the Staats house on the river (plate 136).

Gulick (?)—Ditmars House
Road to Blawenburg, Harlingen
PLATE 130

Little is known of the history of this house. The county road on which it stands, is the division line between the Hart and Harlingen tracts. Unless the course of the road has been changed at this particular point, the house stands on the extreme west end of the 4000 acre tract granted in 1690 to Thomas Hart and Walther Benthal. It extended from the Millstone River near Griggstown westward to the Harlingen tract, and was sold by Hart in 1702 to Gerardus Beekman and his associates. Again, unless the course of the road has been changed here, this house is undoubtedly the same as the one shown on Erskine's Revolutionary map on the northeast corner of the meeting place of the road from Sourland (now Harlingen) to Rock Mill and Ringoes and of the road to Garrison's Tavern, west of Somerset Courthouse (now Millstone), the house being marked on this map Youim Heuleck (? or Heuluk ?, the spelling is not clear). It is probable that this is a phonetic rendition of the name Joachim Gulick.

It is believed that a Joachim Gulick emigrated to this country in 1653 and settled by 1717 at Six Mile Run in New Jersey (some miles to the east of Harlingen and on the opposite side of the Millstone River); he is stated to have had four sons, Benjamin, Henry, John and William, of whom the latter three lived in Franklin Township (of which Harlingen was then a part) at the end of the eighteenth century. This account obviously confuses several generations. The family was very numerous about Rocky Hill to the south.

The hesitancy in ascribing this house to the Gulick family, in spite of Erskine's map, is due to the fact that there yet stands, on the opposite or northwest corner of the county road, a small stone house built in 1752 by Derick Gulick; it is possible that the course of the road has been straightened and that this was the house mentioned by Erskine. Derick Gulick was church master of the Harlingen Church in 1759, but for some reason no member of the family seems to have had children baptized here. We are ignorant of his age; it might have been a son of his, Joachim, who owned his house during the Revolution. It (that is, the stone house) was owned in 1790 by Isaac Amerman, who removed to Cayuga County in 1806.

To return to the frame house in question, our first positive information is that it was owned in 1850 by Peter Ditmars. About this time, Henry Ditmars lived up the mountain to the west, and another Ditmars lived nearby between them on the Revolutionary road to Ringoes, which still exists although impassable at one point. Dutchtown was then the local name for this region. Many of the Ditmars family settled throughout this territory during the nineteenth century. In 1873 the house was owned by H. Stryker and in the 1890s by Enoch Cain. It is now owned by Mrs. Julia Haelig of Bound Brook and is leased out.

The house is built in many units and is an irregular one story frame structure with a small portion of stone. It is still used as a farmhouse. It stands on the northeast corner of the country road to Blawenburg and the road to Harlingen, and is one mile west of the latter village.

House of Gisbert Lane

south of North Branch, Bridgewater Township

PLATE 131

In the division of the fourth Indian deed of Nov. 19, 1681, Lot No. 48 consisted of 1650 acres on the east side of the North Branch of Raritan River, extending from its junction with the South Branch northward beyond North Branch village. Lot No. 48 was surveyed for Lord Neill Campbell and eventually passed into the hands of Daniel D. Dunster, who sold a large portion in the middle of the tract to Gisbert Lane about 1730.

The ancestor of the family, Thys or Mathys Jansen Laenen van Pelt, emigrated in the *Rosetree* in 1663 from the province of Liege in North Belgium, with his wife and four children, and settled at New Utrecht on Long Island. With him was his brother Theunis, whose descendants retained the name of Van Pelt (see plate 21). Adriaen[2] Lane, b. about 1672 in New Utrecht, d. after 1738, was a younger son of Thys, the emigrant, born in this country. He married Martyntje, daughter of Hendrick Smock, and secondly Jannetje, daughter of Ferdinandus Van Syckelen. Adriaen left New Utrecht for Middletown in Monmouth Co., New Jersey, and by 1711 had removed to Hunterdon County. That year he bought 450 acres near Holland's Brook, not far from Readington and west of the confluence of the North and South Branches of Raritan River. Thirteen children have been ascribed to him, including Gisbert (Guisbert, Gilbert), b. ——, d. 1762-63, married by 1723 Johanna or Hannah Loveritz.

In or about 1730 Gisbert Lane purchased the above tract on the North Branch of the Raritan River in Somerset County, not very far from the lands of his supposed father in Hunterdon County. Gisbert Lane built thereon the present stone house in 1737 and settled here. He was a Judge of the Court of Common Pleas in Somerset County in 1742. He had two sons and three daughters. In his will of 1762 Gisbert left the south part of his plantation to his son Arie and the north part to his son William. In 1791 William mortgaged a 300 acre plantation which he had inherited from his father; this and later conveyances show that William's property included the brick house to the north (plate 132), which is known as the Brokaw house. Presumably his brother Arie also received about 300 acres, and the old house evidently stands on the southern portion which Arie inherited. Only William Lane's house is shown on Erskine's Revolutionary map, possibly because the properties of the two brothers were considered as one tract.

Arie[4] Lane, b. about 1726, d. 1780, married his first cousin Lucretia, daughter of Abraham Lane of Middlesex County (will 1760). They had two daughters and one son, the latter inheriting the homestead. He was Guisbert or Gilbert A.[5] Lane of Bridgewater Township, who married and had two daughters, Hannah and Jane. The 1737 house had passed out of the family by 1850 when the owner was Lewis Anderson. He sold it about 1856 to David Dunn, the owner in 1860. The farm passed to his only son John R. Dunn, and is now owned and occupied by one of his children, Matthew H. Dunn.

The house is built of roughly cut, flat fieldstones. It is one story in height, with a gable roof. Iron figures on the south front below the eaves bear the date of erection, 1737, of which the first two figures are shown in the photograph, the last two figures being hidden by the modern porch. The house is on the east bank of the North Branch of Raritan River, one and a quarter miles south of the church at North Branch village, and south of the railway. Formerly the road was nearer the river, between the house and the barns, but now it runs behind the barns.

Lane—Brokaw House
south of North Branch, Bridgewater Township
PLATE 132

Although known as the Brokaw house, because Gen. Washington is supposed to have ridden here in 1779 to condole with the widow of Lt. John Brokaw, it is probable that this family did not own it at this early period. It is possible that William Lane (1727-1797) built the house; he lived here during a part of his life at least and his family cemetery is in the adjoining field. William Lane's house is marked on Erskine's Revolutiony map, although it is not positive whether this is the house referred to or the one just to the south which had previously been owned by his father Gisbert Lane (plate 131), as only one of these two houses is shown on the map.

The ancestor of the Brokaw family was Bourgeon[1] Broucard, a Huguenot, who emigrated in 1675 from Manheim on the Rhine with his wife Catharine Le Febre, and settled on Long Island. Among his sons was John[2] Broka or Brokaer, bap. Nov. 14, 1680 at Flatbush, d. 1740 in Somerset Co., New Jersey, intestate. It is probable that he settled near Millstone at an early date; six of his eight children were baptized at Raritan (then the nearest church) between 1705 and 1717 and his eighth child in 1728 at the new Harlingen Church nearby. Various properties, all in Hillsborough Twp., Somerset Co., are mentioned in the inventory of his estate. One of his daughters, Femmetje Broka, married her neighbor John Staats and lived west of Millstone in Hillsborough Twp.; they were the parents of Abraham Staats, builder of the second portion of the Staats homestead at South Bound Brook (plate 136). John Brokaer was survived by his wife Sarah Van Middlesworth, who renounced the executorship in favor of their eldest son John; in 1787 the latter, then of Bridgewater Twp., and his wife Mary, sold 107 acres on the Millstone River and the Road to Roycefield, property presumably once his father's.

This son John Broecka or John³ Brokaw, Sr., bap. Oct. 26, 1709, d. 1803-04, lived in Bridgewater Township, Somerset County; his homestead consisted of about 325 acres on the south side of the road from Pluckemin to Bound Brook, which he had bought in 1762 and of which he still owned 110 acres at his death which were sold by his executors. The mother of most (or all) of his children was Maretye or Mary, daughter of Benjamin Van Cleave of Freehold (see his will of 1747); she was still living in 1789, when she joined her husband in a sale of land to their son Borgun. John's second wife was Catharine ——. In his will of 1803 John Brokaw, Sr., mentioned his wife Catharine, his grandson John, son of his son John deceased, his sons Benjamin, Isaac (of Woodbridge), Brogun, Richard, his daughters Catharine Van Arsdalen, Hendrecy Lott, Sarah Van Deventer, Mary Van Dyke and Phebe Field. The youngest son, Richard⁴ Brokaw of Bridgewater Township, stated in his pension papers that he was born Sept. 17, 1758, that he served in the Revolution, substituting for his brother Benjamin, and that his eldest brother (unnamed) was killed in the battle of Germantown. The only member of the family killed in this battle was John Brokaw, whose position in the family tree is thus identified. (The D.A.R. papers wrongly state that he was the John Brokaw, bap. 1733, son of Abraham.)

John⁴ Brocka or Brokaw, b. about 1739, was a farmer in Bridgewater Township. On June 23, 1775 he was appointed Lieutenant in the First Regiment of Somerset Co. Militia, Capt. Ten Eyck's Company, and was killed Oct. 4, 1777 at the Battle of Germantown. He died intestate, the inventory of his estate was made by Aurie and William Lane, and his widow Mary was appointed administratrix. She received a small pension allowance during her widowhood, until she married William Lane in 1781. Lt. John⁴ Brokaw's wife was Maretye (Maria, Mary) Van der Veer (her parentage is unknown but indirect proof of her maiden name is shown by a Van der Veer giving bond for the estate and by several children bearing the names of this family). John and Mary Brokaw had nine children (many bap. at Raritan): John, Henry (1761-1834) of Hillsborough Twp., Ferdinand, Michael, Benjamin, Phebe wife of Joseph Stull, Peter, Mary wife of Dr. Bogart, and Ann wife of Rynier Van Nest. By license of Nov. 3, 1781 Mary Brokaw (the widow) married William Lane of Somerset County. In 1796 a suit was brought in the Orphans Court by John Brokaw against William Lane and Maria his wife, late

443

Maria Brokaw, administratrix of John Brokaw, deceased, to force them to render an account of the personal estate of said John Brokaw, deceased.

Lt. John Brokaw, Jr., lived in Bridgewater Twp., either with his father, or on a farm of his own, the location of which is unknown. The strong tradition that General Washington rode to the brick house south of North Branch in 1779 to console the widow of John Brokaw, Jr., suggests that his home was here. However, this was the home of William Lane at the end of the eighteenth century and presumably earlier. His father, Gisbert Lane, built the house a short distance to the south (plate 131) and willed the north portion of his plantation to his son William, who probably thus inherited the land on which the brick house stands; his family burial ground is in the field adjoining the brick house, and his first wife, who died in 1777, is buried here, indicating that he probably owned this property as early as this date. It is very possible that William Lane built this house about the time of his first marriage (1750), that Mary Brokaw went to reside with him (as housekeeper?) when she became a widow in 1777 because his wife had just died and he was a friend of the Brokaw family (William had taken the inventory of John Brokaw's estate), and that she married him in 1781. Even if Washington visited the Widow Brokaw elsewhere, the tradition could have become attached to the brick house since she later lived here for so many years.

William[4] Lane, b. May 27, 1727, d. Oct. 14, 1797, married first June 20, 1750 Jannetje Rappelyea, d. Feb. 7, 1777, aged 46 years, 3 mos., and had two sons and five daughters. He had another son by his second marriage (by license of Nov. 3, 1781) to Mary Brokaw who, according to the above records was Mary (Maria or Marytje) Van der Veer, widow of Lt. John Brokaw. She is not buried on the place with her husband and stepchildren, but is believed to be the Maria Lane on whose estate administration was granted Jan. 7, 1813.

William Lane was a farmer of means; the births of seven slaves are recorded in his family Bible. On Sept. 1, 1791 William Lane of Bridgewater Twp., and Mary his wife, mortgaged a 300 acre plantation "which was devised to said William Lane by the last will of Gilbert Lane, deceased," beginning at the east side of the North Branch of Raritan River at the uppermost corner of the land of Gilbert A. Lane (son of Arie, who was William's brother and seems to have inherited the house built by their father Gisbert—plate 131). In 1796 William's plantation was bounded on the north by Matthias Ten Eyck (whose house is shown on Erskine's map as just south of the highway from Raritan), on the west by Gilbert W. Lane and on the south by Gilbert A. Lane. In 1797 William Lane bequeathed his farm, one half to his son Tunis, and the other half to his wife and eventually to their son Abraham, stating that he had already deeded a farm to his son Gilbert. In 1799 Tunis Lane mortgaged a 90 acre tract, part of the former plantation of William Lane, deceased, on the east side of the North Branch River and north of Abraham Lane; Tunis either inherited more or purchased additional land adjoining on the north as his heirs later sold his farm of 182 acres. In 1804 Abraham Lane mortgaged a 100 acre tract south of Tunis Lane and north of John Bennet's land, formerly William Lane's; Abraham had disposed of it by 1835 when it was owned by Jacobus Staats. In his will dated 1830 and probated 1840, Abraham⁵ Lane divided his lands and estate between his three sons and four daughters, including "the farm where I now live, lying on the north side of the stage road"; thus Abraham did not live on his father's and grandfather Lane's land. These several tracts along the river probably amount to more than 300 acres; thus William Lane (or possibly his son Tunis) may have purchased land in addition to his inheritance. It is therefore possible that the brick house was once John Brokaw's but not probable, especially since William Lane's wife, who died in 1777, is buried on the farm.

The brick house stands on Tunis Lane's tract, where he and others of his family are buried. Tunis⁵ Lane (1763-1834) was a bachelor and bequeathed his entire estate equally to his brother Gilbert W. Lane and his five sisters, Hannah wife of Hendrick Field, Jane wife of Jacob Ten Eyck, Sarah wife of Hendrick Vroom, Mariah wife of George McGowen, and Elizabeth Lane single, and their heirs, stating "to my half brother, Abraham Lane, nothing, because he had the half of all my father's estate when my brother and sisters got little or nothing." On Jan. 3, 1835 the devisees of Tunis Lane conveyed "the farm and real estate of the said Tunis Lane," consisting of 182 acres, "excepting and reserving the graveyard as now enclosed with posts and rails," bounded west by the North Branch of Raritan River, for $1,010 to Albert C. Voorhees of Hillsborough Twp., who had purchased it at public sale the month previous.

In 1837 Voorhees sold most of this land in various parcels, including an 80 acre tract on the river, excepting the Burial Ground, and also 67 acres adjoining this on the east for $6,026.59 to Isaac Polhemus of Montgomery Twp., who the following month conveyed the 80 acre tract, excepting the burial ground, for $5,000 to Court G. Voorhees of Hillsborough Twp. The latter probably moved into the brick house as he was a resident of Bridgewater Township at his death. His executor sold the 80 acre tract on the east side of the river, excepting the burial ground, on April 5, 1848 to James P. Brokaw of Hillsborough Twp., who disposed of it in 1854 to John D. Kershow, and he in turn conveyed it on Jan. 4, 1859 for $6,400 to Dennis and Abraham Voorhees Nevius of Branchburg Twp. They were brothers and settled in the brick house with their parents. On Feb. 10, 1864 Abraham married Anna Maria, daughter of Henry B. Staats and Hannah Field (the latter was a great-granddaughter of William Lane and his first wife). Abraham Nevius bought out the interest of his brother in 1866 but sold the farm in 1883 and removed to Cordova in Maryland. It was later purchased by Chauncey Brokaw, who is stated to have occupied the house formerly William Lane's. The present owner is Harry Sally.

The house is a long, low, brick structure, with brick three-centered arch heads over the windows and a low-pitched gable roof. The old twelve-pane window sashes and old door remain on the south front. The house is on the east bank of the North Branch of Raritan River, one-half mile south of the church at North Branch village.

Middagh (?)—Frelinghuysen House
now at Somerset Street and Wyckoff Avenue, Raritan
PLATE 133

This house (also the Dutch church parsonage and the Coejeman house) stands on Lot No. 7 of the Indian deed of 1681, which was patented Feb. 3, 1683 to Graham and associates. In the subdivision of this lot No. 7, which consisted of 1,904 acres, the third quarter was assigned to James Graham, who sold it Oct. 26, 1693 to Peter Van Nest, who deeded it to his son-in-law Derrick Middagh on May 1, 1709. Dirck or Derrick Aertse Middagh, bap. March 3, 1672 in New York, d. 1716, married Catalina, daughter of Peter Van Nest, and came to Raritan late in 1698 and bought a farm on the Raritan River from his father-in-law ten years later. On this large farm still stand several old houses: from west to east they are the Frelinghuysen house, the Duykinck-Cornell house, the Mann house, the present site of the Dutch church parsonage, and the Wallace-Miller house.

This large farm was inherited by Dirck's eldest son Cornelius Middagh, bap. June 13, 1698 at Breukelen, d. 1778. He served with the New Jersey militia in the colonial wars and was a commissioner of highways. He is believed to have lived in the house later Frelinghuysen's; in his will of 1778, he directed that after the death of his wife, his land should be sold and the proceeds divided between his children. He sold a part of his farm to his brother George in 1734. George Middagh, bap. 1709 at Raritan, lived where the Cornell house stands and kept a tavern there for some years; public meetings were held here 1750-56; the tavern was sold to John Arison in 1765. It is probable that this tavern was the old, low wing of the present Victorian house, which came into the hands of Richard Duykinck, and later of Rev. Frederick Frelinghuysen Cornell; it stands near the river on Granetz Place. In the middle of the eighteenth century a stone house stood at the foot of Middagh Street, where lived another brother Dirck Middagh, bap. 1703 at Raritan, whose son Col. Dirck Middagh lived here until he sold it in 1795. The present house, a two story frame structure with pleasing lines, was probably built about this time or possibly not until the land was bought in 1833 by John M. Mann. George Middagh, mentioned above, sold land in the east part of the tract in 1765 to Rev. Jacob Hardenburgh, who sold it in 1775 to John Wallace of Philadelphia; his son William built his home here in 1778, which was occupied early in the Revolution by Gen. Washington as his headquarters, and sold in 1801 to Dickenson Miller. Still another brother Tunis Middagh, bap. 1705, lived at the opposite or west end of the tract, near the Coejeman property. These were the homes of the sons of the first Dirck Middagh who came to Raritan.

On Erskine's Revolutionary map is a house marked Col. Frelinghuysen's, which stands on the bank west of the island in the Raritan River, west of a stream and of Raritan village. It is probable that the house so designated is the one known as the Frelinghuysen homestead, and may be the one (or on the site of the one) occupied by Cornelius Middagh. The house was probably built about the time of the war. Colonel, later General, Frederick[3] Frelinghuysen, was a son of Rev. John Frelinghuysen, and was born April 13, 1753 at the Dutch church parsonage (see supra) at Raritan village (now Somerville). It is probable that he is the Colonel referred to on the map, since his son John later owned the house. His home was on the Millstone River near Weston, but he may not have removed there until later, one account stating not until about 1787. Frederick was a brilliant lawyer. He was actively engaged in the battles of the Revolution, was a member of the Provincial Congress of New Jersey, of the Continental Congress and the United States Senate. He died April 13, 1804 and lies buried at Weston. He was married twice, to Gertrude Schenck, d. March 1794, aged 41 years, and to Ann Yard.

Frederick's son General John[4] Frelinghuysen was a lawyer, philanthropist, and Brigadier General of the militia, serving in the War of 1812. He was born in 1775 (supposedly at Millstone) and resided after his maturity at Raritan; he died April 10, 1833 in his 58th year and lies buried at Somerville. He married first Louisa Mercer, who died shortly afterwards, and secondly Elizabeth Van Vechten, who as a widow married John I. Gaston. Gen. John Frelinghuysen had six children by his second marriage: his sons Theodorus and Frederick lived nearby; two of his daughters married; his remaining two daughters, Catharine and Sarah, were spinsters and continued to occupy their father's home at Raritan. The estate sold the house in 1924 to Mr. Glazier, whose widow Mrs. Ida Glazier now owns it.

The house is not typical and is a veritable mansion compared to the majority of Dutch houses. It is a two story structure of yellow brick with an early nineteenth century doorway, a neo-classic portico, and a more modern gable dormer. A wide hall is flanked on either side by large rooms with very high ceilings. The roofline at the gable end is the only part of the exterior which suggests that the house is pre-

447

revolutionary. The low, frame wing on the west was built for slave quarters. It is possible that the house was not in existence at the time of the Revolution; it may have been built by Gen. John Frelinghuysen. At one time the house is supposed to have been used as a tavern and also as a prison. The house formerly stood nearer the river bank. It was recently moved back a short distance to the main road, Somerset Street.

House of Johannes Moelich (Mellick)
Road to Peapack, Far Hills
PLATE 134

This house is north of the main Dutch settlements in central New Jersey and east of the principal German settlements; it stands near the Revolutionary road from Pennsylvania to Morristown via Coryell's Ferry. Johannes Moelich was born Feb. 26, 1702 at Bendorf on the Rhine, whither his parents had come from Winningen. He grew up and became a tanner and burgher of good repute. There he married Nov. 1, 1723 Maria Catherina, daughter of Gottfried Kirberger, burgomaster of Bendorf, b. Jan. 6, 1698, d. Oct. 17, 1763. They emigrated in 1735 with four children and his brother Gottfried from Rotterdam to Philadelphia. They settled in New Jersey, in 1747 along the Delaware River, and in 1750 in Readington Township, where he established a tannery.

On Nov. 1, 1751 Johannes Moelich bought from George Leslie of Perth Amboy 367 acres of wild land (part of the tract patented to Johnston and Willocks in 1701), having a frontage of three-quarters of a mile on the North Branch of the Raritan River above Lesser Crossroads (the old name for Bedminster). He paid £324 down, and the balance of £202 and £228 within six months. He immediately took possession, erecting a temporary log structure for winter occupancy. Early the following spring the cellar and foundations for the house were laid across the way. The stone was hauled from a quarry on the tract and roughly dressed; the mortar was carried by the good wife on her head to the masons at work. The building progressed under the direction of Caspar Berger, a German stone mason and redemptioner, who built many of the early houses in the vicinity. Nearby on Peapack Brook was established a tannery and bark mill, which was operated for over one hundred years. Here Johannes Moelich lived the rest of his days with his six children (two more had been born in this country), and died Nov. 16, 1763. He was an active member of the Zion Lutheran Church of New Germantown, which supplied the pastoral needs of the Germans of central New Jersey.

The stone house, tannery and 200 acres were inherited by the eldest son Ehrenreich, whose name was anglicized to Aaron. Aaron[2] Malich, b. Oct. 17, 1725 at Bendorf in Germany, d. April 7, 1809 at Bedminster, married Charlotte Miller, b.

May 14, 1734, d. March 13, 1802. He was a leader of the county, a member of the Bedminster Committee of Observation and Inspection during the Revolution. One of his two sons, Daniel³ Melick, b. Oct. 28, 1763 in the old house, died here July 9, 1815, aided and later succeeded his father as tanner and farmer and owner of the homestead. In 1785 he married Margaret Gaston of Bedminster and had ten children; in 1808 he married secondly Catharine Johnston, widow of Othniel La Rue and had two more children. Again widowed, Catharine bought and settled nearby two years after Daniel's death. Four of her husband's children made their home in the old stone house: Charlotte, a spinster, John, David (1798-1870) who was a bachelor, a man of probity and honor, and the head of the house although not the eldest, and Daniel, also a bachelor and a semi-invalid. Still another child of Daniel's was Mary⁴ Mellick (1796-1833); in 1826 she married Peter Sutphen of Bedminster, a neighbor, and had two sons. The younger was William P. Sutphen, b. Aug. 8, 1832; after the early death of his mother, and the remarriage of his father, he was taken by his Aunt Charlotte to the old stone house, where he continued to live and eventually succeeded his uncle David to the Mellick homestead. The present owner, J. Macy Willetts of New York, occupies the old stone house from time to time.

It is interesting to compare this house of a German immigrant with the stone houses of the Dutch. It is similar and yet different from the style evolved by them in this country. Like theirs, it is a one and a half story structure of undressed stone, covered by a gambrel roof, but there is no suggestion of the beautiful curve and overhang of the roof developed by the Dutch. On the other hand, the arched window openings and the quarter-circle attic lunars emphasized by the rough stone trim give a rugged grace to this house which is absent from the others. The house has been greatly changed by the addition of wing, dormers and porches. It stands on the side of a hill near the northwest bank of the North Branch River, on the west side of the road to Peapack. It is a short distance north of Far Hills village.

Quick House
near North Branch, Bridgewater Township
PLATE 135

Lot No. 58 in the Indian deed of 1681 consisted of 912 acres on the east side of the North Branch River by the bend above the village of North Branch. This lot No. 58 was surveyed Aug. 14, 1693 for Ann West; she was the daughter of Gov. Thomas Rudyard, and married John West as the first of her three husbands. Her land fell to the possession of the Duchess of Gordon, whose agent, Gouverneur Morris, sold 640 acres of it April 1, 1801 to John Van Derveer. He divided it with his son-in-law Abraham Quick. That year they both came from Ten Mile Run near

Kingston; John built and settled on the larger north portion of the tract, and Abraham settled on the smaller south portion (230 acres) where he lived until he died.

Abraham's father, Col. Abraham Quick (1732-1805) was a patriot and served in the Revolution; his home was at Ten Mile Run. One of his children by his first wife, Matilda Wyckoff, was Tunis Quick who bought the Ryerson homestead near Three Bridges, not far from Flemington (plate 160). One of Abraham's children by his second wife Charity was Abraham Quick, Sr., b. 1774, d. Dec. 29, 1866, aged 92 years, 9 months and 17 days, married June 15, 1799 Mary Van Derveer, b. Jan. 10, 1780, d. April 11, 1866, aged 86 years, 3 months, and 1 day. Her parents were John Van Derveer, Sr., b. Oct. 3, 1752, d. June 16, 1811, and his wife Jane Van Pelt, d. Feb. 22, 1813, aged 58 years, 10 months and 15 days. All four lie buried in the family cemetery on the river bank west of the Quick house.

About twenty years after the death of Abraham and Mary Quick in their home, their farm is believed to have been sold by their son partly for payment of his debts. It was bought by Abraham Van Nest, b. Oct. 5, 1806 in Bridgewater Township. He settled in North Branch village in 1840 and kept a store there for many years. On Oct. 22, 1841 he married Mary Ann, daughter of James Ten Eyck. He left the farm to his daughter Esther J. Van Nest, wife of Dr. James Van Derveer. His father was John F. Van Derveer, who built the present house on the Van Derveer tract adjoining the Quick farm on the north. Esther's estate sold the farm about 1930 to Kenneth Schley, the present owner. It is now occupied by tenants.

This road was not surveyed by Erskine during the Revolution, so we have no definite knowledge of the age of the house. But the type of house as well as the wording quoted above (that John built while Abraham settled) suggests that Abraham Quick moved into a house already built. It was probably erected about the time of the Revolution or shortly afterward by a tenant of the Duchess of Gordon, or possibly by a purchaser who fell down on his payments. It is a one and a half story white frame house with gable roof. It is built in two units, the west room having the lower ceilings. The house stands on the east side of a lane following the east bank of the North Branch River; it is by the bend in the river, one and a half miles north of the main highway at North Branch.

House of Hendrick and Abraham Staats; Steuben's Headquarters
Main Street, South Bound Brook
PLATE 136

This property was in the continuous ownership and occupancy of the Staats family and descendants from the time of its purchase by one of them in 1738 until 1935. The original parchment deed is still preserved in the house. Dated Sept. 11,

1738, it reads as follows: "Cornelia Van Dam of the City of New York, Widdow relict of Richard Van Dam late of the same city," conveyed to "Peter Staats of Brookland in Kings County on the Island of Nassau in the province of New York, Yeoman, . . . All that Tracts or Parcells of Land Lying Situate and being in the sd County of Somerset and Province of East New Jersey aforsd, which is Divided into two parts in manner above and after specified, One part whereof begins at the North East Corner of Jacob Walton's Land on the South Side of Rarington River aforesd adjoining thereto and Runs thence South Twenty Eight Degrees West one hundred and fifty-six chains to the Bounds of Land late of Robert Lurting aforssd thence along sd Lurtings line North East Eighty Two Chains to the South Corner of a Twenty nine acre Lott now in possession of the sd. Jacob Walton thence North Thirty two Degrees fifteen minutes East Sixty four Chains to Rarington River aforesd Thence along the sd River Thirty One Chains Twenty Links to the place of beginning. And the other part beginning at a certain place on the Line of said land lately belonging to sd. Robert Lurting, being distant from the South West corner of the sd. Lurtings Land Twenty one chains fifty links and runs thence along the sd Lurtings line towards the sd corner Six chains and a half to the North East Corner of a small Tract belonging to the sd. Jacob Walton thence along sd Waltons line South Twenty Eight Degrees West Forty Five Chains and Ten links thence East So. East Three Chains and a half thence North thirty-two Degrees Fifteen Minutes East Forty two chains to the place of beginning. Both which said Tracts together Do contain Three Hundred and five acres as by the annexed Chart or Draft may more fully appear, Together with all and singular the Houses Edifices Buildings Orchards Gardens pastures Swamps Cripples Woods Woodlands Waters Water Courses Mines Minerals . . . all which premises are now in the Actual possession of him the sd Peter Staats by virtue of one Indenture of Bargain and sale to him thereof made for the term of one year bearing date the Day before Date of these presents and Made between the sd Cornelia Van Dam of the one part and the sd Peter Staats of the other part and by Virtue of the Statute made for transfering Uses into possession." Previously in this deed, it was recited that, "WHEREAS Garret Beekman, late of the City of New York Esqr. Decd, by his deed of Sale bearing Date the Eighteenth Day of April One Thousand Seven Hundred and Twenty two . . . Did give grant Bargain Sell and Convey unto his beloved Daughter Cornelia Beekman now Van Dam widdow relict of Richard Van Dam aforesd All that Certaine Tract or parsell of Land known by the Name of Lott No. 1 containing Three Hundred and five acres Situate Lying and Being in the County of Somerset and Province of East New Jersey on the South Side of Rarington River, being part of a Tract of Land purchased by the sd Garret Beekman and Lefferts Peterson in comn. of William Dochrea and divided into Six Lotts and the part thereof allowed to the sd. Garret Beekman was Denoted and Known by the names of Lott No. 1, 2, 3, which sd Lott no. 1 is bounded on the North by Rarington River aforsd on the West by land of Mary Beekman on the East by the sd William Dockera's Land and on the South by (blank). AND WHEREAS in the Year One Thousand Seven Hundred and Thirty One Coll. Robert Lurting Did by Virtue of a prior patent granted to him Run a Line of Division which did Divide the aforesd Lott No. 1 into two Separate and Unequal parts taking in a certain Quantity of Land on the North East End and cutting off the like Quantity in the South West End which said Tracts or parcells of Land are Situate. . . ." On the reverse of the parchment is the receipt for 350 pounds signed by Cornelia Van Dam. Then follows the record, "Be it remembered that the within Cornelia Van Dam appeared before James Alexander one of his majesties councel for the province of New jersey and acknowledged the within" and that he does "allow that it be recorded" on May 1, 1740. Following this acknowledgment is the "MEMORANDUM That I the within named Peter Staats for the Consideration of the Natural love and affection which I have and bear towards my well beloved Son Hendrick Staats of the within County of Somerset and the further Consideration of Five Shillings . . . have . . . granted . . . over unto my Said son Hendrick Staats . . . with this present and the within written Indenture of Release and Conveyance as also all the lands Messuage Hereditaments within mentioned . . . ," dated April 29, 1740, and signed Peter Staats. Below that is the record of the acknowledgment before the above named James Alexander by the said Peter Staats, likewise dated May 1, 1740. Although the above deeds were evidently recorded, they are not now to be found at the Somerset County seat nor at Trenton.

The land along the southwest side of the Raritan River, from Bound Brook beyond New Brunswick to Lawrence Brook, was bought in 1681 from the Indians by John Inians and associates for Lady Elizabeth Carteret. The following year she sold the Province of East Jersey to the Twelve Proprietors. By 1685 William Dockwra, one of the Proprietors, had come into possession of a large portion of this tract near Bound Brook. On Feb. 2, 1702 he sold 1800 acres here to Gerardus Beekman (for some reason he was called Garret in the deed cited above) and Leffert Peterson jointly for £366. This tract was divided between them, Beekman taking the half to the southeast, and conveying one-third of his portion to his daughter Cornelia Van Dam in 1722, as recited above. This was a triangular parcel of land with its short base on the river, extending some distance into the interior, and was by her sold in 1738 to Peter Staats, as above.

The ancestor of the Staats family was Jan Pieters, who emigrated from Huysen before 1640 and settled at Gowanus in Breuckelen, Long Island. His first wife Elsje died, and he married secondly May 16, 1652 Grietje Jans, and thirdly Nov. 15, 1663 the widow of Frederick Jansen. He was still living there in 1698. His son Pieter Jansen[2] Staats, born in this country and a farmer in Gowanus, had a son Pieter Pietersen[3] Staats, bap. July 8, 1663 at Breuckelen. The latter lived at Gowanus and later on Staten Island. His son Peter[4] Staats, bap. Feb. 16, 1690 at Flatbush, d. 1760-61, was a farmer at Gowanus in Breuckelen (or "Brookland"). On Aug. 29, 1712 at Flatbush he married Lammetje, daughter of Hendrick Claesen Veghte, bap. April 23, 1693, and the mother of his children. In his will of 1760 he mentioned his (second) wife Rebecca, his eldest son Peter and another son John. The above deed shows us that he also had a son Hendrick, whom he did not mention in his will, possibly because the conveyance of this land on the Raritan River was his share of his father's property.

Hendrick[5] Staats was probably the second son, born about 1715, and named after his maternal grandfather according to Dutch custom. He evidently built and settled on his father's Raritan River tract immediately after his father purchased it in 1738, for he was termed a resident of Somerset County when the property was turned over to him in 1740. He probably made his home here until 1769 when he conveyed the property to his brother John. We do not know where he then settled nor when he died. He married Macheltie Van Duyn, a daughter of Cornelius Gerretse Van Duyn of Brookland, who mentioned them in his will of 1752. Possibly they were the parents of the following three: (1) Peter Staats, b. about 1741, d. Oct. 16, 1793 in his 53rd year and buried at Bound Brook; in his will he mentioned his wife Synia, and his children: Hendrick, Mary (b. 1767, d. 1827, married Joseph Blackford and Thomas Coon, both of Bound Brook), Nancy, Tyney, and Jane, and named as his executors his sons-in-law Joseph Blackford and Edward Howell and his cousin Abraham Staats. (2) Cornelius Staats was a witness in the deed of 1769, and may have been named for his maternal grandfather. (3) John Staats, who is said to have been a brother of the above Peter of Bound Brook, married April 19, 1776 Hannah Trembly and had the following children, named in the records of the Orphans Court of Somerset Co. in 1827: John, Peter dec'd, Henry dec'd, Hannah (who married Nathan Van Kirk), Tiney (possibly Dinah who married 1817 Tobias Boudinot) dec'd, Nancey and Susan (who both died in 1812 and are buried in Bound Brook).

By deed of April 5, 1769 (recorded 1786), Hendrick Staats of Somerset County, yeoman, and Maghtel his wife, conveyed to John Staats of Sowerland in the county aforesaid, yeoman, for £1,450 current Jersey money at 8 shillings per ounce, "All that certain tract or parcel of land situate, lying and being near Bound Brook in the County of Somerset and Province of New Jersey, Beginning at the northeasterly corner of land belonging to Jacob Buys on the south side of Raritan River," running southwest along his line "to a stake standing in Hendrick Fisher's line," from thence along his line northeast to a large white oak tree standing in the middle of the road and then northeast to the Raritan River and up the river to the place of beginning, containing 272 acres, signed by Hendrick Staats, Maghtel (her mark) Staats, and witnessed by Cornelius Staats and Hendrick Fisher. This included 90 acres of "land at Raritan near Bound Brook" which had been purchased by Hendrick Staats of Raritan on Dec. 1, 1768 from Christian and Abraham Van Dorn and mortgaged that same day to John Staats of Sowerland.

The John Staats, who thus obtained possession of the property, was a younger brother of Hendrick and son of Peter⁴ Staats of Brookland. He left Long Island about 1740 and settled at Sourland in Hillsborough Twp., Somerset Co., on a 300 acre farm on Royces Brook below the Amwell Road two miles east of Flagtown, where he died in the fall of 1781. He married Femmetje Brokaw, bap. Aug. 3, 1707 at Raritan, still living in 1753, daughter of John Brokaw and aunt of the John Brokaw who was killed at the battle of Germantown (see plate 132). He was survived by his second wife Magdalena or Lena, by four sons and two daughters, all mentioned in his will. To his son Abraham he bequeathed a 300 acre farm near Bound Brook where Abraham was then living; this was the farm in which we are interested, which John Staats had purchased from his brother Hendrick in 1769, and which he probably gave to his son Abraham when the latter married in 1770.

Abraham⁶ Staats was born May 23, 1743 in Hillsborough Twp., and died in this house May 4, 1821* lacking 19 days of 78 years; he married Nov. 8, 1770* Margaret Du Bois, b. Jan. 17, 1749* at Neshanic, d. April 22, 1822,* daughter of Abraham Du Bois of Hillsborough Twp. They were buried with their immediate family in the graveyard in the orchard north of the present barns, from which the remains were removed after 1863 to the Bound Brook Cemetery. In his will of 1819, Abraham Staats of Franklin Twp., Somerset Co., provided for his wife Margaret, bequeathed half the farm where he lived to his son Isaac, including all the buildings and orchard, and the other half to his five daughters "provided that those of my daughters who may be single at the time my wife has done with the farm, shall occupy and possess for their use only the one half of my dwelling house and garden"; the executors were the son Isaac and friend Col. John Frelinghuysen (owner of the house at Raritan—plate 133). The inventory of the estate of Abraham Staats, deceased, taken May 10, 1821, named the rooms in his house, mentioned pastel portraits of Abraham and his wife (which still hang in the "dwelling room"), and listed the personal estate as worth $7,560.66. The extant folio manuscript books in

454

---

* Taken from family Bible.

Abraham's excellent penmanship include treatises on geometry, navigation and surveying, from which it is apparent that he practised land surveying and probably taught a class of scholars. In 1788 and 1795 and probably in the years between, he was one of the Commissioners of the Loan Office for the county; he was also a justice of the peace.

When in 1776 Lord Howe offered full pardon to those who would give up their allegiance to the American cause, he excepted therefrom Abraham Staats, his neighbor Hendrick Fisher and one other, as being beyond pardoning. An "Inventorie of goods and Chattels taken and destroyed of Abraham Staats by the British and their adherents on April 13, 1777" included a cow, five calves, ten articles of apparel, a pewter teapot and a coffee pot, to the value of £22.5s.; in connection with his claim for this amount, he made a deposition in 1782 "that on the approach of the Enemy and their Adherents the 13th of April, 1777, he fled, left his house, and on his return home again the said day he found missing the several goods and chattels contained in the above Inventories and that he verilly believes they were taken by the Enemy and their adherents. . . ." Toward the end of the war, the Queen's Rangers, a British troop of cavalry, raided the Raritan valley, and a dealer in New Brunswick was allowed to hide his stock of china beneath the flooring of the barn, together with the family's china and silver. In gratitude therefor the dealer presented Mrs. Staats with two china figures, probably of Chelsea and Bristol ware, and a Lowestoft mug, which are still in the house. In 1782 Abraham was one of the three appraisers appointed to adjust claims for property losses suffered by Americans in the county during the Revolution.

The house is possibly best known as the headquarters of Baron Steuben in the spring of 1779. Steuben arrived in March and occupied the front room and the adjoining back room, and his staff were quartered in a marquee built in the orchard. In his diary he recorded: "During my stay in Philadelphia, I became intimate with M. Girard, the French minister. . . . He honoured me with a visit to camp . . . (and) was received with all the honours of an ambassador. On (May 2, 1779) the day after his arrival, I ordered a maneuvre with eight regiments of infantry and sixteen guns. After the military display, he in company with the Commander-in-Chief and all the other Generals and Colonels, more than sixty persons, partook of a dinner at my headquarters."

Lossing wrote under date of Sept. 14, 1848 in his *Pictorial Field-Book of the Revolution*, p. 333, which also gives a cut of the house: "We rode to the house formerly owned by Abraham Staats, and now in possession of his son. Three sisters survive, one of whom, Mrs. Jane Doty, nearly 80 years of age, who resided there during the Revolution, has a clear recollection of many events connected with Baron

Steuben's occupancy of the house. Although she was then a child eight or ten years old, she remembers the dignity of his appearance, the urbanity of his manners, for which he was noted, and the elegance and richness of the ornaments with which he was adorned. She spoke of a brilliant medal that hung by a ribbon upon his breast. Mrs. Doty recollected two visits made to the baron by Washington and his lady, one to dine and the other to take tea with him. On the latter occasion several ladies were present. She also remembers an entertainment given by the baron to the American officers and their ladies, on which occasion the table was spread in a grove nearby. This occurred a short time before the encampment broke up, which took place early in June, 1779. This view (see cut) is from the field in front of the house, looking north. The dwelling is at the end of a lane several rods from the main road leading to Middlebrook from New Brunswick. . . ."

Abraham and Margaret Staats had eight children, recorded in her family Bible: (1) Jane, b. May 25, 1773,* d. here Nov. 18, 1859, married Dec. 21, 1808 Joseph Doty as his third wife, and had one child; (2) Phebe, b. Sept. 4, 1775,* d. here Dec. 27, 1863 unmarried; (3) Catherine, b. Nov. 2, 1778,* d. Sept. 1, 1779* in her first year; (4) Margaret, b. Dec. 30, 1781,* d. here Nov. 10, 1821* unmarried; (5) Mary Smith, b. July 26, 1784,* d. here Jan. 23, 1863 unmarried; (6) Sarah, b. March 15, 1787,* d. here Feb. 16, 1870, married May 10, 1814* at Bound Brook William Bayles of North Branch; she left her husband with the approval of her father and returned to her family home to live in 1817 with her only child Margaret Ann Bayles, b. June 24, 1815* at North Branch, d. March 23, 1906 in this house, married first on Nov. 10, 1836 Dr. George Bayles of Kingston (d. 1839), and secondly at Preakness Aug. 18, 1845 Cornelius Wyckoff La Tourrette, b. Nov. 29, 1814 near Neshanic, d. Aug. 3, 1902 in this house; Cornelius went to California via the Isthmus in the Gold Rush and later returned and ran a saw mill on the canal; (7) Magdalene, b. Sept. 19, 1789,* d. March 2, 1790* in her second year; (8) Isaac, the youngest child and only son, b. Dec. 5, 1791,* d. about 1869 in another house in South Bound Brook, married first Martha A. Ross, who d. Nov. 6, 1838, aged 44 years, 3 mos., leaving an only child, Margaret⁸ Staats, b. Feb. 17, 1813, married Reuben H. Freeman who removed about 1854 to Independence, Iowa. Isaac Staats married secondly Nov. 26, 1840 Mary A. Matthews, who survived him and had four sons and a daughter, all of Plainfield, N. J.

By deeds of partition dated Nov. 12, 1823, Isaac Staats of Franklin Twp., and Martha, his wife, and his sisters Jane Doty, Phebe Staats, Mary Staats, and Sarah Bayles, the then surviving children of Abraham Staats, divided the estate half and half, whereby Isaac received 132.42 acres, including the tract between the Raritan River and the New Jersey Turnpike on which the homestead was situated, while

456

---

* Taken from family Bible.

his sisters received the remaining 132 acres directly across that road but retained their rights of residence in one half the old homestead. About this time Isaac Staats made the high-ceilinged addition at the east end of the house and occupied that part separately from his married and unmarried sisters in the older parts of the house. The property evidently passed to Isaac's daughter by his first marriage, and on April 26, 1869 her husband, Reuben H. Freeman of Independence, Iowa, conveyed to his wife's cousin Cornelius La Tourrette of Franklin Twp., the 13 acres of the farm between the turnpike and the canal, "subject to the life right of Sarah (Staats) Bayles to the use of one half the Old House and the whole of the garden." Sarah bequeathed her right to her daughter, Mrs. Cornelius La Tourrette, and the homestead was owned and occupied until 1935 by her son, Eugene Du Bois La Tourette.

A study of the plan (plate 6) will disclose that the house was built at several different times. The deed of 1738 mentions a house, but it is in a legal list giving all forms of possible improvements from swamps to minerals; the owners previous to 1738 resided in New York and it is probable that the oldest unit of the house was not erected until Hendrick Staats settled here between 1738 and 1740. This unit is a deep, narrow house, consisting of two rooms, with corner fireplaces which are fed by one large chimney in the center of the east side, and a hallway running down the west side. According to a family manuscript, the original kitchen was at the east end of the house and was a separate building with the slave quarters over it. This may have been torn down when the kitchen wing on the west was added about 1800; otherwise it was destroyed when the house was enlarged about 1825. Lossing stated that "only the center building was in existence at the time (of the Revolution) and that seems to have been enlarged. Each wing has since been added. . . . The interior of the old part was . . ., like most of the better dwellings of that time, neatly wainscoted with pine wrought into moldings and panels." It was not until about 1800 that Abraham Staats enlarged the house by building two rooms on the other side of the hall and adding a service wing. This wing was formerly clapboarded but is now shingled. In the inventory of his estate, taken in 1821, the rooms of the house are listed: Dwelling Room, Bed Room adjoining, Parlour, Entry, Room back of the Parlour, Bed Room back of the Entry, Upstairs Garret, Cellar, Milk Cellar, Pantry, Linter Room, Kitchen and Kitchen Garret. The son Isaac Staats built the large, high-ceilinged and finely panelled addition on the canal side about 1825. The accompanying photograph (plate 136) shows the central unit of the house, the section on the right built in 1738-40 and that on the left about 1800. There is little difference to be seen from the outside, other than the thickness of the window moldings. It is a typical one and a half story shingled house covered by a steep, gable roof. Old twelve pane window sashes, Dutch double door with oval bull's eyes, low ceilings,

exposed beams, early panelled chimney wall with no mantel shelf in one room, butterfly hinges, are a few interesting items. Judging by the shingles beneath the cellar
hatch, it is probable that the house was originally covered by long shingles with
rounded ends. The interior is unchanged and contains many old family heirlooms.
Two very small dormers were added at one period, and more recently these with a
third one were enlarged and roofed in a slope to the ridgepole of the house. The
present roof extends slightly beyond the walls. A small porch added about 1,870
has been replaced recently by a small pergola. A photograph of the entire house
from the end is reproduced in the vignette. Various views of the exterior and also
of the interior can be seen in *Northwestern New Jersey*, v. 1, p. 64 and 104, in the
Somerset Co. Hist. Quarterly, v. 2, p. 81, and in Lossing's *Pictorial Field Book
of the Revolution*, v. 1, p. 333. The house stands in a field between the road and
the canal in South Bound Brook, one mile below the bridge over the Raritan River.

House of Jacob Ten Eyck
North Branch

The grandfather of the builder was Coenradt Ten Eyck, who emigrated about
1650 and settled at Coenties Slip in New York City. His son Matthias² Ten Eyck
(1658-1741) lived at Old Hurley in Ulster County, where he was a farmer and river
trader. On Nov. 12, 1700 and June 22, 1702 Matthias purchased of the original
grantee, John Johnston, lots Nos. 53 and 61 of 400 and 100 acres on the west side
of the North Branch River in and just north of the present village of North Branch.
He himself never left Hurley; on Oct. 20, 1721 he conveyed this 500 acre tract to his
son Jacob, who built and settled here between 1725 and 1733.

Jacob³ Ten Eyck, b. 1693 at Hurley, d. Oct. 26, 1753 at North Branch, married Jemima Van Nest, d. 1792, aged 92 years, daughter of Jerome Van Nest of
Raritan, and had seven children. The eldest of their four sons, Capt. Jacob⁴ Ten
Eyck was born Aug. 25, 1733 in his father's stone house at North Branch and died
in 1794. He inherited his father's one and a half story stone house and, after the
death of his aged mother, added a second story in 1792. His brothers were: Peter
who settled north of him, Conrad who settled on the Riddle tract on the east side
of the river, opposite the old homestead, and Matthew who settled on Lot No. 48
on the east side of the river, just north of the Lane—Brokaw house (plate 132).
Capt. Jacob Ten Eyck died less than two years after he enlarged his father's house.
By his wife, Margaret Hagaman, he had two sons, Jacob and James, and four
daughters. The brothers bought out their sisters' interest and divided the property
between them in 1800. The old house fell to the share of James⁵ Ten Eyck, b. here
May 2, 1773, d. July 4, 1854, married Esther Hanker. Their son Tunis⁶ Ten Eyck,

b. June 9, 1816, d. Nov. 12, 1895, bought out his brothers' interests but, as he never married, he left the homestead to his niece, Esther Van Nest, daughter of Mary Ann Ten Eyck and Abraham Van Nest (who had purchased the Quick house nearby— plate 135), and wife of Dr. James D. Van Derveer. She willed it to her son, Frank M. Van Derveer, who is the present owner. He now leases it.

The house is a good-sized two story structure of fieldstone, with brick arch heads over the old windows and low ceilings. There is some fine woodwork in the interior; the narrow mantel shelves in the main rooms are only two or three inches wide with semi-circular projections at each end for the support of candlesticks. The house stands on the west bank of the North Branch River, a short distance above the main highway of North Branch village.

House of Jacob Van Derveer; Knox Headquarters
Road to Pluckemin, Bedminster Township

The tract lying north of the North Branch of Raritan River and south of the road from Lamington to Bedminster (until lately called Lesser Crossroads) was at an early unknown date bought by Major Daniel Axtell. Jacob Van Derveer bought part of the Axtell tract by 1756 (probably some years before this date) and built his home here. In 1758 he donated some of his land to the Bedminster Church for a building and cemetery, and his wife, who died in 1759, was the first to be buried here.

Jacob's grandfather, Cornelis Janse¹ Vande Veer, emigrated in 1659 from Alkmaar in North Holland, and settled at Flatbush on Long Island where he became a patentee and magistrate. He married Tryntje Gillis de Mandeville, and had among others a son Jacobes² Van de Veer, bap. Oct. 29, 1686, d. 1726. This Jacobes was a farmer at Reems Hook, Salem County, New Jersey; he was survived by his wife Catharine, his son Jacob, whom he made his executor, and two minor sons, William and Hendrick. Jacob³ Van Derveer, b. March 6, 1704, d. Nov. 17, 1776 aged 72 yrs., 8 mos., 11 days, married Phebe Ditmars, b. about 1706, d. Sept. 11, 1759 in her 53rd year. Both lie buried near their home in the Old Bedminster Cemetery with most of their immediate family. Their home was on the north side of the North Branch River on the west side of the highway between Pluckemin and Lesser Crossroads (Bedminster). Jacob, in his will of 1772, distributed a very large amount of property, including some in Virginia and Maryland, between his various children and grandchildren.

Jacob and Phebe (Ditmars) Van Derveer had five sons and one daughter: (1) Joseph, bap. March 17, 1734 at Readington, d. Jan. 15, 1769 aged 35 years, married Catrina ——, and had two children, Jacob, who died in 1785 aged 22 years, and

Femmetje; this Joseph lived at Sowerland. (2) Femmetje or Phebe, bap. Feb. 28, 1736/7 at Readington, d. June 6, 1872 aged 45 years, married Jacob Van Dorin, d. Sept. 12, 1811 aged 86 yrs., 9 mos., 2 days, and had one son Jacob and three daughters. (3) John or Johannes, bap. 1739 at Raritan, d. 1771 without issue. (4) Lawrence, bap. 1741 at Raritan, d. Dec. 8, 1815 in his 75th year, married Maria ——, d. March 27, 1777 aged 28 years; Lawrence inherited chiefly the 430 acre plantation on which he was living when his father died. (5) Jacobus inherited among other property 560 acres over the river; he is probably the James Van Derveer, d. Feb. 3, 1810 aged 66 yrs., 4 mos., 22 days (i.e., b. Sept. 12, 1743), married first Winche ——, d. March 26, 1777 aged 22 years, and married secondly Maria, daughter of Rev. James Hardenbergh, d. March 12, 1789 aged 32 years; this James had three children who died in childhood, possibly others. (6) Elias, of whom below.

The youngest child of Jacob was Elias⁴ Van Derveer, bap. Nov. 30, 1746 at Raritan, d. Nov. 29, 1778 in his 33rd year. Jacob bequeathed the 435 acre plantation he lived on, bounded north by Peter Perne and south by Jacob Offs, to this son Elias, also two adjoining tracts purchased of Edward and Robert Lucas, where the testator had lived at some time, and several other parcels of land. Elias Van Derveer was a warm patriot and his home, formerly his father's, was placed at the disposal of Gen. Knox and his artillery forces. Gen. Knox had his headquarters here in 1779 (not at the Mehelin house at the main crossroads in Pluckemin, in front of which is an incorrect marker). Elias served in the Revolution; his tombstone states that he died in his 33rd year "in consequence of his cruel incarceration while prisoner to the British army. . . ." In Elias' will of 1778, he left to his wife Catharine £1,000 and all the goods she brought with her at her marriage, mentioned his sister and two surviving brothers, his three brothers-in-law Frederick Frelinghuysen, John Schenck and Abraham Schenck, and his children. Elias and Catharine had three children: Jacob, d. March 6, 1776 aged 9 months, Hendrick or Henry, and Phebe, d. unmarried Sept. 27, 1849. The homestead was inherited by Dr. Henry⁵ Van Derveer, b. 1776, d. May 2, 1868 and buried with all his family at Bedminster. He lived, however, in a large two story frame house nearby on the opposite, or south, side of the river, which he had erected about 1820. As Dr. Van Derveer was a bachelor, his whole farm at his death was subdivided and sold at auction. Henry Ludlow purchased the old Jacob Van Derveer house, and John F. Van Derveer bought the Henry Van Derveer house. Both buildings still stand.

The old house is a one and a half story building covered with wide clapboarding, and having lie-on-your-stomach windows under the roofline. It stands in the fields with its gable end toward the road. A photograph of it may be seen in *Northwestern New Jersey*, v. 1, p. 272. The house has since been stuccoed and remodelled; it is now owned by the Schley heirs. This house stands on the west side of the road from Pluckemin to Bedminster a short distance north of the North Branch River, and the later house is on the east side of this road south of the river.

House of John Van Doren
Millstone
PLATE 137

About 1690 Capt. Clement Plumstead obtained a grant for land on the west side of the Millstone River from Peace Brook south to Blackwell's Mills. On Feb. 28, 1742 he deeded this 2,000 acre tract to William Plumstead, who on May 1, 1752 sold 246 acres of the tract along the river on the south side of the Amwell Road in Millstone to Christian Van Doren for £740. On Dec. 12, 1755 the latter conveyed it to his son John. Christian Van Doren, b. Aug. 11, 1699 near Hillsdale in Monmouth Co., d. July 20, 1781 at Middlebush in Somerset Co., married Dec. 11, 1723 Altje Schenck and had seventeen children. Christian left Monmouth County with his brother Abram about the time of his marriage and settled on a tract of 566 acres on the Amwell Road at Middlebush (east of the Millstone River). Among his children was John Van Doren, b. April 23, 1726 at Middlebush, d. 1815 aged 89 years.

The early county seat of Somerset County was at the village now called Millstone and in Revolutionary days known as Somerset Courthouse. It was here on the Millstone River that John Van Doren built and settled on the tract that his father conveyed to him in 1755. Gen. Washington spent the night here in Van Doren's house after winning the battle of Princeton in January 1777, as well as on other occasions. Although he was the victor, Washington had 8,000 British troops thundering after his small army, so he decoyed Cornwallis into thinking his destination was New Brunswick, but wheeled about and followed the Millstone River, halting at Van Doren's overnight, and marched for Pluckemin early the next morning. The British imprisoned Van Doren's wife and hung her up by the heels in a vain attempt to get some information from her. The Hessians established a hospital for their sick and wounded on the farm here, after clearing off a large piece of woodland.

John Van Doren married Marretje Lott, b. about 1728, d. April 27, 1805 aged 77 years, and had six sons and one daughter. The homestead farm was bequeathed to the son Jacob, except for one lot with a house on it which was occupied by and left to William. Jacob I. Van Doren, b. Dec. 6, 1761 on the homestead, d. July 27, 1828 aged 66 years, married Mrs. Hoagland, née Mattie Ditmars, b. Nov. 10, 1767, d. April 8, 1852. The homestead was inherited by their only son, John Van Doren, b. here Feb. 3, 1804, d. Sept. 15, 1892, married Jan. 7, 1829 Charity, daughter of

Rynear Staats, b. Sept. 24, 1807, d. Nov. 11, 1872. Their three children were Rynier, Jacob who lived on the ancestral farm (he had no issue), and Catharine who married George W. Metlar and lived in the Low house at Raritan Landing (plate 116). The Metlars purchased the old farm from the other heirs, and their son John Van Doren Metlar sold it about 1925 to Charles D. Smith, the present owner.

The house is a two story shingled structure with a gable roof. The ceilings are of medium height and the beams are still exposed in the dining room, formerly the kitchen. Washington is supposed to have slept in the room in the southwest corner of the ground floor; the fireback plaque in this room has the image and name of Gen. G. Washington embossed upon it. An old hatchet mark on a door jamb dates from the Revolutionary forays. The house is in very good condition. Other views may be seen in *Northwestern New Jersey*, v. 1, p. 16, and in *The Van Doorn Family*, p. 356. The house stands on a knoll on the west side of the road running along the west bank of the Millstone River, a short distance south of the Dutch church in the village of Millstone.

House of Philip Van Horn; Sterling's Headquarters
Middlebrook, Bridgewater Township
PLATE 138

This house has historical rather than family interest; it was well known during the lifetime of the builder, but did not become a family homestead. The second Indian deed of 1681 covered a large tract on the north side of the Raritan River west of Middlebrook; Lot No. 3 was surveyed Sept. 25, 1683 for several associates, the easterly part being assigned to Richard Hall. This soon passed to Archibald, son of Lord Neill Campbell, whose place, known as "Kel's Hall," stood on the neck; he died in 1702. The property evidently came into the possession of John Chambers of New York City, who sold it to Cornelius Van Horn on Aug. 28, 1724.

Cornelius Van Horn probably settled here immediately, as in 1724 his place was described as 22 miles northwest of Perth Amboy and in 1749 as 10 miles above New Brunswick on the Raritan River. Cornelius' Van Horn had been a resident of New York City; after removing to New Jersey, he became a member of the Council of this province. He was descended from Jan Cornelis' Van Horn, who emigrated to New Amsterdam by 1645 and was a teacher of the public school there. In Cornelius' will, dated 1768 and probated 1770, he left the farm where he then dwelt in Somerset County, one half (551 acres) to his son Philip and half to his son John, after the death of his wife (Elizabeth French).

The son Philip⁵ Van Horn, bap. April 29, 1719 in New York City, was a merchant living in the town of his birth until about 1754; we first find him at Bound

Brook when he and others offered lands for sale in Morris Co. in 1754. He may have built his home in Somerset County at this time, or possibly not until after his father's death. It was known as "Phil's Hill," or, colloquially, as "Convivial Hall," due to the many festive occasions here. In November 1755 Col. Philip Van Horn was ordered to march with his regiment out of Somerset to repel the French and Indians at Easton, Pa. In 1759 he was for the first time elected Judge of Common Pleas for Somerset County.

Philip Van Horn's patriotism during the Revolution is rather doubtful; like many a rich man with New York affiliations, he was diplomatically cordial to both sides. On April 13, 1777 Cornwallis breakfasted with him. He was under suspicion and put on parole by the Americans but permitted to remain at home. Washington wrote to Sterling: "I am sorry you did not keep old Van Horn under restraint." In the winter of 1778-79 Lord Sterling established his headquarters here, while Greene was at the Van Vechten house nearby and Washington was at the Wallace house in Somerville. In October 1779 Col. Simcoe raided the place to capture the rebel Governor Livingston, who fortunately was not here. Capt. Graydon of the Pennsylvania Line wrote that Van Horn's hospitality ought certainly to have been recompensed by an unlimited credit on the public stores; his house, used as a hotel, seemed constantly full; it was occupied at one time by Col. Bland of the Virginia Cavalry and Capt. Lee, later Gen. Harry Lee; notwithstanding the number of guests that were to be provided for, there appeared no deficiency in accommodation, and we, wrote the Captain, were supped and lodged well. Philip Van Horn married Elizabeth, daughter of William Ricketts, and their many daughters were noted for their beauty. Here on Oct. 12, 1778 their eldest daughter, Mary Ricketts Van Horn, married Stephen Moylan, an Irishman living in Philadelphia, Colonel and later Brigadier General of the American Light Dragoons. Another daughter married Thomas Lansdale; he and Moylan were both original members of the Society of the Cincinnati.

The Marquis de Chastellux wrote of his stopping here with Col. Moylan in December, 1780: "This manor is in a beautiful situation; it is surrounded by some trees, the approach is decorated with a grass plot, and, if it were better taken care of, one would think oneself in the neighborhood of London, rather than in that of New York. Mr. Van Horn came to meet me: He is a tall lusty man near sixty years of age, but vigorous, hearty and good humoured; he is called Colonel from the station he held in the militia under the English government. He resigned some time before the war; he was then a merchant and cultivator, passing the winter at New York and the summer in the country; but since the war he has quitted the town and retired to his manor, always faithful to his country without rendering himself odious

463

to the English, with whom he has left two of his sons in the Jamaica trade, but who, if the war continues, are to sell their property and come and live with their father. Nothing can prove more strongly the integrity of his conduct than the esteem in which he is held by both parties. He has frequently found himself in the midst of the theatre of war, so that he has sometimes had the Americans with him, sometimes the English. It even happened to him once in the same day to give a breakfast to Lord Cornwallis and a dinner to General Lincoln. . . . (I was introduced to his wife and three daughters, including Mrs. Moylan, and to some guests of the neighborhood.) . . . Mrs. Van Horn is an old lady, who from her countenance, her dress, and her deportment, perfectly resembled a picture of Van Dyke. She does the honors of the table with exactness, helps everybody without saying a word, and the rest of the time is like a family portrait. . . ."

It was probably a few years after this that Philip Van Horn died. In February 1786 Benjamin Morgan made a map of "a certain tract of land commonly called Phil's Hill," dividing the tract into fourteen parcels and the homestead lot of 84 acres. On Nov. 1, 1794 John Campbell bought from James Ricketts and his wife Sarah lots Nos. 13 and 14 and the homestead lot, which is described as late the property of Philip Van Horne. In 1810 John Campbell deeded it in trust to his sister Margaret Campbell. She and the trustees sold it in 1831 to John Herbert, who resided here for so many years, that the place is often called the Herbert home.

The house has no resemblance to the typical farmhouse of the Dutch; it is the mansion of a wealthy and hospitable New York merchant. It is an unusually large two story frame house, with a smaller two story kitchen and slave wing on the east end. On either side of a hall, which is 12 feet wide, are very large rooms with high ceilings. The modern shutters and roof detract from its Revolutionary appearance. The house is now an empty shell, with only the wide floor beams, hand wrought nails and a few old doors to denote its age. It is now owned by the Calco Chemical Company, whose factory is opposite. The house stands on a hill on the north side of the Revolutionary road from Bound Brook to Raritan (now Somerville); it is west of the stream called Middlebrook.

House of Derrick Van Vechten; Greene's Headquarters
Finderne
PLATE 139

This house stands on the same tract, Lot No. 3, as the Van Horn house a few miles distant. Lot No. 3 in the second Indian deed of 1681 was surveyed Sept. 25, 1683 for John Palmer and his associates. One of these was Michael Van Vechten, and to him was assigned the western portion, to which he later added considerably both on the north and south sides of the Raritan River. His grandfather Teunis Dircksen[1] Van Vechten emigrated from Vechten in Holland in the *Arms of Norway* with his wife, child, and two negroes, and settled at Greenbush opposite Albany in 1638.

Teunis' grandson Michael[3] Van Vechten, b. Nov. 28, 1663 at Greenbush, is said to have settled on his purchase along the Raritan River as early as 1685. He built a one and a half story stone house here on the north bank, east of Raritan. He gave the land for the first Church of Raritan, which was erected in the fields east of his house, and burned by Col. Simcoe in a raid during the Revolution. On Nov. 21, 1686 Michael married Marytje Parker, d. July 1690, and on April 2, 1691 he married secondly Jannetje De Mont. Among his four children by his first wife was Mary, who married Judge Jeremiah Field, landowner along the Raritan in Piscataway Township (see supra). Of his three children by his second wife, Derrick received from his father 1,000 acres on the north side of the river, and Jane, wife of Jacobus Hageman, the property on the south side of the river. A bridge was erected here at an early date and was called Van Vechten Bridge by 1750.

The son Derrick[4] Van Vechten, b. July 15, 1699 in the Raritan neighborhood, bap. at Raritan Church, d. Nov. 29, 1781, aged 82 years, 4 months and 14 days, and lies buried in the field east of the bridge, where formerly stood the old church. Derrick was married three times: first to Judith, daughter of Anthony Brockholst, secondly on Nov. 2, 1719 to Deborah Antonides, and thirdly, about 1759 to Sarah Middagh, d. Nov. 17, 1785, sister of Cornelius Middagh, owner of the tract, later Frelinghuysen's (plate 133). His third wife was the mother of his four children: Dirck who died in infancy, Margaret who married Joseph Crane, Michael, and Elizabeth who married George Davis.

Derrick Van Vechten was in his 80th year when he acted as host for General and Mrs. Greene in the winter of 1778-79. An entire division of the American army was quartered at this time on his farm; his valuable timber was destroyed for fuel and log huts for the soldiers, but he was so great a patriot that he never asked for nor accepted compensation. Mrs. Greene was a charming young lady of 25, "the favorite lady of the army," when her husband was stationed here. She was fond of social functions and gave many "kettle drums" and minuets. The most notable entertainment here was on Christmas Eve in 1778, of which General Greene afterward wrote that "The Commander in Chief evinces his esteem for Mrs. Greene by dancing with her three hours without sitting down!" When they left, Gen. and Mrs. Greene presented Mrs. Van Vechten with a beautiful carved mahogany table "in grateful remembrance of a bounteous hospitality." It was in the large brick house now standing that all these events took place.

The homestead was inherited shortly after the war by the son Michael[5] Van Vechten, b. Nov. 13, 1764, d. Dec. 29, 1831, married April 10, 1787 Elizabeth La Grange, b. March 1, 1766, d. May 1, 1856. The house passed to their only son and youngest child, Richard[6] Van Vechten, b. Dec. 19, 1808, married Mary Lord and secondly Miriam Betts, an English girl. He was the last of the family to occupy the homestead. It had come into the possession of C. T. Ames by 1873. It was purchased about 1890 by Bernard Meyer, Sr., whose son Bernard Meyer, Jr., now occupies it.

The house is a long two story brick structure covered by a gable roof. According to tradition it was built in 1715 by Derrick Van Vechten, but as he was only 16 years of age then, it was probably erected some years later. Derrick's granddaughter, Mrs. Jane Taylor, wrote in 1887, that the old and stone part of the original building built by Michael Van Vechten in the seventeenth century was still in use in the kitchen part of the present house, and that the brick building adjoining was built by Derrick Van Vechten. The house stands a few fields west of the Manville Road on the north bank of the Raritan River, hidden in a clump of trees. Another view of it can be seen in the *Van Vechten Genealogy*, p. 101.

House of Symen Van Wickle, later Suydam's
Easton Turnpike, Franklin Township
PLATE 140

John Inians and associates bought from the Indians in 1681 for Lady Elizabeth Carteret, widow of the Proprietor, a tract along the south side of the Raritan River from Bound Brook to Lawrence Brook, and laid out the Raritan lots, consisting of ten 500 acre lots, each with a half mile of river frontage. These lots were at first in the hands of Scotch and English speculators. On May 29, 1703 Evert Van Wickle, Gerardus Beekman and Leffert Pieterse, all of Kings County, Long Island, purchased from Thomas Cardale of Jamaica for £200 a tract of 450 acres on the south side of the Raritan River, beginning at Richard Jones' Raritan Lot No. 7, about 3½ miles from Albany Street in New Brunswick (recorded at Trenton). It is probable that Evert bought out the interest of his two partners; he is also believed to have purchased 800 more acres in the vicinity from William Dockwra. In 1713 a road was laid out along this bank of the river, from Hendrick Beekman's to the Millstone River road, showing that settlement had commenced in this region, but we have no evidence that Evert himself ever removed here.

Evert Janse[1] Van Wickelen or Van Wickle emigrated about 1664, probably from Wykel in Friesland. He was a carpenter by trade and was living at New Amersfoort (*i.e.*, Flatlands) on Long Island at the time of his marriage in the Flatbush Church Feb. 27, 1690 to Mettye Symonsen, also of New Amersfoort. They settled in the New Lots of Flatbush, also called Oostwoudt, where he had bought land as early as 1686. It is probable that Gerrit Van Wickelen of New Lots (who had a son Evert bap. 1699) was his brother. Evert and Mettye Van Wickelen had six children: Zytie, born and living at Oostwoudt, married at the house of Evert, her father, in 1711 Hans Jorise Bergen (1684-1726) of Breuckelen and later of Hempstead; Peterneltje, born and married at New Lots, married in 1715 Rem Josephse Hegeman (1685-1767) of Flatbush and Breuckelen; Geertje, born and living at New Lots, married in 1719 Hendrick Jacobs Suydam (1696-1771) of Flatbush; Jan Van Wickle of New Lots married in 1723 Ida Remsen and had two daughters mentioned in his will of 1732; Coevert had a wife Mettje; and Symen in whom we are interested.

Symen[2] Van Wickelen or Van Wickle was named for his maternal grandfather. He married about 1722 Gerrardine Kouwenhoven, bap. Aug. 7, 1705 at Breuckelen, daughter of Nicasius Janse Kouwenhoven. She was generally called Dinah for short. Our earliest record of Symen and Dinah in New Jersey is Nov. 25, 1722, when they acted as sponsors at a baptism in the Dutch church of New Brunswick. It is probable that they settled at this time on his father's tract along the Raritan and built the present house. According to family tradition, which omits Symen and his generation, the house was built by the younger Evert's (1726-1757) father Evert. However, the younger Evert's father was Symen and, with this correction, it is probably true that Evert's father built the house rather than his grandfather Evert, who was living in New Lots as late as 1719 when his daughter was married, and of whom there is no record in New Jersey. Symen Van Wickle was recorded here in the Franklin Township list of 1735. The will of Symen Van Wickle of Somerset Co., yeoman, dated 1753, probated Jan. 3, 1755, mentioned his wife Dinah, his sons Evert (bap. 1726) and Nicholas, his daughters Anne, Mary, Dinah, Elsee, Mettje and Seytje, mentioned his home farm on the Raritan River, and also a 31 acre lot over the River on the north side of Raritan Road bought of his son-in-law Joseph Mount, and listed negroes and plate among his personal estate. These daughters with their husbands are mentioned in the will of their brother Evert, probated three years later: Mettje wife of George Anderson, Jr., Settje, wife of John Boyce, Dinah, wife of John Probasco, Antje wife of Jacob Suydam, and Elsje deceased, late wife of Joseph Mount (Mary may have died unmarried as she is not mentioned).

It is not definitely known who owned the house immediately after the death of Symen Van Wickle. Family tradition states that the uncles of Ann, infant daughter of Evert Van Wickle deceased, lived here. Symen Van Wickle's only other son was Nicholas Van Wickle. By license of Dec. 9, 1752 he married Catrina (Trintie) Buys (Boice) of Middlesex and had at least three children, Gerrardina, Seytie and Evert, bap. 1754, 1757, and 1761 respectively. This Nicholas Van Wickle is believed to have lived near Raritan Landing. The house is not shown on Erskine's Revolutionary map, possibly because this and the adjoining Van Wickle place may have been considered one property. The next knowledge we have is its sale May 18, 1795 by Peter Antonides and wife (unnamed) to Robert T. Kemble, the deed stating it to be the plantation where the said Peter then resided, beginning at the Raritan River at the lower corner of the land of Rev. Abraham Beach; this was a 95 acre tract, and the sale also included a 22½ acre plot on the south side of the road to Middlebush, in the rear of but not adjoining the first plot. The lot between these was bought Feb. 11, 1800 by John Van Deveer from John D. Van Duyn and wife (unnamed) of Somerset; he had received it from his father Dennis Van Duyn, who in his will of 1792 devised to his son John the remainder of the farm unsold whereon he (the testator) then lived, beginning at the line of Abraham Beach and south of the road to Middlebush. From the wording of the will, it is possible that Dennis Van Duyn had sold parts of his farm to Peter Antonides. He may have received it from his father. The will of Willem Van Duyn of Somerset County, probated 1773, left the plantation on the Raritan River, which he bought of Matthias Smock and which of late belonged to Nicholas Van Wickle, to his son Roelef, and left the farm where he lived on the river to his son Denys. John Van Duyn was baptized in 1761 at New Brunswick, son of "De Nis" and Lena Van Duyn; Denys had been baptized in 1724, son of Willem Van Duyn and Sybrech Verkerk.

There is no gap in the history of the farm in the nineteenth century. The lot near the river and the rear lot were purchased May 11, 1797 from Robert Kemble of New York City by Hendrick Suydam of Somerset Co. On June 30, 1802 he also bought the lot in between from John Van Deveer, the transfer stating that it was part of the plantation formerly occupied by William Van Duyn. There were various Suydams in the vicinity of New Brunswick at an early date, and it is probable that this Hendrick was not a direct descendant of Hendrick Suydam, son-in-law of the first Evert Van Wickle. Hendrick Suydam married Aule or Alletta Rappleyea; he died intestate between 1833 and 1838, leaving three adult children: Arriet, wife of Michael Garrish of Middlesex Co.; Ann, bap. 1788, wife of Stephen Mundy of Allegheny Co.; and Ida, bap. 1796, wife of Nicholas Van Wickle of Monmouth Co. This Nicholas was probably a grandson of Symen's son Nicholas. On June 1, 1838 the first two daughters conveyed to Nicholas Van Wickle their two thirds undivided share of the 166 acre farm of their father. Nicholas Van Wickle undoubtedly removed to his father-in-law's farm. He and his second wife Jane Ann, residents of

Franklin Township, sold this farm on Aug. 25, 1862 out of the family, and releases were obtained from the five children of Ida (Suydam) Van Wickle. The property changed hands many times until it was purchased in 1873 by Asher Atkinson. He leased the farm to the Smalley family, who later purchased it from him, and lived on the farm until recent years. It was purchased in 1932 by Mrs. Malcolm Montgomery Donaldson and her two daughters, the present owners.

This is a good example of the one and a half story frame farmhouse of the Dutch. Immense hand-hewn beams, seen in the interior (plate 2), were used for the framework of the walls; the interstices were filled with mud, clay and straw, interlined with brick, and held together by hand-hewn laths. The old, long shingles with rounded ends still cover the side facing the canal, and the balance is clapboarded. The gable roof overhangs one wall, descending in a straight slope with no suggestion of a curve. The cellar beneath is paved with stone flagging and a big batten door separates the compartments where the slaves were quartered. The dining and kitchen wing is later than the main house, although also of an early period; it has very small windows, exposed beams, and low ceilings. In the main house, the wide floor boards, exposed beams, old twelve pane window sashes, simple fanlight, panelling of the fireplace wall, and small enclosed stairway with board rail, are items to be noticed. The Revolutionary road ran along the river bank in the bed of the present canal and in those days the front of the house was the side with the overhanging roof which faced the river. This is now the rear of the building. The house has been restored very successfully by George Howell, architect, and the Highland Park Building Company. The changes in the interior are discussed in the Introduction.

The house stands near the canal on the northeast side of Easton Turnpike, about 3½ miles out of New Brunswick toward Bound Brook. Adjoining it on the north is the Van Wickle—Beach—Lawrence property (plate 141). Between them runs the lane to the old Four Mile Bridge over the Canal; in earlier days there was an important ford here over the river, which connected Middlebush and Piscataway.

House of Evert Van Wickle, later Rev. Abraham Beach's

Easton Turnpike, Franklin Township

PLATE 141

This house is still owned and occupied by descendants of the builder and the land has never been out of the family since it was purchased in 1703. The land along the river was bought from the Indians for the Proprietor of East Jersey in 1681; it was divided and sold to English and Scotch speculators. On May 29, 1703 Evert Van Wickle, Gerardus Beekman and Leffert Pieterse, all of Kings Co., Long Island, purchased from Thomas Cardale of Jamaica for £200 a 450 acre tract on the south side of the Raritan River, 3½ miles from New Brunswick (recorded at Trenton).

One of the purchasers, Evert Janse' Van Wickelen or Van Wickle, emigrated to this country about 1664 and settled in the New Lots of Flatbush on Long Island. His son Symen' Van Wickelen or Van Wickle settled on his father's property along the Raritan River about 1722, building a house still standing (plate 140); a more detailed account of the early period is given in connection with his home.

Symen and Dinah's elder son was Evert' Van Wicklen (as he spelled his name in his will), bap. Jan. 1, 1726 at the Raritan Church. By license of Dec. 9, 1752 he married Cornelia Lupardus of Middlesex County, and they had a daughter Antje or Ann, bap. Sept. 27, 1754 at the Dutch church in New Brunswick. According to family tradition this house was built by or for Evert Van Wickle at the time of his marriage (1752); it stands on the northern part of his grandfather Evert's tract, near the house of his father Symen. Evert and Cornelia had been married only four years when they died. They lie buried in a grove of trees on the property, the grave-stone reading: "On the 3rd Day of March, 1757 Evert Van Wickle and Cornelia his wife accompanied each other to the Land of Spirits. One Grave contains their ashes and this Stone is erected over it by their only Child, then an infant, but now the Wife of Abraham Beach, D.D." The will of Evert Van Wicklen of Somerset Co., probated March 17, 1757, mentioned his wife Cornelia and his daughter Antje, his brother Nicholas Van Wicklen and brother-in-law Ram Lupardus, and his five sisters with their husbands; a codicil dated the day of his death mentioned his wife's father Christianus Lupardus and his wife's sister Anatje wife of Cornelius Duryea. The will of the father-in-law, Christianus Lupardus of Piscataway, Middlesex Co., dated 1767 and probated 1768, mentioned that his wife was deceased, named his three sons and three (surviving) daughters and his granddaughter Ann Van Wickle. This Christianus had lived in early life at Flatbush, Long Island, and was the son of Dominie Gulielmus Lupardus, minister of the Dutch Reformed Churches of Kings County.

The infant Ann' Van Wickle, who inherited the property, was made a ward in chancery by her uncles, who according to family tradition tried to obtain her large estate for themselves. In or about 1772 she married Rev. Abraham Beach, D.D., and had two sons, who died without issue, and four daughters. Abraham Beach, b. Sept. 9, 1740 at Cheshire, Conn., was a son of Capt. Elnathan Beach and his second wife. After graduating from Yale College, he studied for the ministry. Since there was no Episcopal superintendence in this country at that period, he went abroad in 1767 for his ordination. The Society for the Propagation of the Gospel in Foreign Parts sustained most of the Episcopal Churches in Colonial

America with stipends and libraries. Abraham Beach was appointed by this Society to be "missionary" to New Brunswick; he returned to this country and entered on his duties at Christ Church in this "mission" September, 1767. He was a strong believer in the Episcopal faith but was wholly exempt from any persecuting spirit toward those who differed from him and his candor and kindness converted many of his opponents to his beliefs.

Abraham Beach, although attached to his country, did not believe the time was ripe for independence which he thought would come at the proper period without civil war. He did not consider himself absolved of his allegiance by the Declaration of Independence nor free to omit parts of the Liturgy (which directed prayers for King and Government) without the approbation of the Society, and he closed his church for some months rather than violate the vows taken at his ordination. It required great prudence to perform his duties as clergyman of the hated Church of England and yet maintain that neutrality which he deemed imposed by his calling. He was successful in enjoying the respect of both patriots and loyalists, to such an extent that a patriot vestry shortly after the war elected him First Associate of Rev. Samuel Provoost at Trinity Church in New York City. He held this position for twenty-nine years, until he retired in 1813. During this period he was instrumental, as a delegate at various conventions, in organizing the Episcopal Church in the United States and in procuring the consecration of American bishops in this country. He was a liberally educated scholar and was well versed also in doctrinal theology.

The property on the Raritan River remained for many years a part of the Van Wickle estate. Ann Van Wickle and Abraham Beach resided here throughout the Revolution, when it was often between the lines, exposed to depredations from both parties and to balls fired in skirmishes between advance guards. After his appointment to Trinity Church, they lived in New York and only spent their summers on the farm. It was not until Oct. 31, 1799 (recorded 1808) that Robert Boggs, evidently then executor of the Van Wickle estate, conveyed the title of the property to Abraham Beach; in this deed he described it as "the farm whereon . . . Abraham Beach usually resides in the summer season," consisting of a 266¼-acre tract on the south side of the River Raritan adjoining Hendrick Suydam's farm (plate 140), also a 12 acre lot across the river and a 7½ acre lot at the Roundabouts. Ann (Van Wickle) Beach died in January, 1808. Her husband retired in 1813 to the farm on the Raritan, where he dispensed a modest hospitality. With him lived his eldest daughter, Harriet (1769-1848), widow of Rev. Elijah Rattoone.

At the death of Abraham Beach on Sept. 14, 1828, the house was inherited by the daughter Harriet Rattoone, who left it to her niece Julia Beach Lawrence. Her mother Cornelia Beach married Isaac Lawrence of New York; one of Cornelia's daughters married John Adams Pool and lived in the Low mansion at Raritan Landing (plate 116). The daughter Julia Beach Lawrence, who received the Van Wickle—Beach property, married her cousin Thomas Lawrence Wells (1799-1886). Their son Lawrence Wells was the father of the present owner, Miss Julia Lawrence Wells of New York City, who spends her summers here at *Elm Farm*.

The present house is a very large structure built at three separate times. The end toward the canal is the old unit, erected by or for Evert Van Wickle about 1752. It is of brick and sandstone with a shingled gable. It is covered by a gambrel roof of the New England type. There are no overhanging eaves. A central hallway runs the depth of this unit and is flanked on either side by two rooms. Another house was built on the west end in 1810 and became the central portion of the building when another large addition was made on the west in the second half of the nineteenth century. The many alterations have hidden to a great extent the original character of the house. The stone of the south front has been refaced and a large porch added. Balconies, dormers, slatted blinds and various types of windows are other changes. An old slave house formerly stood by the canal bank at the opposite end of the field. A large walnut tree, planted by Abraham Beach at the time of his marriage, still grows by the canal.

The house is on the southwest bank of the canal, which displaced the Revolutionary road along the Raritan River. It stands in an estate of several hundred acres about 3½ miles from New Brunswick toward Bound Brook, and is secluded by its groves of trees from the Easton Turnpike. On the southeast is the first Van Wickle house (plate 140), and between them is the old lane to the ford, which was once an important link between Piscataway and Middlebush.

House of Jacobus Wyckoff, later Voorhees'
Countyline Road, Franklin Park
PLATE 142

The road on which this house stands was laid southwestward from New Brunswick toward Trenton and was an early route to Philadelphia. Every few miles it was crossed by a small brook or run which was early given the name of its approximate distance from New Brunswick. Thus this house stands on the southwest bank of Nine Mile Run. A few miles further up the road was Six Mile Run, which gave its name to an important settlement in early days. The village has gradually spread southward so that Franklin Park, the present name of the Six Mile Run community, lies between that stream and Nine Mile Run. The road was laid along the line between Somerset and Middlesex Counties.

A large tract in this region was granted to Harrison and Willocks in 1700. No house is shown on the southwest side of Nine Mile Run on John Dalley's map of 1745, but a house here is marked C. Wycof on an undated map made by him shortly afterwards, and inscribed to James Alexander (who died in 1756); in most respects these maps are identical. On Azariah Dunham's map of 1766 the house is marked Jacobus Wikoff and on Robert Erskine's Revolutionary map, Cobus Wyckoff. On the map of 1850 it is shown as A. Voorhees' and on the 1860 map as P. Ayers'. The west wing of the house is believed to be over 200 years old and the main part to date from 1745. The above map shows that no house existed here in 1745; the west wing was therefore probably built a few years after this date and the main house at some period before the Revolution.

Jacobus Wyckoff, or Cobus for short, was evidently the builder of the house and lived here until after the Revolution. His connection with the Wyckoff family is unknown. The will of Mariah, widow of Jacobus Wicoff of Nine Mile Run, dated 1799 and probated 1804, mentioned "Peter Wicof, son of my beloved Jacobus Wicof, deceased, with whom I now live," and named as executor "my son-in-law" Peter Wicof. This may be the Pieter, son of Jacob Wyckoff and Sara his wife, bap. Jan. 22, 1758 in the Dutch church at Six Mile Run, although the names Jacob and Jacobus were not generally interchangeable. Peter Wyckoff inherited the north part of the farm, later owned by Garret Nevius; he lived to an old age and died about 1828.

The south part of the farm, on which stands the Jacobus Wyckoff home, was bought about 1797 by the Churches of Millstone and Six Mile Run for a parsonage, and it was occupied for a few years by Rev. Dr. Cannon, and then sold. Abraham Voorhees purchased the property and left it to his only child, Abraham Voorhees, Jr., who died unmarried about 1868. In 1860 it was owned by Peter Ayers, in 1874 by John R. Smith, and in 1910 by his son Peter Smith. The latter sold it to a dealer in real estate, from whom the present owner, Harvey E. Means, purchased it in 1923.

The low one and a half story wing is the original unit. It has only one large room with an immense fireplace at the end, exposed beams, low ceilings, old doors and very small windows. The main house is two stories in height. The gable wall is still covered with the old, long shingles with rounded ends, and the balance of the house is clapboarded. The ceiling beams are exposed in the second story only, the windows are small and narrow, and there is an early mantel and corner cupboard in the main room. There are only two rooms on the ground floor of the main house, one behind the other at one side of the hall, which runs the depth of the house; the room in the wing opens off the other side of the hall.

PLATE 128

House of Judge John Berrien
Rocky Hill

The date on the parlor fireback, 1764, has always been considered the date of erection of this house. John Berrien was living in the township by 1735 and on this site at least as early as 1745, but presumably in the early wing which has since disappeared. He was a Justice of the Supreme Court and a trustee of Princeton University. This handsome two story house was erected on the estate which he called *Rockingham* and was reached from the Princeton side of the river across a ford and up a long private avenue of trees. For an undetermined reason it was only along the Millstone and Raritan Rivers in central New Jersey that the Dutch built two story houses in the country. It will be noted that the old windows in the southeast room have a narrow lower sash while those in the southwest room have sashes of equal size; both are types in common use. Beautiful specimens of old panelling, cupboards and doors remain, especially in the southeast room. Berrien's widow was Washington's host and it is here that he wrote his Farewell Address to the Army and first delivered it from the balcony. This balcony is a very unusual feature for a Dutch house.

PLATE 129

Berrien (?)—Pumyea House
Old Rocky Hill Road, Rocky Hill

This house is believed to stand on the Peter Berrien tract; it was probably built by a Berrien son before the Revolution, and later passed by marriage into the Pumyea family. Most of the Dutch ovens connected with the fireplace and chimney but were built outside the walls of the houses. The photograph shows one of the few still remaining.

476

PLATE 130

Gulick (?)—Ditmars House
Road to Blawenburg, Harlingen

This may be the house owned by Youim Heuleck (Joachim Gulick?) during the Revolution. In the middle of the nineteenth century it was the home of Peter Ditmars. The house is an irregular frame structure built in many units and at different times. A small part of the back and the side walls is of irregular stone roughly laid.

PLATE 131

House of Guisbert Lane
south of North Branch, Bridgewater Township

This stone house was built in 1737 by Guisbert Lane on a tract he purchased in 1730. The ends of the structural tie rods have been shaped to record the date, the first two figures of which still show above the windows. The stones are unusually long and flat. The very wide window frames may have been inserted with the modern four-paned sashes. The house has not the charm of the Bergen County stone houses due to the absence of the curving overhang, which was not characteristic of Somerset County.

478

PLATE 132

Lane—Brokaw House
south of North Branch, Bridgewater Township

This is believed (probably incorrectly) to have been the home of Lieutenant John Brokaw, who was killed at the Battle of Germantown, and whose widow received a visit of consolation from Washington. Brokaw's widow married William Lane and they made their home here. Lane probably had built the house at the time of his first marriage, 1750. It is one of the very few houses built of brick in the region covered by this volume. It also differs in that the masonry is carried up to the roof line with no contrasting use of clapboarding or shingles in the gable. The shallow brick arches over the windows are typical of nearby Hunterdon County. The house has great depth and is covered by a low gable roof.

479

PLATE 133

Middagh (?)—Frelinghuysen House
Somerset Street, Raritan

The date of erection of this house is unknown. It stands on the large Middagh tract and is believed to have been the home of Cornelius Middagh who died in 1778. Erskine's Revolutionary map designates a house in this vicinity as Colonel Frelinghuysen's. The first known owner of the house was General John Frelinghuysen, born 1775, son of the Revolutionary Colonel, and his descendants owned it until recently. The house is not definitely pre-revolutionary in feeling, but this may be due in part to its size and to the neo-Grecian portico, which belongs to the Federal period. However, the gable end has pre-revolutionary proportions and lines. The large gable dormer is of course a later change. The main house is of brick and the more modestly built slave wing is covered with clapboarding.

PLATE 134

House of Johannes Moelich (Mellick)
Road to Peapack, Far Hills

This house was built in 1752 by Johannes Moelich and his wife under the supervision of Casper Berger, German stone mason. It remained the Mellick family home until recent years. Although the builders came from Germany by way of Philadelphia and therefore could not have been influenced by the stone houses of the Dutch in Bergen County, their similarity and differences suggest a comparison. Like many of the Bergen County houses, it is a one and a half story building of irregular stone covered by a steep gambrel roof, but the stonework is carried all the way up the gable, there are fewer windows and the roof has no curving overhang. The most distinctive feature of the house is the stonework over the windows. As in Hunterdon County the tops of the window openings are in the form of shallow arches but they are built of long, irregular stones of varying length laid on end. This gives the house a feeling of ruggedness and defiance of the elements. Porches, dormers, and a large addition at the rear are all later changes.

PLATE 135

Quick House
near North Branch, Bridgewater Township

The date of erection of this house is uncertain. The property was purchased from the Dutchess of Gordon in 1801 by Abraham Quick, who settled here. Accounts suggest that the house was already in existence at this time, and if so it must have been erected by some tenant of the Dutchess. The house is not definitely pre-revolutionary in feeling. It was built in two units, both along similar lines, with lower ceilings in the west half. The small lie-on-your-stomach windows are typical of the post-revolutionary era. The roofline has not been broken by dormers.

PLATE 136

House of Hendrick and Abraham Staats
South Bound Brook

This house is more generally known as Steuben's Headquarters. Until 1935 it was the home of the descendants of his host, Abraham Staats. It is probable that the first settler on the tract was the uncle, Hendrick Staats, and that between 1738 and 1740 he built the original unit. This consists of the right three-fifths of the section in this photograph (see plate 6 for plan). An interesting feature is the very large chimney which feeds the two fireplaces in the corners of the main rooms. Not until about 1800 was this unit enlarged on the west (left) side and a small wing also added. Although the old sashes are typical of both 1738 and 1800, the very thick moldings in the windows to the right of the door can readily be contrasted with the later moldings in the windows to the left of the door. This is the only external difference as the enlargement was carried out in a similar style. The present roof line has been extended slightly beyond all the walls and the sloping dormers have been added. The bottle glass eyes in the old door give a quaint touch; they were generally used in the interior only.

483

PLATE 137

House of John Van Doren
Millstone

This tract was purchased in 1752 by Christian Van Doren and conveyed to his son John in 1755. The house was undoubtedly built by John Van Doren about this time and it continued in the ownership of his descendants until about 1925. It is a handsome two story building which remains practically unaltered to this day. The plan of the main building consists of two large rooms, one behind the other, with a wide hallway running along the side. Adjoining the hall is the wing, formerly the kitchen and slave quarters. The gradation in size of the window openings on the different floors is interesting.

PLATE 138

House of Philip Van Horn
Middlebrook, Bridgewater Township

This was the country mansion of Philip Van Horn, a wealthy New York merchant, which he built in the third quarter of the eighteenth century, where he spent his summers and whither he later retired. It was known as "Phil's Hill" or "Convivial Hall" due to the unlimited hospitality which was dispensed here. Officers of both British and patriot armies were welcomed and Lord Sterling had his headquarters here. The house has nothing in common with the Dutch farmhouses of the period. It is a large, rectangular, two story frame house, through the center of which runs a wide hallway with spacious rooms opening off it on either side. The smaller two story wing was the kitchen and slave quarters. The original roof of the main house undoubtedly ended at the line of the walls in the same manner as the roof over the wing, without cornice or projection over the gable end. The modern shutters and unkempt condition also detract from its original appearance which was probably similar to that of the smaller Van Doren house at Millstone (plate 137).

485

PLATE 139

House of Derrick Van Vechten
Finderne

This is the earliest two story house still in existence. With the exception of the Van Campen house on the Delaware River and the Dey house at Preakness (plates 170 and 144), the only two story houses built in the country by the Dutch before the Revolution were in the Raritan River and Millstone River section, and they were erected in the thirty-five years previous to the war. This house was built by Derrick Van Vechten, supposedly in 1715, but as he was a lad of only 16 years at this time a date a few years later would probably be more correct. It is a two story brick building covered by a gable roof which resembles that on many of the Dutch farmhouses. General Greene had his headquarters here and gave a Christmas Eve dance for his Commander in Chief. The house remained in the Van Vechten family until the middle of the nineteenth century.

PLATE 140

*House of Symen Van Wickle, later Suydam's
Easton Turnpike, Franklin Township*

This house was probably built about 1722 by Symen Van Wickle on land bought by his father in 1703. It passed out of the family, and in 1797 was purchased by Hendrick Suydam whose son-in-law Nicholas Van Wickle later owned it until 1862. This house greatly resembles those in Kings County, the early home of the builder, and is typical of the Dutch farmhouses of this period. Notice the long rounded shingles still remaining on the front wall. The steep gable roof extends in a straight slope over the front (now the rear) wall to form a deep overhang. Until the recent restoration, the plan of the house consisted of a main room and a small bedroom on either side of a central hallway. The wing is unusually long and, although of an early period, was built later than the house. The dormers are more recent alterations.

487

PLATE 141

House of Evert Van Wickle, later Rev. Abraham Beach's
Easton Turnpike, Franklin Township

Family tradition states that the old unit of this house was built by or for Evert Van Wickle at the time of his marriage in 1752. It stands on a tract owned by his father Symen and eventually conveyed to Evert's son-in-law Rev. Abraham Beach, a noted minister of the late eighteenth century. It passed down the female line and is still the home of descendants. The present building is in reality three houses erected at separate times. The original unit is the east end by the canal. It is of stone and brick and is covered by a gambrel roof of the New England type. The stone front of the house has been refaced. Porch, balcony, and dormers are all later changes, as are the shutters and some of the window sashes.

PLATE 142

House of Jacobus Wyckoff, later Voorhees'
Franklin Park

The one and a half story wing is the original unit. It was built by Jacobus Wyckoff between 1745 and 1756. He added the two story building before the Revolution. It was used as the Six Mile Run parsonage for a few years after 1797 and then became the home of the Voorhees family. The wing consists of only one large room with a big fireplace, low ceilings and exposed beams. The hallway runs through the main house on the end adjoining the wing, and off the hall open two rooms each with fireplace, early type mantel and corner cupboard. The small size of the windows in the main unit is to be noted, and also the absence of windows (except in the garret) on the gable end. The old, long, rounded shingles still cover a part of the building. The brackets at the roof line are typical nineteenth century alterations.

WESTERN NEW JERSEY

HOUSE OF JOHN SIP OF ATHENIA

WESTERN NEW JERSEY

including Essex, Passaic, Hunterdon, Morris, Sussex and Warren Counties

Essex and Passaic Counties

THE present Passaic (originally part of Essex) County was settled by men of Dutch descent, most of whom came from the adjoining lands in old Bergen County. The present Essex County was settled largely by Englishmen from New England and Long Island, but there were also a number of Dutch settlements in its northwest and northeast regions.

In the years 1661-63 a group of New Englanders entered into negotiations with Director Stuyvesant for the planting of a Congregational settlement at the Achter Col, but there was a temporary setback to these plans when self government without appeal was denied them. It was not until 1666, when the Province was owned by Carteret, that the project was carried out, and at the Governor's suggestion the people from Milford and Branford commenced their settlement on the Passaic River at the present Newark. In 1667 and 1678 they purchased from the Indians all the land stretching from the Elizabethtown Purchase on the south to the mouth of the Third River on the north and to the top of the mountains on the west; they received a confirmatory deed from the Proprietors on Dec. 10, 1696 and a Town Patent on April 27, 1713. The southern section of old Essex County was settled at the present Elizabethtown in 1665 by four families from Long Island. This lower region remained wholly English and is now incorporated in Union County.

The portion of Essex County west of the mountains was settled by both English and Dutch under many conflicting grants and deeds from the Indians, Carteret and the Proprietors of both East and West Jersey. In 1679 a Dutch company from Bergen purchased from the Indians the lands between Cedar Grove, Pine Brook and Acquackanonk and this deed was confirmed by Carteret in 1684. Sir Thomas Lane and others obtained a patent for a tract at Horseneck in 1701 from the West Jersey Society. In 1702 and again in 1745 the Newark people, disregarding the Proprietors, purchased from the Indians the lands extending to the Passaic River. This confusion of titles resulted in riots and land troubles which were not settled for many years and many lost their homes if they had not the money to repurchase their farms.

Although the Newark Purchase extended as far north as the Acquackanonk Patent, the English made their homes only in the southern portion around Newark and the Oranges. The northern portion was gradually sold to Dutch settlers in the second half of the seventeenth century. The only Dutch village of any size was Second River, now Belleville, situated at the junction of the Passaic and Second Rivers. A Reformed Church was organized here in 1700. A road was laid in 1707 north to Acquackanonk over an Indian trail along the river bank, where several farms had already been opened. Among the earliest settlers were the Speers, Vreelands, and Van Giesens. The Third or Yantecaw River meanders through the northeastern section of the county, and its junction with the Passaic River forms the patent and county lines. The present Town of Nutley includes a group of small Dutch settlements made along the bank of the river in the opening years of the eighteenth century. In the interior, the village of Stone House Plains, now Brookdale, was formed on the headwaters of the Third River in the 1690's; the Van Giesens and Cockefairs were among the early inhabitants here. Further west the Speers and others settled at Upper Montclair, formerly Speertown. These small communities were dependent on the Acquackanonk and Second River Churches until 1795 when a branch church was organized at Stone House Plains.

The northwestern part of Essex County around Fairfield is bounded by a wide loop of the Passaic River, which no doubt gave rise to the old name of Horseneck for the region. This neck was settled mainly by the Dutch. Among the earliest was Simon Van Ness, who was here by 1710. A Dutch Church was organized in 1720.

That part of Passaic County in the bend of the Passaic River, within which the present cities of Passaic and Paterson are located, remained a part of Essex County until 1837. The land here was purchased by a group of Dutchmen from the Indians in 1679; they received a form of government from the Proprietors in 1683 and were granted the Acquackanonk Patent on March 16, 1684/5. Elias Michielsen (Vreeland) was the first settler. He was followed in 1682 by about ten families, who formed the nucleus of Acquackanonk village, now Passaic. The Dutch Church was organized here in 1693.

The portion of Passaic County between the Passaic and Ramapo Rivers was a part of Bergen County throughout most of the eighteenth century. The land here was bought up in large tracts by speculators and gradually sold to settlers. The Wagaraw Patent of 1696 was granted to Marian Campbell, widow, for a large tract of land along the Wagaraw or Goffle Brook above the most northerly bend of the Passaic River. It was purchased in 1706 by the Ryerson family, one of whom settled here. The Totowa Patent of 1696 granted to George Willocks lands along the west side of the Passaic River, a large portion of which was purchased in 1715 by Dirck

494

Van Houten who made his home here. In 1695 Arent Schuyler, Brockholst, etc., obtained an Indian deed and confirmatory patent for 5500 acres along the east side of the Pequanock River from its junction with the Passaic north to the Ramapo River. Arent settled about 1702 at the north end, which remained largely in the hands of his family. The lands in the interior along the Singac or Preakness Brook were mainly granted to Thomas Hart of London; his heirs sold various tracts about 1717-20 to Dutchmen, whose families made their homes here in the next fifty years. These scattered settlements depended on the Acquackanonk Church to the south and the Ponds Church to the northeast. The Pompton Plains Church was organized across the river in Morris County about 1734, the Totowa Church in 1754 and the Preakness Church not until 1804-05.

A county was formed in 1675 out of the Newark and Elizabethtown Purchases; in 1682 it received the name of Essex County and its boundaries were extended as far east as the Hackensack River. In 1710 the Pequannock and Passaic Rivers became the northern and eastern boundaries when a large section was given to Bergen County. In 1837 the western portion of the land thus allotted to Bergen and the northern portion of Essex were formed into the new Passaic County. In 1857 Union County was organized from the southern part of Essex. The present Essex County thus corresponds to the original Newark Township.

There is great variety in the Dutch houses of the present Passaic County and the adjoining lands in Essex County. This may be due in part to the frequent changes in civil organization and to the influence of English neighbors. There were many scattered farms in this territory, the only large village being Acquackanonk (Passaic) at one end, so that there was no center to crystallize architectural forms. Each house standing today has its individual character, although fundamentally a variation of the style evolved throughout the country by the Dutch. The pre-revolutionary houses are all built of stone, two with brick fronts, and all but one with gable roofs. Most of the houses in the section belonging for a time to Bergen County have the curved overhanging eaves so popular there. In two of the houses we find the arched window-heads common in West Jersey. One house far from a village is a two story mansion which shows little Dutch influence except in the characteristic combination of different building materials. In these houses the grouping of the units varies greatly. The "stoep" and the well sweep, formerly such characteristic features, have almost entirely disappeared with the march of time. Examples of these may be seen in plates 145 and 154.

The old roads and houses were located through Erskine's Revolutionary surveys and the owners determined through a series of maps. The genealogical text has been drawn mainly from Nelson's *History of Paterson* and Labaw's *History of*

495

Preakness, although original research work was necessary for a few of the families involved. The photographs in this section were taken partly in 1925 and partly in 1933-34.

Hunterdon County

The greater part of the present Hunterdon County was purchased by the Proprietors from the Indians on June 27, 1703, the deed conveying 150,000 acres on the Raritan River west of the Division Line. The land was divided between the Proprietors in hundredth shares according to their rights. The Proprietors disposed of large tracts generally to speculators. The West New Jersey Society, a stock company organized in London in 1691, made extensive purchases and had 91,000 acres surveyed in June, 1711. They encouraged settlement under leasehold and in 1735 had ninety-eight families as lessees; in 1744 they sold to James Alexander a tract of 10,000 acres embracing the region of Lebanon, Whitehouse and Round Valley. Actual settlement was slow. The 1722 census of Hunterdon County, which at that time included the present Mercer, Morris, Warren and Sussex Counties, recorded only 138 men subject to taxation of whom 16 were single, and only 16,995 acres then in possession.

The earliest settlers, who were mainly Quakers, came from the Delaware Bay on the south and arrived at the Falls of the Delaware about 1676. From the same direction later came the Germans who populated a large part of the county. Other settlers, mainly Dutch and Scotch Presbyterians, came from Raritan Bay on the east, by way of Woodbridge and Piscataway and then along the branches of the Raritan River into Hunterdon County. The Raritan was navigable up to the union of the North and South Branches. The grain crops of West Jersey were gathered here, floated in flat-bottomed boats down to New Brunswick and thence shipped to the larger markets.

The Dutch settlements in Hunterdon County were few in number and size. They were located in the small region between Three Bridges and Whitehouse, near the Somerset County border. This section became Readington Township. It was divided into four proprietary rights: Joseph Kirkbride had the southeast portion, Daniel Coxe of Philadelphia the southwest, George Willocks the northeast, and Budd & Logan the northwest. Adriaen Lane was the first Dutch settler, locating on Hollands Run at Readington village about 1700. Many of his countrymen followed him between 1710 and 1720, settling mainly at White House and along Pleasant Run. Among the most prominent was Abraham Van Horn, in whose barn the congregation worshipped for fifteen years and whose white plastered tavern gave the name of White House to the village. The Reformed Dutch Church of Readington was organized about 1717; the first house of worship was erected the following year near the junction of the North and South Branches of Raritan River, so that in early days it was known as the North Branch Church.

Hunterdon County was organized in 1713 from a part of Burlington County. At that time it comprised all of West Jersey above Trenton. Morris County (including the present Warren and Sussex) was set off in 1738 and Mercer County not until 1838-39. The county seat was at Trenton until 1785 when it was moved to Flemington.

The number of existing pre-revolutionary Dutch houses is too small to establish a type for the county with any degree of accuracy. However, two points stand out. All the houses were built of stone and generally included a certain amount of brickwork. Shallow arches were built above the doors and windows, a style common in West Jersey.

The ownership of the houses in this county was determined through Erskine's Revolutionary surveys and a series of later maps. The photographs were taken in 1933 after the field survey. The author is grateful to Hiram Deats for his aid.

Morris County

An immense tract on both sides of the Pequannock River, extending to the foothills and the Passaic and Pompton Rivers, was purchased from the Indians on June 6, 1695 by Schuyler, Brockholst, and associates. The following year they obtained confirmation from both the East and West Jersey Proprietors of 1500 acres on the west side of the Pequannock River, and settlement was commenced by the Dutch about 1700. John Reading, William Penn and other Proprietors of West Jersey took up tracts of 1200 acres or more further inland, which they sold to settlers. About 1710 a number of men from New England started the villages of Hanover, Whippany and Morristown (then New Hanover). A group of Germans sailed from the continent in 1707, landed in Philadelphia and marched overland toward New York by way of southwestern Morris County, where they stayed in German Valley.

Morris County was a part of West Jersey and in early days was known as Hanover Township in Hunterdon County. Its first assessor was appointed in 1722 and township officers in 1723. That year the first public road was officially laid: the road from Amwell to Hanover through the West Division. On March 15, 1738/9 Morris County (then including Sussex and Warren) was organized and the first court was convened at Morristown in 1740. Three townships, Morris, Pequannock and Hanover, were created. Sussex (including Warren) County was set apart in 1753. After Morris County had become a political division, it rapidly grew in wealth and population and the entire county was opened up for settlement between

1740 and 1775. Grain and cattle were raised, chiefly for the New York market, and timber was cut for export.

The Dutch population of the county was principally in the original Pequannock Township, in the northeastern corner of the county. Schuyler and his associates sold the lower end of their tract in 1702 to Maurice Mourison, one third of the land in 1696 to a group of Dutchmen and another third in 1717 to Symon Vanness and John Le Maitre. These and other Dutchmen from Bergen and New York started settlements here about 1700, centering around Pompton and Pompton Plains on the Pequannock River. The Dutch Church at the latter place was organized about 1734. A short distance to the west a stream flows through the Montville valley into the Rockaway River; in early days it was known as the Uylekill and gave its name to the Dutch settlement, now called Montville. On Oct. 2, 1714 Humphrey Davenport purchased 750 acres here from Thomas Stevenson, Proprietor. He built and settled here and was followed in the next few years by the Hyler, Jacobus, Millege, Parlaman and Van Duyn families, who opened up farms on this and adjoining tracts. A Reformed Dutch Church was organized at Old Boonton nearby about 1753 and was moved to Lower Montville in 1818. Several Dutch families also settled to the east in the Te Wechauw or Towaco valley. Cornelis Doremus located in this neighborhood in the 1740's and so many of his descendants remained here that the locality was known as Doremustown.

The Dutch houses in Morris County were built of the local stone, which varied in character in the different regions. The houses were small, long and narrow and were covered by steep gable roofs, generally with no overhanging eaves.

The houses were photographed in 1933 and 1934 after the field survey was made. As usual, Erskine's Revolutionary maps proved invaluable in determining the old roads and early owners. The text is based largely on county histories and individual researches.

Sussex and Warren Counties

The extreme northwestern portion of New Jersey from the New York border to Lake Hopatcong and Phillipsburg was only sparsely settled before the Revolution. The Dutch located only along the New York border and along the Delaware River south to the Water Gap. This was the Minisink country. The hinterland was mountainous and filled with iron mines which were operated by other nationalities.

There was occasional confusion in the land titles near the state border because the line was run several times and not finally accepted until 1772. Two large Minisink Patents, issued by the Province of New York in 1697 and 1704, extended as far south as Great Minisink Island. From time to time Proprietary rights were located by the Proprietors of West Jersey and sold by them to individuals or groups. The territory, later Warren County, was not purchased from the Indians until Aug. 18, 1713.

The Minisinks were known to the Dutch at an early date. In 1652 the Dutch West India Company sent an inquiry to Stuyvesant concerning the mineral wealth of the Minisink country. Mines were opened in the lower Pahaquarry Township near the Delaware Water Gap, and the Old Mine Road was constructed from there along the Delaware River to Port Jervis, and thence inland through the Neversink valley to Esopus on the Hudson River, a distance of about one hundred miles. This road was abandoned when the English conquered New Netherland in 1664. It was not until the end of the century that Dutch and Huguenot settlers followed this old route from Esopus. The Upper Minisink Neighborhood in the Neversink valley was populated first. The region about Machackemack (Port Jervis) in both states was settled in the 1690's by Willem Tietsoort and others. A joint Church was organized in 1737 for the Reformed Congregations of Minisink and Machackemack, which seem to have been in existence about 1716. Farms were opened on the other side of the mountains in the interior along the state border about the same time, under New York or New Jersey titles. The village of Sussex was not started until 1734 by Peter Decker, and was known until recently as Deckertown. A Dutch church in these back Minisinks was erected in the Clove valley near the Tietsoort farm. On April 18, 1713 Thomas Stevenson, West Jersey Proprietor, sold 2000 acres to Johannes, Claus and Simon Westphalia, Tunis and Romora Quick, and Cornelius Dutcher, all of the West Division of New Jersey. Presumably about this time Thomas Stevenson sold 500 acres, including the Great Minisink Island and the mainland adjoining, to Jacob Kuykendall and Uriah Westfalya, of which they sold 240 acres to Anthony Westbrook. The latter had the village of Minisink platted on April 7, 1725 for himself, Johannes Westbrook, Jr. and Jan Cortreght. Another settlement, known as Walpack, grew up near Flatbrookville and a Church was organized about 1737. Among the early families here were the Schoonhovens, Van Aukens and Rosencrantzes. In 1718 Joseph Kirkbride, West Jersey Proprietor, located 500 acres on the nearby Shapanack Flats, part of which seems to have come into the possession of Isaac Van Campen in 1750, and a church built here before the Revolution. The lower end of the Minisink country was called Pahaquarry and later became a part of Warren County. George Hutcheson, West Jersey Proprietor, sold 1666 acres here on March 8, 1732 to Col. Abraham Van Campen. He was the first permanent settler of this region and is believed to have come here as early as 1725. Across the river at Smithfield, Pa., was another early settlement made by the Du Puys and others; its church, built about 1725, was

499

attended by many of the inhabitants of the lower Minisinks in New Jersey and the same families settled both sides of the river.

In 1769 Richard Smith of Burlington went down the Delaware River in a canoe with Indian guides. He recorded: "The upper part of the Minisink trades to Sopus and the lower to Philadelphia. . . . We lodged last night at Peter Kikendahl's (Port Jervis). He had good Beds but we chose our bear skins as usual. . . . Here the hills on the river open to the right and left and let in some good Flats. . . . From Kikendahl's to Justice Rosencrants (at Walpack) they reckon thirty miles. . . . The lands along the Minisinks are not so rich as I expected; very little meadow is visible, the ground rather fit for the plow and somewhat sandy like ours about Burlington and accordingly they raise more rye than wheat. Not many houses are to be seen and those quite mean, the Flats in many places narrow flanked still by the Range of Hills. The Islands are low and level but the Bushes so thick round them that we could not discover how far they were improved. . . . We quitted Mr. Kikendahl's at seven o'clock and rowed (in the canoe) all the way being fifty-two miles . . . and in thirteen and a half hours reached Otters eighteen miles above Easton. . . . The soil of Sussex as far as we have seen is hilly, stony, broken and indifferent; it is the same on the Pennsylvania side. The timber is . . . shrubby and not fit for sawing for the most part. We had a glimpse of the late Col. Van Camp's place below Walpack; he has a good share of even land and a range of swelling hills proper for sheep pasture as much of all this country would be if it was cultivated. . . ."

Mr. Preston visited the country in 1787 as deputy under John Lukens, Surveyor General. He recorded: "I found Nicholas Dupuis, Esq., son of Samuel (and grandson of the first settlers), living in a spacious stone house in plenty and affluence. He stated that the old mine holes were a few miles above on the Jersey side of the river by the lower part of Pahaquarry Flat; that the Meenisink settlement extended forty miles or more on both sides of the river; that he had well known the mine road to Esopus and used, before he opened the boat channel through Foul Rift, to drive on it several times each winter with loads of wheat and cider, as also did his neighbors, to purchase their salt and necessaries in Esopus, having no other market or knowledge where the river ran to; that after a navigable channel was opened through Foul Rift, they generally took to boating and most of the settlement turned their trade down stream, and the mine road became less and less traveled. This interview with the admirable Nicholas Dupuis, Esq., was in June 1787. He then appeared about sixty years of age."

The Minisinks were claimed for many years by the Province of New York and the boundary was not finally drawn until 1772. Enough settlers had drifted down from Esopus to warrant the organization of a voting precinct by 1701; their votes were counted in Ulster County until 1709 and then in Orange County, New York; as late as 1739 they were taxed for building the gaol at Goshen, the county seat of Orange. For some years, all of northwestern New Jersey was included in Hunterdon County. In 1738/9 Morris County was set off and included all the land to the Delaware River. Walpack Township was formed in 1742 and was organized into Sussex County in 1753. Warren County was not set off until 1824.

These Dutch settlements along the Delaware River were in the wilds far from the larger settlements in central New Jersey. They formed an important line of defence against Indian raids. At the time of the French and Indian War, forts were built at Minisink, Walpack and Pahaquarry and garrisons stationed there. The Old Mine Road was not merely a local highway, but an important thoroughfare between the colonies. As late as 1800 John Adams passed down it as the best route from Boston to Philadelphia.

The number of Dutch houses remaining is too few to determine the average style of architecture in the Minisinks. The extant houses are built of stone, generally limestone, and are covered by gable roofs, which usually have a steep pitch and no overhanging eaves. They vary considerably in size, degree of finish and other details.

The survey of the Delaware River in 1769 by Dennis, articles on the Old Mine Road, county histories, and the records of the Minisink Churches form the basis of the text. The author is indebted to Professor Charles A. Philhower for calling attention to this region.

HOUSES IN WESTERN NEW JERSEY
including Essex, Passaic, Hunterdon, Morris, Sussex and Warren Counties

Houses in Essex and Passaic Counties

House of Albert Berdan
Berdan Avenue, Upper Preakness, Passaic County
PLATE 143

Jan Berdan, Jr. came to this country as a boy with his parents, and settled on Long Island. After his marriage and the birth of his eldest child, he removed to Hackensack, where he built a stone house in 1717 and lived the balance of his life (see supra). He was a large landholder, owning tracts in Hackensack, Maywood, Slooterdam and Upper Preakness. On Nov. 18, 1720 he bought from the heirs of Thomas Hart of London 362 acres on Singac (now Preakness) Brook in Upper Preakness. It was here that his son Albert built and settled. Albert[3] Berdan, b. Jan. 17, 1702 at Hackensack, removed in early manhood to Acquackanonk, where he was living when he married at the Hackensack Church Sept. 29, 1727 Divertje Banta of Acquackanonk, bap. May 24, 1710.

At some date Albert removed to his father's tract in Upper Preakness; he put up a log cabin, and later undoubtedly built a more permanent home (the wing of the present house), which had passed before the Revolution to his son Jacob[4] Berdan, b. March 28, 1746. William Roome, the surveyor, noted that the first story of the main house was built by this Jacob in 1792. Jacob married Rebecca Ryerson, and had a son Albert[5] Berdan (1767-1837) who married Mary Ackerman. This Albert built the second story of the main house. The homestead was inherited by his son Jacob[6] Berdan (1790-1875). He married Catharine, daughter of Rev. John Demarest of the Ponds, and had a son James D.[7] Berdan, who still owned a part of the original farm at Upper Preakness and was occupying the old house in 1902. It later passed to his son Harry M.[8] Berdan who married Elizabeth Berdan of Paterson. The house is now owned by the Berdan heirs, and occupied by tenants.

This is considered the oldest house in the section. The old wing is a small stone unit covered by a steep gable roof having no overhang. The ceilings are low and the windows very small. The main house is now a two story stone structure. The stone of both units is covered with plaster. It is in poor condition. The house stands on the east side of Berdan Avenue, at the end of the straight stretch, over one mile north of the Merselis house (plate 146) on the turnpike. Berdan Avenue was a Revolutionary road leading from Preakness to the Ponds church and settlement on the Ramapo River.

House of Dirck Dey; Washington's Headquarters
Totowa Road, Lower Preakness, Passaic County
PLATE 144

The grandfather of the builder was Dirck Jansen[1] Dey, a soldier in the employ of the West India Company. He emigrated from Amsterdam to New Amsterdam shortly before Dec. 28, 1641, on which date he married Jannetje Theunis, also from Amsterdam. After her death he married secondly Oct. 18, 1659 Geertje Jans Langendyck, from St. Marten in North Holland. He had two children by each wife, and died shortly before Nov. 11, 1687 when his widow married Theunis Gysbertse Bogaert, a widower, who lived in the Wallabocht on Long Island. Dirck's son Thenis[2] Dey of New York City, bap. Sept. 24, 1656, married Feb. 4, 1685 Anneken Schouten. Their only son was Dirck[3] Dey, bap. March 27, 1687 in New York, d. May 11, 1764 in New York, married Dec. 16, 1725 Jeanne or Jane Blanchard, bap. March 21, 1697 in the French church in New York, d. Aug. 14, 1756, a daughter of Jean Blanchard, Huguenot.

Dirck Dey is believed to have settled in Preakness as early as 1707. On Oct. 9, 1717 he bought of the heirs of Thomas Hart of London 600 acres on Singac (now Preakness) Brook in Lower Preakness. The present Georgian mansion is believed to have been built by him about 1740; its superior workmanship is attributed to his being a carpenter. He was a freeholder of Bergen County for many years (this region was then in Bergen Co.), and a member of the New Jersey Assembly 1748-52. He removed to New York City in 1752 for the balance of his life. Only four of Dirck's children lived to maturity, Theunis, Jane, Ann and Margaret; Jane was the mother of Richard Varick, mayor of New York City. Dirck devised all his real estate in East and West Jersey to his only son and left handsome legacies to his three daughters.

The only surviving son of Dirck was Theunis[4] Dey, b. Oct. 18, 1726 (O.S.), bap. at Acquackanonk, d. June 10, 1787. He was an important man in colonial New Jersey, a Colonel in the militia, member of the New Jersey Assembly and of the Provincial Council. He lived in the mansion at Lower Preakness, calling it *Bloemsburg* and later *Bloomsbury Manor*. Washington had his headquarters here twice in 1780. On Dec. 12, 1749 Theunis married Hester Schuyler, b. April 12, 1725, d. Sept. 3, 1784 at the manor. Of their ten children, the eldest was Gen. Richard[5] Dey, b. Nov. 29, 1752, married March 6, 1775 Hannah Pierson and had nine children.

He lived in the mansion until he sold it in 1801 to the Neafies, when he removed to Little Falls and built a house there which burned down in 1848. He was killed Oct. 6, 1811 by a fall from his horse.

John Neafie, Jr. (1779-1869) with his brother Garret bought the Dey Mansion and 355 acres in 1801 and lived here until 1813. Here was born John R. Neafie, the celebrated Shakespearean actor. On April 10, 1813 John Neafie, Jr. sold the property to Martinus Hogencamp. It was inherited by William S. Hogencamp, who sold it on April 4, 1861. Since this time the house has passed through many owners, and is now in the hands of the Passaic County Park Commission.

The house is generally said to have been built about 1740 by Dirck Dey. This was the claim of Sheriff Hogencamp, the owner in 1860. If built by Dirck, it must have been erected before he returned to New York City in 1752. It has been also stated that the house was built by Col. Theunis Dey about 1750-60. It is more apt to have been erected by his father, who was a carpenter and therefore a builder; however, it is known as the house of Col. Theunis Dey since he was the most important owner and Washington's host. The house is 52 feet by 30 feet, and two and a half stories high; the central hallway is twelve feet wide. Huge oaken timbers, pegged with wooden pins, support it. It is built of fieldstone, the front and the eaves faced with brick, the doors and windows and corners of the front trimmed with cut sandstone blocks. The brick was fired on the estate and doubtless the stone was quarried here. The walls are laid with yellow clay, pointed with mortar. The house is surmounted by a cornice and a steep gambrel roof. The dormers were added by a later owner. There was formerly a covered porch with seats on either side of the front door; a stone kitchen a few feet to the east of the house has also disappeared. This house is built in the style of a mansion, and therefore is not typical of the Dutch, who generally built low-lying farmhouses in the country. Dutch influence, however, can be seen in the mixture of building materials and the gambrel roof. It is interesting to compare this house with the mansion of Cornelius Low, built by him at Raritan Landing in 1741 (plate 116). The house is on the north side of Totowa Road, several miles west of Totowa, an early settlement on the Passaic River below Paterson. It stands near a small brook, and east of the Valley Road which runs northward through Preakness and Upper Preakness. The house is also reproduced in *the History of Preakness*, p. 28.

Kingsland House
3 Kingsland Road, Nutley, Essex County

It was a great disappointment that permission could not be obtained to photograph this house. It is run as a roadhouse of some sort, and no doubt publicity of any kind was undesired and feared. Not only is it a good example of Dutch architecture, but it has one of the very few exterior Dutch ovens still in existence and good condition. No information could be obtained about the builder and early owners of the house. It was erected in 1732, if a wooden plaque "1732-1932" over the west door may be believed.

The Kingsland family were one of the patentees and earliest settlers of New Barbadoes Neck, the neck of land between the Hackensack, Passaic and Saddle Rivers, in Bergen County. Joseph Kingsland, Sr., b. 1738 in Bergen Co., d. 1821, married Mary Outwater. They removed to New York City at the close of the Revolution and then to Essex County in 1796, where they purchased and lived in the house in question. Their son Joseph Kingsland, b. 1792 in New York City, d. 1878, married in 1812 Martha Ackerman and had five children. Two of their daughters, Margaret and Martha, were still living in the homestead about 1925. Their son, also called Joseph Kingsland, was born in the old house in Essex County in 1813, and in 1850 married Margaret Stewart.

The house was in Belleville Township, later in Franklin, and now in Nutley, in the extreme northeastern corner of Essex County, a stone's throw from Passaic County. It stands on the south side of what is now called Kingsland Road, on the west bank of Yantecaw or Third River, which is dammed at this point. It is probable that the early owners conducted a mill here. Many Dutchmen settled along the Third River, which empties into the Passaic River, midway between the early settlements of Acquackanonk (Passaic) on the north and Second River (Belleville) on the south.

The house is built in three units, all of stone and covered with gable roofs. The most interesting unit is the south wing, which has a low second story, old window sashes four panes across, and an old Dutch oven, which is still intact and protrudes from the gable end. The central unit is the main part of the house. The garret has been modernized with dormers. A porch has been added to the low north wing.

Lawrence House
formerly on Watchung Avenue, Brookdale, Essex County
PLATE 145

Very little is known that definitely pertains to this house. It stands on the Cockefair tract near Third River, in the locality known for many years as Stone House Plains.

Alexander Coquefaire was a Frenchman who emigrated to this country about 1657. He settled in Bushwick on Long Island, where he bought a plantation in 1663, was a drum major that same year and a patentee in 1687. He is last mentioned when he sold land there in 1698. The name of his wife is unknown, but the town records state that on April 23, 1665 he paid a marriage fee to the Flatbush Church. He signed his name Cokcover; it also appears as Cockefair, the spelling adopted by his descendants.

Another Alexander Cockefair, probably a grandson, settled at Stone House Plains in Essex County, New Jersey. His farm is supposed to have run from a ledge of rock 800 feet west of Third River westward to an oak tree near the present corner of Broad and Watchung Avenues. (Until recently Watchung Avenue bore the name of Oaktree Lane from this landmark.) The first Cockefair house stood on land lately owned by Sylvanus Cockefair; it disappeared about the time of the Revolution. Alexander or Sander Cockefair (Coccifeer, Kokkefeer, Cockefer, etc.) married Johanna Kind (Hanna, Hendrina, Anna Kint) about 1720. He is not mentioned on the church records after 1741 nor she after 1740, so they may have died about this time. They had four children, the eldest two baptized at the Acquackanonk Church to the north, and the youngest two at the Second River Church to the south. (1) Alexander, Jr., b. March 8, 1721, is probably the one who extended the farm eastward to the Third River by purchase of May 27, 1753. No mention of his marriage has been found. (2) Elizabeth, b. March 4, 1724, married Jacob Phillips (Filips), and had four daughters, Aeltje, Saartje, Judick and Antje. (3) Judith, b. April 9, 1731, married John Lawrence. Their only appearance together on the church records is in 1757, when Johannes Lerrens and Judick Kockyefeer acted as sponsors for Alexander, the son of her brother Johannes Kockyfeer. (4) The fourth child of Alexander Cockefair was Johannes or John, b. March 25, 1735. He may be the John Cockkifer who married Jan. 23, 1757 Jennij Swiner, both born and living at Acquackanonk. By a wife unnamed he had a son Alexander in 1757; at the baptisms of his children 1768-74 his wife was called Jannetje Torner. His children were Alexander, Stephanus, Frederick D., Pieter, and Abram, also probably Marytje, John, Thomas, Charity, and Catrina. John Cockefair built the house on the west end of the family tract (No. 901 Broad Street), to which the street front was added in 1817; it remained in the family for many years.

The stone house on the south side of Watchung Avenue was only torn down since the photograph was taken in 1925. It stood near the middle of the Cockefair tract, between Broad Street and Third River. It was undoubtedly built in the middle of the eighteenth century. It is possible that Alexander Cockefair built two houses, but more likely that this house was built by or for Johannes Lawrence when he married Alexander's daughter Judith. Strangely enough there is no record of any children of theirs in the nearby Dutch churches, but they undoubtedly had issue, as the house was owned as late as 1859 by a J. Lawrence. In 1883 it was the prop-

507

erty of W. Stimus and in 1906 of Susan B. Stimus. The house stood in the early settlement of Stone House Plains (now Brookdale), east of Speertown (now Upper Montclair) and some distance west of the settlements along the Passaic River.

House of Edo Merselis
Paterson and Hamburgh Turnpike, Upper Preakness, Passaic County
PLATE 146

This house is marked Marselis' on Erskine's Revolutionary map, and was built in the decade previous to the war by Edo Merselis. His ancestor Pieter Marselis emigrated in 1661 on the *Beaver* from Beest in Gelderland, with his wife, four children and two servants. It is said that he was born near Leerdam, and removed to Beest where his children were born. He settled in Bergen, where he died Sept. 4, 1682 and his wife Aug. 1, 1680. His son Marcelis Pietersen[2] was six years old when he came to this country in 1661; he was the father of Pieter Merselis,[3] bap. July 17, 1687 at New York, lived at Bergen but married in New York Dec. 31, 1717 Jenneke Prior of Bergen. Among their many children was Edo[4] Marselis or Merselis, b. Jan. 27, 1729, d. Oct. 12, 1799, aged 70 years, 8 months, and 15 days, and was buried at Preakness. At Bergen on April 11, 1754 he married Ariaentje Sip, b. May 30, 1732, d. May 20, 1813 at Preakness; both were born at Bergen and living there at the time of their marriage. Her father was Ide Sip, owner of the house in Bergen village (plate 107).

In 1759 Edo Merselis bought 69 acres in Preakness from Robert Hunter Morris; June 1, 1763 he bought a tract in Upper Preakness from Theunis Hennion, whose grandfather David Danielsen (Hennion) purchased it Aug. 30, 1717 from the heirs of Thomas Hart of London; in 1769 he bought 210 acres at Upper Preakness from John Berdan, whose grandfather had purchased it Nov. 18, 1720 from the heirs of Thomas Hart of London. Edo Merselis built his house on the Hennion tract at Upper Preakness on the Paterson-Pompton road, at the point where the road to the Ponds Church begins. Nearby was the Hennion house, and also the Berdan house (plate 143). Edo was an elder of the Totowa Church, and a deputy to the Provincial Congress of New Jersey. In his will he mentioned his nine children, Antje (wife of Simeon Van Winkle), Jannetje (wife of Adrian Van Houten and Enoch Vreeland), Pieter, Edo, Cornelis, John, Catlyntje (wife of Isaac Van Saun), Arreyantje (wife of John Parke), and Gerrit. Three of his sons, Cornelis, John and Gerrit remained at Preakness. The son Gerrit[5] Merselis, b. Oct. 1, 1777, d. April 2, 1843, married May 3, 1799 Lena De Gray, b. Dec. 18, 1780, d. April 20, 1848. He lived in his father's house, which later passed into the hands of his son Peter G.[6] Merselis, b. 1815, d. Aug. 30, 1891. The latter's son Gilbert F.[7] Merselis lived here in 1902, and his son Garret E.⁸ Merselis sold it about 1920 to the present owner Isaac A. Hopper, but continues to occupy the ancestral homestead.

The house is built of stone, plastered and whitewashed, except for the rear which is of stone rubble covered with a coat of whitewash. It has a broad gable roof, extending over the front to form an overhang. The front of the house has been altered with dormers and porch. The house is in Upper Preakness a short distance north of the church; it is on the north side of the Paterson and Hamburgh Turnpike leading to Pompton. The road to Ponds Church, now Berdan Avenue, leaves the turnpike by the house.

House of Johannes Ryerson
367 Goffle Road, Hawthorne, Passaic County
PLATE 147

The grandfather of the builder of this house was Martin Ryerszen, who emigrated from Amsterdam about 1646 and settled at Breukelen, where on May 14, 1663 he married Annetje, daughter of Joris Jansen de Rapalje. Their son Joris Martinse² Ryerse, bap. Sept. 19, 1666, d. about 1749-50, married Aug. 11, 1691 Anneken Schouten, widow of Theunis Dey. At the time of his marriage he lived at the Wallabocht on Long Island. In 1695 he joined Arent Schuyler and others in buying extensive tracts of lands on both sides of the Pequannock River. He settled at Pacquanac (near Mountain View) about 1710. He was a judge and a very prominent man. He had three step-children and eleven children. Of these, Dirck Dey built the mansion at Lower Preakness (plate 144), Marten Ryerson built on the South Branch of the Raritan River near Flemington (plate 160), and Johannes Ryerson built at the Goffle.

On Nov. 11, 1706 Joris Ryerse of Pompton joined with Ryer and Frans Ryerse of New York in buying a tract north of the Passaic River along the Wagaraw or Goffle Brook from Blandina Bayard of New York; this tract was surveyed and divided between the owners on June 7, 1721. In his will of 1744 Joris Ryerse devised his plantation at Wagaraw, on which his son Johannes lived, to this Johannes. The settlement of Wagaraw was on the north bank of the Passaic River at the bend north of Paterson. From here a road led northward along the Goffle Brook to the house and mill of Cornelis Lozier at the present Midland Park (plate 96). As farms were opened up along the brook, this settlement became known as the Goffle. Johannes Ryerse was living here in 1744, and may have removed here shortly after the survey of 1721. He probably built an earlier house no longer existing as well as the present house, if it was built in 1750 as claimed.

Johannes³ Ryerse, also called John G. Ryerson, bap. Aug. 8, 1694, died between

1779-82, married Oct. 27, 1716 Maritie Janse Spier and later married Geertje Hessels, and had nine children in all. He was a Justice of the Peace. He lived at the Goffle on a farm left him by his father, and in 1779 willed one-third of the estate upon which he dwelt to his grandson John, eldest son of his son George. Joris or George I.[4] Ryerson left all his lands in 1801 to his only son John. This John G.[5] Ryerson, b. July 3, 1769, d. 1835, married July 21, 1793 Leah, daughter of Cornelius Westervelt, d. 1861, aged 87 years. He lived on his father's and grandfather's place on the east side of the Goffle Road in the house still standing. After the marriage of his only child, he gave him the farm of 180 acres, and removed to his wife's farm. This son, George I.[6] Ryerson, b. Dec. 17, 1793, d. Dec. 16, 1875, married Sept. 19, 1813 Hillegont, daughter of Gerrebrant Van Houten; after her death June 23, 1847, he married Mrs. Eliza Burtsell of New York, and thirdly Margaret Hanson. He lived on the place occupied by his grandfather on the Goffle Road. His son Henry Garrison[7] Ryerson, b. Dec. 3, 1822, d. 1879, married Martha, daughter of Adam Dater. He was an auctioneer, and continued to reside in the ancestral home. It later passed to his two children, George who died in 1887, and Elizabeth who married John Ackerman of Hohokus. The Ackerman estate owned it until recently. It is at present unoccupied.

It is claimed that the house was erected in 1750. This date could only apply to the wing by the road, as the main house is probably post-revolutionary. The wing is built of roughly cut stone and the main house of dressed stone, whitewashed; the rear of both units is of stone rubble, and both sections are covered by gable roofs, extending to form an overhang on the south front. The photograph shows the rear view. The house stands on the east side of Goffle Road by the Goffle Brook, about one mile north of the Passaic River.

In the fall of 1780 Lafayette had his headquarters in a tent back of the house by the brook; he called his Goffle Headquarters "Light Camp." Why Lafayette did not commandeer the house is not known, but that he did not is additional proof that only the small unit was then in existence. As his host Johannes Ryerse had nine children, some of whom were married, the house was undoubtedly full, and Lafayette may not have wished to disturb them.

Schuyler—Colfax House
Paterson and Hamburgh Turnpike, Pompton, Passaic County
PLATE 148

There seems to be some disagreement as to what member of the Schuyler family built the original unit of this house. On June 6, 1695 Arent Schuyler, Brockholst, and various associates, obtained a deed from the Indians for a large tract on both sides of the Pequannock River, from the Passaic River northward to the bend of the Pequannock River, and on Nov. 11, 1695 obtained a patent for 5500 acres on the east side of the river covered by the Indian deed. Arent's father, Philip Pieterse[1] Schuyler, had emigrated from Amsterdam shortly before Dec. 12, 1650 when he married Margrita, daughter of Brandt Van Slichtenhorst, the director of Rensselaerswyck. Philip became one of the most important of the early colonists of New Netherland. His seventh son Arent[2] Schuyler, b. June 25, 1662 at Beverwyck, d. in or before November, 1730. He was married three times: on Nov. 26, 1648 to Jenneke, daughter of William Teller, by whom he had three sons and three daughters; in January, 1703 to Swantie van Duyckhuysen, by whom he had three sons and two daughters; and in 1724 to Maria Walter, granddaughter of Jacob Leisler. His third wife survived him, and in December, 1736 married Archibald Kennedy. Arent Schuyler was a merchant at Beverwyck in early life, he removed to New York City in 1694 and was still a resident there when he signed a petition to the king in December, 1701. He probably removed to Pompton the following spring, and was living here when he made one of his wills on Oct. 18, 1706. Arent was a fluent speaker of the Indian languages and was often commissioned to treat with the Indians. He was an extensive landowner, purchasing tracts at Kingston, Dan's Chamber, Pequannock, Minisink and New Barbadoes Neck, and later, with his copper riches, buying lands at Bordentown and Elizabethtown for his sons. In 1710 he removed to a tract on New Barbadoes Neck and his homestead there stood until recently; copper was soon discovered there and he became very wealthy.

When Arent Schuyler removed from Pompton, he gave his undivided share in the patent to his eldest son Philip. In his third will, dated 1724, he apportioned his properties between his sons, confirming to Philip his one-third share in the 1200 acres at Pequannock and Pompton, which he held in common with Bayard and Brockholst. Philip[3] Schuyler, bap. Sept. 11, 1687, married Hester, daughter of Isaac Kingsland of New Barbadoes Neck, and had seven sons and five daughters. He occupied the Pompton homestead, and represented this settlement in the colonial legislature. His eldest son Arent, b. 1715, bought the Van Wagenen farm on Ryerson Pond (now Pompton Lakes) in 1739, and was living there during the Revolution; his stone house still stands, but is completely disfigured by a mansard roof; it is now used as an athletic camp. Another son Peter lived on his father's tract near the Pompton River; Erskine shows his house to have been at the corner of the Black Oak Ridge Road and the Hamburgh Turnpike, and his brother Isaac's to have been still further south near the river. Philip's youngest son, Casparus[4] Schuyler, b. Dec. 10, 1735, married Miss Brocas. He also occupied his father's homestead tract, living just north of his brother Peter. His home is marked "Paulus Schuyler" on Erskine's map (Paulus was probably a misunderstanding by the surveyor of the two last syllables of the name).

Casparus Schuyler's property was inherited by his only child Hester or Hetty,[5] who on Aug. 27, 1783 married William Colfax, b. July 3, 1756 in Connecticut, d. Sept. 9, 1838 and was buried on his place at Pompton. William Colfax was a captain of Washington's Life Guards and a great favorite of the Washingtons. He was wounded three times during the war. He was descended from William Colfax, who had come to this country and settled in Wethersfield, Connecticut, about 1643. After the Revolution, William settled on his wife's estate at Pompton as a farmer; he was made a Justice of the Peace, a General, and a member of the General Assembly from Bergen County. Six of William's and Hester's children lived to maturity, three sons and three daughters. The sons were: George Washington Colfax (1784-1811), who built on the Schuyler tract nearby a house which was inherited by his son Major William W. Colfax; Schuyler Colfax (1792-1822), who was the father of Schuyler Colfax, Vice-President of the United States; and Dr. William Washington Colfax, b. April 26, 1797, d. Feb. 28, 1876. Dr. Colfax lived in the old homestead, and practised medicine for fifty years in the vicinity of Pompton. On April 27, 1826 he married Hester Mandeville. Their son was the owner in 1897, and his widow Mrs. Delia Colfax, who approaches her hundredth birthday, is the present owner.

The house was built at three separate times. The north wing is very long, and consists of two similar units. The main part is a typical post-revolutionary house covered by a gambrel roof, and now marred by many dormers. The east front of all the units is of brick, and the rear and sides are of rough fieldstone. The north wing is very interesting; its low exposed beams, rounded door and window tops are distinguishing features; it is covered by a gable roof with no overhang. The main house was probably built after the Revolution by William Colfax who, as an important member of society, wanted a handsome home. The erection of the earlier units presents more of a problem. It has been stated variously that Arent Schuyler, the patentee, lived here in 1697, that he built it about 1700, that Dr. William W. Colfax lived on the site of his house, and that Casparus Schuyler built the present house in 1735. Arent Schuyler probably did not remove to Pompton until the spring of 1702, and it is quite possible that he built one unit of the old wing at this time, giving it to his son Philip when he removed to New Barbadoes in 1710. Otherwise the son Philip probably erected it about 1712, when he set up housekeeping on the Pompton tract. He probably built the second unit. It is of course impossible that Casparus Schuyler, who was born in 1735, should have erected a house the year of his birth; possibly this statement should be interpreted to the effect that Casparus Schuyler, b. 1735, built the house, or more probably that this Casparus inherited the house, a part of which had been built about the time of his birth by his father Philip. It stands on the west side of the Paterson and Hamburgh Turnpike, a short distance south of the Ramapo River and east of the Pompton River, in the outskirts of Pompton.

House of John Sip
Kenyon Street, Athenia, Passaic County

In 1729 Jan Arianse Sip, owner of the house at Bergen village (plate 107), willed to his eldest son Arie the plantation at Acquackanonk, whereon Arie then dwelt, containing 100 acres in the first division on the west bank of the Passaic River, and also 50 acres of the second division adjoining this property on the west. This Arie[2] Sip, b. Oct. 25, 1684 at Bergen and baptized in New York, married at New York April 19, 1711 Gerritje Helmigse, a young girl from Bergen, daughter of Helmig Van Houten. He immediately settled at Acquackanonk, on Lot No. 11 of the patent, which his father had purchased Nov. 6, 1696 from his step-father Hans Didericks. Arie and Gerritje Sip had five children: Annatie, Halmagh, Johannes, Jannitje, and Cornelis. Arie died Dec. 3, 1765,* having devised in 1762 to his son John the 150 acres on which the testator lived and also the 14 acre lots by the highway. Johannes or John[4] Sip, b. March 10, 1715 at Acquackanonk, married there Dec. 12, 1744 Annatje Van Winkle of the same place. They had at least three children, John, Jr., Adrian, bap. 1750, and Cornelius, bap. 1759.

John[5] Sip, Jr., born about 1747, was known as John Sip of Athenia. He is the first one known to have lived here within the memory of an old neighbor; it is probable that he or his father built the present house. He kept a distillery here. John[5] Sip of Athenia married Geertje Van Winckle, and had five children: Annatje, b. 1778, married Aaron Van Houten; John, b. 1780; Catharine, b. 1782, married Abraham Van Houten of Totowa; Adrian, b. 1785; and Eva, b. 1792, married Johannes Ackerman. The elder of the sons was John J.[6] Sip, Jr., b. Sept. 18, 1780 and baptized at Acquackanonk, died about 1865 over 80 years of age. He was a farmer and inherited his father's home at Athenia. His first wife, whom he married May 10, 1807, bore the same name as his mother, Geertje Van Winckle; by her he had but one child John, b. 1808, who lived to the eastward on Van Houten Avenue. John J.[6] Sip, Jr. of Athenia married secondly July 8, 1810 Aariantje Marselis, and had five children born 1811-19: Edo, Geertje, Adrian, Elenor and Ann. The house was sold by the estate of John J.[6] Sip, Jr. after his death.

This house is a large stone structure covered by a gambrel roof, having no overhang. It is now marred by many dormers of different shapes. A view is reproduced in the vignette. It stands on a lane called Kenyon Street, southeast of the juncture of Van Houten and Clifton Avenues, and on the west side of the railway. Athenia is

513

---

* Taken from family Bible.

the modern name for the region just west of Passaic. Until fairly recently there stood a post-revolutionary stone house just east on Clifton Avenue. This was also a Sip house and is believed to have been built by a son of John Sip, the distiller. It is therefore probable that it was erected by his younger son Adrian Sip, b. 1785.

Speer House
614 Upper Mountain Avenue, Montclair Heights, Essex County

There still exists, in a remodelled condition, a small, stone and frame house known as the Speer house, a short distance south of the county border. This region, on the east side of the mountain, was settled by the Dutch from nearby Acquacka-nonk, and came to be known as Speertown, presumably because of the preponder-ance of this family. Hendrick Jansen[1] Spier emigrated to this country on the *Faith* in 1659. Nelson gives a thorough account of his numerous descendants with many of their places of residence but unfortunately assigns none to this particular house. A Jacobus[4] Speer lived on the River Road south of Passaic. Among his sons was Gerrit[5] Speer (1753-1828), who had a son Peter[6] Speer, b. 1789. This Peter lived at Upper Montclair where he owned a large tract of land on the slope of the mountain. Possibly he owned the house in question, but it must have been built before his time.

Stynmets—Sip House
714 River Road, Passaic, Passaic County
PLATE 149

In the Acquackanonk settlement a short distance above the Newark Town Purchase line (now the Essex County border) runs a small stream known as the Min-eral Spring Brook. Lot No. 7 on its south bank, a 100 acre lot in the first division of the patent, fell to a member of the Vreeland family; Dirck Vreeland, bap. 1686, was still living there in 1750, and in 1778 another Richard Vreeland had his home there. Lot No. 6, immediately to the south, was allotted to Gerrit Gerritse Van Wagening, a patentee of Acquackanonk but a resident of Communipaw in the Town of Bergen. His son Hermanus Gerritse settled further north in Acquackanonk, opposite the present bridge at Passaic (plate 154). On Jan. 30, 1698/9 Gerrit Gerritse Van Wagening of the Town of Bergen deeded to Christoffle Stynmets of Essex County Lot No. 6 in Acquackanonk with the house lot and half the patent rights and the commonage pertaining thereto.

Christoffel's parents were Casper Steynmetzen and Jannetje Gerrits; they had six sons baptized in New York between 1650 and 1670. They probably settled in Bergen about the time the youngest was born, as Casper's wife Jannetje was buried in Bergen in 1670. Their fourth son Christoffel² Stynmets (Stymets, Stynmetz), bap. Dec. 19, 1660 in New York, married at Bergen Oct. 6, 1684 Jannetje Gerrits, bap. March 19, 1662, daughter of Gerrit Gerrits Van Wagening and Annetje Hermanse of Communipaw. It is probable that Christoffel left Bergen shortly after the birth of his fourth child in 1693 and settled at Acquackanonk in Essex County, building the rear unit of the present house in the 1690s, on the tract conveyed to him by his father-in-law in 1699. He was an elder of the Acquackanonk Church in 1697-98. His young wife died and he married secondly at Bergen 1698-99 Sara Van Nest; it is probable that she was the mother of most of his children. The will of "Christophel Stynmuth" of Acquackanonk, yeoman, aged and infirm, executed in 1732 and probated in 1735, mentioned his wife Sarah and twelve children: Casparus (bap. 1686), Antie (bap. 1692, married Jacob Van Noordstrand), Jannetie (bap. 1693), Benjamin (married secondly in 1731 Sara Emons, both residents of Riddenstown), Judah or Judith (married Harman Jurianse Van Riper), Peter (married 1734 Marietje Brouwer, both of Essex Co.), Hannah, Johannes (born and lived at Acquackanonk, married 1737 Catharine Post), Garret (of Saddle River, wife Susanna), George (probably married 1742 Claertje Van Iderstein), Elizabeth (married 1730 Juri Jurianse Van Riper), and Marya.

In his will of 1732 Christoffel Stynmets mentioned various tracts of land, among which were 299 acres on the Passaic River adjoining the land of Dirck Vreeland. It is on this property that the house stands. When Lot No. 7 was confirmed to Dirck Vreeland in 1750, it was described as bounded on the south by Christoffel Stymets. The will of Arie Sip of Acquackanonk, dated 1762, gave to his son Helmich the 200 acres on which the son lived, which were purchased from Christoffel Stynmetz, and also the land in the common. This Christoffel must have been a grandson of the first Christoffel Stynmets, and evidently sold the land between 1750 and 1762. Present tenure of the house, however, is based on an indenture dated March 21, 1768 from John J. Ludlow of Acquackanonk to Helmich Sip of the same place, which transferred for £100 a dwelling and lot in Acquackanonk, south of the dwelling of Dirck Vreeland, beginning at the river 17 feet north of the house, running west 90 feet, south 100 feet, and east 110 feet to the river, along the river north 100 feet to the beginning, with barn, stable and gardens (original deed in the possession of Mrs. Roberts, a descendant). At the time of the Revolution, Ludlow was living further north on the Passaic River. How he came to own the house is not known; it is possible that this was a release from a claimant, as it is probable that this house and lot were included in the 200 acres with house which Arie Sip had willed to his son Helmich in 1762.

Arie² Sip, whose father owned the house in the village of Bergen (plate 107), settled at Acquackanonk, some distance north of the Stynmets farm. He had twin sons, of whom John[4] Sip inherited the homestead and is the ancestor of the Athenia branch of the family (see supra). The other twin, Helmich or Halmagh[4] Sip, b. March 10, 1715 at Acquackanonk, married here Nov. 14, 1740 Jannetje Van Houten, b. April 19, 1719 at Totowa, a sister of Gerrebrant Van Houten of Totowa (plate 152). They had two children: Adriaen, b. 1746,* and Derrick, b. 1749* and bap. at Hackensack. They undoubtedly settled in the Stynmets house about 1768, if not earlier in the 1750s, and probably built the south unit of the house at this time. Halmagh Sip died about 1807 at an advanced age. His son Adriaen[5] Sip and wife Gerretje were probably the parents of: twins Metje and Gerretje, b. 1763*; Jannetje, bap. 1767; John A. Sip, b. June 6, 1775* and bap. June 15th*; Annatje, bap. 1781; and Halmagh, b. 1784* (the family Bible is not clear as it merely lists various births without stating the parents; it will be noted that four of these six children were recorded in the Bible, and one of the four with the two others are given as Adriaen's children in the Acquackanonk Church records). Halmagh[6] Sip, Jr., b. Oct. 22, 1784,* d. Jan. 28, 1855, aged 71 years, 3 months, and 6 days,* married at Acquacka-nonk March 30, 1806* Margaret Linford, b. Aug. 7, 1791,* d. Nov. 19, 1852, aged 62 years, 3 months and 12 days.* It is probable that he was called "Jr." because his grandfather was still alive at the time of his marriage, rather than because he had a father or an uncle of the same name. Halmagh inherited and occupied the Stynmets —Sip house and farm, and undoubtedly built the north unit of the house. Here his daughter Charity[7] Sip was born Nov. 11, 1820,* and baptized the following Janu-ary, d. Aug. 10, 1896,* married at Passaic Feb. 28, 1839* Richard Romaine, b. Dec. 1820,* d. Dec. 17, 1891.* They lived at Rochelle Park. After the death of her father, the house was no longer occupied by members of the family. She inherited the prop-perty and left it to her son Helmas Romaine, b. Sept. 8, 1840,* d. Nov. 20, 1896. His daughter, Mrs. Kate Romaine Roberts, sold the place about 1900 to Henry Muth, whose widow is the present owner.

The growth of this house is interesting. The original house is the small unit at the rear. It has unusually thick stone walls covered with clapboard, and very low ceilings, over which is a gable roof with no overhang. Like most of the very early houses it faces south. It was undoubtedly built by Christoffel Stynmets in the 1690s. The next unit was erected at right angles to it on the river end, about the middle of the eighteenth century; it is built of roughly cut and dressed stone. The post-revolu-tionary unit was added at the north; it is built of well-dressed stone and is much larger; the Dutch stoop with its swelling columns is interesting. Note how the size of the house, the height of the ceilings and the size of the windows increase with each later unit. The lean-to at the rear of the original house dates from the middle of the

516

---

* Taken from family Bible.

nineteenth century. The house stands on the west bank of the Passaic River, south of Mineral Brook Road and of the Union Avenue Bridge.

Van Dien House
Fairfield Road, Mountain View, Passaic County
PLATE 150

The date 1706 is to be seen in a stone on the east side of this house. It is supposed to stand on a tract of land granted to a Van Dien in 1704. It is probably on the south end of the large tract purchased from the Indians and patented to Schuyler and his associates in 1695, and they may have sold a portion to Van Dien shortly afterwards. The last owner in the family was Peter Van Dien, his wife was Dorcas Kiersted, and his father was James Van Dien. The estate of Peter Van Dien subdivided and sold the farm for building lots fifty-five or seventy years ago. The house is marked but unnamed on Erskine's Revolutionary map. There is an old family Bible owned by a Van Dien widow of a closely related branch of the family, but unfortunately the author could not obtain access to it.

The house is typical of its early date, built of rough fieldstone, one room in depth, with small window openings, and a gable roof with almost no overhang. There was formerly a stone wing on the west end. The house has been owned since 1909 by Miss Rilla Budd. It stands on the southeast side of Fairfield Road between the Pompton-Newark Turnpike and the railway, in the village of Mountain View. Fairfield Road is a Revolutionary road running along the southeast bank of the Passaic River, connecting Two Bridges, where the Dey house stands (plate 161), with the roads to Pompton, to Preakness, and to Totowa.

Van Giesen—Vreeland House
Chestnut Street, Nutley, Essex County
PLATE 151

The English settled only in the southern portion of their Newark Purchase and sold a large part of the land at the north end of the tract to Dutchmen from nearby Acquackanonk and Bergen. Among these were the Van Giesens and Vreelands. Rynier Bastiensen[1] Van Giesen emigrated to this country and settled at Flatbush on Long Island, where in 1660 the officials of the Dutch Church engaged him as schoolmaster, court messenger, reader, and for other duties pertaining to this office. In 1663 he sold his Flatbush land to Jan Strycker and removed to Bergen, where he was Voorlezer and where he died May 15, 1707; he had five sons and three daughters. Among them was Abraham[2] Van Giesen, b. Nov. 13, 1666 at Bergen, d. July 19,

1753 and buried at Acquackanonk; he was married at Bergen by his father, Voorlezer Van Giesen, before the congregation in the presence of the court, on Oct. 25, 1691 to Fitje Andriesse of Communipaw. He settled in northern Essex County, and was selected judge of the county in 1715. In his will he left the plantation on Third River on which he lived to his sons Andries and Isaac, and left to his sons Rynier and Andries land north of the former's home, which recently belonged to the testator's brother Johannes, deceased, and to all of his four sons (the above three and Abraham) he left tracts in Morris County.

It is claimed that the house on the bank of the Third River in Nutley was built by Abraham Van Giesen in 1702 and lettering to this effect has lately been cut in a stone by the door; on an 1850 map the house is stated to have been built in 1700. It is possible that Abraham Van Giesen lived for a time on the Third River near the Passaic River, although Nelson and Folsom (both authorities) state that he lived at Stone House Plains in Montclair Township, which is further inland and through which the Third River also runs. A photograph of the stone house there, which was supposed to have been built by him and which had a cornerstone marked "A. V. G.," may be seen in Folsom's *Bloomfield Old and New*. A study of the land records may ascertain the builder of the house at Nutley.

The later ownership is also obscure. The house remained in the possession of the Van Giesen family until confiscated during the Revolution from Tory Van Giesen. This Tory is believed to be Abraham Van Giesen, but there were many Abrahams. Abraham[2] Van Giesen, Sr. (1666-1753) had four sons: Rynier, bap. Oct. 1, 1694 at Bergen, had a son Capt. Abraham of Newark who was prominent during the Revolution; Andries married May 26, 1727 Martje Dirkje, and died in Essex County intestate, when letters of administration on his estate were granted Sept. 24, 1753 to his only son Abraham Van Giesen, Jr.; Isaac lived at Second River, where he married Lea Spier and had a son Abraham born in 1747; Abraham Abrahamse, b. Nov. 13, 1702 at Bergen, lived at Acquackanonk where in 1733 he married Antje Dirckse, and he is probably the Abraham, widower of Acquackanonk, who in 1769 remarried at Second River. As Rynier's son Abraham was a patriot, as Isaac lived at Second River and Abraham Abrahamse at Acquackanonk, by process of elimination Tory Abraham of Third River was probably the son of Andries. It will be noted that Andries had inherited half of his father's homestead plantation on Third River, and he may have continued to reside here. His only son Abraham[4] Van Giesen, b. May 18, 1728, married at Second River in 1751 Maria Van Voorst.

Michael[4] Vreeland (b. about 1716, d. by 1804), was a son of Dirck Vreeland of Acquackanonk. He settled on Third River in Newark Township, now Nutley, and made his will here in 1782. He married Aeltie Van Giesen, b. 1728, daughter of Johannes and granddaughter of Bastien Van Giesen. They had an only son and three daughters. Their son John M.[5] Vreeland, b. May 31, 1755, d. 1821, inherited his father's home, saw mill and building mill on the Third River, and added to his estate in 1783, by purchasing from Capt. Speer the homestead confiscated from Tory Van Giesen. He married Jannetje, daughter of John Speer of Belleville and sister of Capt. John Speer, Jr.; she died in 1845, aged 80 years. They moved into the old Van Giesen house on the west bank of the Third River, and had four sons, Ralph, Michael, John and Abraham, and daughters. Ralph inherited land on the Kingsland Road near the Essex County border, and the others the homestead property. Abraham[6] Vreeland, b. 1791, d. March 3, 1860, married in 1817 Elizabeth, daughter of John Mason, and had one son and five daughters. Abraham had inherited the west half of his father's home (the Van Giesen stone house), and lived here until 1838 when he built another house, later his son's. His only son Warren[7] Vreeland was born in 1822 in the old stone house and lived here the first twenty years of his life; his grandmother Jannetje (Speer) Vreeland had lived here the last twenty years of her life. The house was still owned by Warren Vreeland in 1906, although not occupied by him. The Woman's Club of Nutley was organized in 1911. It leased the Vreeland homestead and later purchased it, using it for a clubhouse.

The Woman's Club have successfully restored the homestead. It is a long low stone house, consisting of a hallway with one room on either side. The gable roof with no overhang is characteristic of the early period, as are the small windows. Low exposed beams, old doors, cupboards, and steep stairway remain. In the restoration, two stones on either side of the main door were dated: "A. V. G. 1702," "I. V. L. 1783," "A. V. L. 1821," "W. V. L. 1883," to represent the various owners: Abraham Van Giesen who is claimed to have built it in 1702, John Vree Land who bought it in 1783, Abraham Vree Land who inherited it in 1821, and Warren Vreeland who presumably bought out the other heirs in 1883. The house is in the center of Nutley on the north side of Chestnut Street and on the west bank of the Third River, which is not more than a brook at this point.

House of Gerrebrant Van Houten
Totowa Avenue, Paterson, Passaic County
PLATE 152

The ancestor of the builder of this house was Roeloff Cornelissen[1] Van Houten, who emigrated in 1638 to Rensselaerswyck. He married there Gerritje, daughter of Cornelis Van Nes, and later settled at Amersfoort on Long Island. Their son Hellemeg Roelofse,[2] bap. 1648 at New Amsterdam, d. 1729, settled at Slooterdam on the

Passaic River. His son Dirck[3] Van Houten (1687-1769) removed to Totowa soon after he married Metje Gerrebrantse in 1711. The Totowa Patent for land on the northwest side of the Passaic River south of Paterson was granted in 1696 to George Willocks; it changed hands and later came into the possession of Anthony Brockholst, whose heirs sold one-fourth of the patent on Sept. 26, 1715 and Oct. 29, 1724 to Dirck Van Houten. He built a stone house on the northwest side of Totowa Avenue, on the site of which stands a post-revolutionary house known as the Benson homestead. Dirck willed a part of his Totowa tract north of his own house to his son Gerrebrant[4] Van Houten, b. about 1712 at Hoboken, d. by 1789. Gerrebrant married June 23, 1741 Jannetje Sip, born and living at Acquackanonk, daughter of Arie Sip and sister of Halmagh Sip, both of Acquackanonk (see plate 149), and had two sons and two daughters.

Gerrebrant Van Houten (according to Nelson) built the stone house (the present wing) still standing on the Passaic River by the brook. He was a farmer and a large landowner. He is said to have removed from Totowa and in 1769 to have built the east part of the Doremus house (recently torn down) on Water Street in Paterson, which was eventually inherited by his grandson Gerrebrant, b. 1770, son of his son Dirck. In 1783 Gerrebrant[4] Van Houten willed the house and farm of 150 acres where they resided at Totoway to his son Dirck. This Dirck, whose legal name was Richard G.[5] Van Houten, died Dec. 1, 1810, aged 68 years, 4 months, and 20 days. He married Marytje or Molly Van Rypen, daughter of Abraham Van Rypen, bap. 1747, d. May 25, 1816, and had eleven children. One of these was Abraham[6] Van Houten, b. March 23, 1778, married Dec. 22, 1803 Catharine, daughter of John Sip of Athenia. Dirck built a house adjoining his own on the southwest for his son Abraham when he married, and it was there that Abraham's son Richard (1812-1878) later lived; the house has disappeared only recently, and stood on the river in the present ball grounds.

Another of the sons of Dirck was Adriaen[6] Van Houten, b. March 2, 1784, d. July 27, 1855, married June 27, 1813 Margaret, daughter of John Doremus. It was this son who inherited his father's and grandfather's house. The Van Houten family at Totowa was so extensive that it was found necessary to distinguish the various members by attaching their mother's name to theirs; thus this Adriaen was known as "Molly's Yawn." A brook running through his farm by his house was consequently known as Molly's Yawn's Brook, and has been unthinkingly contracted to the present name, Molly Ann's Brook. Adriaen and Margaret had eleven children, doubtless all born here. Some of their relatives also lived or visited here, for Adriaen's sister Jannetje (b. 1775) married Peter Poulese, and their daughter Sophia was born here in 1810. Sophia later married John Outwater of Slooterdam, and their daughter Mrs. Jennie Benson is the present owner of the Benson homestead, on the site of the first Dirck Van Houten's house nearby.

About opposite the Dirck Van Houten—Benson property, the Passaic River makes a sharp bend eastward for a short distance, and it is on this stretch that the Gerrebrant Van Houten house stands and faces south toward the river, and near it runs Molly's Yawn's Brook. The brook and the house now stand in the West Side Park. When the house was built, the Totowa Road followed the bank of the river. About 1870 Totowa Avenue was straightened at this point, and now runs behind the house. This road connected the settlements at Paterson and Wagaraw with Preakness and Pompton. Gerrebrant Van Houten probably built his small stone house shortly after his marriage in 1741. The main part of the present house, covered by a broad gambrel roof, is post-revolutionary in character and was probably built by his son Dirck Van Houten.

Van Ness House
on the Passaic River, near Fairfield, Caldwell Township, Essex County
PLATE 153

Cornelis Hendricse[1] Van Ness emigrated to Beverwyck in 1642 and settled at Greenbush. He married Mayken Hendricks Burchgraeff, and secondly in 1664 Maritie Damen, as her third husband. After his second marriage, they lived in Albany and later in Schenectady. They both died shortly before 1682. Simon Van Ness was probably a son of the emigrant. He was admitted to the Dutch Church of Albany in 1683, and is supposed to have been living in Schenectady when it was destroyed in 1690. About 1692 he married Rachel, daughter of Melchert Van Deursen of Rensselaerswyck. They had three children: Anna, bap. 1693 at Albany (sponsors Hendrick and Catryn Van Ness; Hendrick was a son of Cornelis the emigrant), Cornelis and Engeltje, bap. respectively in 1695 and 1697 at New York. Simon Van Es of Albany, widower, married at New York Jan. 15, 1701 Hester de La Mater, bap. April 7, 1683 at Albany, daughter of Isaac Le Maitre and Cornelia Everts. As the baptisms of their children are not to be found, it is presumed that they removed to Horseneck, now Fairfield, in Essex County, shortly after their marriage. We know he was a resident of Essex County in 1710 and a farmer within the Newark jurisdiction in 1716. On May 1, 1701 he, Hans and Jan Spier and others bought from the Indians a large tract at Horseneck lying on the east side of the Passaic River and extending to the hills, and it is probably on this tract that he settled. In 1710 and 1717, he, John Le Maitre and a third party bought a large part of the Schuyler patent on the west side of the Pequannock River above Pompton Plains, on which some of his descendants later lived. The land around Fairfield is almost surrounded by a

521

large curve in the Passaic River which presumably suggested the old name of Horseneck. This territory had been bought up and settled under various patents given by the West Jersey and East Jersey Proprietors and was long in controversy. Simon accepted the terms of the proprietors and on Sept. 3, 1744 a deed of confirmation for his 300 acre tract was granted him by Alexander, Morris and Ogden, and commenced: "Whereas John Johnson and George Willocks, West Jersey Proprietors, granted to Simon Vanness of Essex County . . . the tract with other lands . . ." His property was divided in 1749 between his four sons and his sons-in-law Michael Cook and Cobey Jacobusse. Although Simon is not stated to be deceased in the above deed of 1744, it would seem to be his widow who was married secondly at Acquackanonk on Oct. 4, 1733 to Frans Spier, both being residents of the parish. Frans Spier also lived at Horseneck. She was his second wife and had died by 1767 when he made his will.

Simon[2] and Hester Van Ness probably had eight children: (1) Hendrick, the eldest son, who eventually settled at Pompton Plains. He married May 20, 1726 at Acquackanonk Catryntje Roelofs Jacobusse and had six children baptized at Acquackanonk and Second River between 1727 and 1748: Hester, Simon, Geertruy, Margriet, Cornelis and Annatie. A widower of Morris County, he married secondly Nov. 22, 1759 Jannatje Paulusse of Second River. (2) Isaac Van Ness of Horseneck, of whom more later. (3) Evert who married at Second River Sept. 1, 1736 Catryntje Cadmus of Second River and had four children baptized between 1738 and 1750: Thomas, Symon, Hester, and Engeltje. He lived at Little Falls and owned some of the paternal property at Fairfield. (4) Simon, whose wife may have been Cornelia, and who settled at Pompton. (5) Annatje (possibly a child of Simon's by his first wife) who married Gerrit Jacobusse and had a daughter Rachel, bap. 1727 at Second River. (6) (probably) Rachel who married Johannes Rycke and had a daughter Hester, bap. 1735 at Second River. (7) Fietje who married Cobus Jacobusse and had a son Roeloff, bap. 1735 at Second River. (8) Caty who was married on July 3, 1797 at Caldwell to Michael Cook of Morris County, who ran a mill on a branch of the Rockaway River at Montville.

The son Isaac[3] Van Ness married June 27, 1729, Neeltje Reike, both being recorded as residents of (the parish of) Acquackanonk. They are only known to have had two children, Petrus and Hester, bap. 1730 and 1732 respectively at Acquackanonk. Isaac Van Ness remained on his father's lands at Horseneck, now Fairfield, and bought more land adjoining his inheritance. He and his wife were living in 1756. Their only son, Petrus or Peter[4] Van Ness, b. Sept. 2, 1730, and bap. at Acquackanonk, married Hendrica Pier and had a daughter Neeltje, bap. 1756, and a son Isaac. The house on the Passaic River near Fairfield is marked on Erskine's

Revolutionary map as the home of Capt. Van Ness. Peter Van Ness must be the one referred to. His son Isaac married Sarah Jacobus, and had two sons Isaac and Henry. Henry J.⁶ Van Ness, b. Oct. 1812, d. 1888, married Phebe Ann Spear. He was a member of the Dutch Church of Fairfield, and owned a cider mill and farm adjoining his ancestral home on the west, his farm undoubtedly being a part of the homestead tract. His brother Isaac J.⁶ Van Ness owned and continued to occupy "The Old Homestead," as it was always referred to. He was still living here in 1884. His daughter married Henry Francisco, and was the owner in 1906. She sold the house shortly after this to Tom Pier, but the title was not cleared until she died a few years ago. The house is now run as the Orchard Club Restaurant.

The house stands on the south side of the road running along the south bank of the Passaic River. It is between Pier Lane and Grand View Avenue in Caldwell Township, west of Singac and east of Fairfield and Two Bridges, in the northwest corner of Essex County.

Van Wagening House
formerly on River Drive, Passaic, Passaic County
PLATE 154

The ancestor of the Van Wagening, Van Wagoner, Garritson and Garrison families was Gerrit Gerritse, who emigrated from Wageningen in Gelderland in 1660 on the *Faith* with his wife and son. He settled at Communipaw in the town of Bergen. He was one of the patentees of Acquackanonk in 1685, but sold his interest in 1699. His son Hermanus Gerritse², bap. March 10, 1667, married Oct. 6, 1690 Annetje, daughter of Waling Jacobs (Van Winkle). By 1693 his father-in-law leased to Hermanus a tract of land in Acquackanonk (later called Passaic) on the Passaic River east of the King's Highway, and opposite the drawbridge, the property to be retained by the survivor. His son Gerrit Hermanisse³ Van Wagening inherited his father's interest in Acquackanonk. On Oct. 3, 1713 he married Annetje Sip, born in Bergen and bap. 1693 in New York, daughter of Jan Adriaensen Sip, owner of the house in Bergen (plate 107). They had six children.

Gerrit Van Wagening made his will in 1769 shortly before he died; he devised to his son Hermanus the land where he (the son) dwelt, and to his son Johannis the land where he (the testator) dwelt with the building, stating that if Johannis did not marry the land was to revert to Hermanus at Johannis' death; Gerrit also mentioned his daughters and his second wife Sarah. The younger son Johannis⁴ Van Wagenen, b. Nov. 18, 1728, died unmarried in 1770-71. He occupied the old Van Wagening homestead at the Passaic Bridge. The first bridge had been built here over the Passaic River in 1766. His older brother Hermanus⁴ Van Wagenen, b.

Feb. 4, 1717, d. by 1794, married Dec. 29, 1741 Geertruy Van Houten of Totowa. He lived at the Notch, but inherited all his father's lands on the death of his brother. Hermanus left his property to his sons Ruleff and Garret. The family name later became standardized to Van Wagoner. It is not known when the family sold the house. It was owned by Judge Simmons about 1880, later was a part of the Henry P. Simmons estate, and recently belonged to the Newport Chemical Company. It has been torn down since the photograph was taken in 1925.

The house was in two units, built of rough cut stone and with huge adzed beams, each unit being covered by a gable roof extending to form an overhang. It has been stated that the house was built in 1778, but construction places it in the middle of the eighteenth century. It is also doubtful whether Hermanus Van Wagenen, who inherited it in 1771, ever removed here, consequently its erection at this later time is rather improbable. Erskine's Revolutionary map shows Lashley's Tavern opposite the bridge, so it is possible that Hermanus leased it as a tavern. The small wing was undoubtedly an earlier unit; it consisted of two adjoining rooms each with its separate outside door, an arrangement so characteristic of the earliest houses. It is possible that this was the home of Hermanus Gerritse, and that his son Gerrit built the main house about the middle of the eighteenth century. The house stood until after 1925 on the corner of River Drive and Gregory Avenue, opposite the bridge over the Passaic River leading to Hackensack and other settlements.

House of John Van Winkle
868 Goffle Road, Hawthorne, Passaic County
PLATE 155

The ancestor of the family was Jacob Walingen, who emigrated to this country by 1639, probably from the village of Winkel in North Holland. He died in the summer of 1657, and his widow Tryntje Jacobs married three times before she died May 11, 1677. Their son Symon Jacobse[2] Van Winckel, bap. Aug. 24, 1653 at New York, died 1728-32, married at Bergen Dec. 15, 1675 Annatje Sip of New York, sister of Jan Adriaensen Sip, owner of the house at Bergen (plate 107). He was allotted two tracts in the Acquackanonk patent of 1685, and settled on the west side of the Passaic River in the present Passaic, near the Van Wagenings to the north and the Sips to the south (plates 154 and 149). His son Simeon[3] Van Winkle, bap. Aug. 6, 1686, d. 1775, lived several miles further north near the ford at the Bogt on the west side of the Passaic River (now the eastern part of Paterson). His house of whitewashed stone was often referred to in deeds as the White House; it was torn down in 1828. He had twenty children by his two wives.

John S.[4] Van Winkle, b. 1723, was a son by the first wife, Prientje Van Giesen, daughter of Abraham Van Giesen, probable owner of the house at Third River in Essex County (plate 151). On Feb. 9, 1730 Richard Ashfield sold a tract at Wagaraw to Gerrit Gerritse, who on June 8, 1743 sold 212½ acres to Simeon Van Winkle of Essex County; on Oct. 26, 1774 Simeon Van Winkle, shortly before he died, deeded to his son John the 212½ acre tract where John was then living at Wagaraw. Wagaraw was the name of the region above the most northerly bend of the Passaic River, north of the present Paterson. The settlement in the northern part of Wagaraw along the Wagaraw or Goffle Brook came to be called the Goffle. It was here that John S. Van Winkle settled some time between 1743 and 1774. The old part of the present house is said to have been built by him in 1761. On Dec. 5, 1746 at Acquackanonk he married Janneke Ryerson of New York, and had two sons. He deeded the Wagaraw tract to his son Simeon on May 24, 1783, but lived many years longer, and probably continued to occupy his home until he died in January, 1816. His son Simeon J.[5] Van Winkle, b. Dec. 12, 1749, d. Nov. 4, 1828 aged 78 years, 10 months and 22 days,* married Claesje, daughter of Cornelis Gerritse. Although his father deeded him the Wagaraw homestead, he did not reside here; he was known as Simeon of the Bogt, and lived at Riverside in a stone house destroyed about 1880.

Simeon's son Judge John S.[6] Van Winkle, b. Nov. 13, 1784,* lived on his grandfather's place at the Goffle and built the main part of the present house in 1811. He ran a grist mill here. On March 24, 1805* he married Jannetje, daughter of Pieter Kip, b. Jan. 14, 1788.* He and his wife were foully murdered the night of Jan. 9, 1850 by John Johnson, an English farm hand, whom Judge Van Winkle had sympathetically released from jail, where he had been lodged on some complaint. This murder is still the theme of conversation in the district. Their surviving son Cornelius[7] Van Winkle, b. Sept. 9, 1806,* d. May 26, 1873,* married May 31, 1826* Catrina Leah Van Dean, b. March 4, 1809.* They lived at the Goffle, at Riverside, and later in Paterson. The place at the Goffle was inherited by their only son Simon Peter[8] Van Winkle, b. July 6, 1831,* married Oct. 10, 1852* Maria Ackerman; they lived, however, at Paterson. Their daughter Jennie[9] Van Winkle married Aaron Van Houten of Passaic, and the property at the Goffle was sold by her estate about 1901. It was purchased by Thomas Arnold, whose son Ivan Arnold is the present owner. Until the Arnolds purchased it, the house had been occupied for many years by farm hands, tenants of the Van Winkles.

It has been stated that Judge Van Winkle replaced his grandfather's old house in 1811 by a larger stone dwelling. But the present wing certainly dates from his grandfather's time, and it is probable that the wing formed the whole of the early house, and that Judge Van Winkle greatly enlarged it rather than tearing down

525

* Taken from family Bible.

some of it. The old wing was built by John Van Winkle at some time after his marriage in 1746 and before 1774; the date 1761 has been ascribed to it. The old house is built of rough stone laid in irregular courses, and is covered by a steep gable roof extending in front to form an overhang. The main house has a cornerstone dated 1811; it is characteristic of the period, built of well-dressed stone, and covered by a gambrel roof which has a beautiful curving slope. The main house contains unusually beautiful specimens of carved woodwork of the period and a panelled overmantel. The house is on the northwest side of the Goffle Road, on the opposite side of which runs the Goffle Brook. It stands at the foot of the Goffle Hill Road leading to Sicomac and the Ponds settlements, and is less than two miles north of the north bend of the Passaic River.

Unidentified House
534 East Passaic Avenue, Bloomfield Township, Essex County
PLATE 156

Nothing is known of this house, which is now occupied by uneducated foreign tenants. The house is probably within the region formerly known as Stone House Plains. It is near the east bank of the Third River in Bloomfield Township, southeast of the village of Brookdale and just over a mile south of the Essex County border. It is on a bend in the present East Passaic Avenue on its west side. Early in the eighteenth century the Dutch moved southwards from Acquackanonk and settled along the Third River in the vicinity of the present Nutley and Brookdale. It is probable that the house belonged to the Kierstead family in the third quarter of the nineteenth century. Who owned it before then is not known; Christopher Mandeville lived in this vicinity in 1839, but may not have occupied this particular house. The house was undoubtedly built in the first half of the eighteenth century. It is of rough stone covered by a gable roof.

Houses in Hunterdon County

Fitts House
Stanton
PLATE 157

Nothing is known of this house other than that it is called the Fitts homestead. On a map of the county made in 1873, the house is marked J. L. Fitts. How long it was in the possession of this family is unknown. The date 1741 is on a small stone in the east corner. This is undoubtedly the date of erection of the house, but tradition does not suggest the name of the builder. The house is built of irregular stone partly whitewashed. It is covered by a wide gambrel roof, the upper slope of which is continued over two small dormers. The windows are unusual, being long and very narrow; no others like these have been found in the territory covered by this volume. The flat stone archheads of the door, garret window and cellar window are characteristic of various houses in West Jersey. The house has unusually high ceilings for this early date, but its massive exposed beams, hand pegging, old shutters and old window glass are evidences of its age.

The house is northeast of the Stanton village crossroads on a back lane to Whitehouse. The present country lane skirts along the highlands of the valley; in the mid-nineteenth century the road followed the northeast bank of Chambers Brook (now Pleasant Run). A private road goes down the hill from the lane, crossing Pleasant Run inside the property, to the house which is on the southern side of the stream. This back lane to Whitehouse is best known as the road to the "Bandbox House," an unusual whitewashed stone structure built by a Quaker in 1808; it has no corners, and its pure oval shape suggests its nickname of a bandbox.

Howsel—Wagoner House
Stanton
PLATE 158

On Erskine's Revolutionary map this house is marked William Howzel's. As this was an early family in this locality, it is probable that the house was built by one of its members. The Indian deed of June 27, 1703 to the West Jersey Proprietors for land on the Raritan River west of the Division Line, covered 150,000 acres, most of the present Hunterdon County. The West New Jersey Society, a stock company, was organized in London in 1691; the Society made extensive purchases and had 91,000 acres surveyed for them in June 1711. This tract became known as West Jersey's Great Tract in Hunterdon Co. The policy of the Society at first was to lease farms to settlers; in 1735 98 families were lessees, of whom one was Gasper Hawshill who had 150 acres. It is possible that he was a member of the family in question. There were quite a few German settlements scattered through the county; at Lebanon nearby, Germantown (now Oldwick) to the north, and still further north Long Valley, formerly known as German Valley.

The German name of Hausschild was gradually simplified to Housel. The following are a few scattered references to this name: in 1730 Jacob Houselt and in 1744 Matthias Houshilt were naturalized; in 1735 Gasper Hawshill was leasing 150 acres in Hunterdon County; in the Dutch church at Readington were baptized in 1736 Peter, son of Johannis and Neeltje Housel, and in 1744 Marten, son of Jacob and Catharina Houselt; Jacob Hausschild and his wife Anna had two sons,

William, b. 1784, and John b. 1786, both baptized in 1786 at the German Reformed Church of Alexandria; Johannes Houshell of Amwell Twp. made his will in 1761, as did his brother Jacob, and also a brother Mathias in 1778.

From a series of maps, we find that William Howzel owned the house in question during the Revolution, W. Wagner in 1852, W. Wagoner (probably the same man) in 1860, and A. Lowe in 1873. The owner of the house evidently held the leadership of the community, for the village at various times was called Mt. Pleasant, Housel's, and Wagoner's Hill. It was finally named Stanton, after Lincoln's Secretary of War. The Revolutionary William Howsel may be the one whose will was probated in 1809. The Wagoner family who owned the house in the middle of the nineteenth century was undoubtedly also of German origin. Shortly after the Civil War the house passed through several hands. It has been owned since 1925 by W. E. Wayman, who has been very much interested in restoring it.

A veritable community of stone houses stands on this farm. The old stone barn is dated 1741; new trim now hides the stone in part so that only the century figures show. This is a good approximate date for the erection of the farm buildings. The one and a half story stone house is built on a hill slope and has a full basement story at the rear. The ceilings are low in the basement and of medium height on the main floor. The different floor levels in the basement are probably due to its gradual improvement at various times. The kitchen is here, lighted by very small windows, and a cold spring has been piped to an adjoining closet room. The house has many wall and corner cupboards, and all forms of old hinges. There was formerly a Dutch oven on each end of the house, but they were torn down about twenty years ago. The brick archheads of the windows are interesting. The colonial doorway and benches at the entrance are modern pieces of work, but blend very well. A broad gable roof covers the house and is unbroken by dormers. The house has been recently repainted, but the very irregular stonework still shows to advantage. On the east end is a wing which is of later date, although its ceilings are lower than the main house and its windows smaller. This wing was formerly covered with long red shingles secured by hand-made nails; they were removed and the wing has been clapboarded and painted white. The old barn is similarly built of irregular stone. About fifty years ago it was used as a blacksmith shop, and the central third of the side by the road was cut out up to the rafters for a large entrance way, so that wagons could pass straight through. This section has been rebuilt and a small window inserted, but the lines can be seen easily. A frame addition was made at some later period on the end of the barn toward the house, thus tying it architecturally with the main house. Near the frame wing of the house stand two small stone structures, one of which is the stone spring house. The other is the kitchen of a small two story house, which was torn down recently, and which consisted of only one room on each floor. It is unusual to find two houses on the same property. The theory is that this was the temporary structure in which the family lived while the main house was being erected. As a two story building requires the hewing of good-sized beams and a great deal of labor, it is more likely that this house was built for permanent use, possibly by another member of the family. The hillside at the rear has been utilized to great advantage by the present owners in the formation of very attractive terraces and gardens. It is interesting to compare the similarity and yet subtle differences between this German house and the Dutch houses of the period.

The house is on the south side of the road, west of the four corners of Stanton village. Behind it is Round Mountain, and in front lies Round Valley. The road on which the house stands is a pre-revolutionary road leading from Raritan and Readington in a general westerly direction, crossing the road to Coryell's Ferry over the Delaware and the road to Whitehouse, skirting Round Valley, then crossing the South Branch of the Raritan River at the present village of Hamden, and finally passing north of the settlement at Pittstown to Johnson's Forge, now called Bloomsbury.

Reynolds—Van Syckel House
Van Sickle's, near Clinton
PLATE 159

Although the actual builder of this house was an Englishman, his ownership was of short duration, and the house has been in the hands of a Dutch family ever since, thus warranting its inclusion in a book on Dutch houses and Dutch families. A stone on the southwest corner above the first story window is marked "D.R.: 1763: A   ," standing for the initials of the builder and the date of erection: David Reynolds 1763 Anno. Thus we know that Reynolds built this large two story stone house over a decade before the Revolution. He conducted it as a tavern. Evidently he did not have much faith in the American cause as he was a counterfeiter of Continental money at the beginning of the Revolution. He was caught and speedily hanged. His family ran the tavern for a short while after his death. By the time Erskine's Revolutionary maps were being made (1778-79), a man named Buskirk kept the tavern, and was running it until 1800. That year Aaron Van Sykel, Sr., bought the hostel, and he and his son continued to conduct it as a tavern. It is still in the possession of the Van Syckel family.

Their ancestor Ferdinand[1] Van Sycklin emigrated to America in 1652. When he took the oath of allegiance in Flatlands in 1687, he registered that he had been in the country for 35 years. He later removed to Gravesend, where he died about 1712. About 1660 he married Eva, daughter of Antonis Jansen Van Salee, and had eight children. His grandson Reinier[3] Van Syckelen, Jr., left Long Island and settled in the upper Raritan valley before 1723. By his wife Henah he had a son Reinier[4] Van Syckel, born in Hunterdon County, N. J., bap. Nov. 17, 1723 in the Dutch church at Readington. About 1746 he married Maayke or Mercy Langstraat, and had ten children according to their family Bible. He was a farmer and owned 304 acres in Hunterdon Co. In his will dated 1802, he styled himself a resident of Kingwood Township, in southern Hunterdon Co., and left the plantation of 240 acres on which he then dwelt to his son Aaron.

This son Aaron[5] Van Syckel, Sr., spent his whole life in Hunterdon County, where he was born July 8, 1764 and died Nov. 28, 1838. In 1800 he bought the Reynolds tavern, and in 1802 was already domiciled here, in what was then part of Bethlehem Township. He built a store opposite the tavern, and ran both with the aid of his Aaron, Jr., when he grew old enough to help. It was the best-known tavern in Aaron, Sr.'s, day en route to Schooley's Mt., the health resort of the time. Aaron was very wealthy, and a large landowner, farming his lands. He was the High Sheriff of the county. About 1785 he married Catharine Opdyke, b. Aug. 11, 1762, d. Sept. 9, 1851, and had eight children. Their son Aaron[6] Van Syckel, Jr., b. May 26, 1793 in Hunterdon Co., bap. with his five brothers March 3, 1800 in the German Church of Alexandria, married Nov. 30, 1816 Mary, daughter of Joseph Bird, and followed his grandfather's footsteps in raising a family of ten children. He continued to conduct his father's tavern and store until 1855, when he discontinued the store and the tavern also shortly afterwards. His son Joseph[7] Van Syckel, b. June 18, 1818, married first June 16, 1842 Catharine I. Smith (1823-1855), and second Feb. 9, 1858 Cyrena Martin, b. March 5, 1830. He was a farmer, merchant and banker. He had two children by each marriage but only his daughter Kate survived him. Kate[8] Van Syckel, b. Aug. 11, 1860, married Sept. 10, 1889 Robert S. Martin. Mrs. Martin still owns the ancestral tavern. It is unoccupied. Her family reside in a house next door.

The tavern is a two story structure built of irregular, random-laid stone and covered with a gable roof. Brick arches top the door and windows of the first story, and narrow flat-brick lintels the windows above. The house stands on the bank of a stream probably to obtain plenty of clear drinking water for the patrons of the hostel. The hamlet of Van Sickle's is six miles northwest of Clinton. The tavern is on the east side of its only street, a pre-revolutionary route up the Musconetcong River to Hackettstown, or southward to Pittstown and Coryell's Ferry over the Delaware River.

House of Martin Ryerson, later Quick's
near Three Bridges, Readington Township
PLATE 160

The builder of this house was named for his grandfather Martin Ryerszen, who emigrated from Amsterdam about 1646 and settled at Breuckelen. There on May 14, 1663 he married Annetje, daughter of Joris Jansen de Rapelje, b. Feb. 8, 1646 in Breuckelen. Her parents were among the original settlers of New Netherland, crossing in the first ship, and her sister was the first white girl born here. Their son Joris Martinse² Ryerse was a farmer in New York City and later in Bergen County, New Jersey. By his first wife Hannah Schouten, widow of Teunis Dey, he had ten children. One of these was Mary³ Ryerson, bap. July 19, 1699 in New York City, d. 1774, married Nov. 30, 1720 John Reading (1686-1767). Her husband rose to political prominence, acting as Governor of the Province of New Jersey. About 1715 they settled on the South Branch of the Raritan River near Flemington on their estate, *Walnut Grove*, where they died.

Col. Martin³ Ryerson, bap. Oct. 9, 1698 at New York City, followed his brother-in-law John Reading to Hunterdon County and settled on the South Branch of the Raritan River on the opposite bank—the north bank. The land here in the curve of the South Branch was a part of the Lotting Purchase, the Indian deed of June 20, 1708. Martin is said to have joined the Dutch Church at nearby Readington in 1726; he was on the building committee for the new church in 1738 and a deacon in 1744. He may not have settled here until about 1737, as the birthplace of his eldest child in 1736 is unknown, whereas his eight other children were baptized at Readington from 1738 to 1755. Unfortunately there is no dated stone on the house, but Martin Ryerson probably built it at the time of his removal here, 1726-37. He became very prominent in judicial, military and church circles, was an excellent surveyor, a Colonel in the King's Militia, and a Judge of the Court of Common Pleas. He acquired from time to time large tracts in West Jersey which may have proved his undoing, for on Dec. 13, 1771 a petition was presented to the Governor's Council setting forth his good character and distressed circumstances, and praying that he might be relieved by the legislature. The desired relief was not afforded him. It is possible that there was a forced sale of his estate as his wife and three of their sons removed 1772-75 to a tract of her mother's at Myrtle Grove in Sussex County. He is said to have died before his family's removal; administration was granted on his estate Sept. 2, 1790. His wife was Catharine Coxe (Cockas or Cock), bap. Jan. 2, 1713 at Kingston, daughter of Thomas Cock and Elinor Ashfordby.

The Ryerson farm was bought by Tunis Quick about 1790, and remained in the possession of his family for almost a century. Tunis Quick, b. April 11, 1762, d. May 4, 1836, was a son of Col. Abraham Quick of Ten Mile Run, Somerset County, and his wife Matilda Wyckoff. A brother of his, Abraham Quick, Jr., settled in the house near North Branch (plate 135). Tunis married Alletta, daughter of Jacques Voorhees, b. June 20, 1766, d. Feb. 10, 1845. Two daughters of theirs were baptized in 1786 and 1787 at Six Mile Run Church, so they had not removed to the South Branch at this time. Tunis was a farmer and a miller. In early life he had mills near the New Brunswick Water Works. He later established mills on the Ryerson farm near Flemington, and the place became known as Quick's Mills. When he died here he owned about 1,000 acres. At one time he was a Major in the militia. His son Jacques Voorhees Quick was born Nov. 10, 1793, no doubt shortly after the family had removed to the Ryerson farm, as he was baptized Jan. 19, 1794 in the Dutch church of nearby Readington. He continued to operate the mill, which was on the south side of the river. Three mortgages, given by Jacques V. Quick, Jr., in 1855, suggest a family arrangement whereby he had control of the property subject to a life annuity to his father, who died about 1876 in Flemington. On Jan. 24, 1870 J. V. Quick sold to George W. Bateman a tract of 129½ acres with the farm buildings thereon, and also a wood lot. He disposed of it the same year to George A. Rae. The latter's executors sold the property in March 1895 to J. Smith Richardson, and the present owner is his granddaughter, Miss Edith Jones of Elizabeth, who makes her summer home here.

The three units of the house were erected at different times. The main house, which is the central portion, was built by Martin Ryerson presumably about 1726-37. It is built of stone and is covered by a broad gambrel roof. The south front is faced with brick; the overhanging eaves are deeper on this side; the old fanlight here and the arched brickwork over the windows are interesting features. The large, old, twelve-pane windows remain on the north front. The house is flanked on either side by frame wings built by the Quick family. The east wing belongs to the post-revolutionary period and the two story west wing is somewhat later; it is probable that the former was added by Tunis and the latter by Jacques Quick. The interior of the house of Martin Ryerson conforms to the usual plan of rooms on either side of a wide hall. In the dining room, originally the kitchen, is a huge fireplace topped by a simple mantel shelf, and nearby was formerly a Dutch oven. The ceilings are of medium height with exposed beams. In the parlor there is a mantel of a simple early type. The garret of the house was open attic until twenty years ago, when it was improved and the dormers added. The house, surrounded by the fields of the farm, stands on the north bank of the South Branch River, in the curve of the river not far (as the crow flies) from Flemington Junction. It is in Readington Township, several miles west of the village of Three Bridges and an equal distance from Flemington.

Houses in Morris County

House of Thomas Dey
Two Bridges, Pequannock Township
PLATE 161

On June 6, 1695 a huge tract was obtained from the Indians by a company of associates, headed by Arent Schuyler, Brockholst, and Mandeville, extending from the Passaic River on the south up along both sides of the Pequannock River between the foothills on the east and west. They received a patent for it Dec. 2, 1696, and sold the lower end to Maurice Mourison. Derrick Dey probably bought from him and settled almost immediately in the extreme southeastern tip of the township, bounded on the east by the Pequannock River and on the south and west by the Passaic River. This locality early acquired importance, as the two rivers could be crossed separately before they joined to become the broad Passaic River just below. Here was one of the few bridges over the Passaic River before the Revolution.

Derrick Dey came from Wesel on the Passaic River (now eastern Paterson) and settled on a large farm at Pequannock. He also owned land on the east side of the Passaic nearby, mainly to the south; in 1730 he bought a triangular plot of 200 acres to the south from Peter Sonmans, in the deed to which he is styled Derrick Dey of Pachgannick. His house stood a few rods northwest of the present house; it was a stone building of great depth. On Dec. 11, 1736 at Hackensack he married Sarah, daughter of Thomas Laurensen Toers, and had two sons and five daughters. He died at the age of 91 years and was buried on the farm. His son John inherited his father's house and kept a public inn here; he married Jane Doremus on Dec. 19, 1771. In 1823 this older house was owned by Simeon Doremus. It burned down in 1846-47.

Thomas Dey, b. Dec. 8, 1747 and bap. at Hackensack, was an elder son of Derrick and Sarah. In 1779 he built his stone house adjoining his father, and recorded the date in iron figures across the front of the house (later taken off when a piazza was added). It is marked Thomas Dye on Erskine's Revolutionary map. He had a tannery nearby, also a fur hattery and a store. By his wife Abigail Lewis, Thomas had a daughter Sarah Dey, b. May 18, 1769, who married first Cornelius, son of Frans Post, and secondly a Mr. Hughes. Her only child Dirck Dey Post, b. May 6, 1791, was the father of C. Henry Post, who was born in the family homestead in 1820 and still owned it in 1900, dying a few years later. The house passed

533

to Henry's son Abram Post, whose widow sold it out of the family to McGlinn about 1917. The present owner is the Twin Rivers Club.

The house is the usual one and a half story structure, the front of dressed stone and the sides and rear of very irregular stone. The roof on both the wing and the main section has a steep gable and no overhang. Gables and porches now rather mar its appearance. The house is situated on the west bank of the Pompton River within a stone's throw of the junction of the two rivers, which are spanned by bridges, thus giving the name of Two Bridges to the small settlement.

Dodd House
near Chapel Hill Road, Lincoln Park
PLATE 162

This house undoubtedly stands on the huge tract which extended along both sides of the Pequannock River between the foothills on the east and west, which was bought by Arent Schuyler and associates from the Indians in 1695 and patented to them in 1696. The Dodd (Dod, Dods) family settled in the lower valley at an early date. This house on the brow of the hill is marked John Dodd on Erskine's Revolutionary map, and another stone house (still existing but greatly remodelled) on the corner in the village below is marked Dodd's Tavern. There was a prominent Dod-Dodd family which left Branford, Conn., and settled in Newark village in 1668 and on Watsessing Plain in 1679. There are only three generations of John Dodds recorded in this family, and all lived at Orange or Bloomfield, but it is probable that the Dodd family of Pequannock Township is in some way connected with the Newark family of the same name.

According to an old neighbor and relative, the house on the hill was owned before 1847 by John Dods and his wife Polly. Their daughter Lea Dodd married John Hennion, who acquired the house from his father-in-law. In the 1860s he sold it to William Maines. After Maines had owned it many years he sold it to his son-in-law Jesse Richards. His widow, née Maines, later married Mr. Salmon and sold the house about 1920 to Joseph Black, the present owner.

The house is built of roughly cut multi-colored fieldstone. The east wing is covered by a steep gable roof, its south slope extending in a straight line to form a deep overhang. Below are two old windows with the typical small lower sash. The main section of the house probably dates from the Revolutionary or post-revolutionary period; its ceilings are fairly high and it has interesting old cupboards and carved mantels, but a row of cheap modern dormers spoils its appearance. The house stands on the brow of a high hill overlooking the village and the Pompton River valley. It faces south on a lane which runs into the east side of Chapel Hill

534

Road, the present name for the road which traverses Pequannock Township, south-ward from Lincoln Park to Two Bridges. Beavertown was the former name for Lincoln Park.

House of Henry Doremus
Road to Boonton, near Towaco, Montville Township
PLATE 163

The exact date of purchase and settlement of the Doremus family in this neighborhood is not known, but the family became so numerous that the locality was long known as Doremustown. The ancestor of the family is Cornelis[1] Doremus who emigrated from Middleburg in the Province of Zeeland by 1687, and had settled at Wesel (now eastern Paterson) by 1708, and died about 1715. His son Thomas[2] Doremus, bap. April 11, 1687 at Bergen, settled near Cedar Grove on the Peckamin River, in Essex County. In 1743 he bought a tract of 727 acres lying east of the Bog and Vly, and deeded one third of it to his son Golyn in 1748, and the other thirds to his sons Abraham and John, all of whom settled on these tracts in Jacksonville, northeast of Towaco valley. There is no deed on record for the Towaco farm of Cornelis, still another son of Thomas Doremus, but it is probable that the latter bought a farm for this son also. Cornelis[3] Doremus, b. April 16, 1714 at Acquackanonk, d. March 8, 1803, married in 1738 Antje Yong, born in Morris County, daughter of Peter Yong of "Te Wechauw." Cornelis settled on a large farm in the Towaco valley less than two miles east of Montville. In 1745 the road was laid from Cornelius Doremus to Michael Cook's mill (in Upper Montville). Erskine's Revolutionary map shows that Cornelius' house was on the south side of the road. In his will of 1791 he styled himself a resident of Pequanack, the name then applied to the whole region in the southeastern corner of Morris County near the Pequannock and Passaic Rivers. By his wife Antje Yong, Cornelis had four sons and five daughters.

The eldest son, Henry[4] Doremus, b. Feb. 19, 1739, d. Feb. 10, 1817, married by license of Sept. 25, 1760 Peggy Van Winkel, both at that time of Morris County. Her brother John built the house at the Goffle (plate 155). Henry was a tanner on his father's farm at Wechauw until near the end of the Revolution when he sold out, and in 1782 bought a farm at Slooterdam near Wesel Bridge, where he lived. Cornelis' second son Capt. Thomas[4] Doremus, b. Aug. 4, 1740, d. May 9, 1810, married Sept. 20, 1764 Rachel Spier, b. Aug. 6, 1745, daughter of Cornelis Spier of the Notch. He lived in the house in Doremustown on the west bank of a stream and on the north side of the road to Boonton; his descendants recall that George Washington had his headquarters for a time in the east room of the ground floor and entertained his French officers in the orchard. As this is the house marked

Henry Doremus on Erskine's Revolutionary map, Thomas probably lived with his brother at that time and later purchased it from him. Capt. Thomas Doremus had five sons: Cornelis (1765-1859) married Lena Mandeville and lived in Doremustown in the building formerly occupied as a parsonage of the Montville Reformed Church, and on the death of his wife in 1846 removed to New York City; Petrus settled at Mountain View on the other side of the Pompton River, and Francis in New York City. The two remaining sons, Benjamin (1781-1828) and Johannes (1785-1828), remained at Doremustown and may have continued to occupy their father's homestead. Wilson Jacobus bought the property from a Doremus about 1840-50, and his son S. W. Jacobus, the present owner, was born here in 1858.

This valley was in early days referred to as Te Wechauw. The western end acquired the name of Doremustown from this numerous family descended from Cornelis Doremus, who had settled here in the first half of the eighteenth century. The name was later changed to Whitehall. The village nearby is now called Towaco, a corruption of the original name of the valley. The house stands on the north side of the road to Boonton, a scant mile west of Towaco village and east of the railway crossing.

Farmhouse, at one time Demarest's
Changebridge Road, Lower Montville
PLATE 164

The chain of ownership of this stone farmhouse is known back to Lawrence Demarest, who owned it about the end of the eighteenth century. Nothing is known of this Lawrence Demarest, but the house was probably not erected by his family. On Oct. 2, 1714 Humphrey Davenport of Kingston bought from Thomas Stevenson of West Jersey, a 750 acre tract on the east bank of the Rockaway River, extending east to the top of the mountain. He settled here and built south of the Demarest house. Among his children were John Davenport, Humphrey Davenport, Jr. who married in 1731 Elizabeth, daughter of Peter Hyler, and Rachel Davenport who married in 1733 Nicholas, son of Peter Hyler. The Hylers, Parlamans, and Davenports were amongst the earliest settlers of Lower Montville about 1716. Construction of the Demarest house shows it was built about 1720-30; as it seems to stand on the Davenport tract, it was probably built by one of the sons or sons-in-law of Humphrey Davenport.

In 1745 the road from Pompton Plains was laid out westward from the house of Cornelius Doremus in the Towaco Valley (see plate 163) to Michael Cook's mill in the present Upper Montville, and in 1749 the road was continued southward from his mill to the Rockaway River, and then down the river as the path ran to the bridge near John Davenport's. This was the important Rockaway Bridge at the time of the Revolution. The Changebridge Road is further east, but more or less parallels the road from Michael Cook's Mill; it commences nearer Cornelius Doremus' farm and ends near the Rockaway Bridge. From the west end of the bridge a road leads southward to Troy Hills, Whippany and Morristown; further north another road went southwestward from the road to the mill through the settlements of old Boonton and Parsippany, and eventually also reached Whippany. From the east end of the bridge a road runs eastward and was called the Road to Horseneck (the name given to the neck within the bend of the Passaic River in Essex County); it forked, one branch going on to Newark, and the other traversing the Neck to Two Bridges on the Pompton River. Jinning's Tavern was on the Road to Horseneck one mile east of Rockaway Bridge. These were the roads existing at the time of the Revolution, and still to be followed today, with the exception of the Old Boonton-Parsippany Road which is mainly beneath the reservoir. Thus we get an idea of the ramifications of the little community, of the importance of the Rockaway Bridge as a thoroughfare linking roads from all directions, and of the large territory dependent on the Dutch Church of Old Boonton (organized about 1756, and removed in 1818 to Lower Montville). A creek flows southward between the Road from Michael Cook's Mill and the Changebridge Road, and empties into the Rockaway River near the bridge. This creek with its valley was in early days called Uylekill, and lent its name to the settlement, later called Montville. The Changebridge Road obtained its name in the days of stage coaches, when the horses were changed near the bridge.

Thomas Doremus lived in the stone house over two miles away at Doremustown, which had been Washington's headquarters for a time (plate 163). He also owned the stone house at the lower end of the Changebridge Road near the Rockaway Bridge. He died in 1810; in his will dated 1809 he mentioned the latter house as the place he bought of Lawrence Demarest, and stated that it was to be sold and the money divided between his five sons. The property was sold to George Shepard. He was a lunatic; his guardians sold it to Helmah Mandeville, and he sold it to Dr. George Wurts. In 1829 it was sold by a judgment back to Mandeville, and by another judgment to William Meredith, whose executors sold it July 20, 1848 to Dr. Ezekiel Gaines. He sold it in 1857 to Daniel Howard. It was later owned by Alexander McNair, Jr., who sold the house and four acres on April 1, 1921 to Johannes Jacobus Broes Van Heekeren, a Hollander. His widow, Mrs. Van Heekeren, now owns it and runs a charming antique shop here.

The description of the property in the William Meredith deeds runs as follows: Beginning at a red oak tree formerly a corner of the land sold by John Salter to

Lawrence Demarest, also a corner of land sold by Robert Gould to said Demarest, in a line of lands belonging to John Doremus, then extending with his line north 88° to a stone on the west side of the road leading from Richard Duryea's tavern to Pompton Plains, thence along the west side of the road southward to a line of Richard Duryea's land, then north 86° by the lands of Silas Cook, Richard Duryea, and Christian Miller, then with Miller's line south 2 chains to Joan Morgan's corner, then with the line of his land and by Jacob Mourison's line north 87° to Mourison's corner, then north 14 chains with Peter Courter's line to the corner of the lands belonging to the heirs of Thomas Doremus deceased, then along various lines of their land, and along the land of John Doremus south 4° and then north 88°.

The house changed hands frequently but the many owners did little in the way of so-called improvements and the house remains practically in its original condition. A date 1714 scratched on a stone by the doorway is not original, but construction shows the house belongs to this early period and was probably built about 1720-30. It is built of roughly cut fieldstone; its steep gable roof has no overhang worthy of the name, and is unmarred by dormers. The interior consists of two rooms unequal in size, separated by a small hallway in which is an enclosed stairway. As it was unusual for the Dutch to build different sized rooms in this manner, it is possible that the door originally led immediately into one of the rooms, and that the other room adjoined it with no intervening hallway. The windows in front have the usual narrow lower sash, and the rear windows are very small in size; the floors slope unequally, the ceilings are very low, the mantel is of a very simple type, consisting of only a shelf; all these are characteristics of the early eighteenth century. The house is on the east side of the Changebridge Road, less than one mile south of the crossroad to the Dutch church; this section of Montville Township is known as Lower Montville.

House of Johannes Parlaman
Lower Montville
PLATE 165

Various units of this house have been built by different members of the Parlaman family. It is still owned by descendants of the original settler. Johannes, son of Jacob Berleman of Partenheim in Paltz, Germany, married Anna Catharina, daughter of Hans Wendel Hassenberger. In 1709 they declared their intention to emigrate to America, where they first settled at Hackensack and about 1714 on the Ramapo tract. Four of their children were born in Germany and six here in America. One of their elder sons is believed to be Walter[2] Parlaman, and his widow is supposed to be the Barber Parlaman who obtained the tract at Lower Montville.

John Reading, Deputy Surveyor General, took up a large tract on the Rockaway River about 1715. On March 23, 1736/7 Daniel Worms, cordwainer of Hanover, sold to Barber Parleman, spinster of Hanover, 100 acres on the Rockaway River, beginning at the river corner of John Miller's land, along his line north to his other corner, then north 42° east to another corner, then south to the river and up the river, the same 100 acre tract which had been sold to Daniel Worms by Michael Schurts (or Short) on April 14, 1730, and granted to Michael Schurts by John Reading Sept. 13, 1728 (deed recorded Oct. 8, 1804 Morris Co.). This deed shows us that Barber at this early date was already an unattached woman (in this case spinster is said to mean widow) and had already settled in Morris County (then Hanover Township, Hunterdon County). In 1736 (exact date not given, must be Old Style, 1737 in New Style) Barber Parlaman, widow, married Jacob Tymouth, widower, at the Pompton Plains Church. It is probable that she settled on her 100 acre purchase, and she may have built the first house here, which was a small one formerly on the south side of the road overlooking the river.

Barber's son Johannes' Parlaman, b. Aug. 18, 1730, was the first person after her to own the 100 acre tract. He undoubtedly built the early west unit of the house and possibly also the later east unit for one of his married children. Johannes Parlaman married at the Dutch Church of Second River (Belleville) April 19, 1755 Marytie, daughter of Nicholas Hyler, both being recorded as living on the Uylekill. The early name for the creek flowing through the Montville region was the Uylekill, and it gave its name to the settlement, later called Montville. Marytie Hyler's mother was Rachel, daughter of Humphrey Davenport, who had bought a tract nearby on the east side of the Rockaway River in 1715, built and settled there. Johannes Parlaman was prominent in the Revolution. He died April 13, 1805 and was buried in Lower Montville; his widow died in 1818. They had three sons and three daughters. The homestead passed to their son John' Parlaman, b. Sept. 7, 1760, d. Dec. 26, 1829. He was married twice, first to Marytie Hiler, d. in March 1791 aged 30 years, having borne one daughter. He married secondly Oct. 22, 1793 Sarah Miller, b. Jan. 4, 1770, survived him many years and died Feb. 7, 1852. By his second wife, John Parlaman had two daughters. The elder, Barbara, b. Jan. 20, 1797, married Feb. 1815 Thomas Edward Bowlsby who died in 1829, and she married secondly Benjamin Crane; Barbara had two daughters by her first husband, one of whom was Ariadne who married Josiah P. Huntoon but died soon afterward on Jan. 26, 1844.

The homestead was owned by John Parlaman's youngest daughter Ann,[5] b. Feb. 2, 1799, d. Oct. 31, 1889, married 1818 at Montville James[5] Doremus, b. Sept. 18, 1796 at Te Wachauw (Doremustown), d. March 16, 1853. He was a son of Johannis Doremus of nearby Doremustown and a nephew of Henry and Thomas

Doremus, who owned the house there in which George Washington stayed (plate 163). James Doremus raised the roof of the house and added a half story of frame over the two earlier stone units; he also built the older half of the frame wing. James and Ann had three sons and two daughters. The house passed to the daughter Sarah Margaret⁶ Doremus, b. Aug. 20, 1827. On May 24, 1845 she married Josiah P. Huntoon, b. July 16, 1816 at Montpelier, Vt., d. June 11, 1891. He had married previously her first cousin Ariadne Bowlsby. Josiah Huntoon was in the grocery trade at various places, lived at Montville for a while, and removed to Paterson in 1841 for the balance of his life. The house is now owned by their daughter Ada Huntoon, b. Aug. 14, 1849, married April 13, 1870 Henry I. Clark. She lives in Paterson, and the house is at present unoccupied.

The house has been built at several different times. The west unit of the main house is of very irregular fieldstone. The east unit is similar in size, but the front is of roughly dressed stone and lintels have been placed over the door and window. Each unit has its own outside door. The west unit is pre-revolutionary; the east half may not have been added until about the time of the war. The half story of frame was added in the second quarter of the nineteenth century, as was a part of the frame wing. The old windows, with the smaller lower sash, and the old fanlight still do duty, and no dormers break the slope of the roof.

The house overlooks the Rockaway River valley. It is on the north side of the road, which formerly took its course along the river valley from Old Boonton (a Revolutionary village, now under the reservoir) eastward and joined the road from Michael Cook's Mill to Rockaway Bridge. It was later extended across this road to the Dutch Church of Lower Montville, which was moved here in 1818 from Old Boonton. A fuller discussion of the various roads and the locality can be read in the text for plate 164. The house is in Montville Township south of the village of that name, in the locality known as Lower Montville.

House of Lucas Van Beverhoudt
Troy Hills

On March 2, 1772 Lucas Van Beverhoudt, late of the Island of St. Thomas, now of London, bought property from William Kelly, late of New York in America and now of London, the transfer being made in London. The deed was for a 2,000 acre tract in Morris County, New Jersey, which Kelly had bought from John Barlow, Stephen Tuttle, John Marsh, Patrick Darcy and Daniel Cooper. This original parchment deed is in the possession of the present owner of the house. Van Beverhoudt settled on this purchase, then in the township of Hanover, Morris County. It is said that the place was originally named Red Barracks from the hay ricks, and that he changed it to *Beaverwyck*, the place of origin of his family in Holland. His manager was Abraham Lott and the place is marked Mr. Lott's on Erskine's map.

The house was quite a mansion and here Lucas Van Beverhoudt entertained officers of both armies during the Revolution. Born in 1737, he is said to have been married twenty-five years in 1795, and was accidentally killed on the road from Hanover to Troy when thrown from his chaise. He married Maria, eldest daughter of Mr. Malvill of the Danish Islands, and widow of Christian Suhm, Governor of St. Thomas. By her first marriage his wife had a daughter Maria Suhm, who later married President Wheelock of Bowdoin College in Brunswick, Maine. Lucas Van Beverhoudt had a daughter Adriana, b. 1781, married 1796 Tobias Boudinot. She lived at *Beaverwyck*, but died at the home of her daughter Mrs. Col. Amos Brewster at Hanover, N. H., in 1855. Adriana had two sons and four daughters, many of whom lived at *Beaverwyck*. Her daughter Ann Boudinot married William Bibby. She was the last of the family to own the place, but lived in Paterson. As her son was uninterested and extravagant, she sold the house about 1855 to her neighbor John Condit. He had come from Orange and in 1800 bought the property immediately to the south from a descendant of Lucas Van Beverhoudt, and built the large two story frame house on the roadside, erecting the street wing in the 1840s.

It is a question how much of Lucas Van Beverhoudt's home still stands. The house is said to have been destroyed by fire after his death, but Mrs. Condit was told by a descendant that only the kitchen wing burned, and that the present front is part of the original house. If much of the old building still remains, it was greatly changed by the builder's daughter, Mrs. Boudinot. The house is a very large, two story, white frame mansion, with the usual wide hall running down the center between two rooms on either side. The architectural window trim is typical of the period around 1800, there is a large Palladian window in the center over the door, and a mid-nineteenth century roof. The house is in Troy Hills, south of the main highway from Newark to Parsippany and Dover. It is on the east side of the Revolutionary road which led from Rockaway Bridge in Lower Montville southward to Whippany and Morristown. The present owner is Mrs. Sarah Condit.

Van Duyn—Jacobus House
Changebridge Road, Montville
PLATE 166

Very little is known of the history of this house. The property is said to have been a grant to a Van Duyn. We know that several branches of this family settled in this township at an early date (*Biog. Hist. of Morris and Sussex Co.*, pub. 1899). It is said that the last Van Duyn who owned this house hanged himself, and his widow could not pay the taxes. By a sheriff's sale about 1864 the property was deeded to Timothy Jacobus. At one time the Jacobus family owned the land on the west side of this road and the Vreeland family on the east side of the road. Timothy married a sister of John P. and Peter I. Vreeland, his neighbors. He died about 1890 aged about 70 years, leaving three children, Ephraim, Alfred, and Rachel, who inherited the property jointly. They sold it to the present owner, H. B. Van Cleve.

At a rough glance the house would appear to be the usual type of one and a half story house with gable roof. Closer inspection shows that the house was built in two unequal units. The south two-thirds of the house (to the middle chimney) is the oldest section, and the north third was added about a hundred years ago. The three chimneys are unusual. The larger unit is probably pre-revolutionary, its ceilings are low and the old beams are still exposed to view. No dormers mar the roofline. The house is on the west side of the Changebridge Road, south of the road from the Pompton River valley to Boonton. The Changebridge Road leads southward past the Demarest farm (plate 164) to the Rockaway Bridge. The house is in Montville Township about two miles east of the village of that name.

Houses in Sussex (Including Warren) County
House of William Ennes
Old Mine Road, Sandyston Township
PLATE 167

On Sept. 23, 1703 William Ennes, Sr., a Scotchman, bought a tract of 200 acres at Marbletown in Ulster County and settled there. By his wife Cornelia Viervant he had a son William Ennes, b. Jan. 10, 1711, bap. Jan. 27, 1712 at Kingston, who married Elizabeth Quick. They came to the Delaware River valley in 1738, where the younger William became prominent as an early school teacher of the Minisink region and an elder of the Church. On Oct. 5, 1753 he bought a farm on the river in the present Sandyston Township from Richard Gardner, one of the Proprietors. Here he lived and died. He is said to have had eleven children. Eight were baptized at Minisink: Cornelia, b. 1741, Benjamin, b. 1743, m. 1769 Magdalena Van Etten, Daniel, b. 1745, married Elena Hornbeck, Margriet, b. 1748, married Jacobus Hornbeck, Joseph, b. 1751, m. 1770 Grietje Van Etten, John b. 1754, Cornelius b. 1757, Alexander b. 1759. The father of these children may be the William Ennes whose will was probated in 1804. One of the sons, Daniel Ennes, conducted the first tavern in the vicinity, also a store and a smithy. The caption under a photograph of the house, taken in 1890, describes it as the Alexander Ennes house, for what reason is not elucidated. It is not likely that William's son Alexander Ennes, b. 1759, ever inherited the house, as the next known owner was Simon Cortright, b. 1764, who inherited it from his Ennes father-in-law, and Alexander was too young to be the father of Simon's wife.

Petrus Cortreght's son Simon Cortright, bap. July 20, 1764 at Minisink, d. 1824 in his 60th year, married Catharine Ennes and had a daughter Maria, b. Nov. 10, 1784. Simon is said to have inherited the property on the death of his father-in-law William Ennes. Presumably this is the William who purchased the farm in 1753, although there is no church record showing that he had a daughter Catharine, nor an older son William, Jr. who might have been her father. Simon Cortright was a justice of the peace, served three terms in the Legislature and fifteen years as Judge of the Court of Common Pleas. In addition to this inheritance he purchased 1000 acres in the vicinity. At his death the estate passed into the hands of Jacob Kyte, who died in his 82nd year, leaving it to John Kyte, the owner in 1881. Mark Sigler was in possession before Hiram C. C. Snook of Hainesville, who has owned the house for the last twenty-five years, but does not occupy it. The house is vacant at present.

Between the two windows of the house shown in the photograph is a stone marked 7.3.1751, which undoubtedly records the date of its erection. As Richard Gardner, the Proprietor, never occupied the farm, the house may have been built by a tenant of his. No tradition of his identity has been handed down. It is very plausible that the builder was William Ennes, who may have leased the farm before buying it, or purchased it under a several years' contract, not receiving the deed until late in 1753. Although Ennes was of Scotch descent on his father's side, his mother, wife and sons-in-law were all Dutch by blood, so the house warrants inclusion in this volume. The house is very interesting, small in size and almost square in shape, with a steep gable roof. The stonework under one of the two small windows shows that the doorway was formerly here, before the frame lean-to was added. The house is on the west side of the Old Mine Road, several fields from the Delaware River, about one mile south of Great Minisink Island, and west over the mountains from Hainesville. A view of the house from the north can be seen in *Northwestern New Jersey*, v. 2, p. 575.

House of Stephanus Tietsoort (Titsworth)
Road to Port Jervis, north of Sussex, Wantage Township
PLATE 168

The Minisink territory in the interior back of the present Port Jervis was settled at an early date, before the nearby village of Sussex (which was founded in 1734 by Peter Decker and called Deckertown until recently). One descendant of the Titsworth family states that the house was built in 1701, another descendant states that the original log house was built in 1701 and the present stone house about 1710, and also that it was built by William Tietsoort who married Sarah Decker. As this particular William was not born until 1706, he is naturally eliminated as the builder in 1710; he is the first known owner, but his father Stephanus lived in this general vicinity and probably built it at the traditional date, for construction of the house shows it to belong to the very beginning of the eighteenth century.

Abraham Willemszen van Amsterdam married in the Dutch church in New Amsterdam April 27, 1647 Aechtje Jans van Naerden, and had a son Willem bap. Aug. 2, 1648. The latter is undoubtedly the Willem Abrahamse Tietsoort who is the ancestor of the Titsworth family. Willem settled in Schenectady by 1676, where he was a landowner and blacksmith, and was wounded in the frightful Indian massacre. He located at the Forks of the Delaware River, now Port Jervis, before 1698, when he obtained a government license to purchase his lands from the Indians. In a petition to the Governor and Council of New York on April 10, 1708, William Tietsoort stated that he was a blacksmith living in Ulster County (this region was then considered a part of Ulster County in New York), that he formerly lived in Schenectady and barely escaped from the massacre of that village in 1689, that as he had friends in the Esopus country he removed there and was invited by some friendly Indians to settle in the Minisink, his Indian friend voluntarily giving him a tract of land; that he sought a legal title for this gift by obtaining a government license to purchase on Oct. 15, 1698, and so purchased it, which land had been subsequently assumed to be included in the Matthew Ling patent, from which he now sought protection. On June 30, 1700 he obtained the legal deed from the Indians above referred to for land on the Delaware River at Machackemack (now Port Jervis) and at Schacheackaminck, and received a patent for the tract. In another affidavit, Willem Tietsoort, then of Dutchess County, declared in 1717 that he had sold two parcels of land at Port Jervis to Jan Decker in 1713. Shortly after this sale he evidenly removed to Dutchess County in New York, where he is recorded in the 1714 Census with a household consisting of himself (over 60 years of age), two younger males and three females. In his will, made in Dutchess County in 1716 and probated at Albany in 1722, he mentioned his wife Neeltje, daughter of Teunis Swart, four sons and six daughters. Two of the sons settled in Poughkeepsie and one in Middletown, New Jersey.

The remaining son was Stephanus W.² Tietsoort, b. about 1680 at Schenectady. He was living in Minisink when he married at Kingston Oct. 18, 1702 Sara Hoornbeck. She was born at Hurley, bap. April 24, 1681 at Kingston, a daughter of Warnaer Hoornbeck of Hurley. They had at least four children, Anna, William, Maria and Jacobus; the first three were baptized at Kingston and the fourth was the first child baptized in the newly organized church at Machackemack nearby. Thus Stephanus had removed to the back country Minisink before his marriage, probably built the log hut in 1701 and the stone house about 1710. In an affidavit concerning a quarrel at Machackemack (now Port Jervis), he signed himself in 1722 as a resident of Orange County, a juryman of Tappan, about 42 years of age, innholder. (This region was then claimed by Orange Co., N. Y.). In 1739 he and his son Willem were taxed at Minisink, for building a gaol at Goshen, Orange County.

Stephanus' son Willem S.' Tietsoort, bap. Sept. 22, 1706 at Kingston, d. March 4, 1791*, is the first of the family definitely connected with the family homestead. He married Sara Decker and had six children, including Stephanus' Tietsoort, b. April 8, 1734*, d. April 17, 1777*, married Catrina Kuykendal, b. May 28, 1737*, d. Nov. 17, 1805*. The house was inherited by their son William⁶ Titsworth, b. Aug. 12, 1758* in Wantage Township, d. March 3, 1837*; he married Margaret Middagh, b. Oct. 8, 1757*, d. March 31, 1841*. Their son Dr. John⁷ Titsworth, b. April 19, 1793*, d. Feb. 1, 1873*, married May 31, 1819* Abigail, daughter of Deacon Nathan Beers, b. April 10, 1795, d. Dec. 27, 1863. Dr. John Titsworth inherited the homestead and built the large house in the rear. The property passed to his son William⁸ Titsworth, b. July 12, 1824, and it was sold by William's widow Kate about 1902 to Jason House. The present owner is E. Korn of Hackensack; the old stone house is rented out as a refreshment stand.

It is a one and a half story house of rough slaty stone rubble, with a steep gable roof and very small windows. As it stands on a hill slope, a basement story of whitewashed stone is exposed on one side. In the interior at one end there is a panelled fireplace wall with a huge cupboard. Very wide floor boards, exposed beams, low ceilings, old hinges and doors, are authentic details. Although now used as a refreshment stand, the exterior has not been marred, nor the interior very much altered. The house stands above Clove Creek on the northeast side of the road to Port Jervis. It is two and a half miles northwest of Sussex in Wantage Township, and less than ten miles south of the state border. The original log house formerly stood a short distance northward, and the first church in this section was built on a hill near the stone house.

House of Abraham Van Campen
Old Mine Road, Calno, Pahaquarry Township, Warren County
PLATE 169

This house was built by Abraham Van Campen far from any settlement in the wilds north of the Delaware Water Gap. To reach civilization he had to make a

---

* Taken from family Bible.

long and arduous journey over the Old Mine Road northwards along the Delaware River to the present Port Jervis and then strike inland northeastward to Esopus on the Hudson River.

Abraham's grandfather Gerrit Jansen[1] Van Campen emigrated to New Amsterdam, where he was a soldier at the time of his marriage Jan. 17, 1659, to Macktelt Stoffels, widow of Anthony Lodewyck. They settled at Esopus. Their son John[2] Van Campen, bap. April 18, 1661, at Kingston, married there July 23, 1687, Tietje Jans Decker, and survived most of their eleven children. They were living at Shawangunk when two of their children were born in 1694 and 1696, and by 1703 had settled in Marbletown Township, Ulster County, where they were living as late as 1728. He removed to New Jersey and died in Somerset County in 1745 shortly after making his will (in which he does not mention his son Abraham). Of his sons, John, Gerrit and Abraham settled along the Delaware River.

Col. Abraham[3] Van Campen, bap. Oct. 9, 1698, at Kingston, was the first and most prominent settler of the river region, now Pahaquarry Township. This land was included in the Indians' release of 1713 to the West Jersey Proprietors. On March 8, 1732, Abraham bought from the heirs of George Hutcheson, one of the Proprietors, a tract called Pahaqualin, consisting of 1666 acres with a stretch of seven miles along the Delaware River, for £735. This tract was the upper half of the present township; it could not have been his first purchase, as he is said to have had a survey made for him in 1712 and to have settled here about 1725. John Reading, Jr., surveyed the country as far as the Minisink lands in May of 1715 and recorded no white settlers at this time, but the valley was thickly settled for over thirty miles north of the Water Gap by 1730, according to the surveyors Scull and Lukens. Abraham Van Campen at one time owned more than 3000 acres, of which he sold a great deal, leaving 1600 acres to his sons. Richard Smith of Burlington rowed down the Delaware River in a canoe with Indian guides in 1769, and recorded that "we had a glimpse of the late Col. Van Camp's place below Walpack; he has a good share of even land and a range of swelling hills proper for sheep pasture, as much of all this country would be if it was cultivated." On the map of the Delaware River Survey in 1769 by Dennis are shown Van Camp's House and Grist Mills on a stream.

Abraham's home was the headquarters of the settlers in the Delaware River valley during the Indian wars; a fort was built nearby for a garrison of 250 men, and the officers were fed at his table. He was a Colonel of the West Jersey troops in the French and Indian War of 1755-58, and ordered by Gov. Belcher to have his regiment ready to march into Pennsylvania and repel the Indians before they had the opportunity to march into New Jersey. The Indians stood in great dread of him.

As Justice of the Peace he performed many marriages in this section. He was a Judge of the Court of Common Pleas and by far the most prominent man in the Delaware River region.

Abraham was married twice, first to Susanna Depue, bap. Jan. 9, 1698 at Kingston, still living in 1754, a daughter of Moses De Puis and Marretje Wynkoop, and sister of Nicholas and Benjamin Depue who were the first settlers of Smithfield on the Pennsylvania side of the Delaware River. On Oct. 29, 1761 he married secondly Rachel Van Aker widow (probably spouse of Isaac Van Aken), by whom he had no issue. He died in May, 1767, having made his will the year previous as a resident of Walpack in Sussex County (Walpack Township at this time included the whole region along the river south to the Delaware Water Gap). Abraham and Susanna's three daughters were: Maria, b. 1732, wife of John Depui, Catharine wife of Benjamin Depui, and Susanna wife of Thomas Romine. Of their four surviving sons, John, b. 1726, and Benjamin, b. 1728, settled on the opposite side of the river at Smithfield on tracts willed them by their father, and the other two, Abraham, b. 1736, and Moses, b. 1743, lived on their father's homestead. Moses' Van Campen (1743-1819) was a Major; he was captured one night in 1777 by three Indians, who planned to take him to the headquarters of the Susquehanna and murder him by a lingering torture, but he was able to burst his fetters asunder, kill two of the Indians with a tomahawk and put the third to flight. Moses married Sarah Westfaal but had no children and willed all his property to his nephew Abraham III, son of Abraham, Jr., after the decease of his wife Sarah.

Abraham' Van Campen, Jr., bap. Feb. 22, 1736, at Kingston, d. May, 1811, married first about 1752 his cousin Maria, daughter of Moses Depue, and secondly Elizabeth Schoonmaker. Only two of his children matured: Abraham by the first marriage, b. July 12, 1770, d. Nov. 28, 1848, married Sarah Cape and had six children; James by the second marriage, b. Nov. 17, 1781, d. 1826, married Cecilia Decker and had eight children. Abraham' Van Campen, Sr., had made no mention of the homestead in his will of 1766, but by deed of Nov. 26, 1766 he conveyed it to his son Abraham, Jr., who in his will of Feb. 23, 1808 bequeathed the home in which he lived to his son James. It was at the home of James Van Campen that a town meeting was held March 14, 1825 to establish the civil organization of Pahaquarry Township.

In the first half of the nineteenth century the place passed into the Ribble family: to William Ribble, then to his son George, then to the latter's son William R. Ribble. The latter's widow, Cecilia Van Campen Ribble, a descendant of the original owner, died in May 1932 leaving no children, and the house was sold at auction July 8, 1932 to the present owner, Mrs. Julia Orthwein of New York City.

The house is built of red sandstone, until recently covered by the usual lime and sand wash. Since it was purchased in 1932, it has been covered with a heavy concrete mixture and the roof newly shingled with short red shingles; the photograph shows it in its present condition. Modern gable and porch prevent its unusual length from being satisfactorily emphasized in a photograph. The low ceilings and the small size of the windows are both characteristic of the early period. The slave quarters were in the south basement.

Van Campen Brook, on which stood the family mills, has been renamed Milbrook Brook, and meanders southward from the present sleepy hamlet of Milbrook along the Old Mine Road until it empties in the Delaware River. The house stands near the south bank of the brook, on the east side of the Old Mine Road. It is in Pahaquarry Township, in a hamlet called Calno, two miles south of Milbrook and five miles north of Shawnee.

House of Isaac Van Campen
Old Mine Road, Shapanack, Walpack Township
PLATE 170

Isaac Van Campen was a leader of the community as had been his uncle Abraham. It is interesting to compare their two houses, built within twenty-five years of each other in similar and nearby regions. Such a comparison clearly shows the progress in ideas for the housing of wealthy and prominent men.

John' Van Campen, bap. April 30, 1693 at Kingston, was an elder brother of Col. Abraham Van Campen of Pahaquarry (plate 169). John' Van Campen, Jr., of Marbletown married at Kingston Sept. 22, 1711 Madalena Van Garden of Rochester, and settled along the Delaware River near Milford, Pa. One of their sons was Isaac' Van Campen, bap. July 30, 1721 at Kingston, d. late in 1801; he was living at Smithfield, one of the lower Minisink settlements on the Pennsylvania side of the River, at the time of his marriage in the Minisink Church on Oct. 20, 1741 to Madalena Rosenkrans of Walpack, who was still living in 1772; he married his second wife Sarah —— by 1781.

On July 31, 1750 Isaac Van Campen bought a tract on the Jersey side of the Delaware River at Walpack from Joseph Stout of Hopewell, who may have purchased it from Joseph Kirkbride, who in 1718 had located here a 500 acre tract, embracing the Shapanack Flats seven miles above the mouth of Flat Brook. Count Zinzendorf travelled over the Old Mine Road in 1742 and wrote of coming to Samuel Depui and going to church at Walpack; he did not mention any house on the future Van Campen tract so it was probably not built at this time. Neither did the Rev. Henry Muhlenberg make any mention of a house here in his scanty diary, in which he recorded traversing this region on Aug. 10, 1750. It is probable that Isaac Van Campen built here this summer after purchasing the tract. In 1752 he was drawn for the Grand Jury in Northampton Co., Pa., but did not appear, probably because he had settled recently in Walpack. We know he had removed here by the time of the French and Indian War of 1755-58, as his place was one of the headquarters of the army during this war. A series of forts was built along the Delaware River at this time, one on the hill above his house, another near his uncle's home to the south in Pahaquarry, and a third near the Westbrook house to the north in Minisink village. On the map of the Delaware River survey of 1769 by Dennis are shown two houses here, owned by "Isaac Van Comps" and "Rosigrants."

Early in the Revolution all of eastern New Jersey fell into the hands of the British, and Gen. Gates, marching from Ticonderoga to reinforce Washington, had to make a wide detour from Kingston down the Old Mine Road. He arrived at Isaac Van Camp's in Walpack in a snow storm on Dec. 10, 1776 and wrote from here to Washington, heading his letter "Dec. 12, 1776 Van Kemp's, 15 miles from Sussex Courthouse." He joined Washington in time for the victory at Trenton on Christmas Day. Isaac Van Campen was a member of the Continental Congress. John Adams, while attending Congress in Philadelphia went down the Old Mine Road as late as 1800, as the best route from Boston! He was accustomed to lodge at Squire Van Campen's in the Jersey Minisinks.

Isaac Van Campen had many children, of whom only three are said to have matured: Abraham, Jr., Isaac, Jr., and Catharine Rosenkrans. On June 15, 1799 Isaac Van Campen of Walpack deeded to his son Abraham Van Campen, Jr., 111 acres on the Delaware River, part of the land he had bought July 31, 1750 of Joseph Stout of Hopewell. Isaac had owned about 700 acres in all. The son Abraham[5] Van Campen married Coriany or Rosanny Rosenkrans and had two daughters, Lena, b. 1789, and Margaret, b. 1792. He became involved financially and sold the homestead to the De Witts about 1812, removing to the adjoining place, formerly Col. Rosencranz'.

Henry De Witt of Rochester bought the property for his son John H. De Witt, who died in 1827. He had the last slave in Sussex County when slavery was abolished in the state. The property has changed hands many times during the nineteenth century. It is now owned by B. F. Tuthill and leased to Tex Howard as the Diamond T. Ranch.

The house is sixty feet long and two stories high. The front is of dressed limestone and the rear of very irregular cut stone. There is an ornamental cornice and a steep gable roof. The lines of a lower two story wing can still be seen in the stucco of the north end; it was torn down many years ago. This was formerly the slave quarters. The house stands on the east side of the Old Mine Road, opposite a small island in the Delaware River, directly over the mountains from Walpack Center, and five miles south of Dingman's Ferry. This locality is called Shapanack. Nearby are the sites of the fort and the Shapanack Church.

House of Johannes Westbrook
Old Mine Road, Minisink, Sandyston Township
PLATE 171

The children of the present owners are the eighth generation resident on this farm, which has never been out of the family. Their ancestor Johannes Westbroeck, Sr., was born in Albany and living in Kingston when he married May 12, 1687 Magdalena Decker of Kingston. He was one of the original settlers of the upper Minisink region, owning a farm there and voting there in 1701. In his will he called himself a resident of Knightfield (in Wawarsing Township), Ulster County. He died in 1727, survived by wife, four sons and two daughters. Three of his sons settled in the Minisink region along the Delaware River in New Jersey: Anthony lived above Milville in Montague Township until he bought the Minisink Island tract, Johannes, Jr. settled in Minisink village south of the stream, and a third son Cornelius built a house (now remodelled) still further south about opposite Hainesville in Sandyston Township. In 1739 Johannes, Johannes, Jr. and Anthony Westbrook were all taxed at Minisink for building a gaol at Goshen in Orange County (the Minisink region was claimed by New York, its inhabitants voting in Ulster County 1701-09 and later in Orange County).

At an unknown date (about 1724) Anthony Westbrook bought 120 acres on Minisink Island and 120 acres opposite on the Jersey mainland, from Kuykendall and Westfaal, as recited in Kuykendall's sale of the remaining land in December 1731: "Whereas Thomas Stevenson (one of the Proprietors), late of the County of Bucks, Province of Pennsylvania, gentleman, did grant to Jacob Kuykendall of Minisink, farmer, and Uriah Westfalya, late of the County of Hunterdon, yeoman, also deceased, a certain tract of 500 acres in the Province of New Jersey jointly and equally, whereas said land was taken up and surveyed within the Indian purchase of the Council of Proprietors, and whereas said Kuykendall and Westfalya did convey unto Anthony Westbrook 120 acres of lowland on Great Minisink Island and 120 acres of upland opposite, and the remainder of the 500 acres was divided between said Kuykendall and Westfalya . . ." On April 7, 1725 Cornelius Low surveyed and platted the above 240 acre purchase, marking off three 5 acre house lots along the river bank, for Jan Cortreght, Johannes Westbrook, Jr. and Anthony Westbrook. It is probable that Anthony had represented the two others in his purchase of the tract, which in 1725 was bounded on the north by the land owned jointly by Uriah Westphall and Jacob Van Kuykendall and on the south by the land of Matthewes Van Kuykendall. The settlement was formed opposite the lower end of Minisink Island on the site of an Indian village. Three houses, one marked Westbrook, are shown here in the 1769 survey of the Delaware River.

Johannes Westbrook, Jr. settled here in Minisink village, south of the stream which separates the present Sandyston and Montague Townships; he is believed to have built the present house, which is still owned and occupied by his descendants. In 1731 he sold part of his land for a cemetery and a schoolhouse. William Ennes, who lived to the southward (plate 167), undoubtedly taught here. Johannes Westbrook, Jr. was born in Kingston, bap. there Jan. 9, 1698, and married there Dec. 19, 1715 Antjen Roosa of Hurley, who was still living in 1756. Their six children were baptized at Kingston and Rochester between 1716 and 1728: Lena, b. at Hurley, living at Minisink, m. 1738 Johannes Westbrook, Jr., son of Anthony and therefore her first cousin, Maria, Heyltjen (died young), Benjamin, Heyltjen and Cornelius. Another son, Abraham, has also been attributed to them but he may have been a grandson. This Abraham Westbrook married Maria Helm about 1751 and had three children, Michel, Martynus and Johanna, bap. from 1752 to 1755. He was killed shortly afterward in the War of 1755-58. His infant son Martynus Westbrook, bap. March 24, 1754, grew up to become a captain and lived on the farm given him by his father. He married Margaret Lowe and had a son and a daughter. The only son was Abraham Westbrook, b. Nov. 15, 1775, bap. Aug. 24, 1777, d. Aug. 7, 1811; he married Ann, daughter of Reuben Buckley, b. Oct. 11, 1778. Among their seven children were Eliza Westbrook, b. Aug. 29, 1806, who was living in the old homestead in 1881, and Reuben Buckley Westbrook, b. March 26, 1805. The latter was the father of Clementina Westbrook who married Benton Bell. The present owner is their son Burson Bell.

The house was undoubtedly built shortly after the village of Minisink was platted in 1725. It is a very low house of rough gray stone, repointed on the east end. The high and steep gable roof is now covered with tin tiling. The farm is between the Old Mine Road and the Delaware River, opposite the south end of Minisink Island and south of a stream. A willow tree guards the entrance to the farm lane. Nearby is the site of Fort Minisink, a similar stone building, which is undergoing restoration.

PLATE 143

House of Albert Berdan
Berdan Avenue, Upper Preakness

Albert Berdan settled here some time after 1727, at first making his home in a log cabin and later (before the Revolution) building a permanent dwelling, which is the wing of the present house. The first floor of the main house was not built until 1792 by his son Jacob and the second floor added later by the latter's son Albert Berdan. The house is still owned by the family, although it has not been occupied by them in recent years. Both units are built of stone, covered with plaster. The roof of the wing has no overhang in front and extends in a long slope over a lean-to at the rear. Although there was an occasional two story mansion built by the Dutch prior to the Revolution, it was not until after the war that two story farmhouses were erected.

PLATE 144

House of Dirck Dey
Totowa Road, Lower Preakness

It is believed that this house was erected about 1740 by Dirck Dey, whose son Theunis was Washington's host here. It is almost the only two story house in the country built by the Dutch prior to the Revolution except in the Raritan River section. The superior workmanship is attributed to the builder's being a carpenter (that is, a builder) by trade. The house is Georgian rather than Dutch in style. The Dutch influence is mainly seen in the combination of materials: it is built of huge oaken timbers pegged with wooden pins and of rough sandstone blocks, the front and eaves are faced with brick, and the jointing of corners, windows and doors is made with carefully cut and finished sandstone, while the cornice is of wood. The steep gambrel roof is an adaptation of the Dutch roof without the overhang. The shallow arches over the windows on the side wall are unusual in this region. The dormers are later additions. There was formerly a detached stone kitchen a few yards to the east.

PLATE 145

Lawrence House
formerly on Watchung Avenue, Brookdale

This house stood on the homestead tract of Alexander Cockefair and was probably built by or for his son-in-law John Lawrence about the middle of the eighteenth century. The absence of overhanging eaves in both front and rear is more characteristic of the Staten Island houses but the rough stonework and the moderate slope of the roof are typical of the northern New Jersey Dutch houses. The dormers are later additions. Notice the old well sweep near the front door. The Dutch houses were generally built facing the south to obtain the maximum sunlight regardless of the position of the road. This is a good example of such a custom as the road runs past the back corner of the house.

PLATE 146

House of Edo Merselis
Paterson and Hamburgh Turnpike, Upper Preakness

This house was built a few years before the Revolution by Edo Merselis and has remained the home of his descendants ever since, although sold by them about 1920. The stonework of the house has been covered with plaster except in the rear where a coat of whitewash does not conceal the rough character of the stones. The front of the house has been changed by the addition of roof supports and of dormers. A broad gable roof of this type was occasionally used over a deep house although the gambrel roof was more common.

556

PLATE 147

House of Johannes Ryerson
367 Goffle Road, Hawthorne

Johannes Ryerson was living on this tract by 1744 and may have settled here as early as 1721. As it is claimed that the house (presumably the wing only) was erected in 1750, it is probable that Johannes Ryerson's first home here was a temporary structure, which was followed by a permanent home (the present wing) after his father had bequeathed him the property. The main house was probably built by his son or grandson shortly after the Revolution, and later passed by marriage into the Ackerman family. The rear view of the house is reproduced to show the slaty rubble with which the back walls were built and the smallness and sparsity of the windows even at this late period. The front wall of the wing is of roughly cut stone and that of the main house is of dressed stone. The gable roof extends to form an overhang over the south fronts of both units. An unusual feature is the string course of carefully cut and finished sandstone at the floor level of the main story of the house and also the rare type of fanlight. The double Dutch doors and solid shutters have typical panelling.

557

PLATE 148

Schuyler—Colfax House
Paterson and Hamburgh Turnpike, Pompton

This house stands on a tract bought from the Indians in 1695 by Arent Schuyler, and it is still occupied by his descendants, having passed by marriage into the Colfax family. The main house is typical of the post-revolutionary period and was erected probably by William Colfax, Captain of Washington's Life Guards, shortly after his marriage to Hester Schuyler in 1783. The pre-revolutionary wing consists of two separate units, the earliest of which was erected in 1702 by Arent Schuyler or about 1712 by his son Philip; the second and similar unit was added some years later by Philip or possibly by his son Casparus Schuyler. All three units of the house are built of rough fieldstone and their front walls faced with brick. The low ceilings, steep gable roof and absence of overhang in the wing are typical of the earliest houses. The shallow brick archheads of the doors and windows of the wing are unusual in this vicinity and can be compared with those in Hunterdon County. The sloping dormers are later additions which blend with the roofline.

PLATE 149

Stynmets—Sip House
714 River Road, Passaic

This house stands on a tract conveyed by the patentee in 1699 to his son-in-law Christophel Stynmets, who had settled here a few years previously. It was sold between 1750 and 1762 to Arie Sip whose descendants owned it until about 1900. The home of Christophel Stynmets is the small unit at the rear of the house, with one door, one window, and chimney. Like all the earliest houses, it faces south. Its very thick stone walls are faced with clapboarding on the outside and roughly plastered in the interior. The next unit, built by Halmagh Sip, was added at right angles and faces the river and the road. Its dressed stone front and trapezoidal stone lintels are typical of certain houses built a short time before the Revolution. The largest section of the house was probably built a few years after the war. The stonework in the side wall of this unit is as carefully cut and finished as in the front wall. The gradual increase in length, depth and height of the units is typical of Dutch houses and of the periods represented.

PLATE 150

Van Dien House
Fairfield Road, Mountain View

This house was built in 1706 on a tract which is believed to have been purchased in 1704 by a Van Dien, and it remained in this family until the third quarter of the nineteenth century. It is typical of many of the small houses of this early period. The roughly cut, many colored stones with which it is built vary in texture and hue from the reddish sandstones of the houses in the counties further east.

PLATE 151

Van Giesen—Vreeland House
Chestnut Street, Nutley

It is believed that this house was built 1700-02 by Abraham Van Giesen and confiscated from his Tory grandson Abraham during the Revolution. It was purchased by John M. Vreeland in 1783 and owned by his descendants until about 1915. The photograph was taken after its successful restoration. The stones are more carefully cut and finished than in most houses in the frontier settlements of this early period. The steep slope of the roof is characteristic.

PLATE 152

House of Gerrebrant Van Houten
Totowa Avenue, Paterson

Gerrebrant Van Houten is believed to have built the small unit of this house on his father's tract at some period after his marriage in 1741. He may also have erected the main house, but this was more probably built shortly after the Revolution by his son Dirck. Even the wing is not pre-revolutionary in feeling, but this may be due to the refacing of the walls, the modern windows and tin roof.

562

PLATE 153

Van Ness House
by the Passaic River, near Fairfield

This house may have been built by Simon Van Ness, who settled in this vicinity between 1701 and 1710, or by his son Isaac Van Ness, who remained on the homestead tract. It was owned by the family until the early years of the twentieth century. Notice that some of the stones have been cut in almost square dimensions. The second half story of frame belongs to the early nineteenth century.

563

PLATE 154

Van Wagening House
formerly on River Drive, Passaic

This property was acquired conditionally by Hermanus Gerritse (Van Wagening) from his father-in-law before 1693. It passed to his son Gerrit Hermanisse Van Wagening who specifically mentioned the building in his will of 1769. The small unit of the house has the typical early arrangement of two adjoining main rooms each with its separate outside door: possibly it was the home of Hermanus Gerritse or it may have been built by the son Gerrit after his marriage in 1713. The main house was undoubtedly erected about the middle of the century by Gerrit. A building of such great depth was seldom covered by a gable roof. The overhanging eaves in both front and rear are typical of nearby Bergen County. In general there was at least one window in the side wall of such a large house. An interesting feature is the small Dutch stoop, with its railings and benches.

PLATE 155

House of John Van Winkle
868 Goffle Road, Hawthorne

John S. Van Winkle was living in the original unit of this house in 1774 and had erected it at some date following the purchase of the tract by his father in 1743. The date 1761 has been ascribed to the old unit, now the wing. The steep slope of the roof is more typical of an earlier period. This is one of the few examples in which the gable end is built entirely of stone. The varying sizes and finish of the stonework on this end wall add considerable life to the building. The deep jamb of the doorway is not panelled in this instance. The main house was erected in 1811 by the grandson, Judge John S. Van Winkle. Built along pre-revolutionary lines, it is nevertheless typical of this late period in its smoothly cut and finished stonework and in the panelling and carving of the woodwork. The house was not occupied by the family after the murder here in 1850 of the Judge and his wife, but it continued in the ownership of his descendants until about 1901.

PLATE 156

Unidentified House
534 East Passaic Avenue, Bloomfield Township

The history of this house is unknown. It was probably built in the second quarter of the eighteenth century. Like many of the Essex County houses it differs from those in Bergen County in the absence of overhanging eaves.

PLATE 157

Fitts House
Stanton

This house was erected in 1741, but the name of the builder and early owners are unknown. The rough stonework is carried up to the roofline even on the gable end. The shallow stone arches over the door and some of the windows are typical of the pre-revolutionary houses still standing in this county. The long, narrow windows are interesting; they are three panes in breadth rather than the usual four. Markings on the end wall indicate that there was once a low wing. The lower slope of the gambrel roof is shorter than usual; it has a slight curve and extends to form a shallow overhang. The continuation of the shingling over the roof edge gives an odd appearance to the house.

PLATE 158

Howsel—Wagoner House
Stanton

The old stone barn, dated 1741, and the house may have been erected at the same time. The property was owned during the Revolution by William Howzel, a member of a German family which had settled in this vicinity before 1735. The different atmosphere which pervades the house may be due to the racial origin of the builder. The stone structure is the original unit. Its length is less than average, the main floor consisting of a large room at the rear from which opens a small room at the front, and a wide hallway running the depth of the house along the east end. Due to its erection on a hillside the basement is a full story in height at the rear; it contains the kitchen and various larder and storage rooms. The shallow brick arches over the windows add contrast to the irregular stonework and wood trim. The architectural doorway and high-backed benches are modern but blend well as there was originally some form of stoop with benches. The wing on the east end was probably added before the Revolution; its ceilings are lower and its windows smaller than in the main house. The present clapboarding replaces a covering of long, red shingles which were secured by hand-made nails.

568

PLATE 159

Reynolds—Van Syckel House
Van Sickle's, near Clinton

This building was erected in 1763 and conducted as a tavern by David Reynolds, who was later hanged for counterfeiting. About 1800 it was acquired by Aaron Van Syckel and was run as a tavern by the family until after 1855. It is still owned by his descendants. All walls of the two and a half-story building are of irregular stonework. Notice the very large size of some of the stones, especially at the corners. The shallow brick arches over the door and windows of the first story are varied by the use of flat brick lintels over the second story and attic windows. The narrow lower sash is unusual in such long windows. The frame addition belongs to a later period.

569

PLATE 160

House of Martin Ryerson, later Quick's
near Three Bridges, Readington Township

The original unit is the central section, erected by Martin Ryerson probably about 1738. It is of fieldstone, the south front faced with brick. The gambrel roof has a curving lower slope and overhang reminiscent of the houses of Bergen County, the early home of the builder. The arch-shaped wooden lintels framed in a row of brick are an unusual feature. The old twelve-paned window sashes remain in the north front. The garret was open attic until twenty years ago when it was improved and dormers added. The two frame wings were built at different times by the Quick family after their purchase of the house about 1790.

570

PLATE 161

House of Thomas Dey
Two Bridges, Pequannock Township

This house was built in 1779 by Thomas Dey on his father's homestead tract. It passed by marriage into the Post family and was owned by descendants of the builder until about 1917. The very carefully cut and finished stones in the front wall of both units in contrast with the irregular stonework of sides and rear wall are typical of this period, as is the use of stone lintels. The addition of gable dormers, porch, and wide cornices and gutters detract considerably from the original appearance of the house.

PLATE 162

Dodd House
near Chapel Hill Road, Lincoln Park

The multi-colored rock of Morris County is different from the reddish sandstone of Bergen County, and was generally cut in larger blocks, thus giving the houses a different effect. This was the home of John Dodd or Dods at the time of the Revolution. He or his father probably erected the wing early in the eighteenth century. The steep pitched roof extends in front in a straight slope to form a deep overhang. The main house belongs to the Revolutionary period; its floor level is several steps higher than the wing. Porch and a cheap row of dormers now alter its appearance.

PLATE 163

House of Henry Doremus
Road to Boonton, near Towaco

This house was built in the third quarter of the eighteenth century by Henry Doremus, who sold it after the Revolution to his brother Thomas. They were Washington's hosts here. It is typical of the unpretentious houses of this county. There is no hallway since outside doors open directly into each of the two main rooms.

573

PLATE 164

Farmhouse, at one time Demarest's
Changebridge Road, Lower Montville

Construction shows that this house was erected about 1720-30. It is built of roughly cut stone and is covered by a steep, gable roof with a slight overhang on the south front. The door and hallway are not in the center of the house as the room on the west (left) end is smaller than average. The old windows with narrow lower sashes, the very small windows in the rear, enclosed stairway and simple mantel shelf are details characteristic of the early period. The unknown builder may have been a relation of Humphrey Davenport, who purchased a large tract here in 1714. The first known owner of the house was Lawrence Demarest about the end of the eighteenth century. Unlike most of the old houses which were family homesteads, this was a farmhouse which changed hands continuously.

PLATE 165

House of Johannes Parlaman
Lower Montville

The tract on which the house stands was acquired by the family in 1737. Various units of the house were built by different members of the family and it is still owned, although not occupied, by descendants. It can be easily discerned that the main house was built at two separate times; the west half of irregular stonework without lintels and the east half of carefully cut and laid stonework with trapezoidal stone lintels were built respectively about 1750-55 and about the time of the Revolution by Johannes Parlaman. His grandson James Doremus raised the roof and added the half story of frame and also built the older half of the frame wing in the second quarter of the nineteenth century. The various units of the two centuries are plainly differentiated but blend into a harmonious whole.

PLATE 166

Van Duyn—Jacobus House
Changebridge Road, Montville

The early history of this house is unknown, but tradition states that it was first owned by a Van Duyn. The house was built in two units, the division line shown by the middle chimney. The south two-thirds is the original section and was probably erected at some period before the Revolution. The house is a variation of the early type farmhouse which was generally erected in two equal sized units or all at one time. The gable roof extends in front to form an overhang and in the rear is continued in a long curving slope until near the ground.

PLATE 167

House of William Ennes
Old Mine Road, Sandyston Township

This tract was sold in 1753 by Richard Gardner to William Ennes, who had come to this vicinity from Marbletown some years before. As the house was built in 1752, it was erected by some unknown tenant of Richard Gardner's, the absentee owner, or possibly by William Ennes, who may have purchased the land under a several years' contract. Ennes was the early schoolmaster of the Minisink region. On his father's side he was of Scotch descent but both his mother and wife were Dutch. This difference in racial strain may account for the unusual character of the building. It is a small, almost square house built of long, narrow, roughly cut stones and covered by a very high and steep gable roof. The top of the window openings is in the form of a shallow arch surmounted by a row of narrow stones set on end; it varies from the West Jersey type since these stones were chosen so that their tops would form a straight line instead of a shallow curve. The small window openings are unusual, being of greater breadth than height. The northern (right) window supersedes the original door, the lower half of which has been blocked up.

577

PLATE 168

Tietsoort (Titsworth) House
Road to Port Jervis, north of Sussex

This house is believed to have been built about 1710. It was probably erected by Stephanus W. Tietsoort, who lived in this vicinity, and whose son William is the first known owner. It remained in the family until about 1902. It is typical of a frontier house of this early period. Built of very irregular stone rubble, it is covered by a steep gable roof which extends in a long, straight slope to form an overhang beyond the front wall. As it is on a hill, a low basement story is exposed on the south front. The early plan was followed, the main floor consisting of two adjoining rooms each with its outside door. Notice the sparsity and small size of the windows, for better protection against the Indians. The east wall of the interior is panelled.

PLATE 169

House of Abraham Van Campen
Old Mine Road, Pahaquarry Township

This house was built in the wilderness about 1725 by Abraham Van Campen, who became a large land-owner and the most prominent man in this region along the Delaware River. A pioneer house, it yet reflects the station of the builder in its great length. It is built of red sandstone, covered until recently with a lime and sand wash now replaced by a heavy concrete mixture. Notice the very small windows used in the early frontier houses for better protection against the Indians. The porch and dormers are later alterations. The house was the home of the Van Campen family for a century and then of the Ribble family for another hundred years.

579

PLATE 170

House of Isaac Van Campen
Old Mine Road, Walpack Township

This house was built by Isaac Van Campen shortly after he purchased the tract in 1750. Isaac was a member of the Continental Congress, and John Adams was accustomed to spend the night with him on his way from Boston to attend Congress at Philadelphia. How completely different are the houses of Isaac and his uncle Abraham Van Campen (plate 169)! Both were prominent men and the houses were erected only twenty-five years apart, but the uncle's house was built when the region was an absolute wilderness and the nephew's not until this road was an accepted route of travel between the eastern and middle states. Isaac's is a large two story mansion. The front wall is of roughly finished limestone and the rear of very irregular stone. It is surmounted by an ornamental cornice and by a steep gable roof reminiscent of the earlier houses. The shallow arches over the first story windows are typical of West Jersey. There was formerly a low two story wing on the north end, which was the slave quarters.

PLATE 171

House of Johannes Westbrook
Old Mine Road, Minisink

This house was built by Johannes Westbrook shortly after the village of Minisink was plotted in 1725. It has passed by marriage into the Bell family and is still the home of the builder's descendants. The outstanding feature of the house is its close-to-the-ground feeling. It is built of roughly finished limestone and has a steep gable roof. The roof now extends beyond the gable end and is covered with a modern composition but its long slope has never been broken by the addition of dormers. The modern one-paned sashes give the house a vacant expression. Notice the small size of the window openings and the lowness of the ceilings.

BIBLIOGRAPHY

Types of sources will be enumerated below, rather than attempt a complete list of authorities, which would run into a considerable number of pages.

Family Bible Records

Asterisks throughout the volume denote records taken from family Bibles. The author was fortunate in obtaining access to an unusually large number of Bibles. The great majority of these are in the possession of owners of the houses dealt with in this volume, especially in the Rockland and Bergen County regions, and hence definitely record the dates of previous owners in these branches of the family. The great value of these original sources is unquestionable.

Church Records

All available records of the Dutch Reformed Churches were scanned. The majority of these have been published in the Somerset County Quarterly, by the New York Genealogical and Biographical Society and by The Holland Society of New York. Others are still in manuscript form.

Cemeteries

Church cemeteries and numerous family graveyards amplified the above records.

Maps

Of inestimable use were the series of maps drawn by or under the direction of Robert Erskine, Surveyor General 1778-79. They cover most of the territory treated in this volume, and minutely record the various roads, the houses in existence, and in some cases the names of their owners. The originals of these maps are in the possession of the New York Historical Society.

The frequent change of the division line between Somerset and Middlesex Counties resulted in several eighteenth century surveys, which also marked the houses. The plan of Staten Island 1780-1783, in the Archives of the French Government, and the 1769 survey of the Delaware River were of value for these regions.

The collection of miscellaneous early maps at the New York Historical Society was consulted.

The atlases of various dates in the mid-nineteenth century proved valuable.

Contemporary Travels

Contemporary diaries and travel accounts were occasionally full enough to give information as to the existence of houses along the route and their owners at that time.

BIBLIOGRAPHY

Genealogical Works

Countless family genealogies in book, article, and manuscript forms, were consulted, and excerpts culled where they seemed authoritative. The sketchy and obviously inaccurate accounts were not used.

Of value were general works such as Bergen's *Early Settlers of Kings County*, Beekman's *Early Dutch Settlers of Monmouth County*, Nelson's *History of Paterson*, and the various genealogical quarterlies. Historical society publications, county histories, etc., often contained important genealogical sections.

Architectural Works

This section of the country has not been adequately treated in architectural works. Among the articles in print on the so-called Dutch Colonial style, those on the Bergen County houses are the most valuable and have been listed in the introduction for that county.

The few books on the houses of these regions are mainly of a general nature, Ditmas' *Historic Homes of Kings County* being an exception.

County Histories

The county histories were written for the most part in the last quarter of the nineteenth century, while children or grandchildren of many of the early settlers were still alive. Hence they record a large amount of material not available elsewhere and contain a surprising amount of valuable information, both as to land records and families.

Slightly different in form are books such as Gilman's *Story of the Ferry*, which deals exhaustively with the region around Palisades, N. Y., its houses and families.

For sources refer also to the county introductions.

GENEALOGICAL INDEX

GENEALOGICAL INDEX

181; Gerret (Gerrit), 181, 182; Gerret Joseph, 184, 185, 208; Gerrit Hendricksen, 211; Gilbert D., 204; Gitty, 183; Hannes (Johannes Joseph), 181, 182; Harman, 181; Helena (see Tallman), 231; Helena Pullen, 223; Hendrick, 181, 211; Hendrick (Gerritse Gerritsen), 175, 180, 181, 183; Huybert, 183; Isaac, 181, 183, 187; Isaac Jacobse, 229; Jacob, 183, 205, 229, 319; Jacob A., 183, 184, 186, 187, 192, 193, 199, 229; Jacob J., 183, 186, 192; Jacobus, 187; James, 183, 184; Johannes, 183-186, 205; Johannes, A., 199; Johannes Isaac, 223; Johannes J., 182, 183; John A., 185; John Calvin, 185; John I., 185; John Melanchthon, 185; Joseph, 182, 184, 185; Joseph Hendrickse, 181; Lenah Fowler, 204; Letty, 183; Margaret (see Haring), 294; Margaret (see Lydecker), 204; Margaret Clark, 183; Margrietje, 182; Margrietje (see Haring), 182, 296; Margrietje (see Smidt), 182, 211; Margrietje Minnelay (see Tallman), 183, 222; Maria, 182; Maria (see Haring), 294; Maria (see Wood), 187; Maria Ann, 183; Maria Gerrits (see Haring), 293; Maria Talama, 319; Maria Van Houten, 186; Marretje, 181; Marretje (Martha) (see Sickels), 208; Marritje (see Cuyper), 188; Marretje Josephs Waldron, 181; Martha, 182; Mary, 199; Marya Mabie, 204; Mary Adelaide, 184; Mary Ann, 185; Nettie Burr, 185; Peter, 183, 186; Pieterje (see Haring), 183, 184, 186; Rachel (see Du Puw), 193; Rachel Demarest, 183; Richard, 183; Richard R., 183; Sara (see Mabie), 199; Sarah (see Cooper), 189; Sarah De Pew (see Du Puy), 181; Sarah Van Dolsen, 183; T. J., 199; Trina, 186; Tunis, 199; Vrowtye, 182; Will B., 193

Blish
Maggie Peppard Nevius, 394; William, 394

Board
Cornelius Z., 330, 331; Frederick, 330, 331; Nathaniel, 330; Peter, 330

Bodine, Boden
Ann, 124; Dorcas, 124; Elsje, 124; James, 124; Jane Blake, 124; John, 124; John, Jr., 124; Martha, 124; Mary Egberts, 124; Rachel, 124; Vincent, 123, 124; Vincent, Jr., 124

Boeg
Conradus, 127; Jannetie (see Dusochay), 127

Bogert, Bogaert, Bogart
Albert, 295; Angenitie Jansen (see Durie), 290; Ann Westervelt, 325; Catharine (see Terheun), 310; Christina (see Voorhees), 320; Cornelia Haring, 295; Cornelis, 436; Cornelius, 210; David, 199; Dr., 443; Geertje Jans Langendyck Dey, 504; Henry, 325; Isaac, 279; Johannes, 293; John, 279; Maria Jane (see Van Emburgh), 274; Marretje Haring, 293; Mary (see Salyer), 199; Mary Ann, 295; Mary Brokaw, 443; Peter, 310; Stephen, 279; Theunis Gysbertse(n), 282, 504; Willemetje Van Voorhees (see Sloat), 210

Boggs, Robert, 471
Boice (see Buys)
Bond, William, 314
Boudinot
Adriana Van Beverhoudt, 541; Ann (see Bibby), 541; Dinah (? Tiney) Staats, 453; Tobias, 453, 541

Bowlsby
Ariadne (see Huntoon), 539, 540; Barbara Parlaman, 539; Thomas Edward, 539

Bowne, John, 386, 398, 399, 401, 406, 409

Boyce
John, 467; Settje Van Wickle, 467
Boyd, John T., Jr., 267
Bradley, Alvin C., 124
Braecke, Metje Dircks (see Michaelsen), 324
Branford
John E., 317; Robert, 317

Brat
Antony, 130, 138; Nelly (see Hagewout), 130, 138
Brearley, Harry, 220
Breisacher, Marie, 284
Brewster, "Mrs. Col. Amos" (Boudinot), 541
Breyant
Antje (see Kip), 301; Pieter, 301
Brickers, Weyntie (see Terheun), 309
Brickman (see Brueckeman)
Bries
Dinah (see Dusochay), 128; Hendrick, 128; Volkert, Hendrickse, 439
Brinkerhoff, Brinckerhof, Brinkerhof
Albert, 270, 281; Albert, Jr., 271; Altia Hopper, 271; Antje (see Verbryck), 281; Catharine Jane (see Cortelyou), 271; Elizabeth Kip, 281; George, 272; Harriet B., 271; Hendrick Jorisse, 265, 281; Hendrick, II, 281; Henry, 272; Henry H., 281; Jacob, 270, 272, 281; Jacob A., 281; Jacob G., 272; Jacob J., 281; Jacobus, 281; Jacobus H., 281; Jane (see Doremus), 289; James H., 281; Joris, 281; Joris Dircksen, 281; Lavina (see Vreeland), 325; Margaret Bartholf, 272; Nickasi, 281; Rachel (see Westervelt), 327; Rachel Romeyn, 281; Sarah (see Demarest), 281

Britton
Eliza (see Perine), 151; Elizabeth, 121; Elizabeth Gertrude Knight, 122; Frances (see Stillwell), 150; Harriet (see Lord), 122; James, 128; Martha (see Moore), 150; Mary, 121, 150; Nathaniel, 121, 150; Nathaniel, Jr., 121, 150, 151; Nathaniel Lord, Dr., 122; Nicholas, 130, 150; Rachel (see Dongan), 130, 150; Rachel (see Stillwell), 150; Violetta (see Dissosway), 128; William, 121, 150; William, Jr., 150

Brocas, Miss (see Schuyler), 511
Brocka (see Brokaw)
Brocker, Mrs. F., 292
Brockholst
Anthony, 465, 520; Judith (see Van Vechten), 465
Brokaw, Broucard, Brocka, Brokaer, Broka
Ann (see Van Nest), 443; Benjamin, 443; Benjamin, II, 443; Bourgeon, 442; Brogun, 443; Catharine (see Van Arsdalen), 443; Catharine (see Fisher), 439; Catharine ——, 443; Catharine Le Febre, 442; Chauncey, 446; Femmetje (see Staats), 442, 454; Ferdinand, 443; Hendrecy (see Lott), 443; Henry, 443; Isaac, 439, 443; James P., 445; John, Sr., 443; John, 442, 443, 454; John, Lt., 442, 443, 445, 454; John, Jr., Lt., 443, 444; Mary (see Bogart), 443; Mary (see Van Dyke), 443; Mary (Maretye) Van Cleave, 443; Mary (Maretye, Maria) Van der Veer, 443; Michael, 443; Phebe (see Stull), 443; Phebe (see Field), 443; Richard, 443; Sarah (see Van Deventer), 443; Sarah Van Middlesworth, 443

Broucard (see Brokaw)
Brouwer, Brower
Abraham, 137; Abram, 327; John, 405; Lea Dema-

Johannes (John), 287; John, 325; John (Johannes), 287; John, Rev., 503; Joost (George C.), 281; Joost, 295; Lawrence, 536, 537, 538; Lea, 287; Lea (see Brouwer) (see Westervelt), 327; Leah De Groot, 286-287; Margaret (see Banta), 277; Margaret (see Van Emburgh), 274; Margaret Haring, 295; Margaret Holdrum, 281; Margrietje, 288; Margrietje (see Perry), 288; Margrietje Haring, 287, 293; Maria, 287; Maria (see Durie), 290; Maria (see Eli), 285; Maria (sec Haring) (see Demarest), 296; Maria (see Oblenis), 202; Maria Smith, 285; Marie Dreuyn, 286; Marie Sohier, 284; Mary A., 267; Mary Elizabeth Vreeland, 281; Peter, 285; Peter, Jr., 285; Philip, 202; Pieter, 287; Rachel, 287; Rachel Banta, 278; Rachel Cresson, 286; Rachel Vorhase, 281; Rachel Zabriskie, 287, 288; Rebecca (see Westervelt), 327; Samuel, 285-286, 287, 290; Sarah Brinkerhoff, 281; Saretta, 267.

De Mayer, Nicholaes, 84

De Mont, Jannetje (see Van Vechten), 465

Denise, Nyssen
Catharine (see Hendrickson), 404, 410; Elsye Teunise (see Snedeker), 216; Mary (see Schenck), 408; Teunis, 404, 408; Tunis, 216

Depew, De Pew, Depue, Depui, De Puis, Dupuis, Du Puy, Du Puw
Abraham, 193, 195; Abraham C., 193; Annetje, 194; Annetje (see Van Dalsen), 193; Annetje Gerretse, 193; Annie Elsten, 192; Benjamin, 547; Brechje (Bridget) (see Smith), 195; Bregje, 194; Cornelis, 193; Elizabeth, 193; Elizabeth (see Blauvelt), 193, 195; Elizabeth (see Holdrum), 195; Elizabeth White, 193; François, 181, 192; Garret, 193; Geertje Williams, 192; Isaac, 193, 194, 195; Johannes, 194; John, 547; Margrietje, 194; Maria (see Van Campen), 547; Maria Van Campen, 547; Marretje Wynkoop, 547; Marritje (Martha) (see Cooper), 195; Mary, 193; Moses, 547; Nicholas, 176, 500; Peter, 192, 193, 195, 199; Peter, Jr., 193; Peter P., 194; Petrus, 194; Pieter, 194, 195; Rachel (see Blanch), 194; Samuel, 500, 548; Sarah (see Blauvelt), 181; Susanna (see Van Campen), 547; Theunis, 194; Willem, 192

De Rapalje (see Rapelyea)

Derfuss, John, 184

De Ronde, Maria (see Tallman), 231

De Ryck, Abraham, 198

Deshler, Charles, 386, 429

De Sille, Nicasius, 81, 82

Des Marest (see Demarest)

De Vouw
Catharina Ecker(son) (see Blauvelt), 181; Nicholas, 181

De Wint
Anna (Antje) Kermer, 191, 212; Anna Maria (see Blauvelt), 191; Jemima (see Smidt), 212; Johannes, 212; John, 190, 191

De Witt
Henry, 549; John H., 549; Katrena (see Lott), 63

De Wolf, De Wolfe
Catharine Haring, 294; Charles, 294; John Haring, 294; Maggie Cleveland, 294; Martin, 294

Dey, Dye
Abigail Lewis, 533; Ann, 504; Anneken Schouten, 504, 509; Derrick, 533; Dirck, 504, 505, 509; Dirck Jansen, 504; Geertje Jans Langendyck, 504; Hannah Pierson, 504-505; Hannah Schouten, 531; Hester Schuyler, 504; James Hanse, 133; Jane (see Varick), 504; Jane Doremus, 533; Jannetje Theunis, 504; Jeanne (Jane) Blanchard, 504; John, 533; Margaret, 504; Richard, Gen., 504-505; Sarah (see Post) (see Hughes), 533; Sarah Toers, 533; Teunis, 531; Thenis, 504; Theunis, Col., 504, 505, 509; Thomas, 533

Diderick, Didericks, Diederick
Grietje Warnaerts Sip, 323; Hans, 306, 323, 513

Diehl, H., 94

Dirckse, Antje (see Van Giesen), 518

Dirkje, Martje (see Van Giesen), 518

Dissossway, Dissosway, Disosway, Du Sauchoy, Dusochay, Dusosway, Dusway
Ann (see Guyon), 128; Ann (see Winant), 129; Ann M. (see Cole), 129; Annetje (see Beadel), 128; Catharine (see Van Brunt), 128; Catharine Corsell, 128; Charity (see Prall), 128; Cornelius, 128; Cornelius, Jr., 128, 129; Daniel W., 129; Dinah (sec Bries), 128; Elizabeth (see Barberie), 128; Elizabeth Rossignol, 127; Gabriel, 128, 140; Geertruy Van Deventer, 128; Israel, 128, 129; Israel, Jr., 128, 129, 140; Israel R., 128, 129; Jane, 127; Jannetie (see Boeg), 127; Jean, 127; Job, 128; Magdalenc (sec Hardewyn), 127; Marc, 127; Marcus, 127, 128, 129; Maria, 127; Mark, 127, 128; Mark, III, 128, 129; Mary, 128; Mary Baldwin, 128; Sarah, 128; Sarah Denis, 128; Susanna, 127; Susanna Hendricks, 128; Susanna Totten, 129; Violetta (see Britton), 128

Ditmars, Ditmas
Henry, 440; John, 85; Maria Elizabeth (see Van Pelt), 85; Marytje (see Voorhees), 399; Mattie (see Hoagland) (see Van Doren), 461; Peter, 440; Phebe (see Van Derveer), 459

Dobbs, William, 196

Dockwra (Dochrea, Dockera), William, 437, 452, 466

Dodd, Dod, Dods
John, 534; Lea, 534; Polly ——, 534; Donaldson, Mrs. Malcom Montgomery, 468

Dongan, Duncan
Abigail (see Simonsen), 148; John, 130; Magdalena (see Charlton), 130; Rachel (see Britton), 130, 150; Thomas, 129, 130, 138, 149, 150, 293; Walter, 130, 148, 150

Doremus
Abraham, 535; Albert, 289; Anna Berdan, 289; Ann Parlaman, 539, 540; Antje Yong, 535; Benjamin, 536; Cornelis, 289, 498, 535, 536; Cornelis (Cornelius), 535, 537; Cornelis, III, 536; Elizabeth (see Van Alen), 312; Francis, 536; George, 289; George, Jr., 289; Golyn, 535; Harriet Zabriskie, 289; Henry, 312, 535, 536, 539; James, 539, 540; Jane (see Dey), 533; Jane Brinkerhoff, 289; Johannes, 536; Johannis, 539; John, 289, 520, 535, 538; John, II, 535; John B., 289; Joris, 289; Lena Mandeville, 536; Margaret (see Van Houten), 520; Maria (see Hopper), 289; Maria Lutkins, 289; Marretje, 289; Peggy Van Winkel, 535; Peter, 289; Petrus, 536; Rachel Spier, 535; Richard, 289; Sarah Margaret (see Huntoon), 540; Simeon, 533; Thomas, 535; Thomas, Capt., 535-540

Doty, Doughty
Jane Staats, 455, 456; Joseph, 456; Joshua, 436, 437; Joshua, Jr., 437

Dreuyn, Maria (see Demarest), 286

John, Jr., 123; Magdalena Jans, 152; Magdalena Morgan, 152; Maria (see Kroesen), 152; Mary, 153; Raymond M., 153; Richard, 151, 153; Sarah, 152

Titsworth, Tietsoort
Abigail Beers, 545; Abraham Willemszen van Amsterdam, 544; Aechtje Jan van Naerdan, 544; Anna, 544; Catrina Kuykendal, 545; Jacobus, 545; John, Dr., 545; Kate ——, 545; Margaret Middagh, 545; Maria, 544-545; Neeltje Swart, 544; Sarah Decker, 544, 545; Sarah Hoornbeck, 544; Stephanus, 545; Stephanus W., 544, 545; Willem, 499; William (Willem Abrahamse), 544; William, II, 545; William S. (Willem), 544, 545

Titus
Mary, 72, 86; Teunis (Tunis), 72, 85, 87

Toers
Arent, 307; Catlyntje (see Newkirk), 307; Sarah (see Dey), 533; Thomas Laurensen, 533

Torner, Jannetje (see Cockefair), 507

Torr, John M., 223

Tourneur, Terneur, Turnure
Aefie, 226; Daniel, 225; Hendrick (Henry), 226; Jacobus, 225; Jacobus, Jr., 226; Jacomina (see Oblenis), 225; Jacqueline de Parisis, 225; Jacques, 225; Jannetie, 226; John, 226; John (see Hutton), 226; John L., 290; Margrietje Blauvelt, 226; Maria (see Oblenis), 226; Marritie Kuyper, 226; Michail, 226; Riker, 290; Sarah, 226

Tonnette, Mary, 221

Townsend, Elizabeth J. (see Terheun), 310

Trembly, Hannah (see Staats), 453

Truwer, John, 334

Tuthill, B. F., 549

Tuttle, Stephen, 540

Turnure (see Tourneur)

Tymouth
Barber Parleman, 539; Jacob, 539

Tysen (see Tison)

Underhill, John, 75

Valleau, Magdelene Franconier, 279

Vallenburgh, John, 148

Van Aken , Van Aker
Isaac, 547; Rachel —— (see Van Campen), 547

Van Alen, Vanalen, Van Ale, Van Allen
Andrew, Dr., 312; Elizabeth Doremus, 312; Gerret (Garret), 312; Hendrick, 313; Henry, 312, 313; Henry (Hendrick), 312; Hessel, 312; Jannetje Lozier, 313; John, 313; John H., 312; Peter, 279, 312, 313; Pieter Gerritse, 312; Thomasina Earle Hallenbeck, 312; William, 312; Wyntie, 313

Van Amsterdam, Abraham Willemszen, 544

Van Arsdalen, Catharine Brokaw, 443

Van Bergh
Dinah (see Frelinghuysen) (see Hardenburgh), 436; Louis, 436; Mrs. Louis, 436

Van Beverhoudt
Adriana (see Boudinot), 541; Lucas, 540, 541; Maria Malvill Suhm, 541

Vanblercom, Mary (see Youmans), 319

Van Bommel, Hendrick, 176

Van Borsom, Van Borsum
Anna, 61; Cornelius, 76; Egbert, 61; Sara Roeloffs (see Stoothoff), 76

Van Boskerk (see Van Buskirk)

Van Broeckhuysen, Michael Jansen, 324

Van Brunt
Abigail (see Vanderbilt), 83; Abraham, 83; Adriaense, 82; Adrian, 83; Aletta, 83; Bennet, 82; Catharine (see Berre), 83; Catherine (see Dissosway), 138; Cornelis, 82, 83; Cornelis Rutgers, 82; Elizabeth Alberts Van Voorhees, 83; Engeltie Rapalje, 83; George, 83; Gretian, 82; Jane Maria, 83; Jeremiah, 83; Joost, 82; Nicholas, 82, 83; Rutger (see Joosten), 81, 82; Rutgert, 82, 83; Rutgert A., 83; Tryntje, 82; Tryntje Class (see Harmensen), 82; William, 128

Van Buskirk, Van Boskerk
Abraham, 314; Andries, 314; Catharine (see Osborn), 314; Fitje, 314; Geertruy, 314; Isaac, 314; Jannetje Jans Van Hoorn, 314; Johannis, 314; Laurens, 314; Laurens Andriessen, 265, 314, 317; Margrietje, 314; Margrietje Hendrick Van der Linden, 314; Michael, 314; Peter, 314; Rachel Hopper, 314; Thomas, 265-266, 314; Thomas, 314, 315, 316, 317

Van Campen, Van Camp
Abraham, Col., 499, 545-548; Abraham, Jr., 547, 549; Abraham, III, 547; Benjamin, 547; Catharine (see Depew), 547; Catharine Rosenkrans, 549; Cecilia (see Ribble), 547; Cecilia Decker, 547; Corianny (Rosanny), 549; Derricke Smidt, 183; Gerrit, 546; Gerrit Jansen, 546; Hendrick, 183; Isaac, 499; 548, 549; James, 547; John, 546, 548; John, Jr., 548; John, II, 547; Lena, 549; Mackelt Stoffels Lodewyck, 546; Magdalena Van Garden, 548; Margaret, 549; Maria (see Depew), 547; Maria Depue, 547; Moses, Maj., 547; Rachel —— Van Aker, 547; Sarah ——, 548; Sarah Cape, 547; Sarah Westfaal, 547; Susanna (see Romaine), 547; Susanna Depue, 547; Tietje Jans Decker, 546

Van Cleave
Benjamin, 443; Mary (Maretye) (see Brokaw), 443

Van Cleef, Van Cleve, Van Cleaf
Benjamin, 399; Engeltje (see Pietersen), 84; H. B., 542; Jan, 84; Neeltje Couwenhoven, 399

Van Cortlandt
Jacobus, 87; Jacobus, Col., 328; Sophia (see Van Enden), 87; Stephanus, 87

Van Couwenhoven (see Couwenhoven)

Van Dalsen
Alltye (see Haring), 293; Annetje (see De Pew), 193; Dirckje Theunis Tallman, 194; Johannes, 194

Van Dam
Cornelia Beekman, 451, 452; Richard, 451

Van Dean, Catrina Leah (see Van Winkle), 525

Van den Ende (see Van Ende)

Vandenhoff, Henry, 279

Vanderbeek, Van der Beek, Van der Beck
Abraham, 315; Annatje De Boog, 316; Barent, 316; Coenradt, 315; Conradus, 316; Dorthea (Dorothea) Coteleau (see Cortelyou), 143, 144; Elsie (see Kip), 301; Elsie Kip, 316; Elsje Jans, 315; Isaac, 278, 315, 316; Isaac, Jr., 316; Jacob, 316; Jannetje Springsteen Colve, 315; Mary Thomas Badie Verdon Bennet, 315; Paulus, 315, 316; Rem, 143, 144; Salomon, 316; Sarah Remsen (see Adriance), 65; Solomon, 316; Walter, 280

Vanderbilt, Van Der Bilt, Van Der Belt
Abigail (see Van Brunt), 83; Aeltje (see Hogenkamp), 209; Annatje, 227; Annatje (Ann) (see

Dover Books on Art

Dover Books on Art

ART ANATOMY, Dr. William Rimmer. One of the few books on art anatomy that are themselves works of art, this is a faithful reproduction (rearranged for handy use) of the extremely rare masterpiece of the famous 19th century anatomist, sculptor, and art teacher. Beautiful, clear line drawings show every part of the body—bony structure, muscles, features, etc. Unusual are the sections on falling bodies, foreshortenings, muscles in tension, grotesque personalities, and Rimmer's remarkable interpretation of emotions and personalities as expressed by facial features. It will supplement every other book on art anatomy you are likely to have. Reproduced clearer than the lithographic original (which sells for $500 on up on the rare book market.) Over 1,200 illustrations. xiii + 153pp. 7¾ x 10¾.

T908 Paperbound $2.00

THE CRAFTSMAN'S HANDBOOK, Cennino Cennini. The finest English translation of IL LIBRO DELL' ARTE, the 15th century introduction to art technique that is both a mirror of Quatrocento life and a source of many useful but nearly forgotten facets of the painter's art. 4 illustrations. xxvii + 142pp. D. V. Thompson, translator. 5⅜ x 8.   T54 Paperbound $1.50

THE BROWN DECADES, Lewis Mumford. A picture of the "buried renaissance" of the post-Civil War period, and the founding of modern architecture (Sullivan, Richardson, Root, Roebling), landscape development (Marsh, Olmstead, Eliot), and the graphic arts (Homer, Eakins, Ryder). 2nd revised, enlarged edition. Bibliography. 12 illustrations. xiv + 266 pp. 5⅜ x 8.

T200 Paperbound $1.75

THE HUMAN FIGURE, J. H. Vanderpoel. Not just a picture book, but a complete course by a famous figure artist. Extensive text, illustrated by 430 pencil and charcoal drawings of both male and female anatomy. 2nd enlarged edition. Foreword. 430 illus. 143pp. 6⅛ x 9¼.   T432 Paperbound $1.45

PINE FURNITURE OF EARLY NEW ENGLAND, R. H. Kettell. Over 400 illustrations, over 50 working drawings of early New England chairs, benches, beds, cupboards, mirrors, shelves, tables, other furniture esteemed for simple beauty and character. "Rich store of illustrations . . . emphasizes the individuality and varied design," ANTIQUES. 413 illustrations, 55 working drawings. 475pp. 8 x 10¾.   T145 Clothbound $10.00

Dover Books on Art

MASTERPIECES OF FURNITURE, Verna Cook Salomonsky.
Photographs and measured drawings of some of the finest examples of Colonial American, 17th century English, Windsor,
Sheraton, Hepplewhite, Chippendale, Louis XIV, Queen Anne,
and various other furniture styles. The textual matter includes
information on traditions, characteristics, background, etc. of
various pieces. 101 plates. Bibliography. 224pp. 7⅞ x 10¾.

T1381 Paperbound $2.00

PRIMITIVE ART, Franz Boas. In this exhaustive volume, a
great American anthropologist analyzes all the fundamental
traits of primitive art, covering the formal element in art, representative art, symbolism, style, literature, music, and the dance.
Illustrations of Indian embroidery, paleolithic paintings, woven
blankets, wing and tail designs, totem poles, cutlery, earthen-
ware, baskets and many other primitive objects and motifs. Over
900 illustrations. 376pp. 5⅜ x 8.   T25 Paperbound $2.25

*AN INTRODUCTION TO A HISTORY OF WOODCUT, A. M.
Hind.* Nearly all of this authoritative 2-volume set is devoted to
the 15th century—the period during which the woodcut came of
age as an important art form. It is the most complete compendium
of information on this period, the artists who contributed to it,
and their technical and artistic accomplishments. Profusely illustrated with cuts by 15th century masters, and later works
for comparative purposes. 484 illustrations. 5 indexes. Total of
xi + 838pp. 5⅜ x 8½. Two-volume set, T952-3 Paperbound $5.00

ART STUDENTS' ANATOMY, E. J. Farris. Teaching anatomy
by using chiefly living objects for illustration, this study has
enjoyed long popularity and success in art courses and home-
study programs. All the basic elements of the human anatomy
are illustrated in minute detail, diagrammed and pictured as they
pass through common movements and actions. 158 drawings,
photographs, and roentgenograms. Glossary of anatomical terms.
x + 159pp. 5⅝ x 8⅜.   T744 Paperbound $1.50

COLONIAL LIGHTING, A. H. Hayward. The only book to cover
the fascinating story of lamps and other lighting devices in
America. Beginning with rush light holders used by the early
settlers, it ranges through the elaborate chandeliers of the Federal period, illustrating 647 lamps. Of great value to antique
collectors, designers, and historians of arts and crafts. Revised
and enlarged by James R. Marsh. xxxi + 198pp. 5⅝ x 8¼.

T975 Paperbound $2.00

GREEK REVIVAL ARCHITECTURE IN AMERICA, T. Hamlin. A comprehensive study of the American Classical Revival, its regional variations, reasons for its success and eventual decline. Profusely illustrated with photos, sketches, floor plans and sections, displaying the work of almost every important architect of the time. 2 appendices. 39 figures, 94 plates containing 221 photos, 62 architectural designs, drawings, etc. 324-item classified bibliography. Index. xi + 439pp. 5⅜ x 8½.

T1148 Paperbound $3.00

CREATIVE LITHOGRAPHY AND HOW TO DO IT, Grant Arnold. Written by a man who practiced and taught lithography for many years, this highly useful volume explains all the steps of the lithographic process from tracing the drawings on the stone to printing the lithograph, with helpful hints for solving special problems. Index. 16 reproductions of lithographs. 11 drawings. xv + 214pp. of text. 5⅜ x 8½.

T1208 Paperbound $1.65

TEACH YOURSELF ANTIQUE COLLECTING, E. Bradford. An excellent, brief guide to collecting British furniture, silver, pictures and prints, pewter, pottery and porcelain, Victoriana, enamels, clocks or other antiques. Much background information difficult to find elsewhere. 15pp. of illus. 215pp. 7 x 4¼.

Clothbound $2.00

THE STANDARD BOOK OF QUILT MAKING AND COLLECTING, M. Ickis. Even if you are a beginner, you will soon find yourself quilting like an expert, by following these clearly drawn patterns, photographs, and step-by-step instructions. Learn how to plan the quilt, to select the pattern to harmonize with the design and color of the room, to choose materials. Over 40 full-size patterns. Index. 483 illustrations. One color plate. xi + 276pp. 6¾ x 9½. 　　　　　T582 Paperbound $2.00

THE ENJOYMENT AND USE OF COLOR, W. Sargent. Requiring no special technical know-how, this book tells you all about color and how it is created, perceived, and imitated in art. Covers many little-known facts about color values, intensities, effects of high and low illumination, complementary colors, and color harmonies. Simple do-it-yourself experiments and observations. 35 illustrations, including 6 full-page color plates. New color frontispiece. Index. x + 274 pp. 5⅜ x 8.

T944 Paperbound $2.00

Dover Books on Art

LANDSCAPE GARDENING IN JAPAN, Josiah Conder. A detailed picture of Japanese gardening techniques and ideas, the artistic principles incorporated in the Japanese garden, and the religious and ethical concepts at the heart of those principles. Preface. 92 illustrations, plus all 40 full-page plates from the Supplement. Index. xv + 299pp. 8⅜ x 11¼.

T1216 Paperbound $2.75

DESIGN AND FIGURE CARVING, E. J. Tangerman. "Anyone who can peel a potato can carve," states the author, and in this unusual book he shows you how, covering every stage in detail from very simple exercises working up to museum-quality pieces. Terrific aid for hobbyists, arts and crafts counselors, teachers, those who wish to make reproductions for the commercial market. Appendix: How to Enlarge a Design. Brief bibliography. Index. 1298 figures. x + 289pp. 5⅜ x 8½.

T1209 Paperbound $1.85

WILD FOWL DECOYS, Joel Barber. Antique dealers, collectors, craftsmen, hunters, readers of Americana, etc. will find this the only thorough and reliable guide on the market today to this unique folk art. It contains the history, cultural significance, regional design variations; unusual decoy lore; working plans for constructing decoys; and loads of illustrations. 140 full-page plates, 4 in color. 14 additional plates of drawings and plans by the author. xxvii + 156pp. 7⅞ x 10¾.   T11 Paperbound $2.75

1800 WOODCUTS BY THOMAS BEWICK AND HIS SCHOOL. This is the largest collection of first-rate pictorial woodcuts in print—an indispensable part of the working library of every commercial artist, art director, production designer, packaging artist, craftsman, manufacturer, librarian, art collector, and artist. And best of all, when you buy your copy of Bewick, you buy the rights to reproduce individual illustrations—no permission needed, no acknowledgments, no clearance fees! Classified index. Bibliography and sources. xiv + 246pp. 9 x 12.

T766 Clothbound $10.00

THE SCRIPT LETTER, Tommy Thompson. Prepared by a noted authority, this is a thorough, straightforward course of instruction with advice on virtually every facet of the art of script lettering. Also a brief history of lettering with examples from early copy books and illustrations from present day advertising and packaging. Copiously illustrated. Bibliography. 128pp. 6½ x 9⅛.   THE1311 Paperbound $1.00

Dover Books on Art

THE HISTORY AND TECHNIQUE OF LETTERING, A. Nesbitt. A thorough history of lettering from the ancient Egyptians to the present, and a 65-page course in lettering for artists. Every major development in lettering history is illustrated by a complete aphabet. Fully analyzes such masters as Caslon, Koch, Garamont, Jenson, and many more. 89 alphabets, 165 other specimens. 317pp. 7½ x 10½.   T427 Paperbound $2.00

LETTERING AND ALPHABETS, J. A. Cavanagh. An unabridged reissue of "Lettering," containing the full discussion, analysis, illustration of 89 basic hand lettering styles based on Caslon, Bodoni, Gothic, many other types. Hundreds of technical hints on construction, strokes, pens, brushes, etc. 89 alphabets, 72 lettered specimens, which may be reproduced permission-free. 121pp. 9¾ x 8.   T53 Paperbound $1.35

THE HUMAN FIGURE IN MOTION, Eadweard Muybridge. The largest collection in print of Muybridge's famous high-speed action photos. 4789 photographs in more than 500 action-strip-sequences (at shutter speeds up to 1/6000th of a second) illustrate men, women, children—mostly undraped—performing such actions as walking, running, getting up, lying down, carrying objects, throwing, etc. "An unparalleled dictionary of action for all artists," AMERICAN ARTIST. 390 full-page plates, with 4789 photographs. Heavy glossy stock, reinforced binding with headbands. 7⅞ x 10¾.   T204 Clothbound $10.00

ANIMALS IN MOTION, Eadweard Muybridge. The largest collection of animal action photos in print. 34 different animals (horses, mules, oxen, goats, camels, pigs, cats, lions, gnus, deer, monkeys, eagles—and 22 others) in 132 characteristic actions. All 3919 photographs are taken in series at speeds up to 1/1600th of a second, offering artists, biologists, cartoonists a remarkable opportunity to see exactly how an ostrich's head bobs when running, how a lion puts his foot down, how an elephant's knee bends, how a bird flaps his wings, thousands of other hard-to-catch details. "A really marvellous series of plates," NATURE. 380 full-page plates. Heavy glossy stock, reinforced binding with headbands. 7⅞ x 10¾.   T203 Clothbound $10.00

BASIC BOOKBINDING, A. W. Lewis. Enables both beginners and experts to rebind old books or bind paperbacks in hard covers. Treats materials, tools; gives step-by-step instruction in how to collate a book, sew it, back it, make boards, etc. 261 illus. Appendices. 155pp. 5⅜ x 8.   T169 Paperbound $1.45

Dover Books on Art

HAWTHORNE ON PAINTING. Vivid re-creation, from students' notes, of instructions by Charles Hawthorne at Cape Cod School of Art. Essays, epigrammatic comments on color, form, seeing, techniques, etc. "Excellent," Time. 100pp. 5⅜ x 8.
T653 Paperbound $1.00

THE HANDBOOK OF PLANT AND FLORAL ORNAMENT, R. G. Hatton. 1200 line illustrations, from medieval, Renaissance herbals, of flowering or fruiting plants: garden flowers, wild flowers, medicinal plants, poisons, industrial plants, etc. A unique compilation that probably could not be matched in any library in the world. Formerly"The Craftsman's Plant-Book." Also full text on uses, history as ornament, etc. 548pp. 6⅛ x 9¼.
T649 Paperbound $3.00

DECORATIVE ALPHABETS AND INITIALS, Alexander Nesbitt. 91 complete alphabets, over 3900 ornamental initials, from Middle Ages, Renaissance printing, baroque, rococo, and modern sources. Individual items copyright free, for use in commercial art, crafts, design, packaging, etc. 123 full-page plates. 3924 initials. 129pp. 7¾ x 10¾.　　　　T544 Paperbound $2.25

METHODS AND MATERIALS OF THE GREAT SCHOOLS AND MASTERS, Sir Charles Eastlake. (Formerly titled "Materials for a History of Oil Painting.") Vast, authentic reconstruction of secret techniques of the masters, recreated from ancient manuscripts, contemporary accounts, analysis of paintings, etc. Oils, fresco, tempera, varnishes, encaustics. Both Flemish and Italian schools, also British and French. One of great works for art historians, critics; inexhaustible mine of suggestions, information for practicing artists. Total of 1025pp. 5⅜ x 8.
Two volume set, T718-9 Paperbound $4.50

BYZANTINE ART AND ARCHAEOLOGY, O. M. Dalton. Still most thorough work in English on Byzantine art forms throughout ancient and medieval world. Analyzes hundreds of pieces, covers sculpture, painting, mosaic, jewelry, textiles, architecture, etc. Historical development; specific examples; iconology and ideas; symbolism. A treasure-trove of material about one of most important art traditions, will supplement and expand any other book in area. Bibliography of over 2500 items. 457 illustrations. 747pp. 6⅛ x 9¼.　　　T776 Clothbound $8.50

FOOT-HIGH LETTERS: A GUIDE TO LETTERING, M. Price.
28 15½ x 22½″ plates, give classic Roman alphabet, one foot
high per letter, plus 9 other 2″ high letter forms for each letter.
16 page syllabus. Ideal for lettering classes, home study. 28 plates
in box.   T239 $6.00

A HANDBOOK OF WEAVES, G. H. Oelsner. Most complete
book of weaves, fully explained, differentiated, illustrated. Plain
weaves, irregular, double-stitched, filling satins; derivative,
basket, rib weaves; steep, broken, herringbone, twills, lace, tricot,
many others. Translated, revised by S. S. Dale; supplement on
analysis of weaves. Bible for all handweavers. 1875 illustrations.
410pp. 6⅛ x 9¼.   T209 Clothbound $5.00

*JAPANESE HOMES AND THEIR SURROUNDINGS, E. S.
Morse.* Classic describes, analyses, illustrates all aspects of traditional Japanese home, from plan and structure to appointments, furniture, etc. Published in 1886, before Japanese architecture was contaminated by Western, this is strikingly modern
in beautiful, functional approach to living. Indispensable to every
architect, interior decorator, designer. 307 illustrations. Glossary.
410pp. 5⅝ x 8⅜.   T746 Paperbound $2.25

THE DRAWINGS OF HEINRICH KLEY. Uncut publication of
long-sought-after sketchbooks of satiric, ironic iconoclast. Remarkable fantasy, weird symbolism, brilliant technique make
Kley a shocking experience to layman, endless source of ideas,
techniques for artist. 200 drawings, original size, captions translated. Introduction. 136pp. 6 x 9.   T24 Paperbound $1.65

COSTUMES OF THE ANCIENTS, Thomas Hope. Beautiful,
clear, sharp line drawings of Greek and Roman figures in full
costume, by noted artist and antiquary of early 19th century.
Dress, armor, divinities, masks, etc. Invaluable sourcebook for
costumers, designers, first-rate picture file for illustrators, commercial artists. Introductory text by Hope. 300 plates. 6 x 9.
                                               T21 Paperbound $2.00

VITRUVIUS: TEN BOOKS ON ARCHITECTURE. The most
influential book in the history of architecture. 1st century A.D.
Roman classic has influenced such men as Bramante, Palladio,
Michelangelo, up to present. Classic principles of design, har-
mony, etc. Fascinating reading. Definitive English translation by
Professor H. Morgan, Harvard. 344pp. 5⅜ x 8.
                                               T645 Paperbound $2.00

Dover Books on Art

HANDBOOK OF DESIGNS AND DEVICES, C. P. Hornung. A remarkable working collection of 1836 basic designs and variations, all copyright-free. Variations of circle, line, cross, diamond, swastika, star, scroll, shield, many more. Notes on symbolism. "A necessity to every designer who would be original without having to labor heavily," ARTIST AND ADVERTISER. 204 plates. 240pp. 5⅜ x 8.　　　　　　T125 Paperbound $2.00

THE UNIVERSAL PENMAN, George Bickham. Exact reproduction of beautiful 18th-century book of handwriting. 22 complete alphabets in finest English roundhand, other scripts, over 2000 elaborate flourishes, 122 calligraphic illustrations, etc. Material is copyright-free. "An essential part of any art library, and a book of permanent value," AMERICAN ARTIST. 212 plates. 224pp. 9 x 13¾.　　　　　　T20 Clothbound $10.00

AN ATLAS OF ANATOMY FOR ARTISTS, F. Schider. This standard work contains 189 full-page plates, more than 647 illustrations of all aspects of the human skeleton, musculature, cutaway portions of the body, each part of the anatomy, hand forms, eyelids, breasts, location of muscles under the flesh, etc. 59 plates illustrate how Michelangelo, da Vinci, Goya, 15 others, drew human anatomy. New 3rd edition enlarged by 52 new illustrations by Cloquet, Barcsay. "The standard reference tool," AMERICAN LIBRARY ASSOCIATION. "Excellent," AMERICAN ARTIST. 189 plates, 647 illustrations. xxvi + 192pp. 7⅞ x 10⅝.　　　　　　T241 Clothbound $6.00

AN ATLAS OF ANIMAL ANATOMY FOR ARTISTS, W. Ellenberger, H. Baum, H. Dittrich. The largest, richest animal anatomy for artists in English. Form, musculature, tendons, bone structure, expression, detailed cross sections of head, other features, of the horse, lion, dog, cat, deer, seal, kangaroo, cow, bull, goat, monkey, hare, many other animals. "Highly recommended," DESIGN. Second, revised, enlarged edition with new plates from Cuvier, Stubbs, etc. 288 illustrations. 153pp. 11⅜ x 9.
　　　　　　T82 Clothbound $6.00

VASARI ON TECHNIQUE, G. Vasari. Pupil of Michelangelo, outstanding biographer of Renaissance artists reveals technical methods of his day. Marble, bronze, fresco painting, mosaics, engraving, stained glass, rustic ware, etc. Only English translation, extensively annotated by G. Baldwin Brown. 18 plates. 342pp. 5⅜ x 8.　　　　　　T717 Paperbound $2.00

Dover Books on Art

ARCHITECTURAL AND PERSPECTIVE DESIGNS, Giuseppe Galli Bibiena. 50 imaginative scenic drawings of Giuseppe Galli Bibiena, principal theatrical engineer and architect to the Viennese court of Charles VI. Aside from its interest to art historians, students, and art lovers, there is a whole Baroque world of material in this book for the commercial artist. Portrait of Charles VI by Martin de Meytens. 1 allegorical plate. 50 additional plates. New introduction. vi + 103pp. 10⅛ x 13¼.
T1263 Paperbound $2.25

PRINTED EPHEMERA, edited and collected by John Lewis. This book contains centuries of design, typographical and pictorial motives in proven, effective commercial layouts. Hundreds of the most striking examples of labels, tickets, posters, wrappers, programs, menus, and other items have been collected in this handsome and useful volume, along with information on the dimensions and colors of the original, printing processes used, stylistic notes on typography and design, etc. Study this book and see how the best commercial artists of the past and present have solved their particular problems. Most of the material is copyright free. 713 illustrations, many in color. Illustrated index of type faces included. Glossary of technical terms. Indexes. 288pp. 9¼ x 12. T1037 Clothbound $15.00

DESIGN FOR ARTISTS AND CRAFTSMEN, Louis Wolchonok. Recommended for either individual or classroom use, this book helps you to create original designs from things about you, from geometric patterns, from plants, animals, birds, humans, landscapes, manmade objects. "A great contribution," N. Y. Society of Craftsmen. 113 exercises with hints and diagrams. More than 1280 illustrations. xv + 207pp. 7⅞ x 10¾.
T274 Clothbound $4.95

ART AND THE SOCIAL ORDER, D. W. Gotshalk. Is art only an extension of society? Is it completely isolated? In this delightfully written book, Professor Gotshalk supplies some workable answers. He discusses various theories of art from Plato to Marx and Freud and uses all areas of visual arts, music and literature to elaborate his views. "Seems to me the soundest and most penetrating work on the philosophy of art to appear in recent years," C. J. Ducasse, Brown Univ. Addenda: "Postscript to Chapter X: 1962." Bibliography in notes. Index. xviii + 255pp. 5⅜ x 8½.
T294 Paperbound $1.65

THE STYLES OF ORNAMENT, A. Speltz. The largest collection of line ornament in print, with 3750 numbered illustrations arranged chronologically from Egypt, Assyria, Greeks, Romans, Etruscans, through Medieval, Renaissance, 18th century, and Victorian. No permissions, no fees needed to use or reproduce illustrations. 400 plates with 3750 illustrations. Bibliography. Index. 640pp. 6 x 9.   T577 Paperbound $2.50

THE ART OF ETCHING, E. S. Lumsden. Every step of the etching process from essential materials to completed proof is carefully and clearly explained, with 24 annotated plates exemplifying every technique and approach discussed. The book also features a rich survey of the art, with 105 annotated plates by masters. Invaluable for beginner to advanced etcher. 374pp. 5⅜ x 8.   T49 Paperbound $2.50

EPOCHS OF CHINESE AND JAPANESE ART, E. Fenollosa. Classic study of pre-20th century Oriental art, revealing, as does no other book, the important interrelationships between the art of China and Japan and their history and sociology. Illustrations include ancient bronzes, Buddhist paintings by Kobo Daishi, scroll paintings by Toba Sojo, prints by Nobusane, screens by Korin, woodcuts by Hokusai, Koryusai, Utamaro, Hiroshige and scores of other pieces by Chinese and Japanese masters. Biographical preface. Notes. Index. 242 illustrations. Total of lii + 439pp. plus 174 plates. 5⅝ x 8¼.

Two-volume set, T364-5 Paperbound $5.00

OF THE JUST SHAPING OF LETTERS, Albrecht Dürer. This remarkable volume reveals Albrecht Dürer's rules for the geometric construction of Roman capitals and the formation of Gothic lower case and capital letters, complete with construction diagrams and directions. Of considerable practical interest to the contemporary illustrator, artist, and designer. Translated from the Latin text of the edition of 1535 by R. T. Nichol. Numerous letterform designs, construction diagrams, illustrations. iv + 43pp. 7⅞ x 10¾.   T1306 Paperbound $1.25

DESIGN MOTIFS OF ANCIENT MEXICO, J. Enciso. Nearly 90% of these 766 superb designs from Aztec, Olmec, Totonac, Maya, and Toltec origins are unobtainable elsewhere. Contains plumed serpents, wind gods, animals, demons, dancers, monsters, etc. Excellent applied design source. Originally $17.50. 766 illustrations, thousands of motifs. 192pp. 6⅛ x 9¼.

T84 Paperbound $1.85

Dover Books on Art

A HANDBOOK OF ANATOMY FOR ART STUDENTS, Arthur Thomson. This long-popular text teaches any student, regardless of level of technical competence, all the subtleties of human anatomy. Clear photographs, numerous line sketches and diagrams of bones, joints, etc. Use it as a text for home study, as a supplement to life class work, or as a lifelong sourcebook and reference volume. Author's prefaces. 67 plates, containing 40 line drawings, 86 photographs—mostly full page. 211 figures. Appendix. Index. xx + 459pp. 5⅜ x 8⅜. T1163 Paperbound $3.00

WHITTLING AND WOODCARVING, E. J. Tangerman. With this book, a beginner who is moderately handy can whittle or carve scores of useful objects, toys for children, gifts, or simply pass hours creatively and enjoyably. "Easy as well as instructive reading," N. Y. Herald Tribune Books. 464 illustrations, with appendix and index. x + 293pp. 5½ x 8⅛.
T965 Paperbound $1.75

ONE HUNDRED AND ONE PATCHWORK PATTERNS, Ruby Short McKim. Whether you have made a hundred quilts or none at all, you will find this the single most useful book on quilt-making. There are 101 full patterns (all exact size) with full instructions for cutting and sewing. In addition there is some really choice folklore about the origin of the ingenious pattern names: "Monkey Wrench," "Road to California," "Drunkard's Path," "Crossed Canoes," to name a few. Over 500 illustrations. 124 pp. 7⅞ x 10¾. T773 Paperbound $1.85

ART AND GEOMETRY, W. M. Ivins, Jr. Challenges the idea that the foundations of modern thought were laid in ancient Greece. Pitting Greek tactile-muscular intuitions of space against modern visual intuitions, the author, for 30 years curator of prints, Metropolitan Museum of Art, analyzes the differences between ancient and Renaissance painting and sculpture and tells of the first fruitful investigations of perspective. x + 113pp. 5⅜ x 8⅜. T941 Paperbound $1.00

TEACH YOURSELF TO STUDY SCULPTURE, Wm. Gaunt. Useful details on the sculptor's art and craft, tools, carving and modeling; its relation to other arts; ways to look at sculpture; sculpture of the East and West; etc. "Useful both to the student and layman and a good refresher for the professional sculptor," Prof. J. Skeaping, Royal College of Art. 32 plates, 24 figures. Index. xii + 155pp. 7 x 4¼. Clothbound $2.00

Dover Books on Art

STYLES IN PAINTING, Paul Zucker. By comparing paintings of similar subject matter, the author shows the characteristics of various painting styles. You are shown at a glance the differences between reclining nudes by Giorgione, Velasquez, Goya, Modigliani; how a Byzantine portrait is unlike a portrait by Van Eyck, da Vinci, Dürer, or Marc Chagall; how the painting of landscapes has changed gradually from ancient Pompeii to Lyonel Feininger in our own century. 241 beautiful, sharp photographs illustrate the text. xiv + 338 pp. 5⅝ x 8¼.

T760 Paperbound $2.00

THE PRACTICE OF TEMPERA PAINTING, D. V. Thompson, Jr. Used in Egyptian and Minoan wall paintings and in much of the fine work of Giotto, Botticelli, Titian, and many others, tempera has long been regarded as one of the finest painting methods known. This is the definitive work on the subject by the world's outstanding authority. He covers the uses and limitations of tempera, designing, drawing with the brush, incising outlines, applying to metal, mixing and preserving tempera, varnishing and guilding, etc. Appendix, "Tempera Practice in Yale Art School" by Prof. L. E. York. 4 full page plates. 85 illustrations. x + 141pp. 5⅜ x 8½.   T343 Paperbound $1.50

GRAPHIC WORLDS OF PETER BRUEGEL THE ELDER, H. A. Klein. 64 of the finest etchings and engravings made from the drawings of the Flemish master Peter Bruegel. Every aspect of the artist's diversified style and subject matter is represented, with notes providing biographical and other background information. Excellent reproductions on opaque stock with nothing on reverse side. 63 engravings, 1 woodcut. Bibliography. xviii + 289pp. 11⅜ x 8¼.   T1132 Paperbound $3.00

A HISTORY OF ENGRAVING AND ETCHING, A. M. Hind. Beginning with the anonymous masters of 15th century engraving, this highly regarded and thorough survey carries you through Italy, Holland, and Germany to the great engravers and beginnings of etching in the 16th century, through the portrait engravers, master etchers, practicioners of mezzotint, crayon manner and stipple, aquatint, color prints, to modern etching in the period just prior to World War I. Beautifully illustrated —sharp clear prints on heavy opaque paper. Author's preface. 3 appendixes. 111 illustrations. xviii + 487 pp. 5⅜ x 8½.

T954 Paperbound $2.75

DECORATIVE ART OF THE SOUTHWESTERN INDIANS,
D. S. Sides. 300 black and white reproductions from one of the
most beautiful art traditions of the primitive world, ranging
from the geometric art of the Great Pueblo period of the 13th
century to modern folk art. Motives from basketry, beadwork,
Zuni masks, Hopi kachina dolls, Navajo sand pictures and
blankets, and ceramic ware. Unusual and imaginative designs
will inspire craftsmen in all media, and commercial artists may
reproduce any of them without permission or payment. xviii +
101pp. 5⅝ x 8⅜.   T139 Paperbound $1.00

PENNSYLVANIA DUTCH AMERICAN FOLK ART, H. J.
Kauffman. The originality and charm of this early folk art give
it a special appeal even today, and surviving pieces are sought
by collectors all over the country. Here is a rewarding introductory guide to the Dutch country and its household art, concen-
trating on pictorial matter—hex signs, tulip ware, weather vanes,
interiors, paintings and folk sculpture, rocking horses and children's toys, utensils, Stiegel-type glassware, etc. "A serious,
worthy and helpful volume," W. G. Dooley, N. Y. TIMES. Introduction. Bibliography. 279 halftone illustrations. 28 motifs
and other line drawings. 1 map. 146pp. 7⅞ x 10¾.
                                                   T1205 Paperbound $2.00

DESIGN AND EXPRESSION IN THE VISUAL ARTS, J. F. A.
Taylor. Here is a much needed discussion of art theory which
relates the new and sometimes bewildering directions of 20th
century art to the great traditions of the past. The first discussion of principle that addresses itself to the eye rather than to
the intellect, using illustrations from Rembrandt, Leonardo,
Mondrian, El Greco, etc. List of plates. Index. 59 reproductions.
5 color plates. 75 figures. x + 245pp. 5⅜ x 8½.
                                                   T1195 Paperbound $1.75

GRAPHIC REPRODUCTION IN PRINTING, H. Curwen. A
behind-the-scenes account of the various processes of graphic
reproduction—relief, intaglio, stenciling, lithography, line
methods, continuous tone methods, photogravure, collotype—
and the advantages and limitations of each. Invaluable for all
artists, advertising art directors, commercial designers, adver-
tisers, publishers, and all art lovers who buy prints as a hobby.
137 illustrations, including 13 full-page plates, 10 in color. xvi +
171pp. 5¼ x 8½.   T512 Clothbound $6.00

Dover Books on Art

THE COMPLETE BOOK OF SILK SCREEN PRINTING PRO-DUCTION, J. I. Biegeleisen. Here is a clear and complete picture of every aspect of silk screen technique and press operation—from individually operated manual presses to modern automatic ones. Unsurpassed as a guidebook for setting up shop, making shop operation more efficient, finding out about latest methods and equipment; or as a textbook for use in teaching, studying, or learning all aspects of the profession. 124 figures. Index. Bibliography. List of Supply Sources. xi + 253pp. 5⅜ x 8½.

T1100 Paperbound $2.00

A HISTORY OF COSTUME, Carl Köhler. The most reliable and authentic account of the development of dress from ancient times through the 19th century. Based on actual pieces of clothing that have survived, using paintings, statues and other reproductions only where originals no longer exist. Hundreds of illustrations, including detailed patterns for many articles. Highly useful for theatre and movie directors, fashion designers, illustrators, teachers. Edited and augmented by Emma von Sichart. Translated by Alexander K. Dallas. 594 illustrations. 464pp. 5⅛ x 7⅛.

T1030 Paperbound $2.75

CHINESE HOUSEHOLD FURNITURE, G. N. Kates. A summary of virtually everything that is known about authentic Chinese furniture before it was contaminated by the influence of the West. The text covers history of styles, materials used, principles of design and craftsmanship, and furniture arrangement—all fully illustrated. xiii + 190pp. 5⅝ x 8½.

T958 Paperbound $1.50

THE COMPLETE WOODCUTS OF ALBRECHT DURER, edited by Dr. Willi Kurth. Albrecht Dürer was a master in various media, but it was in woodcut design that his creative genius reached its highest expression. Here are all of his extant woodcuts, a collection of over 300 great works, many of which are not available elsewhere. An indispensable work for the art historian and critic and all art lovers. 346 plates. Index. 285pp. 8½ x 12¼.

T1097 Paperbound $2.50

Dover publishes books on commercial art, art history, crafts, design, art classics; also books on music, literature, science, mathematics, puzzles and entertainments, chess, engineering, biology, philosophy, psychology, languages, history, and other fields. For free circulars write to Dept. DA, Dover Publications, Inc., 180 Varick St., New York, N.Y. 10014.